Regulating Undercover Law Enforcement: The Australian Experience

Brendon Murphy

Regulating Undercover Law Enforcement: The Australian Experience

Springer

Brendon Murphy
Thomas More Law School
Australian Catholic University
Sydney, NSW, Australia

ISBN 978-981-33-6380-9 ISBN 978-981-33-6381-6 (eBook)
https://doi.org/10.1007/978-981-33-6381-6

This Springer imprint is published by the registered company Springer Nature Singapore Pte Ltd.
The registered company address is: 152 Beach Road, #21-01/04 Gateway East, Singapore 189721, Singapore

For Mike Cowled (1974–2004)

In the wavering, dimly lit recesses of memory, I remember sitting on the prow of a wooden rowboat, being propelled gently through the still waters at Salamander Bay by my grandfather. Here I was, a boy of seven, with an insatiable curiosity. I was gazing headlong into the waters below, watching the surface part as we moved. The boat came to a slow halt, and Pop remained silent while I stared into the waters. He let me take in all I could see. He knew (but I did not) that I saw things differently. But what I saw troubled me. For there, in the waters, I looked across several planes of perception. I could see the reflection of my face and the clouds above. I could see the surface of the water. I could see the beaded weed and ripples of light distorted on the sand bed below. I could see the horizon around in the world above and knew there was an equivalent horizon in the world below. Four ways of seeing, and five ways of imagining the same thing. A world of the seen and unseen, and endless questions. For here I was troubled by the presence of complexity, and the challenge of how to explain it.

Preface

Law is saturated with discourse. In this respect, it is virtually impossible to separate rule structures from associated practices and the policies that inform them. The tendency, much of the time, is to regard law as something separate from discourse, primarily because of the complexity of relationship and the problem of explaining something of how it works. This book aims to present a study of that complexity, through an analysis of a discrete area of regulation: undercover investigation. In this respect, the book sits at the intersection of several disciplines: law, criminology, history and philosophy. Drawing on Foucault and Agamben, this is an ambitious project that aims to illuminate the knowledge systems operating in this field of law specifically, shed some light on some of the complex ways in which public law evolves, and understand aspects of an emerging society of control, surveillance and exception.

The book is written through an interdisciplinary prism. It deploys both the doctrinal legal method, as well as the theoretical and interpretive technique of the humanities. Throughout I have consciously tried to avoid a strictly "legal" approach, preferring instead to use the core logic of legal reasoning and research as a foundation, deploying alternative knowledge systems in an attempt to open new perspectives and insights into law and regulation. It is a book that explores a powerful transformation that has taken place in criminal investigation practices and associated legal frameworks, strongly influenced – if not outright governed – by epistemic forces that have come to typify much of the rationality of contemporary law and governance. Those forces, broadly, are characterised by the practices of audit, surveillance, exception and risk. These rationalities and their associated practices, it will be argued, constitute a distinct governmentality that has transformed citizenship in liberal democratic states, locating the subject within what I call a zone of impeachment. This zone is characterised by a complex grid of surveillance, law, power and exception that opens a window into some of the ways in which rationalities of governance directly shape legal architectures, and serve to regulate and control populations.

This book began life as a doctoral thesis (Murphy 2015). It incorporates some materials that have been published in journal articles during the writing of the thesis and soon after it (Murphy and Anderson 2007; Murphy 2014, 2016, 2020), as well as content contained within the thesis. While I have added new content, and made numerous changes to the thesis, this book is the final published edition of that project. In its embryonic phase, this book started as a "black letter" thesis, and nothing more. But after several months of research, the materials began to take on a different form. It began with a contradiction and a failure. The contradiction was the presence in law of a legal mechanism that granted immunities for law enforcement to engage in unlawful activity for the purposes of investigating crime and corruption. In an ostensibly liberal democracy such as Australia, the presence of what was effectively an authorised crime was a remarkable contradiction in a nation with a clear commitment to the "rule of law" and a general intolerance for criminal conduct by the State.[1] The failure was the apparent inability of legal literature to satisfactorily explain the reason for changes that took place over a decade towards a national framework effectively codifying authorised crimes beyond questions of public policy. Something more than a mere shift in public policy was evident.

Things began to change as the literature review expanded into sociolegal thinkers and philosophers. Persuaded by Professor Norrie that contradiction and antinomies are often portals into new perspectives (Norrie 2001, 2005), and by Professor Cotterrell that law must be understood through its social and epistemic components (Cotterrell 1983, 1992, 1995, 1998), I embarked on a study that consciously decentred law and turned to the knowledge systems operating through it that ultimately led to Foucault (notably *The Order of Things* (Foucault 2005) [2] and *The Archaeology of Knowledge* (Foucault 2003))[3] and Giorgio Agamben's work, notably *Homo Sacer* (Agamben 1998, 1999, 2000, 2005, 2011). We will return to the theory in due course. The great value of theory, in this context, was it provided an explanatory framework to start making sense of the research findings in ways that a traditional legal analysis could not. This is the genesis of this book.

Terms

Before embarking on the work, it is useful to outline three of the important terms used. First, there are frequent references to the concept of "architecture", with reference to law and rationalities. The term is used deliberately. *Architecture* imports the idea of intelligent and purposeful design and organisation. Law is, of course, a complex phenomenon. It includes legislation, case authorities, regulations, norms, and

---

[1] Eg: *A v Hayden* (1984) 156 CLR 532

[2] *Les Mots et les choses* was first published (in French) by Editions Gallimard in 1966, and later in English by Tavistock in 1970 and subsequently by Routledge in 1989. The identity of the translator is by no means clear, as he or she is not identified in the English edition.

[3] *L'Archeologie Du Savoir* was first published (in French) by Editions Gallimard in 1972. The English translation was undertaken by Alan Sheridan in 1976, published by Tavistock and later by Routledge in 2002.

more nuanced jurisprudence that transcends the text of law. For the purposes of this study, I suggest there is a distinction to be made between two broad types of law. The first type is an intentional and purposeful design of general application; the second type is a situational and case-specific instance. The classic example of the former is legislation, while the latter is the judicial decision. Both types form part of the complex bricolage of law. Each kind of law necessarily has linkages with the other. To speak, then, of *legal architecture* is to speak of the composite of intentional and unintentional structures that govern specific areas and sites at the intersection of law, policy and human behaviour. Legal architectures support, facilitate and orchestrate interventions in the social world, becoming visible through the analysis of documents and the real-world interventions of state investigations and associated prosecutions.

The second term overlaps with the former and is fundamental. That is the idea of "law". As is well known to legal readers, "law" has numerous manifestations, which includes the declared forms of law in legislation and cases, as well as the private treaties of individuals and corporate actors. And yet law also has an equally set of "forces" beyond formal written articulation. Law has metaphysical, coercive, and normative force arising out of theoretical constructs, psychological influence, and social practices. "Law" can involve both the "hard" law of formally expressed rules and institutional enforcement, as well as "soft" law arising out of various forms of influence of compulsion in the absence of formal rule structures (Cotterrell 1992; Deflem 2008; Dworkin 1988; Ehrlich 1922, 2009; Hart 2012). As observed by Sellers, law is further complicated by the overlapping idea of command and compulsion, as well as related norms. What *must* be done, as well as what *ought* to be done, often with an associated affective (emotional) domain (Sellers 2017). For the purposes of this book, the term "law" is used in its primary sense, that is, with reference to the essential *source* of authoritative statements of command, procedure, and resolution. In this case, the primary sources are sourced in the commands of the legislature, executive and judiciary. This includes the delegated commands of executive actors. As the essential source of law in this study is grounded in a "command and control" model linked to a sovereign power, we may assume that references to "law" are references to primary commands located in documents derived from the state. This is aligned with positivist jurisprudence (Hart 2012; Kelsen 2009; Aarnio 2011; Austin 1995). However, for reasons that will become apparent, this book goes well beyond the analysis of rule structures, leaving behind the structures posited in Part 1.

The third term to clarify is the idea of "rationalities". Rationalities are what might be understood as "ways of knowing", or rules for reasoning. They embody both a substantive body of knowledge (ranging from the mythological to the empirical), and a *technique* of knowing. In this respect a rationality is a mechanism for interpretation and the production of certain truths. In law, for example, "the criminal law" constitutes a distinct body of knowledge and categories. But it is not concerned with the production of itself. The substance of those categories is determined by something else – judicial interpretation, public policy as determined by government, intersecting bodies of knowledge, such as criminology. The aspects may be understood as the "should" statements (X conduct *should* be criminalised in this way). Rationalities not only contain mechanisms for determining categories, they also contain mechanisms for *application*. So, in the context of the criminal law, the categories of fault (is person X guilty of category Y?) are determined by their own set of intersecting rules concerned with application and the production of truth. In this way rationalities are distinct from a "settled" body of knowledge. They are *ways of knowing*; what we might call epistemic "technologies". This conception draws heavily from the work of Foucault and Deleuze and will be discussed in full detail in later chapters.

Methodology

Broadly, this book deploys the regulation of undercover investigation in Australia as exemplar and metaphor to illuminate the knowledge systems and the power relationships effected and mobilised in the metaphysical world of law, and the social and cultural lives of its subjects. In doing so, something of the patterns, relationships and structure of knowledge systems and legal architecture may be uncovered. Those patterns are nuanced and complex, but tend to crystallise around ideas of risk, accountability, crime control and exception. These discourses have a transformative effect on law and policy, which has the effect of altering the rights and presumptions available through law into mechanisms of invasive surveillance, authorisation, legitimation, and prosecution. This transformation is not necessarily controversial, since law has always, to some extent, been concerned with state empowerment, risk, and accountability. What appears to be changing, however, are the techniques used in law enforcement and the willingness of legislators to re-design the law in ways that facilitate investigation, prosecution, and contain the inhibiting and frustrating systems found within legal structures. There are signs that contemporary forms of sovereign power are being transformed, as are contemporary forms of rights and citizenship. Ultimately, we move to consider the emergence of a new form of citizenship: the ordinary citizen, who occupies a contradictory space that at once attaches rights, but, under the right conditions,

Scholars have recognised the beginnings of transformation for some time now. Stan Cohen, in his brilliant book *Visions of Social Control* (Cohen 1985), recognised a trend of governments to take greater interest in systems of control and surveillance. Gilles Deleuze, in his apocryphal *Postscript on the Societies of Control* (Deleuze 1992), suggested that the western world was at the beginning of *something* – a transformation difficult to precisely identify, but necessarily linked to a program of control, surveillance and enclosure, perpetual training, specialisation and rationality. David Garland, in *The Culture of Control* (Garland 2001), synthesised many of these themes in his study of the transformative power of late modernity on the criminal justice system. The rapid social and international changes taking place destabilise the existing social order and replace it a new one – wiping away some old problems of governance, only to replace them with new ones. Risk, insecurity and control have taken on a new imperative at the dawn of the twenty-first century. I would contend that the *something* hinted at by Deleuze, and considered by an emerging body of literature, is a society in which the ability to surveil, interrogate and investigate crime is reaching into a "totalising gaze", able to penetrate, almost completely, every aspect of social life. Indeed, the ability to deploy apparatus of control that reach into the very soul through the practice of virtue testing.

Law plays a major role in this transformation. Ashworth, for example, expressed grave concerns about the impact of political pressures based on risk and danger – arguing that "risk society" was reshaping laws in ways that imported temptations to introduce harsher and more "effective" law (Ashworth 2006). Ericson argued that the transformation of law was quite radical, suggesting that the new legal landscape was now characterised as a legal framework in opposition to the rights-based models centred on due process, and was being replaced with a utilitarian model characterised by surveillance and prosecution (Ericson 2007). The role of law in social transformation is necessarily a complex one, enlivening concerns about shaping law in ways that undermine fundamental principles of human rights in the face of state power. It involves mechanisms that both facilitate and accelerate social change as well as retard and refract it. Law constitutes its own distinct knowledge formation but is also constituted by others. It is a multiplicity of discourses, directed to the orchestration of power relations. Law at once functions to enable relations and systems of domination, as well as resistance. Law shapes and ruptures existing social relations. It is an active ingredient in the transformation of sovereignty. The *something* suggested by Deleuze is not yet clear, but this study argues that one of the dynamics of the new social order is a transformation of sovereignty and the legal relationships between citizens and the state, characterised by the conscious transformation of legal architectures that permit a decisive authorisation by state law enforcement to engage in invisible surveillance, assume false identities, manufacture false realities, penetrate the veil of privacy, displace and restructure the laws of evidence, and participate in criminal activity with the suspect. The information collected, in turn, becomes a powerful repository of criminal intelligence, law enforcement methodology, and prosecution evidence. The legal architectures that normally provide some protections against this level of executive power are being transformed and reconfigured. The sovereignty of state is less visible, but more decisive. This new form of sovereignty, it seems, is an evolutionary phase that effectively facilitates the strong neoliberal demands for a powerful, but minimalist state, populated by the rights baring subject. Everywhere freedom reigns, within a legal and investigative system that deploys a precision sovereign power able to kill, or let live; able to make law, or change it; able to extend rights, or qualify them. The need to understand the juridico-legal mechanisms of power is greater than ever.

The extent to which this form of power is desirable or not is another question. My intention here is not to engage with the normative questions about good and evil, right, and wrong. The ability to decisively investigate and prosecute serious crimes is highly desirable, and it is undoubtedly the case that the first duty of government is to protect people from crime and violence. Rather, the intention here is to present a study of some of the ways in which law captures and is captured by knowledge systems and articulates technologies of power. In this respect the study is informed by Foucault but departs from him. Foucault's brilliance did not extend to a focussed examination of the complexities of law, power and the juridico-legal. While critical, the study does not set out to argue that the techniques or legal architectures are necessarily problematic. It is a fact of the human condition that certain kinds of conduct are impervious to the ordinary forms of criminal investigation, and that certain devices within law do have the effect of intentionally or unintentionally frustrating the successful prosecution of individuals and groups who are a manifest threat to the communities in which they dwell. Indeed, it may be the case that much of the transformation in law and associated knowledge systems is largely driven by the manifestation of specific kinds of problems and behaviours within those groups that governments attempt to police and control. While critical, this book should not, therefore, be seen as adopting either an alarmist or an overtly critical position on the dynamics observed.

The general orientation of this book is essentially inductive, moving from specific instances and examples towards a more generalised theory. The specifics in this case relate to a species of law unique to Australia: the law regulating and authorising controlled operations. Controlled operations is the term used in this jurisdiction to refer to undercover investigations that authorise the officer to engage in certain conduct that would otherwise be unlawful in the absence of a warrant. The legal architecture emerged in Australia between 1996 and 2020. The Australian Commonwealth, and each State and Territory, now authorise and deploy these special forms of investigation.[4] They form part of a complex web of surveillance and undercover policing legislation that includes telecommunications interception,[5] access to telecommunications "meta data",[6] covert and overt surveillance, including the use of listening devices,[7] and manufacturing false identities.[8] These legal architectures orchestrate

[4] *Crimes (Controlled Operations) Act 2008* (ACT); *Crimes Act 1914* (Cth), Part 1AB; *Law Enforcement (Controlled Operations) Act 1997* (NSW); *Police (Special Investigative and Other Powers) Act 2015* (NT), Part 2; *Police Powers and Responsibilities Act 2000* (Qld), Chap 11; *Crime and Corruption Act 2001* (Qld), Part 6A; *Criminal Investigation (Covert Operations) Act 2009* (SA); *Police Powers (Controlled Operations) Act 2006* (Tas); *Crimes (Controlled Operations) Act 2004* (Vic); *Criminal Investigation (Covert Powers) Act 2012* (WA), Part 2.

[5] *Telecommunications (Interception and Access) Act 1979* (Cth); *Telecommunications (Interception and Access) (New South Wales) Act 1987* (NSW); *Telecommunications (Interception) Northern Territory Act* (NT); *Telecommunications Interception Act 2009* (Qld); *Telecommunications Interception Act 2012* (SA); *Telecommunications (Interception) Tasmania Act 1999* (Tas); *Telecommunications (Interception) (State Provisions) Act 1988* (Vic); *Telecommunications (Interception and Access) Western Australia Act 1996* (WA)

[6] *Telecommunications (Interception and Access) Amendment (Data Retention) Act 2015* (Cth) assented to 13 April 2015 and will commence operation on 13 October 2015.

[7] *Surveillance Devices Act 2007* (Vic); *Surveillance Devices Act 2007* (NSW); *Surveillance Devices Act 2008* (WA); *Crimes (Surveillance Devices) Act 2010* (ACT); *Surveillance Devices Act 2007* (NT); *Police Powers and Responsibilities Act 2000* (Qld); Chap 13; *Police Powers (Surveillance Devices) Act 2006* (Tas)

[8] *Crimes (Assumed Identities) Act 2009* (ACT); *Crimes Act 1914* (Cth), Part IAC; *Law Enforcement and National Security (Assumed Identities) Act 2010* (NSW); *Police (Special Investigative and*

certain practices of the modern state. In this respect the controlled operation is not unique. Only the legal architecture in Australia is unique. It is representative of a *rationality* and a *technique*; a *technology* that goes beyond an odd-shaped land mass in the southern hemisphere. It represents one manifestation of a practice that has equivalents throughout the world.[9] What is different is the form of regulation within that jurisdiction, rather than the phenomenon. It is the phenomenon, ultimately, that is important.

The broad intention of the book is to contribute to our understanding of some of the complex ways in which law, especially legislation, is shaped by discursive forces, both in terms of the governing policies that shape legal architectures, but also the ways in which doctrine is actively shaped by knowledge systems that are perhaps subconscious. Linked to the interrogation of knowledge structures are larger consequences flowing from the transformation of law that appears to be taking place; the role of risk and accountability; the intensification and expansion of sovereign power at the very time the state appears to be receding; the reconfiguration of the relationship between the citizen and the state.

A book of this kind will necessarily require some attention to developing an analytical theory, as well as an approach to doctrine. This is an exploratory work, with both a legal and explanatory dimension. It will therefore begin with developing and explaining something of theory and method, before turning to doctrine, policy, and associated literature. It is an ambitious undertaking, but one I hope the reader will indulge as we endeavour to explore some of the complexities of the frontiers between law and power.

Beyond the theorists and scholars referred to in this book, my thinking in this project was very much shaped by three academics whom I must acknowledge. *Professor John Anderson* at the University of Newcastle has been a long-standing friend and colleague. He worked tirelessly on reading numerous drafts, as well as coping with my theoretical bent and tendency to write excessively. *Professor Lisa Adkins*, now at the University of Sydney, introduced me to a world of social theorists, and was instrumental in encouraging my "sociological turn". I cannot thank Lisa enough for encouraging my climb of the theoretical fence. Finally, *Professor Simon Bronitt*, Dean at Sydney Law School, has been a long-time friend and influence. His breadth of knowledge of law, humanity and encouragement have been invaluable and will not be forgotten.

Other Powers) Act 2015 (NT), Part 3; *Police Powers and Responsibilities Act 2000* (Qld), Chap 12; *Crime and Corruption Act 2001* (Qld), Part 6B; *Criminal Investigation (Covert Operations) Act 2009* (SA), Part 3; *Police Powers (Assumed Identities) Act 2006* (Tas); *Crimes (Assumed Identities) Act 2004* (Vic); *Criminal Investigation (Covert Powers) Act 2012* (WA), Part 3

[9] In the UK this type of investigation is governed largely by the *Regulation of Investigative Powers Act 2000* c. 23 (UK), with additional powers within the *Police Powers Act 1997* c. 50 (UK)); in Canada the equivalent controlled operations provisions are found in *Criminal Code* RSC 1985 c C-46, ss 9, 10, 25; in New Zealand *Misuse of Drugs Act 1975* (NZ), s34, s34A; *Evidence Act 2006* (NZ), s108; in the United States 19 USC § 2081

In addition, I am indebted to many colleagues whom I have come to know over the years, including Randy Lippert (University of Windsor), Ben Golder (University of New South Wales), Tyrone Kirchengast (University of Sydney), Mark Nolan (Charles Sturt University), Jay Sanderson and Clive Harfield (University of the Sunshine Coast), Ben Sheehy and Bruce Arnold (University of Canberra), Neil Foster, David Tomkins and Kate Lindsay (University of Newcastle), and Jeff McGee (University of Tasmania). All of them have helped shape my development as a scholar.

I cannot put into words what is owed to my wife and children. Without them, I would not have remained grounded, thoughtful or diligent. I am ever mindful of the large clan of broadly Irish descendants that make up my extended family. I give thanks to my parents, who know early I was a problem child when I began to ask "why?". Love to you all.

Sydney, NSW, Australia Brendon Murphy

References

Aarnio, A. (2011). *Essays on the doctrinal study of law*. London: Springer.

Agamben, G. (1998). *Homo Sacer: Sovereign power and bare life* (D. Heller-Roazen, Trans.). Stanford: Stanford University Press.

Agamben, G. (1999). *Remnants of Auschwitz: The witness and the archive* (D. Heller-Roazen, Trans.). New York: Zone Books.

Agamben, G. (2000). *Means without end* (V. Binetti, & C. Casarino, Trans.). Minneapolis: University of Minnesota Press.

Agamben, G. (2005). *State of exception* (K. Attell, Trans.). Chicago: University of Chicago Press.

Agamben, G. (2011). *The kingdom and the glory: For a theological genealogy of economy and government* (L. Chiesa, & M. Mandarini, Trans.). Palo Alto: Stanford University Press.

Ashworth, A. (2006). Four threats to the presumption of innocence. *South African Law Journal, 123*(1), 63–97.

Austin, J. (1995). *The province of jurisprudence determined*. Cambridge: Cambridge University Press.

Cohen, S. (1985). *Visions of social control*. Cambridge: Polity Press.

Cotterrell, R. (1983). The sociological concept of law. *Journal of Law and Society, 10*, 241.

Cotterrell, R. (1992). *The sociology of law* (2nd ed.). London: Butterworths.

Cotterrell, R. (1995). Sociological interpretations of legal development. *European Journal of Law and Economics, 2*(4), 347–359. https://doi.org/10.1007/BF01541072.

Cotterrell, R. (1998). Why must legal ideas be interpreted sociologically? *Journal of Law and Society, 25*(2), 171–192.

Deflem, M. (2008). *Sociology of law: Visions of a scholarly tradition*. New York: Cambridge University Press.

Deleuze, G. (1992). Postscript on the societies of control. *October, 59*, 3–7.

Dworkin, R. (1988). *Law's empire*. Cambridge MA: Harvard University Press.

Ehrlich, E. (1922). The sociology of law. *Harvard Law Review, 36*(2), 130–145.

Ehrlich, E. (2009). *Fundamental principles of the sociology of law* (W. Moll, Trans.). London: Transaction Publishers.

Ericson, R. (2007). *Crime in an insecure world*. Cambridge: Polity Press.

Foucault, M. (2003). *The archaeology of knowledge* (A. S. Smith, Trans.). London: Routledge.
Foucault, M. (2005). *The order of things*. London and New York: Routledge.
Garland, D. (2001). *The culture of control: Crime and social order in contemporary society*. Chicago: University of Chicago Press.
Hart, H. (2012). *The concept of law* (3rd ed.). Oxford: Oxford University Press.
Kelsen, H. (2009). *Pure theory of law* (M. Knight, Trans.). Clark: The Lawbook Exchange.
Murphy, B. (2014). Retrospective on Ridgeway: Governing principles of controlled operations law. *Criminal Law Journal, 38*(1), 38–58.
Murphy, B. (2015). *Zone of impeachment: A post-foucauldian analysis of controlled operations law and policy*. PhD Thesis, University of Newcastle, Newcastle.
Murphy, B. (2016). Deceptive apparatus: Foucauldian perspectives on law, authorised crime and the rationalities of undercover investigation. *Griffith Law Review, 25*(2), 223–244. https://doi.org/10.1080/10383441.2016.1194956.
Murphy, B. (2020). Regulating undercover policing: Subjects, rights and governmentality. *Critical Criminology, 28*(1), 65–84. https://doi.org/10.1007/s10612-020-09504-6.
Murphy, B., & Anderson, J. (2007). Mates, Mr Big and the unwary: Ongoing supply and its relationship to entrapment. *Current Issues in Criminal Justice, 19*(1), 5–33.
Norrie, A. (2001). *Crime, reason and history: A critical introduction to criminal law* (2nd ed.). Cambridge: Cambridge University Press.
Norrie, A. (2005). *Law and the beautiful soul*. London: GlassHouse Press.
Sellers, M. (2017). Law, reason, and emotion. In M. N. S. Sellers (Ed.), *Law, reason, and emotion* (pp. 11–31). Cambridge: Cambridge University Press.

Contents

About the Author

Brendon Murphy is senior lecturer in law at the Thomas More Law School, Australian Catholic University. He has previously been appointed as senior lecturer at the University of Newcastle and associate professor at the University of Canberra. As an academic, his doctoral research examined the regulation of covert investigation in Australia, with emphasis on the legal, policy and theoretical aspects of controlled operations. His PhD was given honourable mention by the Royal Society of New South Wales as an outstanding thesis in 2016. Dr Murphy has published widely in the field of criminal law and procedure, law and society, and legal theory. He was contributing author to *National Security, Surveillance and Terror* in Palgrave MacMillan's Crime Prevention and Security Management Series, and *Criminal Law Perspectives* published by Cambridge University Press. Dr Murphy is the current serving academic member of the New South Wales Law Society's Specialist Accreditation Board for Criminal Law.

Part I
Covert Investigation Law and Practice

Chapter 1
Operation Decade

> *...the Australian Federal Police, acting in conjunction with the Malaysian Police, set up "Operation Decade", which involved what has been described as a "controlled" importation and delivery of heroin. The starting point was the purchase...of heroin in Malaysia.*
>
> Mason CJ, Deane and Dawson JJ in Ridgeway v The Queen (1995) 184 CLR 19 at 25–26

An understanding of covert investigation and its regulation begins in understanding a case. In Australia covert investigation has been part of law enforcement since the early nineteenth century. Plain clothes police were, in fact, the norm rather than the rule in the English legal tradition up until the Peel Reforms in the mid nineteenth century (Emsley 1996, 2010; Radzinowicz 1956). For the most part undercover investigations were largely unregulated and limited mainly by tort. Provided the conduct of investigators was not otherwise unlawful, police were at liberty to deploy whatever methods they liked in the investigation of crime, and where those actions might breach law, a system of warrants empowered investigators to engage in those activities. Over time, however, new forms of investigations began to evolve that involved officers in the commission of crimes, usually in conjunction with suspects, to secure arrest and conviction. Policing had now entered a new phase. In Australia this became known as the *controlled operation*. This development involved a new system of regulation, attendant public policy, and the new implications. We begin with law.

Understanding of controlled operations law requires an examination of its genesis. The genesis is found in a decision of the High Court: *Ridgeway v The Queen* ('*Ridgeway*'). This case was the cause of a seismic shift in Australian law and policing. While there have been some analyses of *Ridgeway* (Galbally and Walters 1995; Gurney 1995; Grevling 1996; Hocking 1996; Nash 1996; Corns 1997), these analyses have not attempted a thorough and detailed legal analysis of the kind offered

B. Murphy, *Regulating Undercover Law Enforcement: The Australian Experience*, https://doi.org/10.1007/978-981-33-6381-6_1

here,[1] which is surprising given the extensive use of *Ridgeway* in Australian and international law.[2] What follows is a detailed reconstruction of the case based on the accepted facts and the reasoning of the courts, a consideration of the legal context at the time of the decision, and finally a consideration of the major legal and conceptual themes.

A Note on Legal Method

For readers who are not familiar with legal methodology, the examination that follows is based on a close reading of multiple documentary sources, known in legal circles as doctrinal method. This involves, inter alia, systematic reading of text, historical genealogies of legislation and cases, as well as deep understanding of legal context. A discussion on the details of legal methodology has been presented admirably elsewhere, to which the reader is referred if interested (Aarnio 2011; Van Hoecke 2011; Hutchinson and Duncan 2012; Hutchinson 2013; Murphy and McGee 2015; Samuel 2016).

For present purposes, legal method typically involves a narrow focus on a range of specific primary legal sources. This approach will be familiar to scholars in the humanities who must pay close attention to documentary sources. A key point of difference with law is the heavy presence of case reports, which present reconstructions of events with legal consequence. Reliance on case reports brings with it specific problems, which are not often understood by those outside the discipline of law. In this case we approach *Ridgeway* as a legal *event*. That is, a historical event interpreted through intersecting rule structures. The event outlined is assembled from the reported decisions of the South Australian Supreme Court[3] and the High Court of Australia.[4] The extent to which these decisions accurately reflect the precise

[1] The exception was written by the author in 'Retrospective on Ridgeway: Governing Principles of Controlled Operations Law' (2014) 38(1) *Criminal Law Journal* 38

[2] *Ridgeway* has been reported in several Australian law reports: *Ridgeway v The Queen* [1995] HCA 66; (1995) 129 ALR 41; 69 ALJR 484; 78 A Crim R 307; 8 Leg Rep C1. There is also considerable variation in the frequency of reporting. Much depends on the publisher of the respective report. Thomson Reuters' FIRSTPOINT identifies over 620 references in reported cases. LexisNexis CASEBASE identifies 380. AUSTLII's LAWCITE identifies over 650. *Ridgeway* is cited in a diverse range of courts, from the High Court of Fiji (*State v Pal* [2008] FJCA 117; *Takiveikata v State* [2008] FJHC 315), the Supreme Court of Nauru (*Republic of Nauru v Batsuia* [2018] NRSC 46), to the House of Lords (*Attorney General's Reference (No 3 of 1999: R v Looseley)* [2000] 2 AC 91). It has also been the subject of an inquiry by the United Nations Human Rights Council (*Communication No. 1080/2002: Australia* [2004] UNHRC 8). Ridgeway's impact continues to ripple through the common law, not only for its position on entrapment, but also its procedural controls through the stay order and the judicial control over abuse of process.

[3] *R v Ridgeway* (1993) 60 SASR 207 (notably in the reasoning on Matheson J at 219–223); *R v Ridgeway* (1998) 72 SASR 73

[4] Ridgeway v The Queen (1998) 184 CLR 19

events is open to debate. "Facts" in law are a complex amalgam of agreement and dispute, physical evidence, interpretation, inference, perceptions, and the constant threat of distortion and perjury. As Karl Llewellyn observed, in common law systems courts depend on the evidence presented by the parties in the construction of events, and then analyse the resulting collage for facts with *legal significance* (Llewellyn 1930). In the absence of facts that are agreed between the parties, the record of "facts" in a case is always to be regarded with caution. Unless the fact is relevant to the case it may never appear in the record at all, as it would normally be rejected by a judge in the application of accepted laws of evidence. Accordingly, we must assume there is a great deal about *Ridgeway* that is known only to the parties directly involved, and that knowledge may not be shared between all the actors. What is recorded in a case is what is left after the information nominated by the parties is filtered through the laws of evidence, heavily structured by the requirements of specific laws that require satisfaction to make out the case. A case is simply a ripple of information. Reported cases must be recognised as contested and incomplete narratives. They remain, however, a *legal fact* once determined. By default, they import into history a construct of events, which requires cautionary analysis. There is a lot about *Ridgeway* we simply do not know. There is, however, enough material to gain some insights about the event, and certainly sufficient information as to the *law* involved.

Examples of the problems in *Ridgeway* include the following. We know that a major figure, an informer called Lee, did not give evidence at trial. He was, by all accounts, a dishonest and disloyal character, described by Justice Legoe as "the Scarlet Pimpernel"![5] Immediately after John Ridgeway was arrested, Lee returned to Malaysia and disappeared. Detective Chong (Lee's controller) gave evidence at committal, but not at trial. He was killed in a car accident in 1991.[6] Ridgeway himself did not give evidence at trial.[7] Indeed, the full facts alleged in evidence were never put to a trial court. Understanding the factual events is further complicated by the usual practice in criminal prosecutions of agreement between the parties to certain facts, and disagreement on others.[8] During a trial the main focus is not so much the background history, but whether or not the accused has actually done the prohibited act(s) with the relevant state of mind. Once that has been determined, the focus then shifts to the personal and surrounding circumstances to evaluate culpability for the purpose of sentencing. Again, what is relevant for that purpose is directed by the laws of sentencing. Consequently, the focus at trial tends to be matters that have direct legal consequence, rather than the parties engaging in discussion with a view to agree on an archival account of what happened. In ordinary practice, unless there was an agreement to plead guilty, competent legal advice would involve remaining silent on all matters put to the accused. In the Anglo-Australian legal tradition, the

[5] *R v Ridgeway* (1993) 60 SASR 207, 210

[6] Ibid, 223

[7] Ibid, 219

[8] Ibid, 209

accused has the right to remain silent during the trial, while the prosecution has the burden of proving the case. As it transpired, not only was the case itself legally complicated, but even getting the case to trial was a major challenge. The pre-trial history was something of a litigation disaster, involving changes in counsel and multiple adjournments in the lead-up to trial.[9] Despite these limitations, there is evident in *Ridgeway* an important ecology that provides insights into the individuals involved, the nature of controlled operations, its legal framework, and the context in which it took place. The primary legal sources remain the only publicly available records that provide some account of what happened in the context of an undercover police investigation, involving multiple jurisdictions, actors, and institutions over time. What follows is a reconstruction of an extraordinary train of events that began in hushed conversation in a prison cell and ended up in the High Court. The critical moment was the arrest of John Anthony Ridgeway at the Old Adelaide Inn, Adelaide, in 1989.

Part 1: The Old Adelaide Inn

The Old Adelaide Inn sits in O'Connell Street, nestled between Gover Street and Roneo Place in North Adelaide, South Australia. On a hot New Year's Eve, 1989, John Ridgeway and Murray Harvey walked out of Room 188 at 10.37 am. Ridgeway was carrying a beige camera bag. Both were undoubtedly elated, having made what they thought was a very profitable drug deal. Elation vanished almost immediately as both men were confronted by plain clothes officers of the Australian Federal Police ('AFP'). Ridgeway dropped the bag. Farcically, he denied any knowledge of its contents. The denial was pointless. They had been under surveillance for some time. Police knew the bag contained 200 g of heroin;[10] they knew who Ridgeway and Harvey were. They knew where to find them. In fact, the men who sold the drugs to them were working for the AFP. They were both immediately arrested, caught in a perfectly executed sting operation. Both men were later charged with being in possession of a prohibited import[11] and convicted. Ridgeway was sentenced to a 12-year prison term.[12] From a law-enforcement perspective the operation was a complete success. Two men clearly implicated in heroin trafficking had been

[9] Ibid, 209–210

[10] There is an error in the reported cases on the exact quantity. The South Australian State Reports have conflicting amounts: both 230 g (60 SASR 221) and 203 g (60 SASR 222), while the Commonwealth Law Reports state the amount was 203 g (184 CLR 26). This amounts to 8 oz. (1/2 lb) and 7 oz. respectively. The amount of pure heroin, essential for conviction under the *Customs Act*, was 140.4 g. That figure is otherwise correctly replicated. It would seem to be a typographical error.

[11] At the time this was an offence pursuant to s233B of the *Customs Act 1901* (Cth) but would now be dealt with in accordance with the *Criminal Code 1995* (Cth).

[12] Murray Harvey was initially indicted as a co-offender with John Ridgeway.

arrested, with compelling evidence supporting the conviction. And yet in what many regarded a failure of the legal system, the triumph would not last. Five years later the High Court quashed the conviction, setting in train a series of events that resulted in major changes in covert investigation in Australia. To understand how that happened, we need to go back in time. It all began when two men met in prison.

John Anthony Ridgeway and Kim Chuan Lee

John Ridgeway was born in 1950. By the time of his arrest in Adelaide in 1989 he was well-known to police. He had a string of minor convictions in his youth for "behavioural" and "dishonesty" offences. In 1983 he was convicted of cultivating, possessing and trafficking cannabis. He was part of a syndicate that attended three plantations, which yielded an estimated 11,000 cannabis plants. He was sentenced to a term of 10 years, with an 8 year non-parole period, increased from 4 years following a successful Crown appeal.[13] It was during his time in prison (1983–1989) that Ridgeway came to know a Malaysian national, Kim Chuan Lee. Lee was serving time for importing heroin. Lee was subsequently released from prison in 1987 and deported to Malaysia. Ridgeway was later released on parole in February 1989. Evidently the pair had shared their knowledge about the drug trade and expressed some desire to remain in contact after release. Despite parole requirements that required weekly reporting and a prohibition against overseas travel, Ridgeway travelled to Singapore using his brother's passport in September 1989. The visit was timed between reporting obligations and intended to re-establish a relationship with a simple design: to get rich fast through heroin trafficking.

What Ridgeway did not know was that Lee had been a police informer for the Royal Malaysian Police (Anti-Narcotics Branch) the moment he returned to Malaysia in 1987.[14] After Ridgeway's return to Australia on 29 September 1989, Lee contacted his controller, Thian Soo Chong, and reported the encounter. Chong then contacted the Australian Federal Police liaison in Kuala Lumpur, Superintendent Butler. The authorities were now alert to Ridgeway's interest in buying heroin from Lee. On 4 October Ridgeway sent Lee a telegram, which effectively sketched out an arrangement whereby Lee would source heroin in Malaysia, then arrange for a friend to travel to Adelaide for a "holiday", import the heroin, and then sell it to Ridgeway. In subsequent telegrams and phone calls, Ridgeway put pressure on Lee to either take steps to make this happen, or confirm his withdrawal so Ridgeway could go elsewhere.[15] Ridgeway made another trip to Singapore on his brother's passport in late October, again timed to comply with his reporting requirements. He again met with Lee. The details were relayed to Lee's controller, who subsequently

[13] *R v Ridgeway* (1998) 72 SASR 73, 106; See also *Ridgeway v South Australia* (1987) 47 SASR 109
[14] *R v Ridgeway* (1993) 60 SASR 207, 220; *Ridgeway v The Queen* (1998) 184 CLR 19, 25
[15] *R v Ridgeway* (1993) 60 SASR 207, 220–221

met with both Lee and Butler on 31 October.[16] It is not clear, but it seems that on or around this day a decision was made to facilitate a "controlled purchase". As will be discussed later, by this stage the use of controlled purchases had become a normal and accepted part of drug investigations. This would involve the purchase of heroin by investigators and facilitating its movement to Australia to identify, arrest and charge Ridgeway and any others involved in the distribution. Telegrams and phone calls were exchanged during November and early December. Lee assured Ridgeway of his imminent journey to Australia. Ridgeway was becoming increasingly impatient. Then, on 18 December 1989, Lee and his controller purchased heroin from northern Malaysia (possibly Haddyai in Thailand),[17] for the explicit purpose of bringing heroin to Australia under the supervision and approval and supervision of Malaysian and Australian police. The stage was now set for *Operation Decade*.[18]

Operation Decade

The next day, Ridgeway sent a telegram inviting a phone call from Lee. Ridgeway was informed during that call that the purchase had been made, and that Lee would bring the heroin to Australia; or, at least, that he was planning a "holiday" in Australia. Behind the scenes, arrangements were made for Lee and his controller (presumably by Malaysian authorities) to travel to Singapore, and then flown from Singapore to Adelaide. Australian visas were issued, coupled with a written authorisation for the possession and movement of heroin from Malaysia into Singapore and then into Australia.[19] In Singapore the heroin went into the custody of Singapore police, who then returned it to Lee and his controller on their departure to Australia.[20] These activities took place through the various authorities liaising with one another. In Australia the liaison between Federal Police and the Australian Customs Service took place via letter, pursuant to a 1987 Ministerial Agreement, enlivened in a letter dated 28 December 1989.[21] When Lee and his controller arrived in Adelaide on the

---

[16] Ibid

[17] Ibid, 225

[18] *Ridgeway v The Queen* (1998) 184 CLR 19, 25

[19] Ibid, 26, 67

[20] *R v Ridgeway* (1998) 72 SASR 73, 76

[21] The contents of the Agreement are set out briefly in decision of Mason CJ, Deane and Dawson in these terms: "That Ministerial Agreement is directed to defining the relationship between, and areas of responsibility of, the Australian Customs Service and crime enforcement authorities, including the Australian Federal Police, with respect to "Narcotic Drug Law Enforcement". By par D7, it provides, among other things, for a request to be made for the transfer of Customs control from the Australian Customs Service to the Australian Federal Police in circumstances "where certain persons, goods, ships or aircrafts, suspected or known to be carrying or having an involvement in drugs, are required by the Australian Federal Police … to be exempted from detailed Customs scrutiny and control". The Australian Federal Police's letter of request of 28 December 1989 was made pursuant to par D7." See *Ridgeway v The Queen* (1995) 184 CLR 19, 26

morning of 29 December they were met by Australian Federal Police, who facilitated their clearance through Customs without their bags being checked.[22]

Once through Customs, Lee and his controller were taken by undercover police to the O'Connell Inn in Adelaide.[23] Lee called Ridgeway by phone. The pair met and had lunch. Lee returned mid-afternoon and obtained a sample of the heroin from his controller. He then met with Ridgeway in the late afternoon on a park bench opposite the Hilton Hotel and had a conversation. Lee subsequently returned to his hotel without the sample. The following day Ridgeway met Lee in the late morning, this time with Murray Harvey. Lee again returned to the hotel to obtain another sample, before meeting up with Ridgeway and Harvey and another (unnamed) male in a vehicle at Victoria Square. While Lee was obtaining the sample, Ridgeway and Harvey were observed to drive to premises in Wayville, where they collected a white plastic shopping bag. They then returned to collect Lee. After a brief drive around the city, Lee was dropped off and returned alone to the hotel.[24]

The following morning (31 December), Lee and his controller went to the Regional Headquarters of the AFP in Adelaide, where Lee made a telephone call (probably to Ridgeway), after which Lee, his controller and detectives from the AFP booked a room at the Old Adelaide Inn. At about 10.15 am Ridgeway and Harvey drove into a service station at an adjacent intersection. Lee and his controller then met with Ridgeway and Harvey, and then walked back to the Old Adelaide Inn. The four men then went into Room 188. Lee and Chong were paid $9000 cash.[25] Justice Gaudron later observed that $9000 was "much less than it was worth".[26] The obvious inference is that Ridgeway would make a significant gain on the heroin, especially if it was cut. Ridgeway and Harvey stood to make a huge return. Some 10 min later they emerged with the camera case containing the heroin, at which point they were arrested.[27] Ridgeway, having dropped the camera bag and being clearly implicated in soliciting its importation through Lee, was charged, and convicted in

---

[22] *Ridgeway v The Queen* (1995) 184 CLR 19, 26, 67–68; *R v Ridgeway* (1998) 72 SASR 73, 76

[23] A separate hotel at the north end of O'Connell Street, easily observed from the opposite park.

[24] *R v Ridgeway* (1993) 60 SASR 207, 221–222

[25] *Ridgeway v The Queen* (1995) 184 CLR 19, 26

[26] Ibid, 68. The street value of heroin is highly variable. A contemporary evaluation of an ounce of "cut" heroin in 1990/1991 was $6500–$7000, with an uncut purity of 60% carrying a value of $8000–10,000 per ounce. In the present case there was some 200 g of heroin (about 7 ounces) of approximately 70% purity. Zahra and Arden suggest this amount of heroin had a conservative street value of $40,000. Given that street-level heroin is often cut to down to 10–20% purity, the heroin in this case may well have converted to $80,000–$90,000, if not more. See Peter Zahra & Robert Arden, *Drug Law in New South Wales* (Federation Press, 1991), 217 and Zahra et al., *Drug Law in New South Wales* (2nd Ed., Federation Press, 1998), 285. Contemporary values also vary. According to the Australian Criminal Intelligence Commission *Illicit Drug Data Report 2017–2018*, the street value for 1 gram of heroin in South Australia is $400; amounting to about $80,000.

[27] *R v Ridgeway* (1993) 60 SASR 207, 222

August 1992 for being in possession of a prohibited import.[28] He was sentenced to 12 years imprisonment, with a non-parole period of 8 years. Ridgeway, no stranger to appeals against conviction and sentence, began an appeal process that, like the operation that snared him, took the better part of a decade to resolve.

Ridgeway v The Queen

Ridgeway's contact with Australian courts would not end until November 1998. The ripple effect is ongoing. For almost a decade his case occupied trial and appellate courts alike. Following his conviction in the Adelaide District Court, Ridgeway appealed to the South Australian Court of Criminal Appeal. This appeal, heard in February 1993, was not directed to denial of the elements of the offence (that Ridgeway was knowingly in possession of a prohibited drug). In that case personal liability was unarguable. This case demanded something else: how the evidence was obtained. What made this case controversial was a sting operation across international boundaries involving systematic cooperation of law enforcement in the importation of heroin into Australia. The purpose was, in effect, to deliver a prohibited drug to Ridgeway, and then arrest him for being in possession of it. At the heart of the trial was a live question about whether the importation was unlawful. Nowhere was the operation authorised as a matter of law. In effect, agents in several government departments in Australia, Malaysia and Singapore had effectively been part of an agreement to purchase and deliver heroin. The basis for that action was a series of formal arrangements between law enforcement, customs and the Commonwealth government. If the importation was unlawful, the evidence of its importation was unlawful and, it was argued, should be excluded either because of entrapment, or the evidence was tainted by the unlawful conduct of authorities. Counsel for Ridgeway, Mr. Michael Abbott QC,[29] argued, inter alia, that the trial judge fell into error either (1) by failing to order a permanent stay of proceedings[30] because the evidence was procured either by unfair or illegal means; or (2) the trial judge failed to exclude evidence that had been obtained unlawfully. The essential basis of these submissions was the heroin that Ridgeway was ultimately in possession of was actually imported by the investigating authorities, who in effect had facilitated the crime (through a paid informer) for which Ridgeway was now being prosecuted. The gist of the argument was this constituted a form of entrapment, an abuse of process, and/or the improper admission of unlawfully obtained evidence.

---

[28] Section 233B(1)(c) of the *Customs Act 1901* (Cth) provided (at that time): "(1) Any person who-(c) without reasonable excuse (proof whereof shall lie upon him) has in his possession any prohibited imports to which this section applies which have been imported into Australia in contravention of this Act,…shall be guilty of an offence."

[29] There were preliminary issues with representation. Mr. Abbott had to withdraw at an early stage of the trial due to a commitment with a Royal Commission. A series of pre-trial adjournments followed. The details are not presently relevant. Suffice to say Mr. Abbott later resumed his role in the management of the case. See *R v Ridgeway* (1993) 60 SASR 207 at 223–225

[30] A "stay" order is a power of courts at common law to order the temporary or permanent "freeze" of a case in the list, if satisfied that judicial process is being exercised for an improper purpose.

The Supreme Court of South Australia

The appeal was heard by Matheson, Duggan and Legoe JJ in February 1993.[31] The appeal was dismissed by 2:1 majority on 17 June. Justice Matheson found that the failure of the trial judge to make a ruling about whether or not a stay should have been granted was an error. His Honour focussed on the question of the illegality of the investigators, because in doing so that would answer both the stay and the admissibility question. In His Honour's reasoning, the illegality was, in fact, a technical failure on the part of law enforcement to obtain a license to import the heroin, rather than a fundamental breach of the criminal law. Although the *Customs Act* prohibited the importation of prescribed substances, the *Customs (Prohibited Imports) Regulations 1956* actually enabled the issue of an import license for otherwise prohibited drugs.[32] In other words, heroin was a substance that could be lawfully imported under certain conditions, and was not prohibited in all cases. The illegality of the import could have been corrected prospectively by the simple issue of a license to the investigating authorities. Here it seems that the whole case ultimately turned on the failure of the investigating officers to apply for a license. Matheson J then considered the totality of the illegality involved, and while "not condoning" the actions of the police,[33] he concluded there was an "inescapable inference" that Ridgeway was the instigator of the importation.[34] This was not a case where police unilaterally imported heroin in the hope of trapping some unsuspecting party. The police were not engaged in activity that induced Ridgeway into conduct he was not otherwise clearly involved in. On balance, His Honour agreed with the prosecutor that the seriousness of the conduct and Ridgeway's involvement in it supported the admissibility of evidence and against granting a stay. In a separate judgment, Justice Duggan agreed.[35] Duggan J concluded that both appeal points demanded consideration of the role of the police in the importation, compared with the role of the offender. While His Honour was critical of the conduct of the police in this case, His Honour found that Ridgeway "needed no persuasion to become involved", and that "the informer did not initiate [or] pursue the matter in the manner of an agent provocateur."[36] Accordingly, Duggan agreed with Matheson J and dismissed the appeal.

---

[31] *R v Ridgeway* (1993) 60 SASR 207 (17 June 1993)

[32] *R v Ridgeway* (1993) 60 SASR 207, 229. Regulation 5(1)(a) at that time provided: "... the importation into Australia of a drug is prohibited unless: (a) the person importing the drug is the holder of: (i) a licence to import drugs granted by the Secretary of the Department of Health, Housing and Community Services or an authorised person under this regulation; and (ii) a permission to import the drug granted by the Secretary of the Department of Health, Housing and Community Services or an authorised person under this regulation;". That provision is virtually identical to regulation 5(1)(a) of the 2010 Regulation currently in force.

[33] *R v Ridgeway* (1993) 60 SASR 207, 239

[34] Ibid, 238

[35] Ibid, 239–240

[36] Ibid, 239

Justice Legoe disagreed.[37] His Honour raised a concern about the nature of the actual evidence of Ridgeway's involvement, because the evidence of his involvement was largely based on inferences raised during argument about the stay and admissibility of evidence. Much of it had not been put to the jury.[38] His Honour also raised questions as to why the police did not charge Ridgeway with offences prior to the actual importation, as there was evidence of parole violations and conspiracy that was open on the evidence. From this perspective, Justice Legoe had some sympathy for the entrapment argument, as the police were focussed on pursuing a particular charge rather than prosecuting criminality that was clearly already evident. For example, why not charge conspiracy as opposed to going to the extravagant lengths of importing heroin? Once the telegrams and evidence of Lee was available there was a case to answer. Justice Legoe was prepared to accept the conduct of law enforcement, provided there was a legal foundation for it. His Honour found there was none. The only potential legal foundations evident in this case were International Conventions on Illicit Drugs, a Ministerial Agreement between Customs and the Federal Police, and a rather informal relationship between the AFP and police in South East Asia. His Honour found that none of these sources had operational function as a source of law permitting the importation of a prohibited substances. The *United Nations Single Convention on Narcotic Drugs 1961* made no reference to the authorisation of "controlled deliveries". The *United Nations Convention Against Illicit Traffic in Narcotic Drugs and Psychotropic Substances 1988* did, but this Convention was not endorsed as part of Australian domestic law until 1992 – *after* the events in question, and otherwise inoperable in domestic law.[39] The Ministerial Agreement (June 1987) had been invoked immediately prior to the arrival of the drugs at Adelaide Airport. Basically, a member of the Executive branch of government had authorised another branch of the Executive to commit a breach of the criminal law across international borders. In a forceful dissent, Legoe J held this was a power the Executive did not have.[40] Like the Majority, Legoe J considered the key issue to be the question of illegality, although His Honour focussed on the question of the admissibility of the evidence. Unlike the Majority, Legoe J concluded that the illegality was so significant the conviction was unsafe. It was accordingly a trigger for applying the exclusionary rules of evidence. In effect, the evidence of the importation should have been regarded as inadmissible. Because these issues

[37] Ibid, 208–219

[38] Ibid, 213

[39] The United Nations' Single Convention on Narcotic Drugs (1961, as amended by the 1972 protocol), and the United Nations' Convention Against Illicit Traffic in Narcotic Drugs and Psychotropic Substances (1988). The latter was specifically ratified and adopted as Australian law through the *Crimes (Traffic in Narcotic Drugs and Psychotropic Substances) Act 1990* (Cth), subsequently proclaimed on 14 February 1992. A discussion on its limits and application in *Ridgeway* is located at (1993) 60 SASR 207, 210–212

[40] Following *A v Hayden (No 2)* (1984) 156 CLR 532

had never really been dealt with at trial, Legoe J would have allowed the appeal, and ordered a new trial.[41]

Ridgeway in the High Court

Given the issue in the case, and the dissent of Justice Legoe, it is no surprise that the High Court granted special leave to appeal in August 1994. In April 1995, a 6:1 majority[42] of the High Court *allowed* the appeal,[43] quashing the conviction, and ordering a permanent stay to the charges against the *Customs Act*. The decision is complex, involving four plurality opinions and a dissent,[44] with differing views on the role of a stay, a unanimous view on the defence of entrapment, and a significant majority on the merits of the appeal. By this stage, the appeal had evolved into three connected issues, all concerned with whether a remedy would be offered to Ridgeway in light of the conduct of the AFP: was he entitled to a stay? Should the evidence of the importation be excluded? Was the High Court prepared to accept the existence of a defence based on entrapment? Any of these possibilities were arguably available where the illegal conduct of law enforcement was substantial.[45] The reasoning varied on each point.

Mason CJ, Deane, Dawson JJ

After considering the known facts, Mason CJ, Deane and Dawson JJ found that Lee's controller, Chong, had actually imported the heroin through Australian Customs, and that his conduct was effectively aided by the Australian Federal Police. The importation was effectively authorised through arrangements between Executive agencies in the absence of any legislative authority. This was done in good faith, but nevertheless the effect was that in the absence of lawful authority the investigators were complicit in the importation of a prohibited substance. Indeed, the parties had effectively engaged in a conspiracy to import heroin. The result was that the personnel involved had committed a serious indictable offence separate to any crime committed by Ridgeway, since it was an offence under the *Customs Act* to import a prohibited substance, or to "aid, abet, counsel or procure" the importation of a prohibited substance.[46] The act of importation was an element of the charge with which Ridgeway was actually charged. Consequently, the evidence was procured in contravention of Australian law, notwithstanding any unfairness towards

---

[41] *R v Ridgeway* (1993) 60 SASR 207, 216

[42] Mason CJ, Brennan, Deane, Dawson, Toohey, Gaudron JJ. McHugh J in dissent.

[43] *Ridgeway v The Queen* (1995) 184 CLR 19 (19 April 1995)

[44] Mason CJ, Deane & Dawson JJ (at CLR 24–44), Brennan J (at CLR 44–54), Toohey J (at CLR 54–65), Gaudron J (at CLR 65–78) and McHugh J (at CLR 78–94).

[45] *Ridgeway v The Queen* (1995) 184 CLR 19, 21–22

[46] *Ridgeway v The Queen* (1995) 184 CLR 19, 27

the accused. This illegality was fundamental, requiring consideration of the appropriate remedy in a case where a person had been convicted based on unlawfully obtained evidence. Entrapment was rejected as a remedy, since there was no such defence in Australian law,[47] and was not regarded as the basis for a stay on this ground alone.[48] The solution was found in the exercise of discretion to admit or reject evidence, based on public policy. It was held that the scope of judicial discretion extended to both illegally and improperly obtained evidence.[49]

While it was recognised that deception was a legitimate aspect of effective investigation, such activity could result in illegal or improper conduct that required a clear statutory footing. In those cases, it was open to the trial judge to reject otherwise relevant evidence where the weight of impropriety rested with the prosecutor rather than the accused. Accordingly, the mere fact of illegality or impropriety was not the basis of an automatic exclusion – rather, the courts must undertake a comparative evaluation of the conduct.[50] Only then, if the rejection of evidence was fatal to effective prosecution of a case, was a stay an appropriate remedy. In those cases it would be vexatious and oppressive to proceed with a case that was doomed to fail.[51] Their Honours concluded that the police conduct in this case was "extreme", and favoured rejection of the evidence connected to the importation.[52] The exclusion of evidence of the importation meant that one of the elements of the charge was no longer supported by evidence, and was doomed to fail. Accordingly, the stay order was triggered. The appeal was allowed, and a permanent stay ordered with respect to the *Customs Act* offences.

Justice Brennan

Justice Brennan also rejected entrapment as a defence, holding that (excepting duress) the fact that a person was induced to commit a crime did not factually deprive a person of their intention to commit the offence charged. The common law requirement for *mens rea* was met, despite the deceptive character of the act. The fact that a person decided to act, in the knowledge they were committing an offence, was the key issue, rather than the underlying matters influencing that choice. This fact also meant that it was not an abuse of process to prosecute a person in a criminal court for an act they had knowingly committed, even if induced by another.[53] For

[47] *Ridgeway v The Queen* (1995) 184 CLR 19, 27–29

[48] *Ridgeway v The Queen* (1995) 184 CLR 19, 40

[49] *Ridgeway v The Queen* (1995) 184 CLR 19, 30–36

[50] *Ridgeway v The Queen* (1995) 184 CLR 19, 36–40

[51] Ibid 40–41

[52] Ibid 43

[53] *Ridgeway v The Queen* (1995) 184 CLR 19, 45–46. This was a point also discussed by Mason CJ, Deane and Dawson, stating (at CLR 28: "…it is a central thesis of our criminal law that a person who voluntarily and with the necessary intent commits all the objective elements of a criminal offence is guilty of that offence, regardless of whether they were induced to act by another, whether private citizen or law enforcement officer."). See also McHugh J at CLR 80–82

Brennan J, the notion that entrapment was a defence was inconsistent with common law, despite the evolution of a substantive defence in the United States.[54] His Honour disapproved an emergent line of Australian authorities that held that entrapment was the basis of a judicial stay of proceedings. Brennan J emphasised the ultimate question in these cases was based on public policy: very simply, the reception of tainted evidence was "too high a price"[55] for the judicial system to pay for prosecution of crimes. Brennan J agreed with the majority that entrapment was properly the basis for the judicial discretion to exclude evidence, drawing the distinction between cases involving the "unwary innocent" induced into committing a crime and the "unwary criminal", otherwise provided with a routine opportunity to offend.[56] Procedurally, a stay was a matter to be determined on the merits of the case and at the stage in which the prosecution evidence was rejected or identified as fatally flawed. However, in such cases the usual result of a flawed prosecution case was an acquittal, not a stay, and in some cases the fact some evidence was rejected did not necessarily mean the prosecution case was inconsequential.[57] In this case, Brennan J concluded that the prosecution evidence should have been excluded at trial, with the result of a verdict of acquittal.[58] In an obiter comment with profound implications, His Honour was critical of the fact that Operation Decade was basically mandated by the Executive arm of government, then confirming that the Executive had no power or authority to authorise its agents to break the law. If the "controlled operation" was to be formalised as an effective technique of law enforcement, it would require the endorsement of the legislature.[59] As will be discussed later, it was clear someone took notice.

Justice Toohey

Justice Toohey noted the grounds of appeal had expanded to include entrapment, and was critical of the at times vague nature of the appeal and the changing nature of the issues argued before the respective courts.[60] Notwithstanding that criticism, Toohey J confirmed his opinion that the issue ultimately concerned the admissibility of evidence improperly or illegally obtained. His Honour agreed with Gaudron J

---

[54] Brennan J referred to seminal decisions of the US Supreme Court on entrapment: *Sorrells v United States* (1932) 287 US 435, and *Sherman v United States* (1958) 356 US 369. See *Ridgeway v The Queen* (1995) 184 CLR 19, 46–48

[55] *Ridgeway v The Queen* (1995) 184 CLR 19, 50

[56] Ibid, 49–50. This was, in fact, am expression used in *Sherman v United States* (1958) 356 US 369 at 372 per Warren CJ

[57] *Ridgeway v The Queen* (1995) 184 CLR 19, 52

[58] *Ridgeway v The Queen* (1995) 184 CLR 19, 53. Justice Brennan gave orders allowing the appeal, setting aside the conviction, and ordering acquittal. In the end the orders of the majority were adhered to.

[59] *Ridgeway v The Queen* (1995) 184 CLR 19, 53–54

[60] Ibid, 54

that entrapment was not a substantive defence in Australian law. The correct position, in Toohey's J opinion, was that two remedies were available: a stay in the prosecution as an abuse of process; or the exclusion of evidence.[61] These remedies overlapped, and rested on analysing the conduct of the prosecution and the accused. Justice Toohey found that Ridgeway had failed to prove (on balance) that he was actually induced into committing the offence charged.[62] Despite that, Toohey J turned his mind to whether or not the conduct of the Australian Federal Police was sufficiently serious to merit a stay order for abuse of process.[63] In some instances, such as this, a person may have a serious case to answer and as such a stay of proceedings was not ideal, because a stay order was effectively a form of judicial censure for unacceptable conduct,[64] which may or may not be appropriate, depending on the circumstances. An investigator should not normally be censured for doing what they are otherwise required to. In these cases, the discretion to exclude or admit evidence on policy grounds was also available. Here Justice Toohey would not have ordered a stay but agreed with the plurality that evidence of the importation should have been excluded because the police had effectively facilitated a specific element of the offence charged. Accordingly, in the absence of any admissible evidence for the importation, the prosecution case would have failed at trial. His Honour allowed the appeal and ordered a verdict of not guilty be entered.

Justice Gaudron

Justice Gaudron, after detailed review of the facts, began with an analysis of entrapment. Her Honour drew a distinction between covert investigation as an exercise in infiltration, and situations where an agent, authorised by the state, incites or participates in the commission of an offence in the course of the investigation.[65] Her Honour concluded that there was no defence in Australian law of entrapment; rather, the conduct of the investigating authority was a relevant consideration in either the exclusion of evidence, or for stay orders. Her Honour concluded that a stay was the appropriate remedy, because ultimately the discretion to exclude evidence was based on public policy grounds that would enliven the court's discretion to halt proceedings as an abuse of process.[66] Evidence of entrapment could constitute an abuse of process, which Gaudron J held was detrimental to public confidence in the legal system. Like Brennan J, Justice Gaudron paid careful attention to drawing a

---

[61] Ibid, 57

[62] Ibid, 58

[63] *Ridgeway v The Queen* (1995) 184 CLR 19, 61. At CLR 62 Toohey J stated: "A stay can be warranted only on the footing that the charge against the appellant was the result of actions by police officers, involving breaches of the [*Customs*] Act, and that to proceed against the appellant in those circumstances was to bring the administration of justice into disrepute."

[64] *Ridgeway v The Queen* (1995) 184 CLR 19, 63

[65] *Ridgeway v The Queen* (1995) 184 CLR 19, 70

[66] Ibid, 74

conceptual boundary between offences committed by an accused resulting from the illegal conduct of law enforcement, and instances where law enforcement provided opportunity to commit an offence. Only the former could be characterised as entrapment, and in Her Honour's opinion, such activity was an abuse of process. Here a distinction was drawn between entrapment as a defence (in the American tradition), and entrapment as grounds for a stay order as an abuse of process. Although law enforcement officers may be conducting themselves with the legitimate purpose of prosecting crime, the effect of prosecuting a person using tainted evidence was to undermine public confidence in the courts.[67] In this case Gaudron J concluded that although Ridgeway was predisposed to commit the offence, and had acted on his own initiative in soliciting the heroin, the crime charged actually depended on the unlawful importation of heroin by law enforcement agents. Her Honour joined the majority judges and allowed the appeal, quashed conviction, and ordered a permanent stay on proceedings.[68]

Justice McHugh Dissents

Justice McHugh agreed there was no defence of entrapment in Australian common law.[69] His Honour also agreed prosecution evidence unlawfully or improperly obtained enlivened the public policy discretion of the trial judge to reject or admit evidence. McHugh J agreed with Gaudon J, that public confidence in the administration of justice could be undermined by the admission of such evidence.[70] In essence, his Honour agreed on the law as stated by the plurality. However, his Honour differed on its application in this case. There was a fine line to be observed regarding covert investigation where law enforcement was involved in offering opportunities to commit offences. These deceptive investigative practices, in McHugh's J opinion, did not necessarily offend the public perception of justice.[71] The proper focus of enquiry in entrapment cases was something quite specific, unlike the public policy discretion. For McHugh J the focus was the nature of the inducements offered to a suspect, the reasons for that inducement, and its effect. McHugh J was influenced by the reasoning of the Canadian Supreme Court in a series of entrapment cases between 1977 and 1988, particularly *R v Mack*,[72] which provided a framework for identifying conduct that may be regarded as 'entrapment'. McHugh concluded that in cases of entrapment,[73] the general remedy of excluding

[67] Ibid, 76–78

[68] Ibid, 78

[69] Ibid, 80–82

[70] Ibid, 84

[71] Ibid, 85

[72] *R v Kirzner* (1977) 38 CCC (2d) 131: *R v Jewitt* (1985) 21 CCC (3d) 7: *R v Mack* (1988) 44 CCC (3d) 513.

[73] Justice McHugh discussed the tests for entrapment at CLR 88–92.

evidence was insufficient; the appropriate remedy was a stay.[74] His Honour included a lengthy critique of the practice of entrapment, although recognised that it was open to law enforcement as a method, provided it was tightly controlled. That control involved a strict focus on individuals based on "reasonable suspicion",[75] provided the strategy adopted was as close to "the ordinary temptations and strategems that are likely to be encountered in the course of criminal activity."[76] In cases where a stay was contemplated, McHugh J devised a 4 part test, concerned with an evaluation of whether the administration of justice was brought into disrepute by law enforcement effectively inducing the offender to commit a crime they otherwise would not commit.[77] This test will be considered further below. In this case Justice McHugh found there was nothing in the facts to suggest Ridgeway was so induced. While law enforcement officers had breached the *Customs Act*, McHugh J concluded they were acting for a legitimate purpose, and in the belief their conduct was lawful because of the existence of a Ministerial Agreement between government agencies. Justice McHugh concluded the unlawful conduct of the investigators here was outweighed by the gravity of the offending on Ridgeway's part. Accordingly, the evidence was correctly admitted at trial, and Ridgeway was not entitled to a stay. McHugh J affirmed the conviction at trial and dismissed the appeal.

Summation and Postscript

The High Court upheld Ridgeway's appeal. His conviction was quashed, and a permanent stay ordered against the *Customs Act* charges. The decision attracted considerable media attention,[78] and was subsequently the trigger for legislative intervention that continued for two decades. Ironically, Operation Decade was an accurate prediction of the time required for the law to settle. Ridgeway, in turn, did not enjoy the fruits of a successful appeal. Soon after the decision the South Australian Parliament introduced the *Criminal Law (Undercover Operations) Act 1995*. The Act indemnified law enforcement officers engaged in authorised activities from criminal liability under state law and preserved the admissibility of evidence. John Ridgeway did not, however, escape the long arm of the law. An obiter comment in *Ridgeway* suggested that the accused was prima facie liable under State law.[79] Ridgeway was soon after arrested, charged and convicted for a deemed supply

[74] *Ridgeway v The Queen* (1995) 184 CLR 19, 87

[75] Ibid, 91

[76] Ibid, 92

[77] Ibid

[78] Eg: Farah Farouque, 'Drugs ruling dismays Kerr', *The Age* (Melbourne), Thursday, 20 April 1995, 5; Bernard Lane, 'Judges question police conduct in heroin sting', *The Australian* (Melbourne), Thursday, 20 April 1995, 7; AAP, 'Ruling may hobble police drug ploy', *The Newcastle Herald* (Newcastle), 20 April 1995, 4; Rod Campbell, 'Government slates court as heroin trafficker goes free', *The Canberra Times* (Canberra), 20 April 1995, 1

[79] *Ridgeway v The Queen* (1995) 184 CLR 19, at 44 per Mason CJ, Deane & Dawson JJ

offence under the South Australian *Controlled Substances Act*, and sentenced to a 9 year prison term. A subsequent appeal to the South Australian Court of Criminal Appeal failed.[80]

Part 2: Intersecting Legal Principles

The reasoning in *Ridgeway* involved several themes. Fundamentally, this case turns on the intersection of complex sets of legal principles concerned with the power of the State to investigate certain kinds of crimes, the methods used to do so, and the control that courts exercise over both. The case begins with the criminalisation of heroin and ends with the recommendation to Parliament to regulate an exceptional power.

The Importation of Heroin

Liability in this case was based on contravention of the *Customs Act 1901*. The *Customs Act* was (and remains) a Commonwealth Statute. This Act (No. 6 of 1901) commenced operation on 4 October 1901. It was enacted in the wake of the Federation of Australian States in January 1901. Immediately we are struck with a Constitutional dimension. The Federal composition of Australia meant the concurrent operation of law from different sources. Unlike the Legislatures in the United Kingdom and the Australian States, which essentially have plenary powers over any matter,[81] the Commonwealth has specific and limited law-making powers. In some areas powers are exclusive; some concurrent with the States; in some areas by implication; and in some areas there is no power at all. One of the paradoxes of Australian criminal law is the fact there is no explicit Constitutional power of the Commonwealth to make criminal laws. The generally accepted position is that the imposition of criminal liability is a matter incidental to some other head of power. The Commonwealth Constitution contains a provision (s51(xxxix)) extending law-making powers to matters that are incidental to any powers vested in the

---

[80] *R v Ridgeway* (1998) 72 SASR 73

[81] State Constitutions contain provisions that extend power of make laws "for the peace, welfare and good government" of the State. For example, see the *Constitution Act 1902* (NSW), s5, and the requirements of State Constitutions set out in the *Australian Act 1986* (Cth), s2(1). That formulation was held by the High Court in *Union Steamship Co of Australia v King* (1988) 166 CLR 1 as extending plenary powers to the States. For a general discussion on the scope of State Constitutions, see Tony Blackshield and George Williams, *Australian Constitutional Law and Theory* (Federation Press, 5th ed, 2010), 426–465

Commonwealth.[82] That position was clearly stated by Griffith CJ in *The King v Kidman* in 1915.[83] However, consistent with many areas of Commonwealth power, Customs is a matter that involves several sections of the Constitution, including powers over trade and commerce (s51(i)), taxation (s51(ii)), and customs, excise and bounties (s90). Although ostensibly for the purpose of controlling the movement of goods and services across borders, the Customs power quickly became a matter of interest in criminal cases, both with respect to the criminal jurisdiction of the Commonwealth, and in the importation of prohibited goods.[84]

Over time the scope of Commonwealth criminal jurisdiction over the importation of narcotics came to rely more on the external affairs power (s51(xxix)). Since Australia is a signatory to numerous international treaties and conventions concerned with drug trafficking, the external affairs power is certainly enlivened in drug interdiction. As it happened, the *Customs Act* contained no references to the importation of heroin when it was first enacted. Indeed, heroin was legal at that time. The *Customs Act* contained delegated authority for the Governor-General to proclaim certain goods as prohibited imports. The first prohibition of a "recreational drug" (opium) took place in January 1906 by proclamation in December 1905,[85] greatly strengthened by the introduction of statutory offence provisions in the form of s233B into the *Customs Act* in 1910,[86] and the expansion of the 1905 prohibitions by proclamation in 1914.[87] Heroin made its first appearance as a prohibited import in 1953.[88] It has been a prohibited import ever since.[89]

The *Customs Act* is closely connected with excise and has been the subject of considerable amendment during its life. When Ridgeway was arrested in 1989, the *Customs Act* was a very complex statute with numerous subordinate regulations. The desperate need to "modernise" the law to engage with an increasingly

---

[82] The *Commonwealth of Australia Constitution Act* (63 & 64 Vic Chap 12). Section 51(xxxix) provides: "The Parliament shall, subject to this Constitution, have power to make laws for the peace, order, and good government of the Commonwealth with respect to:... matters incidental to the execution of any power vested by this Constitution in the Parliament or in either House thereof, or in the Government of the Commonwealth, or in the Federal Judicature, or in any department or officer of the Commonwealth."

[83] In this case the Chief Justice stated at CLR 434: "In my opinion the power of the Commonwealth Parliament to enact criminal laws is to be found in pl. XXXIX. and nowhere else, and is a power to enact them as sanctions to secure the observance of substantive laws with respect to matters within the legislative, administrative, or judicial power of the Commonwealth, and in that sense incidental to the execution of such powers."

[84] Early cases on the scope of the Commonwealth's power to criminalise Customs Act offences had to consider this exact issue. See *Irving v Nishimura* (1907) 5 CLR 233 and *Baxter v Ah Way* (1909) 8 CLR 626, both concerned with the importation of opium.

[85] Opium Proclamation 1905, Commonwealth of Australia Gazette No, 64, 30 December 1905.

[86] *Customs Act 1910* (Cth) (Act No. 36 of 1910)

[87] Opium Proclamation 1914, Commonwealth of Australia Gazette No. 71, 12 September 1914.

[88] Customs (Prohibited Imports) Regulations 1953 (Cth). See also the compilation on prohibited and regulated imports in the Customs (Prohibited Imports) Regulations 1956 (Cth).

[89] For a more detailed review of the evolution of heroin prohibition, see Desmond Manderson's *From Mr Sin to Mr Big: A History of Australian Drug Laws* (Oxford University Press, 1993), esp. 125–131

internationalising economy prompted the Federal Government to engage the Australian Law Reform Commission to review the law concerning Customs and Excise. The report, published in 1992, contained a recommendation (also recommended by the concurrent Gibbs Committee Enquiry) that offence provisions should be taken out of the *Customs Act*.[90] Importation offences have since been located in the *Criminal Code Act 1995* (Cth). However, at the time Ridgeway was charged, the relevant offence provisions were contained in s233B of the *Customs Act 1901* (Cth).

When Ridgeway was arrested, section 223B(1)(c) provided: *"Any person who ...without reasonable excuse (proof whereof shall lie upon him) has in his possession, or attempts to obtain possession of, any prohibited imports to which this section applies which have been imported into Australia in contravention of this Act ... shall be guilty of an offence."*

Characterisation of a criminal statute ordinarily rests on the identification of component elements, which become requirements of proof in law through the reception of evidence to establish the element as fact "beyond reasonable doubt".[91] In *Ridgeway* Mason CJ, Deane and Dawson characterised s233B(1)(c) in these terms:

> *Heroin is included among the narcotic goods to which s.233B applies. The allegation of the quantity of heroin being not less than the trafficable quantity was included in the information for the purposes of penalty. That means that the objective elements of the offence of which the appellant was convicted were: (i) possession of heroin; (ii) absence of reasonable excuse; and, (iii) prior importation of the heroin into Australia in contravention of the Act.*[92]

Technically there are five elements, not three since the provision requires the establishment of a "prohibited import" (a defined term). That element requires attention to the requisite quantity and quality of the substance, relevant to sentence and the jurisdiction of the court. In addition, as discussed below, there is a further question here as to the required level of knowledge and intention (*mens rea*) that was not stated in the section at all, raising the question as to whether mere physical possession of a prohibited import was sufficient. In this case there was no doubt that Ridgeway was in "possession" of a trafficable quality of a prohibited import (heroin), and that there was no "reasonable excuse". There was no contest on the question that the drug had been imported into Australia. And there was no doubt Ridgeway knew the substance was heroin and intended to deal in it. In Ridgeway's cases there is no analysis of the component elements of liability, simply due to the fact these were not contested or contestable issues at trial or on appeal. A momentary digression on liability will provide insight into some of the components of that process.

In ordinary cases, establishing the nature of a chemical substance is a matter of scientific evidence, ordinarily in the form of an analyst's certificate or testimony.

---

[90] Australian Law Reform Commission, *Customs and Excise*, Report No 60 (1992). See Volume 2, 9 [1.17].

[91] A fundamental common law principle. See *Woolmington v DPP* [1931] AC 462; *Keeley v Mr Justice Brooking* (1979) 143 CLR 162. The common law is now embedded in the various Uniform Evidence Acts in s141.

[92] *Ridgeway v The Queen* (1995) 184 CLR 19 at 24–25

Section 233BA of the *Customs Act* facilitated that exact process.[93] Inserted in May 1989, this provision was operational when Ridgeway was before the courts. There is no evidence in the cases of the method of confirmation of the nature of the heroin, but it is likely that any analysis of the drug at that time was in accordance with international standards recommended by the United Nations on the testing of illicit drugs. Those recommendations (which remain current) advised analysis based on at least two methods involving colour tests, chromatography and/or spectrometry.[94] Analysis confirmed not only the substance, but the quantity of pure drug (140.4 g), which according to Schedule VI of the *Customs Act* at the time made this a trafficable quantity. Quantum was/is directly concerned with the penalty, which in this case was a maximum prison term of 25 years and a fine of $100,000.[95]

The charge required "possession". Ridgeway had physical custody of the heroin. However, in Australian drug law the fact of physical possession is insufficient. Physical custody or control is essential, but it was categorically held in a contemporaneous decision, *He Kaw Teh* (1985),[96] also concerned with contravention of s233B(1)(c), that "possession" required both physical custody *and* knowledge of the existence (or likely existence) and nature of the substance.[97] Where the offender denies that knowledge, inferences about knowledge can be drawn from the surrounding circumstances.[98] Given there was direct observation of Ridgeway in the negotiation of the exchange, a history of direct solicitation from an informer, the supply of samples, exchange of cash and physical possession of heroin in the

---

[93] Relevantly, this provision stated: "(2) Subject to subsection (4), in any proceedings for an offence against section 233B, a certificate of an analyst in an approved form stating, in respect of a substance in relation to which the offence is alleged to have been committed: (a) that the analyst signing the certificate is appointed under subsection (1); and (b) when and from whom the substance was received; and (c) what, if any, labels or other means of identifying the substance accompanied it when it was received; and (d) what container or containers the substance was contained in when it was received; and (e) a description, and the weight, of the substance received; and (f) when the substance, or a portion of it, was analysed; and (g) a description of the method of analysis; and (h) the results of the analysis; and (j) how the substance was dealt with after handling by the analyst, including details of: (i) the quantity retained; and (ii) the name of the person, if any, to whom any retained quantity was given; and (iii) measures taken to secure any retained quantity; is admissible as prima facie evidence of the matters in the certificate and of the correctness of the result of the analysis." Subsection (4) required service of the certificate to the defendant at least 14 days prior to the submission of it to the relevant court.

[94] Peter Zahra and Robert Arden, *Drug Law in New South Wales* (Federation Press, 1991), 230–234; United Nations International Drug Control Programme, *Recommended Methods for Testing Opium, Morphine and Heroin* (United Nations, 1988)

[95] Customs Act 1901 (Cth), s235.

[96] *He Kaw Teh* (1985) 157 CLR 523

[97] *He Kaw Teh* (1985) 157 CLR 523 per Brennan J at 648: "On a count of possession under par. (c) the onus is on the prosecution to prove that an accused, at the time when he had physical custody or control of narcotic goods, knew of the existence and nature, or of the likely existence and likely nature, of the narcotic goods in question and that onus is discharged only by proof beyond a reasonable doubt.".

[98] *He Kaw Teh* (1985) 157 CLR 523 per Dawson J at 596

camera bag, his subsequent denial of knowledge of its contents was absurd. An inference of actual knowledge was certain. Accordingly, there could be no doubt that Ridgeway was in possession for the purpose of the offence charged.

Finally, the heroin needed to be "imported". The gist of the law around the meaning of "import" at the time proffered a wide interpretation of what otherwise appears to be a simple concept. The act of "importation" is something of a continuing process with a geographic connection. At a minimum, to "import" required that prohibited goods to be brought onto Australian land across some international boundary, ordinarily for some commercial purpose.[99] That is, the carriage of the goods had ended with the physical landing of the goods in Australia, or the chain of delivery involved physical connection with Australia. A line of authorities between 1970 and 1990 held, however, that an "import" did not cease at the moment of landing. A period of time extended after landing that meant that a person could still be liable for importation even after the goods had physically landed.[100] After an object has been imported it is often subject to change in nature and quality, and as such the legal quality of an import is subject to a temporal and qualitative limitation. There is no question that the heroin in this case was "imported", and that it remained an "import" at the time of Ridgeway's arrest. Indeed, it was the express finding of the goods being an "import" that was central to the subsequent question of legality. What became an issue was whether the importation was lawful, and as the authorities were actually involved in that process, this would be a central issue.

The Question of Lawful Excuse or Authority

Section 233B of the *Customs Act* provided for a defence of "reasonable excuse". A great deal of the problem in *Ridgeway* revolves around the apparent unlawful conduct of the investigators, but there was no consideration of the availability of this important statutory defence. Liability is assumed as the necessary consequence of the investigators involved. The High Court dismissed any suggestion that Ridgeway himself was in possession for anything other than an unlawful purpose.[101] At the time Ridgeway was decided the scope of "reasonable excuse" in drug importation cases had been considered in *He Kaw Teh* in 1985.[102] Fundamentally, a "reasonable excuse" was held to depend on the circumstances of the case, the particular provisions being enforced, and the interpretation of those provisions. The existence of a defence, reasonably open to law enforcement, was not considered. *Ridgeway* is silent on the question of liability of the officers. It seems highly likely that the

---

[99] *Wilson v Chambers* (1926) 38 CLR 131; *He Kaw Teh* (1985) 157 CLR 523

[100] *Forbes v Traders Finance* (1970) 126 CLR 429, 432

[101] *Ridgeway v The Queen* (1995) 184 CLR 19, 25. See also McHugh J at CLR 93.

[102] *He Kaw Teh v The Queen* (1985) 157 CLR 523. For the current leading authority, see *Taikato v The Queen* (1996) 186 CLR 454

officers involved would have had a reasonable excuse in the conduct of a bona fide criminal investigation, and from this perspective the assumption of criminal liability seems misplaced. Of note is a statement by Gibbs CJ in *He Kaw Teh* that where "an officer of Customs…[who] has confiscated [drugs],…may provide him with a reasonable excuse."[103] This aspect of Ridgeway was never developed, nor argued, but it seems a compelling argument that an investigator engaged in the bona fide investigation of drug trafficking would have a reasonable excuse for both importing and being possession of a controlled object. Ridgeway may well have been wrongly decided on that point.

In the first South Australian appeal, Justice Matheson made the astute observation that the *Customs (Prohibited Imports) Regulations 1956* contained express provisions that permitted the importation of a prohibited substance under licence. These regulations commenced on 14 December 1956, serving to repeal and consolidate 52 previous statutory rules. Regulation 5 was contained in the original 1956 regulation.[104] At that stage the provision concerned nominated substances contained within the Fourth Schedule. Heroin was included within that Schedule in 1974.[105] The scope of regulation 5 was broadened in 1980 to include any defined "drug".[106] Otherwise, the essential substance of regulation 5 had been in operation for more than 30 years at the time Ridgeway was arrested, and remains the current law in Australia.[107] No explanation is reported as to why a licence was not sought or granted. Very simply, it appears that the case itself involved a failure to obtain a licence. The reasons why that is the case remain a mystery. It may simply have been overlooked.

What the regulation does indicate is that the prohibition against the importation of narcotics is not set in absolute terms. Rather, the Parliament of Australia had long operated a policy of controlled movement of certain narcotics, rather than absolute prohibition. In the absence of a licence from the relevant Minister, the importation of heroin into Australia in this case was not something done at the level of individual or small-scale decision-making between maverick investigators. In this case the importation was undertaken in the context of a Ministerial Agreement between the Australian Customs Service and the Australian Federal Police, in co-operation with the Royal Malaysian Police. The exact terms of that Agreement are not known. Based on the fragments set out in the Ridgeway cases, it appears that the Agreement was entered into during the Hawke Labour Government in June 1987 by then Minister for Industry, Technology and Commerce, the Hon. Senator John Button, and then Special Minister of State, the Hon. Senator Michael Young. This Agreement appears to have crystallised at the time when the National Crime Authority, Australian Customs and the Australian Federal Police were developing intervention strategies aimed at transnational drug law enforcement in the late 1980s.[108] The

[103] *He Kaw Teh v The Queen* (1985) 157 CLR 523, 541

[104] Customs (Prohibited Imports) Regulations 1956 (Cth) (No. 90)

[105] Customs (Prohibited Imports) Regulations Amendment 1974 (Cth) (No. 249)

[106] Customs (Prohibited Imports) Regulations Amendment 1980 (Cth) (No. 382)

[107] Customs (Prohibited Imports) Regulations 1956 (Cth) r.5

[108] *Ridgeway v The Queen* (1995) 184 CLR 19, 67 fn 171

1987 Agreement was specifically invoked by the AFP the day before Lee and Chong arrived in Adelaide.[109] The scope of the agreement was not, however, unlimited. The operation and nature of the Agreement, and its limits, were set out by Gaudron J in *Ridgeway*. In effect, the Agreement permitted the AFP to limit the scrutiny of baggage checking by Customs officers. However, Gaudron J also noted that the terms of the agreement were limited to following identified drugs and suspects into the country, not to actively engage in the importing of heroin.[110] It appears, then, that although there was an agreement between branches of Government to co-operate in the course of drug law enforcement, the terms of that agreement were still limited by the agreement itself. The Agreement did not authorise actual importation of heroin. Rather, the agreement contemplated what was known as a "controlled delivery" of drugs that had been identified and mobilised by others, not the police themselves. This indicates that the terms of the agreement may well have been contravened.

Of more importance, however, was the limitation imposed at common law. In 1984 the High Court held in *A v Hayden (No 2)* that an officer of the Crown had no defence of "superior orders" to crimes ordered by the State, because the Executive arm of government has no power to authorise a breach of laws mandated by the Legislature.[111] That position was affirmed in *Ridgeway*.[112] In this case what is evident is, in fact, a separation of powers issue, and at the core of Constitutional law. Very simply, regardless of whether or not the investigators in this case were acting with the authority of their superiors, the reality was that as a matter of law the Executive arm of government was not empowered to act in the way they did. *Ridgeway* must be seen not just as a decision about remedies, but as a major decision concerned with the limitation of executive government. The Ministerial

[109] *Ridgeway v The Queen* (1995) 184 CLR 19, 26

[110] *Ridgeway v The Queen* (1995) 184 CLR 19 at 67–68: "Assistant Superintendent Chong was advised by officers of the Federal Police to bring the heroin to Australia in a camera bag. He was instructed to complete a Customs Declaration on the basis that he had nothing to declare. In the meantime, Detective Sweeney of the Federal Police prepared an Authority for Exemption from Detailed Customs Scrutiny ("Customs Exemption Notice"), had it signed by his superior officer, Superintendent Guest, and handed it to Customs officers at Adelaide International Airport. A Customs Exemption Notice is a document which members of the Federal Police can present to Customs officers so that persons carrying drugs can be "exempted from detailed Customs scrutiny and control" in accordance with a Ministerial Agreement with respect to narcotic drugs. If Customs officers agree to the exemption, "total responsibility for compliance with all Customs statutory requirements (rests) with the Australian Federal Police" (par D8). It seems that the Ministerial Agreement is intended to operate to enable members of the Federal Police to pursue drug importers and their contacts, not, as it did in this case, to enable members of the Federal Police to become involved in illegally importing drugs. The effect of the Customs Exemption Notice in this case was that, although Customs officers were aware of the heroin in Assistant Superintendent Chong's possession, he was directed to the "Nothing to Declare" barrier and his baggage was not checked."

[111] *A v Hayden [No. 2]* (1984) 156 CLR 532. See also *Clough v Leahy* (1904) 2 CLR 139 and *Yip Chiu Cheung v The Queen* [1995] 1 AC 111

[112] *Ridgeway v The Queen* (1995) 184 CLR 19. Justice Brennan captured the concept simply at CLR 54: "The Executive branch of government cannot dispense its officers from the binding effect of the laws prescribed by the Parliament."

Agreement could not authorise an operation of this kind without the authority of the Legislature, or in the absence of a judicial warrant. The Executive branch of government cannot engage in criminal activity and immunise itself in the process. To do so strikes at the heart of fundamental principles of the separation of power and the rule of law.

The Stay Remedy

The finding that the heroin in this case had been unlawfully imported demanded consideration of an appropriate remedy. *Ridgeway* gives primary focus to an evidential remedy, but the decision also considered the role and function of a "stay of proceedings". A *stay* is a power of the courts, ultimately sourced in the inherent jurisdiction of the Supreme Courts to supervise proceedings, although this power has been codified or supplemented in some statutory rules of court.[113] A stay is a power (express or implied) to temporarily or permanently suspend part or all of the proceedings brought before the court. The practical effect of the 'stay' is that the matter basically stays in the list for a limited or unlimited time. The purpose of the power is to preserve the integrity of the administration of justice by preventing an abuse of process. Typically, an abuse of process will be found where the prosecution makes improper use of the courts through oppressive or malicious prosecution; the attempt to manipulate the judicial office; cause undue delay in bringing the matter before the courts; fabricate or destroy evidence; or exhibit serious misconduct during the pre-trial stage of prosecution. Entrapment may straddle some or all of these components. The goal is one of public policy, concerned with the preservation of public confidence in the courts. The precise grounds for a stay are contextually dependent, and not closed.[114] At the time *Ridgeway* was decided, stay orders had materialised in cases involving delay affecting the conduct of a fair trial,[115] where alternative charges were laid against a person acquitted of an offence where considered oppressive to do so,[116] and in cases where the prosecution of a criminal matter was essentially invoked for an improper purpose.[117] The remedy is discretionary,

[113] During the trial the specific provisions were found in the *District Court Rules 1992* (SA). Contemporary examples may be found in, for eg: *Civil Procedure Act 2005* (NSW), s67; *Supreme Court Act 1935* (SA), ss25, 39.

[114] The definitive work on the origins and application of the Stay is Andrew Choo, *Abuse of Process and Judicial Stays of Criminal Proceedings* (Oxford University Press, 1993). The leading authorities in Australia are *Jago v District Court of New South Wales (NSW)* (1989) 168 CLR 23; *Barton v The Queen* (1980) 147 CLR 75; *DPP v Shirvanian* (1998) 44 NSWLR 129; *Williams v Spautz* (1992) 174 CLR 509. The most recent deployment and variation on the doctrine is *Moti v R* [2011] HCA 50

[115] *Jago v District Court* (NSW) (1989) 168 CLR 23

[116] *R v Kite* (1992) 60 A Crim R 226

[117] *Williams v Spautz* (1992) 174 CLR 509

and has an extremely powerful effect: it "freezes" a case, either temporarily or permanently. A judge who makes such an order is effectively declaring their refusal to hear the case because to do so is an affront to justice.

The purpose of this remedy is grounded in the maintenance of public confidence in the administration of justice, but can properly be seen as one of the more powerful mechanisms through which the judiciary is able to enforce the separation of powers and discipline the legislature and executive in cases where there is a overt or implied usurpation of power. Justice Toohey in *Ridgeway* summed upon the scope and purpose of the stay in these terms:

> *There is no doubt that a court may intervene to prevent an abuse of its process, in criminal as well as civil proceedings. The concept of abuse of process is not a precise one. Nor can it be; it gives effect to a concern on the part of courts that may arise in a variety of circumstances. But at the heart of the concept lies the legitimate power of the courts to stay prosecutions brought in exercise of the prerogative of the Crown.*[118]

As a discretionary remedy triggered by a cluster of possible incidents, it is no surprise that the High Court in *Ridgeway* differed as to when and if a stay was an appropriate remedy. As we have seen, opinions varied on whether a stay could be triggered by the act of a controlled import. There was no question in this case as to the existence of the power, but opinions differed on the timing and application of it. The majority suggested that the fact the law enforcement officers had committed offences in the course of investigating a suspect who was also liable to be charged did not constitute an abuse of process for that reason alone.[119] A stay in these cases was normally only appropriate in cases where the Crown case was fatally flawed by the exclusion of evidence.[120] Hence the stay remedy was, functionally, applicable *after* the evidential remedy was applied. Gaudron, McHugh and Toohey JJ were prepared to accept that the misconduct or inducement of law enforcement officers *may* constitute an abuse of process of itself, and in this respect the stay order is conceptualised as a distinct remedy applicable *prior* to the application of any evidential remedy.[121] Importantly, the deployment of a stay prior to the commencement of a trial was not ruled out by the plurality judgment either. Evidence could be ruled inadmissible at a preliminary hearing.[122] Consequently, the stay was maintained as a remedy of maximum flexibility; deployed as and where required, based on the factual matrix of a given case. *Ridgeway* can be seen as a 4:3 split on the application of the stay.

---

[118] *Ridgeway v The Queen* (1995) 184 CLR 19, 60

[119] *Ridgeway v The Queen* (1995) 184 CLR 19 at 40–41 per Mason CJ, Deane & Dawson

[120] Ibid.

[121] *Ridgeway v The Queen* (1995) 184 CLR 19 at 59–60 and 62 per Toohey J; at 74–75 per Gaudron J; at 87 per McHugh

[122] *Ridgeway v The Queen (1995)* 184 CLR 19 at 40 per Mason CJ, Deane & Dawson: "Ordinarily, the question whether evidence of an offence or of an element of an offence should be excluded pursuant to the discretion to exclude evidence on entrapment grounds should be raised and determined in the course of a preliminary hearing."

Entrapment as Defence?

Much of the decision in *Ridgeway* was concerned with the question of entrapment in Australian law. One of the lines of arguments raised by counsel for Ridgeway was that a "limited defence of entrapment should be available", along the lines of the entrapment defence in the United States.[123] That argument was unanimously rejected. However, all judges turned their attention as to why entrapment was not a defence in Australian law.

Entrapment has been recognised as a substantive defence in the United States since 1932, after the US Supreme Court held in *Sorrells v United States* that an accused person was entitled to an *acquittal* if the evidence indicates that "the criminal design originates with the officials of the government, and they implant in the mind of an innocent person the disposition to commit the alleged offense and induce its commission in order that they may prosecute."[124] Subsequent US authorities have maintained the general rule that a successful defence triggers grounds for an acquittal. The Federal Courts and most American States prefer a subjective approach, with the focus on whether the offender was actually induced to commit the crime, coupled with a requirement to prove "predisposition" to commit that or similar offences. Alternatively, some States utilise an objective test, which is essentially concerned not so much with the effect on the mind of the offender, but on whether the conduct of law enforcement created "substantial risk" that an ordinary person could be induced to commit the offence charged.[125] The position in the United States, before and after Ridgeway, is one where the scope and nature of entrapment as a doctrine contains divergent paths to the same point, with the important dimension of being matters for a jury. As will be seen in Chap. 5, entrapment is a complex problem for the common law, with a lot of variation and subsequent evolution in the decade after *Ridgeway*. It is really a hybrid doctrine that achieves a variety of purposes.

Entrapment was rejected by the High Court for two reasons. First, the conceptual foundations of the defence were criticised. In *Sorrells* and cases following, the US Supreme Court based their reasoning on a presumption of "legislative intent" – that it could not be presumed that the Congress of the United States, *the* model democracy, intended that "detection and enforcement should be abused by the instigation by government officials of an act on the part of persons otherwise innocent in order

---

[123] *Ridgeway v The Queen* (1995) 184 CLR 19 at 22

[124] *Sorrells v United States* (1932) 287 US 435 at 442. In *Ridgeway* the decisions in *Sherman v United States* (1958) 356 US 369 and *United States v Russell* (1973) 411 US 423 were also invoked and considered.

[125] The literature on entrapment in the United States is extensive, and beyond the scope of this chapter and thesis to address. For current cases and commentary, see Markus Dubber and Mark Kelman, *American Criminal Law: Cases, Statutes and Comments* (Foundation Press, 2nd ed, 2009), 586–598

to lure them to its commission and to punish them."[126] The "presumption of legislative intent" was, according to the plurality judgment in *Ridgeway*, offensive to ordinary principles of statutory construction. The High Court was critical of judges inserting presumptions of the intention of the Legislature.[127] Related to this position was the second point of rejection; the weight of authorities across the common law world had rejected a defence in the form recognised by the United States. The definitive answer was explained by the plurality judges in *Ridgeway*:

> *The question whether the common law of this country recognises a substantive defence of "entrapment" to a charge of a criminal offence has not been directly addressed in any case in this Court. It has, however, been considered on a number of occasions by State Supreme Courts which have consistently and emphatically answered it in the negative. Similarly, the courts of England, Canada and New Zealand have denied the existence of such a substantive common law defence. The decisions to that effect are not surprising since it is a central thesis of our criminal law that a person who voluntarily and with the necessary intent commits all the objective elements of a criminal offence is guilty of that offence regardless of whether he or she was induced to act by another, whether private citizen or law enforcement officer. And that is so even if the inducement involved criminal conduct on the part of a law enforcement officer. Where that is so, the result is not that the induced person is not guilty of the crime. It is that the law enforcement officer is also guilty of an offence.*[128]

In essence, it would have been a substantial departure from the common law to recognise a defence in a system which placed emphasis on the weight of existing authorities and a reluctance to read into the law the "legislative intent" of the Parliament. Entrapment, as an event, was not the basis for a defence. It could, however, form the basis of some other remedy. One of those, as we have seen, was the stay. The other was the exclusion of evidence. In this reasoning and its emphasis on intention and knowledge of the offender we see a further implication: the liability of the instigator. What began as an argument excusing the conduct of the accused was inverted to incorporate the conduct of the "trapper".

The dismissal of entrapment as a defence did not dispose entrapment to the conceptual scrapheap. Ironically, although entrapment was no defence, evidence of entrapment was still relevant to the application of the stay for the minority judges, although specifically rejected by Brennan J.[129] As will be seen in following chapters, entrapment, while not defence in the common law world outside of the US, is relevant to the question of other remedies and processes. Accordingly, *Ridgeway*

---

[126] *Sorrells v United States* (1932) 287 US 435 at 448. See also *Sherman v United States* (1958) 356 US 369 at 372.

[127] *Ridgeway v The Queen* (1995) 184 CLR 19 at 29: "...it is a very long step to the conclusion that, if a person does in fact commit a crime as a result of such inducement, he or she is nonetheless not guilty of it for the reason that there should be read into the express terms of every provision creating a statutory offence an unexpressed qualification establishing an applicable defence which is unknown to, and quite contrary to, our common law. Whatever may be the position in the United States, the principles of statutory construction provide no warrant for the taking of such a step by our courts."

[128] *Ridgeway v The Queen* (1995) 184 CLR 19 at 27–28. (Footnotes omitted).

[129] Ibid, 48

remains an important authority on what entrapment is, or could be. The difficulty, again, is variations in what actually constitutes entrapment.

"Not a Term of Art"[130]: A Test for Entrapment?

The majority reasoning of Mason CJ, Dean and Dawson JJ referred to the reasoning of the US Supreme Court on the elements of the defence as it stood in the US referred to above:

> *The elements of the defence are essentially subjective, namely, that there was an absence of previous intent or purpose on the part of the accused to commit an offence of the kind charged and that the accused actually did what is alleged to be the offence "only because he was induced or persuaded by some officer or agent of the government"*[131]

The test was a question of fact, with a further caveat that merely providing an opportunity to commit an offence, or facilitating it, is not, as a matter of law, entrapment. Deceptive techniques were recognised as legitimate law enforcement methods in some cases, and it was only those cases where the investigator "implanted" the criminal design into the mind of the offender that it was accepted as constituting entrapment.[132] However, these judges went on to reject the defence as valid Australian law, focussing instead on unlawful and improperly obtained evidence. Here an *objective* review of the facts centred on questions of *public policy* relating to the fair and just administration of the criminal law was critical.[133] Entrapment was seen as a matter critical to the admissibility of evidence, enlivening as "judicial discretion to exclude evidence of an illegally procured offence",[134] *and* evidence that was not illegal, but obtained "improperly". In both cases a central consideration was the connection between the conduct of the investigators and whether it caused the accused to commit the offence. A precise test, however, was consciously avoided as both undesirable and impractical.[135] In this case the question of unlawful or improperly obtained evidence is dependent on the framework provided by the laws of evidence rather than a distinct test on entrapment.

Justice Brennan referred to the concept of entrapment considered by Gleeson CJ in *R v Sloane*,[136] based on the idea that a person would not have committed the offence, or been unlikely to commit in the absence of the conduct of the investigators. Such conduct is expressed in general terms, based on the "general criminal

---

[130] Ibid per Gaudron J at 70

[131] *Ridgeway v The Queen* (1995) 184 CLR 19, 28 (Footnotes omitted).

[132] Ibid, 28–29

[133] Ibid, 34

[134] Ibid, 34–37

[135] *Ridgeway v The Queen* (1995) 184 CLR 19, 37

[136] (1990) 49 A Crim R 270

intentions of the offender".[137] The core idea made a distinction between the "unwary innocent" and the "unwary criminal". This assessment was not, however, useful for the determination of any defence – rather it was factored into the application of an evidence-based remedy, recognising that conduct amounting to entrapment could be unlawful, improper, unfair or all of these. Entrapment, per se, was not determinative of the issue. What was key was the exercise of a discretion on evidence, based on the "nature and gravity of the offence…and the nature and gravity of the unlawful conduct engaged in by the law enforcement agency in order to obtain the evidence"[138] In this context entrapment conduct was just one of the factors relevant to the evaluation of the admissibility of evidence.

Justice Toohey conceptualised entrapment as being relevant to the application of a stay remedy on the principle that prosecution based on entrapment evidence is an abuse of process. In this case His Honour referred to Samuels JA in *R v Hsing*,[139] finding that the test for entrapment was "conduct offensive to the administration of justice".[140] This, in turn, was conceived in relation to the reasoning of Justice Estey in the Canadian Supreme Court in *R v Amato*:

> *The principal elements or characteristics of [entrapment] are that an offence must be instigated, originated or brought about by the police and the accused must be ensnared into the commission of that offence by the police conduct; the purpose of the scheme must be to gain evidence for the prosecution of the accused for the very crime which has been so instigated.*[141]

In essence, Toohey J held that entrapment conduct may trigger the application of a stay remedy where that conduct constitutes an abuse of process.

Justice Gaudron recognised that entrapment is a doctrine with a variety of meanings, incapable of precise definition. The concept excluded "mere" undercover investigations and imported to principle conduct where the investigator improperly incited the accused to actually commit the offence.[142] After some discussion of a range of authorities, Gaudron J concluded:

> *the word "entrapment" is used in various different situations. For present purposes it is sufficient to concentrate on the situation in which the accused person could not or would not have committed the offence with which he is charged if law enforcement agents or those acting on their behalf had not acted illegally, whether by aiding, abetting, procuring or inciting him to commit the offence or by participating in some more positive way in its commission. (The theoretical possibility that an offence might be committed as a result of the lawful actions of police or other law enforcement agents can be considered if and when a case of that kind occurs.) It may be convenient to refer to cases involving offences committed as a result of the illegal acts of law enforcement agents as "entrapment", but the critical*

[137] *Ridgeway v The Queen* (1995) 184 CLR 19, 49

[138] Ibid, 51

[139] (1991) 25 NSWLR 685 at 696

[140] *Ridgeway v The Queen* (1995) 184 CLR 19, 57

[141] (1982) 69 CCC (2d) 31 at 61 cited in *Ridgeway v The Queen* (1995) 184 CLR 19 at 58

[142] *Ridgeway v The Queen* (1995) 184 CLR 19, 70

consideration, in my view, is whether the offence results from the criminal acts of law enforcement agents or those acting on their behalf.[143]

Fundamentally, the central principle for Gaudron was the concept of drawing a distinction between providing "mere opportunity", and those cases where the offence itself can properly be recognised as one "where the offence results from the illegal actions of those whose duty it is to uphold the law".[144]

It was the dissenting opinion of McHugh J that involved the clearest consideration of a test for entrapment. This test drew on a synthesis of cases in Australia, the US and Canada. While recognising that a prescriptive test for entrapment was unlikely, he offered a four-part test based on the governing principle of entrapment as conduct bringing the administration of justice into disrepute:

The ultimate question must always be whether the administration of justice will be brought into disrepute because the processes of the court are being used to prosecute an offence that was artificially created by the misconduct of law enforcement authorities. That question should be determined after considering four matters:

Whether conduct of the law enforcement authorities induced the offence.

Whether, in proffering the inducement, the authorities had reasonable grounds for suspecting that the accused was likely to commit the particular offence or one that was similar to that offence or were acting in the course of a bona fide investigation of offences of a kind similar to that with which the accused has been charged.

Whether, prior to the inducement, the accused had the intention of committing the offence or a similar offence if an opportunity arose.

Whether the offence was induced as the result of persistent importunity, threats, deceit, offers of rewards or other inducements that would not ordinarily be associated with the commission of the offence or a similar offence.[145]

As discussed above, McHugh J broadly agreed with the majority about the relevant legal principles, but differed in the application. For Justice McHugh, the application of these principles resulted in a conclusion that Ridgeway was not induced to commit the offence charged. Rather, he was a willing and eager participant who was the prime mover in the chain of events resulting in his arrest and subsequent prosecution. And yet, fundamentally, *Ridgeway* fails to provide consensus on what actually constitutes entrapment. *Ridgeway* affirms that there is no single test. Rather, there are *indicia of entrapment*. Justice Gaudron concluded that the complexities of cases brought before courts are such that the entrapment question is determined by "common sense and experience, not by some hard and fast test".[146] It appears, as suggested by Gaudron, that the ultimate legal issue in entrapment is a question of *causation*, with regard to the governing question of minimum acceptable standards of law enforcement. The problem is *Ridgeway* was that there are different views on what actually constitutes entrapment, even though it is a matter relevant to triggering remedies outside of a substantive defence.

---

143 *Ridgeway v The Queen* (1995) 184 CLR 19, 76–7

144 Ibid, 77

145 Ibid, 92

146 Ibid, 78

Criminal Liability of Law Enforcement Officers

More than any other aspect of *Ridgeway*, it was the finding that investigators engaged in the operation, and operations like it, could be liable for criminal prosecution that had the greatest impact. Since there was no law that authorised the importation of heroin operative at the time (notwithstanding the availability of a licence), no defence of "superior orders", and no statutory defence (other than reasonable excuse) applicable at the time, the investigators in this case were, in theory, criminally liable for the importation of heroin and for effectively aiding and abetting the activities of Ridgeway. That was, in fact, conceded by the Commonwealth DPP during the High Court proceedings.[147] That conclusion was partly the result of the absence of lawful authority discussed above, and partly a product of foundation principles of criminal liability:

> *it is a central thesis of our criminal law that a person who voluntarily and with the necessary intent commits all the objective elements of a criminal offence is guilty of that offence regardless of whether he or she was induced to act by another, whether private citizen or law enforcement officer. And that is so even if the inducement involved criminal conduct on the part of a law enforcement officer. Where that is so, the result is not that the induced person is not guilty of the crime. It is that the law enforcement officer is also guilty of an offence.*[148]

The centrality of reason, manifested in the voluntary and intentional commission of a crime, even when induced, or even when undertaken for a genuinely held belief in its propriety, is a fundamental issue in the *Ridgeway* case. It was the essential basis for the rejection of a "defence" of entrapment at common law; it was also the basis for the conclusion that investigators were themselves criminally liable for crimes committed in the course of an investigation committed independent of the suspect, or in conjunction with them. As will be seen later, the concern of the Parliament in the aftermath of *Ridgeway* was squarely focussed on the consequences of this aspect of the decision more than any other. It had serious implications not only for this investigation; it had significant ramifications for law enforcement generally.

Emerging International Law

Ridgeway refers to an emerging international law concerned with drug law enforcement. Counsel for the Commonwealth, Michael Rozenes QC,[149] located the controlled operation in the context of servicing Australia's international commitment to

---

[147] *Ridgeway v The Queen* (1995) 184 CLR 19, 27

[148] Ibid, 28

[149] Mr. Rozenes was then Commonwealth Director of Public Prosecutions. At the time of writing he is presently Chief Judge of the County Court of Victoria.

the investigation of drug offences.[150] The International dimension was largely ignored in the High Court, but as we will see in due course, the international dimension was, and has become, a fundamental aspect of covert law enforcement. Only Justice Toohey specifically examined the issue, but found that regardless of the framework, there was no domestic law authorising the action, and accordingly concluded that International law was not a basis for securing authorisation.[151] This is in stark contrast to the Supreme Court of South Australia Court of Criminal Appeal, where Legoe J analysed the international dimension in some detail. Australia became a signatory to the *United Nations Single Convention on Narcotic Drugs* in 1961, with an amending Protocol adopted in 1972. This Convention was given effect in domestic law through the introduction of the *Narcotic Drugs Act 1967* (Cth). The Convention required signatories to not only introduce prohibitions to control the trafficking of narcotics; the Convention also required signatories to actively assist and co-operate in the control and investigation of narcotics offences.[152] In 1989 Australia became a signatory of a supplementary Convention; the *United Nations Convention Against Illicit Traffic in Narcotic Drugs and Psychotropic Substances*, a convention that extended the operation of the 1961 Convention, and also enhanced international law enforcement protocols. Article 11 of that Convention specifically endorsed "controlled delivery" as a mechanism for international law enforcement.[153] This Convention was introduced into Australian Federal domestic law in 1992 via the *Crimes (Traffic in Narcotic Drugs and Psychotropic Substances) Act 1990* (Cth). In effect, in the 30 years from 1961, Australia had become an active participant in an emerging international context involving both legal architectures and law enforcement concerned with suppressing domestic and international drug trafficking. It was in this context that John Ridgeway was an unwitting agent for change.

The outcome in *Ridgeway* was shaped by two issues directly linked to the international context. The first was a matter of timing. The second was the character of the operation itself. Justice Legoe rightly observed that the 1988 Convention did not become effective law in Australia until 14 February 1992, well after Ridgeway had been arrested and prosecuted.[154] The problem with that was a well-established prin-

[150] *Ridgeway v The Queen* (1995) 184 CLR 19, 23

[151] *Ridgeway v The Queen* (1995) 184 CLR 19, 59

[152] United Nations Single Convention on Narcotic Drugs 1961, Art. 34–36

[153] Article 11 provides: "1. If permitted by the basic principles of their respective domestic legal systems, the Parties shall take the necessary measures, within their possibilities, to allow for the appropriate use of controlled delivery at the international level, on the basis of agreements or arrangements mutually consented to, with a view to identifying persons involved in offences established in accordance with article 3, paragraph 1, and to taking legal action against them. 2. Decisions to use controlled delivery shall be made on a case-by-case basis and may, when necessary, take into consideration financial arrangements and understandings with respect to the exercise of jurisdiction by the Parties concerned. 3. Illicit consignments whose controlled delivery is agreed to may, with the consent of the Parties concerned, be intercepted and allowed to continue with the narcotic drugs or psychotropic substances intact or removed or replaced in whole or in part."

[154] *Ridgeway v The Queen* (1993) 60 SASR 207, 216

ciple that international instruments were not domestic law unless and until they had been effectively incorporated by an Act of Parliament.[155] As a result, the UN Conventions to which Australia was a signatory could not be regarded as a law authorising controlled operations. Even if they had been specifically endorsed, neither the 1961 Single Convention, or the 1988 Convention contained provisions that provided any clear statutory authority for what had been undertaken. Article 11 itself was conditioned by the requirement that controlled delivery was subject to the law, ("If permitted by the basic principles of their...domestic legal systems...") while "controlled delivery" was (and remains) a technique characterised by *interception* and *supervised transit* of an identified narcotic already in transit.[156] It did not contemplate the purchase or importation of heroin for sale to a suspect by domestic law enforcement. The International Conventions did provide a basis for criminalisation and investigation, but not require direct participation by investigators in crime. As a result, the law contemplated by international agreement neither authorised the kind of operation undertaken, or had been fully introduced into domestic law at the time Ridgeway was charged.

Evidence at "Too High a Price"

Perhaps the most significant legal consideration in *Ridgeway* was the question of a remedy in the context of illegal activity by authorities. In this case that remedy was centred on the question of judicial control over evidence. That control took the form of the assertion of the discretionary exclusion of otherwise relevant evidence on the grounds of *public policy*. The principles applied in *Ridgeway* were sourced primarily from two earlier High Court authorities: *R v Ireland* (1970) and *Bunning v Cross* (1978).[157] In these cases the High Court (led primarily by Barwick CJ) held that part of a court's inherent power included the reception or rejection of evidence (both real and confessional) that had been obtained unlawfully or improperly, even where it was otherwise relevant to a fact in issue. The governing rationale for this discretion was a concern that the administration of justice would be tarnished by the reception of evidence that had been obtained through the unlawful conduct of those agencies charged with the enforcement of the law. In *Ireland* then Chief Justice Barwick

[155] At the time *Ridgeway* was determined both by the Supreme Court of South Australia (1993) and the High Court (1995), the High Court had recently affirmed that principle in *Dietrich v The Queen* (1992) 177 CLR 292, 360

[156] "Controlled Delivery" is defined in Article 1(g) as: ""Controlled delivery" means the technique of allowing illicit or suspect consignments of narcotic drugs, psychotropic substances, substances in Table I and Table II annexed to this Convention, or substances substituted for them, to pass out of, through or into the territory of one or more countries, with the knowledge and under the supervision of their competent authorities, with a view to identifying persons involved in the commission of offences established in accordance with article 3, paragraph 1 of the Convention;"

[157] These cases were part of a succession of cases on this issue. See also *Cleland v The Queen* (1982) 151 CLR 1; *Pollard v The Queen* (1992) 176 CLR 177 and *Foster v The Queen* (1993) 67 ALJR 550

famously concluded that public policy was a legitimate trigger for the discretionary power where the reception of that evidence was otherwise at "too high a price".[158] The mechanism used in the exercise of the discretion was a qualitative evaluation of the evidence, the offence, and the circumstances in which the evidence was obtained. The mechanism is essentially an attempt to balance two competing interests: the public interest in preserving the integrity of the judicial system by ensuring the courts do not effectively give approval to the unlawful or improper conduct of law enforcement by permitting prosecutions based on tainted evidence, and the public interest in securing the conviction of the guilty.

In *Ridgeway* it was recognised that common law in Australia had diverged from the position in the UK during the 1970s, where the House of Lords rejected the existence of this kind of discretion in *R v Sang*.[159] The English position after *Sang* was that provided evidence was relevant and probative, questions of how it was obtained were irrelevant to the question of reception. *Ridgeway* presented a significant departure from the English position. It was also recognised that there was a distinction between evidence that was *unlawfully* obtained, and evidence that was *improperly* obtained. The discretion applied to both, although *Ridgeway* can be seen as containing two distinct limbs of discretion, one concerned with impropriety, and the other illegality. Those limbs could apply to an offence generally, or an element of it. The exercise of the discretion was conceived as based on the balancing of the relative weight of the factual matrix. Central to that consideration was the *nature*, *seriousness* and *effect* of the illegal/improper conduct, and the distinction between offences induced or facilitated by law enforcement that the offender otherwise commits independently, and those cases where law enforcement actually commit an offence independent of the offender, or concurrent with the offender. Those considerations were to be considered in relationship to the seriousness and nature of the offence for which the accused is charged. The result of this evaluation was conceived as necessarily variable. In some cases it would apply to the totality of evidence against an accused; in some cases would relate to one part of it. The effect of this was recognised as variable. In some cases fatal to the case. In other cases, the effect would be essentially academic, as the prosecution would be obtained through other forms of evidence in any case. However, in *Ridgeway* that High Court marked a clear line that certain kinds of evidence could be obtained at "too high a price", with the effect of eroding public confidence in the system of law and justice in Australia.

In *Ridgeway* the result was almost inevitable. Having found that there was no lawful authority to import heroin, it followed (for the majority opinions) that the act of importing a trafficable quantity of heroin was a serious offence that law enforcement agencies had no power to authorise. The operative remedy in this case was the exclusion of evidence. As the importation of heroin was one of the elements of the offence for which Ridgeway had been charged, the absence of admissible evidence meant there was no case against Ridgeway available through the *Customs Act*. The alternative was to receive evidence that had been obtained by the self-authorisation

[158] *R v Ireland* (1970) 126 CLR 321 at 335 per Barwick CJ

[159] *R v Sang* [1980] AC 402

of an executive agency to import narcotics, justified on the basis of selling it to a suspected drug dealer. That conclusion was simply not an option, because it effectively meant that the executive branch of government would be able to authorise itself to commit breaches of the law with immunity from civil or criminal consequence. There were, simpy stated, significant underlying issues linked to the separation of powers and the function of the courts.

Related Questions of "High Public Policy"

A recurrent theme in *Ridgeway* is a concern for "questions of high public policy". Those questions are, in fact, significant and highly political. The central principle of the exclusion of evidence, the prohibition against executive authorisation of illegality, and concerns over the appearance of "curial approval" of tainted prosecutions are ultimately sourced in ideas of the rule of law and the separation of powers. This theme is woven throughout the judgment. In this case the immediate progenitor is the decision of Stephen & Aickin JJ in *Bunning v Cross*.[160] As discussed above, the notion of "public policy" provided the conceptual rationale for the discretionary exclusion of evidence. But the assertion of judicial control over the prosecution is a powerful ideological and practical manifestation of the judicial arm of government. While the High Court was careful to observe that investigation and the decision to prosecute was a matter for the executive, there was no doubt in the court asserting its command of the judicial "jurisdiction" once matters were before the courts.[161] Reception, restriction and rejection of evidence are fundamental to that process and the practical independence of the judicial arm of government. The rejection of evidence, and the stay remedy, was seen as mechanisms that had the effect, if not intention, of offering judicial *disapproval* of the unlawful conduct of the executive, particularly in cases where there was either the absence of official disapproval, or active encouragement, by the executive. Preservation of the "integrity" of the judicial system was a key value underpinning *Ridgeway*.

Express references to the rule of law were also features of this case. This was not a novel development. Justice Frankfurter (US Supreme Court) was quoted with approval from *Sherman v United States* (1932) in support of the principle that the rule of law as a democratic value was best supported by "fair and honourable administration of justice".[162] In this context the "rule of law" is given effect through, and provided as justification for, the discretionary control on evidence. The ability for the judiciary to throw out evidence that is otherwise relevant and probative is an important judicial tool in maintaining the integrity of the executive arm of government. In addition, the rule of law was invoked as a critique of entrapment-based investigative methods. Cases involving the intentional, unlawful acts of law enforcement were described as a "threat to the rule of law" of a "particularly

[160] (1978) 141 CLR 54 at 74–5

[161] *Ridgeway v The Queen* (1995) 184 CLR 19, 32–3

[162] (1958) 356 US 369 at 385 cited in *Ridgeway v The Queen* (1995) 184 CLR 19 at 34

malignant aspect."[163] A failure on the part of the courts to "set their face against grave criminality…would be to undermine the rule of law itself."[164] The assertion of judicial authority over the prosecution processes in the courts, the capacity to censure the executive, and invoking rule of law rhetoric are core values and principles that provide a significant authority to the reasoning of the court.

Views on Law Enforcement

Ridgeway manifests a pragmatic dichotomy in its attitude towards law enforcement. On the one hand that there is an apparent zealous expectation that investigation be undertaken with "clean hands". On the other is recognition of the need to support investigations by legalising and regulating effective investigation methodologies. The High Court appeared to recognise the first duty of government is to protect the public from threat, which includes crime. The High Court immediately recognised the consequence of their decision. In obiter, the plurality, for example, stated:

> *[I]n the context of the fact that deceit and infiltration are of particular importance to the effective investigation and punishment of trafficking in illegal drugs such as heroin, it is arguable that a strict requirement of observance of the criminal law by those entrusted with its enforcement undesirably hinders law enforcement. Such an argument must, however, be addressed to the Legislature and not to the courts. If it be desired that those responsible for the investigation of crime should be freed from the restraints of some provisions of the criminal law, a legislative regime should be introduced exempting them from those requirements. In the absence of such a legislative regime, the courts have no choice but to set their face firmly against grave criminality on the part of anyone, regardless of whether he or she be government officer or ordinary citizen. To do otherwise would be to undermine the rule of law itself.*[165]

In a similar opinion, Brennan J concluded that the result in *Ridgeway* was "manifestly unsatisfactory from the viewpoint of law enforcement."[166] However, his Honour cautioned the "controlled operation" was a practice that required legislative authority. Not only did it require legislative authority; it also required *regulation*. The reason: "It is manifest that there will be anomalies, if not corruption, in the conduct of such operations in the absence of adequate supervision."[167] Law enforcement was recognised as a necessary, important and desirable function of the executive. But it required regulation to maintain the integrity and legitimacy of criminal investigation. To this end the use of subterfuge, deception and trickery were all recognised as an important part of the arsenal of investigation. This was particularly the case in the investigation of crimes ordinarily impervious or invisible to normal forms of investigation. For this reason, there was a clear distinction made between "mere entrapment" and unlawful entrapment. The dilemma was set out by McHugh J in these terms:

---

[163] *Ridgeway v The Queen* (1995) 184 CLR 19, 39 per Mason CJ, Deane and Dawson JJ

[164] Ibid, 44

[165] *Ridgeway v The Queen* (1995) 184 CLR 19, 43–4 per Mason CJ, Deane and Dawson JJ

[166] Ibid, 53

[167] Ibid, 54

[I]n their increasingly difficult battle against crime – particularly organised crime – law enforcement authorities cannot be criticised for taking initiatives to apprehend those who make a business of crime or are about to embark on a course of criminal activity. Where there are no "victims" or there is none who is willing to co-operate with the law enforcement authorities, the taking of steps to apprehend such persons is often a social necessity. The State is entitled to protect itself against likely criminal activity. Merely setting a trap for and consequently apprehending and charging a person whose business is criminal activity or who is about to commit a criminal offence does not in my view offend the community's sense of justice. Provided there is some basis for the entrapment and the means used have not induced the person to commit an offence that that person would not otherwise have committed, the public interest does not require the condemnation of methods of entrapment that result in the apprehension of those who make a business of crime or are about to embark on a course of criminal activity.[168]

Fundamentally, a majority of the High Court flagged the controlled operation as a methodology that required legislative footing and appropriate governance. But in this context, it was not the question of "entrapment" alone that was the impetus for reform. It was the totality of the potential liability of investigators, the unlawful conduct of the investigators, the deployment of entrapment methods, the perceived effect on public confidence in the judiciary, and the risk of the abuse of power that were critical drivers for the recommendation to legislate. In the dissenting opinion of McHugh J, his Honour was cautious of a blind endorsement of the controlled operation. In an echo of the reasoning of early US decisions on entrapment, and the strong human rights provisions within Canadian jurisprudence, McHugh declared "[i]n a society predicated on respect for the dignity and the rights of individuals, noble ends cannot justify ignoble means."[169] What was a concern for McHugh J were two public effects of the undercover/sting operation: the creation of crime, and the practice of "virtue testing". McHugh J affirmed his opinion that no government in a democratic society had the unfettered right to "test the virtue of its citizens"; and because entrapment was the actual creation and facilitation of crime, it could not be justified otherwise than effectively simulating a crime that was already likely to take place. In this respect Justice McHugh had drawn inspiration from academic commentators[170] – an unusual step in a case heavily characterised by the deployment of case authority.[171] In this decision we have a clear recognition that the questions of "high public policy" were not just questions of the "State" and the separation of powers. Entrapment practices took place on the conceptual battleground by the citizen and government; between the disproportionate powers available to the State and its citizens; and between the powerful liberal values of rights and crime control in liberal democracies.

---

[168] Ibid, 85 (Footnotes omitted)

[169] *Ridgeway v The Queen* (1995) 184 CLR 19, 91

[170] Bennett Gershman, 'Abscam, the Judiciary, and the Ethics of Entrapment' (1982) 91(8) *The Yale Law Journal* 1565; John Dyson Heydon, 'The Problems of Entrapment' (1973) 32(2) *Cambridge Law Journal* 268

[171] There are 2 other references to external commentary in *Ridgeway*: a consideration of David Paciocco's 1991 article on Stay Proceedings in criminal cases (Paciocco 1991) in Justice Toohey's decisions (CLR 63, FN162) and Scott Paton's 1994 analysis of entrapment in the US (Paton 1994) in the decision of Justice Gaudron (CLR 72, FN 193)

Part 3: Beyond Ridgeway

Judicial decisions obviously have significant ramifications for the parties to the case. Occasionally they also have significance for subsequent cases. And sometimes decisions, especially those of national Supreme Courts, have an effect that lasts decades. *Ridgeway* brought together, for the first time, the threads of a new kind of law: the controlled operation and its regulation. The case itself has two perspectives: one essentially legal, the other profoundly conceptual and concerned with power.

The significant legal consequences of *Ridgeway* were numerous. At the individual level, John Ridgeway's conviction for possessing a prohibited import was quashed. In so doing the High Court had effectively entrenched the judicial control over relevant but unlawfully or improperly obtained evidence that had been evolving in Australia at common law since the 1970s. The basis of criminal responsibility as grounded in intentional and voluntary conduct, even in the face of incitement or deception, was affirmed. Entrapment could not be relied on as a defence; but it might be relied on for other purposes. The use of deception, subterfuge, surveillance, and unorthodox investigation practices was normalised and accepted – provided it was *lawful*. What made the conduct of the investigators unlawful in *Ridgeway* was not the technique used. Undercover operations involving drug interdiction across international borders was already a fact of international law enforcement and law. What made the conduct unlawful in *Ridgeway* was the apparent absence of domestic legal structures authorising the activity within the accepted legal architecture operating at the time. The solution to the problem in *Ridgeway* was the recommendation for the Parliament to consider whether to permit investigations of this kind, and if so, to carefully consider the proper form of regulation and control. Investigations of this kind necessarily *required controls*. The capacity of State authorities to be authorised to commit crimes during an undercover investigation or to specifically target citizens into temptation was a concept of no small concern. It was seen by the Chief Justice as a potential "malignancy"[172] Even when it was regulated, it was a power open to abuse. Justice Brennan cautioned that such a power would involve anomalies, abuse and corruption. It was a power that demanded *supervision*. Here are the seeds for controlled operations law. The major consequence of *Ridgeway* was the expansion of just this kind of law.

But there is something else that follows in the shadow of *Ridgeway*. The Old Adelaide Inn offers a curious microcosm of what was to come: a civilian architecture infiltrated by the criminal and the law. The unsuspecting public were left undisturbed by the secret arrival of law enforcement. The unsuspecting Ridgeway was identified, tracked, isolated, and secured: arrested at the very moment that his hopes seemed fulfilled. The invisible, sovereign power of the State is here revealed in all its glory. The resources of law enforcement, across the artificial lines of borders and space, were marshalled and networked in an elaborate architecture of communication, information, and surveillance. The power to criminalise the movement of 200 grams of condensed, fibrous gunk extracted from an easily grown poppy. The power

---

[172] *Ridgeway v The Queen* (1995) 184 CLR 19, 39 per Mason CJ, Deane and Dawson JJ

to isolate, physically detain and imprison. The power of a group of 6 men and 1 woman to join in a polyphony of voices and intellectual variations on a theme to control the judicial process. The referral and recognition of the power of the legislator to *make law* and *change law*. The subtle but present anxiety of crime, surveillance, and security. Authorising this kind of activity, it seemed, was a risky business.

Ridgeway offers a preface for the remainder of this book. For in it we find important dimensions in the life of law, public policy, and theory. The case itself reveals how case and legislation intertwine and evolve. The public policy debates reveal how discourse plays a critical part in the construction of law and legal principle. Finally, the resulting apparatus reveals something of the important theoretical and sociological implications of covert investigation.

References

Aarnio, A. (2011). *Essays on the doctrinal study of law*. London: Springer.

Corns, C. (1997). Judicial termination of defective criminal prosecutions: Stay applications. *University of Tasmania Law Review, 16*(1), 75–95.

Emsley, C. (1996). *The English police: A political and social history*. London: Longman.

Emsley, C. (2010). *Crime and society in England: 1750–1900* (4th ed.). Harlow: Longman.

Galbally, R., & Walters, B. (1995). Entrapment: The serpent beguiled me. *Law Institute Journal, 69*, 913–914.

Grevling, K. (1996). Illegality, entrapment and a new discretion. *Law Quarterly Review, 112*(January), 41–46.

Gurney, K. (1995). Covert law enforcement after ridgeway. *Deakin Law Review, 2*(2), 283–296.

Hocking, B. (1996). Ridgeway. *Criminal Law Journal, 20*(3), 160.

Hutchinson, T. (2013). Doctrinal research: Researching the jury. In D. Watkins & M. Barton (Eds.), *Research methods in law*. Oxford: Routledge.

Hutchinson, T., & Duncan, N. (2012). Defining and describing what we do: Doctrinal legal research. *Deakin Law Review, 17*(1), 83–119.

Llewellyn, K. (1930). *The bramble bush: Some lectures on law and its study*. New York: Columbia University.

Murphy, B., & McGee, J. (2015). Phronetic legal inquiry: An effective design for law and society research? *Griffith Law Review, 24*(2), 288–313. https://doi.org/10.1080/10383441.2015.1041631.

Nash, S. (1996). Australian developments in entrapment cases. *Criminal Law Review, 137*.

Paciocco, D. (1991). The stay of proceedings as a remedy in criminal cases: Abusing the abuse of process concept. *Criminal Law Journal, 15*(4), 315.

Paton, S. (1994). "The government made me do it": A proposed approach to entrapment under Jacobson v United States. *Cornell Law Review, 79*(4), 995.

Radzinowicz, L. (1956). *A history of English criminal law and its administration from 1750: Volume 2: The enforcement of the law* (Vol. 2: The enforcement of the law). London: Stevens & Sons.

Samuel, G. (2016). *Epistemology and method in law*. London/New York: Routledge.

Van Hoecke, M. (Ed.). (2011). *Methodologies of legal research: Which kind of method for what kind of discipline?* Oxford: Hart Publishing.

Chapter 2
Controlled Operations

The Lord God said to the woman, "What is this that you have done?"
The woman said, "The serpent deceived me, and I ate."

Genesis 3:13

Ridgeway transformed Australian law by placing covert investigation, in the form of 'controlled operations', on a statutory footing. And yet, from the outset it is important not to overstate *Ridgeway's* importance. The decision did not shift the entire apparatus of covert investigation; it was part of larger transformation that took place in Australian law enforcement and associated laws between 1975 and 1995. What *Ridgeway* did was trigger the regulation of a system of authorisation for conduct by investigators that would otherwise constitute an unlawful act during the investigation. While it is true that many police powers are unlawful in the absence of lawful authority, the controlled operation functioned explicitly on unlawful activities as the central vehicle of the investigation. In other words, *Ridgeway* transformed a discrete arm of undercover work. Australian investigations law is now characterised by an elaborate web of interconnected legislation, in which the controlled operation is one a several powerful investigation tools. As will be considered in this and subsequent chapters, *Ridgeway* not only stands as the catalyst for legislative reform, but as a testament to an important shift in the *method* of investigation. Those techniques evolved over time, tied to the expansion of surveillance, deception and demands for cost effective outcomes. Controlled operations are linked with the production of knowledge used in the prosecution of suspects, criminal intelligence, and in investigative methods. There is a critical link between controlled operations and knowledge systems, which intersect with and shape legislation. These statutes reflect a knowledge system that is both externally and internally oriented. This chapter is concerned with analysing these structures. As indicated in the introduction, controlled operations in Australia are governed by a confederation of laws that, while not uniform in their wording do have distinct doctrinal and normative principles embedded within. Drawing substantially upon materials published by the author (Murphy (2014, 2015)), this chapter examines those principles, and considers the

B. Murphy, *Regulating Undercover Law Enforcement: The Australian Experience*, https://doi.org/10.1007/978-981-33-6381-6_2

relationship between doctrine, knowledge systems, and the historical contours of late modernity.

Undercover Work

Criminal investigation has two main purposes. The first is the collection of criminal intelligence. The second is the collection of information sufficient to determine whether an offence has been committed, and if so, the identity of a suspect. That information must be of sufficient weight to serve as evidence leading to prosecution. The best kind of evidence is in the form of a confession in words and deeds, directly observed by the investigator. Human experience has shown that in the absence of a confession, the best way to obtain that information is when the suspect is unaware of the presence of the investigator, because the conduct and intention of the suspect can be observed without reservation. Proximity to the suspect frequently enables a picture of true motive and intention. This aspect of investigation, based on intimate surveillance and deception, has ancient origins. Surveillance and deception have been part of the human story from the earliest records, ranging from the "Shibboleth" test found in the Old Testament,[1] to the first exposition on domestic spies in Sun Tzu's *Art of War*.[2] Deception for the purpose of punishment has a long tradition, and rapidly emerged as a problem when the first civilian police began to appear in the 18th and 19th centuries in Europe, both in Napoleonic Paris,[3] and by the "thief takers" in London prior to the Peel reforms in the mid-19th century. Prime Minister of England, William Pitt, was notorious for his use of domestic spies, secret police and agents provocateur in the investigation and suppression of Republican sympathisers (Hilton 2006). As we'll discover, the widespread use of domestic spies, secret police and entrapment quickly results in political unrest, and in the case of England, quickly resulted in demands for reform. It appears that the unscrupulous character of undercover police was a major driver for reforms in England, which gradually placed law enforcement and investigation under legal regulation (Radzinowicz 1956; Rawlings 2002). It is clear, however, that undercover work formed a key part of criminal investigation not only in England, but around the world. In the 20th century it appears that the United States played a major role in the professionalisation of covert policing. Clandestine techniques were used to great effect in uncovering the underground slave rescue network during the Civil War, in border interdiction, and subsequently alcohol prohibition. By the end of the Cold War covert techniques were well established in the US, and subsequently exported as part of international police training out of the US from the 1970s in the "War on Drugs" (Nadelmann

[1] Judges 12:6: "they said, "All right, say 'Shibboleth.'" If he said, "Sibboleth," because he could not pronounce the word correctly, they seized him and killed him at the fords of the Jordan. Forty-two thousand Ephraimites were killed at that time."

[2] Chapter 13 of the *Art of War* is entirely devoted to the use and classification of spies at home and abroad as part of the essential apparatus of sovereign power.

[3] Vidocq (2003)

1990, 1994; Andreas and Nadelmann 2006; Bowling and Sheptycki 2012). It is highly likely that an equivalent development took place in Communist nations during this period, both for domestic and international intelligence and law enforcement.

It has been suggested by at least one author (Donnelly 1951) that the undercover agent became a feature of English law through the medieval practice of *approvement*, a discretionary pardon for capital crimes available at common law to an accused on condition that evidence be provided leading to the apprehension and conviction of accomplices.[4] It appeared very quickly, however, that informants and participation in crime led to the problem of entrapment and incitement to commit a crime. Incitement to commit a crime became an indictable offence at common law,[5] with a further distinction made for the person who enticed another to commit a crime and then informed on them to collect a reward. This person became known as the "agent provocateur". This figure was the subject of derision and suspicion, being associated with the Napoleonic "police state" (notwithstanding the widespread use of them in England). This actor become the subject of Parliamentary enquiry as early as 1833.[6] Subsequent enquiries in 1853,[7] 1929,[8] and again in 1977[9] remained critical of the practice as deeply antithetical to the principles of fairness rooted in the English legal tradition. Indeed, the 1977 English Law Commission inquiry went so far as to recommend an *offence* of entrapment be introduced, although this was never implemented.

Undercover Investigation in Australia

Undercover techniques were used in Australia from an early stage. Deceptive techniques appear in Australian cases from 1826,[10] and are clearly documented in the biographies of 19th-century detectives (Wilson and Finnane 2006). Outside the (limited) use of undercover work in policing, most of the undercover work in Australia

---

[4] Donnelly may have been referring to Blackstones's *Commentaries* (Book IV:5), which described approvement as a "species of confession, which we read much of in our ancient books, of a far more complicated kind, which is called approvement. And that is when a person, indicted of treason or felony, and arraigned for the fame, doth confess the fact before plea pleaded; and appeals or accuses others, his accomplices, of the fame crime, in order to obtain his pardon. In this cafe he is called an approver or prover, probator, and the party appealed or accused is called the appellee. Such approvement can only be in capital offences; and it is, as it were, equivalent to an indictment, since the appellee is equally called upon to answer it: and if he hath no reasonable and legal exceptions to make to the person of the approver, which indeed are very numerous, he must put himself upon his trial, either by battle, or by the country; and, if vanquished or found guilty, must suffer the judgment of the law, and the approver shall have his pardon, ex debito juftitiae. On the other hand, if the appellee be conqueror, or acquitted by the jury, the approver fhall receive judgment to be hanged, upon his own confeffion of the indictment; for the condition of his pardon has failed, viz. the convicting of some other person, and therefore his conviction remains absolute."

[5] There is a good discussion on this in Law Commission (UK) (1973)

[6] House of Commons (1833)

[7] House of Commons (1853)

[8] Secretary of State for the Home Department (UK) (1929)

[9] Law Commission (UK) (1977)

[10] Eg: *R v Cook & Curry* [1826] NSWSupC 70; *R v Finch* (1830) NSW Sel Cases (Dowling) 330

appears to have its genesis in domestic counterintelligence in the 20th century, particularly in the post-war years with the threat of communism. Australia, like many countries in the west, turned to covert surveillance, telecommunications interception, and human covert sources in the investigation of sedition and espionage. By the 1950s, ASIO became heavily involved in domestic counterintelligence, authorised to deploy clandestine methods in the investigation of domestic security threats (Cain 2008; Horner 2014). This activity coincided with the advent of mass telecommunications. In that environment the Commonwealth government introduced legislation prohibiting the unauthorised interception of telephony in 1960, while simultaneously legalising interception by authorised agents.[11] For a long period of time the actual use of that power was largely absent in the public consciousness. That changed in the 1980s, when the Stewart Royal Commission into Telephone Interception (Stewart 1986) began hearing evidence of the use of deception, listening devices and undercover techniques had been a routine part of counter-intelligence operations and criminal investigation since at least the late 1960s. In a number of cases those powers were used without warrant, but rarely prosecuted in Australian courts (Murphy and Anderson 2016). This is not surprising, given that senior officers in State police often served in the army before their appointment to senior leadership roles, tended to form close associations, shared ideas on policing, and were sometimes involved in assisting the Commonwealth in counterintelligence during the period 1920–1945. The Commissioner for Police in NSW, for example, for the period 1962–1972, Norman Allan, was a career police officer who served as the assistant for three Commissioners between 1948 and 1962. He started his career as a telephone technician before joining the police force and was a strong advocate of surveillance (notably telephone interception). He was, in fact, implicated in the unlawful interception of wire taps in 1967, and later dismissed in 1972 after it was discovered he had arranged the falsification of police computer records (Whitton 1993). Commissioner Colin Delaney, Allan's immediate predecessor, is believed to have served with security and intelligence during World War 2 and was also known to endorse the use of undercover policing and telecommunications interception as part of police work. Indeed, he was a known advocate of undercover investigation of homosexuals in the 1950s involving entrapment operations, and instrumental in advocating the passage of homosexual offences in Parliament (Wotherspoon 1993). Most, if not all these laws required surveillance, use of informers and undercover work for their enforcement. There is good evidence to indicate that undercover work has been a major part of Australian law enforcement, particularly in New South Wales, in the post-war years.

The Problem with Undercover Investigation

The central problem with undercover work is that it routinely involves actions by the investigator that would ordinarily be unlawful, either as breach of criminal law, or civil law – particularly tort. It is unlawful to interfere with and intercept

[11] Telephonic Communications (Interception) Act 1960 (Cth)

communications. It is unlawful to enter a person's home and install a listening or surveillance device. It is unlawful to engage in conversations effectively becoming complicit in a conspiracy or incitement to commit an offence. As discussed later, the problems go well beyond the legalities – the operational risks, and the potential consequences when things go wrong make undercover work involving direct contact between investigator and suspect dangerous for all concerned. It is no surprise that the emphasis in these operations is a meticulously planned exercise, which has become known in Australia as a "controlled operation".

By way of recap, a controlled operation is a form of investigation in which a human agent is directly involved in activities that are prima facie unlawful during the investigation. Those activities often involve participation with the suspect in the activities under investigation. This type of investigation is often supplemented with the use of surveillance and listening devices. But the most problematic aspect of a controlled operation is the license for the investigator to participate in crimes *with* the suspect. Prior to the decision of the High Court in *Ridgeway* such activities were not formally regulated. As discussed at length in the opening chapter, *Ridgeway* brought a range of undercover practices to the attention of the High Court, notably the intentional importation of narcotics by police across international borders. Police effectively imported heroin to sell to a suspected heroin dealer and did so with the full knowledge and cooperation of executive government. As a matter of law, the immediate problem was the agreement and intention to commit crimes between executive and international agencies. The problem was not only the absence of legislation; there was a clear line of authorities that prohibited the executive branch of government authorising itself to breach laws.[12] One of the concerns was the Executive acting without the imprimatur of the Legislature. But the operation was otherwise entirely consistent with decades of policing practice and was a demonstrably effective mode of investigation.

Ridgeway was controversial not only because of the result. It set a precedent involving undercover operations, which cast doubt of a raft of other cases. Perhaps more seriously for police, *Ridgeway* confirmed that investigators might now be *criminally or civilly liable* for inciting the commission of an offence, being complicit in the offence, or even through independently committing an offence (such as conspiracy). Parliament was faced with a controversial decision that saw a man heavily implicated in drug importation apparently walk free, the investigators potentially criminally or civilly liable for doing their job, and other cases compromised through the potential exclusion of evidence. This outcome, not surprisingly, was immediately criticised by politicians and the media,[13] and later described as "an obstacle" to law enforcement by the Australian government in its report to the UN Economic and Social Council's Commission on Narcotic Drugs the following year.[14] This result was manifestly unsatisfactory, a fact that was not lost on the High

[12] Eg: *A v Hayden* (1984) 156 CLR 532

[13] Farouque (1995); AAP (1995); Campbell (1995)

[14] United Nations Commission on Narcotic Drugs (1996)

Court, which recommended legislative intervention.[15] This recommendation was the immediate genesis for controlled operations legal architecture in Australia.

Controlled Operations

In its ordinary meaning, "controlled operation" is a composite term, conveying the idea of a process carried out under strict conditions, involving systematic observation, clear terms of execution, and the creation, so far as possible, of a predictable and stable environment. An object is said to be "controlled" when it is *restrained*, or *mobilised under conditions calculated to minimise or preclude error.*[16] An "operation" imports ideas of *purposeful, coordinated* and *pre-planned activity.*[17] Fundamentally, this is a term that in its ordinary meaning is referring to a regulated and coordinated event or process, concerned with precision surveillance, intervention and anticipated variables. In both senses, controlled operation imports the language of industry and medicine, based on precision and control, with the implied application of a risk calculus.

In law, defining an object as "controlled" imports a specific meaning. It is the subject of specific governance, possessing a hybrid character that is lawful in one context, and unlawful in another. A controlled drug, for example, is ordinarily unlawful to possess or trade, unless some exception applies, normally in the form of an official authorisation.[18] Effectively, what functions as a prohibition in one context serves as regulation in another. This concept of "controlled activity" is central to the controlled operation as a concept and is a significant marker for the logic of the exception to be examined in subsequent chapters.

Although the term "controlled operation" is unique to Australian law, similar provisions are found in the UK,[19] Canada,[20] New Zealand[21] and the United States.[22] It is essentially a reference to mechanisms that authorise crimes for the purpose of

[15] *Ridgeway v The Queen* (1995) 184 CLR 19 at 43–44 per Mason CJ, Deane and Dawson JJ and at 54–54 per Brennan J.

[16] See "controlled, adj." OED Online. Oxford University Press. March 2014. Contra. "control, v" Macquarie Dictionary Online. Macmillan. October 2013.

[17] See "operation, n." OED Online. Oxford University Press. March 2014. Contra. "operation, n" Macquarie Dictionary Online. Macmillan. October 2013.

[18] Heroin is a "controlled drug" for the purposes of Part 9.1 of the *Criminal Code* (Cth), but may be imported lawfully when a licence is obtained pursuant to the *Customs (Prohibited Imports) Regulations 1956* (Cth)

[19] *Regulation of Investigative Powers Act 2000* c. 23 (UK); (There are also related powers within the *Police Powers Act 1997* c. 50 (UK). For detailed commentary on covert regulation in the UK see Harfield and Harfield (2008); McKay (2011); Harfield and Harfield (2018)

[20] *Criminal Code* RSC 1985 c C-46, ss 9, 10, 25

[21] Misuse of Drugs Act 1975 (NZ), s34, s34A; Evidence Act 2006 (NZ), s108

[22] 19 USC § 2081

law enforcement. The authorisation negatives the criminalisation that occurs through operation of law. "Controlled operation" must be contrasted with "controlled delivery". Controlled delivery is a technique used in drug investigations, where narcotics are identified, intercepted, and often substituted. The goods are then allowed, under surveillance, to proceed to the intended point of receipt and distribution with a view to identifying and arresting those involved. While all controlled deliveries would now fall under the umbrella of a controlled operation, not all controlled operations involve controlled delivery. Controlled operations may have their origin in controlled delivery, but the scope has extended over time. Controlled delivery was found to be highly effective as a method of drug control in the United States from the mid-1970s (Moore 1977), and was subsequently endorsed and promoted internationally by the United Nations (Cutting 1983), eventually finding life in Article 11 of the *United Nations Convention against Illicit Traffic in Narcotic Drugs and Psychotropic Substances* in 1988.[23]

Exactly when the term "controlled operation" began to be used in Australia is unclear, although it began to appear in legal sources in the early 1990s. In *R v Yooyen* (1991)[24] the court accepted evidence that controlled purchase and delivery had become a feature of Australian policing in the late 1980s, particularly through the auspices of the Australian Federal Police. It is certainly the case that the AFP was deploying controlled operations by at least 1989. In January of that year the AFP were involved in a major international controlled delivery involving 2.4 tons of cannabis from Melbourne to the UK (Browne 2009). This is not surprising, given that the UN Convention had recently been signed. It is also worth noting that during the 1970s and 80s undercover techniques were essentially being professionalised and shared between law enforcement agencies internationally, particularly practice models from the United Stated. There the methods used in undercover investigations were professionalised by the FBI during the Cold War, and subsequently applied in domestic anti-war protest disruption and the "war on drugs", only to be exported through training programs among western police agencies in the 1970s and 80s. That transmission was facilitated through a global network of local liaison offices and the creation of an international legal framework aimed at cross-border cooperation, law enforcement and extradition. In this respect Australia was a key ally of the US. The FBI opened its first liaison office in Canberra in 1985, with the

[23] Article 11 refers to "Controlled Delivery". It provides: "**[1.]** If permitted by the basic principles of their respective domestic legal systems, the Parties shall take the necessary measures, within their possibilities, to allow for the appropriate use of controlled delivery at the international level, on the basis of agreements or arrangements mutually consented to, with a view to identifying persons involved in offences established in accordance with article 3, paragraph 1, and to taking legal action against them. **[2.]** Decisions to use controlled delivery shall be made on a case-by-case basis and may, when necessary, take into consideration financial arrangements and understandings with respect to the exercise of jurisdiction by the Parties concerned. **[3.]** Illicit consignments whose controlled delivery is agreed to may, with the consent of the Parties concerned, be intercepted and allowed to continue with the narcotic drugs or psychotropic substances intact or removed or replaced in whole or in part."

[24] (1991) 51 A Crim R 226

Commonwealth entering into a Mutual Legal Assistance Program in 1987 (Nadelmann 1994).[25]

This kind of investigation, once established as effective in the context of narcotics, was easily adapted to other kinds of crime. In *Nicholas v The Queen* (1998)[26] Kirby J observed that controlled operations were emerging in the 1980s in both national and international legal systems as a power required by police to deal with the problem of narcotics trafficking, but also observed that his kind of investigation model was no longer confined to drug interdiction. It was also recognised by Commissioner Fitzgerald in 1989 (Fitzgerald 1989) as a highly effective technique in the investigation of corruption, a conclusion later echoed during the Wood Royal Commission in the mid-1990s (Wood 1997). It is clear that the techniques involved in drug investigation were easily adapted to any context that were difficult for ordinary investigations to produce results.

Thus although we cannot identify exactly when controlled operations began to be used in Australia, it seems likely they emerged in the late 1970s, proliferating during the 1980s and early 1990s, coinciding with the demands of drug interdiction and corruption investigation during this period. By 2020, the technique was well established. As a technique, it has proven to be demonstrably effective. However, as already discussed, and will be examined further in Chap. 3, the use of deception by police in the investigation of crime and corruption has a lengthy history. The technique preceded the regulation. Attempts to regulate this mode of investigation followed the practice. Deceptive investigation practices have been evident in the English-speaking world for centuries. What changed is the legal architectures designed to regulate them. As we have seen, following the decision in *Ridgeway*, there was a push towards placing controlled operations on a statutory footing. But this was not a rapid development. As discussed in detail below, it was an evolution that took some 20 years to complete. By 2015, the Commonwealth and all Australian states and territories had enacted controlled operations statutes. These statutes authorise an exclusive group of Australian law enforcement agencies to participate in controlled operations, including State and Federal Police, Customs, Anti-corruption Agencies, and Wildlife and Fisheries. (Table 2.1).

These developments were not in isolation. They substantially overlap with a systemic shift towards the general regulation of law enforcement powers, and to put undercover policing on a statutory footing. Consequently, controlled operations law is one part of a much larger legal framework concerned with the expansion of covert law enforcement methodologies, ranging from telecommunications interception, the legalisation of false and assumed identities, surveillance and listening devices.

Confirming the exact number of controlled operations in Australia over time is impossible. Controlled operations, as they are now known, were deployed for some time prior to 1995. One of the major changes in the statutory regulation of them has been the requirement for transparency through reporting obligations. However,

---

[25] See also *Mutual Assistance in Criminal Matters Act 1987* (Cth)

[26] (1998) 193 CLR 173 at [177]

Table 2.1 Australian controlled operations statutes and related agencies

Australian Capital Territory	Commonwealth
Crimes (Controlled Operations) Act 2008 (ACT)	Crimes Act 1914 (Cth), Part 1AB
ACT Police; Seconded State Police; Australian Crime Commission	Australian Federal Police; State Police; Australian Customs (Border Force); Australian Crime Commission; Australian Commission for Law Enforcement Integrity
New South Wales	**Northern Territory**
Law Enforcement (Controlled Operations) Act 1997	Police (Special Investigative and Other Powers) Act 2015 (NT)
NSW Police; Independent Commission Against Corruption; NSW Crime Commission; Australian Federal Police; Australian Crime Commission: Australian Customs	NT Police; Australian Crime Commission; Independent Commission Against Corruption
Queensland	**South Australia**
Police Powers and Responsibilities Act 2000	Criminal Investigation (Covert Operations) Act 2009
QLD Police; Crime and Misconduct Commission; Australian Crime Commission	SA Police; Australian Crime Commission; Independent Commissioner Against Corruption
Tasmania	**Victoria**
Police Powers (Controlled Operations) Act 2006	Crimes (Controlled Operations) Act 2004
TAS Police; Australian Crime Commission	Victoria Police; Independent Broad-based Anti-Corruption Commission; Vic Fisheries
Western Australia	
Criminal Investigation (Covert Powers) Act 2012	
WA Police; Australian Crime Commission; WA Fisheries	

because these were introduced at different rates across the country, and are variable in terms of what is reported, an accurate picture is limited. Unlike the standard reporting requirements for telecommunications interception,[27] there is no uniform reporting system for controlled operations in Australia. This is primarily because telecommunications interception is primarily governed by the Commonwealth, and controlled operations law is across the Federation. Statutory reporting requirements did not commence until 1998 in NSW and staggered throughout other jurisdictions. In some cases, there have been changes in the institutional authorities. The National Crime Authority, and Special Investigations Monitor, for example, were disbanded soon after their formation. The information that is available is in a patchwork of annual and ministerial reports located in a variety of places, notably the annual reports of Ombudsmen or Parliament. This information is variable in detail and

[27] *Telecommunications (Interception and Access) Act 1979* (Cth), Parts 2–7, 2–8

sometimes inconsistent. Reports vary in the period of scrutiny, and the inclusion or exclusion of current or completed operations. In some cases reports were not tabled at all, or presented in compilations.[28] Not only that, the number of warrants issued is no indicator of the number of operations undertaken, because multiple warrants can be issued for the same investigation, including cross-border investigations, that may also involve State and Federal authorities. In addition, the expansion of controlled operations to other agencies, such as Wildlife, Fisheries and specialist commissions, also means a multiplication of reports, not all of which are available. Consequently, the information is difficult to collate and interpret with any precision. This is compounded by the fact that the very term "controlled operation" does not appear in statute until after 1995 and is known as "undercover" and "covert" in other jurisdictions. While all controlled operations may be characterised as an undercover operation, not all undercover operations are a controlled operation. Classifying any investigation as a controlled operation prior to 1995 is at best an approximation. Finally, these investigations are necessarily clandestine. They are generally not matters of public information, with the exception of those rare cases that go wrong and become media spectacles, and the controlled release of information through the various media officers of those agencies. With these limitations in mind, a picture can be mapped out.

Based on the available information, we know that there have been at least 10,000 controlled operations warrants issued in Australia since 1998. Given the general absence of Victorian data, and the patchy information from South Australia and Queensland, a figure in excess of 12,000 is a conservative estimate. Indeed, if Victoria follows a pattern similar to NSW, the figure may exceed 15,000. (Table 2.2).

These figures indicate that controlled operations warrants reached a peak in 2005 (n = 530), stabilising at 400–500 per year. There was a sharp increase in 2013, with a minimum of 700 warrants per annum since 2015. By 2015 the average number per year had increased to 791. As indicated above, we need to be cautious about assuming this as an increase in actual numbers or an increase in reporting. To put that in context, we know that in the same period there have been in excess of 64,000 telecommunications interception warrants issued,[29] a ratio of approximately 6:1. Indeed, this data suggests that telecommunications interception is far more significant as an investigative tool than controlled operations, and that the real area of growth in investigation is the invisible surveillance of communication. However, it is highly likely that many controlled operations also make use of telecommunications and surveillance device warrants, so there is a degree of overlap. To what extent the data is silent. Of the 10,000 warrants issued since 1998, 60% (n = 6160) of those warrants were issued to the New South Wales Police ('NSWP'). The NSWP is by far the largest user of controlled operations warrants. When combined with the Australian Federal police (n = 1354) and the Victorian Police (n = 729), it appears that about

---

[28] Joint Standing Committee on the Corruption and Crime Commission (WA), *Annual reports prepared by the Corruption and Crime Commission on the use of covert powers by WA Police, the Department of Fisheries and the Australian Crime Commission* (2016)

[29] Based on a collation of TI Warrants by the author documented in the Commonwealth Attorney General's *Telecommunication (Interception) Act 1979 Reports* (1998–2018)

Table 2.2 Reported Australian Controlled Operations Authorities 1998–2018

AGENCY	ACC	ACTP	AFP	ICAC	NCC	NSWP	PIC	QCMC	QP	SP	TP	VP	WCC	WAP	TOTAL
1998				2	23	123	11								159
1999				2	23	142	14								181
2000				2	45	144	2								193
2001				1	14	148	0		36						199
2002			35	4	6	206	3		45	39					338
2003	3		60	7	18	206	3		0						297
2004	21		39	7	11	334	9		28						449
2005	9		22	3	25	416	10		31				14		530
2006	15		18	2	12	381	7		0				5		440
2007	10		18	7	12	342	2	0	20	26			11		448
2008	4		62	6	30	345	0	0	0	27			9		483
2009	26		45	6	8	310	1	3	23	27			6		455
2010	24	7	49	2	24	292	1	1	18	40			8		466
2011	20	9	90	0	3	280	4	3	7	32	1		4		453
2012	15	2	142	1	2	279	2	7	7	29	2		2		490
2013	5	1	103	0	3	298	1	3	15	31	0	114		20	594
2014	7	8	128	0	1	330	0	0	10	34	0	100		49	667
2015	13	9	165	0	2	372	2	0	11	46	0	106		47	773
2016	18	6	174	0	0	412	1	1	14	57	0	131		44	858
2017	0	7	110	0	0	412	0	3	14	38	0	141		44	769

(continued)

Table 2.2 (continued)

AGENCY	ACC	ACTP	AFP	ICAC	NCC	NSWP	PIC	QCMC	QP	SP	TP	VP	WCC	WAP	TOTAL
2018	0	7	94	0	2	388	0	0	8	75	0	137		56	767
TOTAL	190	56	1354	52	264	6160	73	21	287	501	3	729	59	260	10,009
Source	NO; CO	AO	NO; CO; ACO	NO	NO	NO	NO	CC	CR	AG; CPSA	TO	SIM; VI	CA	CA	

ACC Australian Crime Commission, *ACTP* ACT Police, *AFP* Australian Federal Police, *ICAC* Independent Commission Against Corruption, *NCC* NSW Crime Commission, *NSWP* NSW Police, *PIC* NSW Police Integrity Commission, *QCMC* Queensland Crime and Misconduct Commission, *QP* Queensland Police, *SP* SA Police, *TP* Tasmanian Police, *VP* Victoria Police, *WAP* West Australian Police. These figures were compiled by the author using the annual reports of the statutory inspection authorities: New South Wales Ombudsman, *Law Enforcement (Controlled Operations) Annual Reports* (1998–2016)('NO'); Commonwealth Ombudsman, *Annual Reports* (2002–2017)('CO'); Australian Federal Police, *Controlled Operations Annual Reports* (2010–2019)('ACO')' ACT Police, *Controlled Operations Reports* (2007–2018)('AO'); Law Enforcement Conduct Commission, *Annual Report* (2017–2018); Queensland Crime and Misconduct Commission, *Reports to Parliament* (2007–2018)('CC'); Queensland Controlled Operations Committee, *Reports* (2001–2019)('CR'); Attorney-General for South Australia, *Report to Parliament* (2002–2012)('AG')(Incomplete); Commissioner of Police (South Australian), *Criminal Investigation (Covert Operations) Annual Report* (2010–2018)('CPSA'); Tasmanian Ombudsman, *Reports* (2010–2012)('TO'); Special Investigations Monitor, *Annual Reports* (2010–2012)('SIM'); Victorian Inspectorate, *Report to Parliament on Controlled Operations* (2014–2018)('VI'); Western Australian Corruption and Crime Commission, *Annual Reports* (2004–2018)('CA'). [As at 5 March 2020]

82% (n = 8243) of warrants are deployed by *three* agencies in Australia. Exactly why that is the case is by no means clear. The absence of data from Victoria, and the patchy character of South Australian and Queensland sources make any conclusion tentative at best – but it does suggest that controlled operations are more heavily used in the south-east of Australia, and does suggest the allocation of resources, operational norms, and expertise clustered in that region.[30] This is not necessarily controversial, given most of the population is located in that part of the continent, as are the major international importation routes, and certainly where the largest markets for organised crime are located.

The exact behaviours involved in a controlled operation are difficult to ascertain from the reports. Details as to operations are necessarily classified, although statistical and descriptive information is contained in some of the reports. Overall, it appears[31] that more than 75% of warrants issued are concerned with drug offences. The remainder generally concern property, firearms, homicide, and corruption. Given the connection between these types of offences it is reasonable to conclude that most controlled operations warrants are issued for the investigation of drug or drug-related crime. These reports also indicate that in the vast majority of cases a controlled operation involves a small team of police working in conjunction with a single informant, but can involve very large operations involving hundreds of personnel.[32] Controlled operations typically involve conversations with the suspect negotiating criminal conduct, entry to premises and land, seizing or interfering with property, purchasing and possessing controlled objects (such as drugs or firearms), and manufacturing and using fake identities. It is undoubtedly the case that these types of investigations *also* involve routine use of telecommunications interception and surveillance device warrants.

The most recent high-profile controlled operation in Australia involved the investigation of the death of Daniel Morcombe in Queensland in 2013. As a result of the investigation Brett Cowan was arrested and subsequently convicted of Morcombe's murder. The operational details have never been published, but media reporting of the trial indicated that undercover police manufactured a series of false identities and a fictitious crime syndicate to earn the trust of Cowan, offered him money and status for confessing to involvement in serious crimes, and eventually led police to the location of the skeletal remains of the victim. This ruse allegedly involved undercover police being involved in the consumption of drugs and soliciting prostitutes.[33] Although never identified as such, this was undoubtedly a controlled

---

[30] This information was published and commented on by the author in Murphy (2014)

[31] The following segment is based on the NSW Ombudsman's *Law Enforcement (Controlled Operations) Act Annual Reports* (1999–2012), and the *Review of the Law Enforcement (Controlled Operations) Act 1997* prepared by the Police Integrity Commission in 1999 (The "Finlay Review"). The following part presents a synthesis of this material.

[32] Eg: in 2008 an operation concerned with drug investigation authorised 240 police officers to engage in "conversations and negotiations concerning supply, purchase and possession of prohibited drugs". See warrant 2008/271PS, NSW Ombudsman, *Law Enforcement (Controlled Operations) Act 1997 Annual Report 2007–2008*, 26.

[33] Kyriacou et al. (2014)

operation, which also deployed a sophisticated undercover method known as the "Mr Big" technique.[34] Such was the outrage in the community about the death and apparent sexual assault of a school boy in a relatively quiet part of the Sunshine Coast that there was never any real concern about the technique or method used in the investigation. A legal challenge to the admissibility of evidence was dismissed.[35]

The Evolution of Controlled Operations Law 1995–2015

Although there was immediate pressure to introduce controlled operations law, the current structure did not happen overnight. It took 20 years to evolve, passing through three distinct phases. The first phase (1995–1996) was a crisis response to *Ridgeway,* confined to South Australia and the Commonwealth. The second phase (1997–2003) was a period characterised by adjustment and expansion, with an increasing sophistication in the form of law as controlled operations law began to crystallise, with New South Wales and Queensland introducing their own models during this period. It was a period that coincided with the terrorist attacks in the United States on September 11, 2001, with the result that the foundation laws linked to surveillance, telecommunications and controlled operations suddenly took on new meaning with the added concern for the investigation of domestic and international terrorism and organised crime. This was a period marked by operational expansion of controlled operations law, and the blurring of boundaries between law enforcement and domestic counter-intelligence. It was a period that culminated in recommendations for a *Model Law* in 2003, involving not only controlled operations, but also assumed identities, telecommunications, and surveillance device reform. The final phase (2004–2015) is characterised by the steady consolidation and expansion of controlled operations law across Australia, involving the incorporation and adoption of provisions from the Model Law, notably the cross-border framework.

Pre-Ridgeway Regulation

Prior to 1996 controlled operations were largely unregulated. At this stage regulation consisted mainly of a residual framework consisting of a limited range of statutes, tort, and the internal governance structures of the agencies involved. At this stage police and investigators were basically regarded as "citizens in uniform". They possessed the same powers as ordinary citizens, except where specifically empowered or limited by law. The regulation of investigations and interagency cooperation was primarily a matter of agreement between agencies, and the internal governance structures of those agencies. Cases of impropriety were largely a matter

[34] Discussed further in Chap. 3.

[35] *R Cowan; Ex parte Attorney General (Qld)* [2016] 1 Qd R 433

of internal discipline, with the occasional tort action by citizens aggrieved by the excesses of police power. Where police were involved in technically unlawful conduct during the investigation, reliance was placed upon the discretion of prosecutors not to file charges as a bona fide activity. It seems very likely that cases involving civil action against the state were never recorded as cases, as instances of clear liability would likely have been settled.

As observed by Alderson (2001), this "permissive model" began to change in the 1970s, when an increasing number of cases began to appear in Australian courts principally concerned with the abuse of police powers, improper investigation tactics and admissibility of evidence. The public mood shifted, as did the courts', with a growing concern about the absence of accountability and the potential for the abuse of power. By 1975 the Australian Law Reform Commission made recommendations for the extensive regulation of police powers,[36] later echoed by Royal Commissions that not only confirmed the existence of systematic abuses, but also corruption within the police force, especially concerned with collection of evidence, the use and extent of surveillance, and entrapment. These cases clearly indicate that *Ridgeway* was not the only case of its kind. It was, in fact, one of a succession of cases where improper law enforcement conduct had come before the courts over many years.[37] Ironically, the success of the Royal Commissions was largely facilitated by the same undercover tactics. The Wood Royal Commission into Police Corruption was decisive because of its use of undercover tactics. Of note in that inquiry was not only the utility of undercover techniques and their deployment against police officers, but also the major insights into the nature of corruption among law enforcement. What was revealed was a division between corrupt behaviours: between those interested in profit, and those interested in breaking rules to enforce the law. The findings indicated instances where the integrity of law enforcement was under siege in two directions: from those engaged in crime for personal gain, and those prepared to break the law in order to achieve results in the public interest. These claims of "justifiable" wrongdoing were based on the express purpose of securing convictions against suspects seen as impervious to ordinary methods of investigation.[38] In other words, investigators would sometimes deviate from

[36] Australian Law Reform Commission (ALRC) (1975)

[37] Commonwealth of Australia et al. (1983); Stewart (1986); Wood (1997) Cases include *R v Hsing* (1991) 25 NSWLR 685; *R v Thompson and Thompson* (1992) 58 A Crim R 451; *R v Steffan* (1993) 30 NSWLR 633; *R v Coward* (1985) 16 A Crim R 257; *Hunt v. Wark* (1985) 40 SASR 489; *R v Vuckov and Romeo* (1986) 40 SASR 498; *R v Romeo* (1987) 45 SASR 212; *R v Papoulias* (1987) 31 A Crim R 322; *R v Venn-Brown* (1991) 1 Qd R 458; *R v Weston and Lee*, unreported, Supreme Court of Tasmania, Crawford J, 11 July 1991; *R v Sloane* (1990) 49 A Crim R 270; *R v D'Arrigo* (1991) 58 A Crim R 71

[38] Justice Wood described a range of "noble cause" activities (without endorsing the practices): "This is the kind of corruption whereby unnecessary physical force is applied, police powers are abused, evidence is fabricated or tampered with, or confessions are obtained by improper means. It is often directed at those members of the community who are least likely or least able to complain, and is justified by police on the basis of procuring the conviction of persons suspected of criminal or anti-social conduct, or in order to exercise control over sections of the community." See Wood (1997)

the law to secure a conviction. The undoubted effectiveness of these techniques, coinciding with the realities of hard-case investigations and the corrupting effect on ordinary police, resulted in the Royal Commissions advocating *in favour* of covert investigation, but also calling for statutory regulation.

These domestic developments took place in the context of a global shift from *reactive* to *proactive* policing, as part of in a deeper cultural shift towards increasingly powerful systems of surveillance. This will be considered in more detail in the next chapter. Consequently, while controlled operations law is undoubtedly the reaction by government to the decision in *Ridgeway*, it must also be understood as taking place within a polyphony of voices calling for the regulation of policing powers, statutory frameworks facilitating the controlled operation as an investigative apparatus, located in a larger historical and cultural shift. *Ridgeway* must be understood as being only one of several triggers in the move to controlled operations regulation.

Reaction to Ridgeway: 1995–1996

The "crisis response" to *Ridgeway* predictably involved those jurisdictions immediately affected by the decision. South Australia introduced the first specific controlled operations law, less than two months after *Ridgeway*. The *Criminal Law (Undercover Operations) Act 1995* (SA), was a simple Act consisting of six sections, permitting a senior officer to authorise an undercover operation if satisfied on reasonable grounds that the suspect was, or was about to engage in 'serious criminal behaviour'. Those behaviours were defined, and included not only drug offences, but also prostitution and offences under gaming and fishery statutes. No provisions were made regarding evidence, but the declaration of authorisation meant that the operation was lawful, and consequently the threshold risk of exclusion of evidence was corrected. There were no serious challenges to the constitutional validity of the Act, beyond an appeal launched by Ridgeway in his subsequent prosecution,[39] and the Act remained largely unaltered until its repeal and replacement in 2009.[40] This Act was the simplest controlled operations Act operating in Australia, was clearly rushed, and contained virtually no scrutiny or accountability mechanisms outside of the requirement for authorisation and reliance on judicial examination on matters coming before the courts.

The Commonwealth also introduced legislation soon after *Ridgeway*. The passage of this legislation was far more controversial, complicated by a Federal election that delayed the introduction of the Act. The *Crimes Amendment (Controlled Operations) Bill 1995* (Cth) was initially introduced into the House of Representatives on 29 June 1995 by then Labour minister for justice, the Hon. Duncan Kerr. On the

[39] *R v Ridgeway* (1998) 72 SASR 73

[40] *Criminal Investigation (Covert Operations) Act 2009* (SA), Sched 1, Pt 2

eve of a Federal election, the bill was referred to the Legal, Constitutional and Legislative Affairs Committee for scrutiny, but lapsed when Parliament was prorogued in January 1996. The Act was subsequently reintroduced, passed by both Houses with amendments in May 1996, and received Royal assent in June. This Act amended Part 1AB of the *Crimes Act 1914* (Cth) and was at that stage confined to "serious drug offences". It was not a general investigative power. Over time, however, the scope of Federal controlled operations law would expand well beyond its initial mandate. Part 1AB remains the relevant Commonwealth law, but like most controlled operations legislation, has been the subject of various amendments since then.

Expansion and Experimentation: 1997–2003

Unlike the crisis response that took place in South Australia and the Commonwealth, New South Wales introduced a more considered and detailed Act in 1997. As outlined above, this was partly due to the concurrent Wood Royal Commission, and also recent efforts to strongly regulate police powers. In 1997 the NSW Government introduced the *Law Enforcement (Controlled Operations) Act*, a comprehensive controlled operations framework. This Act consisted of 33 sections, extending the scope of the investigation to any form of criminal or corrupt conduct. This model extended a general investigative power, undoubtedly influenced by the success and recommendations of the Wood Royal Commission into police corruption.[41] The success of that Commission was largely achieved through a variety of covert and undercover investigative methodologies that allowed the Commission, and the public at large, to witness first-hand a range of corrupt transactions by police. The utility of this methodology was clear. Not only was covert investigation an effective method for investigating crime; it was equally effective at investigating the executive. The New South Wales model offered a comprehensive and carefully designed legal architecture mindful of the needs of police, but also concerned with accountability and the abuse of power.

With a legal framework in operation, a process of monitoring and review soon followed. The reviews that did take place not only confirmed the success of the law in achieving their respective goals of regulation, they also indicated the powers were *not* being abused by those authorities empowered to use them, and should be expanded. In NSW the *Finlay Review* recommended a series of administrative alterations to consolidate the operational and bureaucratic dimensions of controlled operations, including an extension in the lifespan of the warrants, mechanisms to enable Federal collaboration with State police, and the capacity for urgent authorisations (Finlay 1999). Similarly, the utility of controlled operations was part of the considerations at the Commonwealth level. Following a review by the *Commonwealth Joint Committee into the National Crime Authority* in 1999, recommendations were

[41] Wood (1997)

made in the *Street Legal Report*[42] that extended the scope of controlled operations to include a broader array of offences amenable to investigation under the Act. Significant reforms were consequently introduced in 2001 in the form of the *Measures to Combat Serious and Organised Crime Act 2001* (Cth). These amendments expanded the scope of Commonwealth investigations beyond drug investigations to a broad range of offences specifically linked to Constitutional heads of power.[43]

In Queensland, the then recently elected Beattie Labour government introduced a series of significant policing reforms, including the *Police Powers and Responsibilities Act* (2000). Queensland, at that time, had emerged from national scandals involving police and political corruption, in the wake of the Fitzgerald Inquiry that had made sweeping recommendations for police reform and regulation (Fitzgerald 1989). In May 2000 further provisions were introduced to implement a controlled operations framework.[44] Like its NSW counterpart, this amendment contained a broad statutory framework directed to the authorisation, accountability, and immunities of police in engaging in controlled operations. Like NSW, the context of this enactment was a recent history of public enquiries into police and political corruption. Unlike the NSW Act, which retained an internal authorisation mechanism,[45] the QLD Act contained an external authorisation process.[46] It is undoubtedly the case that the reason for a wholly external authority was concern about the potential for abuse by investigators in the wake of the Fitzgerald Inquiry. Unlike NSW, the QLD Act was directed towards the investigation of serious indictable offences carrying a prison term of seven years or more.[47] However, the Act also contained provisions that effectively permitted, without authorisation, controlled operations for minor matters that would otherwise not be able to be investigated through ordinary policing measures.[48]

In the wake of the terrorist attacks on the US in September 2001, the Council of Australian Governments met in April 2002. The agenda included growing anxiety about the capacity of state and Federal police to investigate and prosecute organised and cross-border crimes, in addition to the capacity to respond to international and domestic terrorist threats. The consequent referral to the Standing Committee of Attorneys General and Police Ministers saw the formation of a Joint Working Group that published a *Report on Cross-Border Investigative Powers for Police* in 2003.[49] This report recommended a national framework for covert and cross-border law enforcement incorporating model laws for assumed identities, witness protection,

---

[42] Parliamentary Joint Committee on the National Crime Authority (1999)

[43] *Commonwealth Constitution 1900*, s51

[44] *Police Powers and Responsibilities and Other Acts Amendment Act 2000* (Qld)

[45] *Law Enforcement (Controlled Operations) Act 1997* (NSW), s5

[46] *Police Powers and Responsibilities and Other Acts Amendment Act 2000* (Qld), s8 [s174]

[47] *Police Powers and Responsibilities and Other Acts Amendment Act 2000* (Qld), s8 [s163]

[48] Eg: *Police Powers and Responsibilities and Other Acts Amendment Act 2000* (Qld), s222 (formerly s164)

[49] Standing Committee of Attorneys-General and Australasian Police Ministers Council Joint Working Group on National Investigation Powers (2003)

surveillance devices and controlled operations. These model laws were intended to be adopted nationally, drawing upon public consultation and review of the present Australian legal architecture. Ironically, those states that had existing controlled operations laws did not repeal existing laws in favour of the *Model Law*, rather, there was adaptation of select provisions, mainly concerned with mutual recognition and cross border cooperation. Consequently, the Model Law resulted in the incorporation of some recommendations among those states that had pre-existing controlled operations law but was successful in offering a model for endorsement and adoption by the remaining states and territories. One of the results of this development was that Australian controlled operations law embarked on a path that is relatively diverse, despite the attempt at a uniform model, although, as I have observed elsewhere (Murphy 2014), these laws are relatively consistent in terms of unifying general principles.

It was during this period that the only serious challenge to controlled operations law appeared in the High Court in *Nicholas v The Queen* in 1998,[50] an unusual case that saw the High Court uplift an appeal against a stay order out of the County Court of Victoria into the High Court to consider the constitutional validity of the Commonwealth Act.[51] The gist of the argument, inter alia, was that the statutory declaration that made controlled operations evidence admissible was a usurpation of judicial power protected by Chapter III of the Commonwealth Constitution. The High Court held that the stay order in that case was wrongly applied, and that controlled operations laws – at least as they applied to the declaration of legality – was not an interference with judicial power. Indeed, McHugh J suggested that "[n]o constitutional reason exists to prevent the Parliament from altering the common law rules of evidence or the rules of practice and procedure enshrined in Rules of Court."[52] In other words, Parliament could not usurp the exercise of judicial reasoning, but could restructure the laws that regulated the exercise of reason.

Consolidation and Co-Operation (2003–2015)

Following the 2003 Leaders' Summit, controlled operations law has consolidated and gradually expanded into a national framework based upon a broad set of governing principles, characterised by a mechanism that authorises unlawful conduct in the course of covert investigations, with a broad-based capacity for cooperation between agencies within and between state borders. Legislation was introduced in Victoria in 2004, followed by Tasmania in 2006, the ACT in 2008, Western Australia in 2012,[53] and most recently in the Northern Territory in 2015.[54] In this same period

[50] (1998) 193 CLR 173

[51] A power available through s40(1) of the *Judiciary Act 1903* (Cth)

[52] (1998) 193 CLR 173 at [123]. For commentary on this case and this point, see Hanks et al. (2012)

[53] *Crimes (Controlled Operations) Act 2004* (Vic); *Police Powers (Controlled Operations) Act 2006* (Tas); *Crimes (Controlled Operations) Act 2008* (ACT); *Criminal Investigation (Covert Powers) Act 2012* (WA).

[54] *Police (Special Investigative and Other Powers) Act 2015* (NT)

South Australia replaced its law with a more detailed framework in 2009,[55] while the Commonwealth, NSW and QLD have continued to introduce amendments to fine-tune the existing framework, particularly with its relationship with other covert investigative statutes and for cross-border policing.[56] The consequence of this period of consolidation is the existence of a national framework that facilitates and recognises the investigative activities of an array of police agencies capable of cross-border cooperation and mutual recognition.

One of the important extensions of controlled operations law in the later part of this period has been the inclusion of additional agencies empowered to use controlled operations. This includes the Australian Border Force, several Crime Commissions, as well as Fisheries and Wildlife. These developments mean that controlled operations are now available for the investigation of crime and corruption, immigration, fishing and wildlife trafficking. These developments must also be understood as being situated in a large regulatory context concerned with a range of covert regulations that overlap and supplement each other. Not every undercover investigation will involve a controlled operation. Indeed, as discussed in Chap. 4, most undercover operations will not involve physical contact between the investigator and the suspect until arrest. Most investigations are undertaken using ordinary police work, surveillance, and telecommunications intercepts – not controlled operations. But when they are mobilised, the controlled operations draw on a range of well-known principles of regulation, such as the warrant, as well as a number provisions that are unique to the controlled operation.

Principles of Controlled Operations Law

Australia does not have a uniform set of criminal laws, either as substantive offences, or in criminal procedure. This is on account of its colonial history and Federal structure. Law enforcement and criminal punishment are largely within the purview of the States, although the Commonwealth has taken on an increasingly important role over the last 40 years. Because of this there is considerable diversity in Australian criminal law, and that includes areas of criminal investigation – something that has been the cause of some difficulty in the context of cross border investigation. However, while controlled operations law is characterised by a degree of diversity, the framework does contain a set of recognisable governing doctrinal and normative principles.

---

[55] *Criminal Investigation (Covert Powers) Act 2009* (SA).

[56] *Crimes Legislation Amendment (Serious and Organised Crime) Act 2010* (Cth); *Law Enforcement (Controlled Operations) Amendment Act 2006* (NSW); *Cross Border Police Legislation Amendment Act 2005* (Qld).

Authorisation

All controlled operations require authorisation, expressed in the form of a warrant. In this respect the mechanism is much the same as other forms of State investigation. Authorisation is primarily an administrative process, involving a formal written application by an officer (often the head of a team), of a specific agency empowered to use controlled operations as a part of an investigation, to a senior officer within the organisation or their delegate. In ordinary cases that application must be in writing and contain sufficient information that enables the authorising officer to approve the warrant. Authorisation is usually vested in a senior officer at the apex of the organisation, although in some cases authorisation is vested in a body outside the agency. In Queensland, for example, controlled operations are authorised by an independent *Controlled Operations Committee*,[57] while there is capacity in the case of Commonwealth warrants for senior members of the AAT to authorise variation warrants in some cases.[58] There is a requirement for this officer to exercise independent judgement, and to make an informed decision based upon the particulars and a sufficient degree of evidence to be satisfied that there are grounds for the issue of a warrant. Authorisations are time limited, with a maximum lifespan determined by the jurisdiction. In some cases this is three months,[59] in other cases six months.[60] Urgent warrants are limited to seven days in most cases,[61] but to 72 hours in NSW.[62] In all jurisdictions a warrant may be varied.[63] It seems that in most instances the basis for variation is an extension of time. There needs to be *reasonable grounds* justifying the warrant.[64]

---

[57] *Police Powers and Responsibilities Act 2000* (Qld), s240

[58] *Crimes Act 1914* (Cth), s15GU

[59] *Crimes Act 1914* (Cth), s15GK(1)(h); *Crimes (Controlled Operations) Act 2008* (ACT), s11(3)(h)(i); *Police Powers and Responsibilities Act 2000* (Qld), ss247–255; *Criminal Investigation (Covert Operations) Act 2009* (SA), s4(4)(c)(iv); *Police Powers (Controlled Operations) Act 2006* (Tas), s11(3)(i); *Crimes (Controlled Operations) Act 2004* (Vic) s19.

[60] *Law Enforcement (Controlled Operations) Act 1997* (NSW), s8(2)(g); *Police (Special Investigative and Other Powers) Act 2015* (NT), s12(3)(i); *Police Powers and Responsibilities Act 2000* (Qld), s245(3)(j); *Criminal Investigation (Covert Powers) Act 2012* (WA), s15(6)(j).

[61] *Crimes Act 1914* (Cth), s15GK(1)(h); *Crimes (Controlled Operations) Act 2008* (ACT), ss13–14; *Police (Special Investigative and Other Powers) Act 2015* (NT), s14; *Police Powers and Responsibilities Act 2000* (Qld), s245(3)(j); *Police Powers (Controlled Operations) Act 2006* (Tas), s11(3)(i); *Crimes (Controlled Operations) Act 2004* (Vic) s19; *Criminal Investigation (Covert Powers) Act 2012* (WA), s15(6)(j).

[62] *Law Enforcement (Controlled Operations) Act 1997* (NSW), s8(2)(f)

[63] *Crimes Act 1914* (Cth), s15GO; *Crimes (Controlled Operations) Act 2008* (ACT), s10(2); *Law Enforcement (Controlled Operations) Act 1997* (NSW), ss10–11; *Police (Special Investigative and Other Powers) Act 2015* (NT), s11(2); *Police Powers and Responsibilities Act 2000* (Qld), s244(1); *Criminal Investigation (Covert Operations) Act 2009* (SA), s4(5); *Police Powers (Controlled Operations) Act 2006* (Tas), ss13–15; *Crimes (Controlled Operations) Act 2004* (Vic) ss20–25; *Criminal Investigation (Covert Powers) Act 2012* (WA), ss17–18

[64] The term used varies between jurisdictions, but this expression captures the essence of the test. *Crimes Act 1914* (Cth), s15GI(2); *Crimes (Controlled Operations) Act 2008* (ACT), s10(2); *Law Enforcement (Controlled Operations) Act 1997* (NSW), s6(3)(a); *Police (Special Investigative and*

Essentially, the authorisation mechanism is an evidence-based decision that imports a requirement for more than a hunch or mere suspicion; rather, there is a requirement for the production of *some* evidence on the part of the applicant.[65] This is a decision that is partly based on the available evidence (or intelligence), and partly based on a consideration of a number of factors stated in the relevant legislation. Although the process of application appears fairly simple, the decision involves a consideration of numerous matters that may be understood in positive, negative and operational terms as follows:

<table>
<tr><th>Positive Considerations</th><th>Negative Considerations</th></tr>
<tr><td>• There a reasonable grounds to suspect criminal or corrupt conduct has, is or will take place
• The conduct falls within the jurisdiction of the agency
• The nature of the conduct being investigated requires controlled conduct
• The proposed controlled conduct is appropriate to the conduct being investigated
• Sufficient accountability measures are in place
• The information justifying the warrant is reliable</td><td>• The operation involves minimal risk that any controlled goods will be lost during the operation
• The operation does not involve inducing or encouraging another person(s) engaging in activity they would not reasonably be expected to engage in unless presented with the opportunity
The operation will not:
• seriously endanger the health or safety of any person
• cause the death or serious injury of any person
• involve the commission of a sexual offence
• result in the unlawful loss or serious damage to property</td></tr>
<tr><th colspan="2">Operational Considerations</th></tr>
<tr><td colspan="2">• The operation is more likely to result in success than ordinary methods
• The duration of the operation
• The number of participants
• Whether or not the operation will involve participants in more than one jurisdiction
• Whether the operation will involve collaboration with other agencies
• The participants have the necessary skills and training for the operation
• Civilian participants are only to be used where it is not practicable for a law enforcement participant to be involved</td></tr>
</table>

Authorisation is normally prospective, although in some jurisdictions there is capacity for retrospective authority.[66] Despite the capacity for retrospectivity in some jurisdictions, the evidence from scrutineers is that applications for retrospective authorities are rare, and closely monitored.

Other Powers) Act 2015 (NT), s11(2); *Police Powers and Responsibilities Act 2000* (Qld), s244(1); *Criminal Investigation (Covert Operations) Act 2009* (SA), s4(2); *Police Powers (Controlled Operations) Act 2006* (Tas), s10(2); *Crimes (Controlled Operations) Act 2004* (Vic) ss14–17; *Criminal Investigation (Covert Powers) Act 2012* (WA), s12(1).

[65] Judicial consideration of what constitutes "reasonable suspicion" or "reasonable grounds" is not particularly well developed. There are no significant authorities on point where controlled operations are concerned. The leading authorities on the term include *R v Chan* (1992) 28 NSWLR 421; *R v Rondo* (2001) 126 A Crim R 542 and *George v Rockett* (1990) 190 CLR 104

[66] *Law Enforcement (Controlled Operations) Act 1997* (NSW), s14; *Police (Special Investigative and Other Powers) Act 2015* (NT), s19; *Criminal Investigation (Covert Powers) Act 2012* (WA), s25

As discussed above, the authorising officer is also required to consider a range of specific limiting criteria, which includes whether the operation may involve serious risk of danger to health and safety, result in the loss or damage of property, the commission of a sexual offence, and whether or not the participants in the operation possess sufficient skills (including the involvement of civilians). An important point of divergence in the law in the respect is the extent of the prohibition. In some cases, the authorising officer *must not* issue the warrant[67]; while in other jurisdictions the officer *may not*.[68] In other words in some cases the prohibition is mandatory, while in other cases discretionary.

Purposeful Controlled Activity

Authorisation is ostensibly concerned with ensuring accountability on the part of the investigator at first instance to the organisation. The authorisation is permission for the operation to engage in what would otherwise be 'controlled conduct', which is unlawful activity. This is a defining feature of controlled operations legislation in all jurisdictions. These are activities cast in broad terms that would ordinarily be categorised as unlawful in the absence of a controlled operations warrant. It is important, however, not to overstate this aspect of the warrant. Many police powers effectively involve either statutory or judicial immunity for actions that would otherwise constitute a crime or a tort. These activities are directed towards a specific purpose, ordinarily the investigation of a suspected offence, and the accumulation of evidence sufficient to arrest and prosecute the suspect. It is clear, however, that the collection of evidence and subsequent prosecution are not the only functions. The extent to which this is recognised within the legislation varies. Section 3 of the NSW Act, for example, contains a broad definition of controlled operations that not only includes collecting evidence – it includes providing opportunities for arrest, disrupting and frustrating criminal activity, and providing the opportunity to engage in other conduct reasonably necessary for these ends. In addition to these statutory functions, the investigations literature also recognises that a large aspect of undercover investigations is the collection of criminal intelligence. Indeed, it may be that domestic intelligence collection is the primary purpose of a controlled operation. This aspect of the investigation is consistent with observations made by Stelfox and others that undercover work routinely produces far more information than is required for individual prosecution ((Stelfox 2009; Association of Chief Police Officers (ACPO) 2005; Bryant 2009; Miller 1987). This is because all evidence used in prosecution is a form of information, and accordingly the purpose of

---

[67] *Crimes Act 1914* (Cth), s15GI(2); *Law Enforcement (Controlled Operations) Act 1997* (NSW), s7; *Police (Special Investigative and Other Powers) Act 2015* (NT), s11; *Criminal Investigation (Covert Powers) Act 2012* (WA), s12

[68] *Crimes (Controlled Operations) Act 2008* (ACT), s10(2); *Police Powers and Responsibilities Act 2000* (Qld), s244(1)(g); *Criminal Investigation (Covert Operations) Act 2009* (SA), s4(2); *Police Powers (Controlled Operations) Act 2006* (Tas), s10(2)(g); *Crimes (Controlled Operations) Act 2004* (Vic), s14

controlled activities cannot be understood simply in terms of the collection of "evidence". The primary purpose is to immerse the operative within a criminogenic ecology in order to collect information that has multiple purposes: the prosecution of an individual, the mapping of networks, obtaining information, being exposed to opportunities for investigation, arrest, and other police ends. These aspects of investigations will be considered in more detail in the following chapters.

Admissibility of Evidence

Ridgeway confirmed the judicial discretion to exclude or limit unlawfully obtained evidence on the grounds of public policy. This was not a radical departure from common law. If anything, *Ridgeway* was the marginal expansion of settled doctrine.[69] However, *Ridgeway* was clear precedent that evidence obtained using undercover policing methodologies was now at serious risk of exclusion or limitation, even though such investigations were genuine and in the public interest. The result was that all subsequent controlled operations legislation contains a provision addressing the question of the admissibility of evidence. These provisions are carefully worded, because the discretion to admit or exclude evidence is a judicial power. As demonstrated in *Nicholas v The Queen*, attempts to direct discretion invite a constitutional challenge to the validity of the legislation and would very likely be rejected by the judiciary is an impermissible usurpation of judicial power otherwise protected by Chapter III of the Commonwealth Constitution. These clauses provide that evidence is not to be excluded merely because it was obtained in the course of the controlled operation that involved controlled activity. Evidence may still, of course, be rejected or limited under the usual rules of evidence. Evidence may still be rejected because it has been improperly obtained,[70] or is unfairly prejudicial to the accused,[71] or through some other infraction of the rules of evidence. But the mere fact the investigation is not grounds to rule the evidence inadmissible in the absence of some departure from the scope of the investigation. The authorisation to engage in unlawful activity means that such actions are technically lawful.

Limitation on Activity

Controlled operations do not provide an open-ended licence to engage in *any* form of unlawful conduct. Controlled operations are limited in scope. In theory, such operations may not be authorised where they are likely to involve serious violence,

[69] *R v Ireland* (1970) 126 CLR 321; *Bunning v Cross* (1978) 141 CLR 54

[70] Improperly obtained evidence is not necessarily unlawfully obtained. See *Ridgeway v The Queen* (1995) 184 CLR 19 at 36–37; *Employment Advocate v Williamson* (2001) 111 FCR 20 at 43–45; *Robinson v Woolworths* (2005) 64 NSWLR 612 at 617–626; See also Uniform Evidence Act 1995, s138. For commentary see Anderson (2016)

[71] *R v Le* (2002) 130 A Crim R 44; *Driscoll v The Queen* (1977) 137 CLR 517

sex offences or significant loss of property. These 'negative' considerations are discussed above. These provisions do, however, appear to permit a degree of violence and loss of property, but are governed by a concern for public safety and the political consequences of authorised unlawful behaviour. This undoubtedly recognises the reality that all undercover investigations involve some risk, simply by virtue of the investigation of the kinds of crimes they do. In addition, controlled operations law prohibits entrapment, something that ties to a normative principle that will be discussed in more detail below. In some cases, the authorising officer is also required to consider the expertise of the nominated officers involved in the operation. This can involve not only consideration of whether the officer has the skills and experience necessary for the kind of operation contemplated in the warrant application, but also a consideration of the role of any civilian participants. These are matters that can affect the power of the authorising officer to lawfully issue the warrant.

One of the important operational controls over the conduct of a controlled operation is the existence of a mandated *Code of Conduct*. This is not, however, a uniform requirement in all jurisdictions. Indeed, only in NSW is a Code of Conduct legislated.[72] As can be seen in the following extract, the Code of Conduct imposes a range of specific duties on all participants in the operation.

Immunities

A key element of controlled operations law is the extension of statutory immunities from criminal, and often civil liability. The existence of immunities appears at one level troubling, but the immunity cannot be understood as unimpeachable. Indeed, the immunities are properly understood as potentialities. They are conditional upon the validity of the warrant and the conduct of the investigator. In both cases questions may be raised. A warrant may be invalidly issued, but this does not necessarily compromise the immunities otherwise extended to the investigator. Conversely, a warrant may be validly issued but the conduct of the investigator(s) so improper that the investigation falls outside the scope of the warrant, and consequently the immunity is lost. In principle, immunities are one of the fundamental doctrinal principles of controlled operations law. At the time of writing, to the author's knowledge, there are no publicly reported instances of an officer, or the state, being sued for an unlawful or improper controlled operation.

[72] *Law Enforcement (Controlled Operations) Act 1997* (NSW), s20; Law Enforcement (Controlled Operations) Regulation 2017 (NSW), Clause 10, Schedule 2

Controlled Operations Code of Conduct (NSW)

1. **Applicants for authorities to act in good faith**

   1. In making an application for an authority, or for a variation of an authority, the applicant must at all times act in good faith.
   2. In particular, the applicant must ensure that the application:

      (a) discloses all information of which the applicant is aware as to the circumstances giving rise to the application, especially those that could affect the way in which the application will be determined, and

      (b) does not contain anything that is incorrect or misleading in a material particular.

   3. If the applicant subsequently becomes aware of information that, had it been known to the chief executive officer when the application was determined, could have affected the way in which the application would have been determined, the applicant must ensure that the information is given to the chief executive officer as soon as practicable.

2. **Disclosure of changed circumstances**

If the principal law enforcement officer for an authorised operation becomes aware of circumstances that are likely to require a variation of the authority for the operation, the officer must ensure that:

(a) information as to those circumstances is given to the chief executive officer as soon as practicable, and

(b) a written application for such a variation is made to the chief executive officer before it becomes impracticable to do so.

3. **Participants to be properly briefed**

Before conducting an authorised operation, the principal law enforcement officer for the operation:

(a) must ensure that each law enforcement participant and each civilian participant:

   (i) has a thorough understanding of the nature and extent of any controlled activities in which the participant may be directed to engage for the purposes of the operation, and

   (ii) is made aware of the terms of the authority to the extent to which it authorises the participant to engage in those activities, and

(b) must ensure that each civilian participant undertakes not to engage in any controlled activities other than those referred to in paragraph (a), and

(c) must make a written record of each undertaking given by a civilian participant as referred to in paragraph (b).

(continued)

4. **Obligations of law enforcement participants with respect to their own actions**

At all times during the conduct of an authorised operation, each law enforcement participant:

(a) must act in good faith, and
(b) must comply with any lawful directions given to the participant by the law enforcement officer who is conducting, and has responsibility for, the operation.

5. **Obligations of law enforcement participants with respect to the actions of others**

Each law enforcement participant in an authorised operation must take all reasonable steps to ensure that the conduct of the operation does not involve any participant in the operation:

(a) inducing or encouraging another person to engage in criminal activity or corrupt conduct of a kind that the other person could not reasonably be expected to engage in unless so induced or encouraged, or
(b) engaging in conduct that is likely to seriously endanger the health or safety of that or any other participant, or any other person, or to result in serious loss or damage to property, or
(c) engaging in conduct that involves the commission of a sexual offence against any person, or
(d) engaging in any activity that, not being a controlled activity, is unlawful.

6. **Reports to be made in good faith**

   1. In preparing a report on the conduct of an authorised operation, the reporting officer must at all times act in good faith.
   2. In particular, the reporting officer must ensure that the report:

      (a) discloses all information of which the officer is aware as to matters required to be included in the report, and
      (b) does not contain anything that is incorrect or misleading in a material particular.

   3. If the reporting officer subsequently becomes aware of:

      (a) information that, had it been known to the officer when the report was prepared, should have been included in the report, or
      (b) information that indicates that anything contained in the report is incorrect or misleading in a material particular,

the officer must ensure that the information is given to the chief executive officer as soon as practicable.

(continued)

7. **Breaches of code to be reported**
    1. If a law enforcement participant in an authorised operation becomes aware that a breach of this code has occurred in relation to the operation, the participant must ensure that notice of the breach is given to the chief executive officer as soon as practicable.
    2. It is sufficient compliance with this clause if notice of the breach is reported in accordance with the internal reporting procedures applicable to the law enforcement agency to which the law enforcement participant belongs.
8. **Relationship to other codes of conduct**

In its application to a law enforcement agency, the provisions of this code are in addition to, and do not derogate from, the provisions of any other code of conduct that applies to that agency.

Accountability

All controlled operations statutes contain requirements that impose tight systems of accountability. These accountability architectures are complicated, bureaucratic processes intended to impose systems of internal and external surveillance to regulate behaviour. Accountability mechanisms include the requirement for authorisation, reporting, and in most cases an external scrutineer with statutory powers to examine the records of the agency. If the controlled operation is intended to hold the public accountable for criminal or corrupt activity, controlled operations legislation also hold the officers deploying this power to account through bureaucratic surveillance and discipline. In all cases the scrutineer is ultaimtely accountable to Parliament through reporting requirements at the highest level of government. The accountability architectures in this case are primarily “front end”, establishing a mechanism that requires prior authorisation and record-keeping before the execution of a controlled operation. However, accountability through surveillance and scrutiny operates on a continuum that begins with these mechanisms, but ultimately ends in the hands of external agents, including the courts. In this respect accountability measures are both front-end and retrospective.

Mutual Recognition and Cross Border Investigations

All controlled operations statutes, particularly after 2003, contain mechanisms allowing mutual recognition of controlled operations statutes across borders that also facilitate cooperation between agencies. This development is essential in a Federal system of law, and is consistent with international trends in cross-border policing that focus on actual collaboration facilitated by mutual recognition and enablement laws, and the sharing of criminal intelligence and electronically stored evidence (Hufnagel 2011, 2012, 2013, 2017; Hufnagel et al. 2012; Watney 2016; Sallavaci 2018).

Normative Principles

Controlled operations law and policy also contains a distinct set of normative principles that govern and shape the doctrinal structures. These normative principles are concerned primarily with respecting questions of civil liberties and human rights, the nature of a fair trial, and the utilitarian logic embedded within legal reasoning concerned with the balancing of competing interests.

Controlling Entrapment

The prohibition against entrapment reflects public and judicial concern with the incitement to commit crimes by the state of its citizenry. Fundamental questions of fairness and public policy are at stake, which controlled operations law purports to regulate through prospective authorisation requirements. As will be considered at length in later chapters, the difficulty with front-end authorisation as a control for entrapment is the fact that investigations are necessarily organic and frequently chaotic, despite the best efforts of investigators to maintain a stable environment and orderly progression. Entrapment can easily be an operational development rather than pre-planned activity. The target may become suspicious or is so experienced that the investigation needs to constantly evolve. Conversely, targets may also be vulnerable, and essentially reluctant to behave in the way that the investigator believes they will, sometimes because they are trying to live a life without crime, and sometimes because of drug addiction or mental illness. Targets may acquiesce to pressure or the manipulation of relationships. In addition to these operational problems, the legal concept of entrapment is far from simple. However, for present purposes it is necessary to emphasise that entrapment refers to a situation where a person is intentionally encouraged or allowed to commit a crime that they would not otherwise have committed. As we will see, entrapment is less clear when that conduct is the result of the instigation or manipulation by the officer investigating. Situations arise where suspects, indeed, *are* prepared to engage in one form of behaviour, but find themselves involved in a more serious form or crime facilitated by the investigators. In these cases, complex questions can arise as to whether the suspect would have committed offence X at all, even though they were prepared to commit offence Y. Consequently, the common law routinely has to deal with questions about whether or not the test for entrapment is subjective or objective, or a hybrid, whether it is a defence, whether it is a pre-trial or post-trial process, whether the correct remedy is a stay, mitigation of sentence, or exclusion of evidence, let alone what the moral framework justifying the process might be. Fundamentally, the normative principle against entrapment is complicated by the dynamics of the operation itself and the individuals involved within it. The existence of this normative principle does mean, however, that the behaviour of the individuals involved in the operation are matters that may enliven several procedural remedies.

Public Safety

The law requires that controlled operations should not, under normal circumstances, involve a risk to public safety or the investigators. Like entrapment, the problem with public safety as a governing principle is that all operations necessarily involve a degree of public and personal risk. It is a question of the magnitude of risk. Concerns for public safety result in the importation of provisions within legislation designed to minimise and control risk. For example, an explicit requirement to maintain control over prohibited goods, the health and safety of individuals, restrictions on the use or abuse of property, and the explicit prohibition against violence and sexual offences. These public safety provisions find express life within the doctrinal architecture.

A Utilitarian Logic: Balancing Competing Interests

The controlled operations literature, considered in more detail in later chapters, reflects four interconnected themes concerned with the balancing of competing interests. First, there is privacy. Second, the idea of fairness reflected in the right to a fair trial and the right to silence. Third, the necessity of empowering police adequately to deal with crime and corruption. Finally, there is the connected right of the public to be protected from crime and corruption. These themes overlap. These themes are dominant and recurrent in the controlled operations literature, with powerful impact on controlled operations jurisprudence. What is important to emphasise, even at this early stage, is that despite the importance assigned to privacy and protection from arbitrary use of state power, the controlled operations architecture is fundamentally based upon a utilitarian logic: the ends justify the means. This utilitarian logic, as we will see later in this thesis, essentially promotes the principle that when crime and corruption reach a sufficient threshold of seriousness, the legislature and the courts are prepared to read down claims to privacy, fair trial and self-incrimination in the face of necessity. In later chapters we will link this utilitarian logic to the logic of the exception.

Risk Management

As will be discussed in more detail in later chapters, one of the overarching concerns with controlled operations regulation is risk management. In this context risk is a multifaceted concept, going well beyond concern with safety. Much of the discourse considered and evident in Parliamentary debates was concerned with risk management of the operation, preservation of evidence, and containing the manifestation of *legal risk* in the process.

Of Doctrine and Counterlaw

Controlled operations law contains a system of rationalities that shape its architecture. This architecture, regardless of the state in which it is enacted, essentially contains manifestations of the principles described above. These principles are partly a reflection of the practices required in investigations set out in the last chapter, and partly a reflection of the specific problems arising out of *Ridgeway*. These principles are also a reflection of the policy imperatives attached to law enforcement. The political and the legal consequences of *Ridgeway* gave rise to fierce political debate, partly reflected in the doctrinal architectures. In Part 2 we will consider, in some detail, the nature of these debates. The debates are important because these discourses govern the law. But here we also consider the way in which the legislature draws upon a range of knowledge formations to crystallise the legal architecture and the principles discussed above. There is a link between doctrine, policy, and knowledge formations. These knowledge formations import knowledge systems concerned with risk management, accountability, rights, and necessity. Controlled operations law and policy provides insights into the diverse ways in which the rationalities constituting law develop and evolve through the intersections of different kinds of knowledge structures – from the values embedded in policy, to alternative technical systems such as risk and accountability, through to integration with established principles, and errors, in the techniques of regulation.

In addition, controlled operations law entrenches a particular form of investigation. This apparatus is concerned with law enforcement, articulated through precision surveillance of individuals and networks. It is an architecture that alters the ordinary rules of evidence to preserve information obtained during an investigation employing ordinarily unlawful means. In effect, controlled operations law caused a rupture in criminal procedural law, intended to facilitate investigations, prosecutions, and the capacity of the nation state to involve itself in undercover and targeted investigations. This is a legal architecture intended to circumvent and create exceptions to general principles of law that would otherwise prohibit unlawful behaviour, defend the right to privacy, and ordinarily exclude unlawfully obtained evidence. In effect, controlled operations may be conceptualised as *a law against law*, fundamentally characterised by systems of accountability, both inward and outward looking. This is an architecture intended to hold populations to account, populations that not only include the public at large, but also the investigators.

This dynamic – a law *against* law – and the facilitation of architectures of surveillance, is indicative of *counter law* (Ashworth 2000, 2006; Bagaric 2001; Ericson 2007): the phenomenon whereby laws are introduced to alter the existing legal architecture where it is regarded as an impediment to law enforcement. Ericson, for example, argued that changes in the structure of the criminal law are driven by political and social changes in the culture of Western societies where fear of crime and terrorism, and the proliferation of perceptions of risk and uncertainty, create a political imperative whereby laws are introduced aimed at maximising security and reducing risk and uncertainty through statutory amendment and the proliferation of laws that entrench a broad-based and systematic "surveillant assemblage" intended to facilitate surveillance and investigation of populations (Haggerty and Ericson 2000; Ericson 2007).

As I have argued elsewhere (Murphy 2014), there are aspects of controlled operations law broadly consistent with the counterlaw thesis. Controlled operations are part of a legal grid that entrenches surveillance and investigative methodologies concerned with breadth and depth of surveillance for the purpose of prosecution. It is also a legal architecture that creates exceptions to the law. But it cannot simply be the case that controlled operations, properly understood, are a manifestation of counter law. The counter law thesis is grounded in the criminological and governmentality literature. What is significant, in my opinion, is that it is undoubtedly the case the controlled operations are located within a space in which risk, uncertainty, surveillance and law intersect with the political. Although aspects of controlled operations possess characteristics indicative of counterlaw, there is more to it. Counterlaw assists in explaining the effect of law in relation to itself and its relationship with surveillance and risk, but does not go far enough in explaining the specific content of authorised crimes – which is not surprising, since counterlaw was never applied to it. As will be examined and argued later, discourses of risk and uncertainty are major factors in the policy debates underneath the controlled operation's doctrinal structure. For present purposes, the doctrinal and normative principles that govern controlled operations law have been articulated. To a large extent the form of words used in statutes is irrelevant. What is important are the broad principles they reflect, and the substance of the doctrine itself. What they reflect is a combination of the realities of investigations, the attempt to regulate them, the historical and cultural shifts willing to endorse this kind of investigative methodology, the impact that risk and the utilitarian logic at play in policy and doctrinal structures.

References

AAP. (1995, 20 April). *Ruling May Hobble Police Drug Ploy*. The Newcastle Herald, p. 4.

Alderson, K. (2001). *Powers and responsibilities: Reforming NSW criminal investigation law*. Ph.D Thesis, University of New South Wales, Sydney.

Anderson, J. (2016). *Uniform evidence law: Text and essential cases* (3rd ed.). Sydney: Federation Press.

Andreas, P., & Nadelmann, E. (2006). *Policing the globe: Criminalization and crime control in international relations*. New York: Oxford University Press.

Ashworth, A. (2000). Is the criminal law a lost cause? *Law Quarterly Review, 166*(April), 225–256.

Ashworth, A. (2006). Four threats to the presumption of innocence. *South African Law Journal, 123*(1), 63–97.

Association of Chief Police Officers (ACPO). (2005). *Practice advice on core investigative doctrine*. Cambourne: ACPO.

Australian Law Reform Commission (ALRC). (1975). *Report no. 2: An interim report: Criminal investigation* (Vol. Report No. 2). Canberra: Australian Law Reform Commission.

Bagaric, M. (2001). The "civil-isation" of the criminal law. *Criminal Law Journal, 25*(4), 184–193.

Bowling, B., & Sheptycki, J. (2012). *Global policing*. London: Sage.

Browne, T. (2009). *Australian federal police: The first thirty years*. Canberra: AFP History Project.

Bryant, R. (2009). Theories of criminal investigation. In S. Tong, R. Bryant, & M. Horvath (Eds.), *Understanding criminal investigation* (pp. 13–33). Hoboken: Wiley.

Cain, F. (2008). *Terrorism & intelligence in Australia : A history of Asio and national surveillance*. North Melbourne: Australian Scholarly Publishing.

Campbell, R. (1995, 20 April). *Government Slates Court as Heroin Trafficker Goes Free*. The Canberra Times, pp. 1–2.

Commonwealth of Australia, New South Wales Government, Queensland Government, & Victorian Government. (1983). *Royal commission of inquiry into drug trafficking*. Canberra: Australian Government Publishing Service.

Cutting, P. D. (1983). The technique of controlled delivery as a weapon in dealing with illicit traffic in narcotic drugs and psychotropic substances. *UNODC Bulletin on Narcotics, 34*(4), 15–20.

Donnelly, R. (1951). Judicial control of informants, spies, stool pigeons, and agent provocateurs. *The Yale Law Journal, 60*(7), 1091.

Ericson, R. (2007). *Crime in an insecure world*. Cambridge: Polity Press.

Finlay, M. (1999). *Report: Review of the Law Enforcement (Controlled Operations) Act 1997*. Sydney: Police Integrity Commission.

Fitzgerald, T. (1989). *Queensland Fitzgerald Commission of inquiry into possible illegal activities and associated police misconduct* (Report of a Commission of Inquiry Pursuant to Orders in Council). Brisbane.

Farouque, F. (1995). *Drugs Ruling Dismays Kerr*. The Age, p. 5

Haggerty, K., & Ericson, R. (2000). The surveillant assemblage. *British Journal of Sociology, 51*(4), 605–622.

Hanks, P., Gordon, F., & Hall, G. (2012). *Constitutional law in Australia* (3rd ed.). Sydney: LexisNexis.

Harfield, C., & Harfield, K. (2008). *Covert investigation* (Blackstone's practical policing) (2nd ed.). New York: Oxford University Press.

Harfield, C., & Harfield, K. (2018). *Covert investigation* (Blackstone's practice policing) (5th ed.). Oxford: Oxford University Press.

Hilton, B. (2006). *A mad, bad & dangerous people?: England 1783–1846*. Oxford: Clarendon Press.

Horner, D. (2014). *The spy catchers: The official history of ASIO, 1949–1963*. Melbourne: Allen & Unwin.

House of Commons. (1833). *Report from the select committee on the petition of Frederick Young and others* (Vol. XIII). London: House of Commons.

House of Commons. (1853). *The speeches of the late right honourable Sir Robert Peel delivered in the House of Commons* (Vol. 2). London: George Routledge & Co.

Hufnagel, S. (2011). Cross-border police co-operation: Traversing domestic and international frontiers. *Criminal Law Journal, 35*(6), 333–344.

Hufnagel, S. (2012). Harmonising police cooperation laws in Australia and the European Union: The tension between local/national and national/supranational interests. *Australian Journal of Forensic Sciences, 44*(1), 45–62.
Hufnagel, S. (2013). *Policing cooperation across borders: Comparative perspectives on law enforcement within the EU and Australia*. Aldershot: Ashgate.
Hufnagel, S. (2017). Regulation of cross-border law enforcement: 'Locks' and 'Dams' to regional and international flows of policing. *Global Crime, 18*(3), 218–236. https://doi.org/10.1080/17440572.2017.1345681.
Hufnagel, S., Harfield, C., & Bronitt, S. (Eds.). (2012). *Cross border law enforcement*. Abingdon: Routledge.
Joint Standing Committee on the Corruption and Crime Commission (WA). (2016) *Annual reports prepared by the Corruption and Crime Commission on the use of covert powers by WA Police, the Department of Fisheries and the Australian Crime Commission*.
Kyriacou, K., Viellaris, R., & Hall, P. (2014, 10 March 2014). *Final Gamble: How Police Got Brett Cowan to Confess to Murder*. Courier Mail. Retrieved from http://www.couriermail.com.au/news/special-features/the-undercover-sting/story-fnl1b568-1226850102402
Law Commission (UK). (1973). Working paper no. 50: Inchoate offences. In L. Commission (Ed.). London: HMSO.
Law Commission (UK). (1977). *Criminal law – Report on defences of general application*. London: Law Commission.
McKay, S. (2011). *Covert policing: Law and practice*. Oxford: Oxford University Press.
Miller, G. (1987). Observations on police undercover work. *Criminology, 25*(1), 27–46.
Moore, M. (1977). *Buy and bust: The effective regulation of an illicit heroin market*. Lexington: Lexington Books.
Murphy, B. (2014). Retrospective on Ridgeway: Governing principles of controlled operations law. *Criminal Law Journal, 38*(1), 38–58.
Murphy, B. (2015). *Zone of impeachment: A post-foucauldian analysis of controlled operations law and policy*. PhD Thesis, University of Newcastle, Newcastle.
Murphy, B., & Anderson, J. (2016). Assemblage, counter-law and the legal architecture of Australian covert surveillance. In R. K. Lippert, K. Walby, I. Warren, & D. Palmer (Eds.), *National security, surveillance and terror: Canada and Australia in comparative perspective* (pp. 99–127). Cham: Palgrave Macmillan.
Nadelmann, E. (1990). Global prohibitions regimes: The evolution of norms in international society. *International Organisation, 44*(4), 479–526.
Nadelmann, E. (1994). *Cops across borders: The internationalization of U.S. criminal law enforcement*. University Park: Pennsylvania State University Press.
Parliamentary Joint Committee on the National Crime Authority. (1999). *Street legal: A report by the parliamentary joint committee on the national crime authority*. Canberra: Parliament of Australia.
Radzinowicz, L. (1956). *A history of english criminal law and its administration from 1750: Volume 2: The enforcement of the law* (The enforcement of the law) (Vol. 2). London: Stevens & Sons.
Rawlings, P. (2002). *Policing: A short history*. Cullompton: Willan Publishing.
Sallavaci, O. (2018). Strengthening cross-border law enforcement cooperation in the eu: The Prüm network of data exchange. *European Journal on Criminal Policy and Research, 24*(3), 219–235. https://doi.org/10.1007/s10610-017-9355-0.
Secretary of State for the Home Department (UK). (1929). *Report of the Royal Commission on police powers and procedure* (Vol. Cmd. 3297). London: H M Stationary Office.
Standing Committee of Attorneys-General and Australasian Police Ministers Council Joint Working Group on National Investigation Powers. (2003). *Cross-border investigative powers for law enforcement report*. Canberra: Leaders Summit on Terrorism and Multijurisdictional Crime.
Stelfox, P. (2009). *Criminal investigation: An introduction to principles and practice*. Collumpton: Willan Publishing.

Stewart, D. (1986). *Royal Commission of inquiry into alleged telephone interceptions* (Vol. Volume One). Canberra: Australian Government Publishing Service.
United Nations Commission on Narcotic Drugs. (1996). *Illicit drug traffic and supply, including reports from the subsidiary bodies*. Vienna: United Nations.
Vidocq, F. E. (2003). *Memoirs of Vidocq: Master of crime* (E. G. Rich, Trans.). Oakland: AK Press.
Watney, M. (2016). Cross-border law enforcement: Gathering of stored electronic evidence. *Journal of Information Warfare, 15*(3), 69–80.
Whitton, E. (1993). Allan, Norman Thomas (1909–1977). In *Australian dictionary of biography* (Vol. 13). Canberra: National Centre of Biography.
Wilson, D., & Finnane, M. (2006). From sleuths to technicians? Changing images of the detective in Victoria. In C. Emsley & H. Shpayer-Makov (Eds.), *Police detectives in history, 1750–1950* (pp. 135–156). Aldershot: Ashgate.
Wood, J. J. (1997). *Report of the Royal Commission into the NSW Police Service*. Sydney: New South Wales Government.
Wotherspoon, G. (1993). Delaney, Colin John (1897–1969). In *Australian dictionary of biography* (Vol. 13). Canberra: National Centre of Biography.

References

Chapter 3
Theory and Practice of Undercover Investigations

Investigation Theories, Strategies and Context[1]

The investigation of crime is a core function of contemporary law enforcement, and critical to any subsequent prosecution. Without it there would little, if any, evidence capable of securing a conviction. Investigation as a technique in law enforcement has evolved a distinct set of strategies and techniques over time. Like policing, investigation methodologies have been the subject of historical transformation. Contemporary forms of investigation by law enforcement have their origins in the 18th and 19th centuries, and over time have progressed through phases that characterise the approach of the investigating agent. That transformation appears to have involved four distinct phases: (i) the detective as "heroic" individual (1829–1878); (ii) bureaucratic organisation and specialisation (1878–1932); (iii) centralisation of leadership (1933–1980), and (iv) centralised control of scientific modalities (1981-date)(Dupont 2003; Grabosky 2001; Milte 1977; Morris 2007; Wilson and Finnane 2006). These developments take place in the context of the necessary evolution of policing to new threats, forms of offending, and technological change (Rousseaux and Campion 2016). It should not be assumed these phases are mutually exclusive. Rather, they are extensions. Investigation still involves the energy and diligence of individuals and teams, although those actions take place in the context of an increasingly sophisticated system of information exchange and surveillance technologies. Contemporary investigation in law enforcement takes place in a highly structured, bureaucratic context, with strong emphasis on accountability and results. As will be discussed later, modern investigation has been transformed by the material and ideological power of risk, audit, and neoliberalism.

Traditionally, the techniques for investigation were learned "on the job", based on experience, and limited primarily by whatever codes of conduct existed. To a large extent this is still the case, although there is a considerable amount of in-house

---

[1] Segments of this chapter have been published in Murphy (2016)

B. Murphy, *Regulating Undercover Law Enforcement: The Australian Experience*, https://doi.org/10.1007/978-981-33-6381-6_3

training and sharing of methodologies by agencies. Investigation methods in law enforcement began to change in the 1970s and 80s in the face of external and internal pressures, as policing became steadily more professionalised, technical, and scrutinised by outside bodies. This has been particularly the case since 2000, with an increasing trend towards standardisation and dissemination of "best practice models" at the local and international level (Morris 2007; Stelfox 2007, 2009; Bryant 2009). These changes coincided with a series of scandals concerning the failures of the police to solve serious crime,[2] national inquiries into police corruption,[3] and increasing demands from governments for demonstrable "market" efficiencies and outcomes (Maguire 2000). In more recent years, policing has witnessed an increasing focus on "market efficiencies", and an increasing trend towards privatisation and outsourcing of police services (White and Gill 2013). The extent to which this is impacting on the core business of investigation is by no means clear. But there is little doubt that increased emphasis on "community engagement" is effectively calling on the public to provide surveillance and information to law enforcement (Morash and Ford 2002). The new frontier in criminal investigation, undoubtedly, is the technological revolution enabled by "big data", artificial intelligence, facial recognition technologies and body cameras, with a proliferation and corporatisation of private investigation of both internal and public misconduct (Shih et al. 2019; Lei 2019; Lander et al. 2018; Harfield 2014; Headley et al. 2017).

The result has been the effective industrialisation and bureaucratic reorganisation of a partially militarised executive power. This change was achieved not only through the standardisation and subordination of knowledge systems previously internal to policing to economic reasoning, it was also achieved through legislative reform and the availability of emerging surveillance technologies and the

---

[2]Typified in the United Kingdom by the Byford Report into Peter Sutcliffe ("The Yorkshire Ripper") in 1981. Sutcliffe was ultimately convicted of 13 murders between 1975 and 1980. The report was in response to widespread public demands for an inquiry into the failure of police to apprehend Sutcliffe. The report was not made public until 2006. It contained significant criticism of the failure of the investigation. Much of that criticism was a combination of inept investigation, and the absence of compatible and standardised systems of investigation between different police districts. In an age when computers were not available, the investigation involved index cards. The failure to adequately manage a vast amount of information, and the lack of training of many officers involved in the case, were serious failures in this investigation. See *The Yorkshire Ripper Case: Review of the Police Investigation of the case by Lawrence Byford* (December 1981). A copy of the report released under FOI is available at < http://webarchive.nationalarchives.gov.uk/20100418065544/http://www.homeoffice.gov.uk/about-us/freedom-of-information/released-information/foi-archive-crime/1941-Byford-report/>. In Australia the death of Azaria Chamberlain in 1980 has been the subject of four coronial inquests (1980, 1981, 1995, 2012), two High Court appeals (*Chamberlain v R* (1983) 153 CLR 514; *Chamberlain v R (No. 2)* (1984) 153 CLR 521), and a Royal Commission (1985–1987). The case continues to attract considerable public attention and controversy. Shortcomings in the preservation of evidence during the investigation were major points of criticism, which led to the initial conviction of the Chamberlains.

[3]A series of Royal Commissions into Police Corruption took place during this period, notably the Wood Royal Commission (1995–1997); the Royal Commission of Inquiry into Alleged Telephone Interceptions (1985–1986); and the Royal Commission Into Drug Trafficking (1981–1983)

reorgainsation of non-state actors to enable private-sector policing. Controlled operations emerged in a context in which investigative methodologies were being standardised globally, augmented by technology, and with the organisation of policing ever more dominated by demands for regulation, efficiency, and results. At the time of writing, investigations methodologies are merging with apparatus of surveillance, control, and the industrialisation of techniques, with an increasing overlap between state and non-state actors.

Policing and investigations literature are primarily shaped by a body of scholarship sourced in the social sciences, and a body indigenous to law enforcement, with little apparent connection between the two. Consequently, a division exists between practice literature and the social and critical literature. Broadly, there are bodies of literature *within* investigative practice and literature *about it*. Practice-based authors tend to focus on documenting practical interventions. Brodeur (2010b), for example, observed that criminal investigation literature is made up of five key sources: (i) textbooks written by police practitioners; (ii) practice manuals and instructions from investigation agencies; (iii) specialist manuals for particular crimes (esp. murder and drugs); (iv) judicial decisions; and (v) evaluative studies. Bryant (2009) observed that practice sources ordinarily contain perspectives on (i) what works locally, (ii) what works elsewhere, and (iii) attempts to synthesise both. Interestingly, a literature review also suggests the perpetuation of a myth that there is not a great deal written about investigative methods. There is, in fact, a great deal written about investigation – at least in the United States and the United Kingdom. The same cannot be said for Australia. With the exception of Horswell (2004), there is virtually nothing written domestically, at least in publicly available sources. As a result, much of the theoretical material that follows is drawn from the United States and the United Kingdom.

Theories of Investigation

The English word *investigation* is derived from Latin through Old French (*investigare / investigationem*). It appeared as early as 1436 in English sources and refers to *systematic and careful research*. This is to be contrasted with more passive forms of perception, which may be cursory or disinterested. Unlike passive forms of perception, investigation is concerned with a more detailed examination of a topic than is ordinarily the case in human experience. "Investigation" is also a term associated with sovereign power, since the declaration or demand for an "investigation" implies an official process associated with formal consequence, typically rectification or punishment. Accordingly, "investigation" imports a meaning associated with applied reason concerned with perceiving what is unknown, the process of perception, and the purpose behind it (Murphy 2014).

"Investigation" was already in use in the English legal context by 1602.[4] The term itself is often invoked in the context of criminal investigation, being "the process of legally gathering evidence of a crime that has been or is being committed." (Brown 2001) It is important to observe that the term investigation is not the prerogative of police. Investigation is an ordinary human activity inspired by curiosity, but a specialty is engaged in by a variety of actors, including State intelligence agencies, private investigators, journalists, and, of course, scientists and academics. In law enforcement, investigation strategies are amenable to a variety of purposes, ranging from prosecution of specific offenders, through to matters of state and international security. There is considerable overlap between investigative powers exercised by police agents and those exercised by state intelligence organisations.

Contemporary police investigations function within a paradox. They are at once highly regulated, but also fluid. All investigations have three essential dimensions: (i) the *actual methods and behaviours* used by investigators; (ii) *compliance* with legal and organisational norms; and (iii) the *purpose* of the investigation. These factors are mutually exclusive, but necessarily related.

The essential purpose of investigation is information. While the central focus in most investigations in law enforcement is evidence of specific crime, all investigations collect a large amount of collateral information of interest to the nation State. Information obtained during an investigation will have different purposes and importance, depending on the focus of the investigation and the agency involved. This information will consist of multiple types, with a variety of uses. Information not only has different types, but differing qualities. Harfield and Harfield (2008b), for example, make a distinction between information as evidence directly connected to a crime, information surrounding the event, and information concerning the social context, while Stelfox (2009) observes that the collection and analysis of information (broadly) is the central purpose of any investigation. In the context of law enforcement, a major focus is information directly connected with criminal activity, and routinely in the prosecution of identified offenders. Either way, the purpose of investigation is the collection of information. Thus, while general intelligence is a necessary by-product of investigations, as Brodeur suggests, the ultimate purpose "is a quest for information that can be used as court evidence to secure the conviction of one or several offenders." (Brodeur 2010a). A drug investigation, for instance, may result in evidence that person X deals in narcotics. That information may be used to prosecute X. At the same time, investigators may also discover that person Y is the supplier (specific intelligence), able to source that drug from an unknown party in Thailand (general intelligence). That general intelligence may then become the subject of future directed investigation. It is open to debate as to whether the real purpose of criminal investigation is really specific evidence for

[4]The *Oxford English Dictionary* defines investigation as "The action of investigating; the making of a search or inquiry; systematic examination; careful and minute research.". William Fulbecke used the term as being part of the quest for "truth" in legal proceedings in *A parallele or conference of the civill law, the canon law and the common law of England* in 1602. See "investigation, n.". OED Online. December 2011. Oxford University Press. 10 January 2012 <http://0-www.oed.com.library.newcastle.edu.au/viewdictionaryentry/Entry/99038>

prosecution purposes, or a broad "drag-net" interested in network information. In this context there is a fine line between prosecution evidence and criminal intelligence. To a large extent the distinction is artificial and unhelpful, since successful policing and prosecution depends upon both criminal intelligence and sufficiently clear and admissible evidence.

The extent to which information is available varies according to the circumstances. An investigation can simply be a matter of collecting physical evidence left at the scene, in circumstances where the perpetrator is known or suspected. In this case the focus is primarily collection of evidence. Intelligence is ancillary to that purpose. Conversely, some investigations require a more active role, particularly in cases where physical evidence is limited, and the identity of the suspect is unknown or confused. In that case the collection of physical evidence is secondary because the primary purpose will depend upon the collection of sufficient intelligence to allow for the identification of parties and the location of relevant evidence. In these cases, evidence capable of supporting a conviction is the end-product of a much broader level of enquiry.

In criminal prosecutions, the information required has a very specific character. The evidence required must address the specific elements of proof located in law, be admissible, and be relevant to a fact in issue.[5] Proof of crime, as a matter of law, depends on satisfying the elements of a particular crime beyond reasonable doubt. This focus on "points to prove" has been criticised because of its capacity for misuse, and for narrowing lines of enquiry (Bryant 2009). Nevertheless, proof of specific elements remains central to successful prosecution, even though investigations generally yield more information than is required for prosecution. The reality of an investigation is that the investigator is immersed in the physical reality and exposed to the full range of information available, whereas the law is only interested in those elements that have legal utility. However, any "surplus" information may be valuable intelligence, retaining its value as providing the foundations for general and specific intelligence able to sustain future investigations (Association of Chief Police Officers (ACPO) 2005; Miller 1987; Stelfox 2009).

Maguire (2008) found that popular media creates misleading assumptions about investigations. Popular television tends to create a belief that police investigations are (1) necessarily reactive; (2) focussed on retrospective crimes; (3) based on the idea that the charge is clear at the outset; (4) primarily motivated as "truth finding" undertakings; (5) carried out by detectives; and (6) the main skill involves discovery of "clues" to find out "who did it". These assumptions distort the complexity of

[5] Eg: *Smith v R* (2001) 206 CLR 630 at 654 per Gleeson CJ, Gaudron, Gummow & Hayne JJ: "In determining relevance, it is fundamentally important to identify what are the issues at the trial. On a criminal trial the ultimate issues will be expressed in terms of the elements of the offence with which the accused stands charged. They will, therefore, be issues about the facts which constitute those elements. Behind those ultimate issues there will often be many issues about facts relevant to facts in issue. In proceedings in which the *Evidence Act 1995* (NSW) applies, as it did here, the question of relevance must be answered by applying Pt 3.1 of the Act and s 55 in particular. Thus, the question is whether the evidence, if it were accepted, could rationally affect (directly or indirectly) the assessment by the tribunal of fact, here the jury, of the probability of the existence of a fact in issue in the proceeding."

police investigations. The character of an investigation is determined by a host of factors, including context, cause, function, information collection methods, purpose, and regulatory landscape.

Typologies and Categories of Investigation

Investigation literature contains a host of typologies and binary distinctions. Caution is required. Typologies and binary categories are apt to mislead. Maguire (2008), for example, is critical of binary distinctions between proactive and reactive methods. All investigations tend to involve elements of different approaches, determined by operational requirements rather than theoretical categories. The reality is there are frequently overlaps between classification typologies. Despite those limitations, typologies are useful models for understanding the different modalities of police investigations.

The main distinction is between *reactive* and *proactive* models. *Reactive* models concern investigating after the fact, including the completed act, apprehension of offenders, asset recovery, and identification, collation, and preservation of evidence. *Proactive* models concern investigations prior to the commission of a crime. Proactive strategies tend to be concerned with preparatory conduct, like event planning, and contemporaneous direct observation. In reactive investigations, the focus is identification and arrest of offenders and locating, preserving, and analysing evidence. Proactive investigations, by contrast, are normally intelligence-led and covert. The identity of the suspect(s) is often known, with emphasis on collating contemporaneous evidence and intelligence. The distinction is that evidence able to sustain a conviction is often not available during the initial stages of a proactive investigation; it is the paucity of evidence that is frequently the key to engaging in this form of investigation. It is important to note, however, that this binary model is misleading, since there is often a relationship between the two modes of investigation. Complex investigations often involve different phases and a combination of covert and ordinary policing.

Although there is a clear relationship between the model deployed and availability of evidence, there are other forces at work. There has been a demonstrable shift in the nature of investigation in the last 30 years from reactive to proactive in the United States, Europe, the United Kingdom and Australia (Fijnaut and Marx 1995; Maguire and John 1996; Marx 1980, 1988; Bacon 2016). Proactive or "intelligence-led" policing has become normalised and, in many ways regarded as more effective. This evolution is well recognised in police practice literature, although other developments are evident (Association of Chief Police Officers (ACPO) 2005; Maguire 2008; Rogers et al. 2011; Wright 2002; Coyne and Bell 2011; Gibbs et al. 2015). Brodeur (2010a) argues that a third category of investigation – the "retrospective investigation" – is distinguishable. In this case the inquiry is into whether a known suspect's conduct was, in fact, criminal or corrupt. This is quite different, in his view, from inquiries concerned with establishing identity of a suspect and evidence of a crime. Brodeur also observes that investigations can be further divided between *event-centred* and *person-centred* inquiries, although he also conceived *hybrid* or *status-centred* investigations that involve both individual and event-based inquiries (2010b). These basic distinctions are central, because they largely determine the kinds of practices adopted by the investigator.

Scholars such as Stelfox (2009) and Harfield and Harfield (2008a) also recognise a binary distinction between *overt* and *covert* methods. An overt method involves an obvious or visible investigator presence, while a covert method does not. Harfield & Harfield define covert investigation as "investigation of which the suspect is assumed to be unaware and which infringes upon the private life of the suspect." (2008a). Overt methods, on the other hand, are characterised by an open and normally public intervention by investigators. Covert methods are characterised by hidden interventions designed to pierce the "veil" of privacy, often placing the investigator inside the ecology of the suspect. These distinctions are different from the proactive/reactive division, although covert methods tend to be associated with proactive approaches, but can be retrospective or reactive (Association of Chief Police Officers (ACPO) 2005).

Kuykendall (1982) has argued that police models are essentially multi-modal, with an emphasis on information gathering and analysis, focussed on *events* or *individuals*, with a view to intervention (normally arrest and prosecution). He argues that the nature of an investigation is necessarily shaped by the trigger for the investigation, based on one of five essential causes; (i) as a response to a reported or directly observed crime; (ii) the result of a series of events with a common pattern; (iii) a response to observing suspicious behaviour; (iv) an intuitive or rational belief that a person(s) was/is involved in crime; or (v) an intuitive or rational belief a person is a "life-style criminal".[6] These causes determine the character of subsequent investigations. The first three are generally *reactive* in character; the latter two often *proactive* in character. The investigation, once started, has a variety of purposes. Kuykendall argues that in most cases the primary purpose is the investigation of past and prevention of future crime, achieved through the apprehension of offenders and their prosecution through collection of admissible evidence capable of securing convictions. Deterrence is a by-product of the process. Where organisations are known to conduct investigations, there is a demonstrable reduction in the overall frequency of offending of certain kinds of crime – especially white collar, financial crimes, and corruption. The reason for this is that the knowledge of likely detection serves as a powerful element in "risk reasoning". Investigations have the function of enhancing the perception of risk, and accordingly the very practice serves as an important ideological factor in crime reduction – which explains the general success of auditing by experts (Loughran et al. 2011).

Kuykendall recognised that investigations had additional purposes: (i) the identification of successful methodologies that may be deployed in future investigation; (ii) asset recovery; (iii) satisfaction of public expectations for action; (iv) satisfaction and assistance for victims; (v) the augmentation of criminal information systems; and (vi) the formation of legal principles and rights afforded to suspects in

[6] Kuykendall's paper is a landmark in investigative scholarship. This paper represents the synthesis of some 70 sources on criminal investigation, 46 of which were published after 1970.

democratic States. Here Kuykendall conceived an investigation as being shaped by three major components: the location of the crime within a "criminal act continuum"; the source of information being used (people; physical evidence and information systems); and the techniques available to the investigator. He further distilled investigative techniques into five essential types: (i) interviewing; (ii) role playing (undercover work); (iii) scientific analysis; (iv) pattern analysis; and (v) monitoring (surveillance). All these basic methods were conceived as amenable to augmentation through technological means. He further conceptualised investigations as distinguished based on being *visible* or *invisible*, *reactive*, or *proactive*, and being *person* or *event* focussed. This typology gave emphasis to kinds of investigative practices based on the location of the investigation relative to the concluded crime. This model, sourced primarily in practice, illustrates the reality that investigations are highly adaptable processes and not well suited to simple typologies. But what he also indicates is that investigations are forms of expert knowledge, produced, and reproduced through practice as much as theory. Investigations must be understood as producing not only situational evidence and information, they produce and replicate expert knowledge systems.

Wright (2002) offers an alternative model, suggesting the real question in investigation methodology is not so much concerned with binary distinctions, but with decision-making and resource allocation. In effect, investigations are actually concerned with the allocation of resources, triggered by two simple factors: either as a reaction to an event or incident where evidence is already present; or as a response to intelligence or event where evidence was not present. The emphasis here is the differences between resources and behaviours that apply, rather than simply on the timing of the investigation and the crime. Maguire has a similar view, suggesting the distinction between reactive and proactive policing is mainly concerned with prioritising resources and managing competing demands from the public (who normally demand immediate responses to crimes) and the executive (who normally demand long-term prevention) (Maguire 2008).

Investigations have become highly specialised, and in many ways shaped by the nature of the offence being investigated and the actors involved. Brown (2001), and Kent and Nelson (2004), for example, detail a range of methodologies that are offence specific. Drug offences, for instance, ordinarily require the deployment of covert methods in supply cases, because the event is normally conducted in secret between willing participants. Sex offences, by comparison, are normally reactive, with particular emphasis on overt forms of evidence gathering, notably interviews and forensic materials (Brown 2001). This is a critical point: undercover investigations evolved out of the demands to investigate particular kinds of crimes.

Undercover Investigations

Undercover investigations involve distinct techniques differing from ordinary investigation (Candelaria and Steffen 2003; Fitzgerald 2007; Lyman 2006). The leading theorist on undercover investigation is Gary Marx.[7] In his landmark work on the topic, *Undercover: Police Surveillance in America* (1988), Marx argues there a basically two styles of policing investigative activity (covert/overt), and two models within in those activities (open/deceptive). Each model involves distinct investigative practices:

		Nature of police activity	
		Overt	Covert
Method used	Open	Uniformed patrol: Investigations conducted by a known investigator	Unobtrusive surveillance
	Deceptive	Trickery by those whose identity is known	Undercover: Intelligence, preventative, Facilitative

Adapted from Table 1 in Marx (1988)

Marx suggests that undercover operations are characterised by covert and deceptive activities as their essential orientation, but also cautions against a simplistic understanding of undercover work, since the very term "undercover investigations" tends to obscure their complexity. He suggests that undercover work involves at least three orientations with overlapping functions and different phases of execution.

Intelligence operations are aimed at gathering information about events that have happened *(postliminary)*, are in progress, or are planned (*anticipatory*). Any information obtained has multiple uses, not all of them with immediate legal utility. Information may simply be of general value on the state of offending or conduct; it may assist in the identification of individuals and networks hitherto unknown; it may provide sufficient information to obtain warrants; and it may lead directly to information used in the prosecution of targets (Marx 1988).

Preventative operations are directed to some intervention. That intervention may be prevention of a crime, or to minimise consequential harm. This may be achieved through the arrest of suspects at the moment there is sufficient evidence of an attempt or conspiracy, or through the twin processes of "suspect weakening" and "victim hardening". Such operations commonly involve "environmental" or "asset structuring" that renders the risk to victims inert (Marx 1988). For example, intercepting imported heroin and switching it with plaster or salt.

The third type of operation is *facilitative*. These operations involve the actual facilitation of the commission of an offence. This may involve the investigator presenting themselves as a target, or becoming a co-conspirator with the suspect (Marx

[7] Marx conducted a major qualitative study of undercover work in the 1980s. His work continues to be referred to as definitive in this field. See Marx (1988); Fijnaut and Marx (1995)

1988). Ordinarily, facilitation of the offence provides both criminal intelligence *and* evidence used in the prosecution of the offender.

Marx also conceptualised ten points of contextual and behavioural variation used for comparison between each of type of operation, with the potential for a multitude of overlapping possibilities for each (Marx 1988):

• The grounds for initiation	• Target specificity
• The degree of self-selection for illegal activity	• Congruence between real world criminal behaviour
• Natural vs. artificial criminal environments	• Capacity for intentional and autonomous behaviour
• Whether the offender carries out the crime or not	• Who plays the undercover role
• Dep vs. light cover	• The use of results

These points encompass complex qualitative variables. At one level an "undercover investigation" is simply one where the identity of the investigator is unknown, and the essential method is deceptive. The essential character is that the suspect does not know they are being investigated. At another level, the qualitative variations between undercover investigations mean that precise typologies break down once attention is directed to qualitative variations.

The activities deployed in an investigation will vary according to operational demands. The key issue, it seems, is whether the investigator intends to make their actual identity and purpose known during the investigation. Covert operations may comprise any number of techniques involving direct and indirect contact with a suspect, event, or place. A "covert investigation" is not a reference to one method of investigation: it is a reference to investigative activity taking place without the knowledge of the suspect. In this context Harfield and Harfield (2008a, 2018) highlight a range of covert activities, including directed surveillance, intrusive surveillance, interference with property (including wireless telegraphy and entry to land), physical and remote access to computers, mobile phone examination, interception of telecommunications, and "covert human intelligence". These are distinct but complementary methods of information collection. In addition, it is rare that any covert investigation will rely solely on one technique.

Covert operations are not simply concerned with surveillance and monitoring. Covert activity often involves direct contact with the investigator, an informer, or both. Surveillance can be direct or indirect, personal, or locational, intrusive, or public. Consequently, covert investigation is not characterised simply by surveillance. As Marx and Kuykendall (above) have both demonstrated, a defining distinction between investigation models is the visibility of the investigator, and the role of deception in the execution of the role. Within that mode of investigation, it is the *facilitative* model that brings together intelligence, prevention, and evidence collection. And it is here that the intersection of policing ethics, law and civil rights are brought into conflict, for as Kruisbergen et al. observe: "undercover operations are different not only because of their covert and deceptive nature, but also because the police participate in the very crimes they are investigating." (Kruisbergen et al. 2011). While this is a useful principle, it is also misleading. Undercover operations do not necessarily involve participation with offenders, although they may, and even then, that activity may not involve breaches of the criminal law – although it can.

The classification of an investigation is highly complex. Rather than conceiving investigations based on binary typologies, it is better to conceptualise investigations as a multi-modal process concerned with the purposeful collection of information. This process not only involves prospective and retroactive focus, it also shifts between the resources and mandate of the investigator(s), the suspect(s), event, and locality. Information collected will have a variety of purposes. In the context of law enforcement, information will have evidential, tactical, and strategic value. Evidence is used in prosecution. Tactical information relates to specific variables within the case. Strategic information relates to contextual variables outside the case. Fundamentally, investigations have a dual purpose: evidence and intelligence (Brown 2001). But the focus on information and classification of activity also distorts several key aspects of all investigations. Criminal investigations are a physical intervention by authority that may involve a variety of direct actions, including arrest, asset recovery, protection, and evidence preservation. These interventions are manifestations of a deployed sovereign power. Second, investigations have a communicative deterrent function. Investigations signal to the offender and the population that detection, apprehension, and prosecution is likely. Investigations signal to the public at large that the nation state is operational. Investigations communicate risk of detection to the offender, while communicating a Janus-faced risk of victimisation and social instability to the public at large, from which they must rely on the state for protection. Third, investigations can also have a significant role in the disruption of unlawful or deviant activities, ancillary to the police function. That disruption has a social effect on the nature of crime, ranging from displacement out of area, through to being the trigger for changes in the nature of the crime itself. Police, through investigative practices, may well provide the incentive for greater levels of secrecy and sophisticated crime. In other words, developments in police techniques may have an evolutionary or amplification effect on the nature of crime and police deviance (Marx 1988). Finally, investigation represents the clinical gaze of power relations. Investigations are not only devices concerned with instrumental evidence and analysis in specific cases. Investigation is a specific practice of surveillance societies.

Undercover Investigation Strategies

Undercover strategies are limited only by imagination in their design, but normally shaped by the behaviour being investigated, the scope of law authorising the forms of investigation, and the context in which they occur. Undercover methods evolved primarily in the context of crimes that routinely involve willing parties who keep their activities secret. Vice, drugs, corruption, white collar crime, and political violence are typical examples where undercover methods are deployed. The highly variable nature of these crimes is one of the reasons for a wide array of techniques evident in the literature. It is important to emphasise that undercover investigations need not involve a single technique. They routinely involve multiple techniques. A typical undercover operation, for example, normally involves observation/surveillance to identify specific targets and localities; informers who provide specific intelligence used in the execution of the operation and, in many cases, direct evidence against a suspect; followed by a buy/bust operation to secure evidence and facilitate arrest.[8] In the following segment some of the strategies used in undercover investigations are outlined.

Observation/Surveillance

Covert physical observation of the suspect is a routine undercover method. This may involve the officer observing the suspect, or an informer. Ideally the suspect is unaware. This strategy is primarily concerned with direct perception of the suspect and the environment. At its most basic this involves watching the target, but may also involve photography, filming, listening to conversations (by direct or electronic means), intercepting and monitoring telecommunications, stationing an observer (physical or electronic) at a static location to watch a person or place, or following a suspect around. This option is often geared towards collecting evidence of offending, but also has the function of developing a profile of activities over time. In some cases intelligence collection is the primary purpose. This strategy is very effective, being critical to the intelligence-gathering function of the investigation, and for positioning the investigator in a location that permits direct observation and early intervention. This activity is undoubtedly intrusive, a fact that sits uneasily with the idea of privacy and the absence of interference by government resting at the heart of liberal democracies. Consequently, surveillance activities are often subject to legal controls and restrictions, typically in the form of the requirement for authorisation and justification in law, although there are also a range of unregulated activities.[9]

[8] For example, the practice of combined surveillance, undercover and high visibility policing in support of direct community-based interventions involving family members is analysed in the context of a "street-level" drug and violence reduction strategy. See Frabutt et al. (2009)

[9] In Australian law surveillance activity operates in a quasi-regulated environment. Broadly, surveillance strategies are generally unregulated, unless they fall within the specific ambit of particular pieces of legislation or involve interference with private property or electronic media. The *Surveillance Devices Act 2007* (NSW), for example, provides for the installation and use of surveillance devices (optics, audio and tracking) on the issue of a warrant by a Judge or Magistrate. Interception of telephone conversations is governed by the *Telecommunications (Interception and Access) Act 1979* (Cth) using a similar system of authorisation. Internal forms of control are also present through the establishment of agency norms and policy, usually directed at compliance with statutory requirements.

Informers

Informers have a variety of roles, typically providing information to police concerning the activities of a suspect, although often not limited merely to providing information. Informers often function as intermediaries and sometimes facilitators of criminal conduct. Their identity may be actual or falsified. They are normally recruited out of the specific context being investigated and offered indemnity from prosecution for their cooperation, although the willingness of the informer to be involved is often questionable. For example, during the Wood Royal Commission into Police Corruption, former police detective Trevor Haken – himself implicated in corruption – became an informer and assumed a central role in the collection of evidence used in the course of the Royal Commission (Wood 1997).

Manufactured Conspiracies

Manufactured conspiracies are deployed in cases where there is considerable risk attached to the completed crime, often in cases where murder and physical violence is the intended activity, although equally in cases involving drug offences with strong flight risk or loss of control of narcotics. The focus is on facilitating sufficient information to arrest and charge for conspiracy, rather than risk the actual manifestation of the event itself. In these cases the investigator is a party to an agreement with the suspect target(s) for some kind of unlawful activity. Well documented examples include agreements with undercover officers to create forged bank notes[10]; soliciting undercover officers to assassinate spouses,[11] or politicians[12]; and conspiracies that involve the importation or manufacture of prohibited drugs.[13]

Manna from Heaven

This strategy involves placing something valued by the suspect in a place where it is accessible and known to be available by the suspect and waiting. Simply stated, this is a "trap" or "honeypot" operation that involves offering attractive bait for a suspect in a place where prior criminality of the anticipated crime has taken place. Strategies of this kind are often used in relation to property offences and vice. Leaving an unlocked van containing visible cartons of dummy cigarettes on a busy street, in an area with high levels of reported vehicle crime, has been successfully

[10] *R v Sang* [1980] AC 402

[11] *R v Winter* [2008] EWCACrim 3493; *R v Smurthwaite & Gill* [1994] 1 All ER 898

[12] *R v Gill and Ranuana* [1989] Crim LR 358

[13] *R* v *Yip Chiu-Cheng*[1994] 3 WLR 514

used in the UK.[14] Other examples include female officers acting as decoys in places where sexual assaults on women have taken place (Marx 1992), or creating a false online identity, frequenting online "chat rooms" and flirting with suspected paedophiles in the investigation of child pornography and sexual offences against children (Urbas 2010).

"Buy/Bust" or "Test Purchase"

The "buy/bust" involves an undercover officer, or an informer, purchasing a prohibited object or service from the suspect, or vice-versa. This kind of activity ordinarily offers conclusive proof of the offence. This is a highly effective method of enforcement, particularly in cases where the gravamen of the offence involves supply or "marketplace" behaviour, such as drug dealing (Moore 1977; Frabutt et al. 2009; Lyman 2006). There are numerous case examples, including undercover officers buying prohibited abortion drugs from vendors[15]; the purchase of narcotics from suspected dealers[16]; undercover officers hiring taxis suspected of operating beyond licensing conditions[17]; purchasing liquor, tobacco or firearms in breach of statutory conditions (Webster et al. 2006)[18]; and undercover officers seeking sexual services in prohibited circumstances.[19]

Facilitation

As discussed by Marx (1988), facilitation operations involve undercover officers taking an active role in the chain of events leading to the crime. Facilitation overlaps with conspiracy and buy/bust strategies, and typically involve prohibited items, such as firearms or narcotics, but go beyond these types of behaviour. The classic example is the "controlled delivery" of drugs across international borders through customs.[20] An offence is facilitated by the operative fulfilling a perceived role.

---

[14] *Williams & Anor v DPP* [1993] 3 All ER 365. See also Robertson (1994)

[15] *R v Birtles* (1909) 2 Cr App R 53

[16] *R v Looseley; Attorney General's Reference (No 3 of 2000)* [2001] 4 All ER 897; *R v Moon* [2004] EWCA Crim 2872; *R v Mandica & Or* (1980) 24 SASR 394

[17] *Nottingham City Council v Amin* [2000] 2 All ER 946

[18] *Sorrells v United States* 287 US 435 (1932)

[19] *Sneddon v Stevenson* [1967] 1 WLR 1051; *Jitjarden v Thompson* [1996] NSWSC 54

[20] *R v Ridgeway* (1995) 184 CLR 19; *R v Latif & Shahzad* [1996] 1 All ER 353

Network Infiltration and Friending

Undercover operations often aim to infiltrate the social networks of suspects, often through the medium of contrived friendships. These investigations involve undercover operatives networking with groups of individuals suspected of criminal or corrupt activity, or frequenting locations known to be the locations of certain crimes. In some cases, the actual identities of the ultimate suspects are unknown, and the purpose of networking in, in effect, to conduct a spy operation to infiltrate and map the network. This "networking" approach is particularly effective for investigating crimes that depend on relationships, such as white-collar crimes (e.g.: insider-trading), drug offences and corruption in public office (Schlegel 1993; Bell 2002). Examples include "nightclub" investigations for local drug suppliers[21]; "network" investigations through known suppliers[22]; soliciting classified information from a suspected leak[23]; soliciting betting information in venues likely to have punters interested in betting (such as pubs)[24]; soliciting bribes from white-collar targets in the form of "business opportunities" (Caplan 1983; Gershman 1982); and repeat purchases from offenders resulting in more serious criminal liability based on supply of increasing quantities.[25] "Mates" strategies can also involve "friending" a known suspect in order to engage in frank discussions about crimes committed by the person, effectively becoming confessions.[26] The scope of this kind of operation has included sexual relationships (Marx 1992).[27]

Online Deception

In recent years technology has permitted the assumption of a fictitious identity online. In this context a digital medium affords opportunities to engage in direct interactions with suspects, with the added advantage of documentary records of the entire interaction. In this forum technology provides a mechanism to deploy tried and tested undercover strategies in an environment where the identity of the investigator is virtually unknowable. This technique is proving to be highly effective in forming 'relationships' with suspected sex offenders, obtaining evidence of

[21] *R v Jolevski* [2002] NSWCCA 472;

[22] *Teixiera de Castro v Portugal* [1998] ECHR 52

[23] *R v Murphy* [1965] NI 138

[24] *Brannan v Peek* [1948] 1 KB 68

[25] *R v Pethig* [1977] 1 NZLR 448; *R v Smiroldo* (2000) 112 A Crim R 47

[26] *Tofilau v The Queen* (2007) 231 CLR 396; *R v Swaffield; Pavic v The Queen* (1998) 192 CLR 159; *R v Suckling* [1999] NSWCCA 36

[27] *R v Stagg* (Unreported, 14 September 1994, Central Criminal Court, Ognall J); *Proulx v Governor of HM Prison Brixton & Anor* [2000] EWHC Admin 381; *AKJ & Ors v Cmr Police* [2013] EWHC 32 (QB);

criminality, and orchestrating subsequent physical contact to execute arrests (Urbas 2010; Mitchell et al. 2010).

"Mr Big" Operations

An emerging technique originating in Canada is the "Mr Big" operation (Smith et al. 2009; Moore et al. 2009; Murphy and Anderson 2016).[28] In this instance a fictitious criminal organisation is constructed by investigators. The technique involves conspicuous displays of wealth, and cash payments for involvement in criminal acts. At some point the recruit is offered the chance to "join" the organisation, but in order to do so is required to confess or boast about something major in order to establish credentials. It is the "something major" that is actually the subject of the investigation; although there is no reason why this kind of strategy could not be used for more than confession evidence. Documented examples of these cases, and the associated issues, can be seen in a series of recent cases in Australia, including *Cowan v The Queen; Ex parte Attorney-General (Qld)*[2016] 1 Qd R 433, *Weaven v The Queen* [2018] VSCA 127 and *Deacon v The Queen* [2019] NTCCA 21.

Shopfront Operations

"Fencing" stolen goods is a well-recognised strategy. At its simplest this involves the purchase of stolen goods off the offender.[29] It can, however, involve far more sophisticated operations. The "shopfront" is a technique that involves the undercover investigator establishing what appears to be a legitimate business, or advertised through the 'criminal underground' as a location where goods can be 'fenced'. It may well have a registered business name and employees. The true purpose of the business is, however, the investigation of some criminal conduct, such as locating stolen goods offered for sale, or tracking money offered for laundering purposes.

Discussion

These examples are not an exhaustive list of undercover techniques. They illustrate a diverse range of techniques that have been brought to the attention of courts over the years. The essential feature is the use of deception to create a false reality for the

[28] For an authoritative examination of the techniques involved and the legalities, see *R v Hart* [2014] SCC 52

[29] *R v McEvilly* (1974) 60 Cr App R 150

purpose of information collection and control of the suspect. The activities of the suspect are under direct observation by police. That focus produces intelligence information and evidence. There is very little to distinguish covert investigation from espionage.

There is, however, an additional dimension of specific interest not well considered in the literature embedded in the techniques outlined above. Some of these strategies are not only deceptive; they also involve active breaches of the criminal law by the investigators themselves. Deception and breaches of the criminal law are specific components of "facilitative" operations. These two features inherent in the nature of covert investigations are significant in law, because these features are directly connected to the character of evidence ultimately presented to a court in the course of a prosecution. The practical *legal* interest in the controlled operation is oriented to what is done with the information adduced as evidence, because this is where the remedial interest of the defence and prosecution operates when such matters are presented in Australian courts.

The Nature of Controlled Operations and their Place in Law Enforcement

Although undercover investigation involves a range of methods and orientations, the defining character of a controlled operation is not the technique deployed. *A controlled operation is defined by the participation of the investigator in an unlawful act during the investigation.* The techniques discussed above may or may not involve unlawful activity, although many of them will. The effect of a controlled operations authorisation is to extend immunity from civil and criminal liability to the investigator, and to alter the legal status of evidence obtained during the investigation. Controlled operations are not defined by the nature of investigation (whether proactive or reactive); nor are they defined by the technique deployed (whether 'friending' or facilitative). *The essence of a controlled operation is the mobilisation of a legal apparatus that alters the legality of activity and evidence.*

Controlled operations are ordinarily reliant on deceptive and invisible processes, and for this reason must be understood as a covert investigation model. The controlled operation is ordinarily employed in the investigation of conduct resistant to conventional forms of investigation. It needs to be emphasised, however, that it is not the method used, as such, but the *unlawful activity* taking place within the investigation that defines the controlled operation. As discussed in the introductory chapter, the public information available on the operational details of Australian controlled operations are limited, but it is known that controlled operations typically involve the investigation of drug and firearms offences, and normally involve (i) clandestine conversations with suspects negotiating criminal conduct (usually recorded); (ii) unauthorised entry to premises; (iii) unauthorised entry to land; (iv) seizing or interfering with goods; (v) purchasing prohibited goods; (vi) possessing or dealing in prohibited goods; and (vii) using fake identities. These are activities that might take place in any number of investigative strategies as outlined above.

It is also clear from the definitions and the investigations literature that controlled operations have several secondary functions. First, controlled operations provide opportunity to obtain a vast amount of criminal intelligence. The investigative process and the close interaction between the suspect and the investigator provide immediate access to the suspect, their networks, and the environment in which they operate. The information obtained during the investigation necessarily extends well beyond the immediate evidence of offending that may or may not be present. New networks may be identified, along with sources, and hitherto undetected offending. A great deal of that information remains hidden and vested in the investigating agency. Even when a controlled operation does not result in an arrest, the immersion of the investigator(s) in the ecology of the suspect is an immediate opportunity for intelligence collection and assessment.

Second, the direct involvement of police provides a significant opportunity to arrest an offender prior to or at the point of committing the offence. From a police perspective this is significant. Not only does it increase the probability of an arrest proximate to the offence, it also provides a significant reduction in public risk. The capacity to effect a preventative arrest, particularly in cases involving violence, firearms, or explosives, is a major operational advantage and one of the important practical dimensions of the controlled operation.

Third, successful operations have the potential to break open and neutralise networks, especially those within public authorities, or among the powerful, such as political parties. Once arrests have been made, and the essential information concerning sources, identities and practices is known, police are presented with the opportunity to move against some or all of the members of that network.

Finally, the controlled operation arguably has a major deterrent effect. The ability to invisibly infiltrate networks, use informers, gather evidence, and be present at a critical moment, undoubtedly creates the optimum conditions for general and specific deterrence. Conversely, these dynamics of detection also have an evolutionary effect on the *avoidance* behaviours of the deviant; rather than being deterred, the criminal becomes more cautious, more devious, creating the incentive for ever more creative and invasive methods of detection. Power, detection, and resistance appear to be connected.

When considered in light of the investigations theory outlined in Chap. 2, the following observations can be made. The controlled operation is an investigative method that has an evidence and intelligence-gathering function. There is nothing distinctive in the legal construct of controlled operations that marks it as necessarily *proactive* or *reactive*. The controlled operation is not characterised by chronological deployment, or the methods used by the investigator. It is the effect of *legal rules* that redefine the conduct and techniques that is critical. The methods used are, however, characteristically *covert* in their nature. Although there is nothing to prevent overt or static methods of police being deployed, the general orientation of the controlled operation is covert. Since infiltration and breaches of law are expected in this kind of investigation, the idea of a "role playing" intervention as described by

Kuykendall (1982) is a defining feature, but not definitive. When approached through the model offered by Marx (1988), the nature of the controlled operation can be most clearly seen. Controlled operations are characterised primarily by a deceptive form of investigation, in instances where the identity of the operative is not known to the suspects/targets. This infiltration is a form of undercover work. The operative is authorised to behave unlawfully, albeit in a limited way. In some cases, they may participate in offending activity as a part of the operation. This falls within the notion of a "facilitative" quadrant of Marx's investigation typology as a covert form of deceptive investigation. It is worth noting, however, that the authority offered by a controlled operation warrant extends to virtually any form of criminal conduct, short of crimes involving serious physical or sexual violence, and serious damage to property. In that context a range of activities disconnected with direct interaction with the suspect are possible, such as trespass, creating false identities, or being in possession of prohibited drugs. But in each case the essential behaviour is unlawful.

References

Association of Chief Police Officers (ACPO). (2005). *Practice advice on core investigative doctrine*. Cambourne: ACPO.

Bacon, M. (2016). *Taking care of business: Police detectives, drug law enforcement and proactive investigation*. Oxford: Oxford University Press.

Bell, B. (2002). Theatrical investigation: White-collar crime, undercover operations, and privacy. *William and Mary Bill of Rights Journal, 11*(1), 151–207.

Brodeur, J.-P. (2010a). *Police investigation*. New York: Oxford University Press.

Brodeur, J.-P. (2010b). Police investigation. In *The policing web* (pp. 186–222). New York: Oxford University Press.

Brown, M. (2001). *Criminal investigation: Law and practice*. Boston: Butterworths-Heineman.

Bryant, R. (2009). Theories of criminal investigation. In S. Tong, R. Bryant, & M. Horvath (Eds.), *Understanding criminal investigation* (pp. 13–33). Hoboken: Wiley.

Candelaria, S., & Steffen, G. (2003). *Drug interdiction : Partnerships, legal principles, and investigative methodologies for law enforcement*. Boca Raton: CRC Press.

Caplan, G. (Ed.). (1983). *ABSCAM ethics: Moral issues and deception in law enforcement*. Cambridge, Mass: Ballinger Pub. Co.

Coyne, J. W., & Bell, P. (2011). Strategic intelligence in law enforcement: A review. *Journal of Policing, Intelligence and Counter Terrorism, 6*(1), 23–39. https://doi.org/10.1080/18335330.2011.553179.

Dupont, B. (2003). The new face of police governance in Australia. *Journal of Australian Studies, 27*(78), 15–24.

Fijnaut, C., & Marx, G. T. (1995). *Undercover: Police surveillance in comparative perspective*. Norwell: Kluwer Academic Publishers.

Fitzgerald, D. (2007). *Informants and undercover investigations: A practical guide to law, policy and procedure*. Boca Raton: CRC Press.

Frabutt, J., Hefner, K., Di Luca, K., Shleton, T., & Harvey, L. (2009). A street-drug elimination initiative: The law enforcement perspective. *Policing: An International Journal of Police Strategies and Management, 33*(3), 452–472.

Gershman, B. L. (1982). Abscam, the judiciary, and the ethics of entrapment. *The Yale Law Journal, 91*(8), 1565–1591.

Gibbs, C., McGarrell, E. F., & Sullivan, B. (2015). Intelligence-led policing and transnational environmental crime: A process evaluation. *European Journal of Criminology, 12*(2), 242–259. https://doi.org/10.1177/1477370815571947.

Grabosky, P. (2001). Crime control in the 21st century. *Australian & New Zealand Journal of Criminology, 34*(3), 221–234.

Harfield, C. (2014). Body-worn POV technology: Moral harm. *Technology and Society, 33*(2), 64–72.

Harfield, C., & Harfield, K. (2008a). *Covert investigation* (Blackstone's practical policing) (2nd ed.). New York: Oxford University Press.

Harfield, C., & Harfield, K. (2008b). *Intelligence: Investigation, community and partnership*. Oxford: Oxford University Press.

Harfield, C., & Harfield, K. (2018). *Covert investigation* (Blackstone's practice policing) (5th ed.). Oxford: Oxford University Press.

Headley, A. M., Guerette, R. T., & Shariati, A. (2017). A field experiment of the impact of body-worn cameras (Bwcs) on police officer behavior and perceptions. *Journal of Criminal Justice, 53*, 102–109. https://doi.org/10.1016/j.jcrimjus.2017.10.003.

Horswell, J. (Ed.). (2004). *The practice of crime scene investigation*. Brisbane: CRC Press.

Kent, K., & Nelson, B. (2004). Drug operations. In J. Horswell (Ed.), *The practice of crime scene investigation*. Brisbane: CRC Press.

Kruisbergen, E., De Jong, D., & Kleemans, E. (2011). Undercover policing: Assumptions and empirical evidence. *British Journal of Criminology, 51*(2), 394–412.

Kuykendall, J. (1982). The criminal investigative process: Toward a conceptual framework. *Journal of Criminal Justice, 10*(1), 131–145.

Lander, K., Bruce, V., & Bindemann, M. (2018). Use-inspired basic research on individual differences in face identification: Implications for criminal investigation and security. *Cognitive Research, 3*(1), 1–13. https://doi.org/10.1186/s41235-018-0115-6.

Lei, C. (2019). Legal control over big data criminal investigation. *Social Sciences in China, 40*(3), 189–204. https://doi.org/10.1080/02529203.2019.1639963.

Loughran, T. A., Paternoster, R., Piquero, A. R., & Pogarsky, G. (2011). On ambiguity in perceptions of risk: Implications for criminal decision making and deterrence. *Criminology, 49*(4), 1029–1061. https://doi.org/10.1111/j.1745-9125.2011.00251.x.

Lyman, M. (2006). *Practical drug enforcement* (3rd ed.). Boca Raton: CRC Press.

Maguire, M. (2000). Policing by risks and targets: Some dimensions and implications of intelligence-led crime control. *Policing and Society, 9*(4), 315–336.

Maguire, M. (2008). Criminal investigation and crime control. In T. Newburn (Ed.), *Handbook of policing* (pp. 430–464). Collumpton: Willan Publishers.

Maguire, M., & John, T. (1996). Covert and deceptive policing in England and Wales: Issues in regulation and practice. *European Journal of Crime, Criminal Law and Criminal Justice, 4*(4), 316–334.

Marx, G. T. (1980). The new police undercover work. *Journal of Contemporary Ethnography, 8*(4), 399–446.

Marx, G. T. (1988). *Undercover: Police surveillance in America*. Berkeley: University of California Press.

Marx, G. T. (1992). Under-the-covers undercover operations: Some reflections on the State's use of sex and deception in law enforcement. *Criminal Justice Ethics, 11*(1), 13–24.

Miller, G. (1987). Observations on police undercover work. *Criminology, 25*(1), 27–46.

Milte, K. (1977). *Police in Australia*. Sydney: Butterworths.

Mitchell, K. J., Finkelhor, D., Jones, L. M., & Wolak, J. (2010). Growth and change in undercover online child exploitation investigations, 2000–2006. *Policing and Society, 20*(4), 416–431.

Moore, M. (1977). *Buy and bust: The effective regulation of an illicit heroin market*. Lexington: Lexington Books.

Moore, T., Copeland, P., & Schuller, R. (2009). Deceit, betrayal and the search for truth: Legal and psychological perspectives on the "Mr Big" strategy. *Criminal Law Quarterly, 55*(3), 348–404.

Morash, M., & Ford, J. K. (2002). *The move to community policing: Making change happen*. Thousand Oaks/London: SAGE.

Morris, B. (2007). History of criminal investigation. In T. Newburn, T. Williamson, & A. Wright (Eds.), *Handbook of criminal investigation* (pp. 15–40). Collumpton: Willan Publishing.

Murphy, B. (2014). Retrospective on Ridgeway: Governing Principles of Controlled Operations Law. *Criminal Law Journal, 38*(1), 38–58.

Murphy, B. (2016). Deceptive apparatus: Foucauldian perspectives on law, authorised crime and the rationalities of undercover investigation. *Griffith Law Review, 25*(2), 223–244. https://doi.org/10.1080/10383441.2016.1194956.

Murphy, B., & Anderson, J. (2016). Confessions to Mr Big: A new rule of evidence? *International Journal of Evidence and Proof, 20*(1), 29–48.

Robertson, G. (1994, November). Entrapment evidence: Manna from heaven, or fruit of the poisoned tree? *Criminal Law Review*, 805–816.

Rogers, C., Lewis, R., John, T., & Read, T. (2011). *Police work: Principles and practice*. Hoboken: Willan Publishers.

Rousseaux, X., & Campion, J. (2016). *Policing new risks in modern European history* (1st ed.). London : Palgrave Macmillan UK: Imprint: Palgrave Pivot.

Schlegel, K. (1993). Crime in the pits: The regulation of futures trading. *The Annals of the American Academy of Political and Social Science, 525*(1), 59–70.

Shih, C.-H., Chen, F.-C., Cheng, S.-W., & Kao, D.-Y. (2019). Using Google maps to track down suspects in a criminal investigation. *Procedia Computer Science, 159*, 1900–1906. https://doi.org/10.1016/j.procs.2019.09.362.

Smith, S., Stinson, V., & Patry, M. (2009). Using the "Mr Big" technique to elicit confessions: Successful innovation or dangerous development in the Canadian legal system? *Psychology, Public Policy, and Law, 15*(3), 168–193.

Stelfox, P. (2007). Professionalizing criminal investigation. In T. Newburn, T. Williamson, & A. Wright (Eds.), *Handbook of criminal investigation* (pp. 628–651). Cullompton: Willan Publishing.

Stelfox, P. (2009). *Criminal investigation: An introduction to principles and practice*. Collumpton: Willan Publishing.

Urbas, G. (2010). Protecting children from online predators: The use of covert investigation techniques by law enforcement. *Journal of Contemporary Criminal Justice, 26*(4), 410–425.

Webster, D. W., Bulzacchelli, M. T., Zeoli, A. M., & Vernick, J. S. (2006). Effects of undercover police stings of gun dealers on the supply of new guns to criminals. *Injury Prevention, 12*(4), 225–230.

White, A., & Gill, M. (2013). The transformation of policing. *British Journal of Criminology, 53*(1), 74–93. https://doi.org/10.1093/bjc/azs049.

Wilson, D., & Finnane, M. (2006). From sleuths to technicians? Changing images of the detective in Victoria. In C. Emsley & H. Shpayer-Makov (Eds.), *Police detectives in history, 1750–1950* (pp. 135–156). Aldershot: Ashgate.

Wood, J. J. (1997). *Report of the Royal Commission into the NSW Police Service*. Sydney: New South Wales Government.

Wright, A. (2002). *Policing: An introduction to concepts and practice*. Cullompton: Willan Publishing.

Chapter 4
Context and Developments in Covert Investigations Regulation

Controlled operations are not the usual form of covert investigation in Australia. They are one tool in many that can be deployed by investigators during undercover work. They are in a legislative and practice context that, of itself, is a worthy subject for a book in its own right. For present purposes, what follows is a discussion of the wider context in which covert investigations take place, before moving on to consider aspects of similar laws in related legal systems in the United Kingdom, New Zealand and Canada.

Australian Covert Investigations Regulation

Covert investigations in Australia have a long history in practice, but as discussed earlier, have only become formally regulated over the last 25 years. This development is broadly consistent with the international evolution in law enforcement in this area (Murphy 2014; Murphy and Anderson 2016). In this respect covert investigations are in two forms. Those that require a warrant, and those that do not. The regulatory framework ensures that certain kinds of investigations require a warrant to be considered lawful. Those actions have a threefold aspect. First, they ensure an accountability mechanism on the part of law enforcement agents. Second, they have the effect of providing some certainty that the evidence obtained during the investigation is admissible, and therefore useful in subsequent prosecutions. Third, the existence of a warrant ensures that the actions of the participants are immune from subsequent liability that might otherwise arise. In addition, the system of warrants also has the effect of making certain kinds of investigations a state monopoly.

As discussed at length in the previous chapter, investigations are not the exclusive activity of the state. Far from it. There is very real evidence that investigations are a normal part of economic activity, ranging from audit to employee misconduct, promotions, and stock protection (Tsukayama 2015; McDermott 2014; Ferraro

B. Murphy, *Regulating Undercover Law Enforcement: The Australian Experience*, https://doi.org/10.1007/978-981-33-6381-6_4

2012). The purpose of it in the private context is not, usually, for prosecution. Insurance companies, for example, routinely make use of private investigators to conduct surveillance and information collection about claimants, and sometimes competitors. Corporate investigations are typically concerned with what is happening "on the ground" within the organisation and to facilitate accountability mechanisms, although there is undoubtedly corporate espionage. Tsukayama, for example argues that undercover investigations provide enormous benefits to large organisations, which include (i) discovery of internal dishonesty; (ii) the identities of the parties involved; (iii) the causes and systems that enabled that dishonesty; (iv) "to purge the organisation of all guilty employees" (or contractors); (v) to correct aberrant behaviours and processes (Tsukayama 2015). The situation gets more complicated where there are effective mergers of private and public investigations, as can sometimes happen in the investigation of activist groups, such as green or animal welfare groups. In Australia, for example, the Royal Society for the Prevention of Cruelty to Animals has a mandate to investigate and prosecute animal cruelty cases. In recent years it appears that some organisations face a two-pronged penetration from both law enforcement and corporate investigators (Lubbers 2015).

The extent to which many of the activities that take place in corporate investigations are unlawful is open for debate. In most instances of the misconduct of employees, the result is dismissal, and governed by contract and employment law. In other cases, the extent of misconduct may be referred to the authorities, with the appropriate investigation findings presented to police. But in other cases, the actions of internal investigators may be unlawful, but because they are rarely adduced in a court the extent of those activities would not be properly ascertained. This is especially the case in workplace investigations where use of surveillance techniques is widespread, including private investigators, email monitoring and integrity testing programs. This phenomena is beyond the scope of the present work but presents an important and emergent field of future research.

Covert investigations regulation may be understood as being governed by boundaries; primarily determined between public and private spheres. As a rule, activities taking place in public spheres do not require a warrant, unless it is activity that is formally prohibited, usually by the criminal law. Equally, activities that take place in the private sphere do require a warrant, either because they are prohibited per se, or because they are taking place where legal remedies are available to those in possession of a private right or interest. The distinctions may be represented in the following diagram:

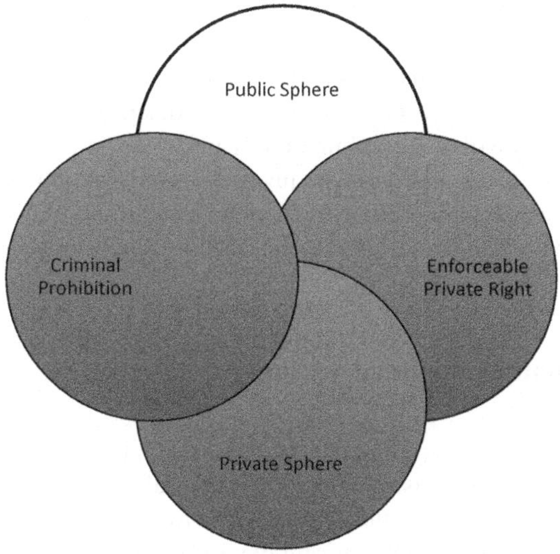

This diagram presents the interests as overlapping and does so intentionally. The various spheres are not always mutually exclusive. Indeed, in many instances the location in which the investigation takes place may have a hybrid character – such as supermarket, where the public are able to move about easily, but only during specified hours, and specified locations. An understanding of this context is important, because it sets the location and shapes the legalities of the investigation.

Unregulated Activities

To speak of "unregulated activities" is something of a misnomer, because in the context of law enforcement investigations all activities are regulated, at least in the sense of being organised and subject to the internal operating standards, norms and regulations of the relevant authority. But a distinction must be drawn between those forms of investigation that require formal authorisation, and those that do not. In the latter case there are additional laters of regulation that possess a greater degree of internal and external governance. For "ordinary" investigations that do not require formal authorisation in the form of warrants, regulation is expressed in a *negative* sense. In other words, it is only where there are specific prohibitions or enforceable common law rights or interests that there is requirement for legal regulation of the proposed activity.

Examples of known techniques in the covert space not normally requiring formal authorisation include observation of suspects, engaging in conversations in public locations, taking photographs in public spaces, forming relationships and so on. These are discussed in more detail in Chap. 3. The basic rule is that an undercover investigator is at liberty to engage in any activity that another member of the public is in the absence of prohibition or private right. Provided the conduct is within that field, a warrant is not required for that activity. However, because investigations often involve a variety of activities or 'modes' of investigation and require movement between a variety of spheres, an application for one or more warrants is routine, especially in complex investigations. As discussed in previous chapters, investigations often involve a combination of information and evidence gathering. Accordingly, many investigations will involve a combination of unregulated and regulated activities, and accordingly will involve warrants. Formal investigations are often preceded by 'informal' one in the opening stages of the investigation.

Telecommunications Interceptions

Telecommunications interception has become one the major forms of investigation and evidence collection in Australia and internationally. Whereas it once concerned only the interception of electronic signals and conversations, it has now evolved to include any form of communication sent electronically. Accordingly, this includes email, digital images, live streaming, meta-data, sound files, browsing histories and especially text-messaging. In Australian law any form of unauthorised access to computing systems is an offence (as well as breach of a private right),[1] and as such requires a warrant. Only specific agencies are authorised to apply for and be granted interception warrants.

Power to make laws with respect to telecommunications is an explicit power of the Commonwealth,[2] and as such telecommunications law resides within the purview of Commonwealth law. However, as most law enforcement takes place through State agencies, there is a requirement for the States and the Commonwealth legislatures to coordinate the legal architecture. Accordingly, telecommunications law involves an interlocking system of State and Federal laws, set out in the following table:

Telecommunications	Interception Legislation
Commonwealth	*Telecommunications (Interception and Access) Act 1979*
NSW	*Telecommunications (Interception and Access)(New South Wales) Act 1987*
NT	*Telecommunications (Interception) Northern Territory Act 2001*
Qld	*Telecommunications Interception Act 2009*
SA	*Telecommunications Interception Act 2012*
TAS	*Telecommunications Interception Tasmania Act 1999*
VIC	*Telecommunications (Interception)(State Provisions) Act 1988*
WA	*Telecommunications (Interception and Access)(Western Australia) Act 1996*

[1] Eg: *Criminal Code Act 1995* (Cth), Part 10.6

[2] *Commonwealth of Australia Constitution Act*, s51(v)

The details of the various Acts are presently irrelevant. Broadly, the legislation provides for a set of authorisation and accountability provisions for access to a range of data to a set of eligible authorities to the exclusion of all others. The starting point is that it is an offence to intercept communications in Australia without a warrant unless some exception applies.[3]

There are two avenues for the issue of warrants. The first is exclusive to the Australian Secret Intelligence Organisation (ASIO). In this case the Director-General of ASIO may seek a warrant directly from the Attorney General. There is a requirement for reasonable suspicion for the issue of the warrant.[4] The second avenue is the more usual, and that is for an eligible agency to make application to an eligible Judge,[5] or a nominated member[6] of the Administrative Appeals Tribunal.[7] Eligible authorities include all police forces, as well as specific organisations that vary according to each state. Those organisations include the state police, as well as specialist anti-corruption bodies work,[8] but can include Royal Commissions.[9]

Warrants are either "telecommunications service warrants", or "named person warrants". The distinction is essentially between a focus on specific providers of telecommunications, and specific individuals.

Fundamentally, the application must contain sufficient information to enable the decision maker to authorise the warrant where there is both reasonable suspicion the subject is likely to use a telecommunications system, and that the person is reasonably suspected of engaging in a serious offence within the meaning of the Act.[10] Warrants enable the interception of communications, but can also be used to access stored data and computer access. There is no requirement on the part of the agency to use any or all of the information obtained in a prosecution, although select parts of that information would usually be used to establish the elements of an offence and to identify the parties engaged in crime or corruption.

---

[3] *Telecommunications (Interception and Access) Act 1979* (Cth), s7. There are numerous exceptions, many of which rely on an intricate interpretation of the legislation. Most of these require a nexus between employment, necessity and consent.

[4] *Telecommunications (Interception and Access) Act 1979* (Cth), ss9, 46

[5] *Telecommunications (Interception and Access) Act 1979* (Cth), s6D

[6] *Telecommunications (Interception and Access) Act 1979* (Cth), s6DA

[7] *Telecommunications (Interception and Access) Act 1979* (Cth), s39

[8] *Telecommunications (Interception and Access) Act 1979* (Cth), s5: *eligible authority*, in relation to a State, means: (a) in any case – the Police Force of that State; or (b) in the case of New South Wales: (i) the Crime Commission; or (ii) the Independent Commission Against Corruption; or (iii) the Inspector of the Independent Commission Against Corruption; or (iv) the Law Enforcement Conduct Commission; or (v) the Inspector of the Law Enforcement Conduct Commission; or (ba) in the case of Victoria – the IBAC or the Victorian Inspectorate; or (c) in the case of Queensland – the Crime and Corruption Commission; or (d) in the case of Western Australia – the Corruption and Crime Commission or the Parliamentary Inspector of the Corruption and Crime Commission; or (e) in the case of South Australia – the Independent Commissioner Against Corruption.

[9] *Telecommunications (Interception and Access) Act 1979* (Cth), s5

[10] *Telecommunications (Interception and Access) Act 1979* (Cth), ss9, 11A, 46, 46A, 48

The Commonwealth Ombudsman provides external oversight of the records of warrants once they have been issued. That information confirms widespread use of telecommunications interception in Australia. Using the Commonwealth Ombudsman Annual Inspection Reports, it has been possible to map out the extent and scale of communication interception in Australia from 1997 to 2019.[11] The results confirm over 64,000 telecommunications interception warrants have been issued since 1997. In that time only 184 applications have been refused (less than 0.002% of applications). This aspect of the warrants system invites an array of important questions. Here the number of refusals, in the context of law enforcement nationally, is so small as to be insignificant. Simply stated, the *overwhelming* majority of warrants are approved. Given the threshold for approval for these warrants is "reasonable suspicion", there is a requirement for the presentation of some level of evidence in the application process. That information would invariably be given in affidavit form on the presentation of the warrant application,[12] unless made as an urgent application. Even then there would be a requirement to provide the authorising officer sufficient verbal information to make a decision.[13] The anomaly here is that the threshold test as a matter of law requires more than a hunch; the information must be sufficient to cause a reasonable person to form the required level of suspicion. As recently stated by the High Court in *Lordianto v Australian Federal Police*, "[a] reasonable suspicion must have a factual basis."[14] The anomaly is that in virtually every case that level of proof has been presented, but it also suggests that the process of approval has become so routine that it is more of a bureaucratic process and less one of judicial scrutiny. This may have something to do either with the notoriously vague nature of "reasonable suspicion", or where the applications are being made. In *Powell and Lenthall* (1930) 44 CLR 470, Rich and Dixon JJ held:

> "The questions what is a suspicion and when it is reasonable are capable of a great deal of subtlety and refinement of argument. Attempts to define such conceptions are seldom helpful. Indeed, it does not seem possible to paraphrase this expression, still less to arrive at any nice definition of the precise stages which the mind must have travelled from complete incredulity to comfortable belief before its condition answers the description "reasonable belief"."[15]

Telecommunications warrants are not uniformly accessed nationally. The same data confirms that just 3 agencies (New South Wales Police; the Australian Federal Police and the New South Wales Crime Commission) account for 65% of all warrants, and that two of them (New South Wales Police (n = 18,942) and the Australian

[11] All inspection reports are available through the Commonwealth Ombudsman website. The relevant reports are published annually, pursuant to the *Telecommunications (Interception and Access) Act 1979* (Cth), s186J

[12] *Telecommunications (Interception and Access) Act 1979* (Cth), s42

[13] *Telecommunications (Interception and Access) Act 1979* (Cth), s43

[14] *Lordianto v Australian Federal Police* [2019] HCA 39 at [89] per Kiefel CJ, Bell, Keane and Gordon JJ

[15] For more recent consideration, see *George v Rockett* (1990) 170 CLR 104; *R v Rondo* [2001] NSWCCA 540; *New South Wales v Robinson* [2019] HCA 46

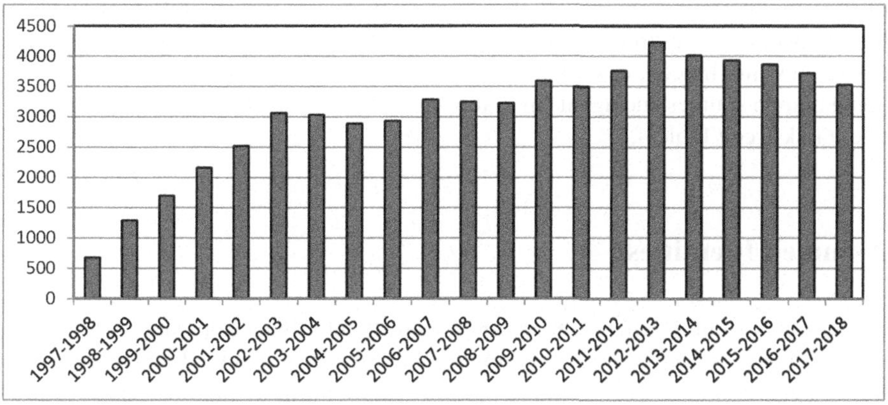

Fig. 4.1 Total telecommunications warrants issued 1997–2018

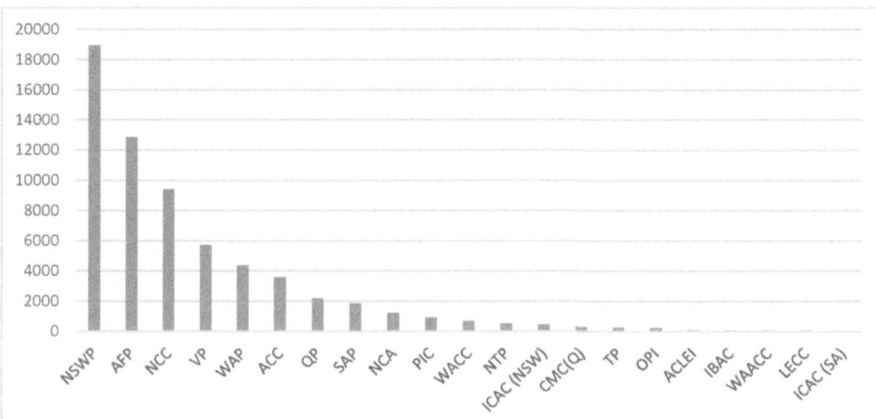

Fig. 4.2 Total number of warrants issued 1997–2018 by Agency

Federal Police (n = 12,873)) account for 50% of all warrants issued. The New South Wales Police are not only the largest users of telecommunications interception warrants, but the trend has been that the use of them doubled between 2009 and 2012, such that the average annual number of applications has increased from approximately 400 in 2003 to over 1400 in 2018. No other agency in Australia has witnessed this increase in the use of warrants. When the overall picture is looked at in basic figures, it appears there is a consistent national use – however, once the two largest consumers of warrants are considered, the numbers are remarkably inconsistent (Figs. 4.1 and 4.2).

The utility of intercepted communications cannot be doubted. In many cases the information, coming as it does directly from the suspect, is highly incriminating and, in most cases, valuable intelligence. There is, of course, no doubt that a large amount of intercepted materials will be mundane and rather boring; but the prospect of sourcing incriminating information from suspects and detailed information about their networks makes the at-time tedious business of filtering through ordinary banter worthwhile. Indeed, in stark contrast to the risks involved in covert investigation using human sources and agents, it is substantially more cost effective and comparatively risk-free (Table 4.1).

Assumed Identities

Australian law enforcement, and national security intelligence operations, are facilitated by the existence of laws enabling the lawful use of assumed identities. These laws emerged out of a 2003 summit on terrorism in multijurisdictional crime, which included recommendations for the lawful use of formal assumed identities and an associated model law.[16] This framework is largely uniform in content, effectively being a national application of the recommendations made in the *Model Law*, although there are some local variations.

Broadly, these laws empower nominated officers of specific organisations[17] to obtain and use official assumed identities. The basis for authorisation varies according to the governing Act, but is broadly concerned with the assumption of a fictitious identity as being necessary for criminal investigation, witness protection, intelligence gathering and/or the training of those involved in those activities.[18] Once granted, the person is entitled to acquire and use a substitute identity for the purposes of the operation. The construction of a false identity may include granting the person fictitious but otherwise legitimate identity papers, including birth certificates, drivers' licenses, and passports. Ordinarily obtaining these documents in a false name would constitute an offence.

Assumed identity authorisations require the authorising officer to not only be satisfied that authorisation is reasonably necessary for the purpose, but also that

[16](Standing Committee of Attorneys-General and Australasian Police Ministers Council Joint Working Group on National Investigation Powers 2003)

[17][Commonwealth: Australian Federal Police; Immigration and Border Protection; Australian Crime Commission; Australian Commission for Law Enforcement Integrity; Australian Taxation Office]; [ACT: Australian Federal Police; Australian Crime Commission; Integrity Commission]; [NSW: NSW Police; Independent Commission Against Corruption; New South Wales Crime Commission; Law Enforcement Conduct Commission; Corrective Services NSW; Australian Crime Commission; Australian Federal Police; Australian Security Intelligence Organisation; Australian Secret Intelligence Service; Customs; Australian Taxation Office]; [Queensland: Qld Police Service; Crime and Corruption Commission]; [South Australia: SA Police; Australian Crime Commission; Independent Commission Against Corruption]; [Tas: Tas Police; Australian Crime Commission]; [Vic: Vic Police; Australian Crime Commission; Independent Broad-based Anti-corruption Commission]; [WA: WA Police; Australian Crime Commission; Fisheries Department]

[18]*Crimes Act 1914* (Cth), s15KB(2); *Crimes (Assumed Identities) Act 2009* (ACT), s9(2); *Law Enforcement and National Security (Assumed Identities) Act 2010* (NSW), s3; *Police Powers and Responsibilities Act 2002* (Qld), s278; *Crimes (Assumed Identities) Act 2004* (Vic), s1

Table 4.1 Outline of telecommunications interception warrants applications by agencies

Issued pursuant to Part 2.5 of the Telecommunications (Interception and Access) Act 1979 (Cth)

Section	Notes
39	An 'agency' is authorised to apply for telecommunications interception warrant from a Judge or nominated member of the AAT An 'agency' is determined by way of declaration[a]
40	An application must be in writing A telephone application may be made by the Chief Officer of the Agency
41	The application must contain the name of the Agency and the person making the application
42	An affidavit must accompany the application, setting out particulars
43	A telephone application must provide particulars
44	The decision maker may request further information
44A	Special provisions for Victorian Agencies
45	Special provisions for Queensland Agencies
45A	State law unaffected by Commonwealth Act
46(1)	Decision maker may authorise issue of telecommunications interception warrant where satisfied: Particulars supplied Reasonable grounds for suspecting the suspect is using the nominated service Information obtained would likely assist in the investigation of a serious offence Decision maker must have regard to matters in 46(2)
46(2)	When deciding to issue a warrant, the decision maker must have regard to: Privacy concerns affecting any person The gravity of conduct being investigated How the information obtained would assist the investigation The use and effectiveness of alternative methods of investigation The extent to which non-suspects are captured by the warrant
47	Warrant requires notification and assistance of carrier provider
48	Warrant may extend to authorisation to enter premises to use, install, maintain or recover equipment on the premises identified
49	The warrant shall be in the prescribed form, containing specific particulars as to the target and premises, not exceeding 90 days in duration

[a]For example, see Telecommunications (Interception) – Declaration of Agency – New South Wales Police Force 2009 (Cth)

there is minimal risk that the authorisation will not be abused by the person so authorised.[19] In addition, the authorisation does *not* permit a person to undertake some action that otherwise requires formal qualifications or training.[20] Once granted,

[19] *Crimes Act 1914* (Cth), s15KB; *Crimes (Assumed Identities) Act 2009* (ACT), s9; *Law Enforcement and National Security (Assumed Identities) Act 2010* (NSW), s6; *Police Powers and Responsibilities Act 2002* (Qld), s283; *Criminal Investigation (Covert Operations) Act 2009* (SA), s7; *Police Powers (Assumed Identities) Act 2006* (Tas), s6; *Crimes (Assumed Identities) Act 2004* (Vic), s5; *Criminal Investigation (Covert Powers) Act 2012* (WA), s48

[20] *Crimes Act 1914* (Cth), s15KT; *Crimes (Assumed Identities) Act 2009* (ACT), s29;; *Law Enforcement and National Security (Assumed Identities) Act 2010* (NSW), s24;

the authorisation enables the nominated person(s) to acquire and use a substitute identity, with associated immunity from liability for doing so.[21]

Given the nature of this legislation, and the Federal context in which it is located, it is no surprise to find that these Acts are exempt from Freedom of Information and State Records legislation,[22] as well as containing provisions for mutual recognition of assumed identities authorisations obtained in other jurisdictions.[23] Assumed identities legislation prohibits the misuse of an assumed identity. In this context "misuse" is a reference to the knowing or reckless use of an assumed identity. Such conduct arises where the actions of the offender exceed the scope of the authorisation, and outside their associated operational duty.[24] As there have not been any reported prosecutions, it can only be surmised that in this context 'misuse' would extend to any purpose other than those actions necessary for the bona fide execution of the operation for which the authorisation was granted, and that any misconduct has otherwise been dealt with under internal disciplinary measures within the relevant organisation. Further, assumed identities legislation restricts a person in court from having their actual identity revealed during judicial processes,[25] and prohibits the unauthorised disclosure of an operative's assumed identity.[26]

Assumed identities legislation is primarily concerned with providing the necessary authorisation to formally construct official identification papers required in cases where the suspect has the capacity to undertake their own inquiries as to the identity of the individual, or where the operation requires what might be described as "deep undercover" work involving immersion of the investigator in a specific

[21] *Crimes Act 1914* (Cth), Part 1AC Div 4; *Crimes (Assumed Identities) Act 2009* (ACT), Part 4; *Law Enforcement and National Security (Assumed Identities) Act 2010* (NSW), Part 4; *Police Powers and Responsibilities Act 2002* (Qld), Chapter 12, Part 3, Div 3; *Criminal Investigation (Covert Operations) Act 2009* (SA), Part 3, Div 2; *Police Powers (Assumed Identities) Act 2006* (Tas), Part 4; *Crimes (Assumed Identities) Act 2004* (Vic), Part 4; *Criminal Investigation (Covert Powers) Act 2012* (WA), Part 3

[22] *Freedom of Information Act 1982* (Cth), s37; *Crimes (Assumed Identities) Act 2009* (ACT), s7; *Government Information (Public Access) Act 2009* (NSW), Schedule 1; *Police Powers and Responsibilities Act 2002* (Qld), s281; *Criminal Investigation (Covert Powers) Act 2012* (WA), s45

[23] *Crimes Act 1914* (Cth), Part 1AC Div 5; *Crimes (Assumed Identities) Act 2009* (ACT), Part 5; *Law Enforcement and National Security (Assumed Identities) Act 2010* (NSW), Part 5; *Police Powers and Responsibilities Act 2002* (Qld), Chapter 12, Part 5; *Criminal Investigation (Covert Operations) Act 2009* (SA), Part 3 Div 4; *Crimes (Assumed Identities) Act 2004* (Vic), Part 5; *Criminal Investigation (Covert Powers) Act 2012* (WA), Part 3 Div 5

[24] *Crimes Act 1914* (Cth), s15LB; *Crimes (Assumed Identities) Act 2009* (ACT), s36; *Law Enforcement and National Security (Assumed Identities) Act 2010* (NSW), s32; *Police Powers and Responsibilities Act 2002* (Qld), s312; *Criminal Investigation (Covert Operations) Act 2009* (SA), s25; *Police Powers (Assumed Identities) Act 2006* (Tas), s31; *Crimes (Assumed Identities) Act 2004* (Vic), s29; *Criminal Investigation (Covert Powers) Act 2012* (WA), s74

[25] *Law Enforcement and National Security (Assumed Identities) Act 2010* (NSW), s34

[26] *Crimes Act 1914* (Cth), s15LC; *Crimes (Assumed Identities) Act 2009* (ACT), s37; *Law Enforcement and National Security (Assumed Identities) Act 2010* (NSW), s33; *Police Powers and Responsibilities Act 2002* (Qld), s313; *Criminal Investigation (Covert Operations) Act 2009* (SA), s26; *Police Powers (Assumed Identities) Act 2006* (Tas), s32; *Crimes (Assumed Identities) Act 2004* (Vic), s30; *Criminal Investigation (Covert Powers) Act 2012* (WA), s75

environment. Normally this kind of target is sophisticated and well resourced, requiring more elaborate and considered investigations than mere representation of a false identity – typically matters concerned with corruption, organised crime, or counter espionage. The extent to which these authorisations are used and deployed in Australia is not known. Unlike controlled operations and telecommunications warrants, these authorisations only require internal reporting obligations and are otherwise not matters of public knowledge. They are not the subject of official reporting.

Surveillance and Listening Devices

As discussed in Chap. 3, surveillance comes in several forms, both overt and covert, passive and targeted. As a general principle, there are no restrictions on surveillance in public spaces that otherwise do not involve a trespass to an individual or their goods. Accordingly, casual observation and consensual discussions of a person in a clandestine manner are not regulated in Australian law. Similarly, taking photographs, or even digital footage, is not unlawful if taken in a public place. However, such conduct is likely to attract attention if noticed, and in some cases likely to result in a hostile response. This aspect of Australian law is controversial, and not without criticism. Harfield (2014a, b), for example, has argued that we all have a right to be anonymous in public places, and that includes the right not to have our images taken without consent simply because we are lawfully going about our business in a public space. The general absence of an explicit right to privacy in Australia is problematic from this perspective. Although there are express rights to privacy reflected in some jurisdictions (the ACT, VIC and QLD), these rights are not absolute, and amenable to both waiver and impeachment by operation of law. Yet even if there was a general right to privacy in this sense, contemporary policing has come to depend on mass surveillance strategies.

Where surveillance involves physical interference with property, or the effective invasion of what would otherwise constitute a private space or interest, the general principle is that intrusive surveillance requires a warrant if the information obtained through the surveillance is to admissible in a court, and its collection lawful. At this point it is important to distinguish the use of human intrusive surveillance and the use of technology to collect sound, electronic or visual images. In Australian law the use of human intrusive surveillance is normally governed by *controlled operations* legislation, while the use of technology is governed by listening or surveillance devices legislation. Like telecommunications interception, intrusive and covert electronic surveillance methods are regulated through a system of warrants in all Australian jurisdictions.[27] Australian courts have shown a willingness to uphold the prohibitions attached to the use of these devices in the absence of a warrant. Recently, for example, in *Kadir v The Queen* (2020) 267 CLR 109, the High Court

[27] *Listening Devices Act 1992* (ACT); *Surveillance Devices Act 2007* (NT); *Surveillance Devices Act 2007* (NSW); *Police Powers and Responsibilities Act 2000* (Qld); *Surveillance Devices Act 2016* (SA); *Listening Devices Act 1991* (Tas); *Surveillance Devices Act 1999* (Vic); *Surveillance Devices Act 1998* (WA). In Queensland see also the *Invasion of Privacy Act 1971* (Qld).

affirmed that surveillance evidence that had been obtained covertly using digital cameras used to investigate illegal greyhound training using live animals was unlawfully obtained and inadmissible, notwithstanding the legitimate public interest in investigating reports of animal cruelty. Like much of Australian criminal law, there is a good degree of variation in the detail of laws in each jurisdiction. Again, this is not an area of law where there are uniform provisions. We can only speak of a set of general principles and refer to the reader to specific Acts for the exact detail.

Surveillance Devices

The starting point to understand the law is understanding what constitutes a "surveillance device". This varies by jurisdiction, and because of rapid technological change, there are numerous instances where the law may not adequately cover the field. The most recent framework, Part 2 Division 1 of South Australia's *Surveillance Devices Act 2016*, makes a distinction between (i) listening devices; (ii) optical surveillance devices; (iii) combined listening/optical devices; (iv) tracking devices; and (v) data surveillance devices. This distinction recognises that surveillance of a person need not involve images or sounds at all; it can include a broad range of devices that collect data *about* the person; their location, their movements, their purchases, biometric information, web browsing habits, what books they read, and whom they interact with. This is an important development, which covers gaps that exists in those jurisdictions that limit the concept of a "device" to visual and audio recordings. These distinctions can be seen in statutory definitions.[28] Fundamentally, the legislation is concerned with the use of a technological instrument or process that enables direct perception of the words and actions of the suspect in the physical world, and the traces of those activities in electronic form. The definitions of "surveillance device" are not limited to those devices whose *primary purpose* is the capture of information, still or moving images, and sound. Rapid and recent advances in technology include numerous devices that have the potential for surveillance use, but as a secondary purpose, such as drones or mobile phones. As a result, the definitions of a "surveillance device" are expressed in broad terms, extending to any device that is *capable* of acting as a surveillance device.

General Prohibition of Unauthorised Surveillance

The starting principle is that the use of surveillance devices, and the communication of information obtained by them, is unlawful in the absence of a warrant or statutory exception. In broad terms, these offences carry a primary and secondary sanction. The primary sanction is a criminal conviction that may involve a fine or prison term,

---

[28] See Appendix A.

or both. The secondary sanction is the prima facie exclusion of evidence if the content is later relied on by the party in any subsequent litigation on the basis the evidence has been obtained unlawfully in contravention of an Australian law. The power to exclude is reflected in both the legislation itself, as well as the overlapping laws of evidence.[29]

Jurisdiction	Use prohibitions	Maximum fine	Maximum prison term	Exclusion of evidence
CTH *Surveillance Devices Act 2004*	Use (s45)	–	2 years 10 years	S45
ACT *Listening Devices Act 1992*	Use (s4)	50pu[a]	–	S10
NSW *Surveillance Devices Act 2007*	Install, use or maintain (s7)	500pu[b] (Corporation) 100pu (Individual)	5 years	S138 *Evidence Act 1995*
NT *Surveillance Devices Act 2007*	Install, use or maintain (s11)	250pu[c]	2 years	S40
QLD *Invasion of Privacy Act 1971*	Use (s49)	40pu[d]	2 years	Common law
SA *Surveillance Devices Act 2016*	Install, use or maintain (Part 2, Div 1)	$75,000 (Corporation) $15,000 (Individual)	3 years	Common law
TAS *Listening Devices Act 1991*	Use (s5)	40pu[e] (Individual) 500pu (Corporation)	2 years	S14
VIC *Surveillance Devices Act 1999*	Install, use or maintain (s6)	240pu[f]	2 years	S138 *Evidence Act 2008*
WA *Surveillance Devices Act 1998*	Install, use or maintain (s5)	$5000 (Individual) $50,000 (Corporation)	1 year	Common law

[a]Valued at $810 for a Corporation and $160 for an Individual. See *Legislation Act 2001* (ACT), s133
[b]Valued at $110. See *Crimes (Sentencing Procedure) Act 1999* (NSW), s17
[c]Valued at $158. Subject to indexation. See *Penalty Units Act 2009* (NT); Penalty Units Regulation 2010 (NT) as amended.
[d]Valued at $110. See *Penalties and Sentences Act 1992* (Qld), s5
[e]Valued at $140. Subject to indexation. See *Penalty Units and Other Penalties Act 1987* (Tas), s4
[f]Valued at $165.22. Subject to indexation. See *Monetary Units Act 2004* (Vic)

[29] *Kadir v The Queen; Grech v The Queen* [2020] HCA 1

As can be seen, the prohibition against the installation, use and/or maintenance of a surveillance device carries with it substantial penalties, although in more jurisdictions these would be regarded as minor matters dealt with in Local or Magistrates' Courts. In NSW the maximum penalty of 5 years technically makes the offence indictable. However, this offence is normally dealt with summarily.[30] In addition to the various offences related to the actual use and installation of surveillance devices, most jurisdictions also prohibit the communication, publication and possession of information obtained in that forum.[31]

Exceptions

Consent

In an age where large numbers of individuals carry mobile phones, most of which are capable of video and audio capture (including remote access), exceptions exist in most jurisdictions with respect to recordings that have been made with the consent of the parties (express or implied).[32] Ordinarily this will not be an issue in the context of a criminal investigation. In cases involving undercover work, it would be highly unlikely that recording devices would be overtly displayed or used in the process, although much depends on the context.

Inadvertent Capture

In most jurisdictions it is an exception to the rule against prohibition where the image or sound capture is inadvertent.[33] That is, unintentional. The scope of these provisions has yet to be fully tested. It invokes complex issues of law and evidence. Turning on an electronic device is normally intentional; but not always. Ordinary experience demonstrates that it is possible to not only turn on a device in a pocket accidentally,

---

[30] The offence is a 'Table 2' indictable offence that may be tried on indictment only on the election of the prosecution. See *Criminal Procedure Act 1986* (NSW), s260, Schedule 1, Table 2

[31] *Listening Devices Act 1992* (ACT), Part 2; *Surveillance Devices Act 2007* (NSW), Part 2; *Surveillance Devices Act 2007* (NT), Part 3; *Police Powers and Responsibilities Act 2000* (Qld), s352; *Surveillance Devices Act 2016* (SA); *Listening Devices Act 1991* (Tas); *Surveillance Devices Act 1999* (Vic); *Surveillance Devices Act 1998* (WA). In Queensland see also the *Invasion of Privacy Act 1971* (Qld). In Tasmania see also *Police Powers (Surveillance Devices) Act 2006* (Tas)

[32] *Listening Devices Act 1992* (ACT), s4(3)(a); *Surveillance Devices Act 2007* (NSW), s7(3)(a); *Surveillance Devices Act 2007* (NT), s11(2)(b); *Surveillance Devices Act 2016* (SA), s4(2)(a); *Listening Devices Act 1991* (Tas), s5(3)(a); *Surveillance Devices Act 1999* (Vic), s6(1); *Surveillance Devices Act 1998* (WA), s5(3).

[33] Ibid

but also make a call. Then there will be cases where the accidental capture actually picks up something that is relevant and probative in the prosecution of a criminal event. Here the absence of a warrant makes the use prima facie unlawful; but the exception excludes that. Ultimately these are complex questions of fact and degree that would need to be determined in a court applying the laws of evidence.

Police Body-Worn/Vehicle Cameras

It is common for police vehicles to be equipped with in-car cameras and recording devices, as well as police officers wearing body cameras. In these cases the capture of sound and images is deemed lawful where the camera is worn openly and the officer is acting in the execution of their duties.[34] These devices do not require the issue of a warrant to authorise their use or authorise the use of evidence collected by them.

Workplace Surveillance

Surveillance in the workplace has been widely practised, but has only recently been placed on a statutory footing. This is contentious because most workplaces are private premises, as well as being sites where numerous parties who are otherwise lawfully engaged in work are going about their affairs and often caught up in the investigation. The legalities of investigations in the workplace are complicated not only because of the privacy aspects, but also the industrial relations implications. This is a space in which there are potentially overlapping internal investigation processes, largely unregulated and the subject of contract, and external investigation processes. In the context of the investigation of crime, the workplace presents investigators with unique legal obstacles primarily concerned with the maintenance of privacy of individuals who are otherwise lawfully going about their business at the workplace. Consequently, the legal landscape for investigations in the workplace is governed by a complex web of private and public law, including workplace surveillance legislation. Simply stated, employers are able to make application for workplace surveillance authorisation involving cameras, audio, computer and tracking devices under certain conditions. In some cases, there are specific prohibitions against certain kinds of surveillance embedded in surveillance device legislation,[35] while in other cases there are specific workplace surveillance Acts.[36]

---

[34] *Surveillance Devices Act 2007* (NSW), s50A; *Surveillance Devices Act 2007* (NT), s14A; *Police Powers and Responsibilities Act 2000* (Qld), s609A; *Police Powers (Surveillance Devices) Act 2006* (Tas), s44A; *Surveillance Devices Act 1999* (Vic), s6(2)(d).

[35] *Surveillance Devices Act 1999* (Vic), Part 2A

[36] *Workplace Privacy Act 2011* (ACT); *Workplace Surveillance Act 2005* (NSW)

What makes this field of legislation controversial, is that although these Acts prohibit surveillance generally, they do, in fact, authorise surveillance by consent (which is rarely, if ever, negotiated – normally it is a condition of employment). In the ACT and in NSW, an employer is able to seek and obtain a covert surveillance warrant to undertake covert investigation of employees.[37] In most cases the consequences of this kind of investigation would be termination of employment for various forms of misconduct, but equally there may be material relevant to criminal charges. However, it appears in all cases that a valid surveillance warrant issued to a law enforcement agency otherwise trumps workplace surveillance laws. As this book is otherwise concerned with law enforcement, further discussion on workplace surveillance is unnecessary.

Applications for Surveillance Warrants

As with any warrant, all surveillance device legislation sets out certain administrative requirements for an application based on reasonable grounds to suspect or believe that a "relevant offence" is, has been, or is going to be committed. These are important threshold limitations. As discussed earlier, "reasonable grounds" requires the existence of some evidence as a matter of *fact* sufficient to satisfy a reasonable person that circumstances are sufficiently indicated by the existing evidence to suggest an offence is, has been or likely going to be committed within the lifetime of the warrant. The second threshold requirement is that the offence is either an offence against a law of the Commonwealth, *or* an indictable offence. Practically speaking, this process normally involves the applicant presenting the decision-maker with affidavit evidence accompanied with the relevant forms.

Although there are variations in legislation around Australia with respect to surveillance warrants, a typical process can be illustrated using the NSW *Surveillance Devices Act 2007* (Table 4.2).

Once a warrant is granted, the warrant authorises a range of activities linked to the use, installation and information obtained by a surveillance device. As set out in the table below, to a large extent the scope of what is authorised depends on the nature of the device. Broadly, the basic principle is that legislation will authorise what is reasonably necessary to ensure the placement of the device in the relevant location, which will include physical access, alteration of structures, technical advice, and operational use of the device in situ.

[37] *Workplace Privacy Act 2011* (ACT), s26; *Workplace Surveillance Act 2005* (NSW), Part 4:

Table 4.2 Outline of surveillance device applications in New South Wales

Section	Notes
15	Declares two kinds of warrants available: Surveillance device warrant (Part 3, Division 2) Retrieval warrant (Part 3, Division 3)
16	Surveillance device warrants may be issued by a nominated Judge Tracking device warrants may be issued by a nominated Magistrate
17(1)	A Law Enforcement officer may apply for a warrant, where: The officer *suspects* OR *believes* on reasonable grounds A *relevant offence* [an Indictable offence, or an offence against a law of the Commonwealth] Has been, is being, or about to be committed, AND An investigation into that offence is, or will likely be conducted, AND The use of a surveillance device is necessary (i) to collect evidence, (ii) identify, or (iii) locate the offender.
17(1A)	Applications may be made to enter correctional centres for surveillance of high risk terrorist offenders
17(2)	Applications may be made to a Judge (in any case), or A Magistrate in the case of a tracking device
17(3)	The application must contain particulars (s20); Details of alternative means of gathering relevant information (if any); Details of any attempts to use alternatives, and results; Details of any previous warrants issued.
17(3A)	The application must be accompanied with a supporting affidavit
17(4)	An affidavit is not immediately required if circumstances are urgent
17(5)	If so, enough information as is reasonably practical is required, with supporting affidavit within 72 h
17(5A)	Requirement to serve notice to the Attorney General
17(6)	Matter is NOT to be heard in open court
18	Matters may be submitted remotely (eg: via email)
19(1)	Applications may be approved where the approver is satisfied there are reasonable grounds for suspicion or belief in the application
19(2)	The approver must also consider: The nature and gravity of the offence being investigated Any privacy concerns Alternative means of investigation The extent the warrant would assist the investigation The value of evidence obtained The existence of any prior warrants
20	Particulars required in the warrant include: The identity of the suspect(s) The type of warrant Details of the premises, vehicle or object subject of the warrant Name of principal investigator(s) The term of the warrant (not exceeding 90 days)

Scope of authorisation			
Vehicle or premises	Objects	Areas/locations	Persons
Use of a surveillance device on or in a specific vehicle or premises	Use of a surveillance device on or in a specific object or class of objects	Use of a surveillance device to record conversations, activities or location of a specific person or person(s) unknown	Use of a surveillance device on or about the body of a specific person
Installation, use and maintenance of a surveillance device on or in the specified premises or vehicle, and	Installation, use and maintenance of a surveillance device in or on the specified object or an object of the specified class, and	Installation, use and maintenance of a surveillance device on or in premises or a vehicle where the person is reasonably believed to be or likely to be in the future, and	Use of the surveillance device on or about the body of the person specified
Entry, by force if necessary, onto or into the premises or vehicle, or other specified premises adjoining or providing access to the premises or the vehicle	Entry, by force if necessary, onto or into any premises or vehicle where the object, or an object of the specified class, is reasonably believed to be or is likely to be, or other premises adjoining or providing access to those premises or the vehicle	Entry, by force if necessary, onto or into the premises or vehicle, or other premises adjoining or providing access to those premises or the vehicle	

Retrieval of the device, and
Installation, use, maintenance and retrieval of any enhancement equipment, and
Use of an assumed identity for the purpose of the installation, use, maintenance or retrieval of the device, and
Disconnection of, or otherwise making inoperative, any security system for the purpose of the installation, maintenance or retrieval of the device, and
Temporary removal of an object or vehicle from premises for the purpose of the installation, maintenance or retrieval of the device and return of the object or vehicle to the premises, and
Breaking open of anything for the purpose of the installation, maintenance or retrieval of the device, and
Connection of the device or enhancement equipment to an electricity supply system and the use of electricity from that system to operate the device, and
Connection of the device or equipment to a telecommunications system or network and the use of that system or network in connection with the operation of the device, and
Provision of assistance or technical expertise to the law enforcement officer named in the warrant in the installation, use, maintenance or retrieval of the surveillance device or enhancement equipment under the warrant.

As can be seen, there are a wide range of powers available on the issue of a surveillance device warrant, many of which are necessarily incidental to the use and installation of the device.

The scale of use of surveillance devices in Australia is by no means clear. Unlike telecommunications interception warrants, there is no single source of reliable information that details the number of warrants issued. Much depends on the recording keeping, reporting and scrutiny requirements in each jurisdiction. In this respect surveillance device records share the same problems as controlled operations warrants. But in addition, the information made available is highly variable. What we do know from the available information is that law enforcement make significant use of surveillance devices in the course of investigation and, like telecommunications warrants, the main consumers of these warrants appear to be the New South Wales Police and the NSW Crime Commission. It is not possible to collate a picture of surveillance device warrants accurately. The most reliable information comes from New South Wales, and even that is patchy. We know, for example, there were over 9500 warrants issued in that state between December 2008 and July 2019, with 199 being issued in between July and December 2008, and 862 between January and June 2019. Based on the available annual reports, we can observe that the number of warrants issued is not an accurate measure of the scale of surveillance device use. A single warrant can authorise many warrants of different types. Indeed, simply focussing on the number of warrants issued distorts the real picture. For example, the 862 warrants issued between January and June 2019 authorised the use of 7856 surveillance devices, of which 3442 were listening devices, 2251 were optical devices, 1821 were tracking devices, 228 involve data surveillance, and 114 were in combined form.[38] This suggests a warrant will authorise, on average, 9 devices.

Covert Search Warrants

In some jurisdictions, Australian law permits the search of premises without the knowledge of the owner /occupier of the premises until after the event. This power exists for a number of purposes, including entry into premises without permission, ensuring a suspect is not able to move or destroy evidence that might otherwise be available during the execution of an ordinary search warrant, or in the case of terrorist investigations, enable early intervention. This class of warrant is an exception to the usual rule that the occupier of the premises must be given notice prior to the search being conducted. In the context of normal search warrants, the search takes place in conjunction with the service of the warrant. In the case of a covert warrant, the occupier may not even be aware of the search until the time of an arrest.

Given the extraordinary nature of this power, warrants of this kind are limited to certain categories of offence types. These vary by jurisdiction.

[38] *Report by the Attorney General of New South Wales Pursuant to Section 45 of the Surveillance Devices Act 2007 for the Period Ended 30 June 2019*, p. 4

New South Wales

Covert search warrants were introduced in NSW in 2009 in the form of an amendment Act to the main police powers Act in that state.[39] This Act provides a series of exceptions to the usual rules that govern entry and search warrants and expectations, going well beyond anything that would have been acceptable at common law. In NSW a senior police officer is empowered to apply to a Supreme Court judge for a covert search warrant.[40] That application must be dealt with in the absence of the public.[41] There must be reasonable grounds for suspecting that within the next 10 days there will be evidence of a "searchable offence", and that it is considered necessary to enter the premises without the knowledge of the occupier.[42] The concept of a "searchable offence" relies on what is now a complex definition involving a consideration of both the *type* of offence, and the *penalty*. Broadly, a "searchable offence" must also be a "serious offence" within the meaning of the Act. The basic threshold here is the offence must fall into a nominated category and carry with it a penalty of at least 7 years.[43] Initially offences of this kind were essentially confined

---

[39] *Law Enforcement (Powers and Responsibilities) Amendment (Search Powers) Act 2009* (NSW). The amendments commenced on 30 May 2009.

[40] *Law Enforcement (Powers and Responsibilities) Act 2002* (NSW), s46C(1). This is located at the rank of Superintendent or above.

[41] *Law Enforcement (Powers and Responsibilities) Act 2002* (NSW), s76A

[42] *Law Enforcement (Powers and Responsibilities) Act 2002* (NSW), s46C(2)

[43] *Law Enforcement (Powers and Responsibilities) Act 2002* (NSW), s46A: Searchable offences (1) For the purposes of this Part, searchable offence in relation to a warrant – (a) means any of the following – (i) an indictable offence, (ii) a firearms or prohibited weapons offence, (iii) a narcotics offence, (iv) a child abuse material offence, (v) an offence involving a thing being stolen or otherwise unlawfully obtained, and (b) if the warrant is a covert search warrant – means a serious offence, and (c) if the warrant is a criminal organisation search warrant – means an organised crime offence. (2) In subsection (1) – child abuse material offence means an offence under section 91H or 578C of the Crimes Act 1900. firearms or prohibited weapons offence means an offence under the Firearms Act 1996, the Weapons Prohibition Act 1998 or a regulation made under either of those Acts, being an offence committed in respect of a firearm, an imitation firearm or a prohibited weapon within the meaning of those Acts. narcotics offence means – (a) an offence under the Poisons and Therapeutic Goods Act 1966, or a regulation made under that Act, being an offence committed in respect of – (i) a restricted substance prescribed for the purposes of section 16 of that Act, or (ii) a drug of addiction within the meaning of that Act, or (b) an offence under the Drug Misuse and Trafficking Act 1985 or a regulation made under that Act. organised crime offence means any serious indictable offence arising from, or occurring as a result of, organised criminal activity. Serious offence means the following – (a) any indictable offence punishable by imprisonment for a period of 7 or more years and that involves the following – (i) the supply, manufacture or cultivation of drugs or prohibited plants, (ii) the possession, manufacture or sale of firearms within the meaning of the Firearms Act 1996, (iii) money laundering, (iv) car and boat rebirthing activities, (v) the unauthorised access to, or modification or impairment of, computer data or electronic communications, (vi) an activity involving theft carried out on an organised basis, (vii) violence causing grievous bodily harm or wounding, (viii) the possession, manufacture or supply of false instruments, (ix) corruption, (x) destruction of property, (xi) homicide, (xii) kidnapping, (b) any offence under Division 10 (Sexual offences against adults and children) of Part 3 of the

to drug supply, firearms offences and money laundering. However, there has been considerable extension of what constitutes a "serious offence", such that a covert search warrant in this jurisdiction includes not only major drug crimes – it extends to terrorism, child pornography and organised crime.

The covert search warrant, once issued, has a lifespan of 10 days before expiry.[44] The covert search warrant authorises additional powers during its execution, including:

- Power to remove a thing named in the warrant from the premises, or any other thing reasonably believed to be connected to an offence;[45]
- Power to substitute a thing found during the search;[46]
- Re-entry to premises to seize or retrieve a thing;[47]
- The search may be executed day or night;[48]
- An occupier's noticed must be served as soon as practical on the execution of the warrant, unless validly postponed;[49]
- An occupier's notice may be postponed for a period of up to 6 months after the search, or up to 3 years on further approval;[50]
- Authorises entry to *adjoining premises* without knowledge of occupier;[51]
- An occupier's notice of *adjoining premises* must be served as soon as practical on the execution of the warrant, unless validly postponed or dispensed with;[52]
- Authorises the impersonation of any person for the purpose of executing the warrant;[53]
- Do anything reasonably practical to ensure the concealment of entry.[54]

Crimes Act 1900 punishable by imprisonment for a period of 7 or more years, (c) an offence under section 80D (Causing sexual servitude) or 80E (Conduct of business involving sexual servitude) of the Crimes Act 1900, (d) an offence under section 93FA (Possession, supply or making of explosives) of the Crimes Act 1900, (e) an offence under Division 15 (Child prostitution) or 15A (Child pornography) of Part 3 of the Crimes Act 1900, (f) an offence under section 308F (Possession of data with intent to commit serious computer offence) or 308G (Producing, supplying or obtaining data with intent to commit serious computer offence) of the Crimes Act 1900, (g) an offence of attempting to commit, or of conspiracy or incitement to commit, or of aiding or abetting, an offence referred to in paragraphs (a)–(f). (3) For the purposes of this section, an activity involving theft is carried out on an organised basis if – (a) it is planned, organised, structured or otherwise carried out in such a manner as to indicate that the activity is carried out on more than one occasion and involves more than one participant, and (b) it is carried out for profit or gain.

[44] *Law Enforcement (Powers and Responsibilities) Act 2002* (NSW), s73(2A)

[45] *Law Enforcement (Powers and Responsibilities) Act 2002* (NSW), s49(1)

[46] *Law Enforcement (Powers and Responsibilities) Act 2002* (NSW), s49(2)

[47] *Law Enforcement (Powers and Responsibilities) Act 2002* (NSW), s49A

[48] *Law Enforcement (Powers and Responsibilities) Act 2002* (NSW), s72(1A)

[49] *Law Enforcement (Powers and Responsibilities) Act 2002* (NSW), s67

[50] *Law Enforcement (Powers and Responsibilities) Act 2002* (NSW), s67A

[51] *Law Enforcement (Powers and Responsibilities) Act 2002* (NSW), s47A(2)(b)

[52] *Law Enforcement (Powers and Responsibilities) Act 2002* (NSW), s67B

[53] *Law Enforcement (Powers and Responsibilities) Act 2002* (NSW), s47A(2)(c)

[54] *Law Enforcement (Powers and Responsibilities) Act 2002* (NSW), s47A(2)(d)

Probably the most extraordinary aspect of the provisions is the capacity for the execution of a covert warrant on premises adjacent to the premises being investigated. The Explanatory Memorandum and Second Reading Speeches provide minimal commentary on these provisions.[55] During the Second Reading Debate, the Opposition Leader reiterated concerns that had been expressed by the Parliamentary Standing Legislative Review Committee about the intrusive nature of these warrants.[56] Despite those concerns, the Opposition did not oppose the bill, guaranteeing its passage with minor amendment. Broadly, while it was recognised the amendment provided significant powers to law enforcement, the judiciary exercised control over the issue of the warrants, in full knowledge of the extensive powers and trespass involved in their exercise.

Queensland

Covert search warrants were initially introduced in Queensland for the investigation of terrorism. Like NSW, the scope of covert search warrants has expanded over time to include specific offences, terrorism, and organised crime. Similar to NSW, Chapter 9 of the *Police Powers and Responsibilities Act 2002* (Qld) authorises a senior police officer to apply to a Supreme Court judge for a covert search warrant.[57] The application is heard in the absence of the public,[58] and requires sufficient

---

[55] New South Wales, *Parliamentary Debates*, Legislative Council, 24 March 2009, pp. 13531 (John Hatzistergos, Attorney General): "Section 67 of the principal Act is amended so as to alter the current requirements for service of occupiers notices in relation to the execution of standard warrants and to provide for service of occupiers notices in relation to the execution of covert search warrants. At present an occupier's notice is required to be personally served on an occupier on entry to premises, or as soon as practicable after, unless service is postponed. Service may be postponed on more than one occasion for up to 6 months at a time. New section 67 subsections (4) to (7) instead require personal service on entry or within 48 h after entry. If this proves impossible an eligible issuing officer may make orders to bring the entry to the notice of the occupier otherwise than by personal service. These changes will create more certainty for both occupiers and law enforcement agencies alike. New section 67 (8) requires service of an occupiers notice in relation to a covert search warrant as soon as practicable after the warrant is executed unless it is postponed under new section 67A. New section 67A enables an eligible issuing officer to postpone service of an occupiers notice in relation to a covert search warrant for an initial period of up to 6 months and on further occasions for up to 3 years in total. An eligible issuing officer may not postpone service for periods exceeding 18 months in total unless satisfied that there are exceptional grounds to justify the postponement. New section 67B requires an adjoining occupier's notice to be served on an adjoining occupier whose property is entered under a covert search warrant within specified periods, unless service is postponed or dispensed with by the eligible issuing officer."

[56] New South Wales, *Parliamentary Debates*, Legislative Council, 24 March 2009, pp. 13532 (John Ajaka, Opposition Leader). See also New South Wales Parliament, Legislation Review Committee, *Legislation Review Digest* No.2 of 2009, pp. 36–42.

[57] *Police Powers and Responsibilities Act 2002* (Qld), s212

[58] *Police Powers and Responsibilities Act 2002* (Qld), s213

particulars to establish there are reasonable grounds for believing a designated offence,[59] organised crime[60] or terrorism[61] is likely to take place within 72 h.[62]

The PPRA requires that the authorising judge must be "mindful of the highly intrusive nature of a covert search warrant", and balance a range of factors in its issue.[63] This consideration is not present in NSW, but it is by no means clear what difference, if any, this caveat makes to the warrants issued in that State. Further, Queensland has since passed a *Human Rights Act*,[64] that must now be considered in making decisions about issuing a warrant. It has yet to be determined the extent to which covert searches are compatible or limited by that legislation. As that is the same situation in relation to Victoria, this will be discussed in more detail below.

Once issued, the covert search warrant authorises a combination of ordinary and extraordinary powers, including authority to:

- Enter the premises, covertly or through subterfuge, as often as is reasonably necessary for the purposes of the warrant and stay on it for the time reasonably necessary;
- Pass over, through, along or under another place to enter the premises;
- Search the premises for anything named in the warrant, or anything else reasonably believed to be evidence of an offence;
- Open anything that is locked;
- Photograph anything reasonably believed to be connected with an offence;
- Inspect or test anything found on the place;
- Power to take a thing, or part of a thing, and send it for testing;
- Power to seize, take, enter, search or modify a vehicle.[65]

---

[59] *Police Powers and Responsibilities Act 2002* (Qld), Dictionary: designated offence means – (a) an offence against any of the following provisions of the Criminal Code – (i) section 300 [Murder]; (ii) section 306 [Attempted murder]; (iii) section 309 [Conspiracy to murder]; or (b) another offence for which a person is liable, on conviction, to be sentenced to imprisonment for life if the circumstances of the offence involve – (i) a serious risk to, or actual loss of, a person's life; or (ii) a serious risk of, or actual, serious injury to a person.

[60] *Police Powers and Responsibilities Act 2002* (Qld), Dictionary: organised crime means an ongoing criminal enterprise to commit serious indictable offences in a systematic way involving a number of people and substantial planning and organisation.

[61] *Police Powers and Responsibilities Act 2002* (Qld), s211

[62] *Police Powers and Responsibilities Act 2002* (Qld), s215

[63] *Police Powers and Responsibilities Act 2002* (Qld), s214: Before deciding the application the judge must, in particular, and being mindful of the highly intrusive nature of a covert search warrant, consider the following – (a)the nature and seriousness of the suspected offence or terrorism; (b)the extent to which issuing the warrant would help prevent, detect or provide evidence of, the offence or terrorism; (c)the benefits derived from any previous covert search warrants, search warrants or surveillance device warrants in relation to the relevant person or place; (d)the extent to which police officers investigating the matter have used or can use conventional ways of investigation; (e)how much the use of conventional ways of investigation would be likely to help in the investigation of the matter; (f)how much the use of conventional ways of investigation would prejudice the investigation of the matter; (g)any submissions made by a monitor.

[64] *Human Rights Act 2019* (Qld)

[65] *Police Powers and Responsibilities Act 2002* (Qld), s219

In Queensland, covert search warrants are included in the mandate for scrutiny by the Public Interest Monitor ('PIM'). The PIM is required to make annual reports direct to Parliament.[66] External scrutiny direct to Parliament is an important safeguard in the use of covert warrants. Surprisingly, there is no jurisprudence to emerge out of the *Human Rights Act* in Queensland at this stage with respect to covert search warrants as being a threat to the right to privacy otherwise guaranteed by section 25.[67] As will be discussed at length in later chapters, it is important not to overstate that right. Like all human rights instruments, these rights are not absolute. They are subject to lawful breach in the sense that provided the right is "lawfully" impeached, there is nothing particularly controversial about a covert search warrant as a privacy breach. The simple fact is that all covert activity is a privacy breach. Provided the warrant is justified and lawfully issued, the breach is absolved by force of law. The privacy and intrusive nature of these investigations are explicitly recognised in the requirements for approving the application, and to a large extent these issues are "front-ended" in the approval process, but also matters that are subsequently examined by the PIM. This can be seen in *R v Riscuta*, where Justice Burns in the Queensland Supreme Court stated:

> The role of the public interest monitor is an important one. Just as the courts have been traditionally regarded as "the guardians of the citizens' right to privacy" and are regularly entrusted by legislation with the oversight of powers such as the power conferred by [the Telecommunication (Interception and Access) Act 1979 (Cth)], the public interest monitor provides another layer of protection for private citizens who, unknown to those citizens, are sought to be made the subject of a surveillance warrant. In cases such as this where there is an application for the issue of a warrant, the public interest monitor is obliged to critically evaluate the material advanced in support of an application in order to determine whether to question the applicant police officer and/or make submissions on the hearing of the application. This will never be a perfunctory exercise; the public interest monitor must give real attention to the question whether the evidence and information offered by the party applying for the warrant is sufficient to satisfy the decision-maker of the existence of all applicable statutory preconditions and that the material is otherwise such as to justify such an intrusion into the privacy of the citizen in question. There is no reason to think that the public interest monitor failed to discharge these obligations in this case, and there is certainly no evidence to that effect.[68]

Victoria

Part 2 of the *Terrorism (Community Protection) Act 2003* (Vic) provides the equivalent Victorian authorisation mechanism and powers for covert search warrants. Unlike NSW and Qld, in Victoria covert search warrants are confined to

---

[66] *Police Powers and Responsibilities Act 2002* (Qld), s743

[67] Section 25 provides: "A person has the right – (a) not to have the person's privacy, family, home or correspondence unlawfully or arbitrarily interfered with; and (b) not to have the person's reputation unlawfully attacked."

[68] *R v Riscuta* [2017] QSC 47 at [23]. Footnotes omitted.

investigations concerned with terrorism.[69] Accordingly, it is not a warrant that is otherwise open to the investigation of other forms of serious crime. These warrants are only available on application by a senior police officer made to a Supreme Court judge.[70]As is the case with all warrants, the basis of the application must be one of reasonable grounds,[71] accompanied by the required particulars. Once granted, the warrant is active for a maximum of 30 days, during which time the warrant authorises:

- Entry, by force or impersonation if necessary, any named premises, or other specified premises adjoining or providing access;
- Search of the premises and seizure for any kind of thing named or described in the warrant;
- Place and substitute any thing on the premises;
- Copy, photograph or record a description of any thing on the premises;
- Access and copy from any electronic equipment;
- Seize all or part of any object and send for testing.[72]

Like Queensland, Victoria has both a human rights Act,[73] as well as a statutory role for a Public Interest Monitor. The PIM is entitled to attend and intervene in applications for a covert search warrant.[74] The applicant must notify the PIM of the intention to make an application.[75] Section 13 of the Charter protects privacy and reputation;[76] but again, such a right is subject to lawful issue of a warrant, and is thereby impeachable through an exception. An important point of departure in contrast the NSW and Qld is the requirement for the matter being investigated to be related to the investigation of a "terrorist act" within the meaning of s4. This includes matters that involve the targeting of a government outside of Victoria, or section of the community.[77] Otherwise, as stated, the covert search warrant is limited to the investigation of terrorism in this jurisdiction.

---

[69] *Terrorism (Community Protection) Act 2003* (Vic), s4

[70] *Terrorism (Community Protection) Act 2003* (Vic), s5

[71] *Terrorism (Community Protection) Act 2003* (Vic), s8

[72] *Terrorism (Community Protection) Act 2003* (Vic), s9

[73] *Charter of Human Rights and Responsibilities Act 2006* (Vic)('Charter')

[74] *Terrorism (Community Protection) Act 2003* (Vic), s4F

[75] *Terrorism (Community Protection) Act 2003* (Vic), s7A

[76] *Charter of Human Rights and Responsibilities Act 2006* (Vic), s13: A person has the right – (a) not to have his or her privacy, family, home or correspondence unlawfully or arbitrarily interfered with; and(b)not to have his or her reputation unlawfully attacked.

[77] *Terrorism (Community Protection) Act 2003* (Vic), s4(1) In this Act, terrorist act means an action or threat of action where – (a) the action falls within subsection (2) and does not fall within subsection (3); and (b) the action is done or the threat is made with the intention of advancing a political, religious or ideological cause; and (c) the action is done or the threat is made with the intention of – (i) coercing, or influencing by intimidation, the government of the Commonwealth or a State, Territory or foreign country, or of part of a State, Territory or foreign country; or (ii) intimidating the public or a section of the public. (2) Action falls within this subsection if it – (a) causes serious harm that is physical harm to a person; or (b) causes serious damage to property; or (c) causes a

The Scope of Australian and Comparative Covert Investigations Regulation

The operational details of covert investigations in Australia are largely unknown to people outside of those specialised units in the respective agencies. Fragments can, however, be pieced together from secondary sources, particularly the annual reports that detail warrants in different jurisdictions.

Most covert investigations are concerned with drug related crimes in Australia, or where Australia is the point of importation. In that context warrants are often concerned with the interception and substitution of large quantities of narcotics, as well as the facilitation of the substitution into Australia, identification of the parties involved in the importation, and their subsequent arrest. These controlled deliveries are entirely consistent with the literature considered in Chap. 3. In this context a variety of surveillance, telecommunication interceptions, physical entry and direct dealing with prohibited goods and suspects is a routine part of policing. Similarly, domestic drug related investigation not involving importation is also a routine part of covert work involving similar kinds of activities facilitated by a complex system of warrants.

Drug related crimes are multifaceted. They are not only concerned with the actual supply, manufacture, and cultivation of prohibited drugs: they also extend to a range of other forms of crimes, including violence, property crimes, money laundering, homicide and corruption. All these activities are reflected in the warrant records.

We should not assume, however, that covert investigations are confined to drug related crimes. That is not the case. Warrants have been issued for a range of crimes, including arson, cold-case murders, firearms, terrorism, and sex offences – especially sex offences involving children. In addition, covert warrant records demonstrate covert methods are also a regular part of corruption and police integrity cases.

Warrant records demonstrate that investigations can range of small teams of investigators through to very large groups operating in sophisticated teams over time. Some of these investigations can involve dozens of different kinds of surveillance technologies, including multiple telephone intercepts, optical and listening devices, tracking devices, remote computer access, as well as direct human covert interaction.

---

person's death; or (d) endangers a person's life, other than the life of the person taking the action; or (e) creates a serious risk to the health or safety of the public or a section of the public; or (f) seriously interferes with, seriously disrupts, or destroys, an electronic system including, but not limited to – (i) an information system; or (ii) a telecommunications system; or (iii) a financial system; or (iv) a system used for the delivery of essential government services by any entity (whether publicly or privately owned); or (v) a system used for, or by, an essential public utility (whether publicly or privately owned); or (vi) a system used for, or by, a transport system. (3) Action falls within this subsection if it – (a) is advocacy, protest, dissent or industrial action; and (b) is not intended – (i) to cause serious harm that is physical harm to a person; or (ii) to cause a person's death; or (iii) to endanger the life of a person, other than the person taking action; or (iv) to create a serious risk to the health or safety of the public or a section of the public.

The extent to which operations of this kind are "successful" is open to debate. Warrant records suggest that in many cases there are no outcomes that result from the issue of different kinds of warrants, at least if outcomes are measured in successful prosecutions. It appears in many reports, in fact, that there are no arrests that follow the issue of surveillance warrants. However, great care needs to be exercised in assuming the issue of surveillance warrants generally produces no results. On the contrary, virtually every act of surveillance will produce some level of information about persons, places, processes, and things – all of which become part of a much larger knowledge system about the nature of crime and policing. It is not unusual in warrant reports for statements of results such as "valuable information was obtained" to be evident. This is also consistent with the literature on investigation, which confirms that in any investigation more information is obtained than admissible evidence; indeed, it may well be the case in many investigations that insufficient incriminating evidence meant that the agency was not able to arrest or charge a suspect, because the standard of proof required would not be met in the matter progressed to court.

Comparative Dimensions

As seen in this chapter, the legislative provisions governing Australian covert investigations are quite technical, and yet governed by a predictable array of checks and balances that include the requirement of authorisation, record-keeping, external scrutiny and reporting obligations, as well as the prospect of judicial censure through control over proceedings should matters proceed to court. These techniques in the regulation of covert investigation are typical of contemporary policing structures. In the following segment we consider an overview of comparative regulation in the United Kingdom, New Zealand, and Canada.

The legalities in the UK are quite different to those in Australia. The UK operates within a unitary system that it not restricted in the same way by its Constitution in a federal compact. Second, although the laws of the UK are not federated as they are in Australia, they are substantially complicated through an elaborate network of regulations, statutory instruments, codes and standards. Third, the UK is a "human rights" jurisdiction, operating both under the auspices of the *Human Rights Act 1998* (UK), and by virtue of the UK's ratification of the European Convention on Human Rights ('ECHR'). The latter is significant, because of the explicit right to privacy enshrined in Article 8 of the ECHR, and the general commitment of the UK to giving effect to human rights. In effect, every covert investigation in the UK enlivens potential breaches of one or more Convention rights. Fourth, Scotland, although part of the UK, also has a substantial degree of autonomy, which includes legislative powers. Accordingly, Scotland has its own legislative framework.[78] Finally, the geographic position of the UK and its links to Europe mean that cross-border investigations are common, with special arrangements in place for their execution.

[78] *Regulation of Investigatory Powers (Scotland) Act asp 112,000* (UK)

In the UK, covert investigation is similarly regulated by the *Regulation of Investigatory Powers Act 2000 c23* (UK). The definitive work on covert investigation in that jurisdiction is Harfield's *Covert Investigation* (2018), which provides extensive commentary for that jurisdiction, to which the reader is referred. Accordingly, lengthy comments in this book are not necessary. By way of overview, in that jurisdiction, a distinction is made between ***directed surveillance***, ***intrusive surveillance*** and ***use of covert human intelligence sources***.[79] Unlike Australia, where the number of agencies authorised to engage in covert investigation is largely confined to law enforcement and anti-corruption, the UK is notable for the large number of agencies that are able to engage in covert activities, which includes numerous government departments and local councils.[80] Authorisation in that jurisdiction is required in all cases, based on the investigation of specified circumstances,[81] as well as a requirement that the operation is both necessary and proportionate to the kind of the activity being investigated.[82] Authorisations are granted at first instance by the relevant authority through written application to a senior officer at the apex of the organisation. However, in an important distinction, authorisations are invalid until such a time as their approval by a judicial officer on the basis of being satisfied on reasonable grounds the criteria for the warrant have been met.[83] This is known as a "double lock". In addition to judicial oversight on the issue of the warrant, an external agency – the *Investigatory Powers Commissioner's Office* – also scrutinises (at least at the administrative level), the number of warrants issued in any given year. Based on the annual reports, we know that between 2009 and 2018 there were 33,723 covert human intelligence sources authorised under warrant, and 10,119 directed surveillance warrants issued in 2017–2018.[84]

One of the important points of distinction between Australian and UK covert investigations law relates to the admissibility of evidence obtained during these operations. The position on evidence is significantly more restrictive than is the case in Australia. This is especially true with respect to the degree to which investigators can encourage suspects to engage in offences, as well as the degree to which they can verbally elicit information during conversations. Admissions that have been obtained through solicited conversations during an undercover operation are routinely inadmissible as they may constitute a breach of the *Police and Evidence Act*

[79] *Regulation of Investigatory Powers Act 2000 c.23* (UK), s26

[80] *Regulation of Investigatory Powers Act 2000 c.23* (UK), Schedule 1

[81] This includes National security; Preventing crime; Detecting crime; Preventing public disorder; Protecting economic interests; Public safety; Public health; Assessing and collecting revenue; and orders of the Secretary of State. See *Regulation of Investigatory Powers Act 2000 c.23* (UK), ss28(3) and s29(3)

[82] *Regulation of Investigatory Powers Act 2000 c.23* (UK), ss28(2) [Directed surveillance] and s29(3) [Covert human source investigations]

[83] *Regulation of Investigatory Powers Act 2000 c.23* (UK), s32A

[84] Investigatory Powers Commissioner's Office (2018), *Annual Report* (House of Commons, HC67). Available at https://www.ipco.org.uk/docs/IPCO%20Annual%20Report%202018%20final.pdf

1984 (UK) Codes of Practice, in addition to the general disposition of the courts in the UK to cases involving an agent provocateur. Fundamentally, undercover operatives may not engage in conduct that encourages a suspect to engage in behaviours they would not otherwise engage in, and similarly may not engage in incriminating questioning in the course of discussion with a suspect.[85]

New Zealand, in stark contrast, has a far more restrictive approach on the use of undercover investigations. New Zealand has a unitary and common law system, and in this respect the legal framework much simpler than is the case of Australia or the UK. Law enforcement officers are able to apply for a surveillance device warrant in accordance with Part 3 of the *Search and Surveillance Devices Act 2012* (NZ), but are also substantially empowered by the common law provisions that recognise the right of police officers to engage in the same activities as ordinary members of the public unless it contravenes a private right or interest. Accordingly, police officers can engage in surveillance and with members of the public provided it does not involve a trespass. However, great care needs to be taken because surveillance and direct engagement with a suspect may constitute breach of a reasonable expectation of privacy, and accordingly be a contravention of the *New Zealand Bill of Rights Act 1990.*[86] In addition, if the purpose of the surveillance is to gather evidence to be used in prosecution, that evidence is prima facie unlawfully obtained unless it has been authorised under warrant, or otherwise falls within a category of being obtained in accordance with the general law. Because of this lacuna of uncertainty, collecting evidence through surveillance or undercover work normally takes place through authorisation,[87] or falls clearly within a circumstance that does not require a warrant.[88]

In this jurisdiction, surveillance is defined in accordance with the method used. Hence there is a distinction between surveillance permitted by circumstances, through using a device, and "trespass surveillance", which is any form of surveillance that involves interference with land or goods.[89] This Act prohibits the issue of surveillance device and trespass warrants, unless the crime being investigated carries a penalty of 7 years or more, involves firearms, or the investigation of drug offences.[90] It is worth noting that although this appears to be fairly limited in scope, the Act in fact authorises warrants for a large number of offences that are not restricted to offences in the *Crimes Act 1961* (NZ).[91] In addition, for the purposes of investigating drug offences, the *Misuse of Drugs Act 1975* (NZ) contains a statutory immunity for constables for drug offences committed in the course of a bona fide

85 *Teixeira de Castro v Portugal* (1999) 28 EHRR 101; *R v Moon* [2004] EWCA Crim 2872; *R v Pettemore* [1994] Crim LR 836; *R v Sang* [1980] AC 402; *R v Smurthwaite and Gill* [1994] 1 All ER 898; *Nottingham City Council v Amin* [2000] 1 WLR 1071; *R v Looseley* [2001] UKHL 53

86 *R v Williams* [2007] 3 NZLR 207; *Hamed v R* [2012] 2 NZLR 305; *Lorigan v R* [2012] NZCA 264; *R v Alsford* [2017] NZSC 42

87 *Search and Surveillance Devices Act 2012* (NZ), s53

88 *Search and Surveillance Devices Act 2012* (NZ), ss 47, 48

89 *Search and Surveillance Devices Act 2012* (NZ), s3

90 *Search and Surveillance Devices Act 2012* (NZ), s45

91 *Search and Surveillance Devices Act 2012* (NZ), s51, Schedule

investigation.[92] The Act provides that a law enforcement officer *must* obtain a surveillance device warrant when involved in 1 or more of the following:

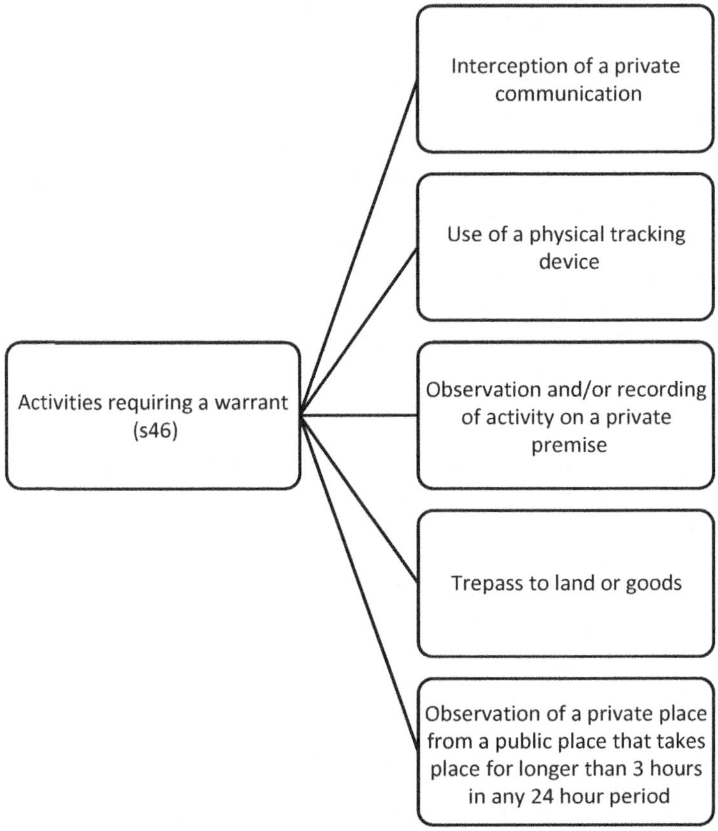

As is to be expected, the warrant process requires the relevant applicant to make a formal application in writing, containing sufficient particulars to enable the authorising officer to make an informed decision as the need for the warrant.[93] In this respect there must be reasonable grounds that an offence was, is or will take place, that investigation will result in 'evidential information', and there are no other restrictions that would otherwise prohibit the operation from being lawful.[94] Those restrictions include the jurisdictional limits set by s45, and a prohibition on such activities being deployed against a suspect and bona fide consultation with

[92] *Misuse of Drugs Act 1975* (NZ), s34A

[93] *Search and Surveillance Devices Act 2012* (NZ), s49. Note that officers of the New Zealand Customs Service and Department of Internal Affairs may also make application for a surveillance search warrant (s50).

[94] *Search and Surveillance Devices Act 2012* (NZ), s51

their legal representative.[95] Warrants of this kind may only be issue with judicial approval.[96] Evidence obtained in the course of an authorised investigation is considered lawfully obtained, including evidence that relates to offending that was not the subject of the investigation but is otherwise captured and observed.[97] External accountability is direct to Parliament in the form of annual reports made by the Police Commissioner.[98] Those reports confirm that the use of surveillance device warrants in New Zealand is very low, with 88 applications granted in 2017, and 75 granted in 2018.[99]

The position in Canada is, to a large extent, similar to the position in New Zealand, notwithstanding Canada is a Federation. In Canada, the Federal government has exclusive jurisdiction over criminal law,[100] meaning that although there are 13 provinces with their own legislatures, there is a single source of criminal law.[101] Canada is also a "human rights" jurisdiction, by virtue of the Charter of Rights.[102] Similar to New Zealand, the starting point with undercover investigation is that any investigation that involves a form of conduct bby an investigator that involves what might be regarded as a trespass to land or goods, or an intrusion into reasonable expectations of privacy, could constitute a Charter violation. One of the major point of distinction between Canada and the others we have examine, is the fact that Canada operates through a Criminal Code (*Criminal Code R.S.C., 1985, c C-46*) that contains relatively few provisions linked the issue of undercover warrants.

The *Criminal Code* contains a broad statutory immunity for investigators engaging in a bona fide way anything that is reasonably in the scope of an authorised investigation.[103] The Code authorises judicial officers to grant warrants that enable intrusive surveillance, video surveillance, telecommunications interception, entry to property, and even covert searches.[104] As a Code jurisdiction, the Canadian position is remarkably lean in terms of the detail relating to the regulation of covert investigations. Apart from the annual reports that are required in relation to the use of covert investigations required for drug offences,[105] there is otherwise no legislative framework to the same extent as the UK, and certain not as is the case in Australia. To a large extent this is the product of the Code, which provides an overarching regulatory framework, but also the way in the focus for regulation in this jurisdiction being residual, in the sense that the main form of regulation is *ex post facto* in

[95] *Search and Surveillance Devices Act 2012* (NZ), s54

[96] *Search and Surveillance Devices Act 2012* (NZ), s53

[97] *Search and Surveillance Devices Act 2012* (NZ), s57

[98] *Search and Surveillance Devices Act 2012* (NZ), s170

[99] New Zealand Police, *Annual Report 2018/19*. Available at https://www.police.govt.nz/sites/default/files/publications/annual-report-2018-2019.pdf

[100] *Constitution Act 1867* (UK) 30 & 31 Vic c 3, s91(27)

[101] There are some exceptions to this, mainly concerned with regulatory offences, but these are not major crimes.

[102] *The Constitution Act, 1982*, being Schedule B to the *Canada Act 1982 (UK)*, 1982, c 11

[103] *Criminal Code Act 1985* (Canada), s25

[104] *Criminal Code Act 1985* (Canada), Eg: ss117, 184, 186

[105] *Criminal Code Act 1985* (Canada), s25.3

the form of judicial control through censure, stay orders, exclusion of evidence, and concerns over Charter breaches. Accordingly, much of the regulation of covert investigations in Canada is in the form of arguments around admissibility of evidence, particularly the lawfulness of confessions, entrapment, and oppressive forms of investigation.[106] What makes Canadian law on covert investigation markedly different to the UK, New Zealand and Australia, is the very location of the Charter. In that jurisdiction the Charter is embedded in the Constitution. The consequence of that is that Charter breaches have the potential to escalate improper use of covert methods directly into a Constitutional issue in ways that are much less likely in other jurisdictions (especially Australia). As discussed in Chap. 3, the literature is somewhat critical of ex post facto controls over covert investigation. However, the fact that misconduct of authorities can bring that action to the attention of the superior courts in Canada very quickly provides an important level of oversight otherwise absent from the Code.

Concluding Remarks

It may seem trite to say that there are is no uniform approach to the regulation of covert investigations. Each legal regime is shaped by a range of local factors including the structure of the various agencies, the constitutional limits of authority, and historical forces. The Australian position is characterised by a highly complex web of legislative provisions, with a minor role for constitutional aspects. This is in stark contrast to the position in Canada, which operates through a light legislative framework, but with a significant role for judicial oversight through Charter and constitutional consideration. That position is similar to the oversight that exists in New Zealand. To a large extent these comparative aspects are to be expected, and really only become (potential) issues in the context of cross-border collaboration between these jurisdictions. Practically speaking, the main point of linkage is between Australia and New Zealand in its trans-Tasman relationship. A central difference between the two is that the Federal architecture that exists in Australia contains no Bill of Rights as it does in New Zealand. To date there have, however, been no significant obstacles in co-operation between these jurisdictions.

[106] Eg: *R v Amato* (1982) 69 CCC (2d) 31 (SCC); *R v Mack* (1988) 44 CCC (3d) 513 (SCC); *R. v. Giles*, 2015 BCSC 1744; *R. v. Oliynyk, Lepage and Ferris*, 2005 BCSC 403; *R. v. Hart* [2014] 2 S.C.R. 544

References

Ferraro, E. (2012). *Investigations in the workplace* (2nd ed.). Boca Raton: CRC Press.

Harfield, C. (2014a). Body-Worn POV technology: Moral harm. *Technology in Society, 33*(2), 64–72.

Harfield, C. (2014b). Law, morality and the authorisation of covert police surveillance. *Australian Journal of Human Rights, 20*(2), 133–164. https://doi.org/10.1080/1323-238X.2014.11882153.

Harfield, C., & Harfield, K. (2018). *Covert investigation* (Blackstone's practice policing) (5th ed.). Oxford: Oxford University Press.

Lubbers, E. (2015). Undercover research: Corporate and police spying on activists. An introduction to activist intelligence as a new field of study. *Surveillance and Society, 13*(3/4), 338–353. https://doi.org/10.24908/ss.v13i3/4.5371.

McDermott, H. (2014). *Investigation and prosecution of financial crime : International readings*. Sydney: Thomson Reuters Professional Australia Limited.

Murphy, B. (2014). Retrospective on ridgeway: Governing principles of controlled operations law. *Criminal Law Journal, 38*(1), 38–58.

Murphy, B., & Anderson, J. (2016). Assemblage, counter-law and the legal architecture of Australian covert surveillance. In R. K. Lippert, K. Walby, I. Warren, & D. Palmer (Eds.), *National security, surveillance and terror: Canada and Australia in comparative perspective* (pp. 99–127). Cham: Palgrave Macmillan.

Standing Committee of Attorneys-General and Australasian Police Ministers Council Joint Working Group on National Investigation Powers. (2003). *Cross-border investigative powers for law enforcement report*. Canberra: Leaders Summit on Terrorism and Multijurisdictional Crime.

Tsukayama, J. K. (2015). *Process of investigation : Concepts and strategies for investigators in the private sector* (4th ed.). Oxford/Waltham: Elsevier/BH.

Chapter 5
Problems in Covert Investigations

> *"Entrapment" is not a term of art; nor is it a term with any precise meaning. It has been used to cover a variety of situations in which law enforcement agents resort to undercover activity. ... It is commonly used when law enforcement agents or persons who are "authorized" by them in that regard incite the commission of an offence or participate in some more positive way in the criminal enterprise giving rise to the offence with which the accused is charged. ... Australian cases favour the view that there is no substantive defence...*
>
> Gaudron J (Ridgeway v The Queen (1995) 184 CLR 19 at 70)

This chapter is concerned with the ways in which covert investigation generally, and controlled operations specifically, are understood in contemporary legal literature. Drawing on unpublished and published materials (Murphy 2014, 2015, 2016), this chapter presents a synthesis of the dominant themes in legal literature concerned with controlled operations. As a general observation, explicit controlled operations literature is rare in Australian legal scholarship. It follows the disciplinary norm of being largely descriptive and normative. It is a field, however, interwoven with diverse and larger bodies of knowledge. The essential dynamic is that controlled operations literature is often connected to an existing knowledge formation outside of law to provide a context and interpretive framework. Basically, controlled operations literature is largely understood within a self-referential epistemology.

Overview of Controlled Operations Literature

Controlled operations regulation is a species of public procedural law. Generally, the doctrinal material on procedural law is limited. Controlled operations literature is no exception. Much of the existing formal literature consists of recommendations endorsing the introduction of this form of law or advising on recommended

B. Murphy, *Regulating Undercover Law Enforcement: The Australian Experience*, https://doi.org/10.1007/978-981-33-6381-6_5

architectures.[1] Outside of this material, there is limited doctrinal content. *Halsbury's Laws of Australia* provides the only substantial current comparative analysis.[2] There is an emerging, but incomplete detailed contextual analysis of controlled operations law in Australian legal writing, covering Queensland, Western Australia, New South Wales and Victoria (Colvin 2002; Colvin and McKechnie 2011; Corns and Tudor 2009; Corns 2014; Douglas et al. 2010; Zahra and Young 2014). Only Bronitt and McSherry (2017) offer a significant analysis in the context of drug investigations. Overall, there is little in the way of deep analysis of the phenomenon. This is not surprising, as the Australian criminal law literature is focussed primarily on doctrine and substantive offences, rather than procedure. And, except for Bronitt & McSherry, rarely engage in interdisciplinary analysis.

As a general observation, the major works on criminal procedure do not consider controlled operations at all (Bishop 1998; Schurr 1996–). This dynamic is replicated in standard criminal textbooks, which frequently do not consider criminal procedure at all (eg Arenson et al. (2011); Bagaric and Arenson (2007); Crofts and Burton (2009); Gans (2017); Lanham et al. (2006)).

Broadly, controlled operations literature emerged in the wake of *Ridgeway* in 1995. Early writings were editorials (Grevling 1996; Nash 1996) or descriptive casenotes, containing limited or no commentary (Galbally and Walters 1995; Howie and Berman 1995; Norberry 1995). These early pieces are important, however, because they emphasised the central issues of entrapment, competing interests and remedial action as the most significant legal themes. These themes have continued throughout the history of commentary on *Ridgeway*, and essentially define the substance of doctrinal commentary.

Commentary began to evolve quickly. The first serious analytical piece, published by Gurney (1995) soon after the decision in *Ridgeway* argued the value in the decision was not what it meant for covert policing, but what it meant for the assertion of an independent judiciary affirming the separation of powers and discretionary controls over evidence. *Ridgeway* was regarded as something of the end statement by the judiciary in insisting on the rule of law in the conduct of law enforcement. This was a view shared by Lancaster (1995) who concluded that there was nothing particularly "revolutionary" in *Ridgeway*. For Lancaster, *Ridgeway* was a minor extension of a line of authorities asserting judicial control over evidence and the conduct of police, suggesting that *Ridgeway* was "a principled synthesis and application of common law exclusionary rules." (1995) Entrapment was never a serious issue. Lancaster expressed surprise, however, that the South Australian and Commonwealth governments had enacted legislation so quickly in a case that was actually quite conservative in its legal character. This opinion was agreed with by

---

[1] Wood (1997); Parliamentary Joint Committee on the National Crime Authority (1999); Standing Committee of Attorneys-General and Australasian Police Ministers Council Joint Working Group on National Investigation Powers (2003)

[2] *Halsbury's Laws of Australia*: Vol 130 *Criminal Law*, 'V General Doctrine', (7) Entrapment and Controlled Operations, [130-10500-130-10520] (LexisNexis, 2018). Compare with the *Laws of Australia* (Thomson Reuters, 2013).

Hocking (1996), who added that the central issue in *Ridgeway* was a *political* rather than a legal one. Echoing Gurney, Hocking emphasised that what was at stake was the competition of interests that had a political dimension – the problem of balancing public interest in crime control at the expense of individual liberties. Hocking observed that the use of controlled operations was creating a divergence in law, for the common law courts had spent much of the preceding decade attempting to restrict and regulate undercover activities, while the Parliaments and law enforcement agencies were favouring their expansion.

Gillies' *Criminal Law* (1997) offered the first consideration of entrapment and new controlled operations laws, concluding that Australian law permitted police to trap a suspect in the commission of a crime, but also made the distinction between active instigation of an offence by investigators, and activities intended to encourage or assist the commission of a crime on the part of a person already suspected or looking for opportunities to commit a crime. Following *Ridgeway*, Gillies affirmed that exclusion of evidence or the stay order was an appropriate remedy in cases of instigation.

A more detailed discussion of entrapment in the context of controlled operations and drug investigations was outlined in the second and third editions of *Drug Law in New South Wales* (Zahra et al. 1998; Zahra and Young 2014). Again, the fine line between instigating an offence and providing opportunities for the commission of an offence was made. Providing opportunities for the commission of a crime was seen as being a necessary aspect of drug investigations. Through a synthesis of the relevant case law, the authors suggested that the common law was manifesting a judicial and general disapproval of undercover techniques, which created a jurisprudence giving heavy emphasis to the recognition and observance of rights and the availability of remedies in the absence of statutory defences. In particular, the remedies that were beginning to evolve in the regulation of undercover investigation were fixed with a cluster of discretionary judicial powers, such as the stay order, exclusion of evidence and mitigation of sentence. However, the authors also recognised that the availability and utility of this form of investigation was sadly necessary, and that controlled operations legislation was largely concerned with preserving the effectiveness of a technique, ultimately in the public interest. Consequently, the general thrust of "entrapment" jurisprudence in Australia was based on the pragmatic requirement to "strike a balance" between the needs of law enforcement and judicial policing of acceptable and unacceptable investigations.

Critical analysis of controlled operations began in earnest with the pioneering work of Professor Simon Bronitt in the late 1990s. Describing the controlled operation as a "licence to deviate", Bronitt raised specific concerns that controlled operations had a disproportionate effect on suspects through entrapment, the impact on a fair trial through confessions obtained through covert means, and the general erosion of privacy through the expansion of telecommunications interception and covert investigation techniques (Bronitt and Kinley 1996; Bronitt 1999). What concerned Bronitt was that entrapment was effectively invisible to the courts. Covert methods were loosely regulated, unpredictable and necessarily executed in a way effectively invisible to the public eye, scrutinised retrospectively, and often only on the basis of paper analyses as opposed to real time observation. Judicial scrutiny was further complicated by the tendency of prosecutors to rely upon public interest immunity and privilege, and the likelihood of suspects pleading guilty in the face of highly probative evidence. Bronitt was also critical of the way Australian remedies for entrapment had evolved. The focus on discretionary exclusion of evidence was unsatisfactory, in his opinion, because of the requirement for the discretion to be exercised on the basis of weighing the public's interest in law enforcement against the accused's right to a fair trial. Bronitt's own work suggested discretion was routinely exercised in favour of the prosecution, a finding subsequently confirmed by an empirical study on the exclusion of evidence by Presser in 2001 (Presser 2001). Drawing on Packer's classic (1964) "crime control/due process" dichotomy (Packer 1964, 1968), Bronitt concluded that controlled operations legislation was a manifestation of crime control values asserting a dominant position within the Australian legislature. The concern was the tendency for crime control rhetoric to trump claims to human rights and the rule of law. Following the work of Gary Marx, Bronitt also identified the link between proactive policing and a global cultural shift in policing practices from reaction to deception. In this way Bronitt presented the initial foray into a contextual analysis linking entrapment and controlled operations with an express concern with human rights and a historical change in policing practices. Bronitt subsequently developed these ideas in work co-authored with Roche (Bronitt and Roche 2000, 2001), essentially arguing that controlled operations statutes created an apparatus whereby questionable policing methods were effectively legalised. Further, they argued similar methodologies were deployed in other jurisdictions, although the result of legal challenges in those jurisdictions was often qualified by the existence of explicit human rights instruments. In particular, the European authority of *Teixiera de Castro v Portugal*[3] illustrated how human rights principles recognised in international law could be compromised but ultimately upheld.

Equivalent concern for the expansion of proactive methods of police was also expressed by Ashworth. Professor Ashworth had been writing for some time on the problems associated with entrapment and undercover policing in Europe and the UK for some time (Ashworth 1977, 1978, 1998, 1999, 2002a, b). It was inevitable that his work would begin to provide insights into developments in Australia and beyond. Of particular concern for Ashworth was the appearance of a political climate favouring crime control through the expansion of greater executive and legislative power that was showing signs of moving towards legal architectures facilitating prosecution at the expense of the public interest in the preservation of rights and liberties. This concern was reiterated by Bronitt (2002) who voiced concern that the legalisation of unlawful conduct has significant implications for the erosion of the rule of law, observing that "[a] judiciary that allows police officials or informers to commit crime with impunity would undermine a central tenet of the Rule of

[3] (1999) 28 EHRR 101

Law - namely, that no-one, especially those tasked with its enforcement, is above the law."(2002).

A slightly different, but no less detailed analysis of controlled operations law was published by Professor Eric Colvin in 2002 (Colvin 2002). By that stage, controlled operations legislation had appeared in New South Wales, South Australia, Queensland and the Commonwealth. Colvin's analysis was a comprehensive doctrinal review of the Queensland provisions, and although largely descriptive clearly linked controlled operations law and entrapment by identifying the kinds of behaviour classically involved in a controlled operation. Like other legal writers, Colvin drew the fine distinction between facilitation and instigation, but highlighted the problem of improper selection of targets. Colvin argued that controlled operations could easily become an entrapment operation, suggesting that even where an operation was properly authorised and executed, there was still scope for entrapment, further complicated by the fact that Australian law, technically, did not recognise any defence of entrapment.

In 2003, following the publication of the *Cross Border Investigative Powers for Police*, Bronitt published an editorial (Bronitt 2003) critical of the failure of proposed model laws to properly regulate undercover investigations, especially the failure to maximise and protect the right to a fair trial and privacy. He was critical of a discretionary and retrospective process that failed to address breaches of privacy, the loss of privilege and entrapment methodologies. He argued that the expansion of undercover techniques was part of a general expansion of police powers emerging in the wake of the "War on Terror", merging with proactive powers of police and the creep of generalised surveillance.

Despite these concerns, the utility and effectiveness of undercover methodologies was reflected in Justice Hall's landmark text, *Investigating Corruption and Misconduct in Public Office* (Hall 2004). Justice Hall brought some 35 years of judicial experience into a textbook that provided a powerful doctrinal and pragmatic assessment of the need for undercover methodologies and the problem of entrapment in the context of controlled operations. Like many practitioners and jurists, Justice Hall had concerns about deceptive methods in investigation, but regarded entrapment and deception as an unfortunate by-product of an essential method for investigating corruption and organised crime. Hall argued that the preservation of evidence available through controlled operations legislation was a powerful weapon in the fight against crime and corruption, and that the administrative framework present within the legislation provided a model system of accountabilities.

Following the introduction of controlled operations law in Victoria in 2004, Corns argued that controlled operations law formed part of a web of regulation extending to assumed identities, powers to compel giving evidence, and the internal surveillance of the executive by the executive (Chris Corns 2005). Corns suggested that controlled operations law represented a "new phase in criminal investigation methodologies" (2005), characterised by forms of regulation, flexible but characterised by multiple layers of accountability. These laws were seen as coercive and undermining well-established common law rights but welcomed as a model of transparency that introduced a system of regulation into an area of police activity hitherto invisible. He concluded that part of this development was a shift in the discourse of law from the investigation of drugs to the investigation of "organised crime". The apparent threat posed by individual criminals was far less than the threat posed by complex criminal organisations.

In the only empirical study of its kind the author, in collaboration with Anderson, (Murphy and Anderson 2007) examined a series of drug supply cases in which entrapment claims had been made in the context of controlled operations. This study found that in the vast majority of controlled operations prosecutions the target was an individual and relatively low-level street dealer. Despite the rhetoric, organised criminals were rarely the actual targets. This study confirmed that entrapment claims were a common feature of drug prosecutions in NSW, despite legislative provisions prohibiting entrapment. Encouragement to offend was found to be endemic, but effective methods of policing. A similar study by Chernok (2011) found a similar dynamic in Victoria. The result was that although much of the rhetoric of controlled operations focussed on "organised crime", the reality was that most investigations were actually focussed on individuals and small, local networks.

Controlled operations literature took on a different complexion in 2010, when Professor Clive Harfield turned attention to broader questions of governance (Harfield 2010). Harfield argued that governance of covert investigation was essentially a three-part dynamic, concerned with internal management, external scrutiny, and judicial examination of prosecution evidence. Controlled operations were a prime example. Harfield argued that the regulation of covert investigation emerged because of a general absence of regulatory systems at common law, and the tendency of the Anglophone legal system to systematise and empower police agencies through statutory powers, particularly intrusive powers of surveillance. Harfield observed that the key points of distinction between covert regulation in the UK and NSW was the explicit English commitment to the European Convention on Human Rights. In the absence of that commitment, NSW focused attention on the integrity of evidence and bureaucratic accountability mechanisms.

Bronitt & McSherry soon after provided an extensive commentary on controlled operations in *Principles of Criminal Law* (Bronitt and McSherry 2001, 2005, 2010, 2017).[4] In their view, controlled operations literature was essentially concerned with (1) the problem of entrapment, (2) the quest for associated remedies, (3) the question of proper forms of regulation, (4) the tension between demands for crime control and due process, and (5) the need to preserve a rights-based focus in law.

These writers all reflect important aspects of controlled operations literature and the focus on entrapment and the balancing of competing rights. Law, as a scholarly discipline, appears to have something of a contradictory relationship with controlled operations. On the one hand writers such as Bronitt present a strong due process theme, with a clear emphasis upon the need to safeguard rights and liberties. On the other hand, writers such as Hall recognise the need and utility of undercover

[4] Bronitt and McSherry (2010) It is worth nothing that the 3rd edition is not substantially different from the commentary in the 1st and 2nd editions. See Bronitt and McSherry (2001) and Bronitt and McSherry (2005)

methodologies in the investigation of crime and corruption. In many ways legal scholarship is reflecting the discourses embedded in cases and political narrative: how do we enable law enforcement to investigate hard cases in ways that do not undermine civil liberties? This is an ancient problem for law, likely to remain unanswered.

Problematic Themes

All knowledge is historically formed, containing a distinct sociology. Controlled operations literature is no different. These writings are not simply a chronological reflection; it is an interpretive undertaking expressing a certain orientation to knowledge. Weber argued that legal writing tends to manifest in three overlapping ways: *dogmatic jurisprudence* (concerned with the source materials of direct application to the practice of law); *moral* or *political* attitude (concerned with normative evaluation); and *sociologies* (interpreting social behaviour, particularly when based on commitment to normative and evaluative standards, including law) (Bodansky 2006; Weber 1978; Kronman 1983; Zeitlin 1985). Controlled operations literature follows this pattern, although it also contains a fourth strand which might be described as *contextual*. Contextual literature is distinct from other categories by its interdisciplinarity, which is not surprising since the linkages between law and other disciplines is a more recent phenomenon than at the time when Weber was writing. Legal scholarship has moved on from the triune categories suggested by Weber, and, as discussed in Chap. 2, exhibit signs of interdisciplinarity.

Controlled operations literature manifests several features. First, the literature is backward looking. The literature is enmeshed with established writing, events and associated legal architectures. Secondly, it emerges primarily after 1995, but is linked with the past through its connections with the established literature, particularly entrapment and surveillance literature. Finally, the third aspect is the prevalence of "Hume's Law". This is a phenomenon that basically involves a conflation of what "is" and what "ought" to be. The dichotomy was famously identified by David Hume in his *Treatise on Human Nature* (Hume 1740). Hume argued that most normative or moral claims tend to begin with a rational or factual proposition of what "is", which tends to drift into a normative and value-based statement of what "should" be. Hume argued that this is a logical fallacy. While I do not propose to engage with the nuances of Hume's Law (MacIntyre 1959; Hunter 1962; Hudson 1964; Mitchell 1968; Allen 1972; Falk 1976), it is worth observing that these characteristics are common in legal reasoning generally (Freeman 2014), and are certainly evident in controlled operations literature, suggesting a powerful interplay between normative and doctrinal knowledge.

Two aspects are worth emphasising. The first is that the literature is primarily constructed through the composite of existing knowledge formations. It is discursive in this respect. The second is that the internal focus emphasises three persistent themes: (1) entrapment; (2) human rights; and (3) remedies. These themes will now be considered.

Entrapment

Entrapment is the "the main event" in undercover investigation literature (McAdams 2005). Entrapment emerges as an issue because the method used in most cases depends upon the direct interaction of the investigator, or an informer, with the suspect for the purpose of investigation, which often involves the facilitation of a crime. Because of the extent of engagement and proximity to the suspect and the evidence, procedural and substantive criminal law is enmeshed with questions of entrapment. Similarly, controlled operations practices are pregnant with concerns for authorisation, protecting the suspect and the availability of remedies to address the problem of entrapment. As it happens, the Anglophone legal tradition is highly variable in its response to the problem of entrapment.

For present purposes it is sufficient to say that entrapment is not a defence outside of the United States.[5] It has been rejected as a defence in Australia[6] and New Zealand,[7] but may constitute an abuse of process. In the UK a detailed framework for the stay remedy exists,[8] while in Canada entrapment enlivens a post-trial examination of the conduct of the investigators that may result in a permanent stay.[9]

Entrapment is a complex issue. There is considerable variation between jurisdictions. Indeed, it may well be the case that it is entirely unhelpful to look for doctrinal principles in allied jurisdictions. Entrapment jurisprudence is jurisdictionally specific. In Australia entrapment has been considered at some length by a variety of authors (Braithwaite et al. 1987b; Chernok 2011; Colvin 2002, 2006; Fisse 1988; Harris 1994; Murphy and Anderson 2007; Roser 1993), of whom Simon Bronitt has left an indelible imprint (Bronitt and Kinley 1996; Bronitt 1999; Bronitt and Roche 2000, 2001; Bronitt 2004). It is, however, Heydon's early work that has left the most enduring mark (Heydon 1973). Virtually all discussions on entrapment in the Anglo-Australian legal tradition refer to Heydon. There is a reasonable body of literature in the UK (M. Allen 1984; Choo 1990; Birch 1994; Robertson 1994; Ormerod and Roberts 2002; McKay 2002; Feinberg 2003; Hofmeyer 2006; Squires 2006; Ho 2011; Levanon 2016), where Ashworth has dominated the field for the last 20 years (Ashworth 1978, 1998, 1999, 2000b, 2002a, b, 2006). In the US, entrapment has

[5] *Sorrells v United States* 237 US 435 (1932); *Sherman v United States* (1958) 356 US 369; *United States v Russell* 411 US 423 (1973); *Matthews v United States* 485 US 58 (1988); *Hampton v United States* 425 US 484 (1976); *Jacobson v United States* 503 US 540 (1992)

[6] *Ridgeway v The Queen* (1995) 184 CLR 19

[7] *Police v Lavalle* (1979) 1 NZLR 45; *Police v Pethig* (1977) 1 NZLR 448

[8] *Attorney General's Reference No. 3; R v Looseley* [2001] 4 All ER 897

[9] *R v Mack* [1988] 2 SCR 903. For a recent discussion of entrapment in Canada see Murphy and Anderson (2014)

been recognised as a defence since at least 1915,[10] but really came to prominence after *Sorrell v United States* in 1932.[11] The reason entrapment emerged early in American jurisprudence is a Constitutional one, based largely on the Fourth Amendment.[12] There is, consequently, a significant amount of material concerning entrapment in US literature (Kent 1933; MacLaughlin 1960; Sagarin and Macnamara 1970; Shafer and Sheridan 1970; Park 1976; Gershman 1982; Altman and Lee 1983; Dworkin 1985, 1987; Carlson 1987; Allen et al. 1999; Deis 2001; Abelson 2003; Colquitt 2004; Dillof 2004; McAdams 2005, 2007; Mekeel 2006; Carlon 2007; Carter 2009; Seidman 1981; Stitt and James 1984; Piccarreta and Keenan 1992; Sinnott-Armstrong 1999; Tawil 2000; Roiphe 2003; Stevenson 2004, 2008; Yaffe 2005; Seidman 2009; Joh 2015; Smith 2017).[13] A good deal of more recent literature in the field relates to allegations of entrapment tactics in terrorism and right and left-wing activist investigation (Norris and Grol-Prokopczyk 2015; Norris 2016; Bejesky 2015; Lubbers 2015; Norris and Grol-Prokopczyk 2018; Norris 2019), as well as the continuation of those tactics in the context of drug interdiction. There is, however, also an emerging thread concerned with the use of undercover and deceptive work in the context of corporate "private investigations", being deployed for a range of purposes including integrity testing and market control (Brockman 2015). Broadly, it appears that what is happening is an expansion of these techniques into any area where intrusive methods are needed to investigate issues of concern that often take place in private spheres.

Entrapment literature is invariably concerned with two problems: definition and practice. How should entrapment be defined as a workable test in law? What limits can and should be imposed on the practice? Roiphe (2003) has argued that the entrapment doctrine emerged at a time of the expansion of Federal power in the US between 1915 and 1970: from prohibition, the Cold War, and eventually the "War on Drugs". This period involved expansion of intrusive domestic investigation methods closely aligned to counterintelligence. Courts in the US began to regulate the growth of State power through a variety of mechanisms, including the entrapment doctrine, which operates as a defence. The problem with the US position is that it is unique in the common law world. English law recognised no such defence. Indeed, provided evidence was relevant and probative of guilt, English law was largely unconcerned with how evidence was obtained.[14] Although English law did

---

[10] *Woo Wai v United States* 223 F. 412 412 (9th Cir. 1915). This is a Californian decision involving undercover agents coaxing a Chinese immigrant to participate in a people smuggling operation.

[11] *Sorrells v United States* 237 US 435 (1932)

[12] The Fourth Amendment prohibits unlawful search and seizure, and the issue of judicial warrants without "probable cause". Evidence obtained through violations of the Amendment is commonly regarded as inadmissible in criminal trials. See *Weeks v United States* 232 US 383 (1914) and *Mapp v Ohio* 367 US 643 (1961)

[13] This is a representative sample. For an extensive bibliography of mainly US sources compiled by Francois Lareau (a Canadian barrister) available at www.lareau-law.ca/entrapment2_.html

[14] Classically, see *R v Sang* [1980] AC 402

contemplate a specific offence of incitement,[15] English authorities evolved in a manner that effectively favoured mitigation of sentence as the major judicial intervention (Murphy and Anderson 2014), and more recently the stay order.[16] These positions constitute a major divergence in entrapment jurisprudence. Australia largely followed the English divergence, but with emphasis on exclusion of evidence.

Part of the difficulty in formulating a useful test for entrapment is the problem of definition. The "boundaries" of entrapment are vague (Ashworth 2002b; Bronitt and McSherry 2017; Hill et al. 2018), partly because of the realities of covert investigation, partly the inherited law, and partly questions of public policy. There are narrow definitions that offer certainty. The ALRC, for example, defined entrapment simply as "inducing the commission of an offence which the person induced would not otherwise have committed" (Australian Law Reform Commission (ALRC) 1975). It is a distinction between "the trap for the unwary innocent and the trap for the unwary criminal".[17] The problem is that even unwary criminals can be trapped into conduct they had not previously contemplated. This distinction is a complex question of fact and degree, involving an examination of the conduct of the investigator and the suspect, with considerable attention on the conduct of the investigator. Consequently, the issue is not simply whether or not the suspect did the act constituting the crime. It extends to the circumstances. Donnelly (1951) argued that undercover operatives tend to manifest one of four behaviours: "informers", "stool pigeons", "spies" and the "agent provocateur". Only the latter is likely to trigger valid entrapment claims. Donnelly's work was influential in the work of other scholars (Jacobs 1963; Park 1976; Rotenberg 1963), but especially Dyson Heydon (1973), who subsequently argued that undercover agents were commonly one of three types: those who *observe*; those who *passively engage* with the target; and those who *actively engage* with the target. Following Donnelly, Heydon argued that only the latter was potentially entrapment, while observation and passive engagement were proper methods of investigation.

These writers identify a process where "acceptable" and "unacceptable" conduct is identified by the judiciary. Entrapment is the label attached to conduct that goes beyond what is acceptable to the courts at the time. It is a construct of law and policy. This is Ashworth's "boundary of entrapment" (Ashworth 2002b). Locating this boundary is a function of the "tests" for entrapment. Historically, these tests tended to manifest a subjective and objective dimension. The *subjective* test is concerned with the question of the predisposition of the suspect. The *objective* test is concerned with the conduct of the investigator. There remains an ongoing debate about which test is to be preferred, or whether they operate concurrently. Throughout the common law world there is no consensus. Even in the US where the defence depends

[15] *DPP v Armstrong* [2000] Crim LR 379; *R v Goldman* [2001] Crim LR 894. It appears that the common law misdemeanour will soon be abolished by changes made by the *Serious Crime Act 2007*. For commentary, see Ormerod (2008)

[16] *R v Looseley* [2001] 4 All ER 897

[17] *Sherman v United States* 356 US 369 (1958) per Warren CJ, repeated by Gleeson CJ in *R v Sloane* (1990) 49 A Crim R 270 at 273

on satisfying the test, there is variation between the States on which test applies (Colquitt 2004). Tests based on predisposition usually succeed where there is evidence of past offending, even when the question is whether or not the accused was engaged in crime on this occasion (Dworkin 1985; Stitt and James 1984). Entrapment models often result in the escalation of conduct involving offenders predisposed to low-level offending or deviant behaviours. Ashworth, for example, is critical of subjective tests because "predisposition" tends to ensnare those who might actually be predisposed to some form of offending or deviant behaviour (such as a drug addict sourcing drugs), but that does not necessarily mean they are predisposed to *this class* of offending in the absence of being effectively resourced by the investigator (Ashworth 2000a).

Conversely, objective tests shift attention away from the suspect onto the investigators. This focus can have the effect of encouraging evidence manipulation, "fit ups" and perjury (Stitt and James 1984), but also shift the focus of enquiry away from the actual suspects. White collar criminals, in particular, are often able to deflect attention away from their conduct by emphasising the "wrongs" and "injustice" of investigators. Such individuals belong, after all, to the "respectable" classes, are frequently politically active, rarely have a record of prior convictions, normally possess substantial resources and status, and are able to focus media attention. The result is that a wholly objective test tends to divert attention and make the investigator the suspect, even in cases when there are serious questions to be asked about the suspect (Braithwaite et al. 1987a; Palmer 1997). The objective analysis tends to be favoured by civil libertarians, because the "real issue" is not that the person was caught, but the manner in which they were caught (Fisse 1988).

As Ashworth rightly observes, in practice the tests for entrapment effectively merge. They become part of the indicia of entrapment, rather than a prescriptive test. Ashworth argued that the test for entrapment is a three-step test based on (i) presentation of an "unexceptional opportunity"; (ii) in the context of a duly authorised and supervised investigation; (iii) based on credible suspicion. When these three factors are present, entrapment claims usually fail (Ashworth 2002b). Similarly, Ho (2011) has argued for a hybrid test for entrapment, requiring five elements: (i) Intentional temptation to commit an offence; (ii) through a covert and deceitful investigation; (iii) for the purpose of obtaining evidence to be used in prosecution of the suspect; (iv) by agents of the State; (v) which causes the suspect to commit an offence they would probably not otherwise have committed.

Entrapment is complicated further by the manipulation of penalties by intentionally aggravating the offence, a practice referred to as sentencing entrapment (Abelson 2003) or manipulation (Mekeel 2006; Carter 2009). Sentencing entrapment involves intentionally exposing the suspect to more serious penalties by manipulating one or more aspects of an offence the suspect is already engaged in. For example, pressing the target to supply larger quantities of drug than they would normally supply, or to convert one class of drug into another (Chernok 2011; Murphy and Anderson 2007). In this sense entrapment can involve not only questions of liability, but also questions of penalty. The problem here is that, as a matter of common law, the coincidence of the prohibited act and the intention to commit a crime results in criminal liability.[18]

Entrapment scholarship is not only concerned with developing a test, but also articulating *why* it is a problem. The problem was expressed by Ashworth as "the Amin Dichotomy" (Ashworth 2002b). Mr. Amin was prosecuted for breaches of his taxi licence after being hailed by an undercover officer and asked to drive to an area that he was not licensed to be in. He claimed entrapment. In the subsequent appeal case, *Nottingham City Council v Amin*,[19] Lord Bingham CJ outlined why entrapment is problematic:

> *[I]t has been recognised as deeply offensive to ordinary notions of fairness if a defendant were to be convicted and punished for committing a crime which he only committed because he had been incited, instigated, persuaded, pressurised or wheedled into committing it by a police officer. On the other hand, it has been recognised that police agencies have a general duty to the public to enforce the law and it has been regarded as unobjectionable if a police officer gives a defendant an opportunity to break the law, of which the defendant freely takes advantage, in circumstances where it appears that the defendant would have behaved in the same way if the opportunity had been offered by anyone else.*[20]

The "Amin Dichotomy" reflects the apparent deep cultural suspicion of plain clothes officers trapping suspects in the commission of crime, but also the pragmatic requirements of crime control. Entrapment offends something deeply rooted in the value system of liberal democracies, but also enlivens the desire for security and safety – which is one of the core components of the "social contract" with government. The public, and the courts, are prepared to accept entrapment models of policing, to an extent, where necessary for public safety and security. The problem is identifying the right combination of circumstances and associated threshold of tolerance.

Objections to entrapment are not just concerned with questions of fairness in the investigation. Objections also concern the subsequent prosecution, based as it is on evidence obtained so close to the suspect. These are questions touching on the fairness of the trial and broader expectations of privacy. *Swaffield & Pavic*[21] is a useful example. In that case both men made statements to undercover agents confessing to serious offences they had formally refused to make when under police caution. In one context they had exercised a right to silence recognised in law; and in another they were unable to exercise that right. Here the issue is that when the suspect is unaware the discussant is an undercover officer, they can make all manner of statements that could be used against them or others. This issue is of particular note, because it has been recognised (Bronitt 1999; Bronitt and Roche 2000) that most entrapment activities are effectively invisible to the courts. Most offenders, faced with a brief of evidence based on an undercover operation, plead guilty in the face of highly probative evidence, effectively by-passing the proof-making model of the

[18] Eg: *Ridgeway v The Queen* (1995) 184 CLR 19 per Brennan J

[19] *Nottingham City Council v Amin* [2000] 2 All ER 946

[20] Ibid at 950

[21] *R v Swaffield & Pavic* (1998) 192 CLR 159

trial process, thereby avoiding questions about fairness, voluntary confessions and the propriety of police action during the evidence collection phase. This is significant because conversations with undercover officers and telecommunications interceptions have immediate implications for the privilege against self-incrimination, confession evidence, and the privacy of those who are not suspects but otherwise connected with the suspect's network. In this environment innocent parties are drawn into the criminal intelligence network without being drawn into the actual prosecution, or indeed are normally unaware they have been identified (Bronitt and Kinley 1996; Bronitt 1996; Colvin 2002, 2006; Sharpe 1994, 2002).

These privacy and fair trial limbs of entrapment are particularly important in those jurisdictions with explicit human rights instruments. English jurisprudence is intimately shaped by the European tradition by virtue of the *Human Rights Act 1998*[22] and its commitment to the *European Convention on Human Rights*.[23] European jurisprudence is particularly strong on observing Convention rights in the context of undercover policing. Bronitt and McSherry (2017) have suggested that it is very likely Australian law will be similarly influenced, given the influence of English law and our commitment to the *International Covenant on Civil and Political Rights* and the recent emergence of human rights instruments with similar provisions. Gans et al. (2011), however, argue that the English/European jurisprudence is distinguishable, meaning that Australia is more likely to develop its own path as it attempts to harmonise its own diversity.

Outside of the strict legalities, entrapment literature is also socio-legal. Entrapment is criticised because it is the "official creation" of crime. The State effectively targets individuals, involving them in the commission of an offence they might not have committed if otherwise left alone, or not provided with the resources needed to execute the crime. It involves, at one level, engineering a crime. This activity raises complex political, ethical and sociological questions (Allen 1984; Ashworth 1999; Choo 2008; Dworkin 1985, 1987; McAdams 2005; Marx 1981, 1982, 1985). Engineering of a crime is a particular issue for weak-willed, impulsive and/or drug addicted targets (Murphy and Anderson 2016). It encourages police to learn how to commit crimes. It entrenches skills that enable official deception and subterfuge, with the potential to erode the ethical and public standing of the police. It creates a climate where the integrity of the officer is routinely subjected to temptation (Ashworth 1998). Ashworth has also suggested that the public and moral authority of the courts may be eroded where courts are seen to receive tainted evidence or fail to censure unlawful executive conduct. In other words, the integrity of the judiciary is linked to how it deals with the problems of entrapment (Ashworth 1999).

The socio-legal imagination on entrapment goes well beyond law, entrapment and associated forms of policing merge with larger questions of the growth of

---

[22] This Act imports the Articles of the European Convention as a part of English law (subject to some modification).

[23] Technically the *European Convention for the Protection of Human Rights and Fundamental Freedoms* (1953)

surveillance and the psychology and sociology of human interaction. Healthy social functioning depends on the existence of large-scale trust and reliability. The trust dynamic is potentially undermined through the deployment of deceptive investigation models. Such forms of investigations not only threaten privacy, they can be deployed as a tool of political oppression by breaking apart the cohesive networks of opposition groups and rival political parties (Braithwaite et al. 1987a). In some cases breaking up social networks, and/or mapping their composition and targeting key players, is an *intended outcome* of the investigation (Bright et al. 2012; Cunningham and Noakes 2008; Marx 1988).

Undercover work also has a significant *personal* cost to those involved. Undercover agents are routinely placed in life-threatening situations, finding themselves acting as a criminal in a situation where they often have strong law-enforcement values, and learn to practise a sophisticated deceit in order to ensure their identities are not uncovered. The risks here are not only personal, but psychological. Retired undercover operatives routinely suffer from long term psychological issues, live in a state of perpetual fear, and are often forced to relocate with their families under assumed identities (Allen et al. 1999; Pogrebin and Poole 1993; Macleod 1995; Miller 2006; Marx 1982).

Undercover operations have also been criticised for their ethical character. The basic model of operation is deception. Some scholars argue that the basic dynamic of undercover work/entrapment is virtue testing that punishes a person for succumbing to temptation. They argue that human beings are imperfect creatures, and in the right circumstances we are *all* capable of deviant or criminal behaviour. This ethical dimension is concerned with the myriad ways in which human reasoning can be corrupted, tending to reinforce the criminological discourse that crime is endemic, and that all decision-making is simply "cost-benefit" reasoning (Dworkin 1985; Allen et al. 1999; Macleod 1995; Feinberg 2003; Deis 2001; Elbaz 1999; Miller 2014).

By far the most significant body of literature on undercover policing is the work of Gary Marx. Professor Marx has made a lasting impression on policing, surveillance and investigations literature, highlighting major aspects of this form of governance throughout his career (Marx 1974, 1980, 1981, 1982, 1985, 1987, 1988, 1992b; Fijnaut and Marx 1995). Marx observed significant sociological impact resulting from undercover operations. Marx found that most targets are not "first time offenders". Undercover models usually target recidivists or suspects with known criminal histories. His research found that undercover models have a *displacement* and an *amplification* effect, tending to shift crime from one locality to another, often escalating the frequency and magnitude of the crime, and sometimes subjecting a new population to forms of offending that have not previously been present. Marx also observed the tendency for criminal networks to *evolve* in direct response to the deployment of undercover method, suggesting that undercover operations may well be active *causes* in the evolution of increasing sophistication in organised crime. Undercover techniques, while at once expanding in use and normalising the creation of crime and corruption as a legitimate technique of crime control and investigation, also has the perverse effect of being an active cause in the *evolution* of crime and corruption.

These criticisms are mainly concerned with when the investigation is directed to a legitimate end. An equally valid criticism is the potential for abuse. Undercover operations offer significant opportunities for overzealous policing, as well as individual or small-group corruption. At the very least, undercover operations are resource intensive, and effectively divert police away from public policing, opening up the potential for criminal conduct in new areas (Heydon 1973). Corruption and abuses are not only the targets of investigations. Crime and corruption can also be caused by investigations. Stress, greed and cultural responses to perceived inadequacies in the law are major contributors to undercover abuses (Marx 1982, 1992a; Dixon 1999; Marx 1980). These observations are entirely consistent with findings of the Wood Royal Commission into Police Corruption, which found that while there were numerous instances of abuses undertaken for greed, "the noble cause" justification was frequently evident, as officers vented frustration in being able to "control the streets" by finding devious methods to ensure prosecution (Wood 1997).

The political dimension of undercover work is also evident in the literature. Some writers are deeply disturbed by entrapment and undercover methods because of what they say about cultural shifts in democratic politics. Carlson (1987) and Carlon (2007) have argued that integrity testing and entrapment is a sign of a slip into totalitarianism, with Carter (2009) suggesting that undercover investigation based on incitement is technically a criminal conspiracy. Carlon goes one step further by arguing that entrapment reflects a shift in the moral character of government towards sadism; for entrapment is ultimately an act by an agent with the power to punish. In his view, entrapment is a form of police brutality, effectively perverting the proper role and function of the police in a democracy. Not only is the liberty of the individual compromised by having their autonomy as rational actors distorted by the creation of conditions that basically offers a choice to obey or not obey the law, but the *purpose* of policing effectively becomes one of punishment as opposed to the prevention of crime. In this thesis the investigator has a particular individual in mind, with a particular offence in mind, and very often a particular punishment in mind. The targeting of individuals is, however, also a manifestation of the targeting of suspect *populations*. Roach (2010), for example, has argued that since 9/11 there has been a proliferation of proactive investigations directed towards population groups, based on racial and religious profiling. Both dynamics challenge and stretch the conception of democracy.

The critique of undercover work is not, however, wholly pejorative. An equally important dimension is the recognition of the requirement for pragmatic and effective police techniques. Indeed, the *necessity* and *effectiveness* of undercover and entrapment techniques offer compelling justifications, and it is this aspect of entrapment that invariably weighs heavily in public debate, policy and judicial evaluation (Wood 1997). These policing methodologies are sometimes the *only* effective mechanism for investigation. Without them, policing would be considerably less able to investigate offences that take place in private, and among powerful networks of careful offenders. Of itself, this inability to investigate certain kinds of crime would be troubling. The Fitzgerald Inquiry made the important observation that the rights and liberties of citizens are just as vulnerable to crime and corruption as they are to the coercive powers of state.[24] In each case, however, a *balancing* rhetoric is plainly evident between respecting the needs of the criminal law on the one hand, with the rights and liberties of citizens on the other. The effectiveness of undercover and entrapment work is undoubted and regarded as legitimate and necessary in the investigation of some types of crime. Ashworth made the observation that despite the tendency of critics to claim that undercover powers are oppressive, the reality was that the vast majority of investigations were professionally executed and focussed on properly identified targets. He suggested that, generally, "...the implication that the police pick on innocent people...is unwarranted." (Ashworth 1978) This is an important observation. While it is true that there has been a progressive and inexorable expansion of proactive policing methods, the policy governing this kind of investigative method has been directed towards the imposition of limits and systems of strict accountability. Although there is the potential for abuse of power, the regulatory framework does provide an effective system of constraint. There can be little doubt that is also the case in Australia. More than a decade of scrutiny records clearly shows that the overwhelming majority of warrants that have been issued have been for a lawful purpose and executed professionally.

Essentially, the entrapment literature highlights three broad themes. The first relates to the *personal costs for suspects*. In most cases these costs are tied to the prospect of criminal prosecution. Specific legal principles and rules are enlivened as a result. The second concern relates to *the social impact* of the deployment and use of undercover and entrapment models. That concern is normally understood in terms of political and civil rights but extends to aspirational ideals about the kind of society being built in the opening years of the new millennium. The third is concerned with *politico-legal tensions* between the executive and judicial branches of government. The cause is primarily the type of investigation. The solution, from the legal perspective, is accountability largely achieved through a focus on respecting rights, and on the development of remedies and legal mechanisms to control the excesses of police. Entrapment, as the major issue arising out of controlled operations, is the springboard for two related legal topics: the preservation of human rights, and the question of remedies.

Human Rights

Controlled operations literature makes routine reference to undercover investigations compromising a variety of human rights. Bronitt (1999), Ormerod and Roberts (2002), for example, argue that entrapment cases compromise the right to a fair trial and the right to privacy. Both rights have force of law internationally, although the

[24] Fitzgerald (1989)

extent to which they operate domestically is less clear. Article 14 of the *ICCPR* and Article 6 of the European Convention both enshrine the fundamental principle of the fair trial. The extent these instruments operate domestically is open to debate. In principle, international instruments do not create actionable rights in domestic law unless enacted locally.[25] However, a patchwork of local laws invoking these principles does exist, suggesting that such principles may be impliedly imported, if not enacted.[26] In addition, the commitment of the Australian government to international convention does create a strong inference that domestic laws should be interpreted in a manner consistent with commitments given by the government.[27] In Australia the right to a fair trial has a long life in common law,[28] although what actually constitutes a fair trial is an open question. It is a broad question of fact and degree, fundamentally concerned with ensuring fairness to the accused during the process, as well as securing the integrity of the courts and maintaining the confidence of the public in the administration of justice.[29]

Similarly, privacy is also protected by Article 17 of the *ICCPR* and Article 8 of the European Convention. Unlike the fair trial, the status of privacy as an enforceable right is less clear and appears to be in a transitional phase. Australian common law does not recognise a general right to privacy.[30] Privacy tends to be fixed to some other cause of action, such as trespass, breach of confidence, or breach of a statutory prohibition.[31] However, a general right to privacy has recently been endorsed in s 13 of the *Charter of Human Rights and Responsibilities Act 2006* (Vic) and s 12 of the *Human Rights Act 2004* (ACT). The difficulty here is that these provisions are jurisdictionally specific and not universally applicable, although their role in the interpretation of law may function as a precedent for other States over time. Where controlled operations are concerned, questions of privacy and a fair trial are broad legal principles that may be invoked on a case-by-case basis but are not an absolute controlling authority. A controlled operation warrant basically nullifies any claim to privacy that might otherwise apply.

In addition to the patchwork nature of Australian human rights law, the legal landscape is complicated by the fact that rights are rarely absolute. Human rights instruments routinely contain mechanisms by which rights may be subordinated or read down, particularly when rights are in conflict with the public interest, or in times of political crisis (Debeljak 2008). Article 8(2) of the European Convention, for example, provides the right to privacy may be abrogated where it "is necessary

---

[25] *Bradley v Commonwealth* (1973) 128 CLR 557 at 582; *Kioa v West* (1985) 159 CLR 550 at 570-1; *Dietrich v The Queen* (1992) 177 CLR 292

[26] Eg: s138(3)(f) of the *Evidence Act 1995* requires a consideration of breaches of the ICCPR when exercising the discretion to admit or exclude evidence adduced in a criminal trial.

[27] Gans et al. (2011). Cf: *Al-Kateb v Cth* (2004) 219 CLR 562

[28] The right is now appearing in domestic human rights instruments. Cf: *Human Rights Act 2004* (ACT), s21

[29] Eg: *Dietrich v The Queen* (1992) 177 CLR 292; *Cesan v R* (2008) 236 CLR 538

[30] *ABC v Leah Game Meats* (2001) 208 CLR 199

[31] *Giller v Procopets* (2008) 24 VR 1

in a democratic society in the interests of national security, public safety or the economic well-being of the country, for the prevention of disorder or crime, for the protection of health or morals, or for the protection of the rights and freedom of others." This facility for derogation during a perceived crisis is an important legal and political mechanism discussed further in Chap. 12 as a manifestation of precautionary logic and the state of exception.

In a forcefully argued essay, Harfield argued that covert operations not only require laws to make them compatible with human rights, but also require a specific ethical framework. In this context covert investigations require *both* law and ethical use in order to be socially and morally justifiable (Harfield 2014). The difficulty with this proposition is that there is no real evidence that there is widespread public concern or moral objection to the use of surveillance and controlled operations in Australian since their inception in 1995. Indeed, in the aftermath of *Ridgeway* there has been almost no media coverage critical of this form of investigation. Concerns, where they exist, are primarily located in academic literature.

The consequence of the human rights jurisprudence is that while entrapment cases can easily fall within the purview of human rights instruments, claims to privacy and the fair trial are no guarantee of protections, because claims to privacy and fairness, where they exist, may be subordinated to a utilitarian analysis favouring crime control, public safety and the rights and freedoms of others. Privacy must, of necessity, be breached in order to conduct a covert operation. Without that capacity human rights frameworks can actively undermine otherwise necessary and successful investigations. In this context human rights appears to be more of a political and value-based discussion, rather than a legal framework that has a precise scope for application in the context of controlled operations. Breach of privacy and fair trial principles can be enlivened in controlled operations cases simply because of the basic character of the investigation. This is a form of investigation that ordinarily involves a direct intrusion into the personal ecology of the suspect, usually relying upon surveillance, public information on the interception of telecommunications. In this context the target is the focus of the investigation, but even then those people interacting with the target become part of the investigation. Privacy is a frustrating and secondary value in the face of necessity. The essential point is that this area of law and the surrounding literature contains a strong dynamic: recognition of the potential for breaches of privacy and a fair trial potentially affecting the admissibility of evidence and the process of the trial itself, competing with strong demands for crime control and security. It seems that if people are given a choice between crime control and security, as opposed to privacy, the choice falls on security.

Remedies and Discretionary Interventions

Controlled operations literature is equally concerned with the question of remedies and the availability of discretionary interventions. In the Anglo-Australian tradition, these arise at multiple and concurrent sites of operation.[32] This is to be contrasted with the position in the US where a defence of entrapment is the relevant remedy, and the position in Canada, where a stay order is the only approved remedy.[33] Such proceedings take place after a determination of guilt but prior to sentence. Broadly, remedial action arises at three key points: pre-trial, trial and at the post-trial stage.

Pre-trial interventions are largely administrative controls imposed by statute and codes of conduct over the behaviour of investigators. Such controls ordinarily involve formal authorisation. Authorisations is a major system of accountability and control for controlled operations. That system requires a sufficient threshold of evidence in order to satisfy the statutory requirements for reasonable suspicion for the issue of the warrant. The behaviour of the investigators is routinely a matter for the internal disciplinary mechanisms of the agency itself. The quasi-military organisation of the police, for example, supplemented with a statutory code of conduct in relation to controlled operations,[34] provides one such example. Breaches of the code of conduct or behaviour expected of officers may result in disciplinary action, which of itself functions as a deterrent to misconduct. The requirement for authorisation and the explicit disciplinary consequences for deviation from the expected standard of conduct function as powerful pre-trial, pre-investigation interventions in controlled operations. But such processes are not remedial as such; rather, these are "front end" controls.

Trial Interventions have branched into five distinct directions: defence, abuse of process, exclusion and control of evidence, estoppel and mitigation of sentence (Ashworth 1999; Friedland 1982); Hunter (1995); (Duff 2002; Carter 2009; Johnston 1980; Yeo 1981; Bates 1982; Choo 1990; Paciocco 1991; Birch 1994; Bates 1994; Presser 2001; Davies 2002; Selway 2002; Abelson 2003; Ormerod and Birch 2004; Bronitt 2005; Hughes 2006; Mellifont 2007; Rogers 2008; Choo 2008; Arenson 2011). In the US the main trial remedy for entrapment is a defence. The defence, where successful, entitles the accused to an acquittal in the face of evidence that would otherwise convict. The US is unique in this respect, as the superior courts of Australia, Canada, New Zealand and the UK have all confirmed that entrapment is not a defence in those jurisdictions. Some have, however, argued for a defence in these jurisdictions (Choo 1990; Fisse 1988; Lippke 2017), but there is no sign of such a defence being accepted by either the courts or the legislature. Outside of entrapment specific defences, Friedland (1982) and Stevenson (2004) have argued that entrapment involves a multiplicity of potential interventions, and

---

[32] Ormerod and Roberts (2002)

[33] *R v Mack* [1988] 2 SCR 903; *R v Pearson* [1998] 3 SCR 620; *R v Meuckon* (1990) 78 CR (3d) 196 (BC CA). For recent commentary see Murphy and Anderson (2014)

[34] Eg: The *Law Enforcement (Controlled Operations) Regulations 2012* (NSW), Sched 2

is not a singular doctrinal rule. Rather, it is a cluster relevant to questions of a defence of entrapment, necessity, estoppel, duress, impossibility, attempt and mistake. Other writers, including Murphy and Anderson (2007) and McAdams (2005) have argued for offence-specific defences based on entrapment, but there is no indication that a general or specific defence of entrapment is likely to gain traction outside of the United States. What has gained traction, however, is a variety of discretionary process remedies.

In Canada and the UK entrapment may constitute an abuse of process,[35] based on the principle that the unlawful conduct of investigators undermines public confidence in the judiciary and the executive. In this context the abuse of process doctrine has emerged as a powerful discretionary remedy enlivening a stay order by the superior courts. In these cases entrapment or improper investigations may enliven the discretionary stay order, effectively freezing a case brought before the courts, even where there is compelling evidence that the offender is guilty of the crime. The stay order has not, however, been accepted as the primary remedy in Australian law. In *Ridgeway* the High Court unanimously rejected the idea that entrapment was a defence,[36] but recognised that a stay order may be appropriate in certain cases. The problem here is that there was divergence of opinion on the timing and the application of a stay order. The plurality held that a stay, while available, was not the primary remedy in an entrapment case. The primary remedy was exclusion of evidence based on public policy.[37] In this context a stay order is the necessary result of some fatal flaw in the prosecution case subsequent to the exclusion of evidence, rather than an option in its own right. Four Justices held that it was *not* an abuse of process for prosecutors to bring a case before a court just because evidence was allegedly obtained through entrapment,[38] while three Justices held that it *could be*, depending on the facts.[39] Consequently, there is no real consensus of opinion in *Ridgeway* on the timing or application of a stay order.

There was consensus, however, on *exclusion of evidence* as the primary remedy in Australian law for entrapment cases. The logic here is that cases of entrapment involve the officer behaving unlawfully or improperly, and perhaps unfairly in the course of the investigation. The jurisprudence holds that there are sound reasons in *public policy* for the careful use of such evidence, which may result in the evidence being wholly or partly excluded, or subject to a variety of warnings about its use. The governing principle, Heydon writes, is "that the law should not be seen as condoning or encouraging unlawful conduct of those whose task it is to enforce it." (Heydon 2013). Australian evidence law had, since the 1970s, evolved a

[35] *R v Mack* [1988] 2 SCR 903; *Attorney General's Reference No. 3; R v Looseley* [2001] 4 All ER 897

[36] *R v Ridgeway* (1995) 184 CLR 19 at 28 per Mason CJ, Deane and Dawson JJ, at 45-46 per Brennan J, at 56 per Toohey J, at 72-73 per Gaudron J, at 82 per McHugh J

[37] *R v Ridgeway* (1995) 184 CLR 19 at 40-1 per Mason CJ, Deane and Dawson JJ

[38] *R v Ridgeway* (1995) 184 CLR 19 at 33 per Mason CJ, Deane and Dawson JJ and CLR 46 per Brennan J

[39] *R v Ridgeway* (1995) 184 CLR 19 at 57 per Toohey J; at 74-5 per Gaudron J, at 92 per McHugh J

discretionary exclusionary rule that permitted the trial judge to exclude evidence unlawfully obtained on the grounds of public policy. This rule, developed in *R v Ireland*[40] and later *Bunning v Cross*,[41] was expanded somewhat in *Ridgeway* by the confirmation that the unlawful conduct of investigators could trigger the exclusion of evidence.[42] Consequently the major trial intervention in Australian law in entrapment cases is concerned with the exclusion of evidence. This is an aspect of law that has been criticised, for the exclusion of evidence requires that such matters are brought to the attention of a judicial officer at the point of trial – a point at which the accused is well and truly engaged in the prosecution process. In addition, Presser (2001), Bronitt and McSherry (2017) have observed that empirical studies indicate that in most cases the discretion is exercised in favour of the prosecution rather than the defendant. In his analysis of the phenomena in the common law world more broadly, Ashworth rightly observes that the reason for this dynamic is that it is arguably in the public interest to admit probative evidence of serious crime, even in cases of impropriety (Ashworth 1998). The remedy also suffers from the fact that it is a remedy of imperfect effect. A person may still be convicted even when evidence is rejected if there is sufficient alternative evidence (Bronitt and Roche 2000).

The key point here is that the Australian position on entrapment is oriented towards a *trial process* focus as the point of challenge and remediation for the accused, with emphasis on judicial discretion over the reception of evidence. This is not to say that other forms of intervention are not available, rather the character of entrapment is that it invites a variety of potential forms of intervention operating at multiple sites.

The final category of remedial action is *post trial*. These cannot be understood as functioning as remedies in the strict sense, because they normally concern the investigator. The only exception to that is mitigation of sentence. The case law on this in Australia is relatively poor,[43] but as I have explained elsewhere, mitigation of sentence is an option in Australian entrapment cases (Murphy and Anderson 2014). This option still results in a conviction, but it permits the judicial officer to import the entrapment claims into the intuitive synthesis involved in determining the punishment of the offender. The extent of mitigation is necessarily a question of fact and degree in all the circumstances of the case. In cases where the investigators have

[40](1970) 126 CLR 321

[41]*Bunning v Cross* (1978) 141 CLR 54

[42]This conclusion was a departure from the English position affirmed in *R v Sang* [1980] AC 402 that there was no such discretion to exclude otherwise relevant evidence. The common law rule was subsequently altered by s138 of the *Evidence Act 1995* (NSW/Cth), which provides that unlawfully obtained evidence is prima facie *inadmissible*, and the discretion functions to admit such evidence.

[43]*R v Birtles* (1969) 53 Cr App R 469; *R v McCann* (1971) 56 Cr App R 359; *R v Sang* [1980] AC 402; *R v Mandica* (1980) 24 SASR 394; *R v Jardine* (1981) 5 Crim LJ 49; *R v Sloane (No 2)* (unreported, Court of Criminal Appeal, NSW, 15 July 1992); *R v Campanella* [2004] SASC 99.

behaved unlawfully, they may become liable for criminal or civil prosecution,[44] in addition to internal disciplinary proceedings. There are, of course, a variety of actions in tort available to the aggrieved, notably misfeasance in public office. But overall the attention of Australian law in entrapment cases is focussed on *pre-trial* and *trial process* interventions.

Conclusion

It is an ambitious undertaking to try to synthesise such a large field of information. The critical point is that the *legal understanding* of controlled operations is situated within an inward-looking disciplinary framework, mainly concerned with the legal consequences of proactive policing, and the associated quest for principled remediation. Those principles are characterised by discourses of entrapment, rights and remedies. It is a framework of tense public policy. On the one hand "the Amin Dichotomy" and its drive for fairness, on the other by a "reluctant" acceptance of necessity: the ends justify the means. As Bronitt and McSherry (2017) have insightfully argued these polarities may be understood through Packer's crime control thesis (Packer 1964, 1968).

In *The Limits of the Criminal Sanction* (1968), Packer argued that criminal law is characterised by two dominant conservative value-sets. One system values crime control, the other due process. *Crime control* emphasises efficiency and power as governing policies. Crime control means detection, apprehension, and conviction of offenders. This perspective competes with loyalty to *due process*, which also values crime control, but emphasises accuracy of outcomes. Here the policy is concerned with ensuring that the public are protected by strong judicial and procedural controls that exclude weak cases and that maximise the legal security of the suspect. Convictions cannot be obtained at the expense of convicting the innocent. Packer's classic analogy is the distinction between an assembly-line and an obstacle course. Although Packer's model has been criticised (Ashworth and Redmayne 2010), it remains a powerful theoretical model. Drawing on the earlier work of McBarnet (1981) and Dixon (1997), Bronitt & McSherry argued that *Ridgeway* provides an example of the competition of these values. The legal and policy tensions in controlled operations law can be understood through Packer's model. They argue that despite the rule of law rhetoric, the reality of the reception of entrapment evidence, and the authorisation of unlawful activity manifested in controlled operations legislation, produced a mechanism where the unlawful conduct of the State was effectively licensed. The result was a system that rarely excludes evidence because such conduct is technically no longer unlawful – a dynamic that efficiently facilitates convictions. They concluded that the Australian position on entrapment effectively

[44] The case of Detective Mark Standon is a case in point. Standon was implicated in cocaine trafficking in the course of the investigation of Gilbert Gedeon and David Dowe. See *Gedeon v Cmr NSW Crime Commission* [2008] HCA 43; *R v Standen* [2011] NSWSC 1422

consolidates the purposes of the two models: the due process requirements within controlled operations law is actually directed at crime control – effective merging crime control and due process values (Bronitt and McSherry 2010).

As I have suggested elsewhere (Murphy (2014), this argument requires clarification. It is easy to misinterpret Packer's model. Packer did not contend that these value systems were antithetical, or binary. While recognising at least two distinct competing "polarities", he also recognised that value systems were complex, and that ultimately "due process" and "crime control" values were working towards the same ends: the suppression and punishment of crime through lawful means (Packer 1968). It does appear that controlled operations law presents a model where due process and crime control value systems are fused within the architecture of law. But there is something more to controlled operations than a simple principled rule structure authorising unlawful conduct. Controlled operations literature is shaped by distinct internal and external rationalities, sourced in both legal and extra-legal sources. It is a phenomenon that cannot be understood simply through the lens of legal scholarship, or through Packer's thesis.

Controlled operations literature presents a network of distinct historical forces at work, a landscape in which controlled operations law is necessarily shaped. The historical national and international shifts towards cross-border and surveillance-based policing concerned with drug interdiction, terrorism and organised crime provide a complex legal context shaping doctrinal architectures and practices. That context is shaped by the legal architectures and policing practices associated with the "War on Drugs", where the "controlled delivery" was born. Associated with this is the transformation of policing methods and practices through professionalization, corporatisation, and technologies promoting expert knowledge systems, based on risk, deception and surveillance. Within that network we find autopoietic developments in caselaw and legislation – the development of specific rules within the courts and within Parliaments directed to the government of the legal architectures. These developments are interlinked with the intersections existing with the laws of evidence, police regulation, the Constitution, and the jurisprudence of the "rule of law".

Despite the appearance of being a specialist limb of criminal procedure, controlled operations literature forms part of a much larger body of scholarship primarily concerned with the legal consequences of undercover investigation. The dominant themes cluster around the problem of entrapment, the implications for human rights, public confidence in the administration of justice, and the quest for suitable remedies. While the controlled operations architecture was a direct consequence of *Ridgeway* in 1995, it was also profoundly influenced by an emergent national and international shift towards broad systems of surveillance and targeted investigations work. It is well recognised that these models have the potential to touch on substantial matters of public policy, but law makers and legal writers condition the critique with the express commitment to a utilitarian rationality: the powers are proper and necessary, subject to certain controls. Legal writers, overall, accept the utility, purpose and legality of the controlled operation. Such powers serve the public good. The "due process" component of the controlled operation aims to emphasise a protective element and a focus on fact integrity and the preservation of evidence, which tends to support Bronitt and McSherry's use of Packer's model.

The legal literature also presents a curious dynamic. In most cases involving a critique of entrapment or undercover investigation the author identifies something objectionable. The author then offers some form of pragmatic or general acceptance, conditioned on the power being tied to distinct legalities. Entrapment, in particular, is problematic because (a) it is difficult in hard cases to properly characterise in law; (b) it involves serious potential costs to the suspect and investigator; (c) it involves serious potential social costs through the creation of exceptions and compromise of rights; and (d) the practice itself is recognised as carrying the prospect of undermining public confidence in the judiciary and the executive. Indeed, there are *critical* questions for democratic/liberal governments at stake in societies which permit unlawful conduct by state authorities. And yet, despite all these problems, the power continues to exist and expand. The "crime control" and "due process" dynamic suggests something more than competing values at work. When law evolves in a way that frustrates the efforts of crime control, the legislator changes the law. It appears that a *categorical imperative*[45] is operating within the criminal law generally and controlled operations specifically – a demand and a desire to make laws and create exceptions to ensure the utility of crime control. Broadly, the law maker is convinced of the merits and virtue of an imagined good, and acts in a way that promotes that good as a universal, even when to do so extends powers to police that the legislature itself recognises is exceptional and dangerous. This aspect is absent in the literature. Controlled operations literature, simply, fails to explain itself beyond the need to empower police while protecting rights. It is apparently blind to the deeply embedded rationalities operating within policy *and* the doctrinal structures of the law itself. Rights are *subject to* the requirements of the State, a dynamic explained based on necessity, rather than an understanding of the dominant role of specific intellectual structures and the project of governance. The law, as a discipline, essentially understands the controlled operation through its own disciplinary orientation, although it draws upon content from outside of law, suggesting that the interpretive and contextual understanding of controlled operations law can only truly be effected through a socio-legal perspective that demands attention to literature external to law. Indeed, in the following chapter the themes of surveillance, risk, and exceptions to the rule of law will be developed and argued as far more significant features of this species of law than the legal literature suggests. Controlled operations are a manifestation of a technique of government, arising out of a central problem in the policing of modernity.

[45] Famously developed as a concept by Kant, who argued that the way we understand rational behaviour in ourselves and others is fixed in relation to what we "ought" to do in pursuit of a particular goal. See Schneewind (1992)

References

Abelson, D. (2003). Sentencing entrapment: An overview and analysis. *Marquette Law Review, 86*(4), 773.

Allen, G. (1972). The is-ought question reformulated and answered. *Ethics, 82*(3), 181–199.

Allen, M. (1984). Entrapment: Time for reconsideration. *Anglo-American Law Review, 13*(4), 57–84.

Allen, R., Luttrell, M., & Kreeger, A. (1999). Clarifying entrapment. *Journal of Criminal Law and Criminology, 89*(2), 407.

Altman, A., & Lee, S. (1983). Legal Entrapment. *Philosophy and Public Affairs, 12*(1), 51–69.

Arenson, K. (2011). Rejection of the fruit of the poisonous tree doctrine in Australia: A retreat from progressivism. *University of Notre Dame Australia Law Journal, 13*, 17–68.

Arenson, K., Bagaric, M., & Gillies, P. (2011). *Australian criminal law in the common law jurisdictions* (3rd ed.). Sydney: Oxford University Press.

Ashworth, A. (1977). Excluding evidence as protecting rights. *Criminal Law Review, 723*.

Ashworth, A. (1978). Entrapment. *Criminal Law Review*, 137–140.

Ashworth, A. (1998). Should the police be allowed to use deceptive practices? *Law Quarterly Review, 114*(Jan), 108–140.

Ashworth, A. (1999). What is wrong with entrapment? *Singapore Journal of Legal Studies, 2*, 293–317.

Ashworth, A. (2000a). Is the criminal law a lost cause? *Law Quarterly Review, 166*(April), 225–256.

Ashworth, A. (2000b). Testing fidelity to legal values: Official involvement and criminal justice. *The Modern Law Review, 63*(5), 633–659.

Ashworth, A. (2002a). Entrapment and criminal justice (R v Looseley and Attorney-General's reference (No 3 of 2000)). *Oxford University Commonwealth Law Journal, 2*(1), 125–131.

Ashworth, A. (2002b). Re-drawing the boundaries of entrapment. *Criminal Law Review, March*, 161.

Ashworth, A. (2006). Four threats to the presumption of innocence. *South African Law Journal, 123*(1), 63–97.

Ashworth, A., & Redmayne, M. (2010). *The criminal process* (4th ed.). Oxford: Oxford University Press.

Australian Law Reform Commission (ALRC). (1975). *Report No. 2: An interim report: Criminal investigation* (Vol. Report No. 2). Canberra: Australian Law Reform Commission.

Bagaric, M., & Arenson, K. (2007). *Criminal laws in Australia*. Melbourne: Oxford University Press.

Bates, F. (1982). Evidence unfairly obtained: Home thoughts from abroad. *Journal of Criminal Law, 46*(1), 49–56.

Bates, F. (1994). Improperly obtained evidence and public policy: An Australian perspective. *International and Comparative Law Quarterly, 43*(2), 379–391.

Bejesky, R. (2015). Sixty shades of terror plots: Locating the actus reus and the hypothetical line for entrapment. *Creighton Law Review, 48*, 393–793.

Birch, D. (1994). Excluding evidence of entrapment: What is a fair cop? *Current Legal Problems, 42*, 73.

Bishop, J. (1998). *Criminal procedure* (2nd ed.). Sydney: Butterworths.

Bodansky, D. (2006). International law in black and white. *Georgia Journal of International and Comparative Law, 34*(2), 284–304.

Braithwaite, J., Fisse, B., & Geis, G. (1987a). Covert facilitation and crime: Restoring balance to the entrapment debate. *Journal of Social Issues, 43*(3), 5–41.

Braithwaite, J., Fisse, B., & Geis, G. (1987b). Overt observations on covert facilitation: A reply to the commentators. *Journal of Social Issues, 43*(3), 101–122.

Bright, D., Hughes, C., & Chalmers, J. (2012). Illuminating dark networks: A social network analysis of an Australian drug trafficking syndicate. *Crime, Law & Social Change, 57*(2), 151–176.

Brockman, J. (2015). The use of undercover operators by professional organizations when gathering evidence to enforce their monopolies: Reprehensible tactics and outright deception. *Manitoba Law Journal, 38*(1), 243.
Bronitt, S. (1996). Electronic surveillance and informers: Infringing the rights to silence and privacy. *Criminal Law Journal, 20*(3), 144–152.
Bronitt, S. (1999). Entrapment, human rights and criminal justice: A licence to deviate? *Hong Kong Law Journal, 29*(2), 216–239.
Bronitt, S. (2002). Sang is dead, loosely speaking. *Singapore Journal of Legal Studies, 1*, 374–387.
Bronitt, S. (2003). Taking privacy rights seriously: Engaging with undercover law reform. *Criminal Law Journal, 27*, 113.
Bronitt, S. (2004). The law in undercover policing: A comparative study of entrapment and covert interviewing in Australia, Canada and Europe. *Common Law World Review, 33*(1), 35–80.
Bronitt, S. (2005). Interpreting law enforcement immunities: The relationship between judicial, legislative and administrative models. In S. Corcoran & S. Bottomley (Eds.), *Interpreting statutes* (pp. 223–249). Sydney: Federation Press.
Bronitt, S., & Kinley, D. (1996). Undercover policing: Detection or deception? In H. Selby (Ed.), *Tomorrow's law*. Sydney: Federation Press.
Bronitt, S., & McSherry, B. (2001). *Principles of criminal law* (1st ed.). Lawbook Co.
Bronitt, S., & McSherry, B. (2005). *Principles of criminal law* (2nd ed.). Sydney: Lawbook.
Bronitt, S., & McSherry, B. (2010). *Principles of criminal law* (3rd ed.). Sydney: Lawbook.
Bronitt, S., & McSherry, B. (2017). *Principles of criminal law* (4th ed.). Sydney: Lawbook.
Bronitt, S., & Roche, D. (2000). Between rhetoric and reality: Sociolegal and republican perspectives on entrapment. *International Journal of Evidence and Proof, 4*(2), 77.
Bronitt, S., & Roche, D. (2001). Entrapment, the art of police deception. *AQ: Australian Quarterly, 73*(1), 20–48.
Carlon, A. (2007). Entrapment, punishment and the sadistic state. *Virginia Law Review, 93*, 1081–1134.
Carlson, J. (1987). The act requirement and the foundations of the entrapment defense. *Virginia Law Review, 73*(6), 1011.
Carter, D. (2009). To catch the lion, tether the goat: Entrapment, conspiracy, and sentencing manipulation. *Akron Law Journal, 42*(1), 135–184.
Chernok, A. (2011). Entrapment under controlled operations legislation: A Victorian perspective. *Criminal Law Journal, 35*(6), 361–375.
Choo, A. L.-T. (1990). A defence of entrapment. *Modern Law Review, 53*(4), 453–471.
Choo, A. L.-T. (2008). *Abuse of process and judicial stays of criminal proceedings*. Oxford: Oxford University Press.
Colquitt, J. (2004). Rethinking entrapment. *American Criminal Law Review, 41*(4), 1389–1438.
Colvin, E. (2002). Controlled operations, controlled activities and entrapment. *Bond Law Review, 14*(2), 227–250.
Colvin, E. (2006). Fairness and equality in the criminal process. *Oxford University Commonwealth Law Journal, 6*(1), 1–26.
Colvin, E., & McKechnie, J. (2011). *Criminal law in Queensland and Western Australia: Cases and commentary* (6th ed.). Chatswood: LexisNexis.
Corns, C. (2005). Combating organised crime in Victoria: Old problems and new solutions. *Criminal Law Journal, 29*, 154–168.
Corns, C. (2014). *Criminal investigation and procedure: The law in Victoria* (2nd ed.). Melbourne: Thomson Reuters.
Corns, C., & Tudor, S. (2009). *Criminal investigation and procedure: The law in Victoria*. Sydney: Law Book.
Crofts, T., & Burton, K. (2009). *The criminal codes: Commentary and materials* (6th ed.). Sydney: Thomson Reuters.

Cunningham, D., & Noakes, J. (2008). What if she's from the FBI?' The effects of covert forms of social control on social movements. In M. Deflem (Ed.), *Surveillance and governance* (pp. 175–197). Bradford: Emerald Group Publishing Limited.
Davies, G. L. (2002). Exclusion of evidence illegally or improperly obtained. *Australian Law Journal, 76*(3), 170.
Debeljak, J. (2008). Balancing rights in a democracy: The problems with limitations and overrides of rights under the Victorian Character of Human Rights and Responsibilities Act 2006. *Melbourne University Law Review, 32*(2), 422–469.
Deis, G. (2001). Economics, causation and the entrapment defense. *University of Illinois Law Review*, (5), 1207–1246.
Dillof, A. M. (2004). Unraveling unlawful entrapment. *The Journal of Criminal Law and Criminology, 94*(4), 827–896.
Dixon, D. (1997). *Law in policing: Legal regulation and police practices*. Oxford: Clarendon Press.
Dixon, D. (Ed.). (1999). *A culture of corruption*. Sydney: Hawkins Press.
Donnelly, R. (1951). Judicial control of informants, spies, stool pigeons, and agent provocateurs. *The Yale Law Journal, 60*(7), 1091.
Douglas, H., Everton-Moore, K., Harbidge, S., & Levy, L. (2010). *Criminal process in Queensland and Western Australia*. Sydney: Lawbook.
Duff, A. (2002). "I might be guilty, but you can't try me": Estoppel and other bars to trial. *Ohio State Journal of Criminal Law, 1*, 245–259.
Dworkin, G. (1985). The serpent beguiled me and I did eat: Entrapment and the creation of crime. *Law and Philosophy, 4*(1), 17–39.
Dworkin, G. (1987). Ethics and entrapment. *Journal of Social Issues, 43*(3), 57–59.
Elbaz, D. (1999). The troubling entrapment defense: How about an economic approach? *American Criminal Law Review, 36*(1), 117–143.
Falk, W. (1976). Hume on is and ought. *Canadian Journal of Philosophy, 6*(3), 359–378.
Feinberg, J. (2003). Criminal entrapment - Instigating the unpredisposed. In *Problems at the roots of law: Essays in legal and political theory* (pp. 57–76). New York: Oxford University Press.
Fijnaut, C., & Marx, G. T. (1995). *Undercover: Police surveillance in comparative perspective*. Norwell: Kluwer Academic Publishers.
Fisse, B. (1988). Entrapment as a defence. *Criminal Law Journal, 12*(6), 367–386.
Fitzgerald, T. (1989). *Queensland Fitzgerald Commission of Inquiry into Possible Illegal Activities and Associated Police Misconduct* (Report of a Commission of Inquiry Pursuant to Orders in Council). Brisbane.
Freeman, M. (2014). *Lloyd's introduction to jurisprudence* (9th ed.). London: Sweet & Maxwell.
Friedland, M. L. (1982). Controlling entrapment. *University of Toronto Law Journal, 32*(1), 1.
Galbally, R., & Walters, B. (1995). Entrapment: The serpent beguiled me. *Law Institute Journal, September*, 913–914.
Gans, J. (2017). *Modern criminal law of Australia* (2nd ed.). Melbourne: Cambridge University Press.
Gans, J., Henning, T., Hunter, J., & Warner, K. (2011). *Criminal process and human rights*. Sydney: Federation Press.
Gershman, B. L. (1982). Abscam, the judiciary, and the ethics of entrapment. *The Yale Law Journal, 91*(8), 1565–1591.
Gillies, P. (1997). *Criminal law* (4th ed.). Sydney: LBC Information Services.
Grevling, K. (1996). Illegality, entrapment and a new discretion. *Law Quarterly Review, 112*(January), 41–46.
Gurney, K. (1995). Covert law enforcement after ridgeway. *Deakin Law Review, 2*(2), 283–296.
Hall, P. (2004). *Investigating corruption and misconduct in public office: Commissions of inquiry - Powers and procedures*. Sydney: Lawbook.
Harfield, C. (2010). The governance of covert investigation. *Melbourne University Law Review, 34*(3), 773–804.

Harfield, C. (2014). Law, morality and the authorisation of covert police surveillance. *Australian Journal of Human Rights, 20*(2), 133–164. https://doi.org/10.1080/1323-238X.2014.11882153.
Harris, W. (1994). Entrapment. *Criminal Law Journal, 18*(4), 197–222.
Heydon, J. D. (1973). The problems of entrapment. *Cambridge Law Journal, 32*(2), 268–286.
Heydon, J. D. (2013). *Cross on evidence* (9th ed.). Sydney: LexisNexis.
Hill, D., McLeod, S., & Tanyi, A. (2018). The concept of entrapment. *Criminal Law, Philosophy, 12*(4), 539–554. https://doi.org/10.1007/s11572-017-9436-7.
Ho, H. L. (2011). State Entrapment. *Legal Studies, 31*(1), 71–95.
Hocking, B. (1996). Ridgeway. *Criminal Law Journal, 20*(3), 160.
Hofmeyer, K. (2006). The problem of private entrapment. *Criminal Law Review*, (April), 319.
Howie, R., & Berman, P. (1995). Ridgeway v R. *Criminal Law News, 2*(3), 17.
Hudson, W. (1964). Hume on is and ought. *The Philosophical Quarerly, 14*(56), 246–252.
Hughes, P. (2006). Temptation and culpability in the law of duress and entrapment. *Criminal Law Quarterly, 51*, 342–359.
Hume, D. (1740). A treatise of human nature. In T. Green & T. Grose (Eds.), *A treatise on human nature* (1898th ed.). London: Longmans, Green & Co.
Hunter, G. (1962). Hume on is and ought. *Philosophy, 37*(140), 148–152.
Hunter, J. (1995). Abuse of process savages criminal issue estoppel. *University of New South Wales Law Journal, 18*(1), 151.
Jacobs, H. (1963). Decoy enforcement of homosexual laws. *University of Pennsylvania Law Review, 112*(2), 259–284.
Joh, E. (2015). Bait, mask, and ruse: Technology and police deception. *Harvard law review forum, 128*, 246–359.
Johnston, E. (1980). The exclusionary rule and other controls over the abuse of police power. *The Australian Law Journal, 54*(August), 466–471.
Kent, A. (1933). The nature of the defense of entrapment. *The University of Chicago Law Review, 1*(1), 115.
Kronman, A. (1983). *Max Weber*. Stanford: Stanford University Press.
Lancaster, R. (1995). Ridgeway and response. *Criminal Law News, 2*(7), 54.
Lanham, D., Bartal, B., Evans, R., & Wood, D. (2006). *Criminal laws in Australia*. Sydney: Federation Press.
Levanon, L. (2016). The law of police entrapment: Critical evaluation and policy analysis. *Criminal Law Forum, 27*(1), 35–73. https://doi.org/10.1007/s10609-015-9271-2.
Lippke, R. L. (2017). A limited defense of what some will regard as entrapment. *Legal Theory, 23*(4), 283–306. https://doi.org/10.1017/S1352325217000271.
Lubbers, E. (2015). Undercover research: Corporate and police spying on activists. An introduction to activist intelligence as a new field of study. *Surveillance & Society, 13*(3/4), 338–353. https://doi.org/10.24908/ss.v13i3/4.5371.
MacIntyre, A. (1959). Hume on is and ought. *The Philosophical Review, 68*(4), 451–468.
MacLaughlin, F. (1960). The defense of entrapment in trial by court-martial. *JAG, 5*, 7–19.
Macleod, A. D. (1995). Undercover policing: A psychiatrist's perspective. *International Journal of Law and Psychiatry, 18*(2), 239–247.
Marx, G. T. (1974). Thoughts on a neglected category of social movement participant: The agent provocateur and the informant. *American Journal of Sociology, 80*(2), 402–442.
Marx, G. T. (1980). The new police undercover work. *Journal of Contemporary Ethnography, 8*(4), 399–446.
Marx, G. T. (1981). Ironies of social control: Authorities as contributors to deviance through escalation, nonenforcement and covert facilitation. *Social Problems, 28*(3), 221–246.
Marx, G. T. (1982). Who really gets stung? Some issues raised by the new police undercover work. *Crime & Delinquency, 28*(2), 165–193.
Marx, G. T. (1985). I'll be watching you: Reflections on the new surveillance. In C. Norris & D. Wilson (Eds.), *Surveillance, crime and social control*. Aldershot: Ashgate.

Marx, G. T. (1987). Restoring realism and logic to the covert facilitation debate. [Article]. *Journal of Social Issues, 43*(3), 43–55.

Marx, G. T. (1988). *Undercover: Police surveillance in America*. Berkeley: University of California Press.

Marx, G. T. (1992a). Under-the-covers undercover operations: Some reflections on the State's use of sex and deception in law enforcement. *Criminal Justice Ethics, 11*(1), 13–24.

Marx, G. T. (1992b). When the guards guard themselves: Undercover tactics turned inward. *Policing and Society, 2*(3), 151–172.

McAdams, R. (2005). The political economy of entrapment. *Journal of Criminal Law and Criminology, 96*(1), 107–186.

McAdams, R. (2007). Reforming entrapment doctrine in "United States V Hollingsworth". *The University of Chicago Law Review, 74*, 1795.

McBarnet, D. (1981). *Conviction: Law, the state and the construction of justice*. London: Macmillan.

McKay, S. (2002). Entrapment: Competing views on the effect of the human rights act on English criminal law. *European Human Rights Law Review, 6*, 764–774.

Mekeel, J. (2006). Misnamed, misapplied, and misguided: Clarifying the state of sentencing entrapment and proposing a new conception of the doctrine. *William and Mary Bill of Rights Journal, 14*(4), 1583–1627.

Mellifont, K. (2007). *The derivative imperative: How should Australian criminal trial courts treat evidence deriving from illegally or improperly obtained evidence?* Queensland University of Technology.

Miller, L. (2006). Undercover policing: A psychological and operational guide. *Journal of Police and Criminal Psychology, 21*(2), 1–24.

Miller, S. (2014). *Investigative ethics: Ethics for police detectives and criminal investigators* (Investigative ethics). Hoboken: Wiley.

Mitchell, D. (1968). Must we talk about "is" and "ought"? *Mind, 77*(308), 543–549.

Murphy, B. (2014). Retrospective on ridgeway: Governing principles of controlled operations law. *Criminal Law Journal, 38*(1), 38–58.

Murphy, B. (2015). *Zone of impeachment: A post-Foucauldian analysis of controlled operations law and policy*. PhD thesis, University of Newcastle, Newcastle.

Murphy, B. (2016). Deceptive apparatus: Foucauldian perspectives on law, authorised crime and the rationalities of undercover investigation. *Griffith Law Review, 25*(2), 223–244. https://doi.org/10.1080/10383441.2016.1194956.

Murphy, B., & Anderson, J. (2007). Mates, Mr big and the unwary: Ongoing supply and its relationship to entrapment. *Current Issues in Criminal Justice, 19*(1), 5–33.

Murphy, B., & Anderson, J. (2014). After the serpent beguiled me: Entrapment and sentencing in Australian and Canada. *Queen's Law Journal, 39*(2), 621.

Murphy, B., & Anderson, J. (2016). Confessions to Mr Big. *The International Journal of Evidence & Proof, 20*(1), 29–48. https://doi.org/10.1177/1365712715613485.

Nash, S. (1996). Australian developments in entrapment cases. *Criminal Law Review, 137*.

Norberry, J. (1995). Police entrapment - The high court's decision in ridgeway v The queen. *Research Note - Parliamentary Research Service, 47*.

Norris, J. (2016). Entrapment and terrorism on the left: An analysis of Post-9/11 cases. *New Criminal Law Review, 19*, 236–437.

Norris, J. (2019). Explaining the emergence of entrapment in Post-9/11 terrorism investigations. *Critical Criminology, 27*(3), 467–483. https://doi.org/10.1007/s10612-019-09438-8.

Norris, J., & Grol-Prokopczyk, H. (2015). Estimating the prevalence of entrapment in Post-9/11 terrorism cases. *Journal of Criminal Law and Criminology, 105*, 609–705.

Norris, J., & Grol-Prokopczyk, H. (2018). Entrapment allegations in right-wing terrorism cases: A mixed-methods analysis. *International Journal of Law, Crime and Justice, 53*, 77–88. https://doi.org/10.1016/j.ijlcj.2018.03.009.

Ormerod, D. (2008). *Smith & Hogan: Criminal law* (12th ed.). Oxford: Oxford University Press.

Ormerod, D., & Birch, D. (2004). The evolution of the discretionary exclusion of evidence. *Criminal Law Review*, (October), 767–788.

Ormerod, D., & Roberts, A. (2002). The trouble with Teixeira: Developing a principled approach to entrapment. *International Journal of Evidence and Proof, 6*(1), 3.

Paciocco, D. (1991). The stay of proceedings as a remedy in criminal cases: Abusing the abuse of process concept. *Criminal Law Journal, 15*(4), 315.

Packer, H. (1964). Two models of the criminal process. *University of Pennsylvania Law Review, 113*(1), 1–64.

Packer, H. (1968). *The limits of the criminal sanction*. Palo Alto: Stanford University Press.

Palmer, A. (1997). R v Elliott. *Melbourne University Law Review, 21*(1), 331.

Park, R. (1976). The entrapment controversy. *Minnesota Law Review, 60*(2), 163.

Parliamentary Joint Committee on the National Crime Authority. (1999). *Street legal: A report by the parliamentary joint committee on the National Crime Authority*. Parliament of Australia Parliamentary Joint Committee on the National Crime Authority.

Piccarreta, M., & Keenan, J. (1992). Entrapment targets and tactics: Beyond Jacobson v United States. *Arizona Attorney, 29*(November), 11–14.

Pogrebin, M., & Poole, E. (1993). Vice isn't nice: A look at the effects of working undercover. *Journal of Criminal Justice, 21*, 383–394.

Presser, B. (2001). Public policy, police and interest: A re-evaluation of the judicial discretion to exclude improperly or illegally obtained evidence. *Melbourne University Law Review, 25*(3), 757–785.

Robertson, G. (1994). Entrapment evidence: Manna from heaven, or fruit of the poisoned tree? *Criminal Law Review, November*, 805–816.

Rogers, J. (2008). The boundaries of abuse of process in criminal trials. *Current Legal Problems, 61*(1), 289–323.

Roach, K. (2010). Entrapment and equality in terrorism prosecutions: A comparative examination of North American and European approaches. *Mississippi Law Journal , 80*(4), 1455.

Roiphe, R. (2003). The serpent beguiled me: A history of the entrapment Defense. *Seton Hall Law Review, 33*(2), 257.

Roser, W. (1993). Entrapment: Have the courts found a solution to this fundamental dilemma to the criminal justice system? *Australian Law Journal, 67*(10), 721–743.

Rotenberg, D. (1963). The police detection practice of encouragement. *Virginia Law Review, 49*(5), 875–903.

Sagarin, E., & Macnamara, D. E. J. (1970). The problem of entrapment. *Crime & Delinquency, 16*(4), 363–378.

Schneewind, J. B. (1992). Autonomy, obligation and virtue: An overview of Kant's moral philosophy. In P. Guyer (Ed.), *The Cambridge companion to Kant* (pp. 309–341). Cambridge: Cambridge University Press.

Schurr, B. (1996–). *Criminal procedure (NSW)*. North Ryde: LBC Information Services.

Seidman, L. (1981). The supreme court, entrapment, and our criminal justice dilemma. *Supreme Court Review, 1981*, 111–155.

Seidman, L. (2009). Entrapment and the "free market" for crime. In P. Robinson, S. Garvey, & K. Kessler Ferzan (Eds.), *Criminal law conversations*. Oxford: Oxford University Press.

Selway, B. (2002). Principle, public policy and unfairness - Exclusion of evidence on discretionary grounds. *Adelaide Law Review, 23*(1), 1.

Shafer, J., & Sheridan, W. (1970). The defence of entrapment. *Osgoode Hall Law Journal, 8*(2), 277–299.

Sharpe, S. (1994). Covert police operations and the discretionary exclusion of evidence. *Criminal Law Review*, 793–804.

Sharpe, S. (2002). Covert surveillance and the use of informers. In M. McConville & G. Wilson (Eds.), *The handbook of the criminal justice process* (pp. 59–73). Oxford: Oxford University Press.

Sinnott-Armstrong, W. (1999). Entrapment in the net? *Ethics and Information Technology, 1*(2), 95–104.

Smith, S. (2017). Policing Hoover's ghost: The privilege for law enforcement techniques. *American Criminal Law Review, 54*, 233–339.

Squires, D. (2006). The problem with entrapment. *Oxford Journal of Legal Studies, 26*(2), 351–376.

Standing Committee of Attorneys-General and Australasian Police Ministers Council Joint Working Group on National Investigation Powers. (2003). *Cross-border investigative powers for law enforcement report*. Canberra: Leaders Summit on Terrorism and Multijurisdictional Crime.

Stevenson, D. (2004). Entrapment and the problem of deterring police misconduct. *Connecticut Law Review, 37*(1), 67–154.

Stevenson, D. (2008). Entrapment and terrorism. *Boston College Law Review, 49*(1), 125–215.

Stitt, B. G., & James, G. G. (1984). Entrapment and the entrapment defense: Dilemmas for a democratic society. *Law and Philosophy, 3*(1), 111–131.

Tawil, D. D. (2000). "Ready? Induce. Sting!": Arguing for the government's burden of proving readiness in entrapment cases. *Michigan Law Review, 98*(7), 2371–2394.

Weber, M. (1978). *Economy and society* (Vol. 1).

Wood, J. J. (1997). *Report of the Royal Commission into the NSW Police Service*. Sydney: New South Wales Government.

Yaffe, G. (2005). "The government beguiled me": The entrapment defense and the problem of private entrapment. *Journal of Ethics and Social Philosophy, 1*(1), 1–50.

Yeo, M. H. (1981). Discretion to exclude illegally and improperly obtained evidence: A choice of approaches. *Melbourne University Law Review, 13*, 31.

Zahra, P., & Young, C. (2014). *Drug laws in New South Wales* (3rd ed.). Sydney: Federation Press.

Zahra, P., Arden, R., Ierace, M., & Schurr, B. (1998). *Drug law in New South Wales* (2nd ed.). Sydney: Federation Press.

Zeitlin, I. (1985). Max Weber's sociology of law. *The University of Toronto Law Journal, 35*(2), 183–214.

Part II
Discourses in Public Policy

Chapter 6
Risk, Threat and Necropolitics

> *In the United Kingdom, South Africa and many other nations, governments are confronted with threats of terrorism and serious crime and naturally wish to take ... steps to reduce the danger and increase public protection. The pressures to increase the severity of penal responses or to widen the net of risk-based strategies grow more urgent when there are dramatic incidents touching the lives of ordinary citizens. In a context such as this, human or constitutional rights are sometimes not mentioned at all or regarded as afterthoughts or minor inconveniences: the main aim is to improve public confidence by taking measures...regarded as decisive. Governments succumbed to the temptation to announce more severe measures which are expressive but are, often dubiously, promoted in the language of effectiveness... a cherished value, with fundamental international recognition and strong justifications, is being undermined through the alleged imperatives of governance in the risk society.*
>
> Ashworth (2006)

Controlled operations law emerged at the intersection of policing practices and public policy. In Part 1, controlled operations law was shown to have evolved as a device to regulate and authorise undercover investigations involving direct engagement with suspects as an intrusive mode of investigation in order to make this activity compatible with the existing legal system. Consequently, the focus of legal literature is concerned with mapping that evolution and its consequences. One of the aspects of law routinely overlooked are the forces that shape public policy. Public policy manifests a complex system of thought: an epistemic code that inscribes the way law is structured and the ends to which patterns of regulation are manifest. These are knowledge systems that are discursive. This chapter, and the ones following, are aimed at analysing the rationality that informs policy. It is argued that key aspects of these rationalities can be identified in Parliamentary discourses. A qualitative examination of controlled operations Second Reading Speeches is presented,

B. Murphy, *Regulating Undercover Law Enforcement: The Australian Experience*, https://doi.org/10.1007/978-981-33-6381-6_6

identifying, and considering the major themes that inform controlled operations debates. Fundamentally, this analysis suggests that a multi-dimensional risk discourse is the key driver of controlled operations policy. Risk discourses not only direct public policy, they actively govern the substance of controlled operations law.

Discourses of Causation, Formation and Risk

This part reports on aspects of a qualitative examination of Second Reading Speeches in Australian parliaments concerned with controlled operations law. Hansard provides a rich source for the analysis of discourse. In order to contain the vast amount of information that a multi-jurisdictional and essentially longitudinal study of text generates, it becomes necessary to concentrate on a combination of breadth and depth, of synthesis and example. This chapter provides something of a macro analysis, while the following two chapters provide more detail examination of two specific related themes, legal risk and accountability.

Discourses of Causation

Hansard clearly demonstrates that controlled operations law is strongly associated with some material cause. A shift in policy has one of more causes. Those causes can change over time. The evolutionary changes to controlled operations law set out in Part 1 are directly connected with identifiable causes, which might be a primary or secondary response to danger, threat or risk. A primary response may be conceived as an event or crisis (acute or chronic) with a consequence for law and policy, while a secondary response may be conceived as a response to developments *within law itself.* These causes change over time, with the evolutionary pattern being one of primary causes, followed by secondary causes.

Ridgeway

As considered in detail in the opening chapter, the decision of the High Court in *Ridgeway* was a major early trigger for change. It was the consequences of *Ridgeway* that were the main concern of legislators from 1995 to 1997. This is not to say that the impact of *Ridgeway* was forgotten. It appears that after 2001 the primary motivation for law reform shifted. In this early phase of lawmaking the legislatures were mainly concerned with the manifestation of a multifaceted *legal risk* that compromised the effectiveness of law enforcement. *Ridgeway* meant that evidence obtained through proactive techniques was now potentially inadmissible. This meant that the prosecution of serious crime was in doubt. *Ridgeway* also meant that investigators could also face criminal and civil liability for engaging in a bona fide undercover investigation. The perverse outcome was that police could be liable, while offenders would be acquitted.

These issues can be seen in the address of then Attorney General for South Australia, Kenneth Griffin MLC:

> *On 30 May, 1995, in a trial in the District Court for the sale of heroin, Bishop J has held that the principle in Ridgeway applies to the trial and has excluded all of the evidence. Inevitably, that will mean that the prosecution will fail. This case concerned what is known as 'controlled buying.' In general terms, when police are given information that a person is selling drugs, they pretend to be a buyer and determine whether the person will sell drugs to them. If so, they may make a number of 'buys' with a view to identifying the seller's source of supply. That was the method used in this case. Bishop J, applying Ridgeway, has held that the purchasing police officers have committed the crime of procuring or aiding the sale, and that therefore the evidence is tainted and should not be admitted.*

> *It is arguable that this is not a correct application of the principles in Ridgeway. But, even if that be so, the doubts about this area of law require clarification. It is intolerable that a principal method by which police obtain evidence against drug sellers should be left in doubt, particularly because it is otherwise very difficult to obtain sufficient evidence in other ways. Obviously, the matter is urgent.*[1]

Ridgeway meant that successful prosecution was now uncertain. Prosecutors had to rely on the discretion of judges in relation to evidence, in the knowledge that controlled operations evidence could be inadmissible. In addition, the investigators had to rely on the discretion of public prosecutors not to press charges for technically unlawful conduct. The uncertainty was clearly unacceptable as a matter of public policy, a fact also recognised by the High Court, which recommended legislative intervention.[2] Curiously, there is also evident a certain mythology about judicial powers over evidence, and of the liability of investigators. The 'rule' in *Ridgeway*, and its subsequent modification in Uniform Evidence Law, does not require *automatic* exclusion of unlawful or improperly obtained evidence. It requires an *evaluation* of that evidence, based on the balancing of competing interests. As observed in the last chapter, studies on the exclusion of evidence by Presser (2001),

[1] South Australia, *Parliamentary Debates*, Legislative Council, 6 June 1995, 2066–2067

[2] *Ridgeway v The Queen* (1995) 184 CLR 19 at 43–44 (Mason CJ, Deane, Dawson JJ) and 53–54 (Brennan J)

Bronitt and Roche (2000), found that the exclusion of evidence was very rare in serious cases. Indeed, it is a well-established common law rule that in serious cases the public interest is "best served" by the reception of relevant, probative evidence, even when it has been obtained unlawfully. Basically, the more serious the offence, the greater the public interest.[3] The appearance of unlawfully obtained evidence is better understood as *a trigger* for judicial scrutiny of admissibility, rather than automatic rejection. Nevertheless, controlled operations law has been careful not to intrude on the judicial discretion over evidence, but qualified that discretion by the Parliamentary declaration that evidence is *not* to be considered as unlawfully obtained simply because it was obtained in the course of an authorised controlled operation.

Harmonisation of Law

Related to *Ridgeway* and its consequences as a driver of change is an associated legal cause, based on *law* being a source of *frustration* to law enforcement. The initial source of frustration was tied to the problems of interstate and international law enforcement and problems of legal and administrative jurisdiction. The rise of controlled operations regulation and international interdiction created a high degree of legal pluralism in the opening years of controlled operations law. The legal landscape was changing rapidly. The initial phase was largely jurisdictionally specific, creating a new problem for police: that of interstate and cross-border investigation. The law was not only problematic procedurally; it also became a source of frustration organisationally. Different laws and regulatory practices made co-operation difficult. This situation was clearly problematic for legislators, and one of the driving forces for law reform. Parliamentarians recognised that the existence of a patchwork legal framework was an impediment to successful and efficient law enforcement in complex investigations involving police in different jurisdictions. Part of controlled operations discourse involved a search for consensus on suitable models of law; ideally, a system of law without borders. Consequently, the drive for reciprocal recognition, and a streamlining of process, have been major causal drivers in controlled operations law and policy.

Crime and Corruption

Closely connected with the *legal causes* of controlled operations law was the apparent *social cause*: drug trafficking, crime and corruption. Although well recognised as driving forces in social policy and law, the controlled operations context shapes

[3] *R v Dalley* (2002) 132 A Crim R 169; *R v McNeill* (2007) 209 FLR 124; *R v Mokbel* (2012) 35 VR 156; Cf: Ashworth (1998)

this discourse in a particular way. Here there are two intersecting concerns. First, is the mere existence of crime and corruption – a discourse that has long been recognised. What is different in this context is *the nature* of crime and corruption, and *the way in which it is to be addressed*. The fundamental belief evident in the transcripts is that there are certain forms of crime and corruption (such as drug trafficking) largely *impervious*, if not immune, to ordinary forms of police investigation. Then Minister for Police, Duncan Kerr, provides an example:

> *Drug crime is peculiarly difficult to combat. Rarely are there complainants about this conduct. The importation of large quantities of drugs is a clandestine criminal activity involving complicity, or participants who will remain silent for fear of retribution. Organised crime does not tolerate complaint.*[4]

These concerns are based on experience. Criminal activity takes place in a number of forums, but is most insidious when it is invisible. Drug crime, in particular, involves participants well aware of the unlawful character of their actions, and who rarely trust one another. The greatest risk to drug offenders is not detection by police, but detection by other criminals. Secrecy is an ordinary part of drug trafficking. Indeed, the ecology of drug society was described by Shadbolt DCJ as a "hermetically sealed culture".[5] Drug crime is not, however, the only crime difficult to police – it extends to any sphere of activity involving willing participants, an absence of direct victims, limited physical evidence, and closed-group networks. The latter is especially hard to investigate where the participants can mobilise effective methods of destroying, controlling and manipulating evidence and veils of secrecy. The "impervious" nature of some types of crime promotes an imperative logic, justifying the need for extraordinary forms of police powers.

Organised Crime

Over the last decade, controlled operations discourse appears to have expanded from drug crime to organised crime as it main target. These themes overlap. Organised crime is presented as an insidious enemy, justifying the expansion of powers and the demands for harmonisation of law. That theme intersects with equally powerful rhetoric concerning national security and terrorism. Terrorist networks, paedophile rings and motorcycle gangs, in particular, are routinely identified as subjects of interest. "Organised crime" is an object of fear and insecurity – a threat to the social order. It is a theme that transcends the ordinary conception of "crime", and transforms it into something far more serious. Organised crime

---

[4] Commonwealth, *Parliamentary Debates*, House of Representatives, 22 August 1995, 4

[5] *R v Salem* (1997) 96 A Crim R 421, 431

confronts liberal rationality not only with a "criminal other"; organised crime presents itself as a behavioural system that organises itself for the purpose of crime, and with the intention of committing crime; an inversion of the liberal citizen, organised for purposes contrary to and outside of the social order. Organised crime comes to represent a major cause and justification for invasive techniques. The discursive construct in Hansard is complex and dense. For example:

> *It is regrettable that in this day and age a lot of criminal activity is highly organised. To combat that organised activity the Police Service and other police agencies have to become equally organised. The legislation will ensure a capacity to infiltrate and a capacity to organise for the right result, thus ensuring that the fight is taken to people on the other side of the fence, that is, these very sophisticated and organised criminals. It is important for the Minister to emphasise that this legislation is directed at serious matters, such as drug trafficking, money laundering, child pornography, organised crime and corruption. Such serious matters warrant this type of legislation. These crimes are so serious to the community at large and often so well organised that police officers have to infiltrate a group in order to make an arrest, break up the activity and bring to justice those involved....*[6]

The intensity of language and rhetoric mobilised in this context is particularly strong. Organised crime is a disease and a threat to the social order, justifying invasive law and practices. An instructive example appeared in the Commonwealth Parliament in 2009:

> *The problem is that organised crime still exists on a grand scale within Australia. It takes the form of drugs, prostitution, standover work and illicit and illegal gambling. It is, in short, a blight and a cancer – an illness – upon our society. As a parliament which by world standards has had a remarkably unblemished record of corruption and engagement with criminal activity, we have a duty to ensure that the standards we set will help protect and preserve community life, economic life and public safety and order over the coming decade and generation.*[7]

---

[6] New South Wales, *Parliamentary Debates*, Legislative Assembly, 26 November 1997, 2644 (Andrew Tink)

[7] Commonwealth, *Parliamentary Debates*, House of Representatives, 24 June 2009, 11,143 (Greg Hunt)

The discursive picture that emerges in Parliament of organised crime may be summarised as:

1. *Well Resourced* – Organised crime is routinely presented as lucrative and able to mobilise a large number of personnel, including lawyers, to preserve and expand the organisation.
2. *Adaptable* – Organised crime adapts and evolves to changing domestic and international developments. This capacity means that crime syndicates are difficult to detect, able to react when detected, and constantly able to exploit legal loopholes. Indeed, law enforcement is commonly presented as being somehow *less* sophisticated, *disempowered*, and constantly "playing catch-up" with a rapidly evolving target.
3. *Invisible* – A defining characteristic of the activities of organised crime in this context is its apparent invisibility. Organised crime is everywhere and nowhere. It possesses the contradictory features of a secretive yet public profile.
4. *Systemic Wariness* – Members of organised crime syndicates are living in a state of constant suspicion. They are presented as ordinarily highly suspicious of their habitat, living in a constant state of vigilance. This dynamic makes routine investigations exceedingly difficult, especially when the suspect is taking great care to ensure their guilt remains undetected.
5. *The Infiltration Imperative* – Because organised crime operates on the basis of closed-system networks, an associated set of investigative practices emerge designed to penetrate and infiltrate those networks through clandestine means. This method is conditioned by the private nature of organised crime and the systemic suspicion involved. The unique character of the environment in which the investigation takes place demands a method based upon infiltration, rather than open collection.
6. *Ruthless* – Organised crime is presented as both dangerous and merciless. It presents a manifest risk to investigators and to society. The criminal is presented as a figure unconcerned with and largely unrestrained by law, their actions routinely violent and at times unpredictable.
7. *Social Risk* – Organised crime is distinguished from other kinds of crime by its association with the more serious forms of crime across society. Not only is organised crime presented as a source of individual harm to victims; organised crime is identified as the source of threat to society. The threat presented by organised crime is strongly tied to demands for security, safety, and intervention, particularly of public safety and the integrity of the economy.
8. *Crime without Borders* – The final major theme concerns the fact that organised crime does not observe or respect borders. In this context "border" refers not only to a geographic border, it also refers to the borders between the private and the public, and the boundaries between lawful and unlawful. This is linked to the expansion of law that facilitates cross-border investigations and police cooperation, and to the architectures that facilitate the infiltration power of investigation. Crimes without borders require a highly dextrous legal and investigative response, a dynamic that can be frustrated within a Federal system of law.

The discourse of organised crime is a complex one but appears to be largely rhetorical and concerned with the presentation of a dangerous, internal enemy. That danger is manifested in a criminal "other"; a subject in need of governance, control and eradication. The ingenuity and relative invisibility of this enemy mobilises law and executive power as a concurrent social force, enlivened within policy debates. Organised crime is a particular kind of enemy; something more than simple deviance. It is the presence of an organised force – a non-state actor operating within for the sole purpose of crime. Organised crime is a manifest threat, which behaves, ironically, in a symbiotic way with the powers of State law enforcement. Law is here mobilised as the force that legalises and legitimates the conduct and behaviour of its target.

Language and Rhetoric

Hansard also demonstrates a remarkable use of language. Undoubtedly much of this language is political hyperbole but is routinely mobilised as a rhetorical device. The purpose of this rhetoric is arguably to manifest a discursive signifier that functions to give emphasis and an emotional character that assists in the moral justification of a proposition. The language used in Parliamentary controlled operations debates involves numerous signifiers. Like the organised crime discourses, rhetorical signifiers are embedded in complex ways throughout Hansard, exemplified in Commonwealth Hansard in 2009:

> *I know this will intrude on various perceived liberties of individuals – there is no question about that – therefore various safeguards have been built in to ensure that, where appropriate, those liberties are suitably protected. If people think that just because we are in the twenty-first century we are winning the fight against crime, it is time to think again. We need to have the tools necessary to compete with and break serious and organised crime enterprises. That is what this legislation will do. It is designed, unashamedly, to be tough – but only to protect our community.*[8]

> *We will ensure that the sort of thing which hurts mums and dads, shopkeepers, people who seek to live a peaceful life in good order is dealt with and that these organised crime syndicates are ultimately crushed.*[9]

[8] Commonwealth, *Parliamentary Debates*, House of Representatives, 27 October 2009, 11,132 (Chris Hayes)

[9] Commonwealth, *Parliamentary Debates*, House of Representatives, 27 October 2009, 11,144 (Greg Hunt)

> *Unless this is an effective law, we will continue to see organised crime syndicates. The outlaw motorcycle gangs will continue to prosper and continue to have their corrosive and destructive influence on society.*[10]

The rhetorical devices in Hansard present their own themes:

1. *War, Security and Safety* – Controlled operations law is routinely presented in the context of a war and state of threat. The social compact, represented in the democratic Parliament and institutions of the State, is in a state of siege from an enemy within. Law enforcement is a struggle, a fight against crime. Crime is a "scourge" that demands control and eradication. Security and safety are mobilised as justifications for legal and policing interventions. This rhetoric is significant, because it invokes notion of a state of emergency, triggering a logic concerned with creating exceptions to the ordinary rule of law. This dynamic is of critical importance and will be examined further in Chap. 11 in the context of derogation and the state of exception.
2. *Disease* – Society, it seems, is poisoned by crime and corruption. Organised crime is a cancerous blight, corrupting the institutions of civilisation. The image of disease and viral infection intersects with ideas of threat, adaptation, and precision excision and intervention involved in law enforcement. The rhetoric of disease enlivens a medical discourse of disease, incision, prevention and cure.
3. *Death* – The rhetoric around crime and corruption invokes images of death, from the violence endemic in crimes, through to the consequence of narcotics abuse and addiction, to the death of legitimate economy. Death operates in the background of discussions concerning not only the individual, but also civil society. Images of this kind suggest a dynamic in which the threat of death and decay is politicised for the purpose of policy justification, and the exercise of power.
4. *Tools and Weapons* – Lawmakers often refer to investigative practices, and the law that surrounds it, as *tools* or *weapons* in a *struggle* or *war* against a dangerous enemy. In this environment "tools" and "weapons" are presented as technological powers, an equalising, if not superior, force to be used in combat in a war against crime, terrorism and corruption. This primitive imagery is undeniably masculine. However, the rhetoric of tools and weaponry is rarely reflected as a simple, Neanderthal technology. The tools and weaponry involved are routinely presented as new, cutting edge, and something superior – an intelligent innovation. Law is presented as a decisive and exclusive weapon – a device that is a symbol, if not power, deployed against the enemies of the people.
5. *Mr Big, Danger, and the Criminal Other* – As discussed previously, the "criminal other" is invariably presented as an intelligent, mysterious, and elusive figure – a danger and threat to the existing order. The criminal other retains the atavistic

[10] Commonwealth, *Parliamentary Debates*, Senate, 27 October 2009, 454 (Nick Xenophon)

qualities of classic nineteenth century criminology, but at the same time is ever present and highly adaptable, and altogether contemporary in thought and action. We are here presented with something more the "organised crime". The criminal other has many manifestations, ranging from outlaw motorcycle gangs, notorious individuals, and the enigmatic "Mr. Big". This character is always presented as a highly intelligent, well-resourced and slippery, something to be feared and the legitimate target of all the resources of the state. This image is, in fact, far more powerful than the reality of the vast majority of those who are serving time in prison. The image of the criminal other is far more sophisticated than the typical offender.

6. *Victims and the Innocent* – The opposite of the "criminal other" is the virtuous public in need of protection and reassurance. Risk and security are strong features of this model. "Young people" and women are often identified as vulnerable and needing the protection of the State. The harm suffered by the innocent, and the ongoing threat of the criminal other, intersect as major justifications for controlled operations. The public is consistently reassured that as they are innocent, they have nothing to fear by the expansion of controlled operations powers. Indeed, the virtuous public and the innocent are specifically identified as subjects whose rights and liberties are to be protected, and ensured, by the law. Only the criminal other's rights and liberties are subject to impeachment.
7. *Evil* – A striking aspect of some of the rhetoric used in these debates is the notion of "evil". In the twenty-first century this seems a strange expression, but it is commonly invoked in Parliamentary rhetoric to intensify the characteristics of the object of discussion and its associated intervention. The identification of a subject as "evil" identifies that subject as requiring a particular socio-legal response. The language of evil is associated with the language of the imperative.
8. *Civil Society* – Aligned with threat and security discourses are the images of a society worth preserving, civil society. Civil society is a fundamental "good" that is the ultimate end; a utopian vision that *must* be protected.

The language used here appears to be symbolic, and indicative of a chain of reasoning. These images are value-laden terms that represent concepts ultimately tied to a logic based on the intersections of *risk*, *security* and *intervention*. The language functions to intensify the debate and compel action. The dynamic evident here is not unlike the dynamics identified by sociologists and anthropologists such as Cohen (2002), Douglas and Wildavksy (Douglas and Wildavsky 1982; Douglas 2002) as "moral panics" and the predictable response to threat.

The Language of Imperative

The language used in Hansard is not only symbolic; it also reflects an imperative logic. This is a form of reasoning where the speaker is normally convinced of a correct course of action. This sense of "right" is expressed as an invitation or demand for consensus, a script of conviction and persuasion that courts alliances and compels agreement, but also generates points of conflict. Imperative rhetoric manifests itself in words indicating that the speaker is compelled and justified in a course of action, and in so doing is compelling others to follow suit. Imperative language is deployed in at least three directions. First, the language is used in *support* of controlled operations legislation, sometimes manifesting as an attempt to trump the "tough" responses of earlier speeches – often in the case of Parliamentarians who not only support the law presented, but also advocate going further than originally conceived. Second, the language may be used as utilitarian method of resolving moral dilemmas, as in the case of Parliamentarians who are reluctant to act but find – on balance – that the response is justified in the circumstances, notwithstanding their concerns. Third is the language of opposition. Opposition tends to flow in two directions – one in total opposition *in principle* to the whole idea of the legal intervention proposed, and the other that is critical but *reformist*, advocating *necessary changes*. In all cases an imperative logic is identifiable by the presence of emphatic verbs or adjectives, notably "must", "necessity", "must not", "ensure", "should", "has to", "requirement" or "obligation". *This is a language of necessity.* This language extends itself into the actual doctrinal fabric of controlled operations law, for the imperative relates not only to the policy behind the law – it also relates to the statutory requirements within it. These concepts can be seen in the following examples:

> *...**we must protect** the persons who are undercover agents in these operations and **must not** jeopardise them.*[11]

> *...chief executive officers **must satisfy themselves** about certain matters before granting a controlled authority.*[12]

> *Application by phone is a significant step. In **extreme** circumstances, judges can accept applications over the phone for an urgent injunction. That provision grants significant power to police to make an application by phone. **We must be extremely vigilant** and **ensure** that proper records are kept. If at any time the rules are not followed, **the most severe and comprehensive punishment should be** imposed.*[13]

[11] Commonwealth, *Parliamentary Debates*, Senate, 27 May 1996, 1150, (Sid Spindler)

[12] New South Wales, *Parliamentary Debates*, Legislative Assembly, 11 November 1999, 2781 (Bryce Gaudry)

[13] New South Wales, *Parliamentary Debates*, Legislative Assembly, 17 November 1999, 3132 (Andrew Tink)

Naturally, the extension of the authority from one officer to some hundreds of officers will ***require careful monitoring and ongoing vigilance****. The* ***danger*** *is that if a controlled operation is compromised in any way, serious criminal cases may be jeopardised.*[14]

*I believe the Senate committee maturely considered all the issues extensively and canvassed the competing principles which I have already mentioned. Those of us on the committee who have a legal background...as defence counsel would not necessarily like this sort of legislation. But when you see the sort of havoc that can be caused within the community by these merchants of death, these peddlers of narcotics, you have to ask, '****What is the worst evil?****' Unfortunately, that is the basis on which I came down on the side of supporting the* ***necessity of this legislation****. It gave me no joy, and I am sure none of the other committee members, to have to do that, but it is a difficult area. When you talk to parents and families that have lost loved ones because of the black market narcotics industry,* ***you have to agree*** *that there should be a balance.*[15]

The Risk Imperative

The language of imperative is intimately connected to a vocabulary of threat and uncertainty. Once the analysis of Hansard is focused on the question of risk, it becomes clear that *risk is one of the major dynamics* circulating in the legislature, driving both policy and the substance of controlled operations law. Risk operates at multiple sites within this discourse, which intensifies the imperative rationality behind the policy.

In this environment, risk manifests in numerous ways. Risk may be explicit or implied and can be attached to a specific object or process, or both. Risk is both precise and fuzzy, and ranges from explicit and quantifiable content, through to vague notions of uncertainty. Risks may be broadly economic, social, political, legal, or hybrids. The risks identified in the course of this research include, but are not limited to, the following:

[14] New South Wales, *Parliamentary Debates*, Legislative Council, 25 November 1999, 3683 (Michael Gallacher)

[15] Commonwealth, *Parliamentary Debates*, Senate, 27 May 1996, 1159, (Eric Abetz)

1. *Operational Risk* is concerned with the inherent dynamics of an undercover investigation. Operational risks may arise through known or unknown factors at any stage of an operation: a suspect may become suspicious; the identity of an undercover operative may become known; the drugs which are the object of an investigation may be stolen by a rival criminal interest or a corrupt investigator; details of the operation may be revealed by a corrupt officer. Fundamentally, operational risks function to disrupt or cause the operation itself to fail. In this sense the execution of the investigation is itself an objective risk.
2. *Economic Risk* is a major consideration in controlled operations discourse. Economic factors can be abstract, such as references to "legitimate", local and national economy. Crime and corruption is often presented as the direct cause of lost revenue and productivity, or as an indirect cost through law enforcement and prosecution. In addition, organised crime presents an alternative "illegitimate" economy outside of the "legitimate" social order. But economic rhetoric also extends to the time consuming and expensive undercover operation. The "failure" of a prosecution is regarded as an unwelcome cost to public finance.
3. *Public Health* is not infrequently cited in controlled operations debates, particularly in relation to drug investigations. The law is sculptured in such a way as to require an assessment of any risks to public health, often associated with the risk of drugs being released into the public realm during an investigation. There have been examples of considerable amounts of narcotics being lost, or distributed, during an undercover investigation.[16]
4. *Public Safety* – Closely associated with public health is public safety. Consistent with the rhetorical imperative to protect the innocent, controlled operations discourses keep the question of the safety of ordinary members of the public firmly in mind. As one of the driving concerns of public policy of the liberal state is to defend the public and society as a whole, controlled operations are shaped by a desire to minimise the risk of death, loss of property, or serious injury.
5. *Occupational Health and Safety* is a major theme in controlled operations debates. These debates present a discourse that is, in many ways, entirely consistent with the investigations literature examined earlier. These risks are very serious, and a sobering reminder of the realities of police work. Not only are police personally at risk of death, sexual and physical assault, and intimidation in the ordinary course of their work, it is well recognised that undercover work carries with it a range of long-term occupational hazards. Undercover work is commonly associated with long-term psychological effects. Officers often find themselves in the contradictory position of having to behave as a criminal, while at the same time retaining a commitment to law enforcement. Undercover work is a high-risk environment. Officer are routinely under suspicion by those being investigated, many of whom regard violence as an ordinary part of life. In addition, undercover operatives, especially those involved in internal investigations,

[16] *Gedeon & Dowe v NSW Crime Commission* (2008) 236 CLR 120

are frequently ostracised and regarded as pariahs by their colleagues, being identified as basically untrustworthy. Not only that, undercover operatives, functioning essentially as domestic spies, are distrusted by the public they serve. In addition to the personal costs and risks involved in undercover work, it is also well recognised that the families and close associates of undercover operatives are themselves at risk of social and psychological harm, not to mention the obvious personal physical dangers that can arise if the identity of the officer and their families becomes known. These personal and psychological risks are augmented by the legal consequences of their work, which in the wake of *Ridgeway* involved the prospect of criminal and civil liability.

6. *Crime* – Crime and corruption are themselves identified as manifest socio-cultural risks. This is not unique to controlled operations, and indeed a preoccupation with the fear and anxiety of crime and corruption is common in criminal legal discourse. This is well recognised in sociological and criminological literature. As discussed above, what makes controlled operations discourse unique is that it is a specific kind of crime, and a specific kind of corruption, that is invoked. This kind of crime is perceived to be impervious and undetectable to ordinary forms of investigation and surveillance, either because of the nature of the crime, or because of the secretive and dextrous character of some suspects. Crime and corruption, undetectable and generally impervious to ordinary investigation is a key driver of controlled operations law and policy.
7. *Political Legitimacy* is a consistent theme in Parliamentary discourse. Hansard frequently manifests references to the consequences for democracy, and the governing party at the time, for the failure to properly address organised crime. Loss of public confidence is a major concern in Parliamentary discourse. The rationality involves a chain of reasoning that involves some kind of crisis of state that the public looks to government to resolve. After *Ridgeway*, with its consequential impact on the prosecution of serious drug crime, politicians were very concerned about the apparent failure of government to deliver security through suppression of drug trafficking and successful prosecution. The failure of government to react to crises of itself constitutes a class of risk is a particular concern to elected officials in a democratic system, a dynamic entirely consistent with Habermas's theory of democratic legitimation (Habermas 1979). Coupled with the failure to respond and react to crime and violence, there is an associated anxiety concerned that the failure to keep up with the evolving nature of crime and corruption. The failure to empower police, and the failure to provide laws that facilitate that empowerment, is of equal concern. Parliament, when presented with a threat or source of uncertainty, is expected to respond by providing security and certainty (Haines 2011). Controlled operations are presented as both a reactive and proactive measure to control, eliminate, and reduce crime and corruption. It provides both certainty and security, and in so doing has the effect of bolstering perceived political legitimacy.

8. *Abuse of Power* is one of the more complicated risk categories evident in Hansard. In this context abuse of power normally relates to the idea of police agents behaving unlawfully or exceeding their mandate. Yet abuse of power is a surprisingly complex concept. The complexity arises out of the motivation underlying the activity. Abuse of power can simply be the use of a lawful power for a criminal purpose. In that case the motivation is often simply greed or self-interest, a classic abuse of power. Alternatively, abuse of power can also arise where police behave in a technically unlawful way, but for the purpose of securing a conviction by behaving in a way regarded by those officers as the "greater good". The Royal Commission into Police Corruption documented many forms of corrupt activity motivated out of a perceived failure on the part of the justice system to properly deal with criminality, so-called "noble cause corruption" (Wood 1997). In this context, investigators resorted to various methods to incriminate the suspect for the purpose of securing conviction. These activities are identified in Hansard are being manifest risks to the legitimacy and stability of the State, which mobilises emphatic demands for accountability and scrutiny of conduct as the solution to the risk.

   This discourse is not just concerned with the activities of individual officers; it concerns the very question of the authorisation of crimes. At every stage of controlled operations debate Parliament was concerned about providing a licence to commit a crime. Abuse of power was seen not only as having implications for individual investigations but having serious and wider implications for the stability of democracy itself. It is undoubtedly the case, and well recognised in the Hansard, that the failure of government to demand and exercise limits and controls on the behaviour of police is a major source of potential social and political instability. The police are, after all, an armed force with considerable resources at their disposal. Social systems can easily break down when the police cease behaving lawfully in the interests and service of the public.
9. *Rights Infringement and Entrapment* are themes closely connected with the abuse of power discourse. The "abuse of power" is not just expressed at the political level; it relates to the abuse of citizens and the legalities that function to protect them. Chief among these is the claim to privacy. Here privacy is conceptualised as the ability, or demand, to live one's life in quiet anonymity, without the arbitrary interference of the State. Hansard recognises that controlled operations and their associated surveillance powers provide an invasive power that most people, at the very least, find uneasy, if not outright reprehensible. In an apparent contradiction, the same discourse also recognises privacy is conditional. In Hansard, the criminal, and the corrupt, lose any entitlement to live privately and anonymously. They are in breach of the social contract, and accordingly subject to a *different* set of legalities. Being able to live privately and anonymously means that a person can behave undetected – a source of frustration to law enforcement. In this place we find the discourse of rights occupies a contradictory space. On the one hand rights of privacy and liberty are celebrated, while on the other we find that the same discourse conditions and erodes those same rights.

Associated with privacy is anxiety about the wrong person being investigated. Again, a contradictory space appears where anxiety is manifested about identifying and targeting the wrong individual, particularly where that targeting results in an investigation, criminal charge, and subsequently a criminal trial, while also recognising that a person may be protected from prosecution by hiding under the rights that protect them. But even here proactive techniques are recognised as problematic, since even an innocent person could be tempted into committing a crime when presented with the opportunity, or the weak-willed may succumb to temptation when presented with the right circumstances. Here the rights infringement discourse overlaps with anxiety about random virtue testing and entrapment.

Conclusion

We find, therefore, a complex of intersecting discourses with strong associations with risk, which I contend are part of the coding of controlled operations law and policy. The identification by the lawmaker of risk amenable to control becomes reified in policy and law. This process is not simply about identification. Rather, law is mobilised as a way of controlling or responding to risk. Law becomes one way in which behaviours are shaped in response to, and in anticipation of, risk. In this way law becomes the instrument by which human behaviours are shaped by risk. One of the extraordinary aspects of this is the conviction in which law is seen as a method of *controlling risk*. It is an entrenched part of the rationality of lawmakers that risk can be contained and controlled. While it is true that risks may be minimised through identification and contingency plans, many of the risks that materialise in the course of undercover investigations are indigenous to the undertaking and outside of the purview of law. Law is simply the text-based instrument that directs and shapes behaviour but text, of itself, cannot eliminate the types of risks present in Hansard. Risk is an operational and critical logic in controlled operations law and policy, an imperative logic that links this species of law with risk as a social and intellectual phenomenon – a topic to which we will return in later chapters.

Yet, underneath the great ensemble of risk discourses is the shadow of death. The fear associated with the death of society through crime, drugs and economic collapse through the proliferation and extension of unauthorised forms of wealth creation, and the corrupting effects on public institutions and family life, suggests that risk is connected to a hidden set of discourses where death is politicised, a phenomenon entirely consistent with Foucault's biopolitics, described by Agamben as *thanatopolitics* (Agamben 1998), and more recently by Mbembe as *necropolitics* (Mbembe 2003). Both conceptions are linked to the power of the sovereign to extinguish life; but in this case the power of sovereignty to extinguish life is inverted – sovereign power is here not concerned with causing the deaths of its subjects, rather sovereign power is used in order to protect its subjects. The relationship between sovereignty and the politics of death is a major line of enquiry in its own right and cannot be undertaken here. It is appropriately reserved for a later time. However, the underlying necropolitics may well explain why risk emerges as such and powerful discourse, for what is ultimately at stake, at least at the rhetorical level, is a social death that civil society must act to avoid. In this context the full apparatus of sovereign, executive and legal power is deployed.

References

Agamben, G. (1998). *Homo Sacer: Sovereign power and bare life* (D. Heller-Roazen, Trans.). Stanford: Stanford University Press.

Ashworth, A. (1998). Should the police be allowed to use deceptive practices? *Law Quarterly Review, 114*(Jan), 108–140.

Ashworth, A. (2006). Four threats to the presumption of innocence. *South African Law Journal, 123*(1), 63–97.

Bronitt, S., & Roche, D. (2000). Between rhetoric and reality: Sociolegal and republican perspectives on entrapment. *International Journal of Evidence and Proof, 4*(2), 77.

Cohen, S. (2002). *Folk devils and moral panics* (3rd ed.). London: Routledge.

Douglas, M. (2002). *Purity and danger: An analysis of the concept of pollution and taboo*. London: Routledge.

Douglas, M., & Wildavsky, A. (1982). *Risk and culture*. Berkeley: University of California Press.

Habermas, J. (1979). *Legitimation crisis*. London: Heinemann.

Haines, F. (2011). *The paradox of regulation: What regulation can achieve and what it cannot*. Cheltenham: Edward Elgar Publishing.

Mbembe, A. (2003). Necropolitics. *Public Culture, 15*(1), 11–40.

Presser, B. (2001). Public policy, police and interest: A re-evaluation of the judicial discretion to exclude improperly or illegally obtained evidence. *Melbourne University Law Review, 25*(3), 757–785.

Wood, J. J. (1997). *Report of the royal commission into the NSW police service*. Sydney: New South Wales Government.

Chapter 7
The Rise of Risk in Australian Federal Legislation

> *We quickly grow used to the way things are. Today more than ever, it is easy to live in the immediacy of the present and to lose all sense of the historical processes out of which our current arrangements emerged.*
>
> (Garland 2001, p. 1)

The policy and practice discourses around controlled operations are saturated with themes concerned with risk. This begs a further question: has risk colonised law more generally? This is a complex question because, to a large extent, law has always been linked to the containment and control of risk. We are so used to risk being a feature of the fabric of law that, as Garland observed, it is easy to lose track of the gravity and impact that risk has had on the architecture of law. The prevalence of risk discourse in the debates around intrusive methods of investigation appear to be part of a larger shift in risk as a feature of regulation and public policy more generally. This change has been gradual, but inexorable. Risk has now assumed a major role in law, public policy, and social consciousness. Despite that development, there have been no large-scale studies of the phenomenon of risk in Australian law as an epistemic thread. Indeed, it is something that is apparently not considered by legal scholarship generally. In the only study of the effect on risk on legislative activity, Sjöberg et al. (1998) found that bills submitted to the Swedish parliament in 1965 and 1995 demonstrated a significant increase in legislation concerned with risk within that period. On the assumption that a similar dynamic is likely in Australia, this chapter explores the extent to which risk has impacted on Australian legislation over an extended period.

To examine this assumption, this research narrowed the parameters by confining the study to the legislation of the Commonwealth but extended the field of enquiry to all Commonwealth legislation between 1901 and 2014. Broadly, this study found that risk has become a significant feature in Commonwealth legislative activity since 1975. It is argued that Commonwealth law is evolving in a manner consistent with the "risk society" thesis proposed by social scientists. The timing of the

B. Murphy, *Regulating Undercover Law Enforcement: The Australian Experience*, https://doi.org/10.1007/978-981-33-6381-6_7

development of risk markers in legislation is entirely consistent with the emergence of postmodernity.

To develop this argument, the chapter is divided into four parts. It is first necessary to locate the study within a general review of the conception of risk. Here we observe that law has, to some extent, always been concerned with the problem of risk and risk management. Concurrently, we observe that risk is a nebulous concept that tends to morph according to disciplinary perspective. Simply put, risk means different things depending on the purpose and disciplinary lens. Lawyers understand risk in ways that are both common to and different from other disciplines. We then turn to the outcome of the study. This study was an exploratory survey using Boolean search logic. The results were compiled, tabulated, and thematically analysed. Although the methodology was basic, this study concluded a significant change in the frequency and sophistication of the regulation of risk over the period studied. In conclusion, we discuss the rise of risk in Commonwealth legislation, finding that risk has assumed a significant role in Australian Federal legislation - but is by no means the dominant feature. Risk is but one of the many objects of regulation but has assumed a greater role in the architecture of Federal legislation. As an exploratory study, it is now open for a more rigorous quantitative study to prove or disprove the hypothesis.

Risk and the Problem of Definitions

When lawyers speak of risk, they are routinely referring to the chance of an undesired outcome. Lawyers tend to regard risk in terms of a negative conception of some harm, injury or danger. This conception is largely sourced from an internal and external aspect of legality: the internal sourced in the jurisprudence and logic of legal reasoning, and the external in the specific legislative architectures of Parliament. Accordingly, the legal understanding of "risk" is usually locked into a precautionary logic directed towards mitigation, compliance, or remediation. This logic is most clearly exemplified in the common law risk calculus set out by Mason J in *Wyong Shire Council v Shirt.*[1] Here, Mason J made explicit reference to an assessment of probabilities and the manifestation of dangers and consequence as central components in the determination of the breach of a duty of care. This kind of logic is typical of the risk "object" of the discipline of law observed by Althaus (2005). Althaus mapped the disciplinary contours of risk, arguing that law tends to conceptualise risk in terms of fault, conduct or loss, and practices a form of rationality largely characterised by the deployment of explicit rules and reasoning intended to prevent injury, loss or danger, remediation and risk shifting. This may be contrasted with other disciplines, such as economics or business, which focus on risk in terms of elements guiding decision-making concerned with wealth generation, opportunities, and loss avoidance. In this context risk is embraced as potential

[1](1980) 146 CLR 40, 47–48.

opportunity and a liberating decision-making matrix. In other words, law tends to look at prevention and consequence, whereas other disciples look at risk in term of future and present action. For the purposes of law, the conception of risk is necessarily narrow, but understanding the complexity of risk as a concept is important because it assists in understanding how non-lawyers think about risk, as well as shedding light on some of the difficulties that legislators have in designing legislation that purports to regulate risk.

Before going on it is important at the outset to indicate that the concept of risk is going to be considered in some detail in the next chapter, but it is important to set out some of the essential components to give context to the empirical work undertaken. There will be a degree of repetition, for which I beg the reader's indulgence.

In the social sciences, risk is well-established as a major school of thought. The pioneering work of Giddens (1990, 1999) and Beck (1992, 1996, 1999) was the genesis of a substantial amount of scholarship on the nature and contours of risk as a contemporary social phenomenon and intellectual force (Zinn 2008). Risk scholarship is not, of course, unique to the social sciences. Risk is a complex phenomenon that transcends traditional discipline boundaries. Risk is a transdisciplinary concept (Althaus 2005) firmly embedded in virtually all disciplinary fields, from pragmatic management, through to statistics, insurance, literature, theology, psychology and, of course, law. It would not be possible to discuss of the divisions and nuances of risk in a paper of this size. It is perhaps sufficient to say that risk theory consists of a loose confederacy of ideas that are united by the intersection of chance, uncertainty and danger. It is a persistent aspect of the human condition and has both positive and negative aspects. Fundamentally, risk concerns itself with uncertainty and attempts to both determine the chance of desired or undesried outcomes, and the costs and benefits of those outcomes. In this respect risk thinking normally has elements concerned with probability, uncertainty and futurity (Mythen 2004; Mythen and Walklate 2006). Beyond the question of chance and calculation, risk has a psychological dimension, affecting how we think about the world, and how we make decisions to behave in it. Risk has a social dimension, affecting how we collectively organise social life, allocate resources, and mobilise events. Risk has a hysterical aspect, feeding into moral panics and accelerating collective and personal mythologies. Risk has a governance dimension, being mobilised as a strategy of political and social control. In other words, risk is a remarkably diverse and complex knowledge system that traverses traditional discipline boundaries. Law is not immune (Zinn 2008).

The extent to which risk is new to law is open to debate. Law has always, to some extent, been concerned with risk. It appears likely that the law of insurance and contract has always been intimately concerned with the management and distribution of risk. More recent legal developments concerned with risk management ranges from the articulation of regulation through statutory instruments to judicial statements of formal tests used to demarcate the boundaries of acceptable and unacceptable risk, as in the laws of negligence. However, if the social scientists are correct that risk appears to be assuming a greater role in public life and consciousness, it is likely that risk is also shaping law more extensively than it has in the past, both as formal law and legal practice. Indeed, Susskind has argued that one of the most profound recent and future transformations of law and legal practice is the transition from litigation and conflict resolution, to compliance and risk management (Susskind 1998, 2008).

Although risk theory is a recent phenomenon, there is a substantial amount of literature that considers law and risk. This is not surprising, given the central role that risk plays in contract, insurance, occupational health and safety, and tort – particularly in negligence, where risk is critical to the assessment of the duty of care and associated breach. Risk is evident in all manner of legal writing, ranging from property, nuclear waste disposal, domestic violence, terrorism, financial regulation, climate change, to dangerous offenders. A macro literature review using the law citator *LawCite* identified 2589 published articles on law and risk, beginning in Australia as early as 1892 with William Harvey's examination of risk and insurance (W. Harvey 1892). Similar early beginnings are evident in the United States with William Douglas' 1929 paper on vicarious liability (Douglas 1929). Overall, the risk literature is primarily sourced in the United States, but there is an equally large of amount of material in the work of European and English scholars. In more recent years, an emergent field of scholarship has begun to specialise in the concept of *legal risk* and the impact that risk, generally, is having on legal systems at an epistemic level (Ashworth 2006; Baldwin 1997; De Giorgi 2009; Febbrajo 2009; Mahler 2007, 2010; McCormick 2010; Priest 1990; Steele 2004). What is noteworthy is that legal scholarship that has turned its attention to risk as a concept shaping law have done so in a manner that tracks with the rise of risk in the social sciences, with the overwhelming bulk of "law and risk" literature emerging after 1990.

Australian scholars have played an important part in the consideration of risk and its relationship with law. There are at least 378 articles published by Australian scholars that expressly consider various manifestations of law and risk. Like their American and English counterparts, publication on risk and law begins early. As mentioned, Harvey considered risk and insurance in 1892, followed by James Meillon's examination of contractual risk management of damage to goods in transit in 1906 (Meillon 1906). The bulk of Australian scholarship in this field is, however, a recent phenomenon, with most publications emerging after 1995.

There are two important observations about the way legal scholars approach the topic of risk. Firstly, almost all examinations of the law and risk tend to approach risk in one of three ways. First, as an object that is a *source or risk* (a risk "of" something "to" something). Second, as an *intellectual construct* that facilitates legal reasoning (often as a comparative standard to assess conduct, fault, and blameworthiness). Third, as a framework to regulate or eliminate risk. Here law is mobilised as a *controller of risk*. This is entirely consistent with Althaus' thesis that law conceptualises risk primarily through an orientation directed towards rules and rationality (Althaus 2005). This is to be contrasted with the ways in which other disciplines conceptualise risk. Sociological accounts of risk conceive risk as cultural and collective behaviours and consciousness. Edgework and business theorists celebrate risk as providing important forms of esteem and wealth creation; for without risk individuals would be less likely to acquire personal and social esteem, and capital would be less likely to grow and circulate. Economic approaches to risk conceive risk in terms of probability and calculations, which play important roles in guiding decision-making (Zinn 2008). In short, it is well recognised that the knowledge systems that constitute the various disciplines tend to conceptualise and model risk in consistent but largely independent ways, and Australian legal scholarship is no different. This is not to say that risk operates in "knowledge silos", but it does suggest that each author tends to operate within the boundaries and limits of a particular knowledge field, drawing on concepts or devices as and where necessary, but normally with a particular conception of risk. The consequence is that only a handful of Australian legal scholars approach risk from a broader perspective, recognising the link between "risk society" and law at what might be called the "socio-epistemic" level (Buth 2008; Cash 2009; Lee and Morgan 2001; Rochford 2007; Shearing and Johnston 2005; Berns et al. 2003–2004; Greig 1997). In this respect O'Malley, in particular, dominates the field (O'Malley 1991, 1992; O'Malley and Palmer 1996; O'Malley 1996, 1997, 1998a, b, c, 1999, 2000, 2001, 2004, 2005, 2008a, b, 2009a, b, 2010a, b, c, 2011).

The second observation is there does not appear to have been any study of the historical impact that risk, as a social and psychological phenomenon, has had on the architecture of Australian legislation. Given the long-standing relationship between risk and law, the absence of such a study is something of an anomaly. An essential element of risk scholarship is that risk assumes a key place in social consciousness as advanced capitalist economies evolve in various ways. This transformation necessarily has an impact on social and intellectual life, and as such has a transformative effect on public policy. Haines (2011), for example, has argued that democratic governments are particularly susceptible to the transformative effect on policy that risk has because of the political energy that certain kinds of risk generate in populations. As policy is directly linked with legal architectures generally, it stands to reason that legislation will necessarily follow the growth of risk in public consciousness, and in the character of mechanisms intended to formally regulate risk. Despite the apparent relationship, the extent to which risk and legislative instruments have been specifically examined remains surprisingly under-studied. To the author's knowledge there have been few international studies on the nexus between legislation and risk, and no specific Australian studies.

The exception to this is the 1998 study of Swedish legislation by Sjöberg et al. (1998), mentioned earlier. This study was a relatively simple comparison of bills presented to the Swedish parliament in 1964/5 and 1993/5, which found (inter alia) that there had been a quadruple increase in the number of bills concerned with risk in the thirty years between 1964 and 1994. The study concluded with an invitation for other scholars to undertake similar studies. In this chapter I present the findings of a similar examination of the prevalence of risk in Australian legislation. It needs to be said at the outset that this was very much an exploratory study, intended to open a space for a more detailed consideration on the topic in due course, and to open dialogue on the extent to which risk has shaped, and continues to shape, public policy through legislation.

A Survey of Risk in Australian Legislation

As an exploratory study, the methodology deployed was aimed at simplicity, designed to answer a simple question: to what extent has risk expanded in Australian legislation? Initially, it was intended to replicate, as far as possible, Sjöberg, Wåhlberg and Kvist's study. This proved to be impossible, as the original study was limited by a vaguely expressed methodology that focussed on bills presented to parliament in discrete periods of time. The decision was made to focus on passed acts, as opposed to bills. Recognising that law has always been interested in risk, the decision was made to extend the survey beyond two annual reviews of introduced bills separated by 30 years to include *all Acts* passed by the Australian parliament between 1901[2] and 2014. This provided a comprehensive sample.

The study of legislation presents its own methodological problems. Traditional legal research tends to adopt a "linear" approach, focused on specific provisions or enactments over time. Consequently, legal scholarship is highly suited to in-depth but precise "deep" analysis. This approach is quite different to what we might understand as a "lateral" analysis of concepts.[3] In this case I was interested in risk as a concept across legislation, rather than any one specific provision. Accordingly, this kind of study required some attention to an array of specific problems.

The first problem related to search markers. In this case the basic technique for identification of relevant law was a simple Boolean search of the well-known Australian legal database, Austlii.[4] A simple word search for "risk" was used in *Commonwealth Numbered Acts*, sorted according to year. The word "risk" was chosen as a marker that would serve as an indicator for multiple things. As the risk literature strongly indicates that "risk" has a variety of meanings, a single concept had the advantage of functioning to capture a variety of legislative purposes and concepts. This technique was intended to provide an opening for exploration of the concept, but also was limited by the fact that the absence of the word "risk" is not necessarily indicative of legislative design that actually has the function of risk management. The search marker would not capture legislative design expressed outside of the "language of risk". However, as this was always intended to be an exploratory study the flaw was not regarded as significant at this stage.

The initial search revealed 1138 instances of "risk" within the sample. Closer examination of each instance revealed the picture was more complex than it appeared. A number of Acts did not fall within the date sorting function because of variations in the name and numbering of the Act, which the required in examination of every instance to identify its correct name and year. This examination uncovered a further complexity, unique to working with statutes: the year in which an Act is

[2] 1901 was chosen because this was the year that the Australian federal government came into existence. This presents a comprehensive sample.

[3] The technique of distinguishing linear from lateral analysis is loosely based on Foucault's discourse analysis. See (Foucault 1972; Scheurich and McKenzie 2005; Threedy 2005).

[4] www.austlii.edu.au

passed by parliament is not necessarily the year in which it commences. The result was that each Act had to be examined and then categorised by its year of commencement rather than the year passed by parliament. This technique reduced the sample to 653 Acts containing at least one reference to "risk" between 1901 and 2014. The result was then tabulated (Fig. 7.1).

Of itself, these figures suggest a clear and emerging trend in legislation. Risk appears to be an increasing element within legislation, becoming more frequent since the early 1970s. This trend is not, however, one of exponential increase. Risk seems to assume different degrees of importance at different points, doubtless linked to the underlying policy objectives of legislation, and responses to situational factors. Legislation is not simply about risk management, and in most instances, there is no need to include risk management provisions. Risk emerges only at those sites within legislation where the attention of the legislature is directed to engaging risk management strategies. Nevertheless, the initial review suggests that risk is now assuming a dominant rationality within Australian legislative design.

The question then emerged as to how this trend could be understood within the broader context of all legislation passed within this period. In Australia there have been 12,206 Acts passed between 1901 and 2014. If the word "risk" is taken to be a marker of risk architectures within legislation, when the totality of legislation is considered risk is, in fact, relatively small, representing only 5.35% of the total sample (n = 12,206/653) (Figs. 7.2 and 7.3).

Like many jurisdictions in the common law tradition, Australian law follows the trend of legislation supplanting judicial decisions as the primary source of law. The Australian Parliament passed, for example, 17 Acts in 1901, and 135 in 2014. It is well recognised that legislation has become the primary source of public law for most common law countries over the last century. Consequently, some care must be

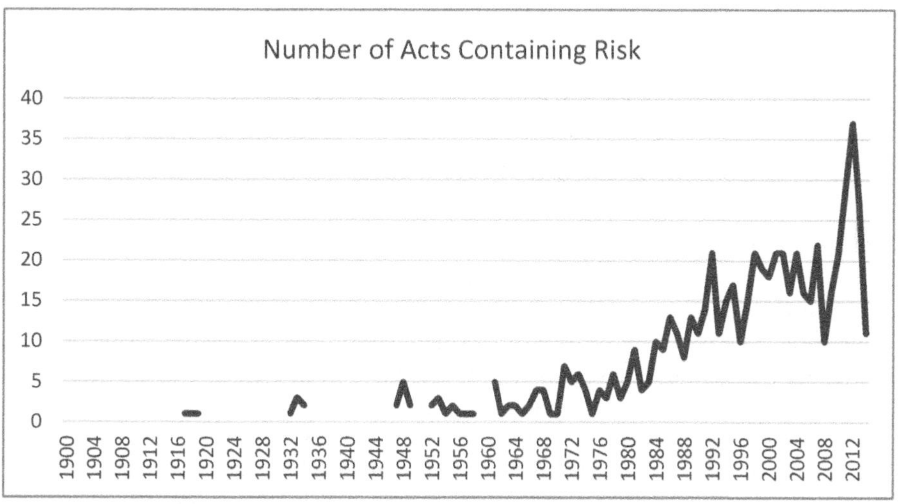

Fig. 7.1 Number of acts containing risk

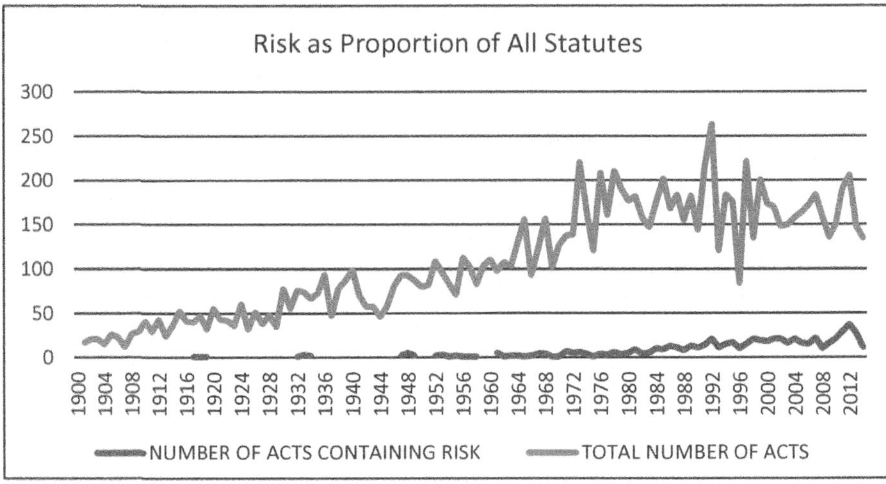

Fig. 7.2 Risk as proportion of all statutes

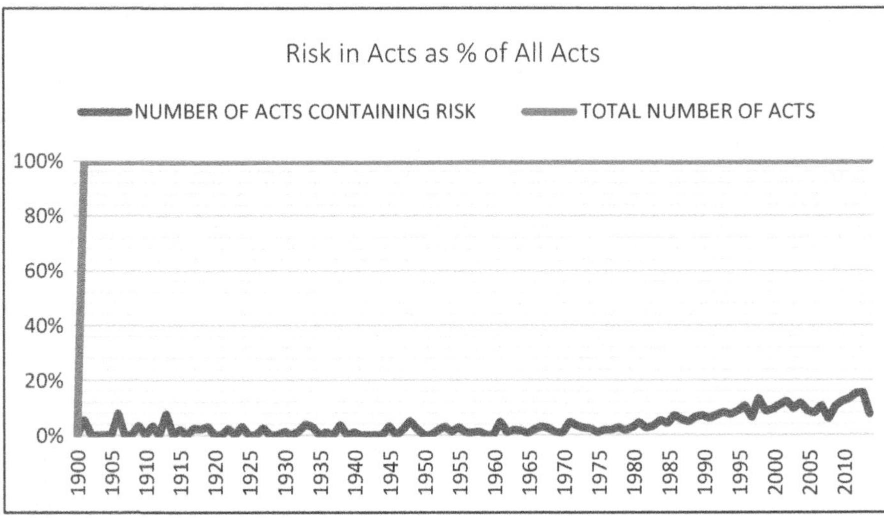

Fig. 7.3 Risk in acts as % of all acts

taken in assuming that risk is growing at some inexorable rate within Australian legislation. The apparent growth of risk may simply be a reflection of the general growth in legislation as a source of law. Has there been a change in the proportion of Acts concerned with risk in the totality of legislation? When the totality of Acts are considered with reference to the decades in which they are passed, it becomes clearer that risk has, in fact, assumed a greater importance in law in the last 40 years. While risk appears in only 5.35% of all statutes since 1901, it emerges in 6.87% (n = 604/8788) since 1960; 7.65% (n = 582/7606) since 1970; 9.15% (n = 542/5922)

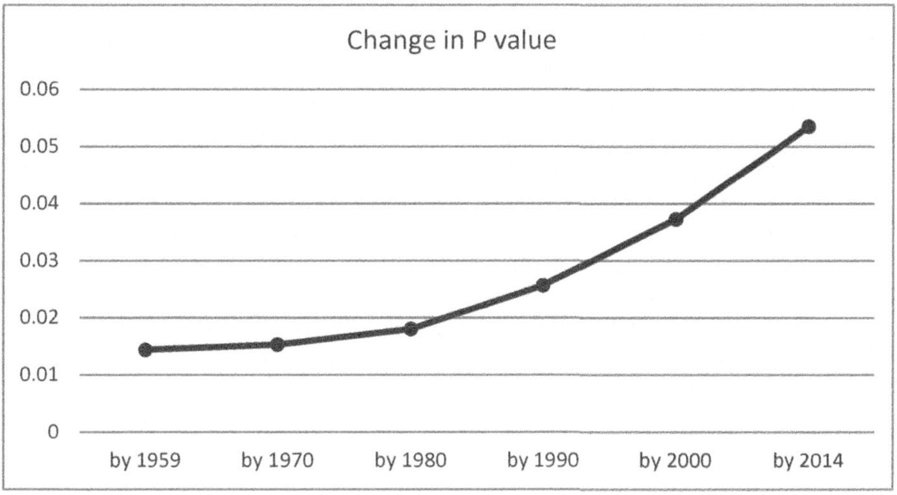

Fig. 7.4 Change in P value

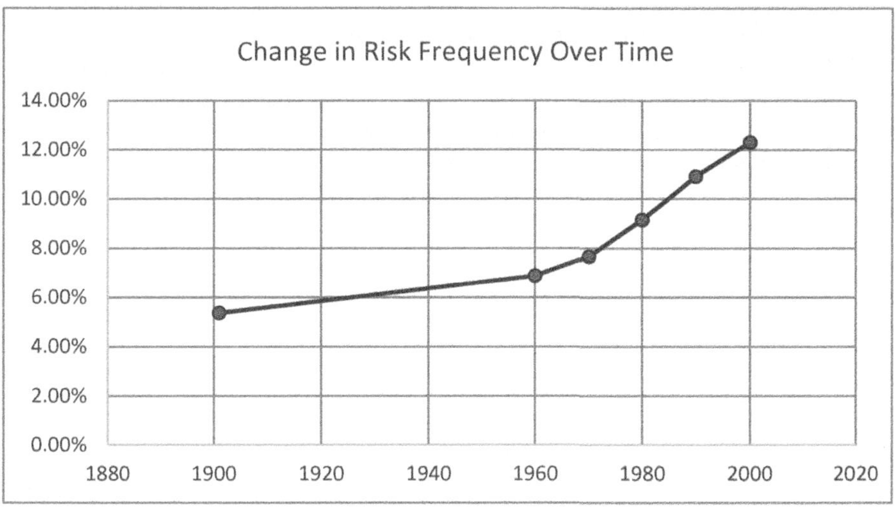

Fig. 7.5 Change in risk frequency over time

since 1980; 10.9% (n = 455/4191) since 1990; and 12.3% since 2000 (n = 301/2444). When considered in terms of probabilities of risk appearing in legislation, it does appear to be a statistically significant change. Between 1901 and 1959 risk appeared in 49 of 3418 statutes (p = 49/3418 (0.014)); by 1970 risk appeared in 72 of 4727 statutes (p = 72/4727 (0.015)); by 1980 risk appeared in 116 of 6461 statutes (p = 116/6461 (0.017)); by 1990 risk appeared in 209 of 8159 statutes (p = 209/8159 (0.025)); by 2000 risk appeared in 370 of 9936 statutes (p = 370/9936 (0.037); and by 2014 risk had appeared in 653 of 12,206 statutes (p = 653/12206 (0.053)). This rudimentary examination does suggest that risk has assumed a greater role in legislation since 1970, with particular growth since 1990. By 2014 risk had become statistically significant in Commonwealth legislation. (Fig. 7.4).

The change over time becomes more apparent when the shift from the baseline totality of 5.35% from 1901 is compared with the proportions by each decade from 1960. Broadly speaking, the frequency of risk as an object or technique of regulation has doubled since 1960 (Fig. 7.5).

It therefore appears that risk has not only expanded as a proportion of all legislation passed by the Australian parliament, but that growth is linked to a historical transition located after 1970. This growth in risk as a concept (or at least term) in law is consistent with Sjöberg, Wåhlberg and Kvist's study, as well as the growth in risk literature, globalisation, insurance and with the idea of shift towards what Beck described as "world risk society".[5]

The picture is, of course, more complex than it appears. Closer examination of the Acts yielded an additional problem: a single Act might contain a single or multiple instances of the word "risk". Accordingly, it became necessary to distinguish both the number of Acts in any given year concerned with risk, and the frequency of "risk" within each Act. Here the consideration related to the extent to which risk was present *within* each statute that contained the word "risk". This information was then tabulated from 1901 to 2014, set out below in Fig. 7.6.

What these figures suggest is that while the number of statutes that include "risk" has increased, the frequency of "risk" within those statutes has *also* increased. Indeed, this dimension is probably more important than the general increase in statutes that include risk as a concept. The broad implication is that risk has increased

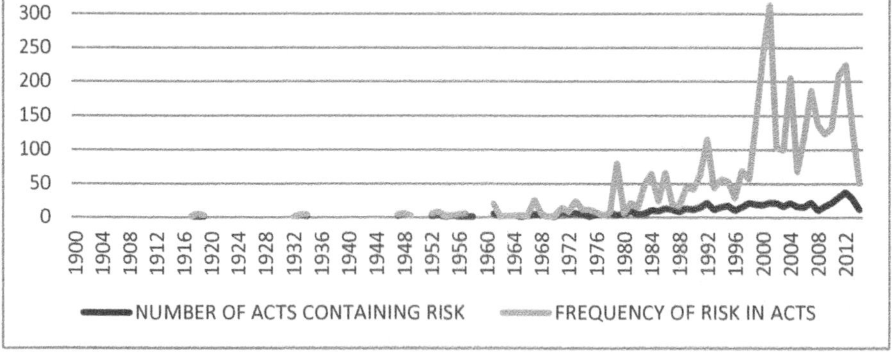

Fig. 7.6 Risk within Australian federal legislation

[5] Beck, above n 6; (Beck 2002).

not only as an element of legislation generally, but also as an element of legislation within itself – most notably since the late 1990s. This suggests that that the regulatory apparatus concerned with risk is becoming not only more frequent, but more sophisticated.

However, it should not be assumed that risk has somehow become *the* major theme of legislative activity. On the contrary, risk occupies specific sites within the broad architecture of legislation. In other words, risk is deployed for specific purposes in specific statutes, rather than being a dominant theme in the totality of legislation. Risk is but one element. What does appear to have happened is that as legislative activity has extended, so has the need to incorporate risk into those areas where risk has been identified as a material reality that requires regulation. The uneven distribution of risk within statutes invites closer examination of the risk objects that law purports to regulate or contain. There would undoubtedly be benefit in an exploration of the major themes of regulation within legislation, as well as a consideration of the obvious "spikes" in legislative activity concerned with risk. The clear spike in 2001/2002, for example, would likely be connected with the legislative responses relating to terrorism in the wake of the September 11 attack on the United States. However, this aspect of research is beyond the scope of the present inquiry.

The Proliferation of Risk?

Are we able to conclude that this shift in legislation is an indication of the proliferation of risk? Was Beck right that risk has expanded with the changes in later modernity? This survey demonstrates quite clearly that although risk has always been an element within the legislation of the Australian Commonwealth, there has been a demonstrable expansion in both the number of Acts that contain provisions concerned with risk, and the number of provisions within legislation concerned with risk. There is no doubt that risk has had a significant effect on the architecture of Australian Federal statutes, particularly since 1990. On that basis it does appear that one aspect of the changes observed by Beck (and others), is that risk has, indeed, expanded in legislative activity. This conclusion forms a hypothesis that is a worthy topic for a more empirically grounded study.

Some caution is necessary when making any conclusions about the presence of the concept of risk within legislation. The increase of risk within legislation could be part of a "linguistic turn" (Rorty 1967), in the sense that legislation is not necessarily reflecting a "riskier" world, but that the language used to regulate loss, attribute responsibility and establish minimum expected standards of conduct has consolidated. In other words, it is plausible that the increase in the word "risk" is a linguistic shift, rather than a change in the purposes of legislation. Similarly, the growth of risk may not be a reflection of social life and economic exchange becoming "riskier", but rather is a reflection of "legislative capture" of new areas that hitherto had been unregulated and left to private arrangements. For example, with the expansion of regulation into corporate activity and commercial dealings, much of the risk management previously embedded in private law – such as contract – is reflected in legislation in ways that had not previously been the case. It may be the case that the dynamic observed is the capture of risk out of the fragments of private law, consolidated into the legislative. The causes cannot be answered at this stage. But whatever they might be, there has been a significant change in the language and the intention of legislation to deal with the problem of risk.

Sjöberg, Wåhlberg and Kvist's study was not only concerned with the distribution of risk over time. It was also concerned with the relationship between economic and political conditions at the time the bills were introduced. The basic argument was that risk-based legislation was "party-neutral", with the exception of the Swedish Conservative Party, which did not demonstrate any particular interest in risk-based legislation. In their study, all parties (except the Conservatives) were associated with an increase in "risk bills", and a decrease in welfare and resource allocation bills in the same period. While recognising that risk may, in fact, occupy a greater consciousness in society as a whole, the authors suggested that the most likely answer as to why this change was evident was not that society was any more "risky" than it had been in the past, but that legislative risk control was cheaper to implement than other forms of policies, and attracted greater political capital than simply funding public interventions. In effect, the political capital lost out of the reduction of public funding and welfare was replaced by a net gain in legislative activity intended to contain and address public risk (Sjöberg and Ramsberg 1997; Sjöberg et al. 1998). In other words, risk management is more efficient and more economical for government to implement through legislative design and public policy mandate, than it is to fund programs intended to do the same.

In the context of the present study, the question of the relationship between Australian governments and risk legislation is not one that can be presently answered. An Act of parliament (unlike a bill) is, to some extent, a collective effort. As the sample chosen was the passed Act rather than a bill over a century, it was not possible in the present study to isolate the sponsoring member/party and the role that amendments played in the passage of legislation. It is worth observing that since 1960 Australian government has been shared primarily between two political parties: The Liberal/National coalition, and the Australian Labour Party. If Sjöberg, Wåhlberg and Kvist are correct, it is likely that risk legislation is not particularly associated with either the Liberal/National coalition, or the Australian Labour Party. It is more likely associated with the economic and political conditions of the time, and particularly the changing rationalities associated with neoliberal economic policies (D. Harvey 2005). If Beck is correct that a key aspect of risk society and reflexive modernization is a systemic interest in risk distribution and allocation, then one explanation is that legislation is the primary vehicle for public risk distribution. A more detailed study would be required to test these relationships. Given the logistics involved in identifying and mapping the legislative party relationship, it is beyond the scope of the present study. As outlined above, Haines (2011) has argued that the regulatory response is often triggered by political anxieties, particularly in the wake of disasters, public violence, and moral panics. It appears, therefore, that the relationship between legislation and risk is grounded in historical, intellectual and material conditions, as much as politics. We should not, however, discount those theorists who recognise the powerful role of epistemic and sociological forces at work in the proliferation and allocation of risk as an economic, political and psychological phenomenon. In that respect it is likely that risk presents a complex and nuanced segment of public consciousness that transcends any one theory. It is no surprise that law and risk have an equally complex relationship.

There are, of course, clear limitations in this survey. The use of "risk" in this case was operating at the level of simple word-search. That operationalization was on the assumption that the simple word "risk" functions as a marker for an array of risk-based conceptions. This approach tells us virtually nothing about what those conceptions are, or about the various ways that risk markers are characterised within the legislation examined. As a research strategy, it fails to capture legislation that has a risk management function, but does not actually use the language of risk, such as "danger", "threat" or "hazard". As Zinn (2008) and Althaus (2005) have observed, risk has a variety of meanings, and not all of them negative. Indeed, in the context of law, risk plays a significant role in the containment, management, and elimination of risks – and in this respect to expansion of risk in legislative design is not to be understood as a negative development. On the contrary, law plays a major part in positive and progressive containment of risk. Legislation need not even use the language of risk to be concerned with it. A deeper examination of risk would necessarily require a closer reading of the legislation, as well as a more nuanced analysis. What this limitation points out, however, is that while risk has clearly expanded in Australian statutes, the nature of that expansion remains to be explored. As Australia has a Federal structure, the extent to which this trend is reflected in State legislation is similarly open to future research.

It should not be concluded that the rise of risk in Australian Federal statutes operates evenly. This study indicates that legislative activity concerned with risk takes place in an ad-hoc manner. This pattern supports Haines' (2011) thesis that risk-based policy shifts tend to track with specific political anxieties and crises. It should not, however, be assumed that legislation is simply a reaction to crisis. Legislation may be in response to crisis; but legislation can also be the modern reformulation of an existing Act, a repeal, an amendment, a consolidation or purely symbolic. It may also be a regulatory architecture for new technologies. What is clear is that even when legislation is not being introduced in reaction to crisis, risk presents itself as an increasingly essential component in 'ordinary' legislative design. Risk management is a core component of Australian legal architecture and has become a routine component of the design and conceptualisation of public law.

In conclusion, we should not assume that legislation is just about risk. That is clearly not the case. The breadth and scope of law is vast and could not reasonably be argued that risk is now the dominant force in legal architectures. It does appear, though, that at the very least the language of risk, and the attempt by the legislature to manage and prevent risk, uncertainty, and danger, is certainly a stronger element, at least in Federal legislation. This exploration invites a window for further study into the intersections between law and risk, since it appears that risk is one of the tectonic plates on which the conceptual mass of law is located.

References

Althaus, C. E. (2005). A disciplinary perspective on the epistemological status of risk. *Risk Analysis, 25*(3), 567–588.

Ashworth, A. (2006). Four threats to the presumption of innocence. *South African Law Journal, 123*(1), 63–97.

Baldwin, R. (Ed.). (1997). *Law and uncertainty: Risks and legal processes*. London: Kluwer Law International.

Beck, U. (1992). *Risk society: Towards a new modernity* (M. Ritter, Trans.). London: Sage.

Beck, U. (1996). World risk society as cosmopolitan society?: Ecological questions in a framework of manufactured uncertainties. *Theory, Culture & Society, 13*(4), 1–33.

Beck, U. (1999). *World risk society*. Malden: Polity Press.

Beck, U. (2002). The terrorist threat: World risk society revisited. *Theory, Culture & Society, 19*(4), 39–55.

Berns, S., Sheehan, G., Banks, C., & Hunter, R. (2003–2004). Reconfiguring post-divorce parenting in a risk society panic. *Newcastle Law Journal, 7*, 13.

Buth, R. (2008). Individualisation and court-connected mediation: Comments from a risk society perspective. *Australasian Dispute Resolution Journal, 19*, 259.

Cash, J. (2009). Negotiating insecurity: Law, psychoanalytic social theory and the dilemmas of the world risk society. *Australian Feminist Law Journal, 30*, 87.

De Giorgi, R. (2009). The risk of risk society and the limits of law. [Article]. *Sociologia del Diritto, 36*(2), 59–67.

Douglas, W. (1929). Vicarious lilability and administration of risk I. *Yale Law Journal, 38*, 584.

Febbrajo, A. (2009). For a socio-legal theory of risk. [Article]. *Sociologia del Diritto, 36*(2), 69–82.

Foucault, M. (1972). *The archaeology of knowledge*. (A. M. S. Smith, Trans.). London: Routledge.

Garland, D. (2001). *The culture of control: Crime and social order in contemporary society*. Chicago: University of Chicago Press.

Giddens, A. (1990). *The consequences of modernity*. Cambridge: Polity Press.

Giddens, A. (1999). Risk and responsibility. *The Modern Law Review, 62*(1), 1–10.

Greig, D. (1997). Professions and the risk society. *Psychiatry Psychology and Law, 4*, 231.

Haines, F. (2011). *The paradox of regulation: What regulation can achieve and what it cannot*. Cheltenham: Edward Elgar Publishing.

Harvey, D. (2005). *A brief history of neoliberalism*. Oxford: Oxford University Press.

Harvey, W. (1892). Risk in sale in relation to insurance. *Juridical Review, 4*, 248.

Lee, R., & Morgan, D. (2001). Regulating risk society: Stigmata cases, Scientific citizenship & biomedical diplomacy. *Sydney Law Review, 23*, 297.

Mahler, T. (2007). Defining Legal Risk. In *Commercial contracting for strategic advantage - Potentials and prospects, Turku, Finland, 13–16 June 2007*.

Mahler, T. (2010). *Legal risk management: Developing and evaluating elements of a method for proactive legal analyses, with a particular focus on contracts*. Oslo: University of Oslo.

McCormick, R. (2010). *Legal risk in the financial markets* (2nd ed.). Oxford: Oxford University Press.

Meillon, J. (1906). The incidence of risk in goods during transit under a CIF contract. *Commonwealth Law Review, 3*(6), 241.

Mythen, G. (2004). *Ulrich Beck: A critical introduction to the risk society*. London: Pluto Press.

Mythen, G., & Walklate, S. (2006). *Beyond the risk society: Critical reflections on risk and human security*. Maidenhead: Open University Press.

O'Malley, P. (1991). Legal networks and domestic security. *Studies in Law, Politics and Society, 11*, 165–184.

O'Malley, P. (1992). Risk, power and crime prevention. *Economy and Society, 21*(3), 252–275.

O'Malley, P. (1996). Risk and responsibility. In A. Barry, T. Osborne, & N. Rose (Eds.), *Foucault and political reason* (pp. 189–207). London: UCL Press.

O'Malley, P. (1997). Policing, politics and postmodernity. *Social & Legal Studies, 6*(3), 363–381.

O'Malley, P. (Ed.). (1998a). *Crime and the risk society*. Brookfield: Ashgate.

O'Malley, P. (1998b). Dangerousness, risk and technologies of power. In *Crime and the risk society*. Aldershot: Ashgate.

O'Malley, P. (1998c). Police strategies and tactics for controlling crime and disorder in England and Wales. In *Crime and the risk society*. Aldershot: Ashgate.

O'Malley, P. (1999). Governmentality and the risk society. [Review Article of Ericson & Haggerty's *Policing the risk society*]. *Economy and Society, 28*(1), 138–148.

O'Malley, P. (2000). Uncertain subjects: Risks, liberalism and contract. *Economy and Society, 29*(4), 460–484.

O'Malley, P. (2001). Risk, crime and prudentialism revisited. In K. Stenson & R. Sullivan (Eds.), *Crime, risk and justice: The politics of crime control in Liberal democracies* (pp. 89–103). Cullompton: Willan Publishing.

O'Malley, P. (2004). *Risk, uncertainty and government*. London: Routledge Cavendish.

O'Malley, P. (Ed.). (2005). *Governing risks*. Aldershot: Ashgate.

O'Malley, P. (2008a). Experiments in risk and criminal justice. *Theoretical Criminology, 12*, 451–469.

O'Malley, P. (2008b). Neo-liberalism and risk in criminology. In T. Anthony & C. Cunneen (Eds.), *The critical criminology companion* (pp. 55–67). Sydney: Hawkins Press.

O'Malley, P. (2009a). *The currency of justice: Fines and damages in consumer societies*. London: Routledge-Cavendish.

O'Malley, P. (2009b). Theorizing fines. *Punishment & Society, 11*(1), 67–83.

O'Malley, P. (2010a). *Crime and risk*. London: SAGE.

O'Malley, P. (2010b). Fines, risks and damages: Money sanctions and justice in control societies. *Current Issues in Criminal Justice, 21*(3), 365.

O'Malley, P. (2010c). Simulated justice: Risk, money and telemetric policing. *British Journal of Criminology, 50*, 795–807.

O'Malley, P. (2011). Security after risk: Security strategies for governing extreme uncertainty. *Current Issues in Criminal Justice, 23*(1), 5–15.

O'Malley, P., & Palmer, D. (1996). Post-Keynesian policing. *Economy and Society, 25*(2), 137–155.

Priest, G. L. (1990). The new legal structure of risk control. *Daedalus, 119*(4), 207–227.

Rochford, F. (2007). The law of negligence in a risk society: Calculating ideas of reasonable risk. *Griffith Law Review, 16*, 172.

Rorty, R. (Ed.). (1967). *The linguistic turn: Recent essays in philosophical method*. Chicago: University of Chicago Press.

Scheurich, J., & McKenzie, K. (2005). Foucault's methodologies: Archaeology and genealogy. In N. Denzin & Y. Lincoln (Eds.), *The Sage handbook of qualitative research* (3rd ed., pp. 841–868). Thousand Oaks: Sage.

Shearing, C., & Johnston, L. (2005). Justice in the risk society. *Australian and New Zealand Journal of Criminology, 38*, 25.

Sjöberg, L., & Ramsberg, J. (1997). The cost-effectiveness of life saving interventions in Sweden. [Article]. *Risk Analysis: An International Journal, 17*(4), 467–478.

Sjöberg, L., Wahlberg, A., & Kvist, P. (1998). The rise of risk: Risk related bills submitted to the Swedish parliament in 1964–65 and 1993–1995. *Journal of Risk Research, 1*(3), 191–195.

Steele, J. (2004). *Risks and legal theory*. Portland: Hart Publishing.

Susskind, R. (1998). *The future of law: Facing the challenges of information technology*. New York: Oxford University Press.

Susskind, R. (2008). *The end of lawyers? Rethinking the nature of legal services*. Oxford: Oxford University Press.

Threedy, D. (2005). Legal archaeology: Excavating cases, reconstructing context. *Tulane Law Review, 80*, 1197.

Zinn, J. (Ed.). (2008). *Social theories of risk and uncertainty*. Malden: Blackwell Publishing.

Chapter 8
Legal Risk

> *Legal Risk: "a situation where the applicable law does not provide for a predictable and sound solution"*
>
> UNIDROIT (Cited in McCormick 2010)

This chapter considers the relationship between risk and controlled operations law evident in Australian Parliamentary discourse. In the previous chapter a complex relationship between risk and public policy was demonstrated through a qualitative analysis of Hansard. The present chapter takes that broad examination one step further by considering *legal risk* as a distinct category. The argument that follows is that risk shapes doctrinal law itself along two intersecting axes. First, law can manifest as a *source of risk*, through its rule systems, the conduct it regulates, its application, and its interaction with the vast web of legal rules and structures. Secondly, law is also mobilised as a *risk controller* to mitigate or eliminate risk. In this respect law is not a source of risk but part of its solution. The result of this internal and external dimension is that controlled operations law is actively governed by risk discourses.

Law as Source of Risk

One of the major concerns of Parliamentarians debating controlled operations law was the law itself being a source of risk. That concern operates at multiple levels: investigators are at risk of criminal and civil liability; judicial discretion over evidence presents enhanced levels of risk and uncertainty into a trial; there is an ever-present risks of abuse of power in the exercise of undercover investigations and surveillance; and even questions concerning the compatibility of statutory functions and the text of the law itself once introduced. In this context law can manifest itself as a source of risk as both uncertainty and threat. These are inherent aspects of law that intensify in the context of controlled operations.

B. Murphy, *Regulating Undercover Law Enforcement: The Australian Experience*, https://doi.org/10.1007/978-981-33-6381-6_8

Law and legal practice, by its very nature, operates within a realm characterised by risk and uncertainty. For this reason, care needs to be taken in concluding that every aspect of law is about risk management. There are, however, aspects of legal practice and reasoning inherently connected to questions of risk and uncertainty. Because of this, the measure of genius in legal practice is the ability to predict the future. Legal reasoning fundamentally depends on two forms of knowledge: fact and law (Gageler 2008-2009; Samuel 2016). When facts are incontestable, and the law unarguable, prediction is relatively easy. When facts are contested, and/or the law arguable, the outcome is uncertain, and accordingly less predictable. Ironically, in both cases legal uncertainty can arise. When laws evolve in a manner that is certain, but inconsistent with a policy directive, then the outcome becomes dissonant with the objectives of government or private interests and consequently a source of uncertainty. While the capacity of government to deliver on its promises of crime control is inherently uncertain, its mission is complicated when law is shaped by courts in ways which are not in alignment with the objects of government policy. Law can become its own source of political and social risk. When facts and law are clear, but subject to discretionary treatment, the outcome again becomes uncertain, because the importation of discretion alters the replication and predictability of outcomes. It appears that within the metaphysical realm of law there is a point where uncertainty becomes a manifest source of frustration, if not actual threat to the functioning and legitimacy of government. Legal uncertainty, when it intersects with risks of a sufficient threshold, becomes unacceptable and triggers an imperative logic for change in order to realign law within the acceptable range of certainty and uncertainty – a retreat *from* that space that might be referred to as a threshold of uncertainty/danger. The controlled operations law debates reflect this dynamic: when law and legal processes constitute a source of unacceptable uncertainty, it creates political demands for its correction. Controlled operations debate consequently manifest a range of discourses where risk and law merge.

Authority and Power

One of the functions of law is to provide authority for the exercise of legitimate power. Legal systems legitimate executive action. The controlled operation provides a range of powers to investigators that service that function. First, it provides authority to engage in unlawful activities. Second, it provides immunities to the investigators and their proxies for that conduct. It is, in effect, a licence to break the law. These aspects of the controlled operation were a source of considerable anxiety for legislators, routinely concerned about the potential for "abuse of power". Hansard manifested a concern for abuse of power in a number of ways. First, it was recognised that the controlled operations power can be abused by investigators through entrapment practices. The power can also be abused as a licence to engage in corrupt activities beyond entrapment. In addition, the controlled operation, even when deployed lawfully and within the scope of any operation, presents a threat to civil liberties. The right to privacy, for example, is essentially neutralised by the practice. The controlled operation, being an extraordinary power, is itself recognised as a source of risk.

There is always a great danger in providing anyone, even a qualified police officer, with immunity from prosecution for breaking the law, since police involvement in a criminal operation always raises some danger of entrapment or other abuse of power.[1]

Despite the coalition's heartfelt support for measures designed to combat organised crime and the fact that these measures will undoubtedly assist our police agencies in this vital task, there is still a real risk that these laws could be open to abuse if not amended.[2]

Liability

Liability is a major source of legal risk. Liability appears to have two manifestations, one intended and the other unintended. Intended liability functions as a control and limitation on the behaviour of investigators. As a matter of law investigators operate in an environment where they face criminal and civil sanctions for breaches of law in the course of their work. This is a rule that applies equally to everyone and is not unique to controlled operations. This principle is sourced in the long common law tradition that police officers are "citizens in uniform" and subject to the same law as everyone else. Unintended liability arises in cases where investigators are unaware that their activities may be the source of liability or are uncertain that their activities may be the source of liability. One of the effects of *Ridgeway* was to create an environment where the legal status of investigators acting in good faith was placed in a situation of legal uncertainty. This uncertainty was recognised as having two primary manifestations, one as a source of *operational risk* where officers might become distracted in the course of an investigation or be exposed as an officer in the course of that investigation, and the other where officers might become the

[1] Australian Capital Territory, *Weekly Hansard*, Legislative Assembly, 3 July 2008, 3099 (Richard Mulcahy, MLA)

[2] Commonwealth, *Parliamentary Debates*, Senate, 4 February 2010, 449 [33] (George Brandis)

subject of prosecution after an investigation through their involvement in a technically unlawful investigation.

> *The bill presents an extremely sensible approach to the pursuit of drug trafficking. It will protect police officers while improving effectiveness by allowing other agencies to conduct controlled operations in New South Wales. I assure the House that tough and effective law enforcement is a priority of this Government. I commend the Minister for Police... for his continued hard work on law enforcement. Giving police officers the powers to do their job to the best of their abilities without fear of prosecution is a necessary reform.*[3]

> *Officers working in this environment need to have their minds on the job, without anxiety about whether they themselves may be the subject of prosecution.*[4]

> *The purpose of this legislation is to enable officers to undertake this undercover work without the risk of prosecution, provided they comply with all the conditions and obligations imposed by the act and also to ensure the acceptability of the evidence obtained through this means.*[5]

Discretion

One of the fundamental powers of the judiciary is a cluster of discretions in the exercise of its function. In the criminal law the primary discretions of the judiciary relate to the imposition of sentence and control over evidence. These discretions are essential to the judicial office, not only because of the pragmatic need to deal with each case on its merits, but also because of the unique role the judicial office plays in a constitutional system of government. The judiciary plays a fundamental role in holding government to account. However, this rule of law function, and the existence of discretionary judicial powers, represents a source of uncertainty and risk to the objectives of executive government. In particular, the judicial discretion relating to the admissibility of evidence was a major part of the justification for the introduction of controlled operations law. As we have seen in earlier chapters, one of the

[3] New South Wales, *Hansard*, Legislative Assembly, 17 November 1999, 3134 (Sandra Nori)

[4] Australian Capital Territory, *Weekly Hansard*, Legislative Assembly, 3 July 2008, 3100 (Richard Mulcahy, MLA)

[5] Tasmania, *Hansard*, Joint Sitting, 21 November 2006, 68 (Ruth Forrest)

effects of the decision of the High Court in *Ridgeway* was to articulate a rule of evidence that meant that evidence obtained in a manner regarded as unlawful would trigger the judicial discretion to refuse to admit that evidence.

> *The bill requires courts, in deciding on the admissibility of evidence, to disregard the fact that evidence was obtained as the result of engaging in criminal activity if the participant is part of a controlled operation. This provision still allows a court the discretion to exclude evidence or stay proceedings on the grounds of Justice, such as in the cases of entrapment or incitement of a crime by police.*[6]

> *It appears that the bill will provide certainty that evidence collected during undercover operations can be presented in court.*[7]

> *[This bill] lessens the risk that evidence might be judicially excluded.*[8]

The consequence of a loss of evidence in a controlled operations case is potentially the loss of the prosecution case itself. In this respect the discretionary powers of Courts is sometimes criticised by lawmakers and the executive because of the way that discretions are applied – particularly in the rejection of evidence concerning notorious and factually guilty offenders in the name of "principle" or "public policy", and in the imposition of reduced sentences. However, for constitutional reasons the High Court has generally defended judicial discretion as a central part of the exercise of the judicial office.[9] Consequently Hansard manifests a discourse that on the one hand aims to restrict the exercise of discretion over the admissibility

---

[6]Australian Capital Territory, *Weekly Hansard*, Legislative Assembly, 3 July 2008, 3100 (Richard Mulcahy, MLA)

[7]New South Wales, *Hansard*, Legislative Council, 3 December 1997, 3046 (Elisabeth Kirkby)

[8]Victoria, *Hansard*, Legislative Assembly, 1 April 2004, 533 (Rob Hulls)

[9]The scope of judicial power has never been defined or limited. It is necessarily fuzzy and critically related to the facts of each case. Classically, see *Huddart, Parker & Co v Moorehead* (1909) 8 CLR 330; *NSW v Commonwealth (Wheat Case)* (1915) 20 CLR 54; *R v Trade Practices Tribunal; Ex parte Tasmanian Breweires Pty Ltd* (1970) 123 CLR 361. There is, however, capacity for Parliament to qualify and condition the exercise of a range of discretionary judicial powers, although the extent of "usurpation" is one of fact and degree. See *Liyanage v The Queen* [1967] 1 AC 259; *Chu Kheng Lim v Minister for Immigration* (1992) 175 CLR 1; *Nicholas v The Queen* (1998) 193 CLR 173

of evidence, while at the same time being careful not to impeach the discretion essential to the constitutional function of the judiciary.

I accept that you may not be able to or want to bring yourself to say, 'yes, it would be unconstitutional.' But, even if the risk is there, the issue is whether you want to, in a sense, give it a run and put at risk what would later be put at risk if a bill were passed in the form that you suggest.[10]

In this environment it is important to recognise that it is not only the judiciary that exercises discretion, but also the prosecution. The Director of Public Prosecutions in the various jurisdictions exercises independent judgement and discretion over the management of indictable cases. This discretion, like judicial discretion, functions as an important limitation and control over the prosecution of criminal cases. Independence and discretion are important components of an independent office. Like judicial discretion, however, the discretion is exercised by the prosecution are also a source of uncertainty. In the case of controlled operations, prior to implementation of a regular true system the investigators and their informers had to rely upon the discretion of the prosecution not to proceed with criminal charges for their involvement in an investigation otherwise undertaken in goodwill.

Historically, covert operations have been a legitimate and common policing method in relation to the investigation of a wide range of offences. However, before 1995, controlled operations were conducted in the absence of any legislative approval. As a result, evidence obtained from those operations was subject to the exercise of judicial discretion to exclude it on the grounds of public interest at any subsequent trial, and the operatives involved had to rely on the favourable exercise of prosecutorial discretion so that they were not charged with any criminal offences arising from their work.[11]

The exclusion of evidence not only carries with it the risk that a case will fail, it also carries with it the risk that the effective prosecution of criminal cases based on controlled operations more broadly is undermined. In this case the legal risk arising from judicial discretion intersects with a broader political and social risk, which is concerned with law functioning as a frustration to the executive. In one sense this is exactly what the rule of law is intended to do. On the other hand, public confidence

---

[10] Commonwealth, *Parliamentary Debates*, Senate, 27 May 1996, 1163 (Amanda Vanstone)

[11] Commonwealth, *Parliamentary Debates*, Senate, 4 April 2001, 26628 (Nick Bolkus)

in the administration of justice can be undermined, and the legislature invited by the executive to extend power and create exceptions to those rules.

> *... Without the passage of this legislation... Trials will have to be abandoned. I believe the community would not see that to be a just outcome.*[12]

> *We are told that there are 10 possible individuals who may face significant charges: three of them for offences which carry penalties with a maximum of 25 years imprisonment, and the other seven for offences which carry penalties with a maximum of life imprisonment. The government claims that the prosecution of these people is in jeopardy if the bill is not passed as the evidence may be inadmissible under the Ridgeway decision.*[13]

> *The longer we delay, the greater the risk that these people will not face justice in the courts. The longer we wait, the greater the risks are that nolle prosequis will be issued. I have heard nothing in this debate today to convince me of any logically legal reason why we should delay the passage of this bill. I urge the house to do the right thing and get it up to the Senate as quickly as possible.*[14]

> *The decision of the High Court in Ridgeway operates retrospectively, because the courts purport to declare the law as it has always been. It follows that all of these past and current prosecutions are now at risk.*[15]

Equally, it is critical that police agencies also have confidence in the support of the public and government. As all police agencies depend upon legal structures as a source of power, legitimacy and even for inception, legal uncertainty can have an

---

[12] Commonwealth, *Parliamentary Debates*, House of Representatives, 22 August 1995, 6 (Duncan Kerr, Minister for Justice)

[13] Commonwealth, *Parliamentary Debates*, House of Representatives, 22 August 1995, 9 (Philip Ruddock)

[14] Commonwealth, *Parliamentary Debates*, House of Representatives, 22 August 1995, 75 (Peter Cleeland)

[15] South Australia, *Hansard*, Legislative Council, 6 June 1995, 2067 (Kenneth Griffin, Attorney General)

impact on the confidence of police agencies themselves. Statutes serve to both empower and legitimate law enforcement.

> *... [B]ringing in legislation quickly and accommodating the police and the prosecutors, who must be terribly concerned about this hiatus that exists as a result of the Ridgeway case.*[16]

Legal Procedure as Risk

In addition to questions of substantive liability and judicial discretion in the exercise of law, the technicalities of law can represent a manifest source of risk. This is particularly the case where fundamental principles of common law are brought into play. These principles have evolved over centuries in the common law tradition and operate as the pre-existing tapestry upon which controlled operations law was subsequently written. In criminal law one of these principles is a presumption against retrospectivity. Like all presumptions, it may be displaced by specific words and necessary intention.[17] Broadly, the presumption against retrospectivity is concerned with fairness. It is manifestly unfair to enact laws that prohibit a course of conduct in the past, and then subsequently hold individuals responsible for behaviours that were, at the time they were manifested, otherwise lawful. This presumption was not unnoticed by Parliament. Ironically, when questions of retrospectivity are enlivened, the tendency is to introduce exceptional or transitional arrangements that address questions of retrospectivity.

> *Without the transitional provisions, the evidence available to prosecute a number of pending cases relating to allegations of serious narcotics trafficking offences will be in serious jeopardy.*[18]

The administrative processes formalised through legal and regulatory mechanisms not only have the potential to create sources of legal risk, they may also intersect with physical operations. The approval mechanisms involved in a controlled operation, for example, has the potential to set authorisation at a threshold so high that it renders practical policing impossible, or creating a threshold of evidence so high that a controlled operation becomes redundant, as an ordinary arrest for a

---

[16] Commonwealth, *Parliamentary Debates*, House of Representatives, 22 August 1995, 71 (Louis Lieberman)

[17] *R v Kidman* (1915) 20 CLR 425; *Polyukhovich v The Queen* (1991) 172 CLR 501.

[18] Commonwealth, *Parliamentary Debates*, House of Representatives, 22 August 1995, 76 (Duncan Kerr, Minister for Justice)

known offence is now available. There would be no need for a covert investigation if there was sufficient, known evidence capable of supporting a conviction.

> *The government opposes the amendment, acceptance of which would make the legislation inoperable. Undercover operations are highly specialised investigations because of the inherent risks associated with investigating criminals involved in serious crime and corruption. Setting up a test whereby chief executive officers must refuse an application for a controlled operation that may involve such a risk would mean that no approvals could be granted because all controlled operations involve some such risk.*[19]

Because controlled operations are such an extraordinary power an administrative system has been implemented tied to the discourse of accountability. In criminal cases adherence to the technicalities of administration becomes a hot topic of legal analysis. There is a long tradition in the common law concerned with impeaching the validity of warrants because of defects that have arisen during the administration of those warrants. The solution to administrative defects is addressed through the creation of two categories of defects. The first category is of a purely technical or administrative nature. In controlled operations cases, cosmetic or technical defects do not compromise the integrity of a warrant, unless the second category is also enlivened. The second category relates to defects concerned with the formal internal integrity and substance of the warrant itself. Broadly, the question is whether the defect is cosmetic, or relates to whether the warrant should ever have been issued at all.

> *The bill also proposes several amendments of a technical nature. First, there is a new provision that will ensure that courts cannot throw cases out of court simply because of a procedural defect in the application, unless it affects the application for the controlled authority in a substantive manner... Police agencies sought this amendment to reduce the risk that courts could declare enabling documentation invalid because it failed to observe all the statutory requirements.*[20]

Procedural risks are not only concerned with the administration of the warrants themselves, but also with other areas of legal process, such as litigation. One area that has been of particular concern relates to the testimony of witnesses in

[19] New South Wales, *Hansard*, Legislative Council, 3 December 1997, 3052–3 (Jeff Shaw, Attorney General)

[20] New South Wales, *Hansard*, Legislative Assembly, 11 November 1999, 2780–1 (Bryce Gaudry, Parliamentary Secretary)

undercover investigations. The identity of an undercover officer or an informer is particularly sensitive in the context of corruption and organised crime. It is an ordinary rule of evidence that a person who is the subject of a criminal allegation is entitled to test the integrity and credibility of the source of evidence being used against them.[21] One of the consequences of this process is that confidential informants and undercover investigators may have their identity revealed during the course of a trial. The disclosure of the identity of a witness may present that witness with specific forms of personal risk. Consequently, the attention of the law has been directed to attempts to maintain the anonymity of witnesses in certain cases.

To gain a conviction and to protect the identity of an investigator during these controlled operations, it may be necessary that evidence is given in court under [an] acquired false identity. This will offer protection but also will ensure that the investigator is able to continue in his or her role for future undercover work.[22]

Putting in place legislation to specifically deal with the police officer engaging in undercover operations and covert surveillance, it is important to ensure that the identities of the officers involved and subsequent prosecutions are not placed at risk.[23]

Law as Symbolic and Actual Legitimacy

One of the essential functions of a legal system is to identify and normalise legitimate behaviour. Controlled operations law is a prime example of the legitimating function in action.

In order to give certainty to the collection of evidence, legitimacy to the actions of the police officers and – arguably, most importantly – transparency and accountability to these operations, the legislative regime was put in place in 1995 by the then Labour government for the conduct of controlled operations in relation to narcotic offences.[24]

[21] *Woolmington v DPP* [1935] AC 462

[22] Queensland, *Record of Proceedings*, Legislative Assembly, 7 June 2005, 3089 (Desley Scott)

[23] Tasmania, *Hansard*, Joint Sitting, 21 November 2006, 69 (Ruth Forrest)

[24] Commonwealth, *Parliamentary Debates*, Senate, 4 April 2001, 26628 (Nick Bolkus)

The result of this bill will presumably have the immediate effect of letting the police know what they can and cannot do legitimately in terms of undercover operations.[25]

Parliamentary intervention is not only concerned with providing a legal architecture to empower and delimit the conduct of the executive, and an extension of the act of legitimation, it also functions as a powerful symbol. Parliament, to address questions of social and political risks, must be seen to act, and to do so decisively. Questions of legitimacy are not only located in the activities of police but are also located in the activities of Parliament in its response to risk and danger.

What happened in Ridgeway was that the police force had carried out an operation which was against the law and had not been approved by Parliament. Therefore, the evidence that would otherwise have been admitted was not admitted, and thereby Ridgeway was acquitted. Indeed, there was a danger that a lot of people would be acquitted as well, but Parliament stepped in at that time and made legislation which protected that position.[26]

Borders

Law operates within and also constructs metaphysical borders with real-world consequences. The existence of legal borders can constitute a risk when attempts are made to transgress them. In the context of controlled operations, real questions began to emerge quite early in relation to jurisdictional borders that exist between governments, and also the function of police agencies. Broadly, jurisdiction refers to the limits of power available to an agency. While an agency may act in a physical way, that activity will be unlawful if the agency has no statutory authority to do so. Queensland Police, for example, could not lawfully investigate a crime in New South Wales in the absence of something that triggered jurisdiction. A substantial amount of legislative activity, particularly after controlled operations law had first been established, related to creating mechanisms by which the risks arising through jurisdictional difference could be addressed. The identified jurisdictional risks ranged from geographic borders through to interagency cooperation. The significance of legal borders ultimately relates to questions of legality, which in turn affects the potential liability of investigators, but more importantly the technical rules that shape the exercise of discretion over evidence. Evidence may be

---

[25] South Australia, *Hansard*, Legislative Council, 7 June 1995, 2128 (Carolyn Pickles)

[26] Commonwealth, *Parliamentary Debates*, Senate, 4 April 2001, 26638 (Bernard Cooney)

inadmissible in some cases because of activities that make the warrant technically unlawful or fail to provide the requisite grounds for authorisation. In addition, the existence of legal boundaries between agencies and the constitutional separation of the Australian Commonwealth, State and Territories, meant that the capacity to conduct complex interagency collaborations was frustrated.

> *This [bill] will enable more effective investigations across jurisdictions and reduce the risk of losing evidence. The availability of consistent sets of powers across jurisdictions also facilitates closer cooperation between law enforcement agencies.*[27]

Legal Precedent as Risk

The outcome of unique cases can also manifest a source of risk. The genius of the common law is its capacity to evolve through decided cases. This capacity is an essential part of the common law legal system. It is also a source of uncertainty because of its organic character. In many cases legislative activity is triggered as a result of cases that interpret law in a manner inconsistent with the desires of the respective Parliaments, where it manifests an unwelcome change in the previously established system of precedent. The inherent dynamics of a common law system are often brought into conflict with the policy agenda of the legislature. This is no surprise, given that one of the actual functions of a system of government based on separation of powers as a political and theoretical principle is to permit courts of law the ability to limit and scrutinise legislative and executive actions. This conflict is evident in controlled operation policy debates, particularly where the fundamental tension points in controlled operations law are considered, notably questions concerning the admissibility of evidence, accountability, and the potential liability of investigators.

> *The bill also responds to concerns arising from the High Court's decision in Gedeon v Commissioner of the New South Wales Crime Commission. Following that case, there is a real risk that there is insufficient protection for persons authorised under state or territory controlled operations law to commit Commonwealth offences.*[28]

---

[27] Commonwealth, *Parliamentary Debates*, House of Representatives, 24 June 2009, 6965 (Robert McClelland)

[28] Ibid

> *... This bills deals with controlled operations, assumed identities and witness identity protection. The bills proposed amendments to the Crimes Act 1914 in response to the High Court's decision in Gedeon v Commissioner of the New South Wales Crime Commission in 2008, which placed in doubt the protection of participants in a controlled operation.*[29]

Lawyers as Risk

In addition to law and the judiciary constituting a potential source of risk and uncertainty, legal practitioners are also identified as a source of risk, for it is they who deploy law and invoke and rely upon the various discretions and defects contained within legal architectures.

> *The bill provides a mechanism that will facilitate controlled operations being carried out in a way that does not compromise their integrity, leave them open to challenge, or allow for attacks by representatives of criminals who have been caught out in various tests.*[30]

Unlike executive agencies that make use of controlled operations, the existence of an independent legal profession is one aspect of the controlled operations ecology that is outside of the immediate control of the legislature. This may explain why lawyers are routinely identified in pejorative terms in Hansard, perceived or presented as manipulators of the legal system. Lawyers are, routinely, a source of uncertainty and risk because it is part of their function to test the integrity of rule systems and the evidence presented in a court. Many of the weaknesses and anxieties attached to the application of rules of evidence and controlled operations law are directly connected to the ordinary practices of the legal profession. This aspect of law as a source of risk is not particularly controversial, or unique to controlled operations law – for the essential task of an independent legal profession is to scrutinise and challenge cases. Lawyers have always been a "source of risk"; but in risk society their role locates them in a highly contentious domain.

---

[29] Commonwealth, *Parliamentary Debates*, Senate, 4 February 2010, 448 (George Brandis)

[30] New South Wales, *Hansard*, Legislative Council, 25 November 1999, 3705 (John Hatzistergos)

Law as Risk Controller

The rule systems of formalised law are also deployed as mechanisms directed towards the control of risk, through eradication or limitation. In this respect law is as much a solution as a problem.

Limitations on Powers

One of the control mechanisms intended to restrict the potential for abuse of powers is the existence of statutory limits on the scope and exercise of powers. The limitations on power are numerous, and in many ways controlled operations regulation is more concerned with establishing limitations on the use of the power as opposed to its authorisation. The first limitation concerns the scope of unlawful activity that may be authorised by the warrant. As discussed in earlier chapters, a warrant may not be validly issued in cases where there is a likelihood of a fatality or serious injury, or an offence involving a sexual assault. Furthermore, the protection of the warrant may well be breached if officers executing a controlled operation exceed their mandate by engaging in conduct in breach of the warrant or the statute itself.

> *The bill provides protection to officers from prosecution for crimes committed in the course of an authorised controlled operation, other than for offences likely to cause death, serious injury or a sexual assault against a person.*[31]

> *Operatives and civilians who breached the terms of the authority do so at their own risk, as they will lose the protection provided under clauses 18 and 19 of this bill.*[32]

The system of limitation of powers evident in legislation forms part of a broader mechanism of regulation that is part of the internal dynamics of the organisation deploying the controlled operation. Organisations are not only regulated by legislation, but also through delegated regulations, internal governance structures, and the accountability mechanisms and operational cultures that exist within those organisations. The limitation on powers evident in legislation is but one part of a larger

---

[31] Australian Capital Territory, *Weekly Hansard*, Legislative Assembly, 3 July 2008, 3100 (Richard Mulcahy, MLA)

[32] New South Wales, *Hansard*, Legislative Assembly, 20 November 1997, 2322 (Richard Amery)

system of regulation that includes both hard and soft law constituting the internal and external structures of governance; that is, the knowledge systems that constitute and standardise the behaviours of institutions. This context is recognised and reflected in Parliamentary discourse.

> *There are risks involved with operating in this twilight zone of infiltration, investigation and the eventual application of Justice. It requires strong safeguards, and I have every confidence that organisations such as the Australian Federal police have the governance measures and the adherence to legislation to carry out these important roles.*[33]

Law as Solution to Risk

While law is often criticised by politicians as constituting a source of risk in various ways, law is also presented as a solution, or at least part of the solution, to the manifestation of identified risks, including legal risk. The solution to a legal risk, ordinarily, is an alteration in the text of law. Very simply, when the law becomes a manifest risk to the objective of government, the solution is to change the laws to either remove the impediment, or redesign law in order to minimise the risk that the law will become a source of frustration as opposed to a source of empowerment for executive action.

> *It was largely as a result of the uncertainty created by the Ridgeway case that the Royal commission into the New South Wales police service recommended that legislation be introduced in New South Wales to overcome the problems for undercover operations presented by the Ridgeway decision. The bill now before the house overcomes the Ridgeway problem.*[34]

In the same way the risk of criminal and civil liability is simply addressed through the declaration that an officer undertaking an approved controlled operation is immune from consequent legal action.

> *In the interests of security, the bill therefore extends protection through to any court proceedings arising from a controlled operation.*[35]

---

[33] Commonwealth, *Parliamentary Debates*, House of Representatives, 24 June 2009, 11137 (Luke Simpkins)

[34] New South Wales, *Hansard*, Legislative Assembly, 20 November 1997, 2322 (Richard Amery)

[35] Ibid

The operational and physical risks inherent in undercover investigations can also be addressed through legal design. The concerns raised about abuse of power, for example, are addressed through accountability mechanisms, whereas the manifest risks and dangers to individuals that arise in the course of the operation itself can be controlled through the careful construction of approval systems. The design of legal architectures intended to address questions of risk is significant. It is significant because it is here at the nexus between policy and doctrine that we can identify the reality that risk directly shapes legal doctrine in addition to risk being a driver of policy.

Clause 7 expressly prohibits the approval of a controlled operation if there is likely to be any undue risk to the operatives involved or to any other person. Clause 7 also prevents approval of operations in which there is a risk of serious damage to the property of others. It is not appropriate to authorise controlled operations when there is a high risk of liability for damages. Similarly, undercover officers cannot be authorised to act as agent provocateurs by enticing targets to commit crimes.[36]

As will be discussed in more detail in the following chapter, law becomes a solution to risk through the creation of norms and procedures concerned with accountability. This is particularly the case in controlled operations, where the problems identified concerning the risk of abuse of process and the risk of inappropriate exercise of discretion, are addressed through specific legal architectures.

As this bill will extend the scope and power to authorise controlled operations from one officer to a great number of officers, it will have to be carefully monitored.[37]

The bill seeks to extend the authority to approve controlled operations to the rank of superintendent, as is the case in South Australia. This improvement will relieve the impossible demand on the Commissioner to process all applications for controlled operations while extending authority to ranks that have sufficient seniority and the best knowledge of daily operations within their areas of command. Naturally, the extension of the authority from one officer to some hundreds of officers will require careful monitoring and ongoing vigilance. The danger is that if a controlled operation is compromised in any way, serious criminal cases may be jeopardised.[38]

---

[36] New South Wales, *Hansard*, Legislative Assembly, 20 November 1997, 2323 (Richard Amery)
[37] New South Wales, *Hansard*, Legislative Assembly, 17 November 1999, 3132 (Andrew Tink)
[38] New South Wales, *Hansard*, Legislative Council, 25 November 1999, 3682–3 (Michael Gallacher)

As outlined above, one of the fundamental effects of *Ridgeway*, and subsequent enactment in controlled operations law, concerned the question of admissibility of evidence obtained during a controlled operation. In this area the law is deployed in a way that reverses the common law assumption that evidence obtained unlawfully is prima facie inadmissible. Here we are presented with another example of the law being used against itself. It does this by declaring the operation is a lawful activity, provided those actions comply with the conditions of the warrant.

> *There is very little point in engaging in some sort of illegal activity that will lead to the conviction of others if because the activity is illegal, the court is able to rule that the evidence collected during that activity is inadmissible. The provisions of this bill seek to overcome that problem as well.*[39]

Law as Empowerment and Shield

Law is frequently identified as a source of power in the fight against crime and corruption. Law here serves the rhetorical function of validating and valorising the agents of police, as well as providing a shield against law being used against those same operatives. In this context law is both sword and shield.

> *With respect to the first initiative of this six-point plan to fight crime, I am sure honourable members have been concerned about recent media reports carrying the tragic tales of undercover police officers who have paid a high personal and professional toll for their undercover activities. Those officers have exposed themselves over a long period to great personal danger and, sadly, without the protection of the law. It is time governments gave these courageous officers the tools they need to do their job properly and with the full backing of the law.*[40]

Risk Shaping Doctrine

In addition to its role in shaping policy, risk also plays a direct role in shaping controlled operations doctrine. In this part we examine the controlled operations act as it stands in New South Wales to provide a specific example of the various ways in which intersecting risk discourses have influenced the specific shape and structure of legislation.

[39] Victoria, *Hansard*, Legislative Council, 12 May 2004, 853 (Andrew McIntosh)

[40] Queensland, *Record of Proceedings*, Legislative Assembly, 17 May 2000, 1817 (Grant Musgrove)

Defined Terms

One of the functions of law is to construct a shared, authoritative nomenclature. Defined terms are central in that function. Such terms have declarative and authoritative meaning. Although all statutory provisions are open to judicial interpretation, the function of defined terms is to provide standard terminology used in constructing a statute. Care needs to be taken, however, for it is erroneous to assume that a defined term operates as a formulaic or "stand-alone" concept in law. Defined terms are not stand-alone principles. Definitions are necessarily read in context, and not necessarily literally, and it is only through reference to the words of the statute, importing the defined terms, that such terminology becomes part of the fabric of law.[41]

In the Foucauldian tradition, this act of determining the meaning of language is a demonstration of the power/knowledge nexus. The ability to determine the meaning of language itself is a significant manifestation of sovereign power – it is the sovereign that determines the meaning to be adopted in statutory language. In this case the power/knowledge nexus functions to distinguish between the lawful and the unlawful use of the power manifested in the controlled operation – for it is only through compliance with the statutory system that the transformation of the contradiction is achieved. Activities taking place outside of the scope of defined may be unlawful. The activities of police must conform to the knowledge system that is controlled operations law to be lawful. This aspect of the intersection between Foucault and law will be considered further in Chap. 10.

Defined terms are nothing new. All statutes possess them. What matters is the question of *whether risk actually constructs the contours of the terminology used*, or *whether risk is operationalized through the linguistic form*. Risk is not a term used in these definitions as an explicit term. In this case risk can only have an implied or oblique role in shaping doctrine. In the following segment we examine the specific relationship between risk and one controlled operations statute, the *Law Enforcement (Controlled Operations) Act 1997* (NSW)(LE(CO)A).

There are six major defined terms within the LE(CO)A, set out in the following table:

Term	Definition
Controlled activity	Means an activity that, but for section 16, would be unlawful
Controlled conduct	Means conduct in respect of which, but for section 20K or 20L, a person would be criminally liable.

[41] *Kelly v R* (2004) 218 CLR 216 at 253 per McHugh J. For commentary see Pearce & Geddes (7th ed., 2011: 247)

Term	Definition
Controlled operation	Means an operation conducted for the purpose of: (a) obtaining evidence of criminal activity or corrupt conduct, or (b) arresting any person involved in criminal activity or corrupt conduct, or (c) frustrating criminal activity or corrupt conduct, or (d) carrying out an activity that is reasonably necessary to facilitate the achievement of any purpose referred to in paragraph (a), (b) or (c), being an operation that involves, or may involve, a controlled activity.
Corrupt conduct	Has the same meaning as it has in the *Independent Commission Against Corruption Act 1988*.
Criminal activity	Means any activity that involves the commission of an offence by one or more persons.
Police agency	Means each of the following: (a) the NSW Police Force, (b) the Independent Commission Against Corruption, (c) the New South Wales Crime Commission, (d) the Police Integrity Commission, (e) such of the following agencies as may be prescribed by the regulations as police agencies for the purposes of this Act: (i) the Australian Federal Police, (ii) the Australian Crime Commission, (iii) the Australian Customs Service.

These terms assist in characterising the fundamental scope of the controlled operation – its aims, and its agents. The controlled operation is one of the myriad *apparatus* of state engaged in law enforcement, directed to the investigation and suppression of crime and corruption. Risk, in this context, shapes doctrine only in so far as it is one of the objects to which the legislation is directed. *Law is here mobilised as a technology of practice.* At the same time, the statute empowers a select group of agencies, while simultaneously excluding all others from that empowerment. This exclusion operates with respect to the world at large; not just the governed. It is an exclusion of all non-State actors – and an exclusion of State actors outside of the jurisdictional scope of the warrant, including domestic military actors. Risk in this context is not only concerned with the corruption/crime object, but also with the contours of sovereignty. Defined terms assist in articulating the object of intervention, and in establishing the lines of authority.

> *...this bill is intended for use only by prescribed law enforcement agencies. These are defined in clause 3....*[42]

[42] New South Wales, *Hansard*, Legislative Assembly, 20 November 1997, 2322 (Richard Amery)

The Exclusionary Rule of Evidence

The first statutory form explicitly shaped by risk in the LE(CO)A is s3A.[43] This section provides that the LE(CO)A is not to be interpreted as affecting "the existence or exercise of any discretions (including any administrative or judicial discretions) that, apart from this Act, may lawfully be exercised in relation to the commencement, conduct or conclusion of legal proceedings." That statement is further qualified (s3A(2)) as referring to the commencement or termination of proceedings, admissibility of evidence, or how a person found guilty is otherwise to be dealt with. These qualifications are primarily concerned with three of the core judicial discretions concerning evidence, the availability of a stay order, and the determination of sentence.

Sections 3A(1)-(3) are carefully worded to ensure that judicial discretions, particularly over evidence, are not impugned. This is a crucial aspect of legislative risk management, since attempts to remove judicial discretions are very likely to invite a Constitutional challenge, particularly in relation to judicial function arising under Chapter III of the Commonwealth Constitution. In the earlier part of this chapter, it was observed that parliamentarians were well aware of the Constitutional implications of attempts to remove judicial discretions, as well as locating the authorisation function with judicial officers.

It is in this section that the uncertainty that emerged in *Ridgeway* was specifically addressed.[44] Rather than remove or redesign the discretion of judges over evidence (likely unconstitutional), the focus was on altering the legal status of evidence. The evidence was simply declared to be lawfully obtained. That status is, however, a 'floating potential' – the status of the evidence remains subject to other intersecting rules of evidence. But that status was effectively brought into alignment with an existing norm: all evidence is subject to a filtering process, and accordingly a degree of uncertainty. The difference was that the uncertainty created by *Ridgeway* had shifted the question of evidence into the realm of certainty/danger and consequently a threat to successful prosecution. By changing the legal status of one aspect of controlled operations evidence the risk of exclusion, with its associated social and political consequences, was immediately addressed. The genius of the provision was its careful locating in relation to existing discretions. In addition, this aspect of the legislation operates to control the risks of Constitutional challenge on the basis

---

[43] Section 3A was originally inserted into the LE(CO)A in 1999 (*Law Enforcement (Controlled Operations) Amendment Act 1999* (NSW), Sch 1 [1]–[3]), and subsequently amended in 2006. The amendment inserted 3A(3A) into the Act, with the intention of clarifying the status of evidence in relation to cross-border investigations. See *Law Enforcement (Controlled Operations) Amendment Act 2006* (NSW), and Law Enforcement (Controlled Operations) Amendment Bill 2006, Explanatory Memorandum.

[44] S3A was not contained in the original Act. It was inserted in 1999 (*Law Enforcement (Controlled Operations) Amendment Act 1999* (NSW)), and subsequently amended in 2006 (*Law Enforcement (Controlled Operations) Amendment Act 2006* (NSW)).

that the attempt to remove judicial discretions would be contrary to the judicial powers of a superior court of record, or the powers of a judicial officer arising under Chapter III.

> *...evidence obtained in a controlled operation may be subject to challenge in court. The admissibility of evidence collected during undercover operations has been under a cloud since the 1995 High Court decision in the Ridgeway case...It was largely as a result of the uncertainty created by the Ridgeway case that the Royal commission into the New South Wales police service recommended that legislation be introduced in New South Wales to overcome the problems for undercover operations presented by the Ridgeway decision. The bill now before the house overcomes the Ridgeway problem. Ultimately, of course, the question of admissibility of evidence will remain an issue for the court to determine in accordance with section 138 of the Evidence Act 1995.*[45]

Authorisation

The authorisation process set out in the LE(CO)A is explicitly and impliedly shaped by risk. This relationship is complex, reflected in the authorisation process. Authorisation involves a rational process, based on evidence. Each step of the process involves an audit trail. Authorisation begins with a general power of any officer within a defined agency[46] to make an application for a controlled operations warrant pursuant to s5.

Authorisation involves a police officer making an application for a warrant, which is then determined by an authorised officer. In NSW that person is identified as the CEO for the agency, but with the notable feature of limited delegated authority to specific senior officers within the agency.[47] The application requires the provision of information, which includes attention to identity. Identity relates to all parties involved: the investigators; the target; the authorising officer; and civilian

---

[45] New South Wales, *Hansard*, Legislative Assembly, 20 November 1997, 2322 (Richard Amery)

[46] In NSW a "law enforcement agency" is defined as (i) the NSW Police; (ii) the Independent Commission Against Corruption; (iii) the NSW Crime Commission; (iv) the Police Integrity Commission; (v) the Australian Federal Police; (vi) the Australian Crime Commission; and (vii) Australian Customs.

[47] *Law Enforcement (Controlled Operations) Act 1997* (NSW), s29

participants. The logistics and geographic locality of the operation is required. These were described by the Hon. Richard Amery (MLA):

> *Clause 5 of the bill refers to the manner in which an application must be made. It requires that an application be made in writing. As applications are to be accountable documents, they must also be signed by the applicant. All applications must contain sufficient detail to allow the authorising officer to make an informed decision. For example, they must be accompanied by a plan that outlines how the investigation will be conducted, what the objective is, and why a controlled operation is necessary. An application must also identify those who are to participate in an operation and the nature of the unlawful conduct in which it is proposed they will engage.*[48]

The identification of specific individuals within the process attaches the responsibility for that operation directly to those involved in its execution. Fixing responsibility aims to ensure that operations of this kind are subjected to formal processes of audit, scrutiny, and consequence. The applicant remains, from the moment the application is made, an identifiable party with attendant expectations of conduct. In this environment risk has two dimensions. The first relates to the potential for the abuse of power. As set out above, abuse of power is a powerful discourse within controlled operations debates and literature. The "tight accountability mechanism for the approval and oversight of controlled operations"[49] is directly attached to anxieties concerned with the abuse of power – a component of the intersecting risk matrix. The second dimension *uses risk as a rationality of disciplinary power*. The risk of abuse of power is managed not only by the mechanisms of approval and oversight – it is also managed by *shifting risk to the investigator*:

> *The importance of the approval, and compliance with its terms, must not be underestimated. The written authority sets clear parameters for the conduct of each controlled operation. Operatives and civilians who breach the terms of the authority do so at their own risk, as they will lose the protection provided under clauses 18 and 19 of this bill.*[50]

Determination of an application is similarly procedural, set out in s6 of the Act. It requires an individual with delegated authority being presented with enough information to enable them to make an informed and defensible decision to make

[48] New South Wales, *Hansard*, Legislative Assembly, 20 November 1997, 2322–3 (Richard Amery)
[49] Ibid
[50] Ibid

the authorisation. In this case the determination is ostensibly made by the "chief executive officer". This term has its origins in business nomenclature, where it forms an integral part of corporations law.[51] The decision itself is discretionary; however, this discretion is shaped by specific conditions – the existence of a 'code of conduct' for the actions of officers involved (an internal governance architecture),[52] and a threshold level of evidence that both justifies the need for the operation and ensures the requirement for audit. These aspects of approval are, again, driven by the demands relating to the risk of abuse of powers, but also questions of legal risk that arise out of legal challenges relating to the validity of warrants. That is partly addressed by compliance with the formality of law, and through attending to the governing rationality of law as being locked in *reason* and *evidence*. The logic at work in this discourse is essentially utilitarian: the ends must justify the means. The justification for action is firmly entrenched in liberal reasoning as evidence-based and considered. Hansard, once again, outlines the controlled rationality at work:

> *When considering whether to approve a controlled operation, the authorising officer must be satisfied of a number of things. These are set out in clause 6. Specifically, the authorising officer must be satisfied that there are reasonable grounds to suspect that criminal or corrupt conduct has been, is being or is about to be carried out. He or she must also be satisfied that this activity is sufficiently serious to warrant a controlled operation being conducted.*

> *Approval may be granted only in circumstances in which the scope of the proposed controlled operation is sufficient to deal with, but not exceed, the conduct being investigated. The use of alternative, more traditional investigative tools should always be considered. Minor matters and matters that can successfully be investigated by traditional means will not be considered for controlled operations. In practice, controlled operations will be used only when traditional methods of investigation are inadequate. This means that they are aimed at the investigation of serious matters like drug trafficking, money laundering, child pornography, organised crime and corruption.*

---

[51] Eg: *Corporations Act 2001* (Cth), s201J

[52] Eg: *Law Enforcement (Controlled Operations) Regulations 2012* (NSW), Sch 2

Clause 6 contains other considerations that are intended as guidelines for authorising officers when determining applications. For example, an authorising officer must have regard to the reliability of any informant involved in an operation. It is to be expected that controlled operations based on intelligence from an unreliable informant would only be approved if supported by some other independent source of information. Importantly, there are limits to what can be authorised.[53]

Reason, evidence, audit and accountability are relied on as effective methods for controlling the decision to issue the warrant, its execution, and its legitimation as an invasive form of investigation. At the same time, there are specific risk-based limitations within the legal architecture that add an additional layer of control over utilitarian reasoning. These limits are set out in s7 as imperatives restricting the conduct of both civilians and investigators alike. These limitations emerge out of explicit discourses of risk considered in Chap. 6: the public occupational health and safety risks; the risk of entrapment; the risk of loss and damage to property; the risk of liability; the risk of compromised evidence; the risk of rogue behaviour. These are limitations that exist at the outset, again clearly described in the Second Reading Speech as based on risk:

Clause 7 expressly prohibits the approval of a controlled operation if there is likely to be any undue risk to the operatives involved or to any other person. Clause 7 also prevents approval of operations in which there is a risk of serious damage to the property of others. It is not appropriate to authorise controlled operations when there is a high risk of liability for damages. Similarly, undercover officers cannot be authorised to act as agent provocateurs by enticing targets to commit crimes.[54]

The approval process allows for *variations* in the warrant once it has been authorised. Variations allow for administrative flexibility, such as changing the names of

[53] New South Wales, *Hansard*, Legislative Assembly, 20 November 1997, 2323 (Richard Amery)

[54] Ibid

those involved, but also permit alteration of the nature of controlled activities that may arise opportunistically. Variations are also subjected to the tight rationality of risk and audit:

> *Clause 10 provides for variations of approvals. An authority may be varied to reflect changes in circumstances. For example, it may add or substitute participants or change the principal police officer. Clause 10 also allows additional or alternative controlled activities to be approved. Variations will ensure that undercover officers can respond to opportunities to investigate, prevent or prosecute serious crime and corruption that they encounter during an operation, for example, in an operation in which an undercover officer is authorised to participate in activities involving drugs and is offered firearms as part of the deal.*

> *Importantly, the same restrictions on approval found in clause 7 apply to applications for a variation. From time to time circumstances will arise in a controlled operation that could not reasonably have been foreseen and which are likely to involve an operative in unlawful activity that has not been authorised. In such circumstances the operative, or another police officer acting on his or her behalf, should make an urgent application to vary the authority in accordance with clause 10. However, it is anticipated that circumstances will arise in which it is neither safe nor possible for an operative to seek such approval. In the normal course of events, this means that the officers should not engage in the additional, unauthorised conduct. Should they do so, they will not have the protections provided by this legislation.*[55]

What is interesting about the variation option is the existence of a specific *exception* to the requirement that authorisation be obtained prospectively. The Second Reading Speech set out the basis for retrospective authority in these terms:

[55] New South Wales, *Hansard*, Legislative Assembly, 20 November 1997, 2323–4 (Richard Amery)

> *The single exception will be when an operative is faced with a situation in which his or her own safety, or the safety of another, is under threat. In such circumstances, clause 14 permits an application for retroactive approval to be made within 24 hours. Retroactive approvals may be granted only when certain conditions are met. Firstly, the operative must at all times have been acting in good faith and in accordance with the agency's code of conduct. Secondly, the applicant must have been operating under a reasonable belief that he or she, or another person, would be seriously harmed should the unauthorised conduct not be undertaken. Whilst unlikely to be used frequently, the provisions of clause 14 are essential. They provide protection for operatives when exposed to the most dangerous of situations. Nevertheless, approvals will be granted only when there is an assurance that the operative acted in good faith.*[56]

Necessity and imperative are again evident within this discourse. It appears that when the legislator is presented with the right combination of risk, threat or danger, it will mobilise a logic of exception that changes the legal architecture in ways that deviate from the existing norm. This is significant, given that in the criminal law abhorrence for retrospectivity is a long-standing principle of law and interpretation. It is noteworthy that this exception is expressed explicitly in terms of risk, both in terms of the risk to the investigator *and* the risk of defective trials. The present s14 contains an explicit concern with risk:

Retrospective Authority

> (1) If a participant in an authorised operation engages in unlawful conduct (other than unlawful conduct that is a controlled activity) in the course of the operation, the principal police officer for the operation may, within 24 hours after the participant engages in that conduct, apply to the chief executive officer for retrospective authority for the conduct.

[56] Ibid

> ...

> (5) Retrospective authority may not be granted unless the chief executive officer is satisfied:

> (a) that the following circumstances existed when the relevant conduct occurred:
>
> (i) the participant who engaged in the conduct believed on reasonable grounds:
>
> (A) that there was a **substantial risk** to the success of the authorised operation, or.
>
> (B) that there was a **substantial risk** to the health or safety of a participant in the operation, or any other person, as a direct result of the conduct of the authorised operation, or.
>
> (C) that criminal activity or corrupt conduct other than the criminal activity or corrupt conduct in respect of which the authorised operation is being conducted had occurred, or was likely to occur, and that there was a **substantial risk** that evidence relating to that criminal activity or corrupt conduct would be lost,
>
> (ii) the participant **could not avoid that risk** otherwise than by engaging in the relevant conduct,...

The section was amended in 2006.[57] The basis for amendment was to incorporate an additional limitation to retrospectivity – that of a requirement that the new event was not "reasonably foreseeable". That requirement imposed an apparently strict requirement for the grant of an exception to an existing warrant, which although expressed as a limitation on the grant of the authority, was expressed not as being sourced in the risk of abuse of power, but concerned with neutralising prosecutions through the exclusion of evidence:

[57] *Law Enforcement (Controlled Operations) Act Amendment Act 2006* (NSW)

Section 14 of the Act has been amended to allow retrospective authority for unlawful activity not addressed in the original controlled operations authority. The principal police officer, the person in charge of a controlled operation, may, within 24 hours of unauthorised conduct being engaged in, apply for retrospective approval for that conduct. Section 14(5) outlines the strict conditions under which a retrospective authority may be granted. For example, the authorising officer must be satisfied that the participant had not foreseen, and could not reasonably be expected to have foreseen, that the circumstances would arise, and that had it been possible to foresee that those circumstances would arise authority for the relevant conduct would have been sought. A retrospective authority is not intended to replace the normal application and approval process and it is expected that retrospective authorisations will be infrequently applied for. However, the new provisions will help to ensure that evidence of criminal activity is not later rendered inadmissible at court.[58]

The capacity for retrospective authority is a pragmatic and arguably necessary feature for police investigations. They are also an exception to the requirement that the controlled operation itself is prospectively authorised. This section is notably shaped by an explicit risk-based logic that is both internal and external. The internal risk logic concerns the shape of reasoning to be applied when an application is made. The external risk logic concerns the limitations imposed on that reasoning, with its requirement for reasonable foresight and the limitation on the activity that may be authorised, notably the prohibition against murder.

The Conduct of Controlled Operations

Controlled operations law is not only concerned with authorisation mechanisms, it also concerns attempts to structure and regulate conduct in the field. The conduct of controlled operations is governed by Part 3 of the LE(CO)A. This part does not, however, go into operational details, leaving such matters to the relevant police agency. The regulatory aim of the legislation is achieved through accountability mechanisms primarily concerned with reporting obligations and the extension of conditional immunities.

Operational accountability is attempted through mandating an approved code of conduct.[59] This code of conduct not only attempts to manage the various entrapment

[58] New South Wales, *Hansard*, Legislative Assembly, 8 March 2006, 21227 (Tony Stewart)

[59] *Law Enforcement (Controlled Operations) Act 1997* (NSW), s20

risks discussed in the previous chapter, it also attempts to manage the occupational health and safety risks to investigating officers. Indeed, it is clear that the drafting of the LE(CO)A involved input from the New South Wales Police Association on this specific point.

> *Before an agency will be able to access the protections provided by this legislation, it will be required to have in place a code of conduct. Codes of conduct for each agency must be approved by the inspector of the Police Integrity Commission, and will be included in the regulations.*

> *At all times operatives and other participants engaged in controlled operations will be expected to abide by the relevant code of conduct. The code is mandatory and will provide guidance for the professional conduct of operatives and participants during controlled operations. Aside from the operational accountability enshrined in this bill, regard must be given to the occupational health and safety risks faced by undercover officers.* ***In order to minimise risk****, authorising officers must be satisfied that operatives are properly trained and are not permitted to expose themselves to unnecessary risk of harm. Whilst on this point I note the Police Association's support for this bill.*[60]

The regulations prescribe that the code of conduct applies to all police agencies deploying controlled operations within New South Wales.[61] Fundamentally, the code of conduct is directed towards the management of the operational risks identified in the previous chapter. The code mandates that investigators must act in good faith,[62] have ongoing disclosure obligations,[63] must be properly briefed,[64] must comply with directives given by the officer in charge,[65] must provide all relevant information in required reports,[66] must report breaches of the code,[67] and must not engage in activities that amount to entrapment or incitement to commit an offence by a person not reasonably suspected of being likely to commit that crime.[68] In addition, the code specifically emphasises the duties and responsibilities of the officers

---

[60] New South Wales, *Hansard*, Legislative Assembly, 20 November 1997, 2324 (Richard Amery)

[61] *Law Enforcement (Controlled Operations) Regulations 2012* (NSW), r10

[62] Ibid, r1

[63] Ibid, r2

[64] Ibid, r3

[65] Ibid, r4

[66] Ibid, r6

[67] Ibid, r7

[68] Ibid, r5

involved, with references to breach of the code as being grounds for disciplinary action.[69]

Provided that the investigators conduct themselves within the scope of the warrant, the critical effect of that warrant, from an operational point of view, is to extend immunity from criminal[70] and civil liability[71] for undertaking controlled activities in the course of that investigation. As discussed in previous chapters, a controlled activity is an unlawful act undertaken in the course of unauthorised investigation. We have seen that investigators are not licensed to engage in any kind of crime, and may not engage in actions that involve homicide, sexual assault or serious damage to property. We have also seen in the last chapter that the extension of this immunity was one of the specific outcomes of the Ridgeway decision. Although risk is not specifically mentioned in any of the relevant sections, it is clear that the prospect of criminal or civil liability for state investigators was an unacceptable risk, if not outright danger to police.

Monitoring of Controlled Operations

The central anxiety attached to the extension of immunity evident in these transcripts was the question of abuse of power. The apparent solution to this problem was the construction of a system of accountability primarily achieved through systems of reporting, scrutiny, internal and external surveillance. Indeed, the controlled operations legislation was celebrated as a model of accountability by the legislature:

> *The distinguishing factor of this bill is its high level of accountability. This bill will ensure that undercover operations continue to be an effective investigative tool and one that is highly accountable...This legislation will be the benchmark for the regulation of undercover operations conducted by police agencies in Australia.*[72]

Internal reporting obligations are simply stated as being the requirement for the investigating officer in charge to provide a report to their superiors within 2 months of completing the operation.[73] At one level this is simply an

[69] Ibid, r8

[70] Ibid, s16

[71] *Law Enforcement (Controlled Operations) Act 1997* (NSW), s19

[72] New South Wales, *Hansard*, Legislative Assembly, 20 November 1997, 2324 (Richard Amery)

[73] *Law Enforcement (Controlled Operations) Act 1997* (NSW), s15

administrative aspect. At another level this has the function of imposing a specific obligation on the part of the officer to document, declare and attest to the substance of the operation. In so doing, the officer is identified and specifically linked, and their decision to authorise the operation becomes, of itself, enmeshed in an accountability process.

External accountability is achieved through the operation of civilian authority, the Ombudsman. The function of the Ombudsman is to provide an independent oversight of the agencies making use of the controlled operation in that State. The various powers available to the ombudsman, and its general duties, were also explained in Parliament:

> *In addition to the rigorous requirements for obtaining approval for a controlled operation, external accountability will be provided through oversight by the Ombudsman. Under clause 21, the Ombudsman must be notified within 21 days of all authorisations, variations and renewals. Authorising officers must also notify the Ombudsman of receipt of reports on completed operations made under clause 15. The Ombudsman must audit and inspect controlled operations of all agencies annually, and report to Parliament on the number of operations conducted, the type of criminal activity against which they were directed and the nature of the controlled activities in which they engaged. In addition, the Ombudsman has the power to make special investigations at any time, and to report any breaches of the legislation to Parliament by way of a special report.*[74]

The Ombudsman's power lies not in any statutory prosecution function, but in its ability to access the records of those agencies that make use of controlled operations, annual reporting, and through its ability to undertake a special investigation in its discretion. In addition, the Ombudsman has direct access to the relevant responsible Minister, and therefore to Parliament. This external scrutiny, with its ability to pass through the boundaries ordinarily erected by bureaucratic structures, is central to the accountability nexus. Although risk is not specifically mentioned in any of the statutory provisions, the internal and external mechanisms of scrutiny and surveillance function as a risk control device, primarily directed towards the fear of abuse of process, and control of it through scrutiny. At the same time this accountability mechanism also functions as a public statement of the control of the executive by the Parliament, and accordingly operates as a system of legitimation.

[74] New South Wales, *Hansard*, Legislative Assembly, 20 November 1997, 2324 (Richard Amery)

Conclusion

Controlled operations law is directly connected to questions of risk. In this context the relationship between risk and law is a complicated one. First, law is created and mobilised in *response to risk*. The risk of abuse of power by police agencies was recognised as a specific risk that required formal regulation. The rule system available through law was mobilised as a method of minimising risk and constructing a mechanism of accountability for the use of its power. Law and accountability intersect at this point. Secondly, law also functions as *a source of risk*. The discretionary application of rule systems and legalised forms of reasoning, combined with the pre-existent norms and rule systems in allied areas of law, can operate to create an environment characterised by uncertainty and sometimes manifest dangers. Finally, controlled operations law is also deployed as a mechanism that aims to *control risk* through creating systems of accountability, prohibitions, and compliance.

It is tempting, at this point, to settle upon risk as the main driving force behind the policy and doctrinal shape of controlled operations law. Certainly, risk plays a major role within the doctrinal structure of controlled operations law, and in the public policy discourses of Parliament. In later chapters we will see that risk in public policy has taken on a major role, and an intensive one, within the rationality of Western policy over the last 30 years. The proliferation of risk is well documented, and certainly the evidence within controlled operations discourse is consistent with that thesis. However, risk cannot be the only force shaping controlled operations policy and doctrine. While there is a strong relationship between risk, legality, and accountability within these discourses, the doctrinal architecture itself makes little mention of the relationship between the controlled operation and the expansion of surveillance and undercover policing practices that have been well documented in the legal literature. This is a mode of investigation that depends upon deceptive practices and surveillance for its execution. These discourses also fail to consider much deeper aspects of the legal system. Risk is just one discourse amid of cluster of discourses. In this respect doctrinal controlled operations law presents us with a *discursive unity*. This will be considered in more detail in subsequent chapters. For the moment, we now turn to the questions of accountability also embedded within these discourses.

References

Gageler, S. (2008-2009). Fact and law. *The Newcastle Law Review, 11*(1), 1–30.

McCormick, R. (2010). *Legal risk in the financial markets* (2nd ed.). Oxford: Oxford University Press.

Samuel, G. (2016). *Epistemology and method in law*. London/New York: Routledge.

Chapter 9
Discourses of Accountability

The princes both make high account of you.
[Aside] For they account his head upon the bridge.

Shakespeare, Richard III, Act 3 Scene 2

In the previous chapters the presence of a complex set of discourses connected with risk and necessity was identified and considered. These discourses have a powerful role in shaping policy and doctrinal law. The intersecting risks evident in parliamentary discourse appeared to be directed towards the justification for legalising and authorising unlawful activity for a designated purpose, with an associated shift in the presumption of admissibility of evidence. At the same time lawmakers remained uneasy about this form of power. It collided with a host of legal and liberal values concerning the limits on executive policing power and curtailing civil liberties. A solution was needed to address the problem. That solution was the invocation of another discourse: accountability. Attempts to justify these actions were based on two forms of reasoning: necessity and accountability. Accountability provided the answer to concerns about the abuse of power, while necessity provided the justification. Both accountability and necessity, in their combination, were intertwined with an imperative reasoning. In the first part of this chapter an examination of the role of accountability in shaping controlled operations law is proposed. The essential argument is that the doctrinal architecture of controlled operations law is profoundly shaped by questions of accountability, both as a claim and a mechanism. Drawing on governmentality scholarship, the second part of the chapter considers the role of accountability in its relationship with the controlled operation as the application of audit rationality to the problems arising out of the risks of abuse of power and the apparent lack of trust in police agencies. The "criminogenic population" being governed *includes* the investigator. The controlled operation, in this sense, becomes a framework through which the behaviours of investigators and suspects are rendered both intelligible and visible through retrospective examination and scrutiny. Accountability, as a rationality and technology of liberal governance, is imported into doctrinal law as a solution to the problem of risk.

B. Murphy, *Regulating Undercover Law Enforcement: The Australian Experience*, https://doi.org/10.1007/978-981-33-6381-6_9

Accountability

Accountability is critical to controlled operations policy. The accountability mechanism provides not only the political justification and the claim for legitimacy by government, it also provides a practical mechanism through which the apparatus of investigation can be implemented and maintained. Accountability in this context is mobilised against suspect populations. In this respect that has an "outward" and an "inward" focus. The outward manifestation is a mechanism through which a suspect population may be closely examined for the purpose of evidence gathering, arrest and collecting intelligence. The inward manifestation is a mechanism through which the activities of police agents may be scrutinised, both in terms of ordinary investigations and for integrity testing. Pragmatically, the layering of accountability mechanisms evident in controlled operations regulation makes it very difficult for corrupt or abusive practices to occur and in this respect the general absence of reported misuse of the controlled operations power outlined in the introduction attests to the success of the model. Controlled operations law is routinely celebrated by politicians as being a complete and successful model of a system of accountability that operates at the intersection of law, practice, and policy.

> *Having a statutory framework for controlled operations improves accountability and in fact makes it harder for corruption to occur ... We have a strong oversight mechanism in place.*[1]

> *Good law enforcement is a citizen's entitlement. It must be borne in mind that loss of confidence in law enforcement will lead governments to measures destructive of civil liberties. This is not such a bill. The choice before us is between a society prepared to accept balanced legislation to counter criminals, and a society poisoned by the conditions created by those criminals and their activities. The bill lays down a full and open system of accountability.*[2]

---

[1]Australian Capital Territory, *Parliamentary Debates*, Legislative Assembly, 3 July 2008, 3102 (Simon Corbell)

[2]Commonwealth, *Parliamentary Debates*, House of Representatives, 22 August 1995, 4 (Duncan Kerr)

The authorisation of breach of law does provide enormous potential for abuse. There is a strong argument to increase the accountability provisions to prevent this. This may be done by extending the information concerning the controlled operation to be provided to Parliament.[3]

This is a discourse that offers assurance. It is an antidote to risk. It is a model that carries with it the latent threat of legal consequences for abuses, with an equally powerful but latent statement that surveillance is continual. Detection is likely.

One of the paradoxes of controlled operations law and practice is the provision of power that undoubtedly carries with it the potential for its abuse, while at the same time recognising that this same power has a distinct public benefit in its capacity to open crime and concealed criminal networks. This paradox is reflected in complex and at times contradictory statements by lawmakers:

It is worth pointing out that if we are to have any hope in bringing narcotics traffickers to justice, we have to give police adequate powers. The way to prevent corruption is not to deny police these powers; it is to build in effective accountability mechanisms and safeguards against abuse of powers. Nobody who supports this bill could possibly be claimed to be supporting a system that will condone any police officer abusing the powers that they have.[4]

The accountability demands within Parliament recognise that the empowerment of the police, which is, in fact, an armed organisation within the state, requires careful management and control that is not only practical but also symbolic and political. For it is well recognised that the authorisation of a controlled operation operates at the conceptual limits between the rule of law and paramilitary activity. Consequently,

... [w]e have seen a number of bills passed through the Senate recently which have been designed to expand the powers of police agencies. We Democrats have approached such legislation with considerable caution. We believe that the Australian people need protection not only from lawbreakers but also from law enforcers. Some of the legislation that has emerged this year has flirted with granting arbitrary power to police agencies. We believe that the powers of such agencies should be limited to what is reasonably necessary to conduct their operations and should be subject to proper accountability regimes to ensure that the powers are not abused.[5]

---

[3] Commonwealth, *Parliamentary Debates*, House of Representatives, 22 August 1995, 9 (Philip Ruddock)

[4] Commonwealth, *Parliamentary Debates*, House of Representatives, 27 May 1996, 1160 (Amanda Vanstone)

[5] Commonwealth, *Parliamentary Debates*, Senate, 27 August 2001, 26,632 (Brian Greig)

One of the key points of disagreement in discussions with the government over this legislation has been the provisions relating to controlled operations .... In such cases, it is clear that officers properly discharging their duties should not be liable to prosecution, despite the fact that they are technically engaged in illegal activity. It is also clear that evidence gathered in proper investigations of this nature should not normally be excluded in court on the basis that it was gathered in the course of an operation involving police criminality. However, there also ought to be restrictions on the extent to which police agencies can break the law in investigating offences. These agencies must be subject to the rule of law along with the rest of the community.[6]

The contradiction and concern for the protection but appropriate balancing of public interests produces a keen interest, and at times distinct eloquence, among lawmakers when presented with the problem of law enforcement and the limits of the controlled operation:

We have a piece of legislation here that extends the powers of the police quite extensively. There are controls such as those from the Ombudsman, who is to look at the way these controlled operations are to be carried out, but clearly there is concern in this area. We are all made up of forces of light and dark. When the forces of light are working, we are very good as police people – if I can use that in a generic sense again and use that term in the sense of the community acting through their police officers, through their police authorities – but, at the same time, there are all sorts of real problems with powers of the sort that we are going to give our police authorities here, and we have to make sure that they are properly controlled. It is appropriate that Parliament make laws giving powers but, at the same time, put tests around those powers which must be met before the powers are exercised. In that way we get good police, we get a good society and we go forward as a community.[7]

---

[6] Commonwealth, *Parliamentary Debates*, Senate, 27 August 2001, 26,632 (Brian Greig)

[7] Commonwealth, *Parliamentary Debates*, Senate, 27 August 2001, 26,640 (Barney Cooney)

The concerns surrounding the dichotomy of public interests police and liberties, and the demands for effective methods of investigations are not just at the level of government- these are concerns from a range of voices recognised as authoritative across the legal profession, particularly those non-government organisations representing the legal profession as an independent class:

> *One of the major concerns that we have with this particular legislation has been raised by a number of organisations, including the Lawyers Reform Association and the new Ridgeway Coalition, a group of interested specialist legal practitioners representing the criminal law committees of the New South Wales Law Society, New South Wales Young Lawyers, the Law Council of Australia and representatives of the Criminal Bar Association, the New South Wales Public Defenders, the New South Wales Council for Civil Liberties, the New South Wales Society of Labour Lawyers, the Lawyers Reform Association and the Australian Chapter of the International Commission of Jurists. I am sure that if the minister were in the House he would recognise the very considerable reputation of all those organisations which have joined together to make submissions on this matter. The bill proposes that senior police officers may authorise the commission of a serious offence without the safeguards of judicial oversight. There is no independent mechanism by which these decisions will be oversighted under the legislation that is proposed by the government.*[8]

The essential substance of the legislation is the attempt to reconcile the competing demands for police on the one hand with expectations and demands for civil liberties on the other. It was in the context of this discourse that accountability and risk merged as distinct concerns mobilised as *techniques* within practice and legislation. The solution to the tensions identified by lawmakers and commentators was to construct a legislative "double movement" (Polanyi 2001) that effectively authorised unlawful activity while entrenching techniques of accountability – a dynamic that imports distinct rationalities of risk and audit into doctrinal law.

The Techniques of Account

Questions of accountability in controlled operations discourses manifest in five major ways: (i) processes of authorisation; (ii) reporting obligations; (iii) the specific identification of individuals at every point of the controlled operations web;

---

[8] Commonwealth, *Parliamentary Debates*, House of Representatives, 22 August 1995, 9 (Philip Ruddock)

(iv) the imposition of restrictions on activities through legal and regulatory provisions; (v) a system of systematic scrutiny by individuals who are, ostensibly, unconnected with the operation itself. These techniques of account make controlled operations one of the most tightly controlled forms of law enforcement within the apparatus of state. It need also be observed that the question of accountability manifested in Hansard is by no means the only mechanism used as a technique of account in this context. Parliament itself has capacity to intervene and hold police agencies to account in a variety of ways, not the least through its ability to functionally eliminate an organisation by removing its finance and its statutory constitution. In addition, the courts play a major role in the supervision of activities, at least in the post operational period, as does the media. However, Parliamentary discourse in the present context is fundamentally concerned with these five dimensions of the techniques of account.

Authorisation

Authorisation is a requirement for legality. It is a precondition for the broad immunities provided by the legislation. The fact that controlled operations must be authorised, prospectively and sometimes retrospectively, simply means that if investigators or their proxies seek to engage in unlawful activities outside the existence or scope of a warrant they lose the protection that might be available under the legislation, and accordingly are placed at risk of criminal and/or civil liability. The requirement for authorisation is a specific component of the rationality of accountability. The existence of authorisation, with its attendant limitations, is a specific aspect of the logic of accountability and audit. In effect, authorisation functions as a risk distribution mechanism.

> *The second component of the bill is the lawful authority to engage in unlawful conduct within the boundaries of the decision to authorise a controlled operation. Protection from criminal or civil liability only applies if the conduct falls within the authority provided to the operations; if the conduct does not amount to inducing a person to commit an offence; and if the conduct does not involve the risk of causing death or serious injury, or the commission of offences against the person of a sexual nature.*[9]

But the authorisation that is required in this context is not simply an authorisation that might otherwise be available through an experienced or senior officer.

[9] Australian Capital Territory, *Parliamentary Debates*, Legislative Assembly, 3 July 2008, 3101 (Simon Corbell)

Authorisation for a controlled operation is located at the apex of the organisation. It is an authorisation that lies close to the personal manifestation of the executive power of the agency itself. The power of authorisation is located within only a few specific and identifiable individuals within the senior levels of agency.[10] Typically, the claim to authorisation at the most senior levels of the investigation agency is presented as a reassurance. The location of authorisation at senior levels within the organisation (and sometimes external to it), in practical terms, creates a dynamic where junior and intermediate level officers necessarily come to the attention of their commanders at any time if a warrant to conduct a controlled operation is applied for. At the same time the process of authorisation also enlivens an accountability dynamic on the part of the authorising officer, who is compelled to demonstrate that the authorisation process was a rational one and properly suited to the investigative task. The logic of account extends itself beyond the applicant, to include the person(s) granting the warrant.

Reporting

The administrative apparatus of the controlled operation produces three forms of knowledge. The first relates to the collection of evidence connected to a suspect that either confirms or contradicts the suspicion that the person is involved in crime or corruption. The second relates to the collection of criminal intelligence, both general and specific. The third relates to the provision of administrative information concerning the nature of the operation itself. All three forms of information are required and tied to the reporting obligations fixed to the controlled operation. The process generates a substantial amount of documentation and information, both informal and formal. Within the context of the operation itself, a register is kept of all warrants issued, which includes the details of the application, the decision concerning the warrant, the operational limitations, a report on the execution of the warrant, in addition to other forms of reporting related to the collection, provision and distribution of criminal intelligence, and that information that may make its way into a prosecution brief to be put before a court of law. Fundamentally, however, the statutory reporting obligations relate to the use of the controlled operation itself. Reporting provides the mechanism through which information, and knowledge, about the controlled operation may be retrospectively examined by those in authority. Such information is both specific to a particular operation and general, relating to the use of the operations as a police device more generally.

---

[10] This location is not uniform. In Queensland the power to authorise a controlled operation is vested in the Controlled Operations Committee – a select body that includes retired judges. It also includes the Commissioner of Police. In this case personality is divided between the agency deploying the operation and external members. See *Police Powers and Responsibilities Act 2000* (Qld), Chapter 11, Part 2

The elaborate character of reporting obligations, and its relationship with the discourse of accountability, is particularly well explained by then Attorney General for the ACT, the Hon. Simon Corbell:

> *The third component of the bill is the accountability of each and every controlled operation. Within 2 months after the completion of every controlled operation, the officer in charge of the operation must provide the chief officer with a report about the operation. The report must articulate the nature of the controlled conduct exercised during the operation, details of the outcome, the nature, quantity and transmission of any illicit goods involved and details of any personal injuries or damage to property occurring as a direct result of the operation.*

> *The chief officer, in turn, must provide my office and me—or the appropriate minister—with a report every year which includes: reporting on the number of operations authorised; the criminal activities targeted by the operations; the nature of the controlled conduct used in the operations; the nature, quantity and transmission of any illicit goods involved; details of any personal injuries or damage to property occurring as a direct result of the operation; and any arrests and prosecutions arising from the operations. In turn, the responsible minister must table a copy of the report in the Assembly within 15 days of receipt.*

> *The chief officer, in addition, must register every application made under the bill, every authorisation made under the bill and details of the completion of every operation. The bill also empowers the Ombudsman to inspect the records made under the bill and requires the chief officer to give the Ombudsman any assistance required by them. In summary, the overarching theme of the bill is accountability and clear lines of authority to engage in a controlled operation.*[11]

In this example reporting is expressed as an imperative; a requirement attached to every operation. Time is asserted as a part of the reporting obligation. The content of each report is standardised through statutory imposition and the bureaucratic

[11] Australian Capital Territory, *Parliamentary Debates*, Legislative Assembly, 3 July 2008, 3102 (Simon Corbell)

knowledge systems of the organisation. The report functions as retrospective surveillance of an operation that the supervising authority is otherwise unable to directly observe in the absence of audio-visual technologies. Accountability is a manifestation of authority – augmented through the power of reporting.

Discourses within Hansard concerning reporting imply that the physical manifestation of the report is paper, or an electronic representation of paper. It is important to note that reports are fundamentally a record of information, and in the present era may take a number of forms that may include digital sound and visual recordings, images, biochemical information, and digital signs and symbols.

The purpose of the report is fundamentally concerned with providing a record of individual activity over time. Being specifically attached to a particular individual, in time and space, produces a historical archive of activity, which in the present context is primarily concerned with ensuring integrity of action. Integrity of action extends to both the investigator and the investigated, as well as the integrity of the authorisation process. In the context of authorisation, the historical archive is concerned with ensuring that the decision to issue the warrant was rational, and in accordance with the statutory requirements. That is, a justified and evidence-based decision. In the context of the investigator, the historical archive is interested in documenting the activities of the investigator are falling within the scope of the warrant, the general law, and the ethics of police. In the context of the investigation this historical archive is interested in documenting those activities that may be corrupt or criminal in nature, as well as that information that may be classified as criminal, and possibly military grade intelligence.

The existence of reports provides a mechanism whereby the activities of the individual identified within them may be examined for any number of purposes. Reporting is essential to accountability because in most cases the examination of legality is not contemporaneous with the event. In complex bureaucratic and politico-legal systems reporting provides the only means by which activities may be retrospectively examined. This is particularly the case when the examination concerns covert and secret activities of individuals and agencies with experience and expertise in remaining out of the public eye. Such systems necessarily involve the individual making the report being aware that they may, at some future point in time, be asked to explain the contents of the report. In the context of controlled operations, the authorising officer and the investigating officer makes these reports knowing that their purpose is for examination. This examination takes place within a hierarchy of authority. The investigating officer reports to their senior officer; the senior officer reports to the responsible Minister; the responsible Minister reports to Parliament. In addition the controlled operations architecture also contains a mechanism whereby reports may be examined and scrutinised by a third party agency, such as the Ombudsman.

Of particular note is the fact that the individual identified with the report may, on the one hand, be the subject of praise or congratulations for their work. On the other, a central purpose of the report is to identify the individuals responsible for when things go wrong. The attribution of blame and the identification of responsible individuals is a central purpose of the controlled operations report, and this is certainly a consideration in the requirement for reporting in cases of controlled operations.

> *I think it is very important to have a system in which responsibility rests with the person who makes a decision. When it comes to whether or not a particular police operation is to be commenced, the decision is one in which we would expect the blame for any failure to be attached to that person responsible for taking the decision.*[12]

> *An officer who sought to deal in narcotics outside the course of duty would face the normal penalties from narcotics trafficking. Federal police officers are already subject to a strict a disciplinary regime. Australian Federal police officers, who will play the leading role in most operations, are subject to disciplinary and criminal penalties for misconduct under both the AFP act and the AFP disciplinary regulations. AFP officers are employed on contract and can be summarily dismissed in cases of misconduct. Authorising operations will be the responsibility of the dozen most senior officers in Federal police. If operations are improperly authorised or as narcotics go astray, responsibility will be brought home to these officers at the very highest level of police.*[13]

The focus on reporting is not simply one that is concerned with attributing blame for failures that might manifest in the course of an operation. The major focus, in fact, is concerned with the prevention of the abuse of power through the existence of a mechanism that identifies specific individuals involved in particular controlled operations activities.

There are expectations that records are kept, particularly in cases where urgent or retrospective applications have been made:

> *We must be extremely vigilant and ensure that proper records are kept. If at any time the rules are not followed, the most severe and comprehensive punishment should be imposed.*[14]

[12] Commonwealth, *Parliamentary Debates*, House of Representatives, 22 August 1995, 76 (Duncan Kerr)

[13] Commonwealth, *Parliamentary Debates*, House of Representatives, 27 May 1996, 1160 (Amanda Vanstone)

[14] New South Wales, *Parliamentary Debates*, House of Representatives, 17 November 1999, 3132 (Andrew Tink)

Ironically, reporting obligations carry with them no actual enforcement provisions. Simply put, it is not an offence to fail to make a report under any of the controlled operations statutes. The only disciplinary mechanisms that exists, outside of the internal censure of the organisation using the controlled operation, are the formal statements made by those external agencies charged with scrutinising the operation. These are, in fact, quite rare, but were evident in the early life of the controlled operation in NSW, when the Ombudsman made numerous observations about the failure of police to comply with the timeliness requirements under the Act.[15] Indeed, the failure to comply with administrative reporting timeframes appears to be the only significant, ongoing criticism that tends to appear in the reports on controlled operations scrutineers.

Identification

Perhaps the most significant aspect of the discourse of accountability in controlled operations debates and law is its association with identification. Individual identity is a core component of the controlled operation at every level. Identity emerges at three critical junctures; (i) the identity of *the authorising officer*; (ii) the identity of *the investigating officer*; (iii) and the identity of *the suspect*. Identification in this respect has an internal and an external component. The internal component involves the interaction between the officer making an application for a controlled operations warrant, and the authorising officer – both of whom are specifically identified through the retention of information relating to the warrant. Locating the source of authorisation at the senior levels of the organisation (either through statutory nomination or through a restricted delegation), imports an organisational gravity within the application process, which of itself is regarded as part of the "rigour" of process. At the same time, from an administrative point of view, the location of authorisation powers at the senior level of the organisation also creates a distinct administrative burden for that officer, which resulted in amendments in NSW as early as 1999[16] to delegate the power to authorise controlled operations. However, even in that case delegations remained strictly limited to senior officers within the organisation, and carried with it the same demands for constant vigilance. In the case of Queensland, the identity of the authorising officer is fractured. In that case the Commissioner of the QLD Police is the initial point of contact for the application,[17] prior to its referral

[15] New South Wales Ombudsman (2007). In this report, then Ombudsman the Hon. Bruce Barbour stated "The major issue of non-compliance with the requirements of the Act is the same as reported in previous years –the failure of Principal Law Enforcement officers to provide a report on the results of the operation to the chief executive officer within the 2 month statutory time frame, despite the failure to do so being a breach of the Code of Conduct. In many cases the delegate does not date the report when received and this adds to the difficultly in ascertaining compliance." (p.11)

[16] *Law Enforcement (Controlled Operations) Amendment Act 1999* (NSW), Sch 1 [23]

[17] *Police Powers and Responsibilities Act 2000* (Qld), s239

to the Controlled Operations Committee[18] – the membership of which varies over time, but necessarily includes the Commissioner as a standing committee member. In this case decision-making is not an individual act, but rather a part of a collective elite, which is intended "to safeguard the process".

> *The bill sets out a rigorous process for authorising controlled operations. In the case of police, a controlled operation may be authorised only by a senior officer of or above the rank of commander ... The senior officer must be satisfied in regard to a number of key controls and safeguards.*[19]

> *The bill seeks to extend the authority to approve controlled operations to the rank of superintendent, as is the case in South Australia. This improvement will relieve the impossible demand on the commissioner to process all applications for controlled operations while extending authority to ranks that have sufficient seniority and the best knowledge of daily operations within their areas of command. Naturally, the extension of the authority from one officer to some hundreds of officers will require careful monitoring and ongoing vigilance.*[20]

As these examples illustrate, individual identity is critical – and what is central in examination is the behaviour of a nominated individual at a juncture determined by statute. For the authorising officer it is the integrity of the decision to authorise. For the investigator it is the integrity of the investigation. For the suspect it is the integrity of conduct filtered through the legal lens of crime and corruption.

Beyond the discourses within Hansard, identification is a central component of doctrinal forms within legislation, forming an essential part of the *required particulars* in any application for a controlled operation, in every jurisdiction. These requirements reveal that particulars concerned with identification are both essential and complex. In short, identity is not just concerned with the mere formality of administration: identity is critical to the investigative apparatus, not only of the actors involved, but also the localities and the activities the subject of the investigation. The process of ***identification and naming*** is a critical aspect of the rationality of the controlled operation, for it provides the legal and conceptual map in which the scope and surface of control is marked and conceptualised. Without this process

---

[18] *Police Powers and Responsibilities Act 2000* (Qld), s240

[19] Western Australian, *Hansard*, Legislative Assembly, 18 August 2011, 6223c-6227a (Rob Johnson)

[20] New South Wales, *Parliamentary Debates*, House of Representatives, 17 November 1999, 3682–3 (Michael Gallacher)

of individuation and categorisation, the legal apparatus supporting the controlled operation would be inoperable. As outlined in the following diagram, a crucial aspect of the technique of accountability involves the explicit identification of the complex institutional and legal context in which the controlled operation takes place. Identification is central in holding all parties, and institutions, responsible for their actions – and critical for the application of surveillance technologies, for without identification the practice of scrutiny is compromised.

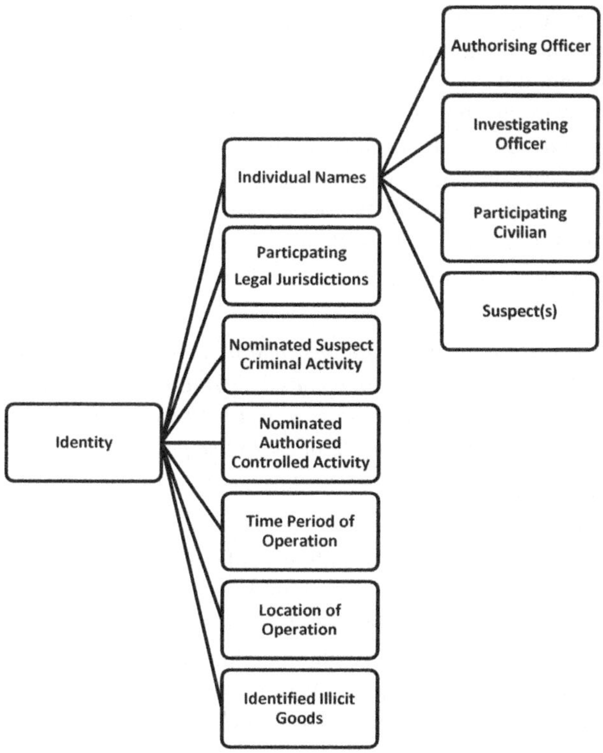

It is through the practice of identification of individuals, localities, jurisdiction and even time that the rationalities of account, surveillance and biopower are articulated – a technique that applies not only to the suspect, but also the investigator. Indeed, this technology is applied to the most senior officers of the organisation as mechanism of power. As examined in Chap. 6, part of the rationale for locating the authorising decision at the apex of the various organisations is concerned with risk management. Part of the rationality of individuation of authorisation is undoubtedly the containment and prevention of intersecting risks identified in that chapter, but also an assurance of accountability through the identification of personnel responsible for the authorisation an execution of the warrant. Accountability, as a discourse, is fundamentally linked to the identification of precise individuals, their actions and a legal and normative comparison. Individual identity is critical to the accountability apparatus of controlled operations, for it is in locating the individual within the surveillance grid that is central to the exercise of the comparative rationalities of law and the disciplinary and biopolitical technologies of governance.

Limitation of Action

Given that an evaluation of action is central to the discourse of accountability, it is no surprise that a legal and normative discourse and structure exists within the law that determines not only the quality and character of decision making, but also the scope and limits of the behaviours undertaken within the operation. Controlled operations law and regulation provides a range of limits over conduct. Those limits include the ordinary law, operating outside the scope of the warrant, as well as the internal disciplinary processes of the agency, and the statutory limits within controlled operations architecture. It is clear that controlled operations law and practice, as the name suggests, is a tightly controlled and highly managed process.

> *In real terms, this means that officers must be constrained in the laws which they can break in the course of their duties, and it also means that the process by which they are authorised to engage in illegality is rigorous and protects the community against the granting of excessive power.*[21]

Limitation of action provides a public declaration of the scope of legitimate activity. A "limited" breach of law is acceptable and justifiable in the circumstances. As observed in the opening chapter, one of the functions of the controlled operation is to transform a breach of law into an application of it. As we will see in Chap. 11, this transformation occurs through derogation from established legality and absorption of the unlawful into the lawful. That mechanism is legitimated and secured through the observance of strict limitation of action. Accountability is based upon the principle that only actions falling within the scope of the law attract the immunities and exceptions available. While individual identity is essential for locating the person responsible for the controlled operation, limitation of action functions to identify the limits of lawful conduct. It constructs the legal space in which the limits of the lawful and the unlawful are inscribed. In this respect limitation of action is connected with accountability as a trigger for closer scrutiny of conduct, with a view to identifying conduct which falls outside of the protections available at law. In this respect accountability is concerned not with identification of the subject, but with identification of action. Here accountability is revealed as involving both legitimation of action through a discourse of limitation, as well as a construction of

---

[21] Commonwealth, *Parliamentary Debates*, Senate, 27 August 2001, 26,632 (Brian Greig)

legality. Consequently, while much of the actual doctrinal architecture is concerned with systems of accountability through scrutiny, specific components of the legislation are concerned with limitation mechanisms that serve a political and pragmatic function by constructing the scope of legality.

Scrutiny

As discussed above, controlled operations law contains complex reporting obligations. Reporting is intended to provide capacity for scrutiny through identification and subordination to increasing levels of authority. In this respect reporting and scrutiny may be distinguished as two distinct but related conceptions – reporting is the technical transformation of events into a form that may be examined. These practices and conceptions are inseparable. Without scrutiny reporting is simply a process of archiving, and essentially redundant. However, both practices are mutually exclusive and arguably more effective when operating concurrently. The relationship between reporting and scrutiny is no accident. It is specifically contemplated by Parliaments. Scrutiny is the practice that gives accountability its essential mechanism. Without the capacity, and perhaps the threat, of scrutiny the identification of individuals and their associated reporting obligations and activities would be ineffective. Indeed, there is a distinct tendency in the critique of controlled operations to demand greater levels of scrutiny:

> *Perhaps more can be done using these record-keeping and accountability provisions to ensure that there is ultimately better scrutiny by the Parliament of the controlled operations contemplated by this bill.*[22]

> *Most importantly the bill will provide a framework of accountability and control which will ensure that the Attorney General (as the responsible Minister), the Parliament and the community have the opportunity to scrutinise the usage of this power by police agencies.*[23]

The capacity to scrutinise is regarded as a major, if not essential, accountability mechanism that on the one hand carries with it the potential for discovering the abuse of power, as well as preventing that activity. In part the reason for the

[22] Commonwealth, *Parliamentary Debates*, House of Representatives, 22 August 1995, 9 (Daryl Williams)

[23] Commonwealth, *Parliamentary Debates*, Senate, 8 May 1996, 469 (Charles Kemp)

expectations and demand for scrutiny is the manifest danger said to be attached to police that is not subject to the oversight of civilian authorities and Parliament.

> *... because controlled operations allow police operatives – sometimes working undercover under assumed identities – to themselves break the law, we have taken the position that they should be strictly managed and never lightly undertaken. With inadequate supervision, they present dangers to both police agencies and to innocent citizens and they provide fertile ground for corruption.*[24]

The *essence* of controlled operations law and practice may be summed up as a technology of scrutiny. Scrutiny is the mechanism of account *par excellence*. It is the practice through which crime and corruption is uncovered; it is the practice through which evidence is obtained; it is the practice through which the assessment of legality of activity and its legitimacy is established.

In summation, the controlled operations policy framework is shaped by a discourse of accountability. Accountability is not a singular concept but constructed through a series of intersecting conceptions sourced in a system of beliefs and ideas at the core of Western liberal rationality. The relationship between controlled operations and accountability is well understood in the existing legal and political literature. What is not so clear is the relationship between the conception of accountability itself and its manifestations within doctrinal law. The discourses concerning controlled operations examined during this research clearly indicate that the relationship between accountability as a concept and doctrinal law is a complicated one, which profoundly shapes the architecture of the law itself. Accountability is mobilised as a specific set of legislated practices and normative declarations that permit for an evaluation of conduct at multiple levels. The idea that an individual is held to account for their actions looms large in this context. But what is associated is the idea of individual identification, and evaluation of specific behaviours and decisions, and the idea that those decisions and behaviours are worthy of protection or sanction. These behaviours and decisions, conversely, may only be held to account through detection. And it is detection that is a major component of the controlled operation as an investigative apparatus. This examination confirms what many within the social sciences have been arguing for close to 30 years, that accountability has taken on a major role in the rationality of governance, and ultimately within legal architectures itself. At this point it is prudent to turn to the question of what role accountability plays within late modernity, and the nature of accountability as a rationality of governance.

[24] Commonwealth, *Parliamentary Debates*, Senate, 27 August 2001, 26,628 (Nick Bolkus)

Accountability as Discourse of Governance in Late Modernity

It is no surprise that accountability is a strong discourse in controlled operations policy and law. Accountability features prominently in the rationalities of liberal governance, and has been recognised as forming a strong component of the rationality of governments since the 1970s (Mulgan 2003). Of course, concerns over the limits and extent of government action is no stranger to law, and indeed the limitation and correction of government action is a central part of the evolution of law, particularly in the common law tradition which has always had a care for holding power to account. The difference, however, is that accountability as a concept, like risk, has emerged as a powerful and dominant discourse in recent history. It is a discourse that features strongly in liberal rationality, and in the present context accountability is invoked as a concept that structures the reasoning and ultimately the doctrine associated with much of controlled operations law and policy. Audit and accountability is a central part of the rationality of late modernity.

Accountability, like most concepts, has a variety of meanings, but tends to be invoked both as a virtue and as a mechanism of governance (Bovens 2010; Braithwaite 1999). The concept of accountability has become so widespread that it is now recognised as being deeply embedded in Western culture, and has assumed a dominant role in the audit cultures and rationalities of organisations (Gibbon and Henriksen 2012; Strathern 2000). Indeed, accountability is seen as an essential part of any form of auditing and risk control process, forming a distinct knowledge system operating internationally as a system of "supreme standards" for transparency and accountability applicable to business and government (INTOSAI Professional Standards Committee 2010). This relationship between linking individual identity and microanalysis of conduct and rationality through comparative analysis of action measured against statutory minimums is a part of the growing neoliberal practice of "responsibilization", an entrenched feature of control and risk societies (Dean 1992, 2010; O'Malley 1996; Steele 2004).

As an ordinary concept, accountability is defined as:

> *The quality of being accountable; liability to account for and answer for one's conduct, performance of duties, etc. (in modern use often with regard to parliamentary, corporate, or financial liability to the public, shareholders, etc.); responsibility.*[25]

The word itself is a composite noun, drawn from "account" and "ability", referring to the quality of being held to account, or able to be accounted. There is a term with dual meaning, one associated with the language of economics, and the other associated with blame, scrutiny and duties. The word appears for the first time in the English language in 1750, and has retained, more or less, the same meaning.

Accountability, as a concept, is more nuanced than the ordinary meaning suggests. Mulgan's analysis of accountability models argues that there are four types of accountability: (1) Political; (2) Legal; (3) Managerial; and (4) Professional.

[25] OED Online – 27 December 2019

Political accountability tends to focus upon the decisions and behaviours of actors within institutions, with a focus upon actions, decisions and public statements of belief and opinion. Legal accountability tends to focus upon the application of specific rules in formal settings, principally concerned with compliance and the quality of application within that setting and its impact upon the subject. Managerial accountability, on the other hand, tends to focus upon the quality of supervision and the associated processes and outputs within organisations, strongly connected with cost/benefit reasoning. Finally, professional accountability tends to focus upon the behaviours, decisions and public statements of belief and opinion through comparison with a closed group of peers, especially in the deployment and use of specialised skill and training. In other words, the nature of accountability as a concept depends upon the context in which it is used, which ultimately shapes the focus of analysis, which may be concerned with finance, compliance with declared norms and rule structures, processes, outputs, questions of efficiency, or a combination of all (Mulgan 2003).

In the context of controlled operations, accountability appears to be focused on issues of legal accountability. That conclusion, however, is misleading because the accountability nexus in this case involves all of the categories identified by Mulgan. Questions of accountability arise in the political context, relating to both government and the relevant policing organisation. They arise, explicitly, in the extent to which the operation itself is compliant with the legal architecture. They arise in a managerial context within the organisation, analysed both internally and externally. And finally, questions of accountability arise in the context of the assessment of professional behaviours within the police organisation. In this way accountability is a complex web of governance, manifested in its strongest form as a legal architecture that demands compliance. That demand is enforced through a system of internal and external scrutiny. Fundamentally the primary vehicles of accountability within the controlled operations legal architecture are concerned with surveillance and the attribution of responsibility to specific individuals within the organisation. The combination of surveillance and responsibility undoubtedly functions as a powerful vehicle for restricting and limiting the potential for the risk of abuse of process identified. Risk is tightly connected to questions of accountability, which is also connected to the legal architecture of the controlled operation and the wider rationalities of liberal governance related to policing.

Prenzler (2013) conceived accountability as a relationship based on two simple mechanisms: performance and conduct. These mechanisms take on a particular aspect when the circumstances involve three further elements – a grant of power, the assumption of responsibility, and discretion in the application of that power. In this context there is a delegation of power and action, in which the party delegating power is unable to be physically present when the power is being exercised – consequently there is an associated demand for ensuring appropriate conduct. Prenzler argues that a "full accountability process" involves six steps:

1. *Delegation of a task*
2. *Articulation of performance measures*

3. *Disclosure of work done*
4. *Reward/punishment depending on quality of the work*
5. *Repair when work is inadequate*
6. *Reform to prevent future failings* (Prenzler 2013)

In addition to these steps in a generic model of accountability, Prenzler also argues that the basic method to "make people accountable" is essentially behaviourist: a system of sanctions and rewards. The goal is for the execution of a task in the manner intended, and in a manner consistent with the ethical qualifications attached to that activity. Prenzler suggests that criminal justice, as a "subset of government", is necessarily subject to demands for accountability by simple virtue of its power as a feature of executive government. This demand arises because policing is a "high risk" occupation, providing significant opportunities for abuse of power, corruption and "just cause" deviance (Prenzler 2013).

In the context of controlled operations law, the investigation is the delegated task. Performance measures arise on the one hand through the statutory limits of the law, and on the other hand through the performance measures of the organisation – ordinarily, operational success, undetected collection of valuable criminal intelligence, and the collation of sufficient admissible evidence to secure an arrest and conviction. The processes of reporting and scrutiny, both internal and external, functions as the disclosure element of the model. Rewards and sanctions are available through the availability or removal of the immunities available under the legislation. The "repair" and "reform" aspect of the model operates not only at the micro level of the investigation, through feedback into the methodologies of the investigation and the internal discipline of the organisation, but also at the macro level through the activity of the legislature in altering law to correct deviations and failure causes by legal architectural defects. In this respect the design of controlled operations law, policy and practice fits neatly into the model proposed by Prenzler.

The demands for accountability of police are not unique to the controlled operation. Indeed, by the time the legal architecture governing the controlled operation had become consolidated in Australia there was a strong discourse, in law and politics, for police accountability in Australia and internationally (Den Boer 1997; Dixon and Smith 1998; Dixon 1999; Chan 1999; Braithwaite 1999; Seneviratne 2004). As identified earlier in this thesis, the controlled operation and its legal architecture emerged in a period following a series of public enquiries into police corruption, a focus upon drug interdiction, and policing across borders. Significant issues had been identified in a series of Royal Commissions relating to the abuse of power by police, and the corrupting effects that drug crime tend to cause within police and the public more generally.[26] The idea of accountability of the police began to emerge in the 1970s and consolidated in the 1980s. By the time controlled operations law and policy appeared architectures and mechanisms for the accountability of police agencies had been established, based upon a web of mechanisms that involved in

[26] Eg: Commonwealth of Australia et al. (1983); Stewart (1986); Wood (1997)

internal and external surveillance, the evolution of statutory and common law rules governing evidence, liability, and police powers. The relationship between police and the discourse of accountability had been established prior to the controlled operation becoming part of the investigation apparatus.

Conversely, the architectures concerned with accountability of police activity also involves a function concerned not only with the limitation of action, but with its opposite: the empowerment of police activity. Broadly, legal and regulatory systems concerned with the powers of police authorities serve to empower and authorise a range of activities, while simultaneously limiting them. This empowerment function is sometimes overlooked, and indeed the legal architecture relating to police investigative powers is far more significant in its empowerment dimension than its limitation dimension. Without the empowerment dimension the activities involved in most forms of investigation would be unlawful, and in the context of controlled operations that is certainly the case. The defining feature of a controlled operation is the lawful authorisation to commit an act that would otherwise constitute an unlawful act. In addition, the legal architectures that empower and authorise a police activities also serve to institutionalise a set of norms and values within the legal system, which has the function of the legitimating the legal architecture and the norms associated with them.

This dynamic was recognised by Morgan and Yeung (2007), who conceptualised legal rules as part of a complex web of regulation in which legal architectures are directly connected with the political practices within which that legal system is constituted. In this environment legal rules, as doctrinal law, have a facilitative and expressive role. Law facilitates those instruments that directly shape behaviour, normally achieved through creating systems that operate as a threat for breaching declared norms, while simultaneously creating a space in which the quality of action may be examined and spaces created that allow for individuals to conduct themselves freely. Law functions to give expression to norms and values by organising and declaring the limits, if any, of certain forms of activity.

In this way the dynamic operating within the accountability structure of controlled operations law and policy can be understood not only as erecting a system of limitation on action, but simultaneously erecting a statement of norms and values and an associated legitimacy within the legal and political spheres. Part of the process of legitimation and the ordering of norms, I would suggest, is the entrenchment of individual responsibility, systems of identification, and the elaborate mechanisms of internal and external surveillance within controlled operations law and policy. Accountability serves as a rhetorical device on the one hand, but also as a clear statement of practices contained within the law itself. Indeed, accountability, in its political form, could not be achieved without accountability in its legal form.

Accountability is a rationality – a way of evaluating, measuring and intervening. It is both rationality and technology. It is a rationality of governance. The relationship between accounting, rationality and governance has been examined by a number of governmentality scholars, notably Feeley and Simon (1994), Miller & Rose

(Miller and Rose 1990; Rose 1999b; Miller 1990), and Power (1994). In effect, the practices of audit so useful in business and economic management over time colonised public policy. Drawing on the work of Power, Rose has argued that the power of audit "derives from its capacity to act upon systems of control themselves". In that case, Rose was referring to financial audit of organisations, but recognised that "Audit … is the control of control." (Rose 1999a) Control is achieved by not only the practice of scrutiny of minutiae; it is also achieved by articulating process and the intellectual schemata in which that scrutiny takes place. It is achieved by articulating a system of norms through which comparisons may be made. It is achieved by erasing the informal social mechanisms of trust that have long constituted traditional structures of governance and behaviour and replaced it with a technology of "mistrust", which entrenches and amplifies suspicion. In the context of audit, the threat of legal sanctions overlaps with the practices of the audit. In that case audit and its associated rationality is augmented and formalised, and becomes an enforceable threat that marks out the intellectual grid in which decisions and practices must be made (Rose 1999a).

In the last chapter it was clear that the invasive power available through the controlled operation, and its concurrent immunity was a source of anxiety for lawmakers. The risk of abuse of power, and the evidence of police corruption that had emerged in recent public enquiries were strong indications that the power itself was not trusted. The question of risk and the absence of trust were problems for which the audit was offered as a solution. The architecture of controlled operations law is fundamentally concerned with articulating a mechanism and regime concerned with the audit. Accountability in this context is achieved through the articulation of a knowledge system that attaches identity to behaviours, practices, and specific individuals. It is a knowledge system that articulates a system of norms through which comparisons may be made for the purposes of establishing legality. The legal structure of the controlled operation becomes both a tool concerned with evaluating legality, as well as a practical device for ensuring accountability. If Rose and Power are correct, controlled operations law becomes a framework through which control at a distance can be achieved.

This dynamic rests, fundamentally, upon two concepts that may be examined further. Accountability rests upon two aspects of power identified by Foucault, one concerned with a pervasive surveillance and the other concerned with the self-regulation achieved through the dynamic of biopower. Accountability rests upon the triad of the identification of specific individuals, scrutiny of their behaviours, and the threat of sanctions for deviations outside of expectations. In the context of controlled operations law, a significant part of the architecture of the law itself is concerned with the identification of specific individuals and the articulation of a set of norms and expectations concerned with the scope and limitations of conduct. Identity and expectations become the subject of systems of internal and external scrutiny of behaviour and decisions made in the course of the operation. In this way a large part of the intention and formal structure of law concerned with controlled operations is about the inscription of accountability is a technology of conduct. To draw on an expression used by Rose (1999a), the accountability discourses enmeshed in controlled operations law and practice construct a grid of visibility which renders the activities of the investigator, and the suspect, visible and comparable.

Conclusion

At this stage it remains tempting to conclude that risk is the ultimate discursive force driving and governing controlled operations law and policy. Risk triggers demands for accountability, and accordingly we find the controlled operation, as a legal architecture, importing risk and accountability as governing rationalities merging as a system of governance. Risk discourses saturate the debates within Parliaments concerning controlled operations. Those debates are enlivened because of the demands for effective methods of the investigation of crime and corruption, and the difficulties arising in that undertaking. In turn, the problems associated with the admissibility of evidence questions of criminal and civil liability arising out of the actions of investigators while conducting a controlled operation are effectively neutralised by the architecture of controlled operations law. In so doing the risks to prosecution presented by the legal system are minimised, or at least brought into alignment within the acceptable range of risks that a tripartite system of government and law normally presents to the conduct of the executive.

But there is something more involved - something deeply embedded and far from obvious. That something more, it appears, is connected to much deeper conceptions of power, knowledge and rationality. The controlled operation, as an investigative apparatus, is a powerful investigative device that has a disciplinary effect on suspect populations, mobilises a significant surveillance and executive gaze, and is constructed through particular conceptions and discourses that are not unique to the controlled operation. The controlled operation, as a practice of investigation, is a technology of power and a rationality of governance importing and bringing together discourses of risk, accountability within a legal space saturated with liberal conceptions of legality and right. While risk is a governing rationality within the architecture of controlled operations law and policy, risk and accountability are only one aspect of a more complicated grid of reasoning that crystallises in the socio-legal space of controlled operations law and policy. In the next part of this thesis we turn to these larger epistemic questions. Here we reach the limits of legal reasoning and thematic description. The conceptual and analytical space that is required must move beyond the doctrinal analytic and move into a deeper consideration of risk, episteme and ultimately questions of sovereignty and the status of the subject.

References

Bovens, M. (2010). Two concepts of accountability: Accountability as a virtue and as a mechanism. *West European Politics, 33*(5), 946–967.

Braithwaite, J. (1999). Accountability and governance under the new regulatory state. *Australian Journal of Public Administration, 58*(1), 90–94.

Chan, J. (1999). Policing culture. In D. Dixon (Ed.), *A culture of corruption* (pp. 98–137). Sydney: Hawkins Press.

Commonwealth of Australia, New South Wales Government, Queensland Government, & Victorian Government. (1983). *Royal commission of inquiry into drug trafficking*. Canberra: Australian Government Publishing Service.

Dean, M. (1992). A genealogy of the government of poverty. *Economy and Society, 21*(3), 215–251.

Dean, M. (2010). *Governmentality: Power and rule in modern society* (2nd ed.). London: Sage.

Den Boer, M. (Ed.). (1997). *Undercover policing and accountability from an international perspective*. Maastricht: European Institute of Public Administration.

Dixon, D. (1999). Issues in the legal regulation of policing. In D. Dixon (Ed.), *A culture of corruption* (pp. 36–68). Sydney: Hawkins Press.

Dixon, B., & Smith, G. (1998). Laying down the law: The police, the courts and legal accountability [1]. *International Journal of the Sociology of Law, 26*(4), 419–435. https://doi.org/10.1006/ijsl.1998.0075.

Feeley, M., & Simon, J. (1994). Actuarial justice: The emerging new criminal law. In D. Nelken (Ed.), *The futures of criminology* (pp. 173–201). London: Sage.

Gibbon, P., & Henriksen, L. F. (2012). A standard fit for neoliberalism. *Comparative Studies in Society and History, 54*(02), 275–307.

INTOSAI Professional Standards Committee. (2010). *Principles of transparency and accountability*. Copenhagen: International Standards of Supreme Audit Institutions.

Miller, P. (1990). On the interrelations between accounting and the state. *Accounting, Organizations and Society, 15*(4), 315–338. https://doi.org/10.1016/0361-3682(90)90022-M.

Miller, P., & Rose, N. (1990). Governing economic life. *Economy and Society, 19*(1), 1–31.

Morgan, B., & Yeung, K. (2007). *An introduction to law and regulation* (Law in context). Cambridge: Cambridge University Press.

Mulgan, R. (2003). *Holding power to account: Accountability in modern democracies*. Basingstoke: Palgrave Macmillan.

New South Wales Ombudsman. (2007). *Law enforcement (controlled operations) act annual report 2006–2007*. Sydney: NSW Ombudsman.

O'Malley, P. (1996). Risk and responsibility. In A. Barry, T. Osborne, & N. Rose (Eds.), *Foucault and political reason* (pp. 189–207). London: UCL Press.

Polanyi, K. (2001). *The great transformation: The political and economic origins of our time*. Boston: Beacon Press.

Power, M. (1994). *The audit explosion*. London: Demos.

Prenzler, T. (2013). *Ethics and accountability in criminal justice* (2nd ed.). Toowong: Australian Academic Press.

Rose, N. (1999a). *Powers of freedom*. Cambridge: Cambridge University Press.

Rose, N. (1999b). *Powers of freedom: Reframing political thought*. Cambridge: Cambridge University Press.

Seneviratne, M. (2004). Policing the police in the United Kingdom. *Policing and Society, 14*(4), 329–347.

Steele, J. (2004). *Risks and legal theory*. Portland: Hart Publishing.

Stewart, D. (1986). *Royal commission of inquiry into alleged telephone interceptions* (Vol. 1). Canberra: Australian Government Publishing Service.

Strathern, M. (Ed.). (2000). *Audit cultures*. London: Routledge.

Wood, J. J. (1997). *Report of the royal commission into the NSW police service*. Sydney: New South Wales Government.

Part III
Theory and Beyond

Chapter 10
Beyond the Boundaries of Risk

Risk: A possibility, chance or likelihood of harm, hazard or loss. A person is at risk when or she is exposed to danger, peril or injury.

Butterworths Concise Australian Legal Dictionary

Risk Everything.

Nike Marketing Slogan (http://www.nike.com/us/en_us/c/football/riskeverything (20 May 2014) (At the time of publication, this marketing campaign had concluded, and the site no longer contains 'risk' as a focus.))

The preceding chapters argued that controlled operations law and policy is governed by risk discourses. Risk was also identified as a complicated web of intersecting concepts. Risk is an intellectual grid that influences and dictates the structure of doctrinal law. Risk discourses saturate controlled operations debates in Hansard, providing justification and the impetus for mechanisms used to control and contain risks arising out of authorised crime. Risk is a multifaceted and dominating discourse surrounding and penetrating law and policy. This present chapter considers risk as a doctrinal rationality in late modernity. The argument is that risk is a social, historical, and intellectual phenomenon with a pervasive effect on public policy, directly shaping law. The controlled operation, properly understood, is not simply an investigations technique – it is a risk technology that depends on a distinct network of knowledge systems. This chapter considers the nature of risk as a rationality embedded in the psyche of Western government and the fabric of jurisprudence, first by considering the role of risk in Australian law, then by considering the nature of risk as an interdisciplinary theory, its links with crime control, and finally as a distinct rationality.

B. Murphy, *Regulating Undercover Law Enforcement: The Australian Experience*, https://doi.org/10.1007/978-981-33-6381-6_10

The Role of Risk in Australian Law

The materialisation of risk in public policy will come as no surprise to social theorists. Risk is an entrenched concept. However, the intersection between risk and law is still in its infancy, although already an important field of emerging legal scholarship, at least in Europe (Priest 1990; Baldwin 1997a, b; Giddens 1999; Steele 2004; McCormick 2004, 2010; Mahler 2007, 2010; Susskind 1998, 2008; Febbrajo 2009; De Giorgi 2009), but has yet to clearly surface in Australian legal scholarship. The idea of "legal risk" and the explicit consciousness of risk in legal theory is a recent phenomenon, despite that fact that risk has always played a major role in law as a knowledge formation (Giddens 1999). Risk has successfully colonised public policy, and in so doing, has been instrumental in transforming law into a primary vehicle for risk management. As observed by Susskind, the effect is profound – shifting the focus away from regulation and problem solving (as reactive activity), towards risk management (as proactive activity) (Susskind 1998). But the effect of risk goes beyond orientation to practice. It extends to reconfiguring the substance of doctrine. Ashworth (2006) expressed serious concerns that risk is shaping criminal law in ways that undermine its rights-based principled core, a concern shared by Ericson (2007) whom, as we observed earlier, argued that risk is a major driver in the manifestation of *counterlaw* – laws designed to act against law by creating exceptions to laws that frustrate law enforcement, which also tend to entrench surveillance practices. This is certainly the case, but it is incorrect to assume that legal scholars are unaware of the role of risk in jurisprudence. Althaus (2005) argues that those who engage in regulation are acutely aware of risk, deploying risk in a particular way, in accordance with its own knowledge system. Legal theory is mainly focussed on the pragmatic intersection between law and risk – especially the attribution of responsibility for the consequences of risk, and the overlap between compliance, public liability, and insurance. Legal scholarship is less concerned with theoretical nuances, and more concerned with the internal rule systems that construct and determine risk and the ways those systems regulate behaviour. This doctrinal perspective is where the bulk of literature on law and risk is located, at least in the UK, the US and Europe. Legal scholarship channels risk in a pragmatic direction and appears to accept risk as a given. Theoretical questions are left to other disciplines. This orientation to risk is entirely consistent with the practical orientation of law as an applied discipline. The problem is that it tends to conceptualise risk as applied pragmatism, an approach that struggles to recognise the complexities of risk as a social, ontological, and epistemological phenomenon. In this part I present a more detailed discussion on risk as a concept, and how it plays a major role in contemporary social life, and why it has such a powerful effect on law and policy.

Risk Shaping Controlled Operations Law?

Hansard suggests that controlled operations law is directly shaped by risk in complex ways. First, the prohibition against entrapment, connected to anxieties about abuse of power and rights infringement, is manifested formally and informally. Authorisation requires the authorising officer to prospectively evaluate the methodology to be used during the course of the investigation, and is required to disapprove an investigation based upon entrapment. In this respect entrapment is not an offence as such, but it is grounds for the refusal of a warrant. By implication the requirement that an authorisation not be given in an entrapment case suggests that even if entrapment actually manifests itself in the course of the operation, such activity may well invalidate the operation itself by compromising the warrant. Retrospective assessment of entrapment takes place when the prosecution is brought before a court. Allegations of entrapment, discussed previously, may well be the basis for the termination of proceedings through a stay order, exclusion of evidence, or reduced sentence on the conviction of the offender.

Second, concurrent with assessment of the methodology, authorisation requires risk assessment of the occupational health and safety of officers, informers, and the general public. Again, there is a requirement to demonstrate minimal levels of acceptable risk on the part of investigators in order to satisfy the authorising officer of the merits and legality of the operation. Here the authorisation requirements within the legislation are directly tied to risk.

Third, the controlled operation, and its legal architecture, presents itself as a multi-layered system of surveillance. The target is under surveillance. The officers involved are under surveillance. The authorising officer is under surveillance. The organisation deploying the controlled operation is also under surveillance. And, arguably, Parliament is under the surveillance of the public. Surveillance is presented as a central mechanism through which accountability is achieved. This relationship between accountability and surveillance will be discussed in more detail in a later chapter, but it is undeniably the case that the accountability provisions within the Act are directly tied to risk. Accountability, as rationality and technology, is mobilised by risk.

Fourth, the question of criminal and civil liability arising in the course of a controlled operation is ostensibly dealt with through the existence of immunity and indemnity clauses contained within legislation. The risk of liability is simply removed. However, like many aspects of law in this field, if the operation is undertaken in the absence of lawful authority, or conducted in a way that the mandate is exceeded, lawful authority may be removed, which invalidates the statutory immunities and indemnities. The duality of immunity is a manifestation of risk. On the one hand the immunity removes the risk of prosecution; and on the other the conditional status of that immunity addresses the risk of abuse of power. A double movement is at work; the availability of an immunity at the same location where potential liability exists. Risk is here mobilised as a device to demand legality.

Finally, the risk of prosecution evidence being inadmissible is addressed by the existence of a provision that declares that evidence obtained during a controlled operation merely because it was obtained during a controlled operation. Closely connected to this are routine statements that the existence of that statutory provision does not alter the judicial discretion over evidence. Consequently, evidence obtained during a controlled operation may still be held to be inadmissible, possibly based on it being unlawfully obtained, despite the existence of the declaratory clause. Again, the mechanisms of risk are directly connected with controlled operations legislation.

Risk in Australian Law

We have considered the role of risk in broad terms in Australian legislation in Chap. 7. We know that risk devices are not unique to controlled operations law. Indeed, risk plays a significant role more generally. What is not clear is the extent, or whether this is a recent phenomenon. There are no studies in Australian scholarship that track the rise and substance of risk as a distinct feature of legal doctrine. Indeed, there are virtually no studies that embark on tracking the rise of risk within law. The exception is a single study in Sweden (Sjoberg et al. 1998). This study confirmed that risk has taken on a major role in legislation in that country, particularly since the 1990s. That is a dynamic that appears to be evident in Australia. In 2014, a simple Boolean search of the well-known Australian legal database Austlii[1] reveals in excess of 41,000 instances of "risk" in Australian legislative instruments, ranging from private health insurance,[2] to gene technology,[3] to road transport.[4] In June 2020, the same search revealed over 54,000 instances of "risk" in Australian legislative instruments.[5] Of particular note is the place that risk has assumed in criminal law. Risk is quickly assuming a major role in the management of people in custody, being critical to the availability of parole for offenders and suspects. Instructive examples include the *Crimes (High Risk Offenders) Act 2006* (NSW). The objects of this Act are:

> *...to provide for the extended supervision and continuing detention of high risk sex offenders and high risk violent offenders so as to ensure the safety and protection of the community...[and] to encourage high risk sex offenders and high risk violent offenders to undertake rehabilitation.*[6]

[1] www.austlii.edu.au

[2] *Private Health Insurance (Risk Equalisation Levy) Act 2003* (Cth)

[3] *Gene Technology Act 2000* (Cth)

[4] *Road Transport (Mass, Dimensions and Loading) Act 2009* (ACT), s110

[5] This represents an increase of 32%.

[6] *Crimes (High Risk Offenders) Act 2006* (NSW), s3

Central to this assessment is the classification of a person as "high risk". These terms are largely defined as "a high degree of probability that the offender poses an unacceptable risk".[7] A similar assessment mechanism can be seen in the recently enacted *Bail Act 2013* (NSW). In this Act the determination of bail *must* consider the existence of an "unacceptable risk" in the determination of bail. An "unacceptable risk" is determined by an evaluation that gives primary consideration to whether:

> *an accused person, if released from custody, will:*
> *(a) fail to appear at any proceedings for the offence, or*
> *(b) commit a serious offence, or*
> *(c) endanger the safety of victims, individuals or the community, or*
> *(d) interfere with witnesses or evidence.*[8]

This focus is wholly objective and concerned with public risk. The risk the offender may pose to themselves is of secondary importance.[9]

Risk not only plays a major role in procedure – it also plays a central role in tort through the "risk calculus" contained in *Wyong Shire Council v Shirt*.[10] Indeed, risk may well be the critical concept in the law of negligence. Broadly, "Shirt" involved questions of liability for a water-skier who suffered serious injury when he fell off his skis at speed. The water at that point was shallow, despite the apparent existence of a sign reading "Deep Water". The injured skier brought an action in negligence against the relevant council. Central to this action was a question about whether the injury was "foreseeable". In this context the perception of likely future injury was critical to the determination of negligence. The awareness of future injury is fundamental to risk, and the failure to act on that knowledge is critical to the question of negligence. In his synthesis of common law authority to that point, Mason J set out a series of proposition that have profoundly shaped the law of negligence:

> *A **risk** of injury which is quite unlikely to occur....may nevertheless be plainly **foreseeable**. Consequently, when we speak of a risk of injury as being "foreseeable" we are not making any statement as to the **probability** or improbability of its occurrence, save that we are implicitly asserting that the **risk** is not one that is far-fetched or fanciful. Although it is true to say that in many cases the greater the degree of **probability** of the occurrence of the **risk** the more readily it will be perceived to be a **risk**, it certainly does not follow that a **risk** which is unlikely to occur is not **foreseeable**.*
>
> *In deciding whether there has been a breach of the duty of care the tribunal of fact must first ask itself whether a reasonable man in the defendant's position would have **foreseen** that his conduct involved a **risk** of injury to the plaintiff or to a class of persons including the plaintiff. If the answer be in the affirmative, it is then for the tribunal of fact to determine what a reasonable man would do by way of response to the **risk**. The **perception** of the reasonable man's response calls for a consideration of the magnitude of the **risk** and the degree of the **probability** of its occurrence, along with the expense, difficulty and*

---

[7] *Crimes (High Risk Offenders) Act 2006* (NSW), ss5B, 5E

[8] *Bail Act 2013* (NSW), s17

[9] *Bail Act 2013* (NSW), s17(3)(j)

[10] (1980) 146 CLR 40

> *inconvenience of taking alleviating action and any other conflicting responsibilities which the defendant may have. It is only when these matters are balanced out that the tribunal of fact can confidently assert what is the standard of response to be ascribed to the reasonable man placed in the defendant's position.*
>
> *The considerations to which I have referred indicate that a* ***risk*** *of injury which is remote in the sense that it is extremely unlikely to occur may nevertheless constitute a* ***foreseeable risk****. A* ***risk*** *which is not far-fetched or fanciful is real and therefore* ***foreseeable****. But, as we have seen, the existence of a foreseeable risk of injury does not in itself dispose of the question of breach of duty. The* ***magnitude of the risk and its degree of probability*** *remain to be considered with other relevant factors.*[11]

As can be seen, the "Shirt Calculus" is saturated with the rationalities of audit, responsibility, and risk. It provides an excellent example of the modes of analysis deployed by risk rationality and is fundamentally involved in the process of the attribution of responsibility (and costs) associated with risk, uncertainty and danger. In setting out a system of reasoning the common law must remain sufficiently adaptable to accommodate the infinite combination of events that may come before the courts. But in doing so, this reasoning exemplifies a dynamic that is a recurrent feature of the intersection of law and risk: risk is conceived in terms of quantifiable objects and events, tied to probabilistic reasoning. The statutes and the common law provide a significant intellectual framework that *identifies* the subject as possessing inherent "risk qualities", the *calculus* used in that reasoning, and the *authority* for intervention. Not only that, law (particularly statute) provides the mechanisms for the logic of the exception, outlined in more detail in Chap. 11. This aspect of law is grounded in material realities. Risk-based regulation is intended to prevent future events, in the full knowledge that past failures have been the source of a variety of social harms. In a real sense risk-based reasoning in law operates with a view to deterrence as much as correction. As these examples suggest, there are complexities to the determination and assessment of risk. What does risk actually mean?

The Anxieties and Rationalities of Late Modernity

Risk is a combination of fact and fiction. It involves the intersection of material events and ideas, resulting in a concept involving subjective and objective characteristics. These dimensions are historically contingent. Accordingly, risk and its social significance are linked to large and small scale social and historical changes. Scholars attuned to questions of social transformation recognise that the traditional institutions that have characterised western societies since the seventeenth century are changing. These changes have a material, social and intellectual character. The nation state, family networks, class, race, capitalist exchange, culture and geography are all in the steady process of evolving. Social theorists described this as a shift

[11] (1980) 146 CLR 40 at 47–48

from *modernity* to *late modernity* (Young 1999; Giddens 1990; Garland 2001), or sometimes *postmodernity* (Harvey 1989; Bauman 1992; Reiner 1992). There is little doubt criminal law and procedure is profoundly shaped by these changes (Norrie 2001). Controlled operations law is undoubtedly affected by this evolution, and accordingly we need to consider the location of this form of law in its global and epistemic context.

The historical transformation manifests itself physically and intellectually. There is an essential relationship between social, material change and intellectual change, including law. The relationship between intellectual, material and historical forces was central to the Marxist conception of history (Marx 1970; Marx et al. 1972), and more recently by Giddens (1990, 1999) and Beck (1992). The gist of the theory is that the transformation of western societies is largely based on material and intellectual shifts linked to the development of productive economic forces and practices associated with the expansion of capitalist economies. These changes unleash significant productive capacities. The associated technologies, productive forces and ideologies assert a hegemonic place in global markets, which, in turn, results in interconnected economic, political and demographic transformation. Giddens, for example, conceives modern national political and social organisation along four axes: (i) the active facilitation and maintenance of capitalist economics; (ii) the promotion of industrialism; (iii) state monopoly over violence and its domestic suppression; and (iv) supervision and information reflexivity as a central feature of government. The facilitation of capitalist economy involves the regulation of a competitive labour market and the expansion of new and existing markets. Industrialism involves creating systems of reward and processes that maximise capital gain and the extraction of surplus value, increasingly achieved through technological innovation, labour efficiencies and wage controls/reduction. State monopoly over violence provides the minimum conditions for capitalist exchange to evolve, and for the expansion and stability of markets and social life. Consequently, a monopoly over the exercise of force has internal and external dimensions. Police provide the necessary internal force and the maintenance of order, while the military is mainly concerned with the external. The fourth dimension – supervision and information reflexivity – primarily involves a complex system of social practices fundamentally concerned with surveillance and the evolution of population knowledge systems. Law is fundamental to each of these developments, and accordingly laws are necessarily influenced by and connected with social and historical change. These changes also produce a variety of intended and unintended consequences, notably a breakdown in traditional familial and social networks, the rise and expansion of bureaucratic organisations increasingly reliant on expert systems of knowledge, and a continuous demand for information and feedback. As societies change, so does law.

Giddens and Beck argue that one of the effects of these changes is the creation and expansion of collective anxieties and uncertainty, as the old social networks that provided a shared sense of security, identity and trust is undermined by repaid social change. Social life is placed under stress in the absence of a shared sense of trust and identity among population groups, which increases personal and familial anxiety about the present and the future, while also increasing a sense of suspicion of others.

In addition to the traditional forms of security being transformed and altered, common symbols and values are displaced, which escalates social anxieties. Accordingly, social life becomes acutely sensitive to objects, people, and events that threaten an ever-decreasing sense of stability. Contemporary life is subject to instabilities both internal and external. Historically, it was primarily external threat and uncertainty that was a source of anxiety and instability. Individuals, families and their communities could normally rely upon the stability and replication of these basic institutions for the resilience needed to react to threat and uncertainty. The nature of contemporary social change is such that the traditional sources of resilience are growing unstable, as they take on a new form.

In this context, Giddens and Beck suggest that risk assumes a key position in social life. Public policy increasingly extends itself to addressing increasing demands for the detection, control and management of uncertainty, risk and threat. Political and social life becomes sensitised to identifying and responding to a variety of threats and uncertainty. In this context risk assumes a key role in public policy in a variety of ways. First, when the intensity and consequence of an identified risk is unacceptable. Second, when the consequences of that risk proliferate. Third, when a new risk emerges out of artificial environments or human intervention. Fourth, when risk-based environments become institutionalised. Fifth, when knowledge formations reach the point that a risk that was previously unknown becomes identified, with its associated gap in knowledge. Sixth, when the knowledge of risk becomes collectively distributed. Finally, when expert knowledge systems become incapable of managing, anticipating or conceptualising risk. Giddens argues that these dynamics are inevitable by-products of capitalist development. In other words, as capitalism evolves and unleashes its productive capacities it simultaneously transforms those populations bound to it. These processes, and the role of risk within it, enables complex social and economic systems to survive and expand, but conversely intensifies actual and perceived risks in public consciousness. So much so, this dynamic now has global reach. Loader and Sparks (2007), for example, observe major international trends connected to these changes in modernity, including the rise and domination of conservative and neoliberal government, promoting market-based rationality and the rhetoric of individual freedom, changing economic, social and cultural patterns centred around economic dependency on consumer economies, the associated reconfiguration of family structure in order to adapt to this environment, global urbanisation, the exponential growth of media and telecommunications technologies, and the increasing "democratisation" of social relations, based on changing conceptions of obedience to authority and a levelling of social status.

Associated with social and physical transformation is an intellectual transformation. Risk not only operates as an externalised source of threat and uncertainty, risk transforms knowledge formations. Karl Marx, for example, recognised this link in his *Contribution to the Critique of Political Economy*, (Marx 1970) arguing that the consciousness of humanity was inextricably linked to the social and historical conditions of the age, later suggesting in *The German Ideology* that the dominant systems of thought in every epoch was the constellation of ideas and rationalities of the ruling classes (Marx and Engels 1974; Marx et al. 1972). When risk and accountability are considered as manifestations of knowledge formations emerging out of late modernity, the transformative effect of ideas, their connection with law through legislation, and their augmentation as specific rationalities within law and regimes of practice, sourced in knowledge systems outside of any single discipline, suggests that Marx was right, at least on this point – a fact that is important to note given that the shadow of Marx lies within the work of Foucault and Agamben, examined in more detail in the next two chapters.

In summation, the sociological literature argues that the major social and intellectual foundations of Western civilisation are in a state of transformation. That change is bound to the power of capitalism as a material and intellectual historical force. The benefits and hazards of capitalism not only shape and reconfigure ordinary social life, it also influences ways of thinking about the management of social life, the role of government, and brings with it new anxieties and a centring of risk in public consciousness. This is the broad historical moment in which law generally, and controlled operations law specifically, is located. The desire to give effect to ideas of human freedom carries with it the need for mechanisms to respond to aberrant uses of that freedom. The materialisation of risk brings with it the demand for legal architectures intended to regulate, react to, and prevent risk. In the context of criminal law, legal mechanisms include an emphasis on surveillance and targeted investigation, with associated mechanisms for punishment, deterrence, and the protection of civil society. When the controlled operation is considered as a specific example, it is clearly influenced by the dynamics of late modernity. The model was born out of a global shift in surveillance and proactive policing techniques. This literature suggests, fundamentally, that legal architectures are influenced not only by the material conditions of society, but by its intellectual conditions. It is these intellectual conditions that assume a particular importance in doctrinal study, because this literature suggests that the controlled operation, and its associated legal architecture, is entrenched in a rationality concerned with risk, crime control and strategies of governance.

Risk Theories

Risk is a term used in a variety of ways for different purposes. It is a concept with a surprising degree of complexity, deployed across the spectrum of formal knowledge systems. Risk is an interdisciplinary or transdisciplinary concept best understood as an ontological and epistemological system of thought rather than a distinct theory or belonging to any one discipline (Adams 1995; Althaus 2005; Thompson 1986). Rothstein et al. (2006) observed that risk has been very successful as a colonising form of knowledge. Consequently, risk is covered by an extensive scholarship, importing both theoretical and pragmatic dimensions. Risk is not, therefore, a singular theoretical model. Risk theory is a diverse federation of theoretical positions, broadly concerned with the effect of risk consciousness in contemporary social life.

Theories of risk place different emphasis upon different aspects of risk, ranging from pragmatic risk management, through to anthropological and sociological studies, and even to the idea of risk as governance. The significance is that each discipline tends to view risk in different ways, incorporating risk and uncertainty as concepts and practices into its own knowledge systems to achieve different ends. Quite simply, risk means different things to different people, and is deployed for different purposes, even though there is a tendency to refer to risk as a singular concept with a simple meaning. Althaus (2005) has persuasively mapped out a typology of risk, adapted in the following table:

Discipline	Risk Object	Orientation of Knowledge
Logic & Mathematics	Risk as calculable phenomenon	Calculations/ Probabilities
Science & Medicine	Risk as objective realities	Principles, Calculations, Probabilities
Anthropology	Risk as cultural phenomenon	Culture/Ritual
Sociology	Risk as social phenomenon	Social constructions
Economics & Business	Risk as decision making; a means of securing wealth and avoiding loss	Decision-making principles
Law	Risk as fault, conduct and a judicable event	Rules/Rationality
Psychology	Risk as behaviour and cognitive process	Cognition
Linguistics	Risk as concept / language	Terminology and meaning
History	Risk as story	Narrative
The Arts (literature; music; poetry; theatre)	Risk as emotion	Emotion
Theology	Risk as an act of faith	Revelation
Philosophy	Risk as conceptual problematic	Logic; Truth; Phronesis

Adapted from Althaus (2005: 569)

Althaus argues that each discipline has something to offer in the understanding of risk and tends to excel in its field of knowledge – but clearly recognises that risk cannot be understood wholly through the prism of a single knowledge formation. As discussed later in this chapter, this aspect of risk is a marker of its role in a larger *epistemic grid.*

As these knowledge formations arise out of intellectual and social practices, it is useful to approach risk through a sociological lens. In his analysis of the social theories of risk, Zinn (2008) argues that risk theories are a sociocultural phenomenon, largely discursive, and formed within particular social networks. Consequently, the concept of risk varies depending upon one's location and disciplinary orientation. In the English tradition risk is primarily conceptualised as a feature of modernity, popularised in the work of Giddens (1990) and Beck (1992, 1999, 2007). Continental theorists, in particular the Germans, emphasise Beck's risk society, but are also strongly influenced by systems theory and the work of Luhmann (1993). By contrast, North American scholars tend to favour cultural and anthropological accounts of risk, such as Douglas and Wildavsky (Douglas and Wildavsky 1982; Douglas 1990, 1992). In Australia, it appears that the social theoretical risk literature follows the English tradition, but tends to favour Foucault's governmentality scholarship, more recently articulated by Dean (2010) and O'Malley (1998, 1999, 2004, 2005). Zinn's observation on the sociocultural and discursive aspects of risk is focussed on social theories of risk, but the insight is likely to be equally valid when the same analysis is applied to other formations concerned with risk. Law, for example, tends to follow the knowledge systems that result from the interplay between local statutory frameworks and the doctrine of precedent. In the Anglophone legal tradition, the reasoning of other common law systems tends to influence local decisions – consequently the discursive and sociocultural aspects identified by Zinn in social theory are clearly evident in law.

Wholly sociological accounts of risk need to be understood cautiously. It appears that much of the risk literature is pragmatic, rather than theoretical. 'Risk pragmatics' is primarily focussed on safety, legal compliance, and investment. This orientation to risk is less concerned with theorising risk, and more interested in decision-making and management. Pragmatic approaches sit comfortably within the Economic & Business class of risk theories identified by Althaus (2005). Within this body of literature, a clear methodology has evolved, to the point where the technique of risk management is now an international standard (ISO3000). The techniques of risk management contained within that standard are replicated in most risk publications. Risk management techniques essentially pass through four phases: (1) Identification; (2) Evaluation; (3) Intervention; (4) Monitoring & Feedback (International Standards Organisation 2009; Standards Australia 2004, 2007). These approaches are undoubtedly useful and offer a practical and simple approach to decision and action. It is this model of risk that dominates "pragmatic" risk literature.

As a concept risk is deceptively simple. Risks are threats to interests, present and future. Risks are also the impact that these threats have on human reasoning, behaviour, and decision-making. The concept is nothing new. Human beings have been making decisions incorporating risk for centuries (Kemshall 2007). What is significant for risk theorists is the proliferation of risk-based reasoning that has taken place globally since the 1970s. It appears that risk has moved beyond being a simple factor in individual or collective decision-making. Risk is now become a dominant force in the late twentieth and early twenty-first century in public policy. It has become a central component of economic and political reasoning. Societies can no longer be characterised along the old lines of race, class, geography, gender, and elites. Contemporary societies are as much about the control, distribution, and allocation of risks as they are about the material conditions that constitute those societies. Risk must be conceptualised as a combination of material event and associated rationality that has extended to become part of contemporary human civilisation. This is the world of risk society.

Beck coined the term "risk society" (*risikigesellschaft*) in his influential work on risk (Beck 1992, 1999, 2007). As outlined above, Beck argued that the transformation of industrial society in the late twentieth and early twenty-first century brings with it new forms of production that not only create material benefits and prosperity, but also material risks that straddle the social, political and intellectual life of advanced capitalism. The intensity of many risks, nuclear, environmental, and economic, has now assumed a global dimension. The breakdown and transformation of traditional social networks and the conscious individualisation of responsibility in the post Keynesian era creates an environment where reflexive risk analysis becomes a personal and political necessity in order to predict, contain and respond to manifest threats and uncertainty. Late modernity is not only about the transformation of society, it is also about the proliferation and distribution of risk. Risk society, in effect, is a reference to that state where populations and their governments employ reflexive risk analysis as a central part of personal and collective decision-making, and actively engage in risk allocation practices.

Dictionary definitions of risk simply refer to the idea of risk as being exposure to a hazard or danger. The *Macquarie Dictionary* defines risk as "exposure to the chance of injury or loss; a hazard or dangerous chance", while the *Oxford English Dictionary* contains a similar reference to chance and danger – but also indicates the word appears in English from 1621, with its origins in French (*risqué*) and Italian (*risio*). An earlier Latin word (*risicum*) imported notions of gambling and opportunity, while an even earlier Greek word (*rhiza*) referred to navigation hazards. These distinctions should not be overlooked. For risk, in one context, can present itself as something undesirable, in another an avoidable danger, while in another context represents an opportunity. This latter meaning of risk is often overlooked by models that focus on the consequences and undesirable aspect of risk. The identification of an object as "risk" allows for informed decision making, mitigation, and, in some cases, significant benefit. Risk is a positive as much as a negative thing. Indeed, Knight argues that the awareness of risk, and the strategies devised to deal with them, marks the transition from a life conceived as fate and divine will, to life conceived as purposeful and rational. The appearance of risk as a concept marks the beginning of the liberation of humanity from disaster and superstition. It allows forward planning, harm reduction, and mitigation of loss (Knight 1921).

Althaus (2005), drawing on Thompson (1986), argues defining risk requires attention to the intersection between conceiving risk as objective, external reality, and conceiving risk as subjective, perception and interpretation. Consequently, there are, in Althaus' view, at least five basic models of risk:

1. *Subjective risk*: the mental state of an individual who experiences uncertainty or doubt or worry as to the outcome of a given event.
2. *Objective risk*: the variation that occurs when actual losses differ from expected losses.
3. *Real risk*: the combination of probability and negative consequence that exists in the real world.
4. *Observed risk*: the measurement of that combination obtained by constructing a model of the real world.

5. *Perceived risk*: the rough estimate of real risk made by an untrained member of the general public.

The quest for simplicity of meaning is manifested in ISO3000 – the International Standards Organisation definition of risk, referred to above. This Standard defines risk simply as "the effect of uncertainty on objectives". ISO3000 is a pragmatic definition, which belies the complexity of risk as a social, material and intellectual construct. It is practically oriented, and aligned with the Bayesian theorem (*Risk = Probably x Consequence*) (Ale 2009; Mahler 2010). This simple conception of risk provides a broad, flexible and practical set of principles that allow for assessment, evaluation and intervention, and is possibly one of the most useful general theories in recent history for saving life and managing public assets. The problem is that this definition makes no distinction between threat, danger, or uncertainty. Some scholars argue that a risk cannot be conceived as such unless it is quantifiable. If the risk object cannot be quantified or predicted, to some extent, it remains in the realm of uncertainty. This is to be contrasted with a manifest danger, which is quantifiable and predictable. The basic difference appears to be one of *quantification* – the steady progression of identification and certainty of outcome. At one end of the spectrum are manifest dangers likely or inevitable, while at the other are possibilities known to sometimes eventuate but basically speculative. While it is possible to quantify and evaluate some events, O'Malley (2004) observes that in most cases risk and uncertainty cannot be seen as binary distinctions. In most cases risk, uncertainty and danger are nebulous concepts that merge and overlap.

This has caused some scholars, such as Ewald (1991), to argue that there is, in fact, no such thing as risk. What does exist is the attachment of a personal or social value to an object or event. Risk is a social and psychological construct, infused with values, importing a complex grid of quantifiable and known dangers, consequence, and perceived futures. Risk effectively politicises values and mobilises practices and intellectual schema that function to construct, control and distribute risk. In a classic definition of risk as a theoretical orientation, Beck (1992) defined risk as:

> *[A] systematic way of dealing with hazards and insecurities induced and introduced by modernisation itself. Risks, as opposed to older dangers, are consequences which relate to the threatening force of modernisation and to its globalisation of doubt. They are politically reflexive.*

Here Beck conceives risk as a complex system that involves the interplay between external objects and events, their causes, social change, and those human actors and institutions subject to them. Risk is not just about chance: it is the combination of realities, interventions, theories and activities that surround risk. This interplay between event, conception and response has caused some scholars, such as Garland (2003), to suggest that risk can be deployed as a form of governance:

> *Risk is a calculation... a commodity... a capital... a technique of government. Risk is objective and scientifically knowable... is subjective and socially constructed. Risk is a problem, a threat, a source of insecurity... a pleasure, a thrill, a source of profit and freedom. Risk is*

the means whereby we colonise and control the future. Risk is our late modern world spinning out of control.

Risk must be understood as something beyond a simple threat. It is a reference not only to an object (the source of risk); it is the process of dealing with that object, and the knowledge systems that relate to both. *Risk must therefore be conceptualised as a problem-oriented, interdisciplinary epistemology and ontology; that is, a way of constructing knowledge and verifiable truth.* Risk appears to be one of those unusual knowledge formations that exist in multiple dimensions: it is a transdisciplinary knowledge system.

Whereas most disciplinary knowledge formations are "vertical" in that they tend to be constructed within existing knowledge systems, risk appears to be a "lateral" knowledge formation, occupying a metaphysical space across and within multiple knowledge formations. Consequently, risk is a concept that has aspects unique to the specific discipline in which it is located, but also possesses universal characteristics. Zinn (2008) for example, suggests that all theories of risk appear to contain the following characteristics:

1. A distinction between past events, present realities and future possibilities;
2. The belief that human intervention can influence the present and the future;
3. A value system that identifies desired and undesired possibilities;
4. Historical knowledge that shapes the perception of the present;
5. The evaluation of the past, present and future based on sociocultural and personal values;
6. An evaluative calculus mechanism based on hazard identification, loss, damage or threat;
7. The distinction between voluntary and involuntary assumption of risk;
8. A distinction between risk as an external object and risk as a subjective or socially mediated interpretation.

It is the way that these concepts are combined, and the emphasis given to one or more of these features, that causes differences between risk theories. Fundamentally, the major divisions lie in the division or intersection of risk as a real and identifiable object, and risk is a subjective or socially interpreted construct.

At a general level, risks can be involuntary, voluntary, personal and public, and range in intensity from the inconvenient to the globally catastrophic. Risk invokes diverse variables of probability ranging from absolute certainty to the totally unique (Kemshall 2007). Mythen suggests that risk analyses normally contain three intersecting elements: probability, uncertainty, and futurity (Mythen 2004; Mythen and Walklate 2006a). The reality is complicated, however, by the fact that, as Renn (2008) has observed, people respond in different ways to risk, even where the probability of occurrence is high. Indeed, some psychological studies have demonstrated that individuals will behave differently to the same probability of risk, and that different personality types may embrace or be quite averse to the manifestation of risk (Slovic 2000). Edgework scholars, for example, suggest that some individuals actively seek risk. Risk-taking is routinely valorised in business dealings, and appears to be associated with certain personality-types who engage in risk-taking activity as part of the active construction of identity in social systems that demand risk-taking behaviours (Lyng 2008). Indeed, in some cases individuals will actively pursue risk for profit, or engineer exposure to risk for their own, sometimes destructive ends. Not everyone behaves "rationally" in the face of risk, and in some cases the "rationality" of one may be the recklessness of another. Cultural theorists, such as Wildavsky and Dake (1990), suggest that individual risk perceptions are socially and culturally biased, while Olofsson and Rashid (2011) suggest that risk perceptions are strongly influenced by gender and ethnicity, especially when a member of a minority group. Essentially, the range of human responses to risk is just as variable as the manifestation of risk itself.

One aspect of risk still emerging in the literature is the relationship between risk and politics in democracies. It appears that because risk involves both objective and subjective elements, it becomes a major site for the deployment or manipulation of risk for political purposes. A recent consideration of the connectivity between risk and politics is the work of Haines (2011). Recognising the multi-nodal character of risk, Haines argues that risk is intimately connected with public policy. In her study of risk and regulation, Haines found that risk tends to cluster around three intersecting typologies: *actuarial risk, sociocultural risk* and *political risk.*

Actuarial risk is "the reality of harm" (Haines 2011) based on empirical knowledge, experience and an identifiable and quantifiable event or subject. Drawing on Renn (2008), Haines draws a distinction between risk as uncertainty, and risk as categorical danger. She argues that some risks manifest a very low probability of occurrence but have catastrophic impact; while others have catastrophic impact and higher probability of occurrence, at which point the risk ceases to be a risk and becomes a manifest danger. Other risks will be highly uncertain in frequency but carry a broad range of consequences. Other risk types will import high frequency and high consequence, but are of no concern to the public or to government, while other risk categories will involve low-frequency and low impact, but carry high levels of political and social anxiety for historical and cultural reasons – a dynamic that makes the assessment of risk and danger problematic.

Sociocultural risk, extrapolated from the work of Douglas and Wildavsky (Douglas and Wildavsky 1982; Douglas 1990, 2002), is focused on collective experience and perception that threaten or challenge a community. This category of risk is concerned with perceived dangers to "the public". As a perception, the actual risk is personally and socially mediated, and as such may import values, distortions, and mythologies. Consequently, sociocultural risks can be irrational, but need not be (Haines 2011). Such risks are not, however, just about collective anxiety. The collective mediation of risk functions as an anthropological marker – a form of meta-communication in which social cohesion is tested and reinforced. Sociocultural filters function to identify collective threats and responses to them, but also reinforce and identify norms. Such risks are much "larger" than actuarial risks; they touch on questions of social order and continuity. In this respect sociocultural risk imports a greater level of emotional and discursive knowledge than actuarial quantification. The purpose of sociocultural risk is concerned not so much with the manifestation of threat itself, but the meaning that risk has for social cohesion and the place of the individual within that community. For example, if actuarial risk is concerned with the manifestation of a particular form of crime, sociocultural risk is concerned with the impact that crime has, or is perceived to have, on the society in which the event is located. Sociocultural risk will often filter the perception of harms in ways that intensify or minimise the actual harms suffered. Sex offenders, for example, mobilise a powerful socio-cultural risk-based imagery based on "stranger danger", even though the empirical evidence consistently demonstrates that most sex crime takes place between parties known to one another (Bronitt and McSherry 2010; Brown et al. 2010).

Political risk is a by-product of risk. Haines argues that because risk and agitates norms and collective values, risk is necessarily politically sensitive. The result, in democratic systems of government, is that the risks are highly political. Drawing on the work of Habermas (1979, 1989), Haines conceives political risk as a relatively straightforward concept. Political risk emerges when certain events challenge or make demands on government to act in response to risk. Failure to do so has an impact on the perceived legitimacy of that government. Legitimacy is achieved through responding to actuarial and sociocultural risk, particularly by providing security and reassurance in times of threat and uncertainty. The failure of government to address actuarial and sociocultural risk generates uncertainty and threats to the acceptance of elected government. Governments in liberal democracies address risk through two principal vehicles. The first is through action, ordinarily the deployment of law and bureaucratic interventions. Interventions can, of course, involve paramilitary and military options, but in most instances are concerned with legal or bureaucratic intervention. The second is the careful management of the economy. Through intervention and management, governments basically respond to risk and uncertainty to contain risk and provide reassurance to the public. However, governments may also provide frameworks that encourage risk-taking for the purposes of economic growth. In this context risk is not necessarily undesirable. Indeed, risk-taking is regarded as necessary. For Haines, these aspects of risk result in the political deployment of risk in policies that involve a combination of containment, reassurance, facilitation and intervention (Haines 2011).

This aspect of risk is important. The Hansard examined during this research clearly demonstrates a powerful association between risk and public policy. Part of the explanation for that is a purpose beyond the immediate response to the legal risk and uncertainty triggered by *Ridgeway*. Part of the response undoubtedly involved the mobilisation of risk and security for the purpose of achieving and maintaining government and the perception of control, order and an effective law enforcement apparatus. Risk is as much about the project of governance as it is about risk management. If anything, risk and security has intensified in the language of government. The mobilisation of risk as part of the techniques of government intersects with crime control. Criminologists have been aware of the role of risk in the *rationalities* and *technologies* used in the regulation and governance of populations for some time. It is here, where risk intersects with crime control and law, that risk theory is able to offer a new perspective on the topic of controlled operations.

From Risk to Crime Control

Risk literature intersects with criminology, creating a body of literature recognising that risk relates to the various attempts of governments in advanced liberal democracies to control, prevent and suppress crime and corruption. This literature suggests that western governments primarily achieve this through related material and intellectual frameworks concerned with surveillance, targeted investigation, and legislative intervention. This is the intersection in which the controlled operation is located. One of the major figures in this field is O'Malley. During the course of his career O'Malley synthesised and extended much of the literature on crime control, governmentality and risk (O'Malley 1992, 1996, 1998, 2000, 2001, 2004, 2005, 2008, 2010), finding that actuarial and insurance-based techniques and rationalities had become widely incorporated into public policy by the early 1980s, which reoriented the practices of control away from direct coercion and reactive policing to forms of control and regulation emphasising a low impact, visible and economically efficient approach, including privatisation of security and emphasis upon individual choice and responsibility in the reconstruction of criminal identity. There remains, however, a residual coercive power contained within specific policies and techniques of government, directed to particular ends. O'Malley was, however, cautious about assuming that risk is the main driving force of policy and social change, and went on in later pieces to advise caution in the adoption and application of risk as a universal or necessarily pessimistic theory, in answer to some scholars, such as Power (2004), who had suggested that risk was central to the management of everything. In O'Malley's view, risk is but one factor in a complex web of crime control rationalities and methods, closely tied to policing, politics and cultural change, equally capable of producing benefits as well as problems.

O'Malley is one of a host of writers who recognised risk as a *major* focus of crime control policy. Risk has been considered as influencing probation (Bullock 2011; Turnbull and Hannah-Moffat 2009), community policing and crime prevention (Kemshall and Wood 2007), drug policy (Brown et al. 2010; Seddon et al. 2008), and terrorism (Mythen and Walklate 2006a, 2006b). Garland's *Culture of Control* traced a major historical shift in the way in which criminal justice has been implemented in the UK and the United States, observing a significant shift away from notions of penal welfare correction and reform, towards incapacitation and punishment as the focus of public crime control policy, based upon surveillance, control and the prevention of crime through early detection and longer periods of incarceration. The overarching crime control policy directive in late modernity is based upon security, containment of danger, the identification and management of risk. Protecting the public has become "the dominant theme of penal policy." (Garland 2001) Probably the most important theoretical synthesis of policing and risk is Ericson and Haggerty's *Policing the Risk Society* (1997). The learned authors argued that a major function of contemporary law enforcement is based not only on the provision of security, but also in the reflexive use and communication of information about crime and insurance. They argued that as societies become increasingly enmeshed in the politics and rationalities of risk, there is increasing demand for intervention and the provision of information concerning risk. In that context modern policing is transformed, and becomes tied to the collection, distribution and maintenance of complex information systems concerned with risk and security. The security function of police becomes a major part of the reflexive character of late modernity.

Fundamentally, the literature suggests that crime control theories have been transformed and reshaped by the intellectual and material forces of late modernity. Globalisation, reflexivity, and risk discourses have transformed the conceptual and physical landscape of criminal justice within contemporary democratic societies. Risk and crime control is a powerful combination in democratic politics, and consequently it is no surprise to find Hansard deeply infused with discourse of risk, crime and the logic of the imperative. It is also no surprise that the rationality evident in discourse, and also in the doctrinal law itself, is infused with the pragmatic risk-intervention reasoning based on surveillance and intervention. The intensive role of the police in surveillance and the collection of information from populations is symptomatic of the reflexive nature of late modernity. The precision and targeted investigation processes are not only a requirement of the nature of the crime being investigated, as suggested by the legal literature, it is also consistent with the drive for efficiency and the rationality of the precise targeting of particular suspects and their networks. The complexity of the risk literature reveals an important problem for law. When attempts are made to formulate exhaustive tests for risk, the result is a complex of indicia rather than a precise formulation. Although Mahler (2007) has proposed a useful typology and definition of legal risk based on ISO3000, ultimately the problem for law is that law is faced with dealing with a combination of precise and idiosyncratic problems, in the context of a highly nebulous constellation of theories united by an idea of "risk". The result is that risk cannot be presented as a single test in law. Those tests that exist remain either at the level of superficial generality or are specific to particular legal problems. Thus, risk emerges in law at specific sites, united by a "language of risk". That language is connected to practices that involve surveillance, reflexive information collection, targeted investigations, and ultimately the question of governmentality.

Late Modernity's Crime Control Fetish

The legal and criminological literature consistently observes one of the significant changes in policing in the last 40 years was the expansion of proactive forms of policing. This was considered in the opening chapters of this book. Some extension is required. Proactive methods rely on surveillance and targeted investigation, and when considered as a feature of late modernity it seems almost inevitable that these methods, and their associated legal architectures, would materialise. Surveillance as a feature of modernity is well recognised (Lyon 2006; Haggerty and Samatas 2010; Newburn 2007). Norris and Armstrong (1999), for example, have suggested that surveillance is now so widespread and sophisticated that a "maximum surveillance society" is forming, a place where the ability of a person to live peacefully anonymous is virtually impossible, and made redundant by a vast array of surveillance technologies, many of the practices ironically both civil and voluntary. It may well be the case that the very idea of peaceful anonymity is disappearing from the cultural fabric of Western society, being inexorably replaced by systems concerned with the intersection of surveillance, risk, crime control and law.

The study of surveillance and its relationship with undercover policing has been at the heart of Gary Marx's work. We first encountered Marx's work in Chap. 5. Broadly, Marx argued undercover investigation is part of the drift into a surveillance society, largely informed by a rationality of government driven by risk and the desire for regulation and control (Marx 1980, 1982, 1985, 1988; Fijnaut and Marx 1995). While recognising that one of the central functions of surveillance is associated with the investigation of crime and evidence gathering, Marx shares the vision that surveillance is part of a much broader cultural set of practices concerned with social control through surveillance. Law is very much a key instrument in this process because it is judicial and legislative activity that formalises and authorises surveillance activity in the practices of undercover investigation. Drawing on surveillance theorists such as Foucault (1977), Cohen (1985) and Goffman (1964), Marx conceived a society where the traditional line between the public and the private is largely rhetorical, subject always to impeachment, classification and documentation:

> *In such a society, the line between the public and the private is obliterated; we are under constant observation, everything goes on a permanent record, and much of what we say, do, and even feel may be known and recorded by others we do not know. Data from widely separated geographical areas, organisations and time periods can be merged and analysed easily. Control is embedded and preventative; informers, dossiers and classification are prominent. The society becomes, in Erving Goffman's words, a 'total institution', and there is no longer a backstage.* (G. T. Marx 1988)

In surveillance societies elaborate processes evolve whereby the public is scrutinised by the State, where the public scrutinises the State, where the public scrutinises the public, and the State scrutinises itself. Internal surveillance becomes a central method for assuring accountability, as an augmentation to external surveillance. The justification for this mode of government is always the collective good. A false consciousness emerges; that the mechanisms of internal account – the gaze of the sovereign turned inward – is somehow its own intimidation. The sovereign regards such things as inconvenient.

Surveillance in late modernity is not only a cultural and policy transformation, it is also a technological transformation. Surveillance is not only characterised by cultural practices and forms of knowledge, it is also characterised by the multiplication of objects, methods and physical technologies that facilitate these practices. We have now moved well beyond the idea of simply physically watching someone, or listening in on their conversations; we have now moved into an age of real-time global positioning, where continuous and total invisible apparatuses of security and surveillance have become normal. Indeed, many of the technologies proliferate not in the arms of the state, but by a willing public, who show an apparent insatiable appetite for recording every aspect of life digitally, who celebrate the capacity to surveil themselves and others as the benchmark of freedom – ignorant of the consequence. The public are leading the charge in the cultural changes that a transforming the power of sovereignty. When Marx wrote his ground-breaking work in the 1980s, the potential for technological surveillance was only beginning. We now live in an age where the totality of surveillance has increased, while the visibility of the investigator has decreased. Surveillance must now be conceptualised at multiple levels. Surveillance can involve both obvious and directed surveillance, such as a CCTV camera. But it may also involve covert direct observation by human observers, electronic capture of data, images or conversation through telecommunications intercepts, voice recognition, and a variety of biometric analyses. Indeed biotechnology has now reached the point where genetic markers may now provide a level of personal identity unprecedented in human history. Because surveillance now involves continuous, real time monitoring of social and individual behaviours, activities, web browsing behaviours, location, actions and even library borrowing, some surveillance scholars are now contemplating an age of "dataveillence" and "überveillance" (Michael and Michael 2007; Bronitt et al. 2009). The vision of Huxley's *Brave New World* (Huxley 2002) and Orwell's *1984* (Orwell 2008) looms large in this environment, shrugged off as irrelevant by the public who are governed by it.

Closely aligned with attempts to theorise and understand the expansion and complexity of surveillance, is the idea of targeted policing. Valverde has observed that traditionally, policing has been concerned with three principal targets: spaces, populations, and activities. Concurrent with the rise of surveillance as a feature of late modernity, the shift into proactive and intelligence led policing, coupled with the reorientation of penal policy away from reform towards retribution, incapacitation and prevention, means that law enforcement has also evolved to incorporate methods of investigation based on the identification and policing of specific targets. Targeted governance is now an entrenched feature of police strategies (Valverde and Mopas 2004; Valverde 2003), although in many respects it is difficult to see how this differs from the traditional role of investigating crime by those agents with a police mandate.

When considered through this lens, the controlled operation and its legal architecture can be understood as an ordinary part of a much broader cultural transformation. When conceptualised as an ordinary part of late modernity, the traditional legal understanding of the cause of controlled operations law – the reaction to *Ridgeway* – is challenged and at the very least extended. The root cause of controlled operations law was the intersection between the legal consequences of the decision, in that case flowing out of a set of practices and cultural drift that was embracing surveillance and targeted investigations that was already an accepted part of the police landscape and the rationality of government. These developments, and the strong theoretical underpinnings concerned with rationality, governance and power inevitably leads us to governmentality.

Governmentality

Following Foucault (1977, 1991, 2007), a number of thinkers have extended a line of inquiry in Foucault's thinking that has become known as 'governmentality' scholarship (Burchell et al. 1991; Gordon 1991; Castel 1991; Dean 2010; Ewald 1991; Feeley and Simon 1992, 1994; Kemshall 2011; Miller and Rose 1990; Rose and Miller 1992; Miller and Rose 2008; Simon 1987, 1988; Rose et al. 2006; O'Malley 1992, 2004, 2005, 2008, 2010). These scholars argue that, since the late eighteenth century, a distinct set of rationalities concerned with the regulation and management of populations has taken shape in Western societies, intensifying in the late twentieth century. During this time the way in which populations have been governed has shifted away from centralised and sovereign centred forms of government and control towards systems of regulation characterised by a diffuse and largely self-governing system of authority in which citizens take an active part in their own government, while the state assumes a residual but necessarily sovereign role. The management of risk, deviance, danger and violence remain within the purview of the coercive branch of government. In these cases the project of government operates in diverse ways that aim to correct or eradicate those subjects and behaviours inconsistent with the project of government. This rationality is given primary effect through the reflexive appropriation of information, mass surveillance, and the careful deployment of sovereign power. Sovereign power has three major dimensions in this context. The first dimension involves the direct application of force. This includes the use of lethal and destructive force. The second dimension involves the removal of the conditions of life. This involves the decision to either withdraw forms of support, or a decision not to intervene at all. The third form of sovereignty is the deployment and reconstruction of legal frameworks. In this case sovereign power involves making, repealing and changing legal frameworks in order to give effect to the project of government. As will be discussed in more detail later in this thesis, in its most extreme form this can involve creating exceptions to the established legalities. The ability to destroy, the discretionary deployment of resources, and the ability to make, break and change the law are fundamental aspects of the new form of sovereignty that retains residual coercive power. Although the modern liberal state promotes the idea of rule from a distance, it is a rationality of government that retains and deploys coercive and destructive power where and when it needs to.

The classic conception of governmentality was outlined by Foucault in a lecture series delivered in Paris in 1978. In this lecture Foucault presented his thesis that governmentality could be understood as a complex system of knowledge and actions:

> *...the ensemble formed by institutions, procedures, analyses and reflections, calculations, and tactics that allow the exercise of... Power that has the population as its target, political economy as its major form of knowledge, and apparatuses of security as its essential technical instrument.* (Foucault 2007)

Dean subsequently extended this conception, arguing that governmentality was identifiable through the existence of distinct vocabularies, models of collecting information, structures for the creation and retention of information relating to government, and physical interventions in the lives of population groups. He suggested that governmentality is identifiable through four intersecting axes: (i) "ways of seeing and perceiving"; (ii) "ways of thinking and questioning", which includes a distinct vocabulary and processes for the production and evaluation of knowledge; (iii) "ways of acting, intervening and directing"; and (iv) "ways of forming subjects" (Dean 2010). Broadly, the governmentality analytic conceptualises power as existing in multiple dimensions, particularly ways of thinking (*rationalities*), and ways of acting (*technologies*) operating among individuals and the various agencies of the state. Miller and Rose described rationalities as "styles of thinking, ways of rendering reality thinkable in such a way that it is amenable to calculation and programming", and technologies as "assemblages of persons, techniques, institutions, instruments for the conducting of conducting." (Miller and Rose 2008). In liberal democracies, the ideal form of governance is self-regulation, which Foucault suggested could be achieved through combinations of disciplinary and "government of the self". This essentially involves willing compliance with policy and economic life, if not an active devotion and defence of the social order. The liberal actor rationally adopts an alliance with the society they are a part of. The citizen is free, within a set of internalised parameters enforced through processes concerned with creating a prudential and responsible citizen (Kemshall 2007). Because there will be deviations from this model, government depends upon elaborate systems of surveillance, information, and expertise in order to detect and correct departures from this alliance. Such systems also depend upon the retention and deployment of sovereign power when self-regulation fails, and where systematic intervention is required in the containment of threat, risk and uncertainty. This is a vision of government in which the state has a minimal, but extremely powerful role in the life of its citizens, because the citizenry becomes the active arms of their own regimentation – while the juridico-legal and executive arms of governance are applied in precise and very powerful ways.

Consequently, when a risk becomes identified through the application of knowledge and experience, a series of rationalities and associated technologies are deployed. Rationalities become a method of organising the variety of knowledge systems and behaviours used as part of the strategy for responding to risk. In this way risk becomes part of the reflexive rationality of contemporary government. Ewald, for example, identifies the practice of insurance as a *risk technology*, importing a knowledge system that identifies and calculates risk, and providing strategies for its containment (Ewald 1991). Of importance to the present work is the recognition that the technologies of government also involve the deployment of various apparatus of security. The police are critical in this role, functioning as agents of compliance, discipline, and the channelling of coercive sovereign powers acceptable, and legitimate, in the liberal democratic state. As observed by Dean (2010), the police function as an apparatus and visible sign of the power of the State, capable of exercising visible forms of policing, but also capable of exercising in visible forms of policing. Invisible forms of policing are not only a direct manifestation of targeted sovereign power, but also a stimulus for self-governance through the deterrent effect of targeted operations, as well as the widespread knowledge of the use and deployment of surveillance technologies. The police are directly connected with the identification and control of those individuals and groups that pose a risk to the interests of the state. The reflective information role of modern policing identified by Ericson & Haggerty (1997) ensures the police, in their various manifestations, are entrenched in this dynamic. This is a dynamic in which law, necessarily, plays a pivotal role in forming the statutory architectures in which contemporary investigations and policing are situated. In this way police also play a role in the objectification of the subjects of intervention, and the development of reflexive knowledge. This role is fundamentally connected to the criminal procedural law, as law is used to both enable and limit the exercise of these powers. Law can be conceptualised as part of the assemblage of procedures and practices formally concerned with the regulation of populations and the deployment of precision sovereignty. Law is critical to governmentality's project. Law shapes the material practices of human actors, and in the context of criminal investigation is predicated upon its own internal logic and rationality. Controlled operations law and policy provides a critical link in reflexive modernity.

Conclusion: Controlled Operations as Risk Technology and Rationality

In bringing this chapter to a close, the significance of risk and its association with government and crime control becomes clearer once it is recognised that risk is part of a historical cultural and intellectual shift connected with, if not a product of, the problems and opportunities presented by late modernity. The controlled operation provides a mechanism through which residual sovereign power may be deployed precisely and invisibly, in ways consistent with the dynamics identified by governmentality theorists. That is, it is the crystallisation of a series of knowledge formations concerned with policing, deviance, and effective strategies of intervention, combined with the political imperatives of rule from a distance and the triumph of the compliant liberal citizen who must be protected. The controlled operation is an apparatus for crime control and accountability. As a legislated set of practices by the executive arm of government it constitutes a technology governed by a distinct rationality based on a risk-based imperative. The rationalities that intersect in controlled operations discourse, doctrinal law and policy are a manifestation of a rationality of government in late modernity. It is a species of governmentality. It is here that the intersection with Foucault begins in earnest. In the following chapter I shall argue that the controlled operation manifests distinct clusters of rationalities, of which risk and accountability are fragments. Controlled operations law is a *discursive unity* in which intersecting and interlocking rationalities crystallise and coalesce. There is more to consider in understanding the true nature of the controlled operation apart from risk and the demands for accountability. Risk and accountability are manifestations of rationalities intended to address threat, danger and uncertainty – but it does not explain the obsession attached to an important contradiction within Hansard related to the role and status of rights and freedoms of the liberal subject, nor does it explain the effect that controlled operations law has on the construction of identities and on the changing nature of sovereign power. It is through the Foucauldian lens that the nature of the controlled operations technology and rationality is uncovered. It is a technology both for producing strategies of discipline and knowledge. It is a device that enlivens not only the reflexive information requirements of late modernity and the rationalities of risk and accountability as doctrinal governing polarities; it is also a marker of shifting conceptions of sovereign power in which the logic of the exception assumes a particular role, altering the ontological character of the liberal subject in possession of rights and liberties – now exposed as a rhetorical construct existing within a zone of impeachment.

References

Adams, J. (1995). *Risk*. London: UCL Press.

Ale, B. (2009). *Risk: An introduction*. Hoboken: Taylor and Francis.

Althaus, C. E. (2005). A disciplinary perspective on the epistemological status of risk. *Risk Analysis, 25*(3), 567–588.

Ashworth, A. (2006). Four threats to the presumption of innocence. *South African Law Journal, 123*(1), 63–97.

Baldwin, R. (1997a). Introduction - Risk: The legal contribution. In R. Baldwin (Ed.), *Law and uncertainty: Risks and legal processes* (pp. 1–18). London: Kluwer Law International.

Baldwin, R. (Ed.). (1997b). *Law and uncertainty: Risks and legal processes*. London: Kluwer Law International.

Bauman, Z. (1992). *Intimations of postmodernity*. London: Routledge.

Beck, U. (1992). *Risk society: Towards a new modernity* (M. Ritter, Trans.). London: Sage.

Beck, U. (1999). *World risk society*. Malden: Polity Press.

Beck, U. (2007). *World at risk* (C. Cronin, Trans.). Cambridge: Polity Press.

Bronitt, S., & McSherry, B. (2010). *Principles of criminal law* (3rd ed.). Sydney: Lawbook Co.

Bronitt, S., Harfield, C., & Katina, M. (Eds.). (2009). *The social implications of covert policing (Workshop on the social implications of national security, 2009)* (Vol. IV, The fourth workshop on the social implications of national security). National Europe Centre, ANU, 1 Liversidge Street, Canberra: University of Wollongong Press, the Centre for Transnational Crime Prevention, Faculty of Law.

Brown, D., Farrier, D., Egger, S., McNamara, L., Steel, A., Grewcock, M., et al. (2010). *Criminal laws: Materials and commentary on criminal law and process in New South Wales* (5th ed.). Sydney: Federation Press.

Bullock, K. (2011). The construction and interpretation of risk management technologies in contemporary probation practice. *British Journal of Criminology, 51*, 120–135.

Burchell, G., Gordon, C., & Miller, P. (Eds.). (1991). *The Foucault effect: Studies in governmentality*. Chicago: University of Chicago Press.

Castel, R. (1991). From dangerousness to risk. In G. Burchell, C. Gordon, & G. Miller (Eds.), *The Foucault effect: Studies in governmentality* (pp. 281–298). Chicago: University of Chicago Press.

Cohen, S. (1985). *Visions of social control*. Cambridge: Polity Press.

De Giorgi, R. (2009). The risk of risk society and the limits of law. [Article]. *Sociologia del Diritto, 36*(2), 59–67.

Dean, M. (2010). *Governmentality: Power and rule in modern society* (2nd ed.). London: Sage Publications.

Douglas, M. (1990). Risk as a forensic resource. *Daedalus, 119*(4), 1–16.

Douglas, M. (Ed.). (1992). *Risk and blame: Essays in cultural theory* (2013th ed.). London: Routledge.

Douglas, M. (2002). *Purity and danger: An analysis of the concept of pollution and taboo*. London: Routledge.

Douglas, M., & Wildavsky, A. (1982). *Risk and culture*. Berkeley: University of California Press.

Ericson, R. (2007). *Crime in an insecure world*. Cambridge: Polity Press.

Ericson, R., & Haggerty, K. (1997). *Policing the risk society*. Toronto: University of Toronto Press.

Ewald, F. (1991). Insurance and risk. In G. Burchell, C. Gordon, & P. Miller (Eds.), *The Foucault effect: Studies in governmentality* (pp. 197–210). Chicago: University of Chicago Press.

Febbrajo, A. (2009). For a socio-legal theory of risk. [Article]. *Sociologia del Diritto, 36*(2), 69–82.

Feeley, M., & Simon, J. (1992). The new penology: Notes on the emerging strategy of corrections and its implications. *Criminology, 30*(4), 449–474.

Feeley, M., & Simon, J. (1994). Actuarial justice: The emerging new criminal law. In D. Nelken (Ed.), *The futures of criminology* (pp. 173–201). London: Sage.

Fijnaut, C., & Marx, G. T. (1995). *Undercover: Police surveillance in comparative perspective*. Norwell: Kluwer Academic Publishers.

Foucault, M. (1977). *Discipline and punish: The birth of the prison* (A. Sheridan, Trans.). London: Penguin.

Foucault, M. (1991). Governmentality. In G. Burchell, C. Gordon, & P. Miller (Eds.), *The Foucault effect: Studies in governmentality* (pp. 87–104). Chicago: University of Chicago Press.

Foucault, M. (2007). *Security, territory, population: Lectures at the College de France 1977–1978* (G. Burchell, Trans.). Basingstoke: Palgrave Macmillan.

Garland, D. (2001). *The culture of control: Crime and social order in contemporary society*. Chicago: University of Chicago Press.

Garland, D. (2003). The rise of risk. In R. Ericson & A. Doyle (Eds.), *Risk and morality* (pp. 48–85). Toronto: University of Toronto Press.

Giddens, A. (1990). *The consequences of modernity*. Cambridge: Polity Press.

Giddens, A. (1999). Risk and responsibility. *The Modern Law Review, 62*(1), 1–10.

Goffman, E. (1964). *Asylums: Essays on the social situation of mental patients and other inmates*. New York: Double Day.

Gordon, C. (1991). Governmental rationality: An introduction. In G. Burchell, C. Gordon, & P. Miller (Eds.), *The Foucault effect: Studies in governmentality* (pp. 1–51). Chicago: University of Chicago Press.

Habermas, J. (1979). *Legitimation crisis*. London: Heinemann.

Habermas, J. (1989). What does a crisis mean today? Legitimation problems in late capitalism. In S. Seidman (Ed.), *Jurgen Habermas on society and politics: A reader*. Boston: Beacon Press.

Haggerty, K., & Samatas, M. (Eds.). (2010). *Surveillance and democracy*. Abingdon: Routledge-Cavendish.

Haines, F. (2011). *The paradox of regulation: What regulation can achieve and what it cannot*. Cheltenham: Edward Elgar Publishing.

Harvey, D. (1989). *The condition of postmodernity: An enquiry into the origins of cultural change*. Oxford: Basil Blackwell.

Huxley, A. (2002). *Brave new world*. New York: Rosetta Books.

International Standards Organisation. (2009). *Risk management - Principles and guidelines on implementation: ISO 31000*. Sydney: Standards Australia.

Kemshall, H. (2007). *Understanding risk in criminal justice*. Buckingham: Open University Press.

Kemshall, H. (2011). Crime and risk: Contested territory for risk theorising. *International Journal of Law, Crime and Justice, 39*(4), 218–229.

Kemshall, H., & Wood, J. (2007). Beyond public protection: An examination of community protection and public health approaches to high-risk offenders. *Criminology and Criminal Justice, 7*, 203–222.

Knight, F. (1921). *Risk, uncertainty and profit*. Boston: Houghton Mifflin.

Loader, I., & Sparks, R. (2007). Contemporary landscapes of crime, order and control: Governance, risk and globalization. In M. Maguire, R. Morgan, & R. Reiner (Eds.), *The Oxford handbook of criminology* (pp. 78–101). Oxford: Oxford University Press.

Luhmann, N. (1993). *Risk: A sociological theory*. New York: de Gruyter.

Lyng, S. (2008). Edgework, risk and uncertainty. In J. Zinn (Ed.), *Social theories of risk and uncertainty* (pp. 106–137). Melbourne: Blackwell.

Lyon, D. (2006). Theorizing surveillance: The Panopticon and beyond. Cullompton: Willan Publishing.

Mahler, T. (2007). Defining legal risk. In *Commercial contracting for strategic advantage - Potentials and prospects*, Turku, Finland, 13–16 June 2007.

Mahler, T. (2010). *Legal risk management: Developing and evaluating elements of a method for proactive legal analyses, with a particular focus on Contracts*. University of Oslo.

Marx, K. (1970). *A contribution to the critique of political economy* (S. Ryazanskaya, Trans.). Moscow: Progress Publishers.

Marx, G. T. (1980). The new police undercover work. *Journal of Contemporary Ethnography, 8*(4), 399–446.

Marx, G. T. (1982). Who really gets stung? Some issues raised by the new police undercover work. *Crime & Delinquency, 28*(2), 165–193.

Marx, G. T. (1985). I'll be watching you: Reflections on the new surveillance. In C. Norris & D. Wilson (Eds.), *Surveillance, crime and social control*. Aldershot: Ashgate.

Marx, G. T. (1988). *Undercover: Police surveillance in America*. Berkeley: University of California Press.

Marx, K., & Engels, F. (1974). *The German ideology* (C. Arthur, Trans., 2nd ed.). London: Lawrence & Wishart.

Marx, K., Engels, F., & Lenin, V. (1972). *On historical materialism*. Moscow: Progress Publishers.

McCormick, R. (2004). *The management of legal risk by financial institutions*.

McCormick, R. (2010). *Legal risk in the financial markets* (2nd ed.). Oxford: Oxford University Press.

Michael, K., & Michael, M. G. (Eds.). (2007). *From Dataveillance to Überveillance and the Realpolitik of the Transparent Society* (The second workshop on the social implications of National Security). Wollongong: Centre for Transnational Crime Prevention.

Miller, P., & Rose, N. (1990). Governing economic life. *Economy and Society, 19*(1), 1–31.

Miller, P., & Rose, N. (2008). *Governing the present*. Cambridge: Polity.

Mythen, G. (2004). *Ulrich Beck: A critical introduction to the risk society*. London: Pluto Press.

Mythen, G., & Walklate, S. (2006a). *Beyond the risk society: Critical reflections on risk and human security*. Maidenhead: Open University Press.

Mythen, G., & Walklate, S. (2006b). Criminology and terrorism: Which thesis? Risk society or governmentality? *British Journal of Criminology, 46*, 379–398.

Newburn, T. (2007). Late modernity, governmentality and risk. In T. Newburn (Ed.), *Criminology* (pp. 320–338). Cullumpton: Willan Publishing.

Norrie, A. (2001). *Crime, reason and history: A critical introduction to criminal law* (2nd ed.). Cambridge: Cambridge University Press.

Norris, C., & Armstrong, G. (1999). *Maximum surveillance society: The rise of CCTV*. Oxford: Berg Publishers.

Olofsson, A., & Rashid, S. (2011). The white (male) effect and risk perception: Can equality make a difference? *Risk Analysis, 31*(6), 1016–1032.

O'Malley, P. (1992). Risk, power and crime prevention. *Economy and Society, 21*(3), 252–275.

O'Malley, P. (1996). Risk and responsibility. In A. Barry, T. Osborne, & N. Rose (Eds.), *Foucault and political reason* (pp. 189–207). London: UCL Press.
O'Malley, P. (1998). Dangerousness, risk and technologies of power. In *Crime and the risk society*. Aldershot: Ashgate.
O'Malley, P. (1999). Governmentality and the risk society. [Review article of Ericson & Haggerty's *Policing the Risk Society*]. *Economy and Society, 28*(1), 138–148.
O'Malley, P. (2000). Uncertain subjects: Risks, liberalism and contract. *Economy and Society, 29*(4), 460–484.
O'Malley, P. (2001). Risk, crime and prudentialism revisited. In K. Stenson & R. Sullivan (Eds.), *Crime, risk and justice: The politics of crime control in Liberal democracies* (pp. 89–103). Cullompton: Willan Publishing.
O'Malley, P. (2004). *Risk, uncertainty and government*. London: Routledge Cavendish.
O'Malley, P. (Ed.). (2005). *Governing risks*. Aldershot: Ashgate.
O'Malley, P. (2008). Neo-liberalism and risk in criminology. In T. Anthony & C. Cunneen (Eds.), *The critical criminology companion* (pp. 55–67). Sydney: Hawkins Press.
O'Malley, P. (2010). *Crime and risk*. London: SAGE.
Orwell, G. (2008). *Nineteen eighty-four*. London: Penguin Books.
Power, M. (2004). *Risk management of everything: Rethinking the politics of uncertainty*. London: Demos.
Priest, G. L. (1990). The new legal structure of risk control. *Daedalus, 119*(4), 207–227.
Reiner, R. (1992). Policing a postmodern society. *Modern Law Review, 55*(6), 761–781.
Renn, O. (2008). *Risk governance: Coping with uncertainty in a complex world*. London: Earthscan.
Rose, N., & Miller, P. (1992). Political power beyond the state: Problematics of government. *British Journal of Sociology, 43*(2), 173–205.
Rose, N., O'Malley, P., & Valverde, M. (2006). Governmentality. In *Annual review of law and social science* (Annual review of law and social science) (Vol. 2, pp. 83–104). Palo Alto: Annual Reviews.
Rothstein, H., Huber, M., & Gaskell, G. (2006). A theory of risk colonization: The spiralling regulatory logics of societal and institutional risk. *Economy and Society, 35*(1), 91–112.
Seddon, T., Ralphs, R., & Williams, L. (2008). Risk, security and the 'criminalization' of British drug policy. *British Journal of Criminology, 48*, 818–834.
Simon, J. (1987). The emergence of a risk society: Insurance, law and the state. *Socialist Law Review, 95*, 61.
Simon, J. (1988). The ideological effects of actuarial practices. [Article]. *Law & Society Review, 22*(4), 771–800.
Sjoberg, L., Wahlberg, A., & Kvist, P. (1998). The rise of risk: Risk related bills submitted to the Swedish Parliament in 1964–65 and 1993–1995. *Journal of Risk Research, 1*(3), 191–195.
Slovic, P. (2000). *The perception of risk*. London: Earthscan.
Standards Australia. (2004). *Risk management: AS4360*. (Vol. AS/NZS 4360:2004).
Standards Australia. (2007). *HB 296:2007 legal risk management*. Sydney: Standards Australia.
Steele, J. (2004). *Risks and legal theory*. Portland: Hart Publishing.
Susskind, R. (1998). *The future of law: Facing the challenges of information technology*. New York: Oxford University Press.
Susskind, R. (2008). *The end of lawyers? Rethinking the nature of legal services*. Oxford: Oxford University Press.
Thompson, P. B. (1986). The philosophical foundations of risk. *The Southern Journal of Philosophy, 24*(2), 273–286.
Turnbull, S., & Hannah-Moffat, K. (2009). Under these conditions. *British Journal of Criminology, 49*(4), 532–551. https://doi.org/10.1093/bjc/azp015.
Valverde, M. (2003). Targeted governance and the problem of desire. In R. Ericson & A. Doyle (Eds.), *Risk and morality* (pp. 438–458). Toronto: University of Toronto Press.

Valverde, M., & Mopas, M. (2004). Insecurity and the dream of targeted governance: Governing international spaces. In W. Larner & W. Walters (Eds.), *Global governmentality* (pp. 233–250). London: Routledge.

Wildavsky, A., & Dake, K. (1990). Theories of risk perception: Who fears what and why? *Daedalus, 119*(4), 41–60.

Young, J. (1999). *The exclusive society: Social exclusion, crime and difference in late modernity*. London: Sage.

Zinn, J. (2008). A comparison of sociological theorizing on risk and uncertainty. In J. Zinn (Ed.), *Social theories of risk and unceraint*y (pp. 168–210). Malden: Blackwell Publishing.

Chapter 11
Governmentality

> *By … "governmentality" I mean three things. First … the ensemble formed by institutions, procedures, analyses and reflections, calculations, and tactics that allow the exercise of this very specific, albeit very complex, power that has the population as its target, political economy as its major form of knowledge, and apparatuses of security as its essential technical instrument. Second … the tendency, the line of force, that for a long time, and throughout the West, has constantly led towards the pre-eminence over all other types of power – sovereignty, discipline, and so on – of the type of power that we can call "government" and which has led to the development of a series of specific governmental apparatuses (appareils) on the one hand, [and, on the other] to the development of a series of knowledges (savoirs). Finally … the process, or rather, the result of the process by which the state of justice of the Middle Ages became the administrative state in the fifteenth and sixteenth centuries and was gradually "governmentalized."*
>
> Foucault (2007)

On the surface, controlled operations appear in two major forms: investigative practices, and the text of law that purports to govern those practices and the relationships between associated rule systems. These forms are built on a distinct cluster of knowledge formations. The design is composed of concepts and rationalities that traverse legal logic. We find, on closer examination, a complex system of formal and informal knowledge systems and discourses embedded throughout those systems: the imperative of crime control; the existence, logic and management of risk; techniques of surveillance; collation and deployment of information; the discipline of suspect populations; and the emergence of unique legalities. These complex and seemingly unconnected elements begin to make sense as a coherent whole when we consider their common link: the exercise of power. Consequently, controlled operations law cannot be understood simply as the legislative response to *Ridgeway* and the drive to govern undercover policing. Controlled operations law is part of an epistemic code based on the rationalities of liberalism in late modernity. Controlled

B. Murphy, *Regulating Undercover Law Enforcement: The Australian Experience*, https://doi.org/10.1007/978-981-33-6381-6_11

operations law and practice provide a paradigm example of a rationality of governance.

In the preceding chapter, risk was identified as a key component of the rationality of contemporary government in advanced liberalism. It was, however, concluded that the practices and architecture of controlled operations law could not be understood solely as a manifestation of risk society. Risk is a key component of something larger and far more subtle. In this chapter we progress the examination of controlled operations law and policy by deploying a series of Foucauldian analytics. As the quote above indicates, governmentality is a technique through which the complex intersections between power, knowledge, discipline, and sovereignty may be teased apart. For present purposes, the analytic consists of five moves. First, we consider the rationalities identified in this thesis as components of an *epistemic grid* that provide markers for the ways in which systems of governance are conceived and deployed in late modernity. We then deploy the analytic for the purpose of developing a typology of the ways in which controlled operations law and practice shapes a field of governance. Third, we consider the controlled operation as *dispositif* – an apparatus of sovereign intervention directed to the tri-fold end of law enforcement, police discipline, and legal settlement. Fourth, we then turn attention to the various ways in which these practices and rationalities produce new forms of truth and subjectivities. Finally, we locate these dynamics within a broader system of rationalities of governance in which power, biopolitics and associated technologies are identified as the critical components of controlled operations legal architecture and practice, providing an important exemplar of the signature of power, opening insight into a hitherto unexplored manifestation of contemporary sovereignty.

The Epistemic Grid

Controlled operations risks present an object of anxiety for regulation and intervention. Controlled operations law emerges out of the uncertainty and threat of crime and iatrogenic developments in law frustrating the political ends of policing. The solution is to prescribe forms of conduct and promote certain ways of thinking about crime, surveillance and evidence. We are here dealing with an imposed system of thought, intersecting with law, authority, the freedoms of the liberal subject and the regimentation of audit and accountability. This is a signature of governmentality (Dean 2012, 2013): an epistemic grid that reifies specific liberal ideas about regulating conduct.

Before examining the idea of "epistemic grid", a brief digression is required to address the threshold test of relevance. For legal readers the concept of an "epistemic grid" may seem unfamiliar at best, and pointless at worst. Embarking on epistemological analysis is apparently the domain of bald continental philosophers, not legal scholars.[1] The tension arises because lawyers are grounded in a tradition that requires obedience to a sovereign source of knowledge and trained to think in particular ways. Lawyers tend to subscribe to the intellectual and theoretical boundaries of the discipline. Outside of socio-legal scholarship, the legal mind is attuned to focus sharply on "relevant" specifics, and to exclude "irrelevant" considerations. A Foucauldian analysis of law offers a powerful tool to disturb these disciplinary boundaries, to make the familiar seem strange. Ironically, although this perspective is one of the essential orientations of the social sciences, art, and the humanities (Brecht 1961), it is a position that appears largely absent from the legal vocabulary. While the legal orientation to thinking is primarily concerned with the identification, characterisation and application of specific, relevant principles (sourced in law) to a limited range of known "facts", a Foucauldian analytic is concerned with disrupting the whole process through techniques intended to uncover the ultimate foundations of its subject, the substance of these "principles", how they operate to create architectures of governance, resistance and new subjectivities. The "relevance" of Foucault in this context is the intentional disruption of disciplinary thinking in order to test the capacity of Foucauldian thinking to open new insights into the way law is understood. This positioning is not incompatible with law. Indeed, an examination of the deep substance and impact of ideas lies at the very heart of legal reasoning. In the following segment we consider law as a formal knowledge system concerned with the project of governance – a consideration made possible through a consideration of three Foucauldian conceptions: archaeology, genealogy, and episteme.

Archaeology, Genealogy and Episteme

Before considering these concepts and their relationship with the present study, a critical observation is needed. Foucault's archaeology has been the subject of serious criticism, not only from linguists (such as Chomsky and Searle), but also philosophers (such as Dreyfus and Rabinow). The critique relates to Foucault's tendency to misconceive the nature of language and the proposition that the discursive regularities within knowledge systems function as *rules* that determine and govern the formation and power of statements and the content of those regularities (Dreyfus and Rabinow 1982). It is further complicated by the fact that Foucault went through distinct transitions in his thinking, giving preference to archaeology in his earlier works, and genealogy later on. Various reasons have been suggested for these transitions, including maturation in thought, theoretical and methodological crises and contradictions, his contact with the French left (particularly the Maoists), and the influence of Nietzsche in his thinking (Scheurich and McKenzie 2005;

[1] When speaking of episteme and Foucault to a respected senior colleague the expression "intellectual masturbation" was used!

Mahon 1992; Foucault 1986; Dreyfus and Rabinow 1982; Behrent 2009, 2010, 2012; Karlsen and Villadsen 2014). In addition, the terminology used by Foucault does not always translate smoothly into English, made worse by Foucault's own inconsistencies and failure to rigorously deploy his own methodologies (Gutting 1989).

Leaving aside the methodological and linguistic criticisms (which are addressed by Foucault himself (Foucault 1980), but also Gutting (1989, 1994), Dreyfus and Rabinow (1982) and more recently Behrent (2012)), the position adopted in this thesis is that Foucault's archaeology and genealogy are not incompatible. On the contrary, both techniques sit comfortably, although the distinction between the two is subtle. Genealogy is basically rooted in a nomadic, historical totality, concerned with the identification and consciousness of regularities and their role in the evolution of knowledge and the exercise of power on individuals and populations, while archaeology is a more structured approach applied to the identification and analysis of specific discursive regularities. The former is something of a historical "macro" analysis, while the latter is something of a "mirco" analysis of discourse and knowledge formations. In *Society Must Be Defended*, Foucault compared the two:

> *genealogy is ... a sort of attempt to desubjugate historical knowledges, to set them free ... to enable them to oppose and struggle against the coercion of a unitary, formal, and scientific discourse ....Archaeology is the method specific to the analysis of local discursivities, and genealogy is the tactic which, once it has described those discursivities, brings into play the desubjugated knowledges that have been released from the them.* (Foucault 2003)

It is important, however, not to regard Foucault as merely interested in historical epistemology. On the contrary, Foucault is acutely interested in the various ways in which the human form is captured and inscribed by knowledge schemas, for the purpose of disrupting the classical assumption that histories are linear. Archaeology is concerned with an interrogation of knowledge, truth and meaning – while genealogy calls attention to power, biopolitics and the deconstruction of historical assumptions. As Dreyfus and Rabinow have observed, a Foucauldian analysis regards both as concurrent modes of thinking about and interpreting the present. The key issue is that Foucault gave preference to genealogy in his later work, but it would be wrong to assume that he abandoned interest in discursive analysis or knowledge formations (Dreyfus and Rabinow 1982).

Because the present thesis is primarily concerned with an analysis of law as a knowledge formation, emphasis is given at this point to archaeology, a methodology Foucault developed in his "early" works. *Madness and Civilisation*, *Birth of the Clinic*, *The Order of Things*, and ultimately *The Archaeology of Knowledge*, draw distinctions between formal ('scientific') knowledge (*connaissance*), and informal ('discursive') knowledge (*savoir*). *Connaissance* "refers ... to a particular corpus of knowledge, a particular discipline", while *savoir* refers to "knowledge in general, the totality of connaissances ... in an underlying way ... the conditions that are necessary for [the] enunciation to be formulated." (Foucault 1972) Foucault argued that formal knowledge structures cannot be separated from the informal, widely held views on a topic and the discursive practices that constitute them. This is a distinction between *knowledge systems as the formal product of a discipline*, and *knowledge systems as a process traversing disciplines*. *Savoir* focuses on a different axis of analysis, and is interested not only in the formal structures and elements of knowledge, but also its informal elements, its contradictions, its voices, the way it captures and defines a field and its social location. In the present context, a useful distinction is between the formal law constituting controlled operations regulation (*connaissance*) and the informal logic informing policy and principles of governance, such as crime control, the practices of undercover policing, and the independent intersections of risk and accountability (*savoir*). Foucault argued there was no knowledge formation (formal or informal), that was not affected by or a consequence of a pre-existent knowledge system and associated discursive practice. The difference between legal enquiry and archaeology is that traditional scholarship is normally focussed on *connaissance* (formal knowledge), while archaeology is concerned with the informal and discursive practices that give formal knowledge its shape (Gutting 1989). The real focus is the *conditions of possibility*, rather than the "authorised" expressions of knowledge (Foucault 1972).

This way of thinking about knowledge challenges us to rethink how we approach formal knowledge systems, such as law. Foucault suggests that formal knowledge structures are composed of an elaborate web of informal and sometimes unconnected network of popular fictions, mythologies, irrational and anecdotal images, of political and reactionary opposition and compromise, of failures and disaster, of imagery and symbols. A formal knowledge structure is typified by the authorised, obvious manifestation of its kind – typically a document, or book. The book, in turn, can be located and ordered in a grand typology – the *oeuvre*. This ordering, classification and interpretation of knowledge is one of the major functions and orientations of all formal disciplines (Foucault 1972). When law is considered as a discipline, it appears to possess these qualities: a formal, authorised knowledge structure enmeshed and formed by a complex field of processes and conceptions. The composition of law is determined by a complex integration of existing 'legal' knowledge structures, political discourse, and a host of components drawn from the wider episteme – such as accountability and risk rationalities. The focus on *connaissance* ignores the components of assembly, while a focus on *savoir* is sensitive to them.

The great strength of this approach is also its weakness. It is a technique that lacks any precise "science", and typically relies on those elements within text that are ultimately of interest to the examiner. It is not, however, the present intention to critique or dwell on the complexities of archaeology or genealogy. Dreyfus and Rabinow capture much of these deficiencies, concluding that Foucault's "methods" were never intended as a complete theory of anything. They were always intended to be complementary and diverse modes of thinking. Foucault's enduring contribution was the articulation of a discrete set of analytical tools through which new perspectives on existing phenomena are opened. That is the position adopted here.

Foucault's 'archaeological' work suggested that knowledge passes through "threshold" phases of development on the road to its formal composition – from the crystallisation of ideas into a distinct form (*threshold of positivity*); to the assertion of that form as a system of verifiable norms, capable of dominating present understanding on the topic (*threshold of epistemologization*). Knowledge, when sufficiently formed and able to pass through pre-existent grids and rules of verification, rationality and organisation (*threshold of scientificity*), goes on to become entrenched and formalised (*threshold of formalization*) when it is able to define the topic and the elements essential to it (Foucault 1972, 1991). Recognising this process has important implications for legal knowledge, because it may help understand the process whereby a phenomenon first emerges as an object of regulation, being initially characterised by a host of non-legal but largely sociological elements and inputs, subsequently passing through the official channels of the legislature and judicial reasoning into formal statements of governing principle.

In addition to presenting a framework for conceiving the development of knowledge and discourse, Foucault also identified something much larger – the potential for knowledge systems to become a dominant and pervasive intellectual force, beyond the confines of any one discipline. Multiple knowledge systems can become expressions of a particular body of knowledge, and a way of thinking characteristic of an age. Knowledge formations can become historical *statements* of the rationality of the societies in which they are formed. This was referred to as *episteme*. For Foucault, episteme

> *... may be suspected of being something like a world-view, a slice of history common to all branches of knowledge, which imposes on each one the same norms and postulates, a general stage of reason, a certain structure of thought that the men of a particular period cannot escape –a great body of legislation written once and for all by some anonymous hand. By episteme, we mean, in fact, the total set of relations that unite, at a given period, the discursive practices that give rise to epistemological figures, sciences, and possibly formalized systems; the way in which, in each of these discursive formations, the transitions to epistemologization, scientificity, and formalization are situated and operate; the distribution of these thresholds, which may coincide, be subordinated to one another, or be separated by shifts in time; the lateral relations that may exist between epistemological figures or sciences in so far as they belong to neighbouring, but distinct, discursive practices. The episteme is not a form of knowledge (connaissance) or type of rationality which, crossing the boundaries of the most varied sciences, manifests the sovereign unity of a subject, a spirit, or a period; it is the totality of relations that can be discovered, for a given period, between the sciences when one analyses them at the level of discursive regularities.* (Foucault 1972)

Episteme was critical to Foucault's early analysis of medicine and psychiatry, and ultimately central in his analysis of the changes in the mode and form of punishment in western societies. These exemplars were symptomatic of major shifts in knowledge, reasoning, social life and government – from the Renaissance through to the Enlightenment, and on into the various forms of modernity. This is not to say that Foucault was suggesting a progressive view of history; rather he was arguing for contested and multivariate histories, where knowledge systems are equally contested and fragmented, but contemplating the potential for certain kinds of rationality to characterise an age of human development, which emerge through the accretion, displacement, dispersion and succession of discourses (Foucault 1991). Episteme assists in explaining the power of ideas around contemporary forms of government, liberal reasoning, surveillance and the apparent obsession with economic decision-making, risk and freedom in the collective consciousness of the western societies. In his own lifetime, Foucault spoke of distinctions between classical and Enlightenment reasoning, followed by the transition into modernity and late modernity. In *The Birth of Biopolitics*, in particular, Foucault began mapping out the particular role that liberalism and neoliberalism played in the development and operation of governmentality (Foucault 1997b [1984]).

One of the effects of episteme is the tendency for human actors to perceive, interpret and act in certain ways. Fundamentally, the rationalities of governing are profoundly shaped by the pre-existing knowledge formations available at a given time and place. Once knowledge has reached the point where it constitutes a *formalised structure*, it functions to determine the shape of that topic. This includes the processes involved in identification, interpretation and *problematisation* (Dean 2010). These are features of an *epistemic grid*. In their analysis of Foucault's paper "What our Present Is" (Foucault 1997a), Schirato, Danaher and Webb explained:

> *[a] particular episteme can be viewed as a 'grid' that consists of a number of interwoven systems, forces, institutions and practices, and of their relationship to each other, to their history, and the collective experiences of individuals and organisations at a particular time and place.* (Schirato et al. 2012)

In a very real sense, an epistemic grid shapes (but not necessarily determines) how the actor perceives, behaves and rationalises. It reveals how context, organisation and the inherited empirical and intellectual history of individuals and groups import such a powerful force in policy. Public policy and its attendant laws can be seen as part of a larger field of the various problems of the government of populations – the "conduct of conduct" (Dean 2010) – because they necessarily draw upon familiar conceptions and rationalities circulating at the time policy is formulated.

Controlled Operations Law and Policy Exemplifies Episteme

How may we apply this to the present enquiry? In Hansard we are witness to a process whereby ideas around crime and legal uncertainty pass through a pre-existent grid (existing legal forms), transformed into declarative statements of conduct. Hansard is a unique space where some, and perhaps all, of the threshold phases of development suggested by Foucault take place – from positivity to formalization. The apparently disconnected fragments of discussion begin to make sense when considered as a part of an *epistemic grid*, constituted by the intersection of (neo) liberal ideas of responsibility, accountability, crime control, the articulation of legitimate and illegitimate activity, and particularly risk as the pursuit and potential frustration of objectives, come to dominate the lawmaking discourse. These elements appear to operate as an epistemic grid that exemplify present understanding and future anxieties, providing moral justification for action, and an answer to one of the principal concerns – the exception that manifests in legalising unlawful activity, authorising breaches of privacy, the widespread deployment and acceptance of surveillance technologies, and subordinating all of these into a legal architecture that transforms these practices into conduct that is lawful and consistent with 'rule of law' values.

These dynamics and concepts contained within the debates examined in Part II appear to be consistent with Miller and Rose' analysis of political rationality (Miller and Rose 2008; Rose and Miller 1992). They argued that (western) liberal rationality tends to manifest three core intersecting features. First, *a moral component*, concerned with articulating a problem and justifying a required intervention. This articulation involves associating a threat with core social institutions (economic, familial, political etc.), with associated identification and assignment of powers to various intervention authorities. In so doing, that articulation functions to identify the values and objects of government, notions of "justice", "freedom", "common sense" and "efficiency". Second, the political discourse and related policy is normally articulated through *a distinct epistemological framework*. That framework imports both pre-existent formal knowledge and the "practical" experiences of those who engaged in the administration of the problem, and those affected by it. The practice of government imports a combination of "the empirical" with "common sense". Third, political rationalities manifest *"a distinctive idiom"*, which goes beyond political rhetoric. This idiom transforms realities into an object that makes the topic thinkable and able to be actioned. In this way "a vocabulary of the 'the State' has come to codify and contest the nature and limits of political power. Political rationalities … are morally coloured, grounded upon knowledge, and made thinkable through language." (Miller and Rose 2008).

There is undeniably a moral component evident in the Hansard. Organised crime, drugs, terrorism, threats to economic life, threats to prosperity, and the uncertainty attached to successful prosecutions are all objects of concern. The "innocent" are subjects to be protected from these evils, but at the same time the existing social relations are preserved and desired. The law is maintained and represented as a powerful weapon to defend the public, while accountability – a system of multilayered forms of surveillance – is presented as the instrument to prevent the excesses of executive power while simultaneously forming the foundations of criminal responsibility. The powers involved in the controlled operation are distributed and fragmented. Only the *responsible* are permitted to use these powers, while those subject to its power are *held responsible*. But even those entrusted with the use of this power are not trusted. It is a power that must be used in a particular way, consistent with the freedom expected of the law abiding. Indeed, the freedom of citizenship is enforced. Freedom must be used in a particular way. Freedom is maintained through an invisible but efficient power. It is also undoubtedly the case that controlled operations law and discourse manifests a particular epistemological framework that imports both the pre-existent and inherited forms of knowledge around crime control and intervention, fundamental to which is both law and police knowledge systems. At the same time Hansard manifests a clear tendency to draw on the personal experiences of parliamentarians, the decisions of courts, extra-judicial writing, submissions from the public and police agents, as well as the sometimes irrational mythologies and political posturing that takes place in that forum. It is also without doubt that these discourses function as a "distinct idiom" – a system of linguistic codification that interprets and re-aligns these diverse conceptions into an intelligible form, characterised primarily by risk, liberties, crime control, and the ends justifying the means. In essence, part of the reason why controlled operations law and policy contains the distinctive and at times contradictory character is because it reflects the attempt by the legislature to exercise sovereign powers in a high risk environment, by deploying specific rationalities of governance compatible with the (neo)liberal order. Controlled operations law and policy is discursive and necessarily epistemic in character. But there is more to it than knowledge formations and discursive regularities. This is a knowledge system that has a distinct purpose, concerned with the material practices of law enforcement and the application of legal interpretation. There are practices associated with knowledge.

Dispositive Analysis

Chapter 3 contained an early observation that controlled operations investigations could be understood as a technology – a working component of an apparatus of power. As outlined above, there is a significant relationship between controlled operations and certain rationalities of governance. At this stage it becomes necessary to reconsider this aspect in more detail. Controlled operations law is more than just procedural law: it represents a rationality of governance, exercised through a multiplicity of discrete moments that include conceptual, legal, institutional and physical elements. We are here concerned with understanding the relationship between knowledge and power (the "assembling" components of power (Dean 2012)) and their physical (and legal) manifestations. The totality of these components are elements of "apparatus"; recognisable through dispositive analysis.

The starting point for understanding the idea of "apparatus" is Foucault's *Discipline and Punish* (Foucault 1977), where Foucault suggests the existence of "disciplinary apparatus" used in the correction and training of criminal and delinquent behaviour. The difficulty is that the concept is interwoven with the work as a whole, without precision of formulation. The concept re-emerges as central to the first volume of "The History of Sexuality" (*The Will to Knowledge*) (Foucault 1998). Here Foucault presents his thesis that power operates in highly complex ways, beyond the crude ideas of "juridical" and "sovereign" power. Power operates through "the uniformity of apparatus" – through myriad "capillary interventions", institutions and the internalised compliance of human actors in the face of formal and informal prohibitions, norms, incentives and reason (Foucault 1998). The problem here was two-fold. First, the idea of "apparatus" was presented in quite broad terms, and therefore vague; and second, Foucault did not actually use the word "apparatus". The French term is *dispositif.* There is no clear English translation that captures the nuances. For present purposes the shortcomings of terminology will be put aside, but the absence of a distinct term may partly explain the struggle of many writers to succinctly state its meaning (Bussolini 2010; Raffnsøe et al. 2014).

Foucault himself later attempted to clarify what he meant by *dispositif* in a recorded symposium later published as "The Confession of the Flesh" in 1977 (Foucault 1980). As a discussion there was no single statement of concept. Rather, dispositif was presented in fragments:

> *What I'm trying to pick out with this term is, firstly, a thoroughly heterogenous ensemble consisting of discourses, institutions, architectural forms, regulatory decisions, laws, administrative measures, scientific statements, philosophical, moral and philanthropic propositions–in short, the said as much as the unsaid. Such are the elements of the apparatus. The apparatus itself is the system of relations that can be established between these elements* (Foucault 1980).
>
> *Secondly, what I am trying to identify in this apparatus is precisely the nature of the connection that can exist between these heterogenous elements. Thus, a particular discourse can figure at one time as the programme of an institution, and at another it can function as a means of justifying or masking a practice which itself remains silent, or as a secondary re-interpretation of this practice, opening out for it a new field of rationality* (Ibid).
>
> *Thirdly, I understand by the term "apparatus" a sort of ... formation which has as its major function at a given historical moment that of responding to an urgent need. The apparatus thus has a dominant strategic function* (Ibid, p. 195)
>
> *... apparatus is thus always inscribed in a play on power, but it is also always linked to certain coordinates of knowledge which issue from it but, to an equal degree, condition it. This is what the apparatus consists in: strategies of relations of forces supporting, and supported by, types of knowledge.* (Ibid, p. 196)

Agamben, whose consideration of the topic was translated as "What in an Apparatus?", later offered a rather more succinct statement of the idea:

> *I shall call an apparatus literally anything that has in some way the capacity to capture, orient, determine, intercept, model, control, or secure the gestures, behaviours, opinions or discourses of living beings* (Agamben 2009).

In one of the more influential contemporary essays, Deleuze presented his own interpretation of the concept, with an important methodological extension in his essay "What is a Dispositif?" (Deleuze 1991, 2006). Here Deleuze presented dispositif as "a tangle, a multilinear ensemble ... composed of lines, each having a different nature." (Deleuze 1991). Deleuze argued that the study of dispositives was similar to "drawing a map ... surveying unknown landscapes" (Ibid). Undoubtedly influenced by Foucault's *Archaeology of Knowledge*, Deleuze identified four specific "lines" of enquiry: (1) "curves of visibility"; (2) "curves of enunciation"; (3) "lines of force"; and (4) "lines of subjectification" (Deleuze 1991). The problem here, again, was the density of terminology and failure to simply explain both what was meant by the term, and its practical application.

In *Governmentality*, Dean incorporates and clarifies Deleuze's work as part of a systematic framework for the analytics of power (Dean 2010). Here Dean prefers the term *assemblage* or *regime of practice*, but specifically deploys the lines of enquiry suggested by Deleuze, with the added advantage of clarifying and arguably simplifying them. Dean argues that when practices of government are understood as assemblage or regimes of practice, a space opens to reconceptualise practices of rule by disturbing the assumed ('self-evident') historical constants, with a new focus on the complex and diverse causes and rationalities embedded within those regimes, contending that practices of government "should be approached as composed of heterogeneous elements having diverse historical trajectories, as polymorphous in their internal and external relations, and as bearing upon a multiple and wide range of problems and issues." (Dean 2010). As a guide to exploring governmental assemblages, Dean contends that at least four domains require examination: (1) *fields of visibility*; (2) *technicalities*; (3) *rationalities*; and (4) *identities*. (Dean 2010).

This "four dimensional" approach has more recently been considered and deployed by Villadsen (2008, 2011), who argues that dispositif analysis is not a methodology as such, but rather "analytical entry points" that allow for an understanding of the strategic logic in institutionalised practices to be identified and their impact on known subjects to be evaluated. Villadsen provides a clear definition:

> *The study of dispositives pays particular attention to the description of practices in which the production of knowledge and the regulation of humans are tightly intertwined. Dispositives can be defined, then, as strategic logics which in retrospect seemed to have had an organizing role within practices where governing individuals intertwines with knowing them* (Villadsen 2011).

Like Dean, Villadsen also draws on Deleuze, describing the analytic in these terms:

1. *'Lines of light': Visibilities are not produced by a general source of light that falls upon pre-existing objects. Rather, each dispositif has a particular way of structuring light, giving life to objects that are dependent on it for their existence.*
2. *'Lines of enunciations': Enunciations do not merely represent objects or subjects. A dispositif rests upon regimes of enunciation; i.e. procedures for the production of truth (derived from the modern sciences).*
3. *Lines of force': Interconnections between seeing and saying, between things and words, are established by power. Power is internal to a dispositif; it passes through all its elements and gives it a certain strategic imperative. In particular, it can be observed in the shape of techniques and technologies.*
4. *'Lines of subjectification': The subject is not pre-determined but is rather in a process of becoming, made possible by particular dispositifs. Moreover, subjects are not determined by the powers and forms of knowledge of one dispositif, but rather 'dispositioned'.* (Villadsen 2008)

We have here three distinct "entry points", with variations in the approach, represented in the following table:

Author	Line of Enquiry			
Deleuze	Curve of Visibility	Curve of Enunciation	Lines of Force	Lines of Subjectification
Dean	Field of Visibility	Technicalities	Rationalities	Identities
Villadsen	Lines of Light	Lines of Enunciation	Lines of Force	Lines of Subjectification

There are notable variations in conceptions here. Dean, in particular, does not dwell on the "enunciation" dimension, preferring to tease out the technicalities and vocabularies of government ("technicalities") from those procedures for the "production of truth" attached to "enunciation", and the separation of "rationalities" from the intervention/rationality dimension in Deleuze's "lines of force". The variation is not surprising, since Dean was not proferring a strict adherence to Deleuze. The great problem, no doubt recognised by Dean, was two-fold. First, the "dispositif", of itself, was an incomplete tool of analysis. Dean rightly illustrates that a significant component of governmentality must devote attention to the question of problematisation (Dean 2010) – something absent from a strict "dispositive" analysis. Second, dispositif relies on some fairly dense conceptual models that have not made the transition into English particularly well and were perhaps too loosely formulated in the original French. Nevertheless, there is value in deploying the analytic, provided that is deployed concurrently with some attention to considerations of both problematisation and the production of truth – subjects that will be examined in due course. For present purposes, we proceed by adopting Dean's terminology in a dispositive analysis.

Fields of Visibility

For Dean, the field of visibility "concerns the forms of visibility necessary to the operation of particular regimes." (Dean 1995, 2010) In this context a field of visibility is established by attending to the combination of actual practices that make a subject visible for examination and rendered into forms of representation. When considered as a mechanism for *visibility*, the controlled operation is principally concerned with the mobilisation, application and extension of the sovereign gaze in specific sites that are ordinarily outside the "public sphere". Controlled operations law, and its associated investigative apparatus, mobilises a field of visibility for the determination of suspect guilt. The legal architecture sanctions multiple instances of surveillance and micro instances of examination. The suspect is examined in the very environment in which their conduct takes place. In many cases that activity is ordinarily out of the routine gaze that might detect crime and corruption. Indeed, the suspect is under observation in the *very act* of breaking the law, for the investigator is with them. Conversations are heard. Email and physical evidence is collected. Social networks are studied. This information is filtered through the process of prosecution into distinct categories – relevant, probative, irrelevant, admissible, inadmissible, intelligence, noteworthy, trivial. It passes through the judicial process, and ultimately is inscribed as a record of the past for the benefit of the future. But the field of visibility is not limited to the suspect; it applies to the conduct of the executive. An elaborate system of documentation and reporting is constructed within the practices of the agency, overseen by a supervisory jurisdiction. In this respect the field of visibility is identifiable not only as the surveillance of actual practices, but the inscription of those practices within a vast array of permanent data sources – reports, notebook and documents. The field of visibility, in this context, is articulated through discourses of accountability, audit and the rights-bearing subject within the architecture of law. In this respect one of the functions of controlled operations law is to construct a field of visibility, mobilised through the concurrent operation of law enforcement and normative vocabularies and the preservation of direct evidence in the form of visual, digital video and audio surveillance, reports and the testimony of witnesses who have observed the activity of the offender. In this respect a key element of the controlled operations dispositif is a power to render the invisible *visible* to the demands of law enforcement – to bring light to those locations in which crime and corruption ordinarily operate undetected.

Technicalities

Dean suggests that a key element of dispositif analysis relates to attending to the "techne of government" (Dean, 2010, p.42) – those technologies deployed in the exercise of government through which forms of regulation and authority are actually exercised. This component is familiar to the legal mind, since a major component of law as a discipline is concerned with mastering the technicalities of forms of regulation – the space between the statements of practice and its implementation. However, the dispositif alerts the legal reader to the fact that law (at least in its black-letter sense), is primarily located within the field of the technicalities of a dispositif. When considered as one of the *technical* aspects of government and police, it is clear that this regime of practice contains a diverse array of techniques and vocabularies that are essential conditions. These are numerous.

The first are *investigative practices* – that body and system of thought and behaviour concerned with the investigation itself – the expertise associated with police work, particularly undercover work. As outlined in Chap. 3, these practices involve their own distinctive methodologies, vocabularies, procedure and tactics that intersect with the legal and regulatory architecture.

Related to this is an equally complex and diverse set of *practices of deviance;* the activities of "the suspect." For every action of police, there is an equivalent reaction on the part of the suspect, and vice-versa. The "criminogenic situation" is a symbiotic and constantly evolving environment. Like policing, the "criminal underworld" has its own culture, language and techniques. This symbiosis contribute are central to the language, practice and habitat of those involved, and constitute a distinct technical knowledge within the crime/policing subculture. In this respect the "techne of government" is informed and shaped by strategies of resistance and the informal, organic characteristics of the sub-cultures being governed.

The third technique of government is *judicial.* The judicial scrutiny of criminality available through the controlled operation offers a profound insight into the conduct of the suspect and the investigator. The judicial/legal process is a complex vehicle and system of practices with its own distinct mechanisms, knowledge systems and cultures, all concerned with facilitating the more obvious techniques of governance. Ironically, the judicial-legal process is also shaped by the specific architecture of controlled operations law through its declaration of conditional immunities and the admissibility of evidence. The normal rules were changed to deal with exceptional circumstances.

A fourth manifestation of governance is *bureaucratic*, represented in documents, such as the *application form*, the *annual report* and the *warrant*. The *document* becomes a technology of practice that performs the function of accountability, imprinting its own vocabulary, both technical and general. This becomes the vehicle through which the insistence on accountability is inscribed and attached to the conduct and identity of individual actors within a complex system. The document becomes a major statement of evidence and legality; the technology through which accountability is given effect; through which the actuarial practices tied to risk and surveillance are mobilised. Controlled operations are bound to the production and articulation of documents that present and inscribe evidence of compliance and deviance for use in the future. These bureaucratic technicalities provide some of the key structures through with the field of visibility is mobilised.

Rationalities

This point of entry is concerned with the intellectual components deployed in the activity of governing (Dean 2010). Controlled operations are comprised of a complex grid of rationalities concerned with crime control, audit, risk, threat and a logic of exception. It is a rationality that emerges out of a specific "urgent need" that demands intervention. Crisis and threat provides the impetus for the crystallisation of these rationalities into a particular socio-legal space, heavily wedded to law enforcement – but at the same time is a rationality that straddles it. It achieves its ends through processes tied to the rational application of investigative expertise, reason, surveillance and the articulation and enforcement of a norm system clustered around trust. At its depths, we are confronted by a rationality that touches on the theological: the knowledge of "good and evil" imports an expectation of virtue and trustworthiness, forming the basis of declarations of criminality, revealed through an invisible sovereign power that presents temptation to suspect and investigator alike. Through the process of a precision analysis of conduct, an assessment is made of guilt or innocence in comparison with the norm. This is a rationality of power that transforms the model of power away from a singular sovereign, closely aligned to Foucault's image of the power/knowledge nexus, a space where "multiple bodies, forces, energies, matters, thoughts and so on are gradually, progressively, actually and materially constituted as subjects, or as the subject." (Foucault 2003).

Identities

Finally, dispositif requires some attention to the construction of specific *identities* at the group and individual level. Because these identities are closely aligned with the typologies that emerge out of the problematisation practices discussed below, the details of these new forms of subjectivity will be considered in detail below. It is sufficient to state that controlled operations law and regimes of practice are very much tied to the construction and inscription of a variety of identities. Controlled operations function to construct a socio-legal space in which the identity of particular subjects is qualified and scrutinised. Identity is contained within a grid of surveillance and normalization, where the particular identity of individual actors is transformed through the practices, rationalities and legalities of controlled operations practices.

In this respect, while it is true to say that controlled operations are a form of *dispositif*, analysis that confines itself to dispositive analysis is incomplete. A more complete picture is available by extending the analysis by a consideration of the role of problematisation, and the intersection between law and dispositif.

Problematisation, Law and Emergent Typologies

Let us develop the analysis by going beyond 'dispositif', and considering the nexus between discourse, policy and law as an instrument of government, and the question of problematisation. In *Governed by Law?*, Rose and Valverde (1998) theorise an approach to the analysis of law and policy based on Foucault's *Archaeology of Knowledge* and Ewald's extension of the operation of norms within legal structures (Ewald 1990). This model dovetails with the dispositif in that Rose & Valverde argue that law presents a framework for the codification of the juridical limb of power, suggesting there is a distinction between processes which articulate the normative and the legal. These are necessarily connected: "[a] rule is external to that which is governed: it is imposed on its subjects … A norm, on the other hand, appears … to emerge out of the very nature of that which is governed." (Rose and Valverde 1998). The relationship between norms and rules is a complex and symbiotic one; law constitutes and is constituted by norm systems. Because of this, attempts to interpret and formulate purely doctrinal, "principled" accounts of law are apt to ignore, minimise, or confuse the relationship between law, norms and power. An alternative approach is suggested: to focus the analysis on "the problem" that law is mobilised to address, and to analyse the discursive regularities that emerge from "the problem" as opposed to the "privileged sites of legal reason", such as legislation and case authority. The proper location for analysis, in their view, is not on law or norms, but an analysis of problematisation. This reorientation decentres law as the mode of analysis and locates law as but one part of a larger system of coding, discourse and practice. In this respect the shortcomings of dispositive analysis can be overcome.

Problematisation

The first step is to consider the nature and identification of "the problem", and to then consider the ways in which the object is characterised as "a problem" and its suggested solutions. Dean argued that problematisation refers to a particular rationality informing practices, consisting of both object and process, located primarily at the beginning of a process resulting in the deployment of formal expressions of power. Problematisation identifies some phenomenon that demands attention, for which the logic and technology of government is applied. This involves the identification of some phenomenon as a "problem", coupled with an analysis of the causes of "the problem", and the formulation of techniques and practices deployed in its management and solution (Dean 2010). Basically, experience and knowledge is applied to an objectified "problem". In this context the "problem" passes through an epistemic grid; pre-existing knowledge formations, ordinarily involving actual experience, applied to an object that carries with it political and real consequences if ignored. Problematisation involves a reflexive relationship with information, experience, engagement with a polyphony of voices and the documentation of events – a *surface of emergence*. Foucault conceived these "surfaces" as an assemblage of actors, events and ideas that constitute and identify subjects and objects, attaching value and normative evaluation of them (Foucault 1972). Within these networks are distinct and recognisable voices – *authorities* – which play a major role in defining the problem and articulating causes, substance and consequence. These authorities often draw upon their own experiences and knowledge formations, which routinely includes a set of *conceptual codes* and *criteria for judgement* which function to articulate "the problem", a process that provides sites and channels of communication between actors, and offers an explanatory logic informing intervention (Rose and Valverde 1998).

The controlled operation provides a clear example of the problematisation of crime control, as an object and process. It is concerned with a particular kind of criminality – forms of conduct that "normal" policing finds difficult to address. The legal architecture emerged out of undercover and proactive practices, and the subsequent uncertainty caused by the law's initial rejection of this model as being incompatible with the existing legal framework. When considered as an example of problematisation, there is no surprise as to why and how this technique crystallised into law. Here the *surface of emergence* is an intersection of significant policing interests directly connected with the apparatus of the State and the Constitutional mandate for "good government".[2] The controlled operation technique was a consequence of the pragmatic demands for crime control – particularly narcotics; the real difficulties associated with investigating crimes that take place in "private" and those involving intelligent, closed-group networks; the problems investigating the crimes of the powerful – particularly white collar offenders; and the need for effective methods for internal investigations. While the law has always exercised a degree of control over proactive law enforcement, these pragmatic and legal tensions came to a head in *Ridgeway*. The main actors in this field became actively involved in the process of lawmaking through submissions to Parliament and the lobbying of sympathetic members. The media, through public reporting, and the judiciary, through obiter comments in decisions and their role in public enquiries, joined the chorus of voices advocating for regulation, acceptance, and accountability. In this way a polyphony of voices constituted a source of *authority* for reform. These were powerful, authorised voices. The accepted wisdom was that there was a very real *need* for proactive, undercover methods based on surveillance and facilitative models of investigation. Need was transformed into a discourse of *necessity*; and necessity justified and legitimated the legislative changes. Not only that, these voices of authority effectively neutralised dissent by presenting failure to reform as a threat. Society was threatened (i) by the potential inability for police to use undercover methods in the investigation of serious crimes, (ii) by the potential for police to be held criminal and civil liability for legitimate investigation actions, and (iii) by the potential for innocent citizens to be framed in the process. The "public interest" demanded law reform in ways that permitted and controlled this form of investigation. Controlled operations and their intersection with legality was effectively problematized. The police, the courts and the legislature became allied at the point where law enforcement was recognised as a necessary and inherently valuable public duty.

Subjectification

The second axis of analysis suggested by Rose & Valverde is concerned with *subjectification*. They argue that "[s]ubjects are constituted in a whole variety of ways in different legal contexts and forums. Each of these … has a history, each is differently suffused by the norms and values of positive knowledge." (Rose and Valverde 1998). From this perspective individual identity is inscribed with a combination of legally imposed, social mediated and psychologically indigenous characteristics. This aspect of analysis overlaps with the "lines of subjectification" outlined by Deleuze and dispositive analysis. Essentially, this is a process where individual actors are influenced by the forces embedded in the matrix of problematisation – in this case law and controlled operations practices. These processes operate at the

[2] Australian Constitutions all provide for a legislative power for the "peace, order and good government" or "peace, welfare and good government". See, eg, *Constitution Act 1902* (NSW), s5; *Commonwealth of Australia Constitution Act 1900* (63 & 64 Vic, Ch 12), s51

intersection of the (liberal) individual actor, and the identity forged by the *role* of the actor in a legal and institutional matrix.

There appear to be five key actors constituted and governed as subjects in the controlled operations nexus. The first is the *target*. The target is normally a "person", or a network of people. For non-legal readers that may sound obvious, but legal personhood is constructed in particular ways. A "person" includes biological *and* incorporated entities.[3] Criminal law further qualifies personhood on the basis of the 'rational actor', possessing knowledge of wrongfulness. Ordinarily, that principle normally precludes children and the insane from criminal liability.[4] In principle, there is nothing within controlled operations law that technically prevents children or the mentally ill from being the targets of an investigation, outside of ethical principles, and the reality that the evidence of these actors is notoriously unreliable. The reason is that the focus is not on personhood, but upon *activity*. It is what the person is *doing*, or *suspected of doing*, that is the issue. In this respect controlled operations law and practice plays a major role in the construction and articulation of specific subjectivities. The ordinary qualities of personhood and identity are irrelevant – the attention is on activity, or *suspected* activity. Personal characteristics ordinarily constituting the subject are relevant only insofar as they provide information as identifying markers – the social coordinates that locate the target in time and space. The target is identified on the basis of conduct and words, information on past criminal or corrupt activity, or expressions and indicia of future criminal intent. But the target is not always identified; the target may be more general, focussed on a network or geographic location (sometimes virtual), where the target is a population within a catchment. The target may then become identified through the application of a focussed surveillance, or information from others within the zone of inquiry. In this respect "personhood" may have no actual identity at all, other than a generalised archetype. Once identified, the target is subject to the application of a perceptual and analytical gaze – a targeted surveillance that draws on existing knowledge formations that evaluate behaviours in the past, present and future. In this space the target's personality and social identity is a secondary consideration – relevant on questions of sentencing rather than liability. Analysis is directed firmly on issues of threat and conduct. In the presence of indicia of a crime, the citizen is transformed from citizen to target. In the presence of evidence of crime, identity is transformed from target to suspect. The investigation imports a "surveillant assemblage" (Haggerty and Ericson 2000) that, ideally, has a totalising aspect – for every aspect of the person may be captured within the web of investigation as part of the intelligence gathering phase. Communications, actions, social networks, web browsing behaviour, prior convictions, and even existing friendships are examined and potentially utilised by investigators. Aspects of social identity that normally affirm and constitute identity are inversed and potential sources of evidence to be used against

[3] Eg: *Crimes Act 1900* (NSW), s4 defines "person" as including "any society, company, or corporation." See also *Interpretation Act 1987* (NSW), s21: "person includes an individual, a corporation and a body corporate or politic."

[4] This varies according to the jurisdiction.

the suspect. The portfolio created becomes its own knowledge formation and is incorporated within a reflexive grid, becoming first criminal intelligence, then a prosecution brief, and ultimately sentencing report. The suspect's identity shifts again, from suspect to accused, and if convicted, is transformed once more into *the offender*. This process takes place through a combination of practices and legislative forms involving surveillance, investigation, arrest, prosecution, trial, formal denunciation, and incarceration. Each of these layers is saturated with distinct legalities. This power is sovereign. At the very least this is a power that incapacitates the subject, for at least the period in custody. But it also has another effect, deterrence. The controlled operation is not just a manifestation of sovereign power on the life of the subject, now transformed into "criminal" or "corrupt". The threat of the controlled operation has a deterrent effect on suspect networks, and the public at large. In this way the controlled operation influences the life of all through the deterrent effect of invisible sovereignty. Sovereignty and disciplinary power are merged – shaping the identity of all. This subjectivity involves both biopower and disciplinary power. In this respect the power deployed through the architecture of controlled operations law functions not so much as a prohibition, but in the productive sense as constituting distinct identities. The success of controlled operations law is not concerned with prohibition and prosecution, rather it is the productive effect of power.

The second transformative identity concerns the *investigating officer*. The officer must *apply* for authority to deploy the controlled operation from their superiors. They must justify, through some evidence, that the target and the circumstances merit the deployment of this degree of assessment. Evidence, and reason, are central to the request. Above all, the officer must present as rational, informed and in possession of reliable evidence. But the decision to *authorise* the power resides elsewhere. In that context the officer has power to request but may not act without ordination. The relationship of the officer with the sovereign is always one of loyal subordination. Once ordained, the officer may then act. But those actions are not open ended. The orders include temporal limitations. The officer may not exceed the mandate; they may not take life or destroy property; they may not expose the unsuspecting and law-abiding to injury or death. And when acting on and in the life of the suspect, their true motive, if not actual identity, must remain *invisible*. They must infiltrate and listen. They must cloak and substitute their personal identity with something else: an assumed identity. They become the perceptual organs of the sovereign. Above all, they must not entrap the suspect. They may facilitate but may not cause the law-abiding to become a criminal. They must present the target with the *opportunity to offend* so the suspect, possessed of reason, may choose. The officer is transformed into an agent of deception, but at the same time a champion – vested with special and unique powers in the fight against crime and corruption. They perform this role with the benefit of special knowledge about the suspect obtained through surveillance and informers, in the knowledge of a legal status of effective immunity and bolstered by a discourse of virtue as an agent of the law. But at the same time the officer is also a suspect; for the power is not trusted. The officer is embedded in the criminal ecology; at constant risk of going rogue, or exceeding powers extended for the public good. They possess a dual identity, at once valorised and suspect. The investigating officer has a unique identity: a mirror image of the suspect, being tested with the opportunity to exceed the limits of law through reason alone.

A third subject is the *authorising officer*, the person superior to the investigator but inferior to the executive. They are the point of contact with the officer applying for the warrant. This subject is possessed with a statutory delegated authority. They are pre-ordained as a trustworthy and responsible officer of the executive. But ordination involves account. Their actions are closely monitored by a more senior authority within the organisation, or outside of it, or both. This officer is, necessarily, an appointed and *rational* actor. They must be satisfied, on the presentation of the application, that there is a sufficient threshold of evidence justifying the application. Invariably, the consideration involves a combination of information that could be adduced in a court of law, as well as inadmissible information constituting "mere" intelligence. The law requires that the exercise of judgement in this respect is evidence-based, but there is undoubtedly a degree of intuition exercised based on professional experience. This subject's organisational authority is augmented by the extension of legal authority to confer extraordinary powers on subordinate officers, professional experience, and the application of reason in the pursuit of the *public interest*. They sit in a privileged position within the centre of an epistemic grid; being able to assess and trap through the nexus of authorised power and knowledge. Unlike the officer, this subject is situated at the first level of internal surveillance, whose function is to scrutinise the subordinate officer, and in this capacity has a disciplinary effect on the subordinate officer. If the investigator's purpose is to scrutinise the suspect, the authoriser's role is to both authorise and scrutinise the investigator.

The fourth identity is that of *scrutineer*; that person or group whose task is to examine the operational activities and decisions of the organisation deploying the controlled operations power. These are Juvenal's "guards" who "guard the guardians". They stand outside the organisation. The extent to which this subject has actual and immediate authority over the authorising officer varies, depending on the legal architecture. In some cases, this subject is a part of the legislature (a responsible minister). In other cases, this subject stands at the apex of an external executive agency. This subject's identity is based on a targeted scrutiny of the actions and decisions of the agency using the controlled operations. The task, fundamentally, is compliance and the detection of deviance, based on a rationality of reporting. This role, over time, incorporates its own history, critique and knowledge-system. It is an evaluative role, which although overtly designed as one of detecting abuses and deviation, is also one of legitimation and normalisation – for the process of evaluating deviation also affirms successes and conformity, actively constructing the limits of the normative. In so doing, this is a process that articulates institutional norms. For it is here, at the nexus between operational activity and legal architectures, that the value of the controlled operations methodology is primarily crystallised – for here the scrutineer is positioned to speak into the ear of the figurative sovereign through the mechanism of formalised reporting on the activities, successes and conformity of those agents deploying this technique. A distinct epistemology is manufactured in the process of scrutiny and reporting ostensibly directed at deviance and abuse, but in reality, based on compliance and normalisation.

The fifth major subject is the *judicial officer*. This figure is constituted in multiple dimensions, drawing upon a vast network of legally constituted epistemologies and formal expertise in a way quite distinct from those involved in the process of authorisation. This subject has two major roles. The first is adjudicative. The second is evaluative. The adjudicative role is concerned with the determination of the legal guilt or innocence of the *target* of the operation. In this respect the judicial officer performs the role of legal denunciation; that part of sovereign power that declares guilt and orders punishment, and in so doing is able to inscribe identities on the person of its subjects. For practical purposes, the judicial officer, and the legal process, is the face of the sovereign in the eyes of the *target* – the power that enforces the normative and inscribes new identities on its targets. But the juridico-sovereign is not just concerned with the declaration of guilt and the ordering of punishments; the judicial officer is also concerned with the process – for violence without law is *unjust*. In this respect the judicial officer also possesses an identity also concerned with evaluation of the controlled operations process, with an eye to the question of excesses, abuses, and the irrational. The disciplined and rational use of an extraordinary power is a critical factor in the evaluation of its legality. As Norrie has observed, "[r]ationality is fundamental to legality." (Norrie 2001). Consistent with the principles of legal reasoning, that evaluation is empirical; it must be based on evidence. But most importantly, the evaluation is based on *admissible evidence*. In this way the factual realities of the event are filtered through a grid of rules to produce and reproduce a legal rationality that aims to discipline the factual matrix to produce a disciplined knowledge. The judicial officer has power to not only inscribe identities on offenders, but also investigating officers, the process, and the the legal architecture itself.

On this reading, controlled operation law and practice plays a significant role in the construction of distinct subjectivities. These are shaped by the norms and posited knowledge inherent in the controlled operations framework, although it cannot be said that these subjectifications are dominated by this architecture. Rather, the controlled operations architecture comes to play a role in a larger juridico-legal field concerned with the attribution of liabilities and the evaluation of a legalised reason and compliance with an authorisation structure. The legal architecture is here concerned with "practices of the self in particular sites and practices" (Rose and Valverde 1998), although these practices vary and need not depend on the controlled operations architecture itself.

Normalizations

One of the defects of Rose and Valverde's model is the absence of a clear statement of what "normalization" involves. They do, however, argue that legal architectures increasingly become enmeshed with the articulation and imposition and authorisation of norms in the regulation of social life (Rose and Valverde 1998). To understand what is meant by "norm" and "normalization", we need to track back to Ewald (1990). Ewald conceived "norm" as a knowledge system involving a combination of valorised conduct and systems for reinforcing and producing them. Norm systems are not only "standards", but also associated mechanisms that allow evaluation and intervention to maintain conformity and reinforce the characterisation of the norm. The intervention mechanisms vary, but often involve State-sanctioned and institutional activities. Thus:

> *Normalization is ... the production of norms, standards for measurement and comparison, and rules of judgment ....[it] produces not objects but procedures that will lead to some general consensus regarding the choice of norms and standards* (Ewald 1990).

In short, Ewald suggests that legal structures possess a distinct relationship with the normative; they are part of the formal systems that express and enforce values and norms. The "Norm" is thus a language, a rationality, valorisation and practice with disciplinary effect, intersecting with law as a formal system of evaluation, procedure and enforcement. This is why Rose and Valverde argue that analysis of normalization involves a study of the *technicalities* of legal procedure, and the intersection between legal and non-legal knowledge systems in the construction of the norm and its associated procedures. The interchange between intersecting knowledge systems creates a "transactional zone of conflict and alliance between forms of expertise." (Rose and Valverde 1998).

Consequently, controlled operations law and practice not only requires a consideration of the technicalities of law and its intersection with knowledge systems, but also with the norms articulated in that matrix. As a strategy of government, the controlled operation is inextricably tied to disciplinary power and biopolitics. This is a technology that necessarily implies obedience to public law as a requirement of citizenship. Compliance with public law is a minimum expectation of behaviour, and accordingly is a valorised concept. The law functions as a codification of a variety of normative statements. These normative statements are not located in controlled operations law *per se*, but in the substantive criminal law. These standards are conditioned, however, by the requirement within controlled operations law that the relevant conduct that will trigger a controlled operation is sufficiently *serious*. In most cases that is an indictable offence. However, there are nuances in this domain, since some of the offences identified in controlled operations law are not indictable, nor are they located in criminal statutes. These are offences that are not so much "serious", as offences that *take place in private*. The subject is compared with a norm system that demands the subject must not engage in criminal or corrupt conduct and may not expect security by hiding in the normally sacred private realm. At the same time, a second normative structure exists, concerned with the conduct of the investigators. The investigator may not misbehave either. Conduct before, during and after the event must accord with parameters set by the norm. Obedience is again an expectation. Both dynamics touch upon another norm: *trust*. The liberal citizen, and investigator alike, is expected to be self-governing, and trustworthy. If the subject cannot be trusted, then the pervasive architecture of the controlled operation can, under the right conditions, be mobilised. In this respect the target is governed by the general law, while the investigator is governed by the procedural. In both instances the critical moment is the conclusion, through evidence, that the subject cannot be trusted, demonstrated through their breach of law. That conclusion is achieved through a test of virtue: the temptation to commit a crime, abuse a power, or satisfy the demands of greed in the face of expectations of duty.

Surveillance and *detection* constitute a third norm system; a particular form of reflexivity, where information and knowledge operate in a continuous circle, from public life to institution and back again. This is a technology – the device through which the conclusion of trustworthiness is obtained. Through accurate detection and deployment of surveillance the technology itself becomes valorised as a successful procedure or technique. Successes reinforce the value attached to the technology, while failure drives the demand to perfect and correct technique. The assessment of trustworthiness is based on evidence, linked to a fourth norm: the possession and use of *reason:* criminal liability rests upon an assessment and evaluation of conduct and the state of mind of the offender, while the authorisation of the controlled operation depends on an evidence-based assessment of the basis for the operation. Evidence adduced in court is inevitably the subject of judicial reasoning that will assess the very *legality* of that evidence and the operation itself. Intersecting with *reason* is the complex array of *risks* that finds their way into the evaluation of criminality and authorisation. A fifth norm system emerges out of controlled operations law overlapping with trust, concerned with an enduring concern of government: the preservation of the virtuous actor. The rights and liberty of the virtuous (obedient) citizen must be preserved, while the untrustworthy are inscribed with a new identity – one that possesses a different and inferior legal status. Here the binary logic of law is called into play: the conviction of the guilty, and the protection of the innocent.

In this way controlled operations rationality and technologies are infused with and produce a plurality of norms and knowledge systems. This is a space in which the controlled operations architecture is informed by a polyphony of norms, allied in ways that produce a system of normalisation with disciplinary and biopolitical effect. The neo-liberal ideal of the *responsible and rational actor* is normalised through this rationality and technology, while the technology and rationality of "virtue testing" and surveillance connects controlled operations law and policy to the project of normalization.

Spatializations

Drawing on the work of Garland (1997), Rose and Valverde describe spatialization as "the ways in which legal practices are involved in the constitution of … 'governable spaces'" (Rose and Valverde 1998). For the purposes of criminal law and public policy, these "spaces" are referred to by Garland as "criminogenic situations" that "constitute a new site of intervention for governmental practices … a domain with its own internal dynamics." (Garland 1997). Criminogenic spaces present a unique problem for government because they are spheres that share two basic characteristics – the presence of something of value, and the absence of effective guardians. Garland suggested that these are locations that can never be completely protected or governed, and accordingly the focus of crime control policy shifts away from investigation of crime and its elimination, to minimising offending behaviour by reducing opportunity and vulnerability through surveillance and self-regulation. The project of government extends beyond the regulation of individuals and the deviant to *locations* where the deviant and the unlawful are known to operate and shifts from a prosecution to a management orientation. Spatialization is the process through which law and enforcement practices mobilise to govern criminogenic locations, including "private spheres" of social life.

Controlled operation law and practice is designed to insert an investigation into criminogenic locations. These locations vary, ranging from public to private spaces – and even beyond physical landscapes into cyberspace. The genius of the controlled operation is its capacity to penetrate invisible criminogenic locations resistant to usual forms of investigation. Controlled operations allow for the construction of a space where the infiltration of the private is a routine method of operating, and where the ordinary rules of law in that context are qualified in ways that allow alliances between investigator and suspect for the purposes of collecting evidence to be used against that suspect. In this way there is no space that is not a potential site for colonisation as a governable space, including the interpersonal and psychological spaces of the suspect who often establishes working relationships with individuals they believe to be allies, but who are actually agents of the State.[5] The controlled operation, as a legal architecture, presents to the world the capacity to transform the hidden and the private into a transparent and governable space; a location that may be opened up for investigation and scrutiny, and, as suggested by Deleuze (1992), is one step closer to a society of control.

Authorisations

The final step suggested by Rose and Valverde is to consider the concept of *authorisations*. This goes beyond the idea of approval mechanisms. It involves considering *the various ways authority is mobilised* that has disciplinary effect within the field of regulation. The scope of authorisation is necessarily broad, but tends to cluster around mechanisms concerned with (i) legal licensure; (ii) liability and punishment; (iii) the encoding and enforcement of standards; (iv) economic control through budget allocation; and (v) the power of the audit (Rose and Valverde 1998).

Controlled operations law provides a powerful example of this kind of authorisation. It is a technology that presents internal and external threats to those who are its subjects. The immunities offered to investigators depend on the issue of a valid

[5] In particular, "Mr Big" and "Friending" operations, discussed in Chap. 3.

warrant – a legal instrument that authorises and limits the investigation. Such warrants are within the purview of a limited range of delegated officers at the apex of the organisation. These organisations have a specific mandate, and invariably operate based on a chain of command. Failure to obtain a warrant, or substantial deviation from the terms of it, will trigger the threat (or fact) of disciplinary and/or legal sanctions, which may involve, at least, the disciplinary power of the organisation, if not criminal and/or civil liability. These organisations operate not only the basis of statutory authority, they are also required to observe regulations and internal Codes of Conduct. One of the defining characteristics of police organisations is the existence of explicit standards of conduct in the execution of duty, and in this respect controlled operations law intersects with the organisation and professionalised norms of conduct indigenous to the organisation. Indeed, one of the essential mechanisms of controlled operations law is to entrench the power of surveillance, audit and accountability within organisational culture. The controlled operation may well provide a mechanism for the disciplining of a suspect population, but it has a major impact on the organisations that use them, as it crystallises an internal surveillance and accountability technology and rationality *within the organisation*, triggered and maintained by the mechanisms of authorisation.

The Production of Truth

Deleuze and Villadsen argue that a key element of dispositive analysis requires attention to those mechanisms concerned with "the production of truth". This is a core Foucauldian strategy. The production of truth is, in fact, a fundamental concern of the law enforcement apparatus and associated judicial practices. In this respect, attending to the production of truth is an important and often neglected element of legal inquiry. For lawyers and police agents, an investigation is concerned with the collection of criminal intelligence and evidence used in the prosecution of an offender suspected of involvement in crime or corruption. Foucault, on the other hand, invites a focus on the ideas and practices involved in that process, and the relationship of those knowledge systems and practices with the exercise of power. That focus has two dimensions. The first, discussed above, relates to the disciplinary effect controlled operations law and practice has on the identity of those involved in the investigation. The second relates to the role of the investigation in the production of truth and knowledge. In this context truth and knowledge relates to the legality of actions by those who use them, and those subject to them. It also relates to the production of knowledge related to the activities of police agencies more broadly, as well as to the decisive power of state in its efforts to control crime. In this respect the controlled operation produces critical information that constitute a variety of "truths".

In a series of lectures published as *Truth and Juridical Forms* (Foucault 1994), and later extended in *Wrong-Doing, Truth-Telling* (Foucault 2014), Foucault argued that political and sovereign power was directly tied to practices that involve the production of knowledge and "truths". Power and knowledge are "woven together" (Foucault 1994). According to Foucault, the nexus between power and legal/juridical knowledge in the west emerged out of practices of State with origins in Roman and Germanic law and custom, ultimately established as a loose set of more or less uniform practices in Europe coinciding with the establishment of national governments in the late Middle Ages. The first of these, *inquisitio,* involved an individual with delegated sovereign power and authority directed to local and regional fact-finding. In essence, the administration of the realm demanded the delegation of power and authority of monarchs to examine specific problems of governance – especially rebellion and corruption. This practice coincided with similar ecclesiastic practices of the (pre-Reformation) Church, where a senior Church delegate (usually a Bishop) would physically visit an area to conduct general inquiries on matters concerning both the administration of the Diocese (*visitatio*), and the transgressions of the faithful (*inquisitio generalis*). If issues were petitioned, or became apparent through inquiry, a second phase (*inquisitio specialis*) was convened to gather evidence and interrogate witnesses. Foucault argues that over time the practices of *inquisitio* and *visitatio* merged, so that the formal investigations of crime and corruption can be traced to the fact finding practices of feudal monarchy, and the ecclesiastic administration of land and souls (Foucault 1994). Guilt or innocence thereby became enmeshed with offending the temporal power of the sovereign, and the ecclesiastic (normative) power of the Christian church. We therefore find a merger of norms, law and morality attached to the production of truths. Indeed, the juncture between law, power, knowledge and morality intersects with the theological (Murphy 2020).

The practice of investigation and examination of individuals charged with crimes and transgressions was (and remains) critical to the exercise of governmental and disciplinary power. It was a technique that not only offered and standardised a distinct technology of practice, it also generated and captured a knowledge system of how to engage in such practices, deployed a knowledge system (*law*) used to determine guilt and innocence, and produced a grid of truth that captured and inscribed itself on the specific targets of the inquiry. Foucault concludes that:

> *... we might say that the inquiry is absolutely not a content but, rather, a form of knowledge ... situated at the junction between a type of power and a certain number of knowledge contents ... The inquiry is precisely a political form ... of power management and exercise that, through the juridical institution, became, in Western culture, a way of authenticating truth, or acquiring and transmitting things that would be regarded as true. The inquiry is a form of knowledge-power* (Foucault 1994).

Foucault's assessment of the knowledge/power nexus is a useful entry point for inquiry. As discussed above, controlled operations are both rationality and technology, an apparatus that articulates the power/knowledge nexus conceptualised by Foucault. What makes the controlled operations apparatus so powerful is not only its power to govern criminogenic spaces: it is its role in the production and inscription of four truths, outlined below.

The Guilt of the Suspect

Controlled operations provide the investigator with direct access to the ecology of the suspect. In that space the investigator is witness to the actions and words of a figure already identified as *suspicious* (a form of *inquisitio generalis*). This observation becomes the *inquisitio specialis* which allows for the collection of evidence subsequently used in prosecution; the temptation presented to the subject is at once a moral and legal transgression. The body and the soul become a site of inquiry. In this site the investigative methodology, the legal structures shaping authorisation, conduct and subsequent scrutiny are knowledge systems intended and designed to produce knowledge of both *legality* and *illegality*. But the inquiry is binary. It concerns the suspect and the investigator but has different tangents. The investigator is shielded by the legality of the investigation, while illegality is transcribed onto the identity of the suspect who now is transformed from suspect to offender. A binary distinction is operating here; a division between an investigation that separates the suspect as guilt-free, and therefore virtuous, or guilty, and therefore corrupt. The production of truth is completed with the formal juridical declaration of guilt and associated sentence. In this sense the inquiry authorised by controlled operations law is a specific form of inquiry concerning potentialities. The person *might* commit an offence. And the investigator will be there when it happens. Conversely, the investigator *might* behave unlawfully, but equally exposed to the explicit threat of detection and removal of protections at law. Here we see something akin to Foucault's political and administrative arms of sovereign power merged with the ecclesiastic and theological – for the very apparatus used to determine guilt is the combination of unlawful act combined with the "guilty mind" – for it is the "knowledge of wrong" that makes the action substantially blameworthy in the eyes of law (*actus non facit reum, nisi men sit rea*).[6] Criminal culpability is assessed in accordance with the coincidence of the unlawful act and the rational choices of the offender. The guilt of the offender is not only fixed to the unlawful act, but further measured in accordance with the knowledge of good and evil. In this way the offender is classified not only as criminal, but also in terms of the moral blameworthiness attached to the unlawful act. The intentional act, voluntarily committed in full knowledge of consequence, is regarded as more blameworthy than an accident or unintended act (Hart 2008; Feinberg 1970). This aspect of the investigation and subsequent prosecution tends to confirm Foucault's argument that one of the dynamics of the power/truth nexus is the inscription of identity to a subject now known as "criminal". This identity is a powerful one, for "the criminal is the social enemy …

[6] A fundamental common law maxim that holds that a person's actions are not criminal unless the mind is also criminal. In other words, an action is not regarded as criminal unless there is a coincidence of action and knowledge of the gravity of that action. A crime is therefore distinguished from an accident to the extent that the individual knew or desired a particular outcome knowing the action was wrong, as opposed to an action undertaken in ignorance or with knowledge or desire. This is a fundamental principle of common law *mens rea*. See, for example, *R v G* [2004] 1 AC 1034 at 1035; *R v Morgan* [1976] AC 182 at 213; *He Kaw Teh* (1985) 157 CLR 523

who has broken the social contract … an internal enemy." (Foucault 1994). The determination of guilt becomes both internal and external process of enunciation, merging the boundaries of the criminal law and legal theory with the theological (Murphy 2020).

A Rational and Lawful Investigation

The controlled operation, as strategy and technique, is produced and reinvented through its acceptance, deployment, and evolution. The legal infrastructure directs the practices of authorisation, limitations and scrutiny that serves to constrain and regulate the potential for abuses. The technology itself is inscribed and reproduced along the knowledge/power axis as rational, controlled, and lawful. The acceptance and longevity of the power is assured and legitimated in the face of its extraordinary potential and its contradictions, because legality ensures its compatibility with law and politics, while rationality, compliance with the rule structures, and demonstrable field successes perpetuate its utility. The structures and the architecture that give the controlled operation its life in law, policy and practice remain solid and largely impervious to critique, repeal or deconstruction. The controlled operation is inscribed and entrenched within the technologies of investigation as effective, accountable, and necessary as a truth characterised as rational and lawful.

The Preservation and Manufacture of Qualified Rights

The legal architectures surrounding the controlled operation, and its precision, intersect with the discourses of rights and liberties within a liberal constitutional democratic monarchy. Accountability, legality, and a deserving social enemy all coalesce as elements within the grid of rationalities produced and recycled in controlled operations law and practice. Freedom, as observed by Rose (1999), is a manufactured conception of late modernity. Law plays a major role in this process. In the present context freedom, as a politico-legal construct, is partially serviced and augmented by the rationalities and knowledge structures enlivened and produced by the controlled operation. The existence of a cluster of rights, freedoms and liberties is an assumed (if not legal) fact, but also constructed within the architecture of controlled operations law and its associated policies and practices. Rights, freedoms, and liberties are actively produced as a part of the theoretical and practical apparatus of the controlled operation. However, the preservation of rights, freedoms and liberties is one of qualification: The State has legal power to extend, qualify and derogate from the rights expected by the citizen *and* the investigating officer. The truth here is that the protections offered by the legal system are qualified at the same time as being preserved. This aspect of the ontology of controlled operations is significant because it rests upon and intersects with the power to make exceptions to ordinary law – a topic that will be examined in more detail in the following chapter.

Epistemic Coding: The Risk/Crime/Account Nexus

Drawing on Foucault, the final truth suggested here is one I call *epistemic coding*. In *The Order of Things* Foucault suggests that one of the key aspects of *episteme* was the existence of regularities of ideas, practices and knowledge systems that function as hidden or cultural codes that are learned and circulate within social systems (Foucault 1972, 2005). Here I am suggesting that a fourth truth emerges out of the controlled operation as a powerful knowledge formation that forms within the grid of risk, crime and accountability. This space offers a combination of information and explanatory networks, intervention techniques, knowledge evaluation devices, control systems and an imperative rationality. This is a complex web of truth that appears to comprise the following logic. The manifestation of certain crimes and corruption poses a manifest social and political risk that demands intervention in the interests of the collective good. That intervention involves legal and executive apparatus needed to investigate, prosecute and suppress those risks. When those apparatuses themselves present a risk, systems of accountability and internal surveillance are deployed in the management and elimination of those risks. The external surveillance and disciplinary apparatus of power so effective in the intervention and governance of the population is equally amenable to internal deployment. It is a power equally effective when turned on itself. However, in the deployment and execution of investigations that penetrate the boundary between public and private life, certain rights and liberties recognised in law may be qualified or removed when the risks involved in not investigating a suspect's activities reach a sufficient threshold of danger. In such cases the liberties and expectations of liberal citizenship become secondary and are exposed to a logic of exception. Similarly, when the legal architectures begin to frustrate the ends of government in the context of a threshold of danger, the rule systems are exposed to a regime of change and to a logic of exception. The epistemic code of risk/crime/account is joined by a fourth conceptual code: a logic of exception. A fourth truth is, simply, the ends justify the means, and the means involves a framework of codes that qualify and alter the existing web of legality.

Controlled Operations as Signature of Power

Thus far we have argued that controlled operations legal architecture functions as the codification of a rationality of governance, characterised by the imperative of action, the management of risk, and the technology of audit. We have seen that the law and practices authorised by it play a key role in shaping subjectivities and the reconfiguration of new spaces of governance. At this juncture we pause for a moment and follow the "line of inquiry" back to a common referent: the role of power.

It cannot be disputed that the controlled operation is an expression of a form of authoritarian power applied specifically to penetrate invisible spaces in the private spheres of life. But we have seen that controlled operations legal architectures are not just about "juridico-sovereign power". It is a form of power with biopolitical effect, equally applicable to the investigator, the investigated and the public at large. It is also a form of power that operates as much outside of the scrutiny of the courts and the eyes of government as it does within it. The legal literature discussed in Chap. 5 clearly indicates that despite much of the attempt to bring the activities of the investigators into the surveillance of the courts and the public, much of that activity remains invisible. Indeed, a substantial amount of information obtained by the state in the course of an investigation never appears within the realms of *public* knowledge systems – but undoubtedly forms a part of the archives of state, forming a (ordinarily) secret system of knowledge in its own right. But there is also an important dimension of controlled operations law and policy that requires explanation and that is the role of contradiction.

As set out in the introduction, a defining characteristic of the controlled operation is the authorisation of a limited range of unlawful activity by an agent of the state. That characteristic operates in the face of the rule of law principle that those who enforce the law are necessarily expected, if not bound, to obey the law. To some extent that problem was neutralised by the exercise of juridical-sovereign power in changing the law so that authorised operations, within the scope of a warrant, were declared not to be contraventions of law. As far as law is concerned, that is the end of the matter. However, the fact that the law actually operates with concurrent legality and illegality (the warrant may be invalid, thereby making the act technically unlawful – or the operative may exceed the mandate of warrant and lose the immunity) results in a conceptual space of floating potentials of persistent contradiction. The unlawful is made lawful; but remains unlawful in the right conditions. How may we understand this profound dynamic within a Foucauldian framework? The answer, it seems, is by taking a step back from *dispositif*, and looking at the connection between sovereign power and law.

As has been discussed previously, Foucault did not articulate a clear theory of law in his analysis of power. He was, undoubtedly, interested in law, but devoted his time to an exploration on the subtle elements of power beyond the sovereign, famously arguing the need to "cut off the head of the king" Foucault (1998). The problem is that the "king", in its contemporary manifestation, is a multi-headed immortal and incorporate entity. The king cannot lose his head, because the monarch exists everywhere and nowhere. Accordingly, a reconceptualization of the relationship between sovereignty, law and power is a pressing need.

The defining feature of the legal dynamic in controlled operations law is the existence of a cluster of oppositional concepts: the recognition of rights combined with the power to suspend or qualify them; the freedom of the citizen, subject to the power of the state; the legalisation of unlawful activity; the transformation of the private into public. These contradictions are antinomies – binary oppositions with powerful evolutionary effect. Norrie has argued that criminal law is replete with antinomies, and in many ways a significant contour of criminal law, generally, is defined by irrational and contradictory elements Norrie (2001, 2005). Recently, in *Signature of Power*, Dean (2012, 2013) has argued that the analysis of power is substantially extended when it begins to attend to the "signature of power". Drawing on Agamben (2011), Dean argues that power can be understood not only through an examination of its internal organisation (such as through *dispositif*), but also be attending to two characteristic signatures. The first is metaphysical, the second material. The metaphysical signature concerns the tendency for power to operate through dualities: binary, oppositional conceptions, or at least fractured distinctions. Agamben uses the example of the division between sacred and profane (Ibid, p.4). It is within and between these conceptions that power and knowledge systems operate to both establish power and provide the seeds for construction of allied conceptions or new oppositions. The second signature relates to the material exemplar of power; the physical or symbolic representation that makes power visible. Dean argued that rather than approaching sovereignty and power as a monolithic form or theory, sovereign power was best approached by a consideration of specific instances of rule and its associated symbolism and expression. These expressions will typically rely upon specific monumental expressions that reveal the "signature" expression of power relevant to the specific instance of rule.

I would argue that in law this metaphysical dynamic is often codified, presented on the one hand by a framework of legal statements of process and prohibition, but held together with exceptions to the ordinary order. In contemporary law the text provides the material exemplar, while the definition of terminology and the exceptions to the norm identify antinomies and the metaphysical signature. The power to change law, the associated floating capacity, and the ability to enforce the will of the sovereign with substantial (but not complete) impunity, are significant markers of sovereign juridical power. These powers are reflected and expressed in the specific text of law and the associated documentation of practice manuals of executive agencies. In this respect, controlled operations law is not only *dispositif*, it is also signature of power.

Conclusion

When controlled operations law and policy is approached through a discursive and archaeological lens, the cause, operation, and effect of this legal architecture is revealed as a complex intersection of law, audit, risk and the politics of legitimation. The shape and purpose of controlled operations law, and its inherent contradictions, become explicable as components of an epistemic grid. Here the law operates along pragmatic and discursive axes. The law's pragmatic axis establishes a system of powers that authorise investigations and provide opportunities for investigating crime and corruption, informed by intersecting rationalities of governance existing outside the law.

The law's discursive axes are multivariate. Controlled operations law is a part of the criminal law's larger mechanism of criminogenic problematisation. Through the application of the rationalities concerning crime, risk and accountability, certain forms of conduct and social systems are problematized as requiring certain forms of intervention. Here the law forms a part of the system of encoding crime, corruption, and intervention. In so doing, controlled operations also function to construct and reconstruct distinct identities and subjects, while simultaneously functioning in ways that produce, articulate, and valorise norm systems. It is a model that functions to construct spaces, persons and places as governable localities, which at once extends the capacity of surveillance and the disciplinary effect of law, and provides a mechanism through which the boundaries between the private and the public spheres become porous. Finally, it creates a system through which contemporary manifestations of authority become entrenched and articulated. In so doing, this is a knowledge formation that augments the role of risk, accountability, and targeted investigation methodologies through the very process of its articulation. At the same time this is a mechanism through which certain forms of knowledge concerned with, or causing, the production of certain truths become manifest: knowledge of criminality and guilt; knowledge of criminal and corrupt networks; knowledge of intervention techniques and rationalities; knowledge of the consequence and effectiveness of the intersection between law, risk and accountability.

Here, within the archaeological and genealogical space available through Foucault's flexible analytic, we find a space where discipline, surveillance and biopower are revealed as tightly connected with the knowledge systems deployed and produced by this form of investigative activity: a linkage between episteme and law, codified in the text of law, leaving the signature of an invisible sovereign open for all to see. The consequences of this dynamic are quite profound. The anxieties that gave rise to controlled operations law became entrenched and reified within the doctrine and practice of precision investigations. The model of undercover participation in crime by police agents expanded through its undoubted utility and successes, which provides the reflexive input required by modernity and its attendant discourses. It suggests that this species of law is necessarily an extension of an epistemic grid, where the intersection of crime control, risk and accountability are revealed as sovereign discourses embedded within it. This has implications for a whole new field of a *jurisprudence of risk and sovereignty*. In addition, it opens a path for a further consideration of a major component of the "sovereign decision to change the law" in the face of crisis. We are now able to step into a consideration of the *logic of the exception*. The character of risk, where it assumes an imperative, relates to the manifestation of a pattern of thinking in which exceptions to the existing legal norms become not only justifiable, they become essential. This dynamic is a part of the logic of the exception that is embedded in the identity of *Homo Civicus* and leads inevitably to *Homo Sacer*.

References

Agamben, G. (2009). *What is an apparatus?* (D. Kishik, & S. Pedatella, Trans.). Stanford: Stanford University Press.

Agamben, G. (2011). *The kingdom and the glory: For a theological genealogy of economy and government* (L. Chiesa, & M. Mandarini, Trans.). Palo Alto: Stanford University Press.

Behrent, M. (2009). Liberalism without humanism: Michel Foucault and the free-market creed, 1976–1979. *Modern Intellectual History, 6*(03), 539–568. https://doi.org/10.1017/S1479244309990175.

Behrent, M. (2010). Accidents happen: François Ewald, the "antirevolutionary" Foucault, and the intellectual politics of the French welfare state. *The Journal of Modern History, 82*(3), 585–624. https://doi.org/10.1086/653042.

Behrent, M. (2012). The genealogy of genealogy: Foucault's 1970–1971 course in the will to know. *Foucault Studies, 13*(May), 157–178.

Brecht, B. (1961). On Chinese acting. *The Tulane Drama Review, 6*(1), 130–136.

Bussolini, J. (2010). What is a Dispositif? *Foucault Studies, 10*(November), 85–107.

Dean, M. (1995). Governing the unemployed self in an active society. *Economy and Society, 24*(4), 559–583. https://doi.org/10.1080/03085149500000025.

Dean, M. (2010). *Governmentality: Power and rule in modern society* (2nd ed.). London: Sage.

Dean, M. (2012). The signature of power. *Journal of Political Power, 5*(1), 101–117.

Dean, M. (2013). *The signature of power*. London: Sage.

Deleuze, G. (1991). What is a Dispositif? In T. J. Armstrong (Ed.), *Michel Foucault: Philosopher* (pp. 159–168). New York: Harvester Wheatsheaf.

Deleuze, G. (1992). Postscript on the societies of control. *October, 59*(Winter), 3–7.

Deleuze, G. (2006). What is a Dispositif? In D. Lapoujade (Ed.), *Two regimes of madness: Text and interviews, 1975–1995* (pp. 338–348). New York: Semiotext(e).

Dreyfus, H., & Rabinow, P. (1982). *Beyond structuralism and hermeneutics*. Chicago: University of Chicago Press.

Ewald, F. (1990). Norms, discipline, and the law. *Representations*, (30), 138–161.

Feinberg, J. (1970). *Doing & deserving; Essays in the theory of responsibility*. Princeton: Princeton University Press.

Foucault, M. (1972). *The archaeology of knowledge* (A. M. S. Smith, Trans.). London: Routledge.

Foucault, M. (1977). *Discipline and punish: The birth of the prison* (A. Sheridan, Trans.). London: Penguin.

Foucault, M. (1980). The confession of the flesh. In: C. Gordon (Ed.), *Power/knowledge: Selected interviews and other writings 1972–1977* (pp. 194–228).

Foucault, M. (1986). Nietzsche, genealogy, history. In P. Rabinow (Ed.), *The Foucault reader* (pp. 76–100). Harmondsworth: Penguin.

Foucault, M. (1991). Politics and the study of discourse. In G. Burchell, C. Gordon, & P. Miller (Eds.), *The Foucault effect: Studies in governmentality* (pp. 55–72). Chicago: University of Chicago Press.

Foucault, M. (1994). Truth and juridical forms. In: J. Faubion (Ed.), *Michel Foucault: Essential Works of Foucault 1954-1984* (Editions Gallimard ed., Vol. 3: Power, pp. 1–89). London: Penguin.

Foucault, M. (1997a). 'What our present is', interview with Andre Berten. In S. Lotringer (Ed.), *The politics of truth* (pp. 129–143). New York: Semiotext(e).

Foucault, M. (1997b [1984]). What is enlightenment? (C. Porter, Trans.). In: P. Rabinow (Ed.), *Michel Foucault: Essential works of Foucault 1954–1984* (Vol. 1: Ethics, pp. 319). New York: Penguin.

Foucault, M. (1998). *The history of sexuality: The will to knowledge* (R. Hurley, Trans., Vol. 1). London: Penguin.

Foucault, M. (2003). *Society must be defended* (D. Macey, Trans., Lectures at the College de France, 1975-1976). New York: Picador.

Foucault, M. (2005). *The order of things*. London/New York: Routledge.

Foucault, M. (2007). *Security, territory, population: Lectures at the college de France 1977–1978* (G. Burchell, Trans.). Basingstoke: Palgrave Macmillan.

Foucault, M. (2014). *Wrong-doing: Truth-telling* (S. Sawyer, Trans.). Chicago: University of Chicago Press.

Garland, D. (1997). 'Governmentality' and the problem of crime. *Theoretical Criminology, 1*(2), 173–214.

Gutting, G. (1989). *Michel Foucault's archaeology of scientific reason*. New York: Cambridge University Press.

Gutting, G. (Ed.). (1994). *The Cambridge companion to Foucault*. New York: Cambridge University Press.

Haggerty, K., & Ericson, R. (2000). The surveillant assemblage. *British Journal of Sociology, 51*(4), 605–622.

Hart, H. (2008). *Punishment and responsibility: Essays in the philosophy of law* (2nd ed.). Oxford: Oxford University Press.

Karlsen, M. P., & Villadsen, K. (2014). Foucault, maoism, genealogy: The influence of political militancy in Michel Foucault's thought. *New Political Science*, 1–27.

Mahon, M. (1992). *Foucault's Nietzschean genealogy: Truth, power, and the subject*. Albany: State University of New York Press.

Miller, P., & Rose, N. (2008). *Governing the present*. Cambridge: Polity.

Murphy, B. (2020). The technology of guilt. *Australasian Journal of Legal Philosophy, 44*, 64–99.

Norrie, A. (2001). *Crime, reason and history: A critical introduction to criminal law* (2nd ed.). Cambridge: Cambridge University Press.

Norrie, A. (2005). *Law and the beautiful soul*. London: GlassHouse Press.

Raffnsøe, S., Gudman-Høyer, M., & Thaning, M. (2014). Foucault's dispositive: The perspicacity of dispositive analytics in organisational research. *The Organ*, 1–27.

Rose, N. (1999). *Powers of freedom: Reframing political thought*. Cambridge: Cambridge University Press.

Rose, N., & Miller, P. (1992). Political power beyond the state: Problematics of government. *British Journal of Sociology, 43*(2), 173–205.

Rose, N., & Valverde, M. (1998). Governed by law? *Social & Legal Studies, 7*(4), 541–551.

Scheurich, J., & McKenzie, K. (2005). Foucault's methodologies: Archaeology and genealogy. In N. Denzin & Y. Lincoln (Eds.), *The sage handbook of qualitative research* (3rd ed., pp. 841–868). Thousand Oaks (CA): Sage.

Schirato, T., Danaher, G., & Webb, J. (2012). *Understanding Foucault* (2nd ed.). Sydney: Allen & Unwin.

Villadsen, K. (2008). Doing without state and civil society as universals: 'Dispositifs' of care beyond the classic sector divide. *Journal of Civil Society, 4*(3), 171–191.

Villadsen, K. (2011). Modern welfare and 'good old' philanthropy. *Public Management Review, 13*(8), 1057–1075.

Chapter 12
The Shadow of Homo Civicus

> *"[T]he decisive fact is that, together with the process by which the exception everywhere becomes the rule, the realisation of bare life – which is originally situated at the margins of the political order – gradually begins to coincide with the political realm, and exclusion and inclusion, outside and inside, bios and zoé, right and fact, enter into a irreducible zone of indistinction."*
>
> Agamben (1998)

This final chapter extends the analysis of controlled operations by locating it within Agamben's conception of *bare life* and *state of exception*. In earlier chapters it was argued that controlled operations discourse and rationality is governed by a risk-based imperative that triggers a drive to create exceptions to "ordinary law". Indeed, that rationality is not unique to controlled operations; exception is a feature of law more generally. This is a manifestation of the deep utilitarian logic operating at the heart of legal policy. Controlled operations law is a composite governance structure that imports the rationality and technologies of discipline, audit and surveillance. This combination transforms social life and constructs mechanisms that legitimate and facilitate exceptions and erect distinct antinomies in legal architectures; the unlawful becomes lawful; the inadmissible becomes admissible; the private becomes public. These legal constructs are justified and realised through legal devices triggered by exceptional conditions. Suspects and investigators are exposed to a grid of exceptional legal principles that authorise covert surveillance and qualify and remove legal protections that might otherwise apply. This insight, I contend, opens a window into the nature of contemporary forms of citizenship, and a window into that space in the politico-legal order that is not yet "bare life" as suggested by Agamben, but a much larger zone of impeachment where ordinary law and rights are qualified by risk. The "bare life" of *homo sacer* proposed by Agamben begins with a rationality fixed within the ordinary legal order – a location occupied by *Homo Civicus*. Authorised crime, and its attendant rationality, has a transformative effect on contemporary forms of citizenship.

B. Murphy, *Regulating Undercover Law Enforcement: The Australian Experience*, https://doi.org/10.1007/978-981-33-6381-6_12

To develop this argument, the chapter has been divided into five parts. Part 1 lays out a critical review of Agamben. As that part indicates, Agamben has not been well received by the legal fraternity either for his conclusions or the at times dense continental philosophy he deploys. In this part *homo sacer* and *state of exception* are considered and employed to suggest important consequences of precautionary logic. Part 2 then turns to theorise the "logic of exception" and argues that this is a powerful rationality in democratic legislative politics, vulnerable to the imperatives of risk and threat. Part 3 extends that discussion to a common exceptional logic operating in law, that of derogation, for the purpose of testing the operation of exceptional logic in the legal context. Part 4 moves the discussion to argue that controlled operations law functions to create a form of exceptional, qualified citizenship – opening a window into the emergence of differing forms of citizenship in the 21st century. This new form of citizenship, *homo civicus*, is the subject of part 5.

Agamben and his Heresies

The decision to segue into Agamben was a considered one, for two reasons. The first was the character of the evidence that emerged during this study. Not only was there a distinct discourse of risk intersecting with audit, there was an important but buried dynamic essentially concerned with the manufacture and application of exceptions to established legality. These exceptions were quite profound and could not be explained through doctrinal analysis beyond the conditions and mechanisms of the exception. The second reason relates to a consideration of the clustering of rationalities within controlled operations policy and discourse. Risk and audit are common elements in liberal and neo-liberal rationalities. But in addition, exception has also been recognised as a major element of neoliberal rationality. In her examination of East-Asian labour and finance relations, Ong has forcefully argued that neoliberalism is saturated with exceptional logic (Ong 2006). Confronted with both empirical and theoretical imperatives, it became necessary to extend the argument one step further by turning to the modern master on the logic of exception: Agamben.

Before developing this argument, it is necessary to understand the Foucauldian extension offered by Agamben. Agamben's later works are concerned with the intersections between law, politics, and philosophy. Here Agamben turned his attention to the ways modern governments attempt to merge life, law, and politics through the creation of a contradictory field of policy. This field recognises rights and liberties on the one hand, while simultaneously erasing and qualifying them on the other. Like most scholars, Agamben's work does not follow a linear trajectory. His work covers a broad range of topics, ranging from metaphysical questions concerning potentialities, aesthetic questions linked to language, representations and "the object", messianic treatises on the nature of happiness, time and utopia, and, of present relevance, the biopolitical nexus between the human subject, law and sovereignty (Mensard 2004; De la Durantaye 2009; Mills 2008). Only the latter is of present relevance.

Agamben's biopolitical project is reflected in two major concepts. The first is the concept of "homo sacer", or "bare life". The second is the power of decision to determine the nature and application of exceptions, a bio-political decision that results in the "state of exception". These concepts are linked and extend Foucault's biopower thesis. In this respect Agamben is a complementary theoretical framework. Indeed, Agamben expressly intended that his work would function to either correct, or complete, aspects of Foucault's work (Agamben 1998). Before turning to the details of these two major concepts, some consideration of Agamben's critics must be presented.

The Critique of Agamben

Agamben has attracted considerable interest in Europe, ranging from the broadly supportive and complimentary, through to outright opposition and hostility. There are, however, only a few authoritative commentaries, notably De la Durantaye, to which the reader is referred for analysis (Lewis 1999; Nikolopoulou 2000; Raulff 2004; Mensard 2004; Mills 2008; De la Durantaye 2009; Humphreys 2006). The extent to which Agamben's work has penetrated Australian scholarship is limited. Although his work has generated a reasonable amount of controversy and commentary in Europe, generally Agamben's work appears infrequently in Australian legal writing (Moran 2001; Jenkins 2004; Bird 2005; Crowley-Cyr 2005; Johns 2005; Bailey 2009), and tends to be concentrated in the work of specific scholars, such as Whyte (2009, 2012, 2013) and McLoughlin (2009a, b, 2012), rather than a widely endorsed theoretical model. Indeed, as discussed below, legal scholars are largely critical of Agamben. Agamben's work is ongoing, and a number of his publications have post-dated much of the commentary on his work, complicated by the fact his work is ordinarily published in Italian first, before translation into English. These limitations are, however, peripheral, as his work on *homo sacer* and *state of exception* are now well known in English.

The legal fraternity is generally highly critical of Agamben. Schotel (2009), for example, offers a scathing critique, arguing that Agamben advocates a "sellout" of legal practice, suggesting that Agamben can only offer a "dangerous" cluster of incomplete theories that lack sufficient understanding of law and its operation, and should be altogether discouraged as a theoretical model for law. For Schotel, Agamben's conclusions are simply untenable. He argues that Agamben fails to address complex questions of law, legal practice and politics because of his heavy reliance on philosophy, particularly Carl Schmitt's theory of sovereignty. Schotel is especially critical of Agamben's assumption that the exercise of executive power is routinely a breach of international or domestic law, or beyond the supervision of the judiciary, rightly pointing out that international and domestic law does operate in ways that offer protections for the vulnerable and of itself has a powerful normative force even in the absence of jurisdiction. In addition, Schotel argues that Agamben also seems to assume that legal professionals are themselves inactive players in the processes that create "homo sacer", when the reality is that lawyers are actively involved, at least in Western democracies, in those locations where Agamben suggests the subject has been abandoned. In short, Schotel argues that the rule of law does operate, and is sufficiently complicated that it cannot be reduced to a single philosophical or genealogical enquiry.

This critique of Agamben is powerful and cannot be ignored. It illustrates one of the difficulties identified at the outset, and that is the problem that arises through approaching a problem through the lens of a single discipline. I agree with Schotel that Agamben's theories do not properly, or accurately, engage with the complexities of legality. They contain a fundamental assumption that needs to be cautiously handled, and that is that all legal systems are necessarily the same, and that the dynamic Agamben identified operates in all legal systems. This is simply not the case. Schotel also correctly indicates that law, properly understood, is a complex phenomenon that includes not only statements of rules, but also jurisprudential principles, norms and precedent that operates in linear and lateral trajectories. Perhaps the most significant issue is Schotel's view that legal problems cannot be answered *primarily* through philosophical or genealogical enquiry. As a legal scholar, I am inclined to agree with this conclusion. The present work illustrates the highly nuanced and complex system of relationships involved in the process of lawmaking, enforcement, and conceptualisation to illustrate this point. The suggestion that executive action is beyond the supervision of the judiciary, even in the more extreme cases such as Guantanamo, is also incorrect.[1] However, as I will argue below, Agamben has identified a dynamic that requires considerable attention: the consequence of a shift in policy and law towards the normalisation of exceptions to ordinary law, of the tendency to authorise locations outside the purview of judicial review, and the consequence of that dynamic for human rights and citizenship. For that reason alone, Agamben cannot be dismissed. Agamben rightly challenges legal scholars and invites reconsideration of established legal norms.[2]

The critique of Agamben is not limited to Schotel. Lewis (1999) has argued that Agamben's reliance on Foucault's theory and method locked Agamben into the same problems as Foucault – in particular, a general failure to provide evidence in support of his claims. The result, Lewis argued, is that Agamben's thesis was basically limited to theory, supported by fragments of citations to other theories. Agamben's argument is a theory built upon theory, as opposed to an evidence-based claim. There is merit to this critique. Any reading of Agamben, or Foucault for that matter, needs to tread carefully in the world of ideas and the apparent absence of "evidence" beyond that which is self-evident, or the ideas found in other theories. Foucault, in particular, challenges the very concept of "empirical evidence",

[1] Eg: *Hamdi v Rumsfeld* 542 US 507 (2004)

[2] In *State of Exception* Agamben begins with a provocation: "Quare siletis juristae in munere vestro?" [Why are you jurists silent about that which concern you?]

observing that very often "evidence" is a privileged or authorised voice or version of events, and in some instances the absence of evidence is just as important as its presence. A core component of genealogy is an alternative vision of "the empirical" and the assumption that histories necessarily have a point of origin.[3] Legal scholars often overlook Foucault's challenge to the use and deployment of evidence because they are trained to locate, interpret and contextualise posited (but contextually qualified) fact. It is also inaccurate to assume that either of these writers produced their work in isolation or in the absence of evidence. Agamben and Foucault's work was clearly based on the identification of specific exemplars intended to demonstrate a specific concept or paradigmatic example. Agamben used, for example, specific laws, Guantanamo Bay and controversially, Auschwitz to illustrate his thinking. Similarly, Foucault's work cannot be understood as absent empirical foundations. Although Foucault's work often assumes of level of knowledge on the part of the reader, (particularly continental philosophy), his work relies on an exhaustive synthesis of original material.[4] The endurance of Foucault arises from the fact that it is deeply rooted within a combination of the theoretical traditions of Europe, and in the rich primary source materials that informed his work. Foucault's work *was* empirically grounded. It was presented in a highly synthesised form, rather than the frenetic obsession with footnotes demonstrated by most legal writers.

Other criticism of Agamben tends to be less forthright than Schotel and Lewis. In most cases the critique tends to be more nuanced. For example, Frost (2010) provides a comprehensive and critical analysis of Agamben's use of Foucault arguing that Agamben's understanding of law is based on what is referred to as the "expulsion thesis", a now discredited reading of Foucault's works.[5] Frost suggests that Agamben is more closely aligned to Foucault than Agamben himself realises. Frost argues that Agamben clarifies and extends Foucauldian conceptions of biopolitics and law, as opposed to establishing a new ontology. In essence, *bare life* and *state of exception* are an extension of Foucault, rather than something new.

In an equally nuanced critique, Passavant (2007) considers one of the fundamental problems with the political dimension of Agamben; his failure to move beyond identifying a problem, without providing any sense of capacity to move forward, other than to engage in an abstract re-imagination of relationships, in the face of an identified state power. Although recognising that Agamben suggests that a new humanity is possible in a future beyond the state, Passavant maintains there is an apparent inability within Agamben's work to articulate the future beyond the

[3] Classically, see *Nietzsche, Genealogy, Morals* in Foucault (1986)

[4] Foucault's three volumes of the History of Sexuality, contains extensive deployment of primary materials, particularly classical texts. It may well be that a great deal of the bibliographic materials was excised from Foucault's work in the translation into English. Jean Khalfa observed in the 2006 reprint of *Madness and Civilisation* that the original translation of *Histoire de la Folie* (1961) was translated into English in 1972, a process which removed some 300 pages of text, including 800 footnotes and the bibliography! The 2006 edition was re-titled *History of Madness*, which restored much of the excised material. See Foucault (2006)

[5] A debate that is neatly captured by Baxter (1995) and Golder & Fitzpatrick (2009).

capacities or reach of the state. Basically, Agamben's thinking is locked into an ontology of power and otherness within in the bounds of the state. We need to treat this argument carefully. While it is true that Agamben is closely tied to a theory of life enmeshed with the state and power, Passavant's argument pre-dated Agamben's later exploration of life beyond the state – particularly the *Kingdom and the Glory* (Agamben 2011) and *Opus Dei* (Agamben 2013b). Nevertheless, the dynamic identified by Agamben is part of the fundamental rationality of governance and is deeply entrenched within the transformation of the nation state underway within late modernity. Simply put, the "public profile" of the nation state is fading, and in some cases invisible, but cannot be said to be "absent". If anything, the institutional and legal apparatus of the modern state is intensifying at the point of is reduced visibility, a conclusion that tends to confirm a future that remains locked into a complex relationship of power between citizen and the state.

Agamben's apparent state-centred pessimism is also identified by Lemke (2005), who suggests that Agamben tends to focus on legal and political "negatives". Lemke argues that Agamben fails to adequately recognise the public good available through the law and the state, tending to focus on the state and law as an instrument of oppression, as opposed to an instrument of liberation and public positive governance. Agamben appears to focus primarily on the negative conduct of the state and law. There is little in the way of clear recognition of the value of government to the advancement of the human condition. Similarly, Lemke rightly identifies Agamben's conception of law is mainly public, as opposed to private. Fundamentally, Agamben's focus is on law facilitating state power, and does little to recognise the value of law in shaping public policy in a positive manner, or the observance and recognition of public exchange operating through private law. It needs to be said, however, that Agamben was not interested in the operation of ordinary law. Agamben's interest is on the expression of law as a manifestation of sovereign power. Although Lemke's criticism needs to be kept in mind, Agamben is interested in the frontiers of law, rather than its core.

Gregory (2006) also challenges Agamben's apparent pessimism. For Gregory, Guantanamo is not only the site for the deployment of political and sovereign power. Guantanamo reveals the Foucauldian observation that all sites of power invoke sites of resistance. Gregory argues that despite the abject poverty of the spirit evidenced in locations like Guantanamo there remained a clear defiance; a location of resistance that invited a deeper consideration of power beyond sovereignty and abject domination. Rather, these locations must be understood as sites of political struggle. The extent to which the "resistance" of a subject under total control is actually meaningful is another question. To suggest that the subject of the kind of extreme violence that exists outside the law is able to "resist" in anything more than a token way is nonsense.

It is worth observing the theme of pessimism in Agamben is perhaps eclipsed, given that Agamben's more recent work explores the possibilities of meaningful life beyond the state, which in many ways is drawing heavily on well-established Christian theology (Agamben 2005b, 2007, 2010, 2011, 2013a, b). Indeed, in many ways the accusation of pessimism is unfair, since Agamben re-opened a space that had already been opened by Hannah Arendt, Walter Benjamin and Foucault. Analysis of the realities of power and totalitarianism are necessarily pessimistic.

More recently, Hauka (2013), drawing on the work of work of Vito (2006), is critical of Agamben's argument that the state of exception is a "lawless void". Hauka argues that the state of exception is fundamentally a creature of law, and refutes the idea it is either a permanent development, or as powerful as Agamben suggests. The dynamics in law and the social world constituting spaces of exception are, in fact "saturated with law rather than devoid of it", and that much of that saturation is concerned with restraining power rather than enabling it (Hauka 2013). Hauka argues, in line with Foucault, that all sites of power import sites of resistance, and that Agamben's conception of "sovereignty" is impliedly monolithic, when the reality is that spaces of exception are the product of a plurality of actors, institutions and laws. Hauka's critique must be considered. Law and sovereignty are symbiotic; and while law can be a channel for oppressive and executive power, it can also function as an important limitation on executive power. Indeed, law is the vehicle through which executive power can be checked and held to account – at least to that point where the legal order remains functional. Once the raw violence that exists outside the constituted legal order dominates, the capacity of law to hold that kind of power in place is doubtful.

Tagma (2010) shares this view, arguing that Agamben basically preferences sovereignty, whereas Foucault's thesis is actually more concerned with a more nuanced analysis of power. Foucault regards sovereignty as a part of a larger project and dynamic of government, conceived as the triangulation of sovereignty, discipline and government management of populations. Biopower is, in effect, the product of the operation of various forms of power, much of which exists beyond sovereignty (Foucault 2007). Consequently, Tagma argues that Agamben's theories need to be further developed and extended in order to position it as a (narrow) advance on Foucault.

To this must be added Ong's critique. Ong challenges Agamben at several levels. First, Ong argues that Agamben's notion of "bare life" and "state of exception" owes much of its character to post-war European thinking, particularly Arendt and Schmitt – a tradition that is indelibly printed with the holocaust. The result is a unified conception of "the human condition" and an ethical ontology that basically provides a binary organisation of humanity – the excluded and the included, those with rights, and those without. Ong argues this bifurcation is flawed, because it excludes the power of non-Judeo-Christian universalising ethical systems (Islam and Buddhism, for example) in providing alternative ethical structures, and denies the possibility of a plurality of concurrent conceptions of life. Ong challenges the idea that the possession, mediation and articulation of rights involve both complex processes of negotiation and expression and is not necessarily dependent on fixed geographies. Finally, Ong argues the very idea of abandonment in the "zone of indistinction" is factually wrong, because even in "failed states" a complex intervention of non-government organisations routinely takes place. What takes place is not "abandonment", but intensive intervention that reorders and reclassifies humanity, in which citizenship and law is only a part of the picture (Ong 2006, pp. 21–25).

While these paragraphs do not set out an exhaustive review of Agamben's critics, it is neither necessary nor prudent to do so. The point is to recognise there are shortcomings with Agamben's theories. Rooted in the Foucauldian and post-structuralist traditions, Agamben often fails to satisfy readers from outside those disciplines – particularly jurists. Agamben tends to operate on the basis of assumptions and pre-existing theories, with an overall theme that is rather gloomy. Yet Agamben invites us to reflect deeply on a powerful dynamic operating within law. This dynamic has two dimensions of present relevance. The first is the construction, through law, of the legal subject. Legal architectures construct human identities. This construction is complex, involving intersections of law, bio-politics, personality, ethnicity, and historical location. This is a socio-legal grid including several temporary and permanent potentialities. Agamben alerts us to the fact that human beings, under certain conditions, may have their identities reconfigured through law and power and become *homo sacer*. Agamben also alerts us to the creeping effect of legal mechanisms that constructs those temporary and permanent potentialities that result in the proliferation of exception laws articulating executive power, and of the conditions where exception develops. This space, within the jurisprudential metaphysic, is necessarily tied to the power of the sovereign to make law and create exceptions, and to discourses of risk and necessity. The second dimension is the operation of the sovereign power to *alter the rules* to capture and exclude new threats to the social and legal order. It is at this intersection that we find an array of conditions that can trigger potentialities. In other words, the logic of necessity and exception is deployed in response to clusters of risk, danger, and threat. In societies in which risk is a key component of social life, the need for the expansion of executive powers increases to address apparent shortcomings in law and policy. Exceptional laws have begun to proliferate. This dynamic, I contend, operates within the legal space we know as controlled operation. At this point we need to turn our attention to *Homo Sacer* and the *State of Exception*.

Homo Sacer

Homo Sacer is a term originating in the laws of ancient Rome.[6] It was a declared identity of a citizen in breach of the criminal or religious law. The person was declared "sacred" – his life consigned to the gods, but ritually unclean. He could not be sacrificed but killing "homo sacer" was a religious act, if not duty. Killing homo sacer was not murder, it was an authorised execution. The person was, effectively, consigned to the gods as "dead man walking" – separated from the people by a

[6] Agamben expressly refers to Pompeius Festus. See Agamben (1998)

religious, legal, and political declaration. Ordinarily, a citizen's body was protected by law unless they broke it; and even then, the death penalty applied only in rare cases. Once the declaration was made, the subject was no longer able to invoke the protection of laws – they had been abandoned by law at the same time they were captured by it (Agamben 1998; Murray and White 2011). Agamben argues this power to protect or excise the citizen from the legal order constitutes a fundamental component of sovereign power, in contrast to Foucault's argument that the biopolitical power of sovereignty changed during the eighteenth century so that sovereign power captured life and death quite late in the history of sovereignty. Agamben argues that the biopolitical power of the monarch over life and death through law is the *original activity* of sovereign power (Genel 2006; Frost 2010). This capacity to include or exclude the person from law constitutes a merger between law, power and politics into a "zone of indistinction". In *Homo Sacer*, Agamben explained the dynamic in these terms:

> *The political sphere of sovereignty was ... constituted through a double exclusion, as an excrescence of the profane in the religious and the religious in the profane, which takes the form of a zone of indistinction between sacrifice and homicide. The sovereign sphere is the sphere in which it is permitted to kill without committing homicide and without celebrating a sacrifice, and sacred life – that is, life that may be killed but not sacrificed – is the life that has been captured in this sphere.* (Agamben 1998)

Agamben argued that the resulting politico-legal capture was the production of a very different type of life. It is life that exists at the intersection between sovereign power, theology, and law, which Agamben called "bare life" (*la nuda vita*):

> *The life caught in the sovereign ban is the life that is originarily sacred – that is, that may be killed but not sacrificed – and, in this sense, the production of bare life is the originary activity of sovereignty. The sacredness of life, which is invoked today as an absolutely fundamental right in opposition to sovereign power, in fact originally expresses precisely both life's subjection to a power over death and life's irrepairable exposure in the relation of abandonment.* (Agamben 1998)

Bare life represents a peculiar status in politics and law, and part of its character can only be understood by tracing the origin of the term. In Agamben's work *bare life* is a composite, drawn from classical Greek and Roman concepts. It refers to the inscription of legal status attached to the notion of what constitutes "life". Agamben observed that the Greeks had no single word for "life". Rather, a distinction was drawn between the life common to all living beings (*zoé*), and a normative concept of life "proper" for human beings (*bios*) (Agamben 1998, 2000). The former are those simple biological processes necessary for the continued existence of the organism, while the latter are concerned with the qualities of civilisation. De la Durantaye (2009) observes that Agamben drew heavily on the earlier work of Walter Benjamin and Hannah Arendt in conceiving bare life as the result of the politicisation of life by the state, with the ultimate result that the qualities of civilised life traditionally attributed to human beings are stripped back to mere existence through the intersections of political, physical and legal power. The result is a biopolitical process where the qualities of life common to all living beings also become a form of life conferred and inscribed by sovereign power. Life itself comes to rely on law, politics and power. In its ultimate form, Agamben argues that the modern manifestation of *bare life* is represented by subjects at the margins of the politico-legal order: refugees, inmates at Guantanamo Bay, prisoners, the mentally ill, and the "muselmann" of concentration camps (Agamben 1999).

Agamben also identifies much deeper social and cultural images rooted in the deep recesses of European consciousness, the *outlaw* and the *werewolf*. The outlaw has been cast out of the group for their behaviour, or for the perceived threat that figure brings to the group. This is a figure that represents danger and threat, who possesses the same qualities as Homo Sacer: the outlaw may be expelled, or killed, because of the threat they represent. This figure is closely associated with the werewolf, an even more dangerous figure because of its capacity to blend in with the "ordinary population", but possesses the heart and soul of the Wolf – a predator, apparently trustworthy, who may be transformed unpredictably under the right conditions into a beast that only extraordinary power and violence can contain. Unlike the outlaw, the werewolf never belonged to the group, but can move within it, and able to infect and subvert the group and individuals within it. The werewolf is "neither man nor beast, and who dwells paradoxically within both while belonging to neither." (Agamben 1998). The image of the werewolf represents a latent archetype – a figure able to be mobilised as the eternal threat within, justifying surveillance, intervention, and law. These archetypes engender anxiety, fear and in some cases panic, mobilising politics, law and power in ways designed to isolate and eradicate these figures – contemporary examples being sex offenders, "bikies" and terrorists. Homo Sacer, inscribed with the identity of outlaw, werewolf, or simply as social threat, is transformed through law into a new social and legal identity.

Homo Sacer, then, may be understood as a legal status conveyed through sovereign power that relies upon formal (legal) processes for its conveyance, and physical violence and intervention for its implementation. As observed by Wall (2005), homo sacer is a form of life perpetually at risk of legal and physical violence. This status functions to provide the social, political and legal legitimacy for the exercise of that power and the moral justification for its deployment. The practical effect of this power is to strip the subject of the qualities of citizenship ordinarily attached to life that is "proper or correct" for human beings (*bios*), and to politicise the life that is common to human beings (*zoé*). In so doing the legal apparatus that operates to construct homo sacer appropriates qualities of existence independent of that apparatus. The qualities of existence, in effect, are transformed so that the individual comes to depend upon the sovereign power for the continuation of life. The qualities of existence that were conferred on the organism at the moment of conception, and continue to be in the possession of the organism until its death, and now owed to the sovereign, rather than being an absolute possession common to the living. It is a status that often begins with the declaration the person is part of a group that threatens the social order (as outlaw or werewolf), and ultimately results in the application of laws authorising forms of intervention not normally applied to "ordinary" and "virtuous" populations. In many ways, homo sacer is a wretched figure, possessed of life, but reliant upon others for its continuation, in the knowledge that the continuation is infused with discretion, legality and violence. It is for this reason that Agamben argued, controversially, that the concentration camp provides the paradigm example as the "nomos of the modern" (Agamben 1998, 2000).

State of Exception

Homo sacer does not happen accidentally. It is the intentional application of law, power, and politics. Indeed, Agamben argues that the process of capture and exclusion of life is the foundation of sovereignty and the political order on which all government depends and has done so since humanity began to live and organise itself in towns and cities. Bare life is the product of the operation of the zone of indistinction; indeed, it is its purpose.

This dynamic has important implications for human rights and democracy itself. Agamben argues that much of the philosophical underpinning of rights-based liberal discourse is concerned with attaching and emphasising an array of rights to protect humanity against the excesses and abuses of sovereign power. The contradiction is that modern democracies rely precisely upon the same source of power to emphasise and recognise human rights, with the result that rights remain politicised and inscribed with the very legality that qualifies and removes them:

> *Behind the long, strife-ridden process that leads to the recognition of rights and formal liberties stands once again the body of the sacred man with his double sovereign, his life that cannot be sacrificed yet may, nevertheless, be killed.* (Agamben 1998)

The result is that Western democratic societies find themselves in a double-bind: despite claims of natural law theorists, human rights *are* attached to the political and legal order. Increasingly, individuals and groups rely upon sovereign power in order to recognise, validate and uphold rights in the face of their abuses and infringement. At the same time, the very mechanisms that recognise, validate and uphold those rights also provide mechanisms for their qualification, derogation or removal. In this environment we encounter the ghost of Bentham and his ardent criticism of "natural rights". Bentham argued that the idea that human beings possess "rights" by simple virtue of being human was absurd: "[n]atural rights is simple nonsense: natural and imprescriptible rights, rhetorical nonsense, – nonsense on stilts." (Bentham 1843). At the same time Bentham made a prophetic statement: "…there is no right, which ought not to be maintained so long as it is upon the whole advantageous to the society that it should be maintained, so there is no right which, when the abolition of it is advantageous to society, should not be abolished." (Ibid). Bentham was clearly inferring the sovereign logic that would later characterise Carl Schmitt's decisional definition of sovereignty in his 1934 treatise *Political Theology*: "[s]overeign is he who decides on the exception." (Schmitt 2010). The capacity of the sovereign to qualify, derogate and, in some cases, suspend the legal order is a fundamental component of sovereign power that is at once within and outside of legal systems. Although law and the history of constitutionalism has been directed to the elimination or restriction of this dynamic, Schmitt was very much aware that the power of the state to depart from the "legal norm" was ultimately political and physical rather than legal (Schmitt 2010).

Drawing heavily on Schmitt, in *State of Exception*, Agamben traced a history of this dynamic, finding that the "state of exception" is linked to the perception or reality of some emergency, crisis or threat. In that environment governments tend to drift into a logic intended to control, reduce, or eliminate that threat. Agamben demonstrated that this dynamic has been evident in all the major European legal systems. Beginning with the idea of a "state of siege" in France following the Revolution in 1791, all European legal systems incorporated provisions that allowed for the alteration and suspension of law in times of crisis (Agamben 2005a). Agamben argues that this same dynamic is evident even in the legal system of the great champion of rights, the United States. Drawing on Rossiter's comprehensive *Constitutional Dictatorship,* (Rossiter 1948) Agamben cited Rossiter's proposition that:

> *in times of crisis a democratic, constitutional government must temporarily be altered to whatever degree is necessary to overcome the peril and restore normal conditions. This alteration inevitably involves government of a stronger character; that is, the government will have more power and the people fewer rights.* (Rossiter 1948; Agamben 2005a)

It is this dynamic, Agamben suggests, that operates within the rationality of the exception, manifested recently and most powerfully by the United States in 2001 in the form of the *Patriot Act,* which provided for the indefinite incarceration of non-citizens suspected of terrorism (Agamben 2005a).

Agamben argues that the logic of the exception, and the associated suspension of the legal order, effectively results in two things. First, it results in the production of a new framework of legal norms at once apparently "illegal", or at least contrary to the existing norm, but at the same time entirely *lawful* through their production and alteration through juridical and constitutional systems (Agamben 2005a). In effect, the conduct proposed is recognised as initially unlawful, but declared to be lawful in the circumstances. Secondly, the state of exception and the suspension of the legal order produces *homo sacer*. This dynamic rests upon the capacity of the sovereign power to both capture and exclude subjects inside the legal order. This process is achieved in two ways. The first is through operation of ordinary law. The second is through the operation of an exception. In both cases the object of governance is captured by law, either through its ordinary application, or through an exception that captures the particular subject. In the most extreme case, the sovereign decision may result in a complete suspension of the legal order. Drawing upon Schmitt's thesis that sovereign power is ultimately traced to the ability to decide upon and determine exceptions to law (Schmitt 2010), Agamben concluded that there was a relationship between the logic involved in the determination of an exception, and the production of bare life.

What concerns Agamben is the proliferation of this logic as an ordinary feature of law and sovereign power. "Exceptional law" has become a routine feature in late modernity (Agamben 2005a). In his view, the state of exception is characterised by the coincidence of ordinary and exceptional law, arguing that:

> *[p]olitical organisation is not regressing towards outdated forms; rather, premonitory events are, like bloody masses, announcing the new nomos of the Earth, which (if its grounding principle is not called into question) will soon extend itself over the entire planet.* (Agamben 1998)

To speak, then, of the "state of exception" is to speak of two things. Firstly, it refers to an individual event characterised by the operation of an exception to laws that would normally apply. Secondly, it refers to the operation of this logic across the whole legal system. Under the right conditions, the state of exception can effectively extend to the whole system of law, becoming a "suspension of the juridical order" (Agamben 2005a). What is critical here is that the latter can overrule the former. In effect, in a "state of emergency" the ordinary operation of law may be suspended, partially or in totality, temporarily or permanently. The state of exception functions to subsume, or compartmentalise, spaces within the legal order in ways that allow the original activity of the state – the production of biopolitical life – to operate. In most cases this production normally applies to a class or groups, but in the most extreme case can apply to the population as a whole (Agamben 2005a). Agamben argues that although this dynamic began during the 19th century, it began to proliferate during the European crises of the 20th century in the conflict between democracy, fascism and communism, and has continued and intensified into the opening decades of the 21st century. Agamben argued that "the state of exception comes more and more to the foreground as the fundamental political structure and ultimately begins to become the rule." (Agamben 1998). The consequence of this dynamic, Agamben suggested, was that legal systems are increasingly characterised by a basic structure composed of exceptional mechanisms, and the condition of humanity was one where an ever growing number of people were living "bare life" as *homines sacri* (Agamben 1998).

The Logic of the Exception

In *State of Exception* Agamben argued that although the "state of exception" has been well recognised and considered by political scientists, "there is still no theory of the state of exception in public law" (Agamben 2005a). Agamben made a considerable contribution to theorising the state of exception and homo sacer, but was less clear about the critical dynamic operating within both that has import for jurisprudence – and that is the nature of the "logic of the exception". What, then, is the "logic of the exception"? What are some of its triggers? How does it manifest?

It appears the logic of the exception is tied to both the legal and executive aspects of sovereign power. There must be a sovereign power possessed with executive and legal power for the dynamic to operate. The logic begins to operate when that sovereign power is presented with a crisis. There must be some emergency or perceived threat. This threat will mobilise a logic of imperative and necessity, typically manifested in a public rhetoric of danger, threat and need. The sovereign must act to preserve the preconditions of existence. The greater the threat, the greater the imperative. Rossiter ominously declared: "[n]o sacrifice is too great for our democracy, least of all the temporary sacrifice of democracy itself." (Rossiter 1948). In this context the sovereign will determine to act according to the magnitude of the threat. Those actions will typically manifest in one of three ways: through the executive limb of power, the legislative, or both. Importantly, when the ordinary operation of those processes is inadequate, there is an associated intensification in the imperative, which drives a demand for novelty and an exception in order to deal with the dissonance between the threat and the inadequacy of ordinary intervention. Legality is achieved when executive, legislative and judicial opinion and intervention are aligned. In the context of law, the logic of exception depends on the existence of a power able to declare the conditions and scope of an exception. Thus, the critical moment is the "sovereign decision" argued by Schmitt and Agamben.

It appears that that the logic of the exception is highly susceptible to the discourses of risk, danger and uncertainty. Risk, danger, and uncertainty are fundamental triggers for the imperative rationality of the controlled operation, and it seems probable that risk, danger and uncertainty are generic factors enmeshed in the logic of the exception. As observed by Douglas (1990, 2002), threat, impurity and danger are powerful drivers of collective behaviour. The inevitable conclusion is that the logic of exception forms a major component in the rationality of governance. The reflexive obsession with information collection and surveillance constitutes the "detection" end of a spectrum that ultimately ends in an intervention, which may draw upon the logic of imperative and exception to achieve the goal of containment.

One of the weaknesses of Agamben (and to be fair this was not his intention), is his failure to examine the ways in which the logic of the exception might manifest in doctrinal law. Part 2 provides some indicators of how the logic of exception can manifest in public policy and doctrinal law. As risk, danger and uncertainty are fundamental triggers for the imperative that gives rise to exceptional logic, imperative reasoning searches for epistemic codes to provide mechanisms that can be used to address those factors giving rise to the imperative. In this case, those epistemic codes reflect the rationalities embedded within the episteme of late modernity concerned with the project of governance. The entrenched neoliberal coding, or episteme, identified by Foucault in *Archaeology of Knowledge* and *The Order of Things* provides some indicators as to the nature of those rationalities. In controlled operations law and policy, we find these codes manifested both in policy and law. One of the vehicles for the logic of the exception is the alteration of existing law, shaped to absorb the contradiction of an authorised crime. In this way exceptional powers are arranged within the framework of legality.

In Part 2 we also observed the rationality of audit presented as a mechanism to ensure transparency in the activities of law enforcement. The rationality of audit draws upon classic conceptions of audit and accountability, through processes of authorisation, documentation, scrutiny, and reporting. This rationality overlaps with another aspect of late modernity, surveillance. The practices associated with controlled operations are saturated with devices and practices of surveillance, ranging from broad spectrum information collection, to precision surveillance of individuals, telecommunications interception, and the manufacture of artificial realities through deception to create a controlled environment where the behaviour of the suspect can be directly observed. Surveillance overlaps with yet another feature of late modernity, reflexivity. Reflexivity, in this sense, is the perpetual collection, evaluation and deployment of information collected from a plurality of sources, both official and unofficial. The effect of these rationalities is to provide a broad disciplinary power that may be applied to deviance behaviour, as well as to ordinary behaviour, both suspect and the investigator. In addition, these rationalities also provide a technology of power, which inscribes itself on the activities of individuals, and provides a mechanism to produce truth about the individual, their behaviours, but also the behaviours of police agencies. It is a system that mobilises both disciplinary and biopower. These rationalities intersect at various points with the rationality of risk. Risk provides a structured rationality and technology for the identification, control, management and ideally, elimination of risk. In the present case, risk rationalities demand mechanisms that allow for the detection, control, and evaluation of risk through the technology of doctrinal law and the apparatus of investigation.

The imperative logic that governs the decision to change the law is not tied to the inability of the existing law to meet the challenge presented at the intersection of existing law and new forms of threat. Part of the drive is the apparent failure of the existing legal structures to deal with novel situations and threat in ways aligned with the preferred agenda of government. Failure and dysfunction, recognised as key aspects of the rationality of governance (Hunt and Wickham 1994), appear to be tied to the logic of the exception. The failure of existing law, the presence of risk and insecurity, and the imperative attached to action, link questions of contingency, exception, and sovereignty. As Arias argues, these demands are primary reasons for the very existence of government. The requirement for exceptional measures is, in fact, one of the reasons for government. The presence of risk, uncertainty and threat demands government action. Emergency and contingencies are necessarily part of the concern of sovereignty (Velasco Arias 2011). The result is that the proliferation of risk and threat becomes a validating exercise for the decision-maker in creating working exceptions able to address the problem.

In addition, the logic of exception is tied to the normative as a reference point. As discussed in the previous chapter, law is intimately connected to the identification and articulation of the normative. In this respect exception is also tied to the production of the normative. Prozorov (2005) and Huysmans (2006), for example, argued that the articulation of exceptions is a necessary part of articulating the ordinary. The contours of the "ordinary" are reinforced by the existence and expression of exceptions to it. The "ordinary" is constituted as much by those objects external to it as it is by those objects part of it. Consequently, the logic of exception plays a critical role in defining the normative. I would argue that while a great deal of attention is directed to the character and nature of the exception, an equally important part of exceptional logic is an associated characterisation of what the exception is a departure from. Ordinary and exceptional law are concurrent states of the legal norm. The existence of exception augments the identity and value of the norm, and functions to determine its constitution.

Ong has argued that the logic of exception operates in complex, often contradictory ways. It may operate at multiple and concurrent sites within the same field of social policy. Exceptions may, on the one hand, be deployed to protect society, but at the same time remove or wind back social, political or economic benefits normally or historically operative in that location. Citizenship may offer certain benefits and entitlements to citizens but be unavailable for non-citizens. Ong links these dynamics to the extension of market rationalities into public policy, an event that results in a fragmentation and rearticulation of citizenship and the state. The logic of exception "allows for a measure of sovereign flexibility in ways that both fragment and extend the space of the nation state" (Ong 2006, p. 7). In other words, the logic of exception provides a mechanism that opens the ordinary confines of law and policy into a flexible technology of governance and a significant component of contemporary sovereignty.

The logic of the exception must therefore be understood as forming part of a complex knowledge system directed to the deployment of sovereign decisions. Controlled operations law, equally, can be understood as the by-product of the agglomeration of intersecting rationalities informed by distinct knowledge systems (risk management, audit, accountability), which form a part of the cultural practices characteristic of late modernity (surveillance and control), which function to produce unique subjects within the neoliberal legal order. The problem in conceptualising the logic of the exception along the lines proposed by Agamben is its abstraction and its exact interface with legal theory. It is fundamentally based upon the idea of decision-making, and that decision rests with the sovereign power vested in the modern state. The decision that Agamben speaks of is fundamentally a part of both the political and the legal order.

Derogation as Diagram of the Exception

One of the problems conceptualising the state of exception in law is that law routinely makes use of a variety of exceptions. The concept that closely matches Agamben's logic is the principle of derogation. Derogation is a formal departure from the ordinary rules that would otherwise apply in those circumstances. Derogation is justified based on crisis or emergency. It is used most clearly in the context of human rights law, and in this respect is most closely aligned to Agamben's theory.

The mechanism and logic of derogation can be seen most clearly in Article 4 of the International Covenant on Civil and Political Rights (ICCPR)[7]:

[7]Australia signed the covenant on 18 December 1972, and subsequently ratified it on 13 August 1980.

1. *In time of public emergency which threatens the life of the nation and the existence of which is officially proclaimed, the States Parties to the present Covenant may take measures derogating from their obligations under the present Covenant to the extent strictly required by the exigencies of the situation, provided that such measures are not inconsistent with their other obligations under international law and do not involve discrimination solely on the ground of race, colour, sex, language, religion or social origin.*
2. *No derogation from articles 6, 7, 8 (paragraphs I and 2), 11, 15, 16 and 18 may be made under this provision.*
3. *Any State Party to the present Covenant availing itself of the right of derogation shall immediately inform the other States Parties to the present Covenant, through the intermediary of the Secretary-General of the United Nations, of the provisions from which it has derogated and of the reasons by which it was actuated. A further communication shall be made, through the same intermediary, on the date on which it terminates such derogation.*

Here derogation is justified because of public emergency. It operates through formal declaration and notification made to other State parties. It is both decision and declaration. In theory, it is limited by a requirement for both a proportional and time limited response, pursued for a legitimate purpose, and subject to compatibility with international law. In particular, the derogation mechanism in this case may not infringe the "personal integrity rights" referred to in Article 4(2), such as the right to life (UN Commission on Human Rights 1984; UN Human Rights Committee 2001; McGoldrick 2004; Higgins 1977; Lillich 1985). In other words, certain rights are, in principle, "non derogable". The immediate problem on the apparently inviolability of certain rights is the extent to which the ICCPR actually has legal force. While the Commonwealth has ratified the ICCPR, the various State governments have not. The extent to which the various State legislatures are actually bound is an open question. At present the only uniform position is the persuasive interpretive principle.

Aside from any requirement to observe non-derogation principles arising under the ICCPR, in Australia, the limited range human rights instruments also present mechanisms for derogation. In Victoria section 7 of the *Charter of Human Rights and Responsibilities Act 2006* provides:

(1) *This Part sets out the human rights that Parliament specifically seeks to protect and promote.*
(2) *A human right may be subject under law only to such reasonable limits as can be demonstrably justified in a free and democratic society based on human dignity, equality and freedom, and taking into account all relevant factors including—*
  (a) *the nature of the right; and*
  (b) *the importance of the purpose of the limitation; and*
  (c) *the nature and extent of the limitation; and*
  (d) *the relationship between the limitation and its purpose; and*
  (e) *any less restrictive means reasonably available to achieve the purpose that the limitation seeks to achieve.*
(3) *Nothing in this Charter gives a person, entity or public authority a right to limit (to a greater extent than is provided for in this Charter) or destroy the human rights of any person.*

In principle, mechanisms of derogation allow for the preservation of human rights, but are mainly concerned with the state being able to protect itself and to preserve the preconditions of civil society by being able to take direct action in the face of serious disturbances. A circular reasoning emerges: rights exist through the existence of the state, which has power to qualify and remove them in order to preserve the state. Like most areas of law, derogation is complicated, particularly where the characterisation of public emergency and proportionality is concerned. Sheeran (2013) argues there are basically two schools of thought. The first favours a constitutional or legislative "rule of law" approach, locating the architecture of derogation within rule systems, designed and intended to restore a state of normality and the ordinary operation of law through the mechanism of the exception. In effect, a conservative outcome is achieved through an extraordinary practice. In this case emphasis is given to the "rule of law" regulating government action even in a crisis. Legality is achieved and maintained by creating legal structures that facilitate responses to an exceptional state of affairs, for the purpose of absorbing it within the ordinary law with a view to restoration of the normal state of affairs as soon as possible. The second school[8] is aligned with Agamben's reasoning, and is rooted in *realpolitik,* emphasising decisive action when are where required, with as little interference from judicial accountability mechanisms as possible. This is a position that argues that the law cannot, in fact, regulate either a discretionary decision, or its implementation, because both exist outside the legal order. In a state of emergency, the law is either a retrospective exercise, or one that involves the radical alteration, qualification or suspension of its own operation in that context. The problem is the challenge that derogation poses for the observance of human rights, because the state of emergency, and the mechanism of derogation, provide "instant legitimacy" (Sheeran 2013) to state action that would otherwise be incompatible with the ordinary law.

These concerns appear to be made out in the emerging literature on derogation by those parties to the ICCPR. Hafner-Burton et al. (2011) found that between 1976 and 2007 there were a total of 586 derogations notified by parties to the ICCPR. They found that "stable democracies" with functioning court systems were *more likely* to derogate than other countries, but at the same time were more likely held accountable by domestic judicial and political processes. In effect, derogation did not mean the absence of accountability structures. This is to be contrasted with states with an unstable government and a weak judiciary, which routinely breached human rights norms and international law, with or without making a derogation declaration. They concluded that stable democracies tended to use derogations for the management of dissent and the maintenance of legitimacy, finding that:

> *derogations are a rational response to domestic political uncertainty...[that] enable governments facing serious threats to buy time and legal breathing space... to confront crises while signalling to [domestic audiences] that rights deviations are temporary and lawful.* (Hafner-Burton et al. 2011)

In other words, derogation appears to be a process that governments use to demonstrate a commitment to legality, rather than a commitment to the observance and

[8] Eg: Gross (2003); Hickman (2005)

strict maintenance of rights. Indeed, the very notion of legality has embedded within it the distinct capacity to mobilise exception as an ordinary part of its exercise.

A similar finding was made by Neumayer (2013) who found that democratic states are more likely to notify derogations than others. However, he also found that the violation of rights, and the manner of violation, varies depending upon the government type. Although democratic states were more likely to notify of derogations, on the whole they took their commitment to the preservation of rights more seriously than other forms of government, particularly autocratic or anocratic states, which may or may not provide any notice of derogation, but routinely breach human rights, particularly those concerned with physical integrity and due process. Neumayer concluded, like Hafner-Burton et al., that in democracies derogation serves an internal political function. That is, voters tend to respond positively to the rhetoric of emergency and threat, and respond by rewarding those leaders and parties who publicly demonstrate a "tough" commitment to the cause and management of that threat by making "strong", "rational" decisions. Basically, autocracies don't particularly care about the notification of derogation, whereas democracies do. The reason is the value of legality and legitimacy amongst the international community, and for the retention of power domestically. The implication here is that the most serious abuses of human rights take place in societies that have an ambivalent commitment to them, while democratic states take that commitment more seriously, but are still prepared to derogate under the right conditions, and prepared to harness the political rewards that derogation can bring. This suggests that it is plausible that part of the reason for the proliferation of exceptional logic is not only the spread of risk in social consciousness, but the political value in being seen to make "tough" choices that extend executive power through legal architectures.

Richards and Clay (2012) analysed the process of derogation and the idea of non-derogable rights across 195 countries between 1996 and 2004. Describing the inviolability of non-derogable rights as both "anemic" and "an umbrella with holes", they found that the special status of physical integrity rights during declared emergencies was routinely ignored, or at least qualified, during the period of declaration. In democratic societies, the only physical integrity right that appeared to be respected was extrajudicial killing. Otherwise even democratic societies were prepared to breach "non derogable" physical integrity rights when and where necessary. Even then, the authors concluded that extrajudicial killing was evident under the right conditions, particularly where it involved non-citizens. They concluded:

> *simply labelling a right as 'non-derogable' is insufficient to protect its respect during the very type of event the label is supposed to provide added protection to – a declared state of emergency... There appears to be very few differences in the way governments behave towards derogable and non–derogable rights in a state of emergency, which points towards the need for increased governmental accountability for rights related actions during these times.* (Richards and Clay 2012)

Derogation provides a mechanism that allows for a departure from ordinary law. In principle, the architecture of derogation provides a lawful mechanism through which the state, through a declared crisis, can depart from ordinary law. Derogation is not, however, unique to human rights law. It is, at its heart, fundamentally concerned with the Constitutional powers and limits of government. Consequently, the power to create exceptions to law in emergency situations is located in a range of statutes and prerogative powers concerned with emergency powers of state. In Australia, such emergency powers are in a host of statutes. In addition, constitutional jurisprudence on the constitutional validity of extraordinary powers expands and contracts. In theory, the courts may read down an expansive mechanism of emergency powers in a statute during peace, but may accept and affirm emergency powers during a declared war or other public emergency.[9] In many ways, the declaration of war or a state of emergency is primarily directed to domestic judicial audiences that the executive is embarking upon a program of creating exceptions through a process of derogation.

The intersection between law, derogation and politics is well articulated by Ferejohn and Pasquino (2004). They provide a useful typology on the logic of the exception arguing that the capacity and practice of sovereign, exceptional powers can be traced in Europe to the Roman Republic in the form of dictatorship. The dictator embodied a power structure outside the constitutional order, but a creature of it. Dictatorship existed to deal with the threat of invasion and significant public disturbance. Absolute authority allowed for a merger of law and violence providing a decisive capacity to address crisis. It could only be achieved through the suspension of citizens' rights and legal process. The purpose was to preserve the existing social and legal order. In other words, the existing social and legal order was so valued that Republican governments were prepared to create a mechanism that allowed for the exercise of autocratic powers to preserve society and the law within it. In this context it was the social and legal norms that were under threat, which triggered a demand for a departure from ordinary law in the form of emergency powers. There is an inextricable link between the systems of norms, derogation, and its associated justification. Ferejohn & Pasquino argue that the essence of the logic of the exception is based upon a dichotomy, the existence of regular government, and the concurrent existence of exceptional government. Regular government is characterised by the ordinary legal order and its associated norm system and practices. It is a political order based upon a plurality of institutions and voices in government. The ordinary legal order is characterised by the extension of rights and liberties. Exceptional government, on the other hand, is characterised by dictatorship. This is a political order based upon singular executive power structures, and a retraction of rights and liberties. For example, regular government would demand and expect due process of law in arrest, investigation and prosecution before a court. Exceptional government would emphasise the value and importance of conviction without trial. These two states, ironically, coexist and necessary preconditions for one another:

> *From the point of view of political and constitutional theory, the exception takes the form of a special threat to the political order. It is the declared existence of an exceptional threat... That triggers the emergency regime. The logic of exceptional government is conservative or*

---

[9] Eg: Communist Party Case

> *preservative. The function of exceptional government is to re-establish ordinary government in its integrity, and as soon as possible.* (Ferejohn and Pasquino 2004)

Ferejohn & Pasquino argue that exceptional powers, in order to retain their legality, must be embedded within the political and legal structures of government. Exceptional, autocratic powers exercised in the absence of legality are a true departure from the legal order. Following the work of Schmitt, they argue that once exceptional government departs from its conservative or preservative mission, it is the beginning of a new legal and political order. In most cases, however, the purpose of the exception is to preserve and restore ordinary law and politics. The principal effect of being embedded within the political and legal structure of government is the requirement for control in the exercise of exceptional powers. They suggest that modern emergencies are managed at three locations; (i) ex ante; (ii) interim; and (iii) ex post facto. At each location systems of law evolve to ensure that the deployment of exceptional, discretionary and autocratic powers remains within the boundaries of legality. It also suggests that emergencies have varying degrees of threat attached to them which alters the tolerance for the scope of derogation. The result of control mechanisms existing at multiple sites is a legal architecture that is flexible, and as such is well adapted and able to confront particular crises as the need arises. They suggest that the essence of control mechanisms within constitutional democracies follows a predictable pattern. First, the identification and declaration of a particular event as a crisis. Second, the introduction and deployment of an exceptional measure justified on the basis of the crisis and the desire for a restoration of the ordinary legal order. Third, the re-establishment of the ordinary legal order. And finally, the deployment of mechanisms of control on those emergency measures.

Derogation, then, is a complex process. It is complicated not only in the mechanism in law; it is also complicated in the circumstances in which it is deployed. Derogations appear to operate on a spectrum ranging from absolutist and tyrannous – the new legal order suggested by Schmitt, Ferejohn and Pasquino – through to conservative and preservative activities that absorb the derogation into the existing legal order.

Fundamentally, the jurisprudence concerning derogation and the state of emergency is concerned with physical threats to the State in the form of invasion, public violence, disasters, and sometimes economic disturbances. It appears, however, that the law itself is capable of generating situations of crisis and uncertainty. Hafner-Burton et al. (2011) argue that derogations are a rational response to political uncertainty. As demonstrated in Part 2, law is also capable of generating periods of political uncertainty. Indeed, it appears that the controlled operations legal architecture was triggered by the intersection of anxieties concerning police, crime, corruption, uncertainty of prosecution and the capacity of police to investigate certain forms of crime. The reaction of politicians was clearly one concerned with perceived need to respond decisively to the decision in *Ridgeway*. The dynamic evident was, however, very similar to the rationalities of the exception discussed above. The threat of crime and corruption coincided with the apparent obstruction to law enforcement presented by the legal architectures that emerged in that decision. *Ridgeway* created a climate in which evidence collected in the course of an investigation was, at the discretion of a trial judge, inadmissible. The behaviour of the investigators could, in the right circumstances, give rise to a criminal charge against legitimate investigations. These preconditions resulted in a declaration by the various parliaments and lawmakers that ordinary law was now in crisis. This justified demands for an alteration in the existing legal architecture. That alteration vested powers in police that were extraordinary, in that it authorised investigators to breach the ordinary law in the routine investigation of crime, with impunity. Indeed, these investigations were prospectively authorised by the state. These extraordinary powers demanded the construction and existence of control mechanisms, based upon surveillance and reporting. These accountability and control mechanisms were located at a variety of sites, before, during and after the investigation. The success of the model resulted in an absorption of the illegality within the body of the normal legal order. This was an example of the logic of exception operating in a paradigm of conservation and preservation. As a problem of government, the crisis was over. It demonstrates, however, the logic and dynamic of the exception operates in a space prior to a state of emergency is ordinarily conceived.

Controlled Operations as Exceptional, Qualified Life

In the above sections we have considered the notions of bare life and the state of exception, and its relationship with a more generalised logic of exception, and its operation in law. The caution proffered by Agamben is the tendency of exceptional logic to proliferate in executive and legislative activity because of its utility and its capacity to mobilise and legitimate flexible instances of sovereignty, and the impact that has on those groups captured by the exception. To what extent, then, can this observation be applied in the context of authorised crime and the controlled operation?

As we have seen, Agamben provides two major conceptual tools which may be used to analyse the controlled operation. As argued in Part 1, the controlled operation is an authorised crime, committed for the purpose of investigating crime and corruption. In this respect the controlled operation stands in contradiction to the legal norm, manifested in the "rule of law" principle that those who enforce the law are bound by it. But, an essential characteristic of controlled operations law is to transform an otherwise unlawful act into a lawful one. In so doing, the activity is not – in law – an unlawful one. A transformation is achieved, or, as Agamben suggests, a new legal norm – a new legality – has been manufactured and produced through a constitutionally valid process.

The preconditions for this transformation are significant. As demonstrated in Part 2, this logic involves the intersection of discourses of *risk* and *necessity*. The ends justify the means. The threat presented by uncontrolled crime and corruption intersects with the problem of the existing legal norm frustrating the ends of police *combined* with the very real risk of judicial opposition and termination of prosecution. *Ridgeway* triggered a crisis in governance. The result was the exercise of a sovereign logic that recognised and politicised the crisis, based on a perceived necessity to restore equilibrium. The combination of risks in this case served to construct the case for an exception to the rule of law, resolved, in an apparently dialectical fashion, by the absorption and inclusion of illegality into the legal order. A logic of exception was (and is) operational in controlled operations law. This appears to be manifested in three ways. First, the initial response was to declare controlled operations unlawful. An exception was therefore created to legalise the unlawful. Second, the ordinary rule of evidence is that unlawfully obtained evidence is inadmissible. An exception was created by declaring evidence from controlled operations was not inadmissible if merely obtained in the course of the operation. Third, a citizen ordinarily has a right to reasonable expectations of privacy. An exception exists so that those expectations are invalidated under reasonable suspicion of crime or corruption.

This logic extends beyond the preconditions for the formation of the substantive law. It also operates within the doctrinal structure. The whole operation is, in effect, a state of exception. The authorisation process depends on the existence of a state of affairs that are, in themselves, of sufficient concern to trigger an extraordinary form of investigation. The target of the investigation, through the controlled operation, becomes the subject of a mechanism of analysis well beyond the ordinary investigative form. The investigator is in possession, in that space, with a variety of intense powers ranging from surveillance and telecommunication interceptions, through to active collaboration and direct communication with the suspect, directed to obtaining evidence and confessions used for intelligence gathering and prosecution. In addition, the controlled operation permits collaboration in the crimes of the offender, and in overt and covert deception. An artificial reality is manufactured; a space in which the reality presented is expressly intended to prosecute the suspect. This is an exceptional space, well beyond the lived experience of ordinary citizenship. In this environment the ordinary legal norm attaches liberal legal values of privacy and non-interference by State actors is suspended through the operation of law. Here privacy, surveillance, telecommunications interception, proactive instigation, the right to silence, and the ordinary rules of evidence are all infused with mechanisms of qualification and exception.

However, it cannot be argued that the exception present in this case represents a total suspension of the legal order. On the contrary, the controlled operation, and the space that is opened up through its operation, is, as Hauka (2013) and Vito (2006) have suggested, saturated with law that operates in diverse ways in particular circumstances. These circumstances do not extend to the population as a whole; rather these circumstances apply to specific targets and localities. The situation here is complex, because there are two spaces present: the applied, and the potential. The controlled operation here presents itself as a specific state of exception for the individual suspect(s), and a floating potential for everyone else. Even when the investigation is concluded and the suspect is engaged in the legal system through prosecution, they are captured by the ordinary force and operation of law. In that environment the exceptional space of the controlled operation is merged with the ordinary "legal" space of the criminal law and its processes. However, even in this context the remnants of the exception continue to operate through the reception and qualification of evidence used in that process. It is a space that it not easily separable; a space where both belong to the other – a "caesurae" which, as Agamben suggests "by means of their articulation and opposition, allow the machine of law to function." (Agamben 2005a).

In effect, what is manifested here is a frontier of law in which the logic of the exception overlaps with law and its associated normative structures. The controlled operation represents a state of exception applied to some, and not all; but *might* apply to all under the right conditions. It is a legal structure that had its genesis in the logic of necessity, risk and exception. It is a frontier, however, that extends well into the ordinary operation of law and the policies of police. Its trigger is not the "state of emergency" that can result in martial law, or the expansion of "war time" powers that might extend executive powers under the Constitution, although this power could undoubtedly be deployed as part of the response to serious instability or unrest. Within this frontier the rights of the subject otherwise manifested as freedoms, liberties and privileges are subordinated or qualified. The controlled operation here manifests itself as an exceptional, qualified life, but has not reached the absolute wretched state of "bare life" that is reflected in "homo sacer". What that suggests is that the "zone of indistinction", where power, politics and law merge and become indistinct, actually begins much earlier in the structure and conception of law than "bare life". There are really two "sacred" figures, rather than one. One, as Agamben suggests, is the human form that has been subjected to the totality of sovereign power and inscription: *homo sacer*. The other figure is far more common; the citizen who lives within the spaces saturated by ordinary law and potentialities: *homo civicus*.

From Homo Sacer to Homo Civicus

Homo civicus is a Latin term revived in modern scholarship by Dahl in his 1961 study of power in the United States. Dahl argued that in democratic societies, human beings basically fall into two types, *homo politicus* and *homo civicus*. The former is politically active, while the latter is not (or at least not effective in that activity). The driving force of "political man" is the pursuit of government and power, while the driving force of "civic man" is personal interests – normally maximising happiness and avoiding pain and inconvenience. The two groups interact in the pursuit of their respective goals. Dahl argued that "civic man" tends to agitate and act politically when personal interests are threatened, reverting to 'ordinary life' when the threat has passed or been addressed, while "political man" is ever vigilant, receptive to opportunities to harness political power and the discourses that flow out of the "ordinary life" (Dahl 1961).

Dahl's thesis was extended and reconciled with governmentality through the work of Cruikshank (1999). In *The Will to Empower*, Cruikshank was critical of Dahl's failure to explain his dichotomy of citizenship in anything but normative terms. Cruikshank argued that Dahl failed to locate *homo civicus* within basic class or racialised politics. Dahl was, in effect, implying that *homo civicus* was basically happy with and consented to their social location. Cruikshank rejected this idea, and argued that democratic citizens are actively produced through technologies of citizenship (Cruikshank 1999). *Homo civicus* was shaped by regimes of power at once coercive and voluntary. Drawing on Foucault's biopolitics, Cruikshank argued that democratic governments operate through the combination of *enlistment* (willing support and participation) and *intervention*. Citizenship involves internalised norms inscribing a distinct code of conduct, coupled with government intervention to police deviations and ensure compliance. For Cruikshank, "the subjectivity of the citizen is the object and outcome of government," (Cruikshank 1999) concluding that the democratic citizen is shaped by:

> *a form of power that promotes rather than represses subjectivity, power that produces and relies upon active subjects rather than absolute subjugation...biopower operates to invest the citizen with a set of goals and self-understandings, and gives the citizen-subject an investment in participating voluntarily in programs, projects, and institutions set up to "help" them.* (Cruikshank 1999)

Homo civicus may be understood as the archetypal democratic citizen – the "ordinary person". This person is distinct from *Homo Sacer* and *Homo Politicus*. Their life is not "bare life". Indeed, for many their life is relatively comfortable, and that state of affairs is a common goal. Homo civicus is distinct from another archetype of modernity: *homo criminalis*. Homo criminalis is the "criminal man" conceived by the classical criminologists, notably Beccaria and Lombroso. Homo criminalis is located within other categories of humanity. Leaving aside the controversies attached the so-called 'classical' conception of criminality (Criddle and Fox-Decent 2012); the point to make is that the various apparatus of biopower – including controlled operations law – is directed towards the containment, detection and suppression of the "criminal type" within a population. It is the presence of crime and corruption *within ordinary populations* that we find the genesis of the reflexive interventions of late modernity. Homo civicus is a population to be governed as much as cared for, for it contains voluntary and involuntary participants, as well as deviations that require enlistment, coercion, correction or elimination. For the most part, the life of homo civicus is characterised by routine, anonymity, the pursuit of happiness, pleasures and avoidance of pain. They are the product of biopolitics. It is a status of belonging and inclusion, rather than containment and exclusion. It is a form of life willingly bound to the existing social order.

At first glance, the ordinary life of homo civicus is largely unexciting and uncontroversial. Homo Civicus is sacred in the sense of being in possession of rights, freedoms and liberties as a citizen in a liberal democracy. In principle, the citizen is inviolable without lawful cause or justification. Their existence is the paramount duty of the nation state. Immediately, once the legal position of the ordinary citizen is considered we are confronted by a simple reality. As Agamben has observed, the citizen is unable to determine questions of law. The citizen is subject, not sovereign. The citizen may not decide upon or determine exceptions to *public* law. Their power is either political, disobedience, or those fixed options provided by the nation state. At best, the citizen may rationalise a decision to act contrary to law, in the hope they will not be detected, or the expectation that their conduct will be excused or fall within some exception to avoid prosecution or liability, or in the context of a private arrangement may negotiate conditions or exception in that relationship – but otherwise the powers over lawmaking are vested in the legislature. In addition, the rights that the citizen possesses are invariably subject to qualification and derogation as a matter of law. Simply put, there is no right that the state cannot qualify, or take away, under the right constellation of conditions.

The life of homo civicus is saturated with law and the inscribed identity it provides. As a legal subject, homo civicus may be subjected to the same rationality of governance as homo sacer, but in most cases will never be reduced to the latter. The exceptional governance involved in the construction of homo sacer is exactly that, exceptional. For the most part citizenship involves a relatively comfortable existence within the boundaries of the normal legal order. As Ferejohn and Pasquino (2004) suggest, there is a dichotomy within the legal order between ordinary government and exceptional government. Indeed, one of the effects of the logic of the exception is to absorb exceptional circumstances and transform them into an ordinary feature of law and government, and in so doing inscribe the circumstances of the exception with a routine part of the legal order. Ordinary law saturates the biopolitical space occupied by homo civicus. In effect, Agamben's homo sacer is produced by a mechanism concerned with containment and exclusion, while homo civicus is produced by a mechanism concerned with absorption and inclusion. In both instances legal architectures cannot be said to have abandoned the subject. Rather, they are bound and qualified by law. As Hauka, Gregory and Tagma suggest, homo sacer and homo civicus both exist in an ecology saturated by laws (Hauka 2013; Gregory 2006; Tagma 2010).

Yet within the confines of ordinary law the dynamic of exception continues to operate. The conditions and operation of the exception are normalised, operative at multiple sites. A key distinction is that the homo civicus' experience of sovereignty exists mainly as an unfulfilled potential in the life of every citizen. Homo civicus, unlike homo sacer, is rarely aware they are the subject of potential extraordinary examination. Once that potential is crystallised, life may be examined at an intimate level, ranging from physical surveillance, interception of telecommunications, and even direct approach by undercover operatives for the purpose of soliciting confessions and criminal intelligence. This power, invisibly deployed, does not disturb the social order and habitus of the general population being governed. Indeed, as Hafner-Burton et al. (2011) and Neumayer (2013) suggest, homo civicus will often applaud the tough stance of government in cracking down on certain forms of crime and corruption. It appears that one of the biopolitical effects of precisely targeted and ostensibly accountable undercover policing mechanisms is that homo civicus generally accepts and supports the rhetoric of necessity that permits a qualified set of civil liberties. While homo sacer and its associated "bare life" exists within a zone in which law, power and politics are indistinct (the zone of indistinction), characterised by exceptional government, homo civicus exists in a zone where law, power and politics are interdependent, and characterised by ordinary government and legality. I suggest that this is a location characterised as a zone of impeachment.

The **zone of impeachment** is a feature of ordinary government and legality, although it shares the same logic of the exception as the zone of indistinction. Indistinction is located with impeachment. The difference, it seems, is that the zone of indistinction and the bare life that it produces is the result of an encounter between ordinary and exceptional law and a set of norms and threats that the existing legal order is unable, or unwilling, to absorb and accommodate. The zone of impeachment, however, is the result of the absorption of events and circumstances that law is able and willing to accommodate. The result is a legal order whereby ordinary mechanisms of government are subject to a process of derogation and qualification. These mechanisms are located at multiple sites within the legal order, ranging from pre-trial investigative apparatus, through to the discretionary decisions of judicial officers in the course of the trial. Within these localities a contradiction emerges, whereby the ordinary rule system is prepared to use a localised exception under certain circumstances. Thus, while the ordinary rule of evidence is that evidence obtained unlawfully is inadmissible, a local exception applies to render that evidence lawful. While the ordinary rule would be that police officers are not permitted to commit a crime in the course of an investigation, a local exception applies to authorise what would otherwise be an unlawful act. Homo civicus may become homo sacer under the right conditions, but already exists within a zone of impeachment. Homo civicus, theoretically possessed with a range of rights and liberties, is perpetually subject to an imperative rationality that, under the right circumstances, will qualify and in some instances remove rights and liberties otherwise available through the rule of law.

One of the effects of legality in this context is that the impact of this qualified life is normalised and uncontroversial. The focus is very much upon questions of exceptional deployment of power, on the abuses of non-derogable rights, and even upon the "bare life" of homo sacer. The ordinary life of the citizen scarcely rates a mention. The exceptional powers able to legally and with impunity operate invisibly within the ordinary social order are effectively absorbed and normalised, and occupy an invulnerable position within public discourse because of the inscription with necessity and the logic of the imperative.

Conclusion

The hero of this chapter, and in many ways the book as a whole, is *homo civicus* – the largely anonymous, ordinary citizen of the modern liberal state. This individual is subject to a powerful mechanism of governance in the form of an extraordinary law that has been absorbed into the heart of the existing legal order. The effect of normalisation is to effectively render this identity as uncontroversial and invisible. I do not argue that the bare life of homo sacer is any less important, but I am arguing that the logic that ultimately leads to bare life begins operating sooner in the political and legal order than is presently understood. Exceptional logic is endemic in legal and policy reasoning at those points where law, sovereign power and risk intersect. The controlled operation, and controlled operations law, provides an example of a process whereby the crystallisation of a series of intersecting risks created a crisis in law and politics that demanded a response. That response involved the introduction of laws that were a departure from a series of deeply cherished norms within the Anglo Australian legal system, namely the rule of law principle that the state is required to observe the laws in the process of enforcement. One of the effects of the controlled operations legal architecture is to present a series of exceptional laws that have the purpose and function of absorbing an exception into the ordinary law. This is quite different from a set of laws whose function is to strip individuals of rights and to contain them through the process of abandonment, as might be argued with refugees or unlawful aliens. In this instance, rather than having an example of a process that creates bare life, we are presented with a process that creates something different: a qualification of citizenship within the liberal order. This qualification is universal and is potentially applied to anyone or any group where there is suspicion of crime, corruption or some other threat to the state. The example presents us with a different form of qualified life to that suggested by Agamben.

The empirical evidence on derogation, particularly with respect to supposedly non-derogable rights, provides something of an amplifier of Agamben's warning one of the problems for contemporary democracies in the opening decades of the 21st century – the potential and the tendency for the logic of the exception to proliferate and become normalised. Indeed, the proliferation of exceptions in statutes, and the deployment of derogation in international law, appears to be increasing in frequency. When one considers the relationship between governmentality and the logic of the exception, it appears that the rationality of the exception forms a part of the liberal episteme discussed in the last chapter. When presented with the right combination of risks and threat, part of the rationality of governance is concerned with mobilising the architectures of exception and derogation in order to both preserve the continuity of ordinary law, but also to capture new subjects and spaces for governance in those instances where ordinary law either fails to do so, or becomes, of itself, an impediment to the need for flexible sovereignty.

References

Agamben, G. (1998). *Homo Sacer: Sovereign power and bare life* (D. Heller-Roazen, Trans.). Stanford: Stanford University Press.

Agamben, G. (1999). *Remnants of Auschwitz: The witness and the archive* (D. Heller-Roazen, Trans.). New York: Zone Books.

Agamben, G. (2000). *Means without end* (V. Binetti, & C. Casarino, Trans.). Minneapolis: University of Minnesota Press.

Agamben, G. (2005a). *State of exception* (K. Attell, Trans.). Chicago: University of Chicago Press.
Agamben, G. (2005b). *The time that remains: A commentary on the letter to the Romans* (P. Dailey, Trans.). Stanford: Stanford University Press.
Agamben, G. (2007). *Profanations*. New York: Zone Books.
Agamben, G. (2010). *The sacrament of language: An archaeology of the oath*. Stanford: Stanford University Press.
Agamben, G. (2011). *The kingdom and the glory: For a theological genealogy of economy and government* (L. Chiesa, & M. Mandarini, Trans.). Palo Alto: Stanford University Press.
Agamben, G. (2013a). *The highest poverty: Monastic rules and form-of-life*. Palo Alto: Stanford University Press.
Agamben, G. (2013b). *Opus Dei: An archaeology of duty*. Stanford: Stanford University Press.
Bailey, R. (2009). Up against the wall: Bare life and resistance in Australian immigration detention. *Law and Critique, 20*(2), 113.
Baxter, H. (1995). Bringing Foucault in Law and Law into Foucault. *Stanford Law Review, 48*(2), 449–479.
Bentham, J. (1843). An examination of the declaration of the rights of man and the citizen decreed by the constituent assembly of France. In J. Bowring (Ed.), *The works of Jeremy Bentham* (Vol. 2). Edinburgh: Simpkin, Marshall & Co.
Bird, G. (2005). An unlawful non-citizen is being detained or (white) citizens are saving the nation from (non-white) non-citizens. *University of Western Sydney Law Review, 9*(1), 87.
Criddle, E., & Fox-Decent, E. (2012). Human rights, emergencies, and the rule of law. *Human Rights Quarterly, 34*(1), 39.
Crowley-Cyr, L. (2005). Contractualism, exclusion and 'madness' in Australia's 'outsourced wastelands'. *Macquarie Law Journal, 5*, 81.
Cruikshank, B. (1999). *The will to empower: Democratic citizens and other subjects*. Ithaca: Cornell University Press.
Dahl, R. (1961). *Who governs? Democracy and power in an American city*. New Haven: Yale University Press.
De la Durantaye, L. (2009). *Giorgio Agamben: A critical introduction*. Stanford: Stanford University Press.
Douglas, M. (1990). Risk as a Forensic Resource. *Daedalus, 119*(4), 1–16.
Douglas, M. (2002). *Purity and Danger: An Analysis of the Concept of Pollution and Taboo*. London: Routledge.
Ferejohn, J., & Pasquino, P. (2004). The law of the exception: A typology of emergency powers. *International Journal of Constitutional Law, 2*(2), 210–239. https://doi.org/10.1093/icon/2.2.210.
Foucault, M. (1986). Nietzsche, genealogy, history. In P. Rabinow (Ed.), *The Foucault reader* (pp. 76–100). Harmondsworth: Penguin.
Foucault, M. (2006). *History of madness* (J. Murphy, & J. Khalfa, Trans.). London and New York: Routledge.
Foucault, M. (2007). *Security, territory, population: Lectures at the College de France 1977–1978* (G. Burchell, Trans.). Basingstoke: Palgrave Macmillan.
Frost, T. (2010). Agamben's sovereign legalization of Foucault. *Oxford Journal of Legal Studies, 30*(3), 545–577.
Golder, B & Fitzpatrick, P. (2009) *Foucault's Law* (Hoboken: Taylor and Francis)
Genel, K. (2006). The question of biopower: Foucault and Agamben. *Rethinking Marxism, 18*(1), 43–62.
Gregory, D. (2006). The black flag: Guantánamo Bay and the space of exception. *Geografiska Annaler. Series B, Human Geography, 88*(4), 405–427. https://doi.org/10.2307/4621537.
Gross, O. (2003). Chaos and rules: Should responses to crises always be constitutional? *The Yale Law Journal, 112*, 1011–1134.
Hafner-Burton, E., Helfer, L., & Fariss, C. (2011). Emergency and escape: Explaining derogations from human rights treaties. *International Organization, 65*(Fall), 673–707.

Hauka, C. (2013). Spaces of exception and suspended logic: Redefining Agamben's biopolitical paradigm on sovereignty, law and space. *Hemisphere, 36*, 67–73.
Hickman, T. (2005). Between human rights and the rule of law: Indefinite detention and the derogation model of constitutionalism. *The Modern Law Review, 68*(4), 655–668.
Higgins, R. (1977). Derogations under human rights treaties. *British Yearbook of International Law, 48*(1), 281–319.
Humphreys, S. (2006). Legalizing lawlessness: On Giorgio Agamben's state of exception. *The European Journal of International Law, 17*(3), 677–687.
Hunt, A., & Wickham, G. (1994). *Foucault and law: Towards a sociology of law as governance*. London: Pluto Press.
Huysmans, J. (2006). International politics of exception: Competing visions of international political order between law and politics. *Alternatives: Global, Local, Political, 31*(2), 135–165.
Jenkins, F. (2004). Bare life: Asylum-seekers, Australian politics and Agamben's critique of violence. *Australian Journal of Human Rights, 10*(2), 18.
Johns, F. (2005). Guantanamo Bay and the annihilation of the exception. *European Journal of International Law, 16*(4), 613–635.
Lemke, T. (2005). "A zone of indistinction" – A critique of Giorgio Agamben's concept of biopolitics. *Outlines, 7*(1), 3–13.
Lewis, S. (1999). Book review: Homo Sacer: Sovereign power and bare life. *Modernism/Modernity, 6*(3), 162–166.
Lillich, R. B. (1985). The Paris minimum standards of human rights norms in a state of emergency. *The American Journal of International Law, 79*(4), 1072–1081. https://doi.org/10.2307/2201848.
McGoldrick, D. (2004). The interface between public emergency powers and international law. *International Journal of Constitutional Law, 2*(2), 380–429. https://doi.org/10.1093/icon/2.2.380.
McLoughlin, D. (2009a). In force without significance: Kantian Nihilism and Agamben's critique of law. *Law and Critique, 20*(3), 245.
McLoughlin, D. (2009b). The politics of Caesura: Giorgio Agamben on language and the law. *Law and Critique, 20*(2), 163.
McLoughlin, D. (2012). Giorgio Agamben on security, government and the crisis of law. [Article]. *Griffith Law Review, 21*(3), 680–707.
Mensard, P. (2004). The political philosophy of Giorgio Agamben: A critical evaluation. *Totalitarian Movements and Political Religions, 5*(1), 139–157.
Mills, C. (2008). *The philosophy of Agamben*. Montreal: McGill-Queen's University Press.
Moran, L. (2001). Gothic law. *Griffith Law Review, 10*(2), 75–100.
Murray, A., & White, J. (Eds.). (2011). *The Agamben dictionary*. Edinburgh: Edinburgh University Press.
Neumayer, E. (2013). Do governments mean business when they derogate? Human rights violations during notified states of emergency. *The Review of International Organizations, 8*(1), 1–31.
Nikolopoulou, K. (2000). Book review: Homo Sacer: Sovereign power and bare life. *SubStance, 29*(3), 124–131.
Ong, A. (2006). *Neoliberalism as exception*. Durham and London: Duke University Press.
Passavant, P. (2007). The contradictory state of Giorgio Agamben. *Political Theory, 35*(2), 147–174.
Prozorov, S. (2005). X/Xs: Toward a general theory of the exception. *Alternatives: Global, Local, Political, 30*(1), 81–112. https://doi.org/10.2307/40645149.
Raulff, U. (2004). An interview with Giorgio Agamben. *German Law Journal, 5*(5), 609–614.
Richards, D., & Clay, C. (2012). An umbrella with holes: Respect for non-derogable human rights during declared states of emergency, 1996–2004. *Human Rights Review, 13*, 443–471.
Rossiter, C. (1948). *Constitutional dictatorship: Crisis government in the modern democracies*. New York: Harcourt Brace.

Schmitt, C. (2010). *Political theology: Four chapters on the concept of sovereignty* (G. Schwab, Trans.). Chicago: University of Chicago Press.

Schotel, B. (2009). Defending our legal practices: A legal critique of Giorgio Agamben's state of exception. *Amsterdam Law Forum, 1*(2), 113–125.

Sheeran, S. (2013). Reconceptualizing states of emergency under international human rights law: Theory, legal doctrine and politics. *Michigan Journal of International Law, 34*, 491–557.

Tagma, H. (2010). Biopower as a supplement to sovereign power. In S. Biswas & S. Nair (Eds.), *International relations and states of exception* (pp. 161–185). New York: Routledge.

UN Commission on Human Rights. (1984). *The Siracusa principles on the limitation and derogation provisions in the international covenant on civil and political rights*. New York: United Nations.

UN Human Rights Committee. (2001). *General comment No. 29: Article 4: Derogations during a state of emergency*. New York: United Nations.

Velasco Arias, G. (2011). The normalisation of exception in the biopolitical security dispositif. *International Social Science Journal, 62*(205–206), 363–375.

Vito, M. (2006). La Morte Come Pena: Law, death, penalty and the state of exception. In E. Bellina & P. Bonifazio (Eds.), *State of exception: Cultural responses to the rhetoric of fear* (pp. 26–32). Cambridge: Cambridge Scholars Press.

Wall, T. (2005). Au Hasard. In A. Norris (Ed.), *Politics, metaphysics and death: Essays on Giorgio Agamben's Homo Sacer* (pp. 31–48). Durham and London: Duke University Press.

Whyte, J. (2009). Particular rights and absolute wrongs: Giorgio Agamben on life and politics. *Law and Critique, 20*(2), 147.

Whyte, J. (2012). Is revolution desirable?: Michel Foucault on revolution, neoliberalism and rights. In B. Golder (Ed.), *Michel Foucault: Law, power, rights* (pp. 207–228). London: Routledge.

Whyte, J. (2013). "The king reigns but does not govern": Thinking sovereignty and government with Agamben, Foucault and Rousseau. In T. Frost (Ed.), *Giorgio Agamben: Legal, political and philosophical potentialities* (pp. 143–162). Abingdon: Routledge.

References

Conclusion: Reconfiguring Sovereign Power

This book has examined the doctrinal rationalities of Australian controlled operations law and policy. The central finding has been that controlled operations are an investigative practice shaped by the pragmatic expertise of undercover investigations, the social and political imperatives of crime control, the logic of surveillance and audit, and the power of risk as rationality and imperative. The Foucauldian analytic has extended our understanding of controlled operations law by shifting the focus beyond entrapment, rights, and remedies, to consider the effect of this kind of law in the production of truth, identity, and governable spaces. Controlled operations laws articulate archetypal modes of contemporary liberal governance: an invisible sovereign power able to invoke exceptional changes to the fabric of rights-based laws. As a legal architecture it embodies these rationalities within doctrine, such that the doctrinal law is actively governed by a triangular relationship characterised by surveillance, audit, and risk. The ostensible unlawful character of a controlled operation creates a rupture in the fabric of law, addressed through the rhetoric of necessity, and the logic of exception and derogation. In this respect the controlled operation goes well beyond a simple investigative licence to engage in controlled activities. It is a knowledge system tightly connected to the exercise of power. It is not only a legal architecture; it is rationality and technology of governance. This book may therefore be understood as revealing not only something of the relationship between ideas and rationalities about crime and legal architecture, but also something of the changing nature of the way sovereign power is deployed and its associated qualification of citizenship in late modernity.

Review of Findings

Analysis of controlled operations law and literature in part 1 demonstrated that this form of law forms part of a large web of laws regulating overt and covert law enforcement investigation in Australia that has evolved since the 1990s. This framework is not uniform, consisting of a patchwork of laws, although this patchwork is

B. Murphy, *Regulating Undercover Law Enforcement: The Australian Experience*, https://doi.org/10.1007/978-981-33-6381-6

governed by a clear set of principles aimed at producing a system of accountability and legality. There are common threads throughout this patchwork system, and these common threads include shared conceptions for the structuring of law, as well as shared conceptions of governance. The socio-legal literature locates the controlled operation as part of a cultural shift in investigative methodologies, tied to the expansion of surveillance and proactive policing throughout the Western world, emerging in the wake of international drug interdiction since the 1970s. In that context the principal concerns of law and jurisprudence have been the interrogation of pragmatic legal and policy directives, largely concerned with the problem of entrapment, the availability and application of judicial remedies and intervention, and the proper mechanisms for balancing competing rights and interests.

This legal understanding of controlled operations is incomplete, although it is an essential part of the picture. Questions about the internal substance of this type of law remains focused on the exposition of rules, doctrinal architecture, and location within the larger ecology of the regulation of law enforcement. The governing principles of controlled operations law are primarily concerned with the design and operation of procedure. Legal thinking on this topic does not extend to larger questions of episteme, or to the dynamics of this form of law as an ideological force within the project of governance. When we expand this understanding through an interdisciplinary lens, sensitive to questions of policy, ontology and epistemology, new images of law merge. Controlled operations law not only facilitates investigative practices; it also changes legal structure within the ecology in which it is located. The principle of evidence law concerning the admissibility of unlawfully obtained evidence, is altered. Liberal demands and internationally recognised rights to privacy and protection from interference by police are qualified and revealed to be conditional. The ethical principle of not being set up by authorities is anaemic. In short, the protective legalities of liberal law are qualified and found to be exceptional. Controlled operations are, in this sense, a law against law, a species of counter law.

But it is more than this. The counter law thesis is located within the criminological tradition which conceives such legal changes within larger sociological and ontological developments associated with surveillance, risk and control. An interrogation of the discourses around this kind of law enforcement outlined in part 2 of the book demonstrates that the purpose and structure of the controlled operation is more than simply facilitating undercover investigations and reversing certain presumptions of the law of evidence. Law and policy governing controlled operations is saturated by a complex grid of risk and audit rationalities. The reaction to Ridgeway is infused with discourses of risk, a space in which the twin devices of exception/derogation and audit were mobilised within the legal architecture. The anxieties and realities of government were mobilised and infused with the great intellectual forces of late modernity concerned with crime control, governance, and the assertion of power. In so doing, one of the challenges of contemporary forms of liberal government – how to extend and apply decisive expressions of sovereign power without disturbing the utopian vision of a residual state – appears to have been overcome. Controlled operations architecture presents itself as a device that may be used on the controlled and accountable conditions, deployed invisibly and decisively against suspects and deviant organisations, in such a way that the surrounding social fabric is undisturbed. In addition, the practices associated with the controlled operation present a significant and powerful deterrent force not only on the larger population, but also upon the agencies of law enforcement. The controlled operation not only facilitates the deployment of judicial legal power, it also captures and extends biopower. The extension was intended.

These intellectual forces connected with episteme serve as the building blocks of legal architecture, purporting to empower and regulate those practices necessary for pragmatic law enforcement. As considered in Chap. 10, controlled operations can therefore be understood as being part of the "surveillant assemblage" – an apparatus of government – or, using the term coined by Foucault, *dispositif*. Controlled operations are part of the rationality of governance, a form of governmentality characteristic of advanced liberalism and late modernity. The controlled operation is a technology of power and governance, deployed in the wake of the problemtisation of crime, the risks associated with the authorisation of crime by state actors, the risks associated by the evolution of law developing in ways antithetical to law enforcement, and, to some extent, the shifting of political risks between the legislature, the executive and the judiciary. This is a reflexive power, which at once articulates and enforces a system of norms and regimes of practice concerned with the production of knowledge and truth in individuals, populations, and government itself. It is a knowledge system that articulates the rationality of governance as licence, surveillance, audit and the sovereign power to create exceptions to law, and in so doing presents us with an image of the post-modern sovereign, a fragmented and immortal process, invisible and flexible, able to exercise the combination of powers traditionally held by the sovereign, but in ways invisible and largely unobtrusive for the majority of the governed.

The controlled operation, as a form of sovereignty, is precision governance, bound within the realms of legitimacy by the necessity attached to risk, and the devices of accountability. This is a power that, when applied, qualifies the legal system in ways that, in extreme cases, overrides and qualifies the rights and legal trappings of citizenship, creating a form of citizenship and laws characterised not by bare life, but by impeachment. The power is one that suggests that citizenship of the now, and the future, is characterised not by non-derogable rights and liberties, but by a qualified life perpetually at risk of impeachment. The bare life of Agamben remains a possibility, but the qualified life is the reality. The qualified life is the lived experience of all. The challenge for law, it seems, is to recognise how fragile the rights and liberties of humanity are in a context in which risk, sovereignty and the logic of exception tends to intensify as imperatives under the right conditions, for in the right circumstances the logic that leads to bare life is implemented within the ordinary legal system, beginning in the regulation of Homo Civicus.

Review of Research Questions

Three broad research questions provided a guide to this book: (i) what is a controlled operation? (ii) what are the rationalities of controlled operations law?, and (iii) what are the conditions of possibility? The extent to which this book has obediently attended to those questions is open to debate. As an exploratory book, heavily infused with theory, and directed by the intersection between the empirical, the discursive and the theoretical, a book squarely focused upon specific questions was necessarily limiting. Nonetheless, I return to those questions.

What Is a Controlled Operation?

As an investigative technique, the true character of the controlled operation can be understood as an example of Foucault's *dispositif*; an apparatus of security and law enforcement that materialised in the wake of crisis. Controlled operations cannot be understood simply as a reaction to Ridgeway. Deceptive law enforcement practices have a long history that extends well beyond the formation of state investigative apparatus. Controlled operations law and practice are a composite of discourses saturated with themes of risk, manifesting both sovereign, disciplinary and biopower. The controlled operation is an apparatus of power and knowledge, a technology of power. As an apparatus, the controlled operation cannot be understood simply as black letter law or technique of law enforcement. It is a complex of discourses, institutional actors, expertise, decisions, legal principles, administrative practices, mythologies, hysteria, ethical principles, normative statements, and practices of denunciation. In this respect the controlled operation clearly aligns with Foucault's statement of the nature of apparatus:

> *...a thoroughly heterogeneous ensemble consisting of discourses, institutions, architectural forms, regular true decisions, laws, administrative measures, scientific statements, philosophical, moral and philanthropic perspectives...*(Foucault 1980, 2007)

This conception is infused with, and influenced by, the epistemic threads of the rationalities of contemporary systems of governance, fundamentally characterised by risk, surveillance, exception, and the logic of precaution. Controlled operations law is a manifestation of governmentality: the rationality of governance crystallised in a triad of sovereign power (in the form of law); individual disciplinary power, and collective biopower. Controlled operations can therefore be understood as concerned fundamentally with biopolitics through the practices and rationalities of contemporary forms of sovereignty in late modernity. Once the rationalities involved in controlled operations were crystallised in law, it became the site of resonance and contradiction with associated socio-legal structures – sites of determination and elaboration, directly connected with the legitimation of law and action, in the production of a constellation of truths, and in the reinforcement and extension of episteme.

What Are the Rationalities of Controlled Operations Law?

Controlled operations rationalities are at once pragmatic and discursive. The pragmatic is linked to the investigative practices and purposes of undercover law enforcement, and its intersection with the legal system. The purpose here is for the collection of evidence and intelligence assisting law enforcement in its mission for crime control and prosecution. In this respect the rationality is directed to the production of truths in the legality of law enforcement, and the guilt or innocence of the subject and suspect. It is a set of practices that at once delivers information concerning the behaviours of specific individuals and their compliance with articulated norms, as well as a set of practices concerned with the production and collection of a broad-based constellation of information from the population being governed.

The discursive rationalities are core legal and epistemic knowledge systems operative within and around the apparatus. In this context risk, audit, the rhetoric of rights and the capacity for derogation plays a central role in informing and shaping controlled operations jurisprudence and pragmatic practices. These discursive elements feed into policy imperatives, the practices of law enforcement, and ultimately the architecture of law itself.

What Are the Conditions of Possibility?

This question involves a further and more specific question. How did it happen that Australian legislators, with an ostensible commitment to the rule of law, legislate to create a legal architecture that effectively authorised crimes by law enforcement agents? The answer seems to involve three factors. First, controlled operations law emerged because of a trigger event, a rupture in which the existing laws were unable to provide the political security and certainty needed by government. That was the effect of *Ridgeway*. That decision was antithetical to the demands and needs of law enforcement and compromised the ability of government to deliver security and certainty through effective prosecution, apprehension, and detection of offenders. The second aspect, was a set of social conditions and practices that became the lived surface of emergence; the practices of law enforcement, the realities of crime and corruption, and the historical shifts in technology, culture and legal architectures that were all pushing towards undercover and proactive policing models as an effective set of practices. Finally, controlled operations law required a set of intellectual, epistemic components that could be applied and adapted in ways consistent with law and policy but were also part of the driving intellectual forces behind law and policy. In this environment risk, audit, surveillance, the rhetoric of rights and the value of exception and derogation are dominant discursive forces intersecting in law and policy. The discursive ebb and flow of the balancing of competing interests, combined with the practices of risk assessment, surveillance and audit formed the major intellectual forces occupying the terrain in which controlled operations law and policy was formed, these complex intersections were all essential conditions of possibility. Without the practices associated with risk assessment and audit, controlled operations law could not have happened. Without a declaration in law that unlawful activities were unacceptable in the absence of the mandate of the legislature, controlled operations law would not have happened. Without the social and political imperatives attached to risk, the willingness of government to introduce such a law may not have appeared in a liberal common law tradition. Without the social and political imperatives attached to a plurality of risks in this particular socio-legal space, the demands to derogate from the existing laws may not have happened.

Is it Desirable?

To these three broad research questions at play in this book, a fourth, normative consideration must be added: is it desirable? All things considered, is controlled operations law desirable? Like many subjects, the answer is not simple. Pragmatically, as an investigative apparatus, the answer to this question is a qualified "yes". Controlled operations permit investigators to penetrate, at a very deep and personal level, environments routinely difficult to obtain sufficient evidence from. In the absence of evidence and intelligence-gathering capacities of this kind, a range of serious criminal and corrupt activities, ranging in scale from the local and innocuous, through to crimes of national and international significance may not be detected, much less prosecuted, disrupted or prevented. In particular, the absence of controlled operations techniques would force investigators to rely on retrospective forms of investigations, potentially meaning loss of life, property and possibly government itself. In that environment governments would likely need to rely on potentially even more pervasive intelligence-gathering strategies. Controlled operations, in themselves, may well be one of the most effective methods of investigating closed groups. As Braithwaite & Fisse rightly observed (Braithwaite et al. 1987a, b), covert methodologies may be the only effective method of investigation and prosecution of serious white collar crime. In the context of corporate and political corruption, controlled operations offer a significant tool for law enforcement.

As a system of regulation, controlled operations law provides a mechanism that effectively imposes operational limitations on the scope of conduct of the operation. In this respect it offers a system of regulation that imposes substantial limitations while also empowering investigative activity. In addition, this form of law also provides mechanisms for accountability by identification and examination of conduct. These mechanisms ostensibly function to provide a degree of transparency and discipline over investigative conduct that, prior to the gradual introduction after 1995, was otherwise invisible. While visibility remains an issue, the capacity for at least retrospective review and account does provide an important system of audit. In this respect the rationality of audit, risk and discipline has positive functions, for, at least in principle, the internal dimension of audit serves to hold executive power to account and provides a system of regulation of conduct that was a regular part of law enforcement prior to the legislation that regulates it.

There remain, however, significant reservations. The mechanisms of accountability are by no means uniform. Controlled operations reporting and scrutiny is variable in form. There are divergent views on the utility, location, and extent of scrutiny within the discourses that shape controlled operations law and policy. One of the problematic aspects of this kind of investigation is the role (or lack of it) of third-party approval. It is also evident that all models effectively hide details through internal or restricted Ministerial reporting. These models offer substantially less transparency. In addition, controlled operations can also be used to target not only serious crimes – but may also extend to the disruption and covert investigation of public dissent. In this respect unions, non-government organisations and green groups are particularly vulnerable. As Marx observed (Marx 1980, 1988), the infiltration of student organisations and political groups has long been a part of the techniques of government. In this respect the controlled operation can easily be adapted to police and criminalise dissent. There is significant potential for controlled operations to be deployed beyond the scope of serious crime. Indeed, in the UK, the equivalent legislation provides authority to numerous government departments and local councils to engage in directed surveillance.[1]

The second area for careful examination is the systems for authorisation. As it stands only Queensland has a mechanism for authorisation located outside of the agencies that use controlled operations, and even then, senior police officers are a part of the authorising body. All other controlled operations legislation provides for authorisation of controlled operations warrants internally, although such authorisations are normally located at the apex of the respective agency. In effect, the authorisation of a controlled operations warrant is located within the organisation that deploys them. This may be contrasted with the mechanisms in place for the issue of search warrants, which ordinarily requires an application to a Magistrate, Registrar, Justice of the Peace or a Judge. Applications made to an external agency have three major benefits. First, a system of internal authorisation for the grant of warrants of this kind enlivens questions about the rule of law. At one level the executive agency is technically exercising a quasi-judicial function by making a decision based on a legal test of reasonable suspicion, a complex question of law and fact. At another level, it invites questions about the role of law enforcement agencies authorising themselves to commit breaches of criminal law based on "necessity". The second benefit is that independent scrutiny has the effect of putting the grounds for the application to independent scrutiny prior to its implementation. In the context of judicial authorisation of warrants, there exists a series of common law presumptions on the issue of warrants requiring both strict compliance with the formalities and caution on the issue of warrants that derogate from common law rights to privacy and freedom from state interference.[2] Finally, such a process would shift the alignment of authorisation into the same conceptual field of authorisation as search war-

[1] *Regulation of Investigatory Powers Act 2000* (UK), ss28, 29, Schedule 1

[2] Eg: *R v Tillett; Ex parte Newton* (1969) 14 FLR 101 at 108 per Fox J; *Crowley v Murphy* (1981) 52 FLR 123 at 144 per Lockhart J

rants, importing both consistency and making the public declaration that law enforcement is subordinate to the legislature and the judiciary.

Outside such pragmatic questions, there remains a frontier of major systemic questions. The cultural and historical shift that is underway is one in which sovereign powers are being transformed. The investigative apparatus as practice and law is an example of the transformation and erosion of the private and the public divisions characteristic of modernity and the popular legal and philosophical models of liberalism. Controlled operations law forms a part of that ensemble of powers that facilitates the erosion of private/public dualism and creates sites of governance that were hitherto invisible and largely impervious to ordinary forms of regulation. These practices correspond with associated cultural and intellectual shifts, presenting new visions and ideas of sovereignty that is at once augmented through institutional and legal connectivity, but also invisible and outside the view and concern of the "ordinary" citizen. This is a form of sovereignty which not only qualifies law; it also qualifies citizenship. While only some may become homo sacer; everyone is already homo civicus. Controlled operations law, and the rationalities that govern it, are symptoms of risk society. The ongoing problem for discussion is the question of legitimacy, and the proper limits and controls over the zone of impeachment.

Theoretical Implications

There are three major social and conceptual implications emerging from the dynamics observed in law and discourse, which is arguably more significant than the crystallisation of investigations practice and associated regulation. These are the principally concerned with the way in which power relations are being reconfigured between the state and the governed.

Bare Life Has its Origins in Ordinary Law

The first observation is that Agamben's conception of *bare life* is more nuanced and complicated than is suggested in Homo Sacer. As a theory, bare life is useful for analysing those situations in which individuals and groups are contained and effectively excluded from, and controlled by, the social order. Bare life as a theory is useful for analysing the frontiers of law, power, and politics. It is less helpful when attention is returned to the core business of law, power, and politics. While it is possible that individuals may be transformed to a state of *bare life*, it is the exception, rather than the norm. It is an alien conception for most, and flies in the face of the fact that within the core of social life individuals are protected by law, although the legal system is necessarily imperfect. What authorised crimes and their associated laws suggest is that the individuals and populations who live within the core of law, as opposed to its frontiers, are necessarily bound by and subject to the laws that govern them. This is not a controversial statement. It is axiomatic of law and government. Agamben's theory, however, emphasises the logic of exception is moving beyond the frontier of law into its core. And it is here that we find that under the right conditions the legal status and rights of citizens governed by the core of law is one of potential persistent impeachment. Under the right conditions, individuals are subject to exceptions to the norm of legality. Legal rights and procedures are qualified and may be subject to exceptions when there is a sufficient threshold of risk and threat. Even "non-derogable" rights can be overridden under the right conditions. My argument here is that Agamben's conception of bare life does not apply to all. But the logic of exception does. *The life of Homo Civicus is a life of potential persistent impeachment. Homo Sacer has a brother: Homo Civicus.*

At this point, it needs to be stated that questions of impeachment of rights are complicated. This is not to suggest that in every case an individual is stripped of all rights. It is rather to suggest that a spectrum of impeachment is the norm. In ordinary cases the law provides a range of statutory and common law presumptions and substantive rights that serve to protect the individual from the abuses of government. The extent to which these are operative is a complex question of fact and degree, determined on a case-by-case basis. But it is to suggest that none of the rights taken for granted, and so cherished by the rhetoric of liberalism, are absolute. This relationship between exception, derogation, rights, and liberties is in itself another book, and at this point I have reached the end of the road for the present work. The problem of derogation, the operation of the dynamic of the exception and its impact on law and those governed by it, are significant questions for future research.

A Vision of Post-Modern Sovereignty

The second major theoretical insight emerging from this book is the question of the changing nature of sovereignty. The ways in which sovereign power is being deployed is changing. In a way, this is a post-modern sovereignty in which sovereign power is fragmented and operating at multiple sites; a form of power involving legal, political, and biopower that is routinely deployed within private and public spheres to create "deep governance". It is also a form of sovereignty in which the capacity to penetrate, observe and dominate the long valued private sphere of liberalism appears to be increasing. The controlled operation, with its associated legal structures concerned with deceptive undercover investigations, the technologies attached to surveillance, and the ability to scrutinise and map all manner of information concerning an individual, area or population, not the least of which is the capacity to intercept and record conversations, does suggest that one of the by-products of the investigative apparatus is the ability to transform privacy into a site of investigation and regulation. Only the "virtuous" are entitled, it seems, to any expectations of privacy, but even then, the individual is necessarily bound by the information gathering demands of social life. The death of the private is one manifestation of contemporary forms of sovereignty. These are questions that have been explored and considered by Hardt & Negri in *Empire* (Hardt and Negri 2000). In that work those authors argue, among other things, that the private and public spheres of life have effectively merged in late modernity. The capacity of sovereign power to exercise legal, sovereign and by political force within the private realms has intensified, such that there is now a fusion of spaces. There is no longer a "private" realm, no "outside"; there are only sites of surveillance characterised by different rules of engagement. This is a dynamic observed in the earlier work of Gary Marx (drawing on Erving Goffman) in *Undercover*, who argued that one of the disturbing developments in the Western world was the capacity of government to interrogate and reach into the private realm of the ordinary citizen. This development necessarily involves the death of the private, where "the line between the public and the private is obliterated." (Marx 1988). In this respect there is an intersection with an established body of scholarship that is a worthy site of future research. In particular, the relationship between sovereignty, power and law may well be an exemplar of the kind of sovereignty identified by Hardt & Negri in Empire.

But there is more to post-modern sovereignty than the ability to saturate private spaces with mechanisms of surveillance and control. Post-modern sovereignty includes the ability to manufacture a set of circumstances in which the individual is directly observed and presented with ethical choices with legal consequences. A basic comparative analysis with the norm may then be undertaken by agents of the state. Either the person does or does not commit a crime or behave corruptly. The virtue testing attached to this form of sovereignty is facilitated by another dimension of the post-modern sovereign, and that is its capacity to exercise power and operate invisibly. The ability to obtain information electronically means that for most people, they will never know that the information repositories and traces of their lives have been scrutinised. The ability to observe at a distance through technology means that individuals will often never know they have been observed, but frequently know that they are in an environment where they may be observed at any time, reminiscent of the *Panopticon*.

In addition, one of the dimensions of relevance and interest to the discipline of law is the willingness and capacity of contemporary sovereignty to transform and change the law in order to facilitate the objects of governance. In earlier chapters we saw that writers such as Ericson (2007) and Ashworth (2006) expressed their concern about the expansion and phenomenon of counter law, of laws designed to circumvent, or create exceptions to ordinary rules in order to achieve specific goals. In a similar way when Deleuze hypothesised about being on the cusp of new forms of society, characterised by surveillance and control (Deleuze 1992), these dynamics were in their infancy. Controlled operations law appears to crystallise these dynamics as an example of the transformation of sovereignty. The extent to which this transformation is local or is in fact part of a larger global transformation of legal systems is a new frontier for consideration and examination.

Zone of Impeachment

The third insight relates to conceptualising the zone of impeachment. This term was chosen to describe a dynamic that is at once operational but variable in its application. It is a dynamic that does not operate in every case. It is a dynamic based on a logic that imports conceptions of risk and exception but is also both evidence-based and speculative. It is difficult to define. The idea of impeachment was chosen in order to isolate a dynamic that imports both a powerful liberal conception of the rights-baring citizen of the liberal legal order, and the primacy attached the protection and preservation of the citizen in relationship with the state. Like the Presidential office, the citizen is possessed with a set of rights, liberties and expectations, but is also subject to a powerful political and legal oversight that may crystallise the remove and wind-back those qualities under the right set of conditions. Those conditions, it seems, are tightly bound to discourses of risk and threat, and are achieved through the application of juridico-legal apparatus. Clearly this ill-defined and rather loose constellation of ideas is presently under-theorised but given the impact of this dynamic in judicial and political reasoning, there is a clear need to develop a line of enquiry based around this dynamic going forward. If we conceptualise *homo sacer* was living in a *state of exception*, we may need to consider the equivalent status of *homo civicus*, as one characterised by a 'zone of impeachment'.

This zone is a metaphysical one, in the sense it exists as a conditional state of potentiality. The ordinary social, legal and moral order is that the citizen has the right to live and prosper in any way they see fit, subject to the rights, liberties and limits of law and convention. However, if the citizen chooses to engage in criminal conduct, the potential for intrusive intervention is mobilised, if not justified. The justification appears to be based around what is being referred to as "liability ethics" (Nathan 2017). The gist of this view is that provided a person remains a compliant citizen obedient to the law, they are permitted to remain in peace and go about their business. However, if they deviate from the law the potential for impeachment of rights and liberties crystallises morally and legally, and accordingly justifies intrusive state investigation and virtue-testing. This potentiality has strong overlaps with moral and political philosophy, as well as theology. Again, we are presented with an emergent area for future consideration and discussion.

The Pragmatic Turn: Some Practical Implications

There are a number of practical questions resting at the juncture between controlled operations theory and practice that demand attention.

Human Rights Are Fragile

The first of these is the fragility of human rights as a legal and political reality. The proliferation of risk, and its connection with the logic of exception exposes rights and the fabric of citizenship to a fragile, and as Richards and Clay (2012) suggest, anaemic status. The issue here is that the protections offered by law are subject to derogation under the right conditions, based on an evidence-based utilitarian logic. This dynamic is well-known in human rights jurisprudence and theory (Clayton and Tomlinson 2009; Gans et al. 2011), but it certainly reinforces the arguments of Bentham (1843) and Rossiter (1948) that there are no rights, liberties or freedoms that may not or should not be qualified or abolished if sufficient necessity exists, or even of the ability of governments to simply ignore them. The reliance on governments to effectively codify and recognise rights, justify military intervention, and engage in cultural hegemony is strongly criticised by Zizek (2010). As observed by Golder (2015), it appears we live in an age in which the validity and utility of rights is far more contested than liberal rhetoric suggests. This is a dynamic that invites a much deeper exploration of the relationship between risk, human rights, utilitarian reasoning and the concept of necessity. This is not to suggest that I am arguing for an unimpeachable rights-based jurisprudence. On the contrary, the libertarian opposite of utilitarianism is equally capable of being the site of injustices and eroding the rule of law. To argue that the rights of the highly culpable and dangerous offenders somehow trump the interests of civil society, with their collective right not to be subject to violence, corruption and abuse is nonsensical. The issue, it seems, is emphasising that the intersection of risk, necessity and rights in the intuitive synthesis of judicial reasoning is one that requires specific and careful application, and to emphasise the tendency of legislatures to change those protective mechanisms of law in favour of processes that facilitate investigation and prosecution, a conclusion that tends to confirm the views of Bronitt and McSherry (2017) and Packer (1968). The appearance of "risk" in legislation and policy should be a flag to the judicial officer to deploy common law presumptions concerning penal law carefully, and to incorporate procedural laws concerned with investigation within the ambit of those presumptions. There is certainly scope here to theorise and explore the expansion of common law presumption touching on investigative powers.

The Logic of Exception Plays an Important Role in Law

The second of these is recognition of the role and value of exception. Agamben's position on the exception is a critical one, and necessarily pessimistic. While Agamben's book presents a cautionary tone on the potential role of law in socio-legal exclusion of populations, there is a positive and apparently essential dynamic in the exclusion that needs to be identified. As Ferejohn and Pasquino (2004) have observed, the capacity of the legislature to create exceptions opens something of a window of understanding on the value of executive powers outside the legal order – a power first vested in the ancient role of Roman Dictator; whose capacity to suspend and reconstruct law allows legal systems to adapt quickly to emergency and social changes – a dynamic that common law is effectively unable to provide. Exception is an ordinary part of the dynamic of change within law. The purpose of exception and emergency is to restore functionality and conformity with policy as much as to preserve the survival and integrity of the social order. In principle, exception allows law to equalise. The danger with exception is for the process of equalisation to be aligned in ways antithetical to constitutional liberal democracies. Political actors routinely forget there is a significant difference between the kinds of emergencies that represent a threat to the social and constitutional order, and threats to policy and executive interests. On the one hand exception provides a useful, practical device that allows for law and law enforcement to respond to novel situations and uncertainty. On the other, exception tends to proliferate, resulting in a system of laws in which ordinary law is a starting point, with the allocation of exceptions and conditions the true nature of legal reasoning. The true nature of "exception" is at once a state in which the unusual conditions the usual, and the usual conditions the unusual.

A Symptom of Primary and Secondary Legal Systems

The third implication is the development of what appears to be the emergence of two distinct legal systems; a primary and a secondary. As common law and equity evolved as concurrent systems of laws in England for several centuries until their eventual fusion under the Judicature Acts (1873–1875), controlled operations law appears to form a part of a dual system: one concerned with the formal processes of adjudication, and the other with a quasi-judicial process concerned with decision-making and accountability. The former is largely ideological as much as legal, while the latter is administrative and process oriented. This dualism is indicative of what is becoming known as "the integrity branch" or "fourth arm" of government (Spigelman 2004; Stuhmcke and Tran 2007; Gummow 2012; Martin 2014). The significance of this development has yet to become clear – but controlled operations undoubtedly form a part of those investigative systems that rely on those processes prior to examination by the courts, and after the operation itself. This is a species of law that firmly entrenches and serves to crystallise these secondary legal systems. Again, this is a significant topic in its own right, which for present purposes may be identified but left untouched.

Conclusion

Controlled operations transformed Australian law at multiple levels. The emergence of this branch of public procedural law empowered law enforcement by facilitating an investigative technique that allowed investigators to open up clandestine activities that traditionally had presented hard targets for ordinary forms of law enforcement. At the same time, controlled operations law provided linkages with a range of other forms of legality, ranging from the internal systems of regulation of law enforcement agencies, through to the laws of evidence, constitutional and administrative law. But controlled operations also provide a vehicle through which the relationship between state and citizen has been transformed. Within the space created by controlled operations law, we find the logic of exception and necessity, intersecting with rationalities of risk and accountability, a space in which modern forms of liberal citizenship are presented as existing within a zone of impeachment, a state of persistent potential impeachment. By adopting an interdisciplinary perspective, characterised fundamentally by the work of Agamben and Foucault, this book extends our understanding of controlled operations law and policy beyond questions of procedure, authorisation and accountability. It extends our knowledge of controlled operations beyond the legal concerns for rights, remedies and entrapment. In this space we find linkages between doctrinal law and the rationalities of late modernity. In this space we find controlled operations fundamentally concerned with the production of truths and the construction of complex subjectivities. In this space we find controlled operations manifesting as an apparatus of post-modern sovereignty. The legal nomad, having traversed the vast landscapes that surround of law and doctrine, plants a banner on the frontiers of the socio-legal imagination, and returns to the threshold of the familiar, in the hope that this reconnaissance has served its purpose of exploration and illumination.

References

Ashworth, A. (2006). Four threats to the presumption of innocence. *South African Law Journal, 123*(1), 63–97.

Bentham, J. (1843). An examination of the declaration of the rights of man and the citizen decreed by the constituent assembly of France. In J. Bowring (Ed.), *The works of Jeremy Bentham* (Vol. 2). Edinburgh: Simpkin, Marshall & Co.

Braithwaite, J., Fisse, B., & Geis, G. (1987a). Covert facilitation and crime: Restoring balance to the entrapment debate. *Journal of Social Issues, 43*(3), 5.

Braithwaite, J., Fisse, B., & Geis, G. (1987b). Overt observations on covert facilitation: A reply to the commentators. *Journal of Social Issues, 43*(3), 101–122.

Bronitt, S., & McSherry, B. (2017). *Principles of criminal law* (4th ed.). Sydney: Lawbook Co.

Clayton, R., & Tomlinson, H. (2009). *The law of human rights*. Oxford: Oxford University Press.

Deleuze, G. (1992). Postscript on the societies of control. *October, 59*, 3–7.

Ericson, R. (2007). *Crime in an insecure world*. Cambridge: Polity Press.

Ferejohn, J., & Pasquino, P. (2004). The law of the exception: A typology of emergency powers. *International Journal of Constitutional Law, 2*(2), 210–239. https://doi.org/10.1093/icon/2.2.210.

Foucault, M. (1980). The confession of the flesh. In C. Gordon (Ed.), *Power/knowledge: Selected interviews and other writings 1972–1977* (pp. 194–228). Brighton: Harvester Press.

Foucault, M. (2007). Lecture: 1 February 1978 (G. Burchell, Trans.). In M. Senellart (Ed.), *Security, territory, population: Lectures at the College de France 1977–1978* (pp. 87–114). London: Palgrave Macmillan.

Gans, J., Henning, T., Hunter, J., & Warner, K. (2011). *Criminal process and human rights*. Sydney: Federation Press.

Golder, B. (2015). *Foucault and the politics of rights*. Stanford: Stanford University Press.

Gummow, W. (2012). A fourth branch of government? *Australian Institute of Administrative Law Forum, 70*, 19–25.

Hardt, M., & Negri, A. (2000). *Empire*. Cambridge, Mass: Harvard University Press.

Martin, W. (2014). Forewarned and four-armed: Administrative law values and the fourth arm of government. *Australian Law Journal, 88*(2), 106–126.

Marx, G. T. (1980). The new police undercover work. *Journal of Contemporary Ethnography, 8*(4), 399–446.

Marx, G. T. (1988). *Undercover: Police surveillance in America*. Berkeley: University of California Press.

Nathan, C. (2017). Liability to deception and manipulation: The ethics of undercover policing. *Journal of Applied Philosophy, 34*(3), 370–388. https://doi.org/10.1111/japp.12243.

Packer, H. (1968). *The limits of the criminal sanction*. Palo Alto: Stanford University Press.

B. Murphy, *Regulating Undercover Law Enforcement: The Australian Experience*, https://doi.org/10.1007/978-981-33-6381-6

Richards, D., & Clay, C. (2012). An umbrella with holes: Respect for non-derogable human rights during declared states of emergency, 1996–2004. *Human Rights Review, 13*, 443–471.
Rossiter, C. (1948). *Constitutional dictatorship: Crisis government in the modern democracies*. New York: Harcourt Brace.
Spigelman, J. (2004). The integrity branch of government. *Australian Law Journal, 78*(11), 724.
Stuhmcke, A., & Tran, A. (2007). The commonwealth ombudsman: An integrity branch of government? *Alternative Law Journal, 32*(4), 233–236.
Zizek, S. (2010). Against human rights. *Revista Mediacoes, 15*(1), 11–29.

The manufacturer's authorised representative in the EU is Springer Nature Customer Service Centre GmbH, Europaplatz 3, 69115 Heidelberg, Germany. If you have any concerns regarding our products, please contact ProductSafety@springernature.com

Printed and bound by CPI Group (UK) Ltd, Croydon, CR0 4YY
30/09/2026
02225296-0014